A DISPENSATIONAL BIBLICAL THEOLOGY

by Elliott Johnson

BOLD
ACADEMIC
GRACE

Bold Grace Ministries
410 N Bonham Dr.
Allen, TX 75013
www.boldgrace.org

Library of Congress Cataloging in Publication Data

Johnson, Elliott (1936-)
A Dispensational Biblical Theology

1. Biblical Theology. 2. Dispensationalism. 3. Biblical
History. 4. Salvation History. I. Title.

ISBN: 978-0-9899665-9-7

Editing: Grant Hawley
Cover Design: Bold Grace Ministries
Typesetting: Holly Melton

Printed in the United States of America

TABLE OF CONTENTS

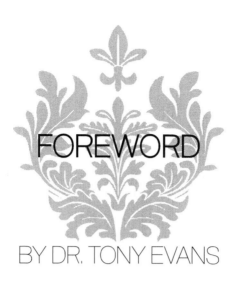

FOREWORD

BY DR. TONY EVANS

There was a time that theology was not limited to the academic arena. Rather, it was the job of pastors to communicate theology to their congregants in a way that taught the content, continuity, and relevancy of theology to life. Today, unfortunately, popularism, liberalism, secularism, and consumerism have left far too many pulpits empty of solid Biblical orthodoxy which inevitably leads to the practice of poor Biblical orthopraxy. This unfortunate dearth also has resulted in people not knowing how the Bible fits together as well as how our theological conclusions are formulated and developed. Systematic theology is not possible without the underpinning of a solid Biblical theology to undergird it, and a solid Biblical theology is best understood through the lens of a dispensational understanding and interpretation of the Biblical story.

At the heart of ministry is a critical need for pulpits to be filled with proclaimers who know how to rightly divide the Word of Truth. This is why my good friend Elliott Johnson's work, *A Dispensational Biblical Theology*, is so timely. It is a comprehensive tool that simultaneously serves both the academic mind and the pastoral heart.

Dr. Johnson has given us a resource that carefully traces, in detail, the purpose of God as revealed in His Word through the various economies that God has established. This work shows the hand of God as it moves through history, giving the reader a clear understanding of the plan and will of God as it is progressively revealed through the inerrant, inspired text of Scripture.

This Biblical theology allows both the student and communicator of Scripture to follow logically and progressively the unfolding of God's dealing with mankind so that history makes sense. It clearly shows the Bible not to be a book of random, disconnected events that are only vaguely related to one another. Rather, it shows the God of history at work in history to accomplish His goal of bringing glory to Himself through the advancement of His kingdom.

A Dispensational Biblical Theology allows the expositor of Scripture to stay tethered to the text of Scripture in its historical context while simultaneously freeing the expositor to bring the Biblical text and its context into the contemporary experience of the audience. This is crucial, since at the heart of a Dispensational Biblical theology is God's partnership with man in both the unfolding and communicating of His divine revelation.

This is a resource whose time has come. It will be an essential tool in the arsenal of those who take seriously the inerrant Word, and who wish to understand it and communicate it effectively, whether in a classroom or in a sanctuary.

I am extremely grateful for the excellent exegetical work and sweat that was obviously put into producing this work. It will certainly serve as the foundation for increasing the theological depth of the pulpit, leading to the greater theological depth in the pew.

Tony Evans
President, The Urban Alternative
Senior Pastor, Oak Cliff Bible Fellowship

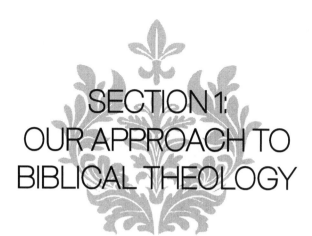

SECTION 1:
OUR APPROACH TO
BIBLICAL THEOLOGY

Biblical Theology features the story of the whole Bible. Our approach is a Dispensational interpretation of the story. As such, Dispensationalism provides a philosophy of Biblical history.

Our interpretation of Biblical history will use the word *dispensation* in three related ways:

> First, *dispensation* refers to the *management* God exercises in salvation history.

> Second, it refers to human partners in God's plan, called to be *stewards* of what God reveals to them.

> Third, it refers to economies of God's management of the stewards, called *dispensations*.

The great mystery of the story is that *God the Father's* management allows evil without directly causing it. Rather, evil challenges God and His creation plan by obstructing mankind in an attempt to thwart God's plan in history. In the end, *God's Son Incarnate* will assume the role of steward to see God's plan to fulfillment. Further, *God the Spirit* is at work with humanity to address their conflict with evil. While the Spirit is a continuing presence throughout history, His presence is more fully displayed following the Son's First Advent.

Thus, the focus of this interpretation is on *God's glory* and *those glorious ways*. It is God's intent to share Himself and His glory with His creation and in particular with those called according to His purpose.

Since this is salvation history, rather than including all of world history, the scope is limited. Yet we may touch upon related issues in the whole world (like creation, nations, races, or gender, etc.)

As salvation history, the focus features two fundamental purposes:

First, Creation Purposes–While creation was completed in seven days, it was designed to set the stage for history to follow. And this history is the realm of time and space in which man would mediate God's rule on earth. This would only be realized in the millennial kingdom of the incarnate Son of God.

Second, Redemption Purposes–The enemy of God quickly challenged God's plan by tempting man to rebel against God and His will. Following man's fall from God, God purposed to use man in spite of the fall and to redeem man from his fallen condition. Further, redemption includes addressing the consequences of man's sin in order to restore His chosen partners to their created role as stewards of His revealed will.

CHAPTER 1: INTRODUCTION

TEACH ME YOUR WAYS—MOSES (EXODUS 33:13)

The proposal that believers are stewards of God's Word may appear strange in this pluralistic age in which contending proposals are often not weighed on the basis of whether they are true. Rather, pluralism incorporates different, if not disparate, points of view for political reasons. As a result, considering whether believers are stewards of God's Word may be outside the pale of what is viable in today's discussion because of its origin. But the issue is too important to set aside. It presents the opportunity for believers to come to know God in a personal partnership with Christ, through the stewardship of His Word and will. For those who share a view of a world originating from the Creator, the idea of stewardship is not unreasonable. As persons created in God's image and as believers in Jesus Christ, we realize that the most crucial aspects of life are received as gifts from God. As a result, we are not the source nor do we control what is given, but we are responsible for making use of what is given. And that use is as a steward according to God's plan.

The idea that believers are stewards of God's Word had its origin in a Dispensational Biblical theology. In a not too distant past, a Dispensational view of God's ways had a significant impact on believers in the Church. George E. Ladd, who himself was a non-Dispensationalist, nonetheless wrote concerning Dispensationalists:

> It is doubtful if there has been any other circle of men who have done more by their influence in preaching, teaching and writing to promote a love for Bible study, a hunger for the

deeper Christian life, a passion for evangelism and zeal for missions in the history of American Christianity.[1]

In view of this significant influence in the past, it seems appropriate, even urgent, to reconsider Dispensationalism, which has been disregarded for so long.

This introduction will focus on the value and the validity of a Dispensational Biblical Theology. Based on the recent literature, two questions will be examined:

1. What is Dispensationalism?

2. What progress in revelation has been reached when New Testament authors use Old Testament texts?

Then based on the discussion, the *validity* and *value* of Dispensationalism will be introduced. The *validity* rests on the unity of a Biblical theology featuring God who governs salvation history from beginning to climax in full realization. As God spoke creation into existence, so God speaks to stewards in history through whom His plan for a fallen creation will be realized. The *validity* highlights a coherence of incorporating both the fall and redemption; both the kingdom lost and restored, the changes necessitated by the power of evil seducing God's own chosen people who in the end will realize what God promised; and God's use of Israel's failure in accomplishing the appointed role for Gentiles. The *value* of Dispensationalism features the distinctive view of the believer's life as a steward of God's will in his appointed time in history. However, the ultimate purpose of telling the story is to have God's story move our hearts to worship. For while it is a story of man in history, that story uncovers the glory of God who shares Himself to accomplish His will for His own people who love Him and are called according to His purposes.

What Is Dispensationalism?

Charles Ryrie has answered this question in a definitive fashion in two works building upon the works of Darby, Scofield, and Chafer.[2] But these two works raise another question. In the forward of Ryrie's *Dispensationalism Today*, Frank Gaebelein asserts that "Dispensationalism is not a theology but rather a method of interpretation helpful in grasping

---

[1] George Eldon Ladd, *Crucial Questions about the Kingdom of God* (Grand Rapids, MI: Eerdmans, 1952), p. 49.

[2] Charles Ryrie, *Dispensationalism Today* (Chicago: Moody, 1966) and *Dispensationalism* (Chicago: Moody, 1995).

the progress of revelation."[3] While he does not explain what he means by it not being a theology, it could be that Dispensationalism does not take the shape of a systematic theology. Evangelicals typically define a systematic theology by its soteriology. But Dispensationalism is not ultimately defined by its soteriology. In its history, there have been Calvinists and Arminians who have claimed to be Dispensationalists.[4] Dispensationalism bears a resemblance to Biblical Theology, an approach dependent on the idea of progressive revelation in Biblical history. Dispensationalism stresses a unique view of the Church and of eschatology in history. What is important is Gaebelien's focus on the role of Dispensationalism in providing a lens for a correct reading of the progress of revelation. One contribution of Dispensationalism is its claim to provide a single and consistent hermeneutic to interpret the whole canon.

On the other hand, Ryrie posits that Dispensationalism provides a philosophy of *history* unified by a doxological goal: "the differing dispensations reveal the glory of God as He manifests His character in the differing stewardships."[5] That glory of God in the broadest perspective is introduced in the two creation accounts. The first creation account introduces the history of the earth as we now know it. In the Biblical perspective, history is viewed as involving conflict at a fundamental level (Gen 3:15). In the conflict, evil is tested for value and for power. Will the serpent and its offspring bring about good and have the power to achieve its ends? At the same time, the conflict will reveal Eve and her offspring as governed by God. And in the conflict with evil, God's glory will be revealed. There will be *grace* for those overwhelmed by evil and *truth* challenging the ways of evil. In the end, the glory of grace and truth will overcome and defeat evil in the conflict.

The new creation holds out hope for a creation free from evil and with the promise of experiencing the fullness of God's glory. Rather than the new creation being a fulfillment of the first creation, it is a fresh start revealing God's glory disclosed in His yet unknown fullness, apart from conflict with evil.

The Biblical story is a theology because it is God's story. The story features dispensations which are distinguishable economies in the outworking of God's purposes.[6] What is distinctive is the sequence of econ-

---

[3] Ryrie, *Dispensationalism Today*, p. 8.

[4] The present construct is based on an Amyraldian view of Calvinistic soteriology.

[5] *Ibid.*, p. 18.

[6] *Ibid.*, p. 28.

omies focusing on the conflict between God's progressive revelation to His stewards, confronting evil and its claim to rule. The sequence of these economies is as follows:

1. Evil in conflict with God's Word of promise;

2. Evil directly confronted by God's law introducing the theocracy in Israel;

3. Evil overcome by Jesus Christ's First Advent yet leaving a world suffering from evil with the gospel;

4. Evil defeated by Christ's return in judgment to rule, yet without removing evil until the evil one is destroyed.

Eric Sauer puts forward that these "new periods always begin only when *from the side of God* a change is introduced."[7] While some things continue, others are annulled, and fresh principles are added.

As a result, Ryrie suggests that Dispensationalism "views the world as a household run by God. In His household-world, God is dispensing or administering its affairs according to His own will and in various stages of revelation in the passage of time."[8] This description explains what Ryrie means by theology. But the phrase "in various stages of revelation in the passage of time," raises another question.

What Is the Dispensational Relationship that Exists between the Old Testament and the New Testament?

Vigorous discussions between Dispensationalists and non-Dispensationalists have occurred over this question. In the late 1980s, a book was published addressing this issue: *Continuity and Discontinuity.*[9] While the title presents the contrast too strongly, it does capture the emphases of the two models.[10] Non-Dispensational models emphasize continuity while Dispensational models stress discontinuity. In order to avoid either/or extremes, care needs to be taken to clarify both discontinuity and a necessary continuity in Dispensationalism.

---

[7] Eric Sauer, *The Dawn of World Redemption* (Grand Rapids, MI: Eerdmans, 1951), p. 194, emphasis in original.

[8] Ryrie, *Dispensationalism Today*, p. 29.

[9] John S. Feinberg, ed. *Continuity and Discontinuity*, (Westchester, IL: Crossway, 1988), p. xi.

[10] Both models have features that express continuity and other features that recognize discontinuity, but both confess to one way of salvation.

Discontinuity

While Ryrie stresses God's dispensing the affairs of governing human history, the term, *dispensation* (*oikonomos*), is based on Paul's use to characterize his life and ministry (1 Cor 4:1-2; 9:17). The Lord also uses the term in response to Peter's question: "are you telling this parable [waiting for the master to return, Luke 12:35-40] to us or to everyone?" (Luke 12:41, HCSB). Jesus responds, "Who then is the faithful and sensible manager (*oikonomos*) his master will put in charge of his household...?" (Luke 12:42, HCSB). Jesus' answer to Peter indicates that He is talking about the manager of the master's affairs rather than everyone. A related term, *entrust*, is used as an act of the master to his servant (2 Tim 2:2; cf. Luke 19:11-27). This *Biblical* concept indicates that it is not God's management of the whole world but of salvation history. These uses are then incorporated into a Biblical theology with a *theological emphasis* on God's management through chosen stewards over salvation history.

John Goodrich investigated the historical origin of this metaphorical use of the term in Paul in light of its use in ancient regal, municipal, and in private administration in the Greco-Roman world.[11] While this is the probable domain of first century uses of the term, a Biblical concept from the Old Testament likely was the antecedent allusion. From the time of creation, Adam was to *mediate* God's rule on earth (Gen 1:26-28). Following Adam's fall into sin, God chose Eve and her seed to do conflict with the serpent and its seed (Gen 3:15).[12] Further, God chose a remnant of Eve's line (Gen 11:10-32) to bless, and through that remnant, to mediate blessings to the nations (Gen 12:2-3; Exod 19:5-6). While God dispenses His providential will over the earth, His dispensing of salvation blessing is through a remnant of *mediating* stewards to whom He entrusts His Word.

Thus, the *theological sense* of *oikonomia*, management, refers to God managing salvation in history. At the same time, God is ruling universally in providence over all creation and nations. The focus of *oikonomia* designates a partnership between God and His elect ones to be stewards of His spoken revelation. Thus, Dispensationalism is a Biblical theology closely tied to salvation history. This is more focused than Ryrie's model.

In this model of Biblical theology, God rules dispensing His Word in history while at the same time acting to choose and to enable stewards

---

[11] John K. Goodrich, *Paul as an Administrator of God in 1 Corinthians* (Cambridge, UK: Cambridge University Press, 2012).

[12] This passage is commonly called the *protoevangelium*, the "first gospel."

of His will on earth. The steward is entrusted with the Word progressively revealed through history. Stewards like Abraham or Paul are to manage their own lives according to the revelation entrusted to them and to mediate God's will to the peoples of their day. So God rules through these chosen stewards, in effect secondary causes, to accomplish His purposes in the history of the creation.

Continuity

The non-Dispensational models stress continuity by constructing normative theological covenants. Yet when these theological covenants are compared to the Biblical covenants, the Biblical covenants are distinct because they are exclusively addressed to Israel as partners (Rom 9:4). In our Dispensational model, the unity features God governing world history, displaying the glory of God as the chief end. We adopt Ryrie's emphasis.

A recent group of Dispensational voices sought to find greater continuity in the historic progress of revelation. Since God governs partners through this progress of revelation, they have called the new model Progressive Dispensationalism.[13] As a result, since all Dispensationalists recognize progressive revelation, the debate among Dispensationalists focuses on what progress has taken place by the time of the present dispensation. Has the Davidic Covenant been fulfilled in some sense with the Church? Does Israel have a distinct future in the kingdom? Has the New Covenant been fulfilled in the Church?

Supporting this emphasis on progressive revelation is "the rise of the discipline of Biblical theology with its focus on interpreting the Scripture in their historical environment which has contributed to a greater appreciation of the development within the historical redemption plan."[14]

So, what is involved in a Biblical theology based on progressive revelation? The debate among Dispensationalists concerns the relationship between Israel and the Church in the progress of revelation. In distinction to finding covenant promises made to Israel having some fulfillment with the Church, continuity is found in promise concerning the Seed of the woman (Gen 3:15), the Seed of Abraham (Gen 12:36), the Son of David (2 Sam 7:12-16). These promises find fulfillment in Jesus Christ.

---

[13] Craig Blaising and Darrell Bock, eds., *Dispensationalism, Israel and the Church*, (Grand Rapids, MI: Zondervan, 1992); Craig Blaising and Darrell Bock, *Progressive Dispensationalism* (Wheaton, IL: Bridge Point, 1993); Robert L. Saucy, *The Case for Progressive Dispensationalism* (Grand Rapids, MI: Zondervan, 1993).

[14] Saucy, *The Case for Progressive Dispensationalism*, p. 13.

Further, as believers were blessed by faith through the promised One (Gen 15:6; Ps 32:1-2), so believers are blessed by faith once the promised One has come (Rom 4:1-8, 22-24; Gal 3:6-9). The Church is then revealed after the coming of Christ (Matt 16:18). It was formed on the Day of Pentecost in the baptizing work of the Holy Spirit (Acts 2:41-47; 11:15-17). In relation to Israel, the Church appeared in history in the time after Messiah was cut off (Dan 9:26) and before Messiah would return (Dan 9:27).

There are two questions that will be considered in attempting to unravel the distinction between these two models: First, what is progress in revelation? Do the Author's/author's speech-acts provide evidence that additional revelation is intended?

Second, does the New Testament use of Old Testament passages give evidence of either model? Does the New Testament *resignify* or transform what the Old Testament *signified* in the original expression and claim fulfillment of such resignification? Or does the New Testament interpret a single, stable meaning expressed in the Old Testament which will be fulfilled with Israel?

Progressive Revelation

"Progressive revelation is the recognition that God's message to man was not given in one single act but was unfolded in a series of successive acts."[15] Further, it is helpful to clarify what acts and what texts are involved in progressive revelation. There is a sequence of books in the Hebrew canon, addressed to Israel. But that sequence of books is not what is at issue in the progress. Rather, within the sequence of that literary corpus, there are themes progressing toward completion. These themes are addressed to historical stewards through whom God unfolds His governance of salvation history. These themes are expressed in speech-acts to do things or to get things done.

In one kind of theme, a *promise*, the Author's intent is to do things according to what He commits Himself to do for, or through, a steward. These performative acts are fulfilled when the Author keeps such commitments. In *prophecy*, the Author's intent is also to do things according to His providential governance of events that would shape the fulfillment.

---

[15] Ryrie, *Dispensationalism*, p. 31.

In another theme, a *law*, the Author's intent is to get things done through the obedience of the steward under the law code. Of course, getting things done is related to the steward's response to the Law—as in obedience fleshing out a theocracy with equity and justice among the people, or in dire situations which arise from disobedience, in which the need for God becomes more evident.

In each of these speech-acts, a setting is established through a *promise* or a *law* in which future acts are expected. When there are intertextual "repetitions that infer some thematic or ideational connection [these] provide a complex structure showing that the Bible…is a unity."[16] So a *promise* may be repeated as God acts on behalf of the steward to whom the *promise* was addressed. Within the whole canon, the fulfillment of the *promise* contributes to that complex structure.

Based on a literal hermeneutic with a stable historic meaning, we expect *added, deepened,* or *replaced* revelation to be included in the progress of revelation. By contrast, Waltke would expect that the progress involves *transformation, expansion,* or *revision.*[17]

In the following consideration of instances of progressive revelation, we will examine what those clues look like in different speech-acts.

Promise of Blessing (e.g., Genesis 12:1-3, 7; 13:15; 15:6)

These promises are divine speech-acts, in which God committed Himself to bless Abraham and to bless the nations through Abraham. But it seems clear these promises are foundational and thus incomplete as first stated. Subsequent revelation can be expected to flesh out what merely appears as a foundation of the plan. Details of that plan do not merely involve deepened understanding, but further revelation may be added which will deepen Abraham's and the readers' understanding of what God will do. This is progressive revelation extending in history to the very advent of Jesus Christ, the Seed of Abraham (Matt 1:1-2 or Luke 3:34).

Typology

Tupos is not a technical word as it is used as an "example" (1 Cor 10:11) or as a theological type (Rom 5:14). Used in a theme which is

---

[16] Waltke, *An Old Testament Theology* (Grand Rapids, MI: Zondervan, 2006), p. 126.

[17] *Ibid.*

progressively revealed, we are interested in the theological meaning of the term. So Goppelt defines type as "divinely ordained types of future realities that will be greater and more complete."[18] There are four qualifications that help to recognize a theological type.

First, a type refers to historical facts—persons, actions, events, institutions which are present in a revelatory narrative.

Second, the divine ordination is recognized as the type corresponds to an antecedent promise. The type partially fulfills the essential implications of the promise.

Third, the antitype then completely fulfills the essential implications of the promise. The heightened or more complete meaning matches the complete fulfillment, rather than a partial fulfillment of the type.

Fourth, this involves interpretation of the same type of meaning, rather than allegorical interpretation that involves a change in types of meaning (Gal 4:24, the two women are two covenants).

Promissory Covenants (Genesis 15:9-21; Second Samuel 7:11-16; Jeremiah 31:31-34)

Covenants are formal partnership arrangements with chosen and specified partners. The role of the partner is thrust into prominence by an oath taken in the ratification of the arrangement. This role of the partner indicates that a change in party cannot be involved if a claim of fulfillment of the original arrangement is made.

In each promissory covenant, God is the primary partner but not the only partner. God alone takes the oath and thus assumes that obligation for keeping the promised arrangement (Gen 15:17-18).

Nevertheless, it is a partnership. The chosen partner is necessarily included as a secondary causative agent with whom alone the covenant will be fulfilled. In the Abrahamic and Davidic Covenants, the final party with whom the covenant will be fulfilled is included as a *situation vacant* party.[19] It will be a Seed of Abraham, a Son of David. As a causative agent, it is not evident what it will take for that agent to receive what the divine Partner has committed to accomplish. Based on the divine Agent's commitment it is certain that it will be kept. Additional revelation is needed

---

[18] Leonhard Goppelt, *Typos: The Typological Interpretation of the Old Testament in the New*, trans. Donald H. Madvig (Grand Rapids, MI: Eerdmans, 1982), p. 18.

[19] G. B. Caird, *The Language and Imagery of the Bible* (Philadelphia: Westminster, 1980), p. 17.

to reveal how that will happen in light of the conflict with evil. There is no indication that the terms of the arrangement will be changed in view of that conflict. It is God who commits to the covenant partnership.

In the New Covenant, the covenant partners are explicitly stated as the Author, the Lord, and the house of Israel and of Judah. In the introduction of the New Covenant, the earlier Mosaic Covenant is declared to be broken (Jer 31:32). So at that point in the progress of revelation, several questions are raised. Although Israel has broken the terms of the original covenant and will experience its curses, who will satisfy Israel's obligation assumed by the oath (Exod 19:7; 24:3, 7)? On what grounds would a New Covenant be ratified? These are both administrative covenants,[20] but what grounds exist for replacing the old with a new?

It seems clear that the promissory covenants set stable ground posts in God's dealing with Israel in history, but in view of the conflict anticipated in history, the revelation is still incomplete. Additional revelation is anticipated to clarify how the conflict will be resolved and the covenant fulfilled (Rom 3:1-4; 9:4-6).

Prophecy Anticipates Future Revelation (Deuteronomy 32)

Moses himself prophesied of the unique role he had, which set the pattern for "a Prophet like me from your midst, from your brethren, him you shall hear" (Deut 18:15). Thus, added revelation will follow. That addition is anticipated in what is often called the Song of Moses. However, Block described it as a sort of national anthem:

> [I]t should really be called 'the song of Yahweh,' because Yahweh inspired it and dedicated it to Joshua and Moses in the tent of meeting (Deut 31:14-21). Whereas in Moses' preaching we hear the voice of God refracted through the orations of a man, this song was composed by God and then performed by Moses precisely as he heard it (31:30; 32:44).[21]

While its anthem character as a hymn accounts for the absence of specific historic references, the people's propensity for idolatry is a dominant theme of the song, which was to be repeatedly experienced in Israel's history prior to captivity.

---

[20] Thomas E. McComiskey, *The Covenants of Promise* (Grand Rapids, MI: Baker, 1985), pp. 163-77.

[21] Daniel I. Block, *Deuteronomy*, NIV Application Commentary (Grand Rapids, MI: Zondervan, 2012), p. 746.

This point is complete even though the particular accounts of the historic instances are not finished. What is incomplete is found at the end of the anthem: "Israel's National Anthem ends on a festive note, appealing to the nations to join in the celebration of Yahweh's gracious acts on behalf of Israel."[22] That is a point in the hymn that is anticipated because of God's election of Israel. But as early as Exodus 32, that point along with all the subsequent instances of idolatry in their history, make this point unexpected. Additional revelation from a righteous God is needed to account for the climax. God's ways with Israel remain unknown as unanswered questions linger. How will Israel as a whole be changed? How will Israel become righteous? The prophecy anticipates that additional revelation will answer these questions.

The Verdict against the Evil One

The verdict is in even though it hasn't been worked out in history. While the plan of God's blessing and the restoration of Israel to a place of honor anticipates added revelation, the verdict against evil has been reached and is completely revealed. This prophecy involving God's providence is certain, yet how it will unfold will be exegeted in history.

The serpent-animal will move on its belly throughout history (Gen 3:14). The verdict is complete. The same is true of the serpent-enemy (Gen 3:15). It is complete because the verdict includes generations of conflict with a final resolution. Yet that resolution remains to be resolved.

Whereas the serpent's temptation introduced conflict between God and the apparent interests of mankind, the verdict indicates that the actual conflict is between the evil one and the human race.

The first generation of conflict is between the woman and the serpent. This interprets the temptation in which the serpent used the woman in his conflict with God. Clarified by the verdict, the woman's true enemy is the evil one.

The next generations are indicated by the use of the collective noun *seed*. The woman will have descendants to do conflict with the serpent's descendants. The first generation involved the conflict between Cain and Abel. Cain, the descendant of the serpent, kills Abel, the descendant of the woman. But God gives Seth and Enosh to Eve (Gen 4:25-26). However, as Genesis 5–11 indicates, the seed of the serpent controls the earth and the early history deteriorates in evil.

---

[22] *Ibid.*

Nonetheless, the final generation of the verdict sees the serpent return to the battle. The conflict of that generation is taken up by the individual Seed (He, Him) of the woman. What is unresolved is that both "strike" death blows, a serpent at the heel and the Man at the head. Since this is a verdict against the serpent, the enemy of God, the outcome is certain even though the experience has not yet happened. The clarification comes in the revelation of the Cross, to which is added the revelation of resurrection. This involves the promise of blessing. And the resurrected Seed will strike the head blow to finally judge the evil one.

Revelation Progressively Fulfilled

The expectations already raised need to be kept in mind as we consider the New Testament's use of the Old Testament prophecy and promise. The issue in question involves the extent of fulfillment in the present age. All agree that the historical Jesus fulfilled to some extent promises and prophecies originating in the Old Testament (Luke 24:25-27). The question is one of extent. Were the promises made to Israel abrogated in their rejection of Jesus the Christ? Or did the Church fulfill or appropriate the promises made to Israel? Did it replace Israel?[23] Or is there some mediating position in which there is a future for both Israel and the Church?

All of the answers to these questions begin with agreement on the meaning of to *fulfill*. Without question, the New Testament authors use the Greek term *plēroō*, often translated "fulfill." Having agreed that there is fulfillment in the First Advent of Jesus Christ, does this fulfillment involve Israel's eschatology (as in Isa 2:1-4 or 4:2-6)? Is there an already fulfillment of Israel's future and a not yet climax for Israel?

Some define the term *fulfill* as a metaphor. A physical object "filled up" is compared to the meaning of the verb. A better way is to think about verbal meaning in terms of speech-acts or performative statements. "Performatives commit the speaker to stand by his words."[24] The *speech* consists of a promise and the performance is the *act* keeping the commitment. Interpretation of promises or prophecies involves what God has committed Himself to do. Have the acts of God completed what He promised or prophesied? This is fulfillment.

---

[23] The view that Israel has been replaced by the Church is called supersessionism or replacement theology.

[24] Caird, *The Language and Imagery of the Bible*, p. 21.

So when Isaac was born, God's promise of an heir to Abraham and Sarah was fulfilled *in part*. Was Isaac Abraham's heir? Yes. Would he inherit all that was promised to the heir? That's not clear yet. The language used to describe what has happened in the progress of revelation can be slippery. That Isaac is born heir has been called fulfillment *in part* or *partial* fulfillment. The first is accurate, the second is not. The first is accurate because *a part* of what was promised has been fulfilled. The second is not accurate because what was promised commits God to more than what had happened.

Fulfillment *in part* refers to the part of the promise that has been kept. *Partial* fulfillment must keep in mind that the whole promise is what is at issue. The fulfillment of *one part* of what is promised is not *partial* fulfillment of *the promise*.

Non-Dispensationalists claim that what was promised to Israel would be fulfilled in a spiritual sense. Does the spiritual component represent fulfillment *in part*? Waltke, who considers "Kingdom Promises as Spiritual,"[25] describes the fulfillment this way: "in the NT, in contrast to the expectation of Judaism, the kingdom's character is 'heavenly' and 'spiritual,' not 'earthly' and 'political.'" Thus, the spiritual is present to the exclusion of the earthly and the political, which existed in the kingdom of David and its promises (2 Sam 7:12-16). The promise had always been heavenly (from God), spiritual (realized by God), earthly (located in Jerusalem), and political (a nation in the midst of other nations).

This earthly and political historical antecedent influenced the expectations of Judaism. Thus, *the part*, spiritual, excludes the earthly and political as necessary components of the self-identity of the kingdom. This is not fulfillment. Rather, the spiritual kingdom resignifies the historic promised meaning of the kingdom. The *resignified* sense cannot be considered a fulfillment of the Davidic Kingdom. We conclude that this is an erroneous claim.

Some Dispensationalists have adopted the same interpretive practice of *resignification or reinterpretation*.

1. Bock contended that "an already fulfillment" involved a *resignification* (expanded meaning) of the promissory covenants (Davidic and New) to be partially fulfilled with the Church.[26]

---

[25] Bruce K. Waltke, "Kingdom Promises as Spiritual" in *Continuity and Discontinuity*, p. 270.

[26] Bock, *Progressive Dispensationalism*, pp. 57-105. The resignified sense is an enlarged sense to include the Church and Israel which is called a complementary sense. His resignified sense claims some level of fulfillment.

Then the "not yet" fulfillment will consist of a normal language usage consistent with the Millennial Kingdom.

2. Saucy contended: "the present salvific operation of God is not in strict accord with the Old Testament prophecies cited…[yet], the apostle does see the fulfillment of these Old Testament texts in the present salvation of both Jews and Gentiles."[27] At the same time, he asserts that "no reinterpretation is necessary to accommodate the New Testament teaching."[28]

The claim that Saucy makes is that "the new covenant promise was fulfilled with the historical work of Christ."[29] This claim seems unsubstantiated because a covenant is only fulfilled when the stated parties to the covenant are both included. Yet the house of Israel and the house of Judah are not included. Rather the New Covenant is ratified by the mediating work of Jesus Christ (Heb 9:15). Claiming fulfillment without the inclusion of the stated parties to the covenant necessarily involves resignification or reinterpretation. If the New Covenant is fulfilled in some sense with the Church in this dispensation, then this is a reinterpretation of Jer 31:31-32.

Grammatical-Historical Hermeneutic

In contrast, Ryrie advocated a hermeneutic of consistent *normal language usage*. It is that hermeneutic that we will contend is what the New Testament uses in quoting most Old Testament promises as fulfilled. This New Testament sense is in accord with what is said in the Old Testament context. There is fulfillment *in part* of two promissory covenants through Jesus Christ's First Advent: the Seed of Abraham is Jesus who received His inheritance upon His ascension (Acts 2:33-35); Jesus is the Son of David who awaits the promised Kingdom at His return (Luke 19:11-27). Jesus represents Israel in fulfilling Israel's role as the Lord's Son (Hos 11:1) and Servant (Isa 49:1-6). Thus, as representing Israel, Christ will enable Israel to fulfill the promises addressed to her. The New Covenant was ratified at the Cross but not inaugurated or fulfilled since Israel rejected the Mediator. The house of Israel and the house of Judah are not

---

[27] Saucy, *The Case for Progressive Dispensationalism*, p. 137 in pp. 39-142.

[28] *Ibid.* p. 136.

[29] *Ibid.* p. 126.

partners in the New Covenant in this age, but will be when fulfilled in the age to come.

Such a normal language hermeneutic considers both the Author/author and the language used. Both will be considered. First, the language may be separated into distinguishable parts which may be called type components. These type components are examined at levels of language context. These levels unfold from a grammatical-historical hermeneutic.

The *word level* shares a field of meaning which may include homonyms. Thus, at this historical level, the meaning is not determinate.

The *construction level* is also historical and shares a field of meaning which is only considered as determinate at a broader textual context.

The *literary genre level* includes historical conventions which are shared by other literary compositions of the same type (e.g., epistles, narrative-histories, prophetic compositions). While conventions share the frame of the type of context, they aren't sufficient to determine a message.

Second, the *author's composition* level is built upon a reading and consideration of all the other type components which the author includes in his composition. The author's *willed-type* composition communicates the message intended in the verbal composition.

E. D. Hirsch[30] correctly contends that communication only takes place as these language type components are *shared* and the meaning to be communicated *determined* in the author's willed-type composition. An *indeterminate* language type does not communicate.

As an example, an evangelist was visiting a West Texas town. Bubba decided to attend. When the evangelist's message was completed, he offered to pray for anyone with a problem. Bubba went forward and asked for prayer in his problem *hearing*. The evangelist put his finger in his ear and his hand on his head and prayed fervently. When he finished he asked about his *hearing*. Bubba responded, "My *hearing* isn't until Wednesday morning."

As a result, the meaning communicated that is *shared* and *determined* is not at the word, construction, or genre level, but the author's type of meaning is expressed in the level of the whole text. Verbal meaning must be sharable and determinate. Otherwise, it does not have a self-identity to be communicated and known. So, the evangelist should have asked Bubba what he meant by *hearing*.

---

[30] E. D. Hirsch, *Validity in Interpretation* (New Haven, CT: Yale University Press, 1967).

In Scripture, the divine Author and the human author are conscious of the same willed type of meaning as a whole. This is the case because it is recognized in the textual composition that is inspired by God. So, the human author is conscious of the type of meaning to be communicated, as is the divine Author. In addition, the divine Author is aware of all intended implications and all intended prophetic references which the human author may not mention nor be aware. The link between the reader and the recognition of the type of meaning is a series of questions that address the *identity* of the meaning:

- What is the *literary genre* of the whole text? This is read in the grammatical and historical context.

- What is the *subject* communicated?

- What is the *complement* completing the message?

So the *identity* of the meaning is the *message* the author intends to communicate. Further, the *literary genre* is the context which entails historical conventions according to which the verbal meaning is to be read and interpreted. Thus, the message is expressed within the conventions of the literary genre and within which the interpreter is to read seeking the message.

The Recognition of Israel's Representative

Israel was called under the Law to serve God. This call was responded to collectively by the people: "all that the LORD has said, we will do" (Exod 19:7; 24:3, 7). This service was spelled out in the promised partnership: "a special treasure," "a kingdom of priests," "a holy nation" (Exod 19:5-6). Each of these is collective, not representative. In the Law (Exodus 20:1–23:33), the reality of these promised titles of partnership was contingent upon keeping God's law. Based on this promise in the Law, one might expect that it was only a matter of time that a generation would arise that would keep the Law and realize the promised role and partnership.

That same call to service had come to Abraham. After promises of personal blessing (Gen 12:2-3a), he was promised the role of mediating blessing to all nations (Gen 12:3b) through service on behalf of God. The scope of that promise (all nations) placed realization outside the reach of any of the patriarchs. Rather, it anticipated the nation who would be "a Kingdom of priests" (Exod 19:5-6).

However, within the canonical context of Scripture, there were clues that in the end an individual descendant of Abraham would fulfill what was promised (Gen 22:16-18).[31] Another clue is found in the individual descendant of the woman (Gen 3:15) who would conquer the serpent.[32]

What was intimated in these texts only became evident in time for Israel; that no generation would keep the Law. This was illustrated in the first generation who demanded an idol (Exod 32:1-6). It also became evident that no individual like Moses would fully obey (Num 20:1-13), even though he had interceded to save that generation (Exodus 32:7–34:35).

In time, the people realized they needed a king (1 Sam 8:1-22; Judg 17:6; 21:25). The recognition dawned on them that they needed a representative to rule but their desire was patterned after the leadership in other nations. As time passed the prophets critiqued the royal representative who didn't serve God's interests or even the people's interests. Isaiah critiqued two kings, Ahaz and Hezekiah, as neither served God nor the people's interests. Then, Isaiah prophesied that a representative (Isa 49:1-6) would arise to serve God and to serve the interests of Israel, God's servant (Isa 41:8-10; 44:1-3).

The Representative Revealed by New Testament Authors

Matthew and his interpretation of Jesus the Nazarene, in the context of Israel's history, traced His early ministry. Incident after incident Jesus recapitulated Israel's history and in those experiences He represented Israel as God's Son and Servant (Matthew 1–4).

First, he quotes Hos 11:1, "out of Egypt I have called My son" as fulfilled in Jesus' flight to Egypt (Matt 2:13-15). Hosea was alluding to the Lord's words to Pharaoh: "Israel is My firstborn son...Let My son go so that he may worship Me" (Exod 4:22). Matthew says that Jesus stayed in Egypt "until Herod's death so that what was spoken by the Lord through the prophet may be fulfilled" (Matt 2:15).

The seeming difficulties are twofold. First, Hosea refers to a historical event. But Matthew treats it as a type-event. Second, Hosea says that the Lord refers to the people, Israel, as the son (cf. Exod 4:21), while Matthew

---

[31] T. Desmond Alexander, "Further Observations on the Term 'Seed' in Genesis" *Tyndale Bulletin* 48:2 (1997): 363-67. And "From Adam to Judah: The Significance of the Family Tree in Genesis" *The Evangelical Quarterly* 61:1 (1989): 5-19.

[32] *Ibid.*

refers to the child, Jesus, as the Son. It was Hosea who had recognized that Israel was called out of Egypt and they dwelt in the land as their inheritance by promise (Gen 15:18). Now some nine hundred years later, Hosea announced that the inheritance they received, they now have lost: "they will not stay in the land of the LORD. Instead, Ephraim will return to Egypt and they will eat unclean food in Assyria" (Hos 9:3). Historically they went to Assyria, but theologically they returned to Egypt, the place from which they had come out as a people. But Matthew recognized that Jesus would go to Egypt to be protected as Israel had. Israel's original exodus was but a *type* of Israel's departure to enter her inheritance, as Jesus' exodus would be the antitype (Matt 2:19-23). Jesus' exodus put Him on the way to claiming the Son's inheritance from the Father (Acts 1:4-5; 2:33). So Jesus is the Representative-Son to receive Israel's inheritance from God and then to enable Israel in the end, as a nation, to enter her inheritance.

Second, in a similar fashion, Matthew also quotes Isaiah to refer to fulfillment found in Jesus Christ as, so to speak, the Representative-Servant. This time, Isaiah himself gives evidence of such a distinction between the Representative-Servant and the people-servant. Oswalt summarizes it this way:

> God has said that the lives of his servants, Israel, would be evident to the world that He alone is the Holy One...But how is it possible? Will God simply ignore the sin that projected Israel into slavery in the first place? How will the blind, deaf, rebellious servant Israel be any different just because Cyrus has sent them home? The answer is: the Servant, ideal Israel, will give himself to be for and in Israel what Israel could never be in itself.[33]

Israel's call to be God's servant came in the giving of the Mosaic Law (Exod 19:5-6). Israel would serve God through obedience to the Law; yet as Isaiah had claimed, the servant's sin resulted in their captivity in Babylon.

So the "LORD formed me in the womb to be his servant to restore Jacob to Him and Israel to Him might be gathered" (Isa 49:5). Only Matthew includes Jesus' directly stated commitment to keep the Law (Matt 5:17-20). Then in two passages, Matthew refers to Jesus as the Servant fulfilling Isaiah: Matt 8:17 in healing fulfills Isa 53:4, and Matt 12:17-18 in His non-confrontational approach fulfills Isa 42:1-4.

---

[33] John N. Oswalt, *The Book of Isaiah: Chapters 40-66*, New International Commentary on the Old Testament (Grand Rapids, MI: Eerdmans, 1998), p. 287.

The roles to which Israel was called—to be the heir in God's plan and to serve under the theocracy of God's rule on earth—were only fulfilled through Israel's Representative Son and Servant. But this doesn't involve fulfillment of Israel's eschatology. Rather, what was fulfilled through Jesus Christ will enable Israel to fulfill her promised destiny.

The Promises to Abraham

Abraham, as Israel's forefather, receives promises of seed, of personal blessing, and of mediating blessings to others (Gen 12:1-3). The scope of mediation was to "all nations" (12:3b). While Abraham experienced initial fulfillment of all these promises, the focus for most of his life was on the seed. As is the case early in the Hebrew canon, the issue of who that seed would be was not clear: *zerah* (seed) is a collective noun, meaning either one or many. There are promises in which it means a single, immediate offspring (Gen 12:7; 13:15; 15:4; 17:16). Other promises directly state that the offspring will multiply into an innumerable number (Gen 13:16; 15:5; 22:17). Alexander has argued that the heir will be One.[34]

However, in Gen 15:1 God promised Abraham reward. This restated promise puzzled Abram because as of yet, Abram and Sarai had no offspring. In fact, Abram had settled in his own mind that Eliezer of Damascus would be his heir (Gen 15:2-3). The Lord corrected this compromise: "This one will not be your heir; instead one who comes from your own body will be your heir" (15:4, HCSB). This clarified a number of issues: in the promise of a seed, *one* would be his heir, his heir would be a physical offspring, and this heir could see a complete fulfillment of the promises given to Abraham (Gen 15:18-21). When Abram took God at His word and believed the fleshed out promise, God declared him to be righteous (Gen 15:6). But the complete identity of the one to be heir remained what Caird called "situation vacant."[35] The situation of what the heir would receive was clarified in the scope of the promises, but the historical identity remained vacant. Would it be Isaac? Would it be Jacob? As a reader read the narrative text, he would attempt to match the situation of each with the promises, but none of the successive immediate descendants fit in with all that was promised, so it remained vacant. Even for Moses, he gives no clues that he knew any more about the "situation vacant."

---

[34] T. Desmond Alexander, "Further Observations," pp. 363-67.

[35] Caird, *The Language and Imagery of the Bible*, pp. 54-61.

The New Testament authors recognized the historical Jesus as the descendant of Abraham who would fit the vacant situation promised (Matt 1:1-2; Luke 3:34). Paul also recognized this when writing to the churches in Galatia. Paul's issue concerned the blessings of God coming to Gentiles: would it be through works of the Law or through faith in Jesus Christ? Paul answered the question from Scripture in Gal 3:6-29. The answer consisted of two aspects.

First, the blessing of justification "Just as Abraham believed God, and it was credited to him for righteousness, then understand that those who have faith are Abraham's sons. Now the Scripture…told the good news ahead of time to Abraham, saying, 'All the nations will be blessed through you'" (3:6-9, HCSB, cf. Gen 12:3; 18:18). As it turned out, it was not through Abraham personally, but through Jesus Christ, Abraham's Seed and Heir (Gen 22:18; Gal 1:3-4).

The blessing of inheritance, including the Holy Spirit (Gal 3:14-24), was considered second. Paul had introduced the issue of blessing: "how did you receive the Spirit?" (Gal 3:3). There are two aspects to Paul's answer which are summarized in the two purpose clauses (*hina*) found in Gal 3:14: "The purpose was that the blessing of Abraham would come to Gentiles by Jesus Christ, that second we [Jews and Gentiles] could receive the promised Spirit through faith" (HCSB). Then to clarify that the promises were addressed to both Abraham and his heir: "Now the promises were spoken to Abraham and to his seed. He does not say 'and to seeds' as though referring to many but referring to one…who is Christ" (Gal 3:16, HCSB). His point does not rest on grammar but on history. The history of Abraham's descendants shows that none matched the situation of blessing all nations until Jesus Christ came. Thus, the Gentiles share Abraham's inheritance because they "have been baptized into Christ (and) have put on Christ like a garment"…they "belong to Christ." As a result, those Gentiles who have been baptized into Christ and in Christ only "are Abraham's seed and heirs according to promise" (Gal 3:27-29, HCSB).

The Church does not replace Israel, who through their Representative-Son will also receive their promised inheritance. Rather, the Church is unexpectedly added along with Israel. Together, they are blessed because of Abraham and because of Jesus Christ. The Church merely receives the down payment of the inheritance, the Holy Spirit (Eph 1:13-14). Thus, the Church is blessed *in Christ* while Israel will be blessed *through their Representative, Jesus Christ* in His Second Advent and receive the complete inheritance.

Promise to David

David, as king in Jerusalem, was promised an eternal kingdom (2 Sam 7:11-16). This promise was identified as incorporated in a covenant according to Ps 89:3. It included the establishing of David's offspring forever and the building up of David's throne for all generations (Ps 89:4). As a *maskil* of Ethan the Ezrahite, the kingdom featured the earthly people of Israel.

> This psalm seizes chiefly on the clause 'forever' which the turn of events seemed to have flatly contradicted…Instead of railing at the promise or explaining it away, it faces the full clash of words and event in an appeal to God to show His hand. Like an unresolved discord, it therefore impels us towards the New Testament.[36]

Matthew saw Jesus as the Messiah, the son of David (Matt 1:1, 6, 16). Luke likewise saw Jesus as He began His ministry as the Son of David (Luke 3:31). In both accounts, Jesus was anointed by the Father with the Holy Spirit at His baptism (Matt 3:13-17; Luke 3:21-22). So He was acknowledged by God in His person as the One who would fulfill the covenant promise, the Messiah.

When Jesus preached the kingdom of heaven was at hand, it was a message that was true because the Anointed One was the Son of David. The kingdom of heaven existed in heaven (Matt 6:10), but the kingdom of heaven was announced on earth by heaven's authorized King. As evidence of heaven's rule on earth, the Messiah performed miracles over the powers of evil as tokens of the heavenly rule (Matthew 8–9). The anointed King laid claim to the Davidic promise in the triumphal entry into Jerusalem in the fashion of Zech 9:9. However, because of His rejection and subsequent crucifixion, the Davidic kingdom did not appear on earth at that time (cf. Deut 17:15).

Earlier in Matthew's account, the Pharisees rejected Jesus' heavenly authority by attributing His exorcisms to the power of Beelzebub (Matt 12:24). This rejection was followed by Jesus' introduction of parables consisting of mysteries of the kingdom of heaven (Matt 13:10-17). This was revelation about the kingdom of heaven that was added to what has been revealed in the Davidic Covenant. The presence of God's rule on earth, inaugurated at Pentecost, was to be seen in the preached Word that germinated and grew in the hearts and lives of those who understood

---

[36] Derek Kidner, *Psalms 73–150* (London: IVP, 1975), p. 319.

(Matt 13:1-9, 18-53), who held on to the Word and by enduring, bore fruit (Luke 8:4-8, 11-15). While the rule of God on earth through the preached Word of Messiah will be real, it is not the Davidic kingdom.

However, Saucy argues that the Davidic kingdom is present in this age. He argues that Jesus' ascension "was in fulfillment of Psalm 110:1 and proved that Jesus had been installed as Messiah (Acts 2:36)."[37] However, this argument for a current Davidic kingdom is misleading for two reasons.

First, Saucy's arguments are not Peter's argument. Peter argues from Ps 16:10 that Jesus' *resurrection* spoke of Him as *Messiah* (Acts 2:29-32). In addition, from Ps 110:1, Jesus' *exaltation* spoke of Him as *Lord* (Acts 2:33-36) rather than Messiah. While Jesus is both David's Son and David's Lord, the two say something distinct about Him (Matt 22:41-46). To be Son is to share David's life and inheritance and to be Lord is to deserve David's worship. So Peter's argument does not claim that His ascension demonstrates that He is Messiah, seated on David's throne.

Second, the reign according to the order of David is distinct from the reign according to the order of Melchizedek. While both occupy God's throne, the thrones are distinct involving different throne rights. From the heavenly throne, the Lord shares the Father's universal reign according to the order of Melchizedek. Accordingly, in His present session, He awaits the LORD who will defeat the Lord's enemies surrounding Zion (Ps 110:1). That, as of now, has not yet come. In His present heavenly session, by oath, He exercises a priestly ministry on behalf of called believers on earth (Ps 110:5). From the earthly throne, Messiah will mediate God's delegated reign on earth and rule with a rod of iron (Ps 2:8-9; Rev 2:27). This reign will silence any rebellion due to evil, even though evil is not eliminated until the end (Rev 20:7-10).

This distinction between an earthly and a heavenly reign is also expressed in Jesus' parables of the mysteries of the kingdom. The pending expression of Jesus' reign is seen in the life and fruitfulness of His planted Word. This realm on earth will also include evil seed planted by the enemy (Satan). Their appearance at stages is indistinguishable from the Lord's seed (Matt 13:24-30, 36-43). This permissive presence of sown evil in the kingdom is distinct from the binding of Satan at the climactic age of the kingdom in history (Rev 20:1-3) and reigning with the rod of iron in the Millennial Kingdom (Rev 12:5; 19:15).

---

[37] Saucy, *The Case for Progressive Dispensationalism*, pp. 69-76.

The New Covenant Promised to the House of Israel and the House of Judah

Since a covenant is an arrangement between stated parties (partners), the author of Hebrews retains the parties stated in the Old Testament (Heb 8:8-12; 10:16-17). The author does not claim that the New Covenant is fulfilled with the Church as the covenant partner. Rather, Jesus was the Mediator of the New Covenant (Heb 9:15). In His death on the cross, the New Covenant was ratified (Heb 9:14). The Lord revealed this in His last supper with the disciples, "This cup that is poured out for you is the new covenant in my blood" (Luke 22:20).

The Book of Hebrews explains the Church's relationship to the New Covenant.[38] It seems preferable to understand that the Church is not party to the covenant thus sharing in the fulfillment of the covenant. Rather, the explanation is fleshed out in the context of Heb 9:15-17 in which the term *diathēkē* is used in two distinct senses.

1. In Heb 9:15, Jesus Christ is the Mediator of a new *diathēkē* (covenant) so that those who are called might receive the promise of the eternal inheritance, because a death has taken place for redemption from transgressions committed under the first *diathēkē* (covenant).

2. In Heb 9:16, in which a *diathēkē* (last will and testament) exists, the death of the will-maker must occur for it (the will) to be enacted. And in 9:17: A *diathēkē* (last will) is valid only when people die, since it is never in force while the will-maker is still living.

So as believers in the Church are called, they become benefactors of the last will and testament (*diathēkē*) through receiving the gospel. They are not shared parties with Israel to the fulfillment of the New Covenant. On the other hand, when all Israel is saved (Rom 11:26), Israel will become party to the New Covenant so that they can realize all that God has promised for them to bring blessings to all Gentiles.

---

[38] The longest single quotation of an Old Testament text in the New Testament is found in Hebrews. The text of Jer 31:31-34 is found in Hebrews 8 and 10 and forms a key point of the argument of the book. See Elliott Johnson, "The Church Has an Indirect Relationship to the New Covenant" *Dispensational Understanding of the New Covenant*, ed. Mike Stallard, (Schaumburg, IL: Regular Baptist Books, 2012), pp. 164-75.

Conclusion

Thus, there is discontinuity between the stewardships Israel and the Church have in history. All models must consider the consequences of Israel's rejection of her Messiah. On the other hand, there is continuity featuring the revelation concerning Israel's Messiah. There is no level of fulfillment of Israel's eschatology already present in the coming of Messiah in the Abrahamic and Davidic Covenants. There is an eschatological fulfillment for Israel in each promissory covenant: the Abrahamic, the Davidic, and the New Covenant (Rom 9:4). Peter, speaking to the Sanhedrin in Israel, said:

> That seasons of refreshing may come from the presence of the Lord [cf. Acts 3:20 with Acts 1:6-7], and that He may send Jesus, who was appointed for you [Israel] as Messiah. Heaven must welcome Him until the times of the restoration of all things, which God spoke about by the mouth of His holy prophets from the beginning. (Acts 3:19-21)

So the everlasting kingdom, promised to David, and Israel's possession of land, promised to Abraham, are included in the eschatology that the New Testament expects.

From this brief response to the issues raised in the recent literature, the introduction will be concluded with an answer to the following question:

What is Dispensationalism? It is a narrative Biblical theology.

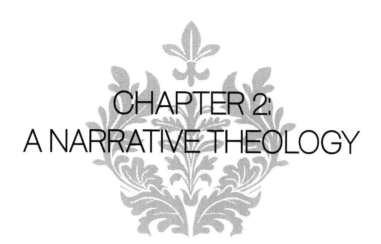

CHAPTER 2:
A NARRATIVE THEOLOGY

Introduction

We who have been exposed to the Dispensational tradition appreciate the heritage in Biblical exposition, yet that interest seems to be waning. While the reasons are varied, the ones related to the text of Scripture are relevant to the task at hand. Perhaps we have lost confidence in the power of the Scriptures. Or it may be that we've found it easier to study a verse alone or a collection of verses. Or we have lost sight that the meaning of a verse is conditioned by the near context. And without considering the whole story, we may only bring our own context to the text. After all, we are the ones who want to hear in our world. And in the new hermeneutic, this is sufficient. Or perhaps most seriously, we have lost confidence that we can receive a Word from God. This volume is intended to recover and to refocus our attention on the issues which will enable us to see the whole of Scripture based on study of individual books. This section will focus on issues from three necessary categories: *theological*, *Biblical*, and *narratival*.

Theological

The principle focus of our study needs to be on God. He is both the initiating Author of the text and at the same time, the primary Actor in the historical account. It is God's story. So His story concerns both what He *says* to historical characters and what the account of each book says that He *does* in history. And based on the creation account of Genesis 1, priority is given to what God says; He speaks and creation comes into existence. So in keeping with this priority, our study needs to be restricted to the Scriptures, which provide a reliable and authoritative foundation to ground our interpretation of salvation history.[1]

The goal of this study of theology is to apprehend what the Scripture says about God, His Person, His message, and His ways. *Apprehension* is to be distinguished from *comprehension*. This distinction is necessary because God is both incomprehensible and yet knowable.[2] We seek to apprehend what is said in the text, which may exceed our ability to understand completely, but is not an unreasonable pursuit.

This phenomenon is illustrated in Jesus' confrontation of His generation's unbelief when He questioned how Scripture could say that Messiah was both David's Son (cf. 2 Sam 7:12-16) and David's Lord (Ps 110:1; Mark 12:28-37). Jesus had just said that the Lord's great commandment involved loving the Lord with *all one's mind* (Mark 12:30). To love with one's mind means to hear and to see all that is written—to apprehend the text as it is written.

That generation's perception of Jesus was represented by a scribe who said he agreed with Jesus, yet he said, you love with *all your understanding* (Mark 12:33). And that is the distinction between *apprehend* and *comprehend*. We can apprehend Jesus' claim to be God yet He appears to be a man. That was also what the Scriptures affirmed but man cannot fully *understand* that. As a result, that generation condemned Jesus of blasphemy (Mark 14:64).

Another way to consider our knowledge of God is to understand that it is both factual and personal. This approach is comparable to how knowledge works in any personal relationship. We can know truths (facts) about a person but our knowledge of the person is so much more than those facts. We enjoy their company. We engage in conversation, agree with some things, and disagree with others. And yet, we often fail to understand what is fully happening at the interpersonal level.

So it is with God. There are facts about who God is and what He does that we only apprehend. This is true in God's predestination and foreknowledge.

God's predestined plan involves mystery built into the creation. The predetermined plan in which God knew every detail included the

---

[1]   See essays by Albert Mohler, "When the Bible Speaks, God Speaks: The Classic Doctrine of Biblical Inerrancy," and Kevin Vanhoozer "Augustine Inerrancy: Literary Meaning, Literal Truth, and Literate Interpretation in the Economy of Biblical Discourse," in *Five Views on Biblical Inerrancy* (Grand Rapids, MI: Zondervan, 2013), pp. 29-58 and 199-235, respectively.

[2]   Charles C. Ryrie, *Basic Theology* (Wheaton, IL: Victor, 1986), p. 25.

participation of chosen human partners created in God's own image.[3] So when God created man, as a person, mankind shared self-awareness and self-determination with God.[4] *The Westminster Confession* (1646) states the combination well:

> Although in relation to the foreknowledge and decree of God, the first cause, all things come to pass immutably and infallibly, yet by the same providence he ordereth them to fall out, according to the nature of the second causes, either necessarily, freely, or contingently.[5]

And those secondary causes feature the partnership with chosen individuals. How this tension between sovereign determination and human self-determination is worked out is an aspect of the mystery.[6] Yet Paul "never had any doubt that the power to which he surrendered was the constraint of love" (2 Cor 5:14; Gal 2:20).[7]

So God's governance is beyond full rational comprehension, a fact that places His governance beyond human attempts at control (Job 38–42). Yet God's sovereign rule does not contradict what is reasonable. This means that partnership involves managing one's life[8] by faith in what God has said; living as a steward in obedience based on what God says in love. And in that partnership, the steward comes to love the One who chose him in love. Finally, it is a partnership in which the partner often

---

[3] Predestination and foreknowledge are difficult terms to grasp. Since God is outside of His creation and thus outside of time, God's determination and knowledge are simultaneous. They exist before the creation. God is omniscient and knows all possible plans of creation in every detail. Upon determining His plan, He has knowledge of every detail in the plan. God then acts in the history of creation as He has determined according to what He knows.

[4] Walter Eichrodt, *Theology of the Old Testament*, vol. 2 (Philadelphia: Westminster), p. 126.

[5] *The Westminster Confession* (Atlanta: John Knox, 1646, 1963), 5.2.200.

[6] Man has creaturely self-determination. This entails limited freedom of choice. He cannot choose to become another person, change his date of birth, or change what talents he has. The mystery concerns how God allows genuine creaturely choice yet maintains His governing predestination. "By the very nature of the case there is not intermediate means between God (the primary efficient cause) and humans (the secondary efficient causes) of free actions. God is the cause of the fact of freedom and humans are the causes of the acts of freedom…God gives people power (of free choice), but they exercise it without coercion. Thus God is responsible for bestowing freedom, but humans are responsible for behaving with it" (Norman Geisler, "God Knows All Things," in *Predestination and Freedom*, ed. Basinger and Basinger [Downers Grove, IL: IVP, 1986], p. 79). At the fall of the human race into sin, man did not lose self-determination, but his self-awareness was darkened. No longer did man see himself as a servant of God, but as one who can be like God in His power. With his awareness fallen, he chose as a slave to lie and sinned.

[7] Caird, *The Language and Imagery of the Bible*, p. 24.

[8] John K. Goodrich, *Paul as an Administrator of God in 1 Corinthians*, Society for New Testament Studies Monograph Series, 152 (Cambridge: Cambridge University Press, 2012).

is surprised by the revelation of God's glory and is in a position of awe as he worships. Thus, the relationship of chosen partners involves a study resulting in personal knowledge including wonder and love.

These realities in the study of Biblical Theology find their place within God's universal kingdom.[9] This kingdom extends over all reality which exists intact without loss or challenge. From His position as universal Sovereign, God created the heavens and the earth. Then in the creation of Adam, He delegated to him the responsibility of mediating God's rule on earth. Yet in Adam's self-determination, God permitted him to rebel and sin entered the world and the human race.

Thus, it was God's mediatorial kingdom on earth that was challenged and lost. Adam had followed the word of the serpent who spoke as the enemy of God (Gen 3:1-6). Now the fallen human race was ruled by the prince of the power of the air (Eph 2:2), the ruler of the world (John 12:31). In God's plan to redeem captive mankind and to restore his mediatorial rule on earth, God chose Eve and her chosen offspring to partner in conflict against God's enemy (Gen 3:15).

Later in the story, Paul saw himself and Apollos as *stewards* of God's revelation (1 Cor 4:1-5). God's governance in a world under Satan's rule featured His progressive revelation. As God had spoken creation into existence (Genesis 1:1–2:3), so in history, God entrusted His historic revelation to *stewards* who were to *manage* their lives according to God's revelation in order to bring blessing to all nations (Gen 12:3; Exod 19:5-6).

But this theological narrative forces us to face a puzzling question: how does the story indicate that God governs the direction of man who is created to determine his own course? How can that be?

Biblical

The answer to our theological question, as Paul later says, will never be fully comprehended: "who are you, a mere man, to talk back to God, Will what is formed say to the One who formed it, 'Why did you make me like this?'" (Rom 9:20). Yet the two perspectives in the relationship can be apprehended—God governs and man either believes or disbelieves. The tension created, complicated by sin is clarified further during the Lord's First Advent and later expanded by Paul. Paul's expansion clarifies aspects of God's governance while Jesus speaks about God teaching

---

[9] Alva J. McClain, *The Greatness of the Kingdom* (Winona Lake, IN: BMH, 1974), pp. 3-64.

individuals who believe. Thus, we will follow the order considering God's broad governance first, and then consider God's particular teaching.

God's Governance

Paul compares God's actions in the lives of vessels of wrath and of vessels of mercy. The comparison features the voice of verbs (active or passive) referring to actions preparing for wrath or for mercy (Rom 9:22-23). God as the Potter has the right over the lump of clay to endure vessels of wrath *made ready* (passive) for destruction (Rom 9:22). He endures some to make known the riches of His glory in others, whom God *prepared* (active) vessels of mercy beforehand for glory (Rom 9:23). While God governs providentially in all people's lives, He endures some who are being made ready and He prepares others to be recipients of mercy. The absence of the subject of being made ready implies that there may be many influences toward evil. On the other hand, unequivocally God is the cause from the beginning to prepare people to receive mercy. While God may include other secondary causes, He is the primary cause in bringing mercy. This raises another question: what does God do to be merciful?

God's Teaching

What God does to *prepare* vessels of mercy (Rom 9:23) had been summarized in Rom 8:30, "those he *predestined*, he also *called*, and those he *called*, he also *justified* and those he *justified*, he also *glorified*" (emphasis added). This work of preparation that we consider involves what God does between His *call* and His work of *justification*.

Jesus explored these preparatory works when He considered the many disciples who were complaining that Jesus' teaching was hard to accept (John 6:60-70). The words were demanding because they could not be comprehended (John 6:60). Earlier, Jesus had distinguished those who would come to Him, they would be drawn by the Father to Him (John 6:44). This work of drawing was a work revealed by the prophets: "they will *all* be *taught* by God" (John 6:45, emphasis added; cf. Isa 54:13). Then Jesus clarified what was necessary to be taught: "Everyone who *has heard* and *learned from* the Father comes to me" (John 6:45, emphasis added). In similar language, Moses spoke about his generation: "to this day, the LORD has not given you a mind *to understand*, eyes *to see*, ears *to hear*" (Deut 29:4, HCSB, emphasis added). So in the work of preparation, God gives this gift. God's Spirit illumines (Isa 52:15; 64:4): giving eyes to see, ears to hear, and a mind to apprehend. Then the Father's teaching, heard in the words of Jesus, persuades. Being persuaded, the hearer *believes*. And by faith, God *justifies*.

That response of faith is illustrated by the twelve. As many other disciples were leaving, Jesus asked the twelve: "you don't want to go away too, do you?" (John 6:67, HCSB). Peter speaking for the group asked, "Lord to whom shall we go? You have the words of eternal life" (John 6:68).

Peter's response did not include the current discussion: eating Jesus' flesh or drinking His blood. Rather it referred to what Jesus had said earlier, "I tell you the solemn truth, the one who believes has eternal life" (John 6:47, NET). Then Peter added: "we have come to *believe* and to *know* that you are the Holy One of God" (John 6:69, NET, emphasis added). Thus, learning begins with believing in the One whose words need to be heard. In time, believing will bring one to apprehend in the Spirit's illumination of what Jesus says.

So the answer to our question of the resolution of the tension between a holy God and fallen human creatures is clarified. This tension is further intensified by the active opposition of evil. Jesus' answer remains within the parameters of humans created "in the image of God" (Gen 1:26; 9:6). Stewards of God's Word respond because they are persuaded to believe, having listened and been convinced by God's Word. God remains in control as He governs salvation history even as He spoke creation into existence. God remains God. Man is called who shares God's image. But would man, even though drawn by God's Word, be sufficient to resolve the conflict between God and the enemy Satan? That question remains to be answered as the story continues.

Narrative

The canon of Scripture consists of sixty-six books, yet the combination tells a complete story. This story has a beginning, middle, and end. In a Dispensational telling of the story, the progress is measured by a series of dispensations.

The number of dispensations measures the stages in the fulfillment of God's purposes until these purposes are completed. Ryrie follows that traditional pattern of seven dispensations although he concedes that "the number of the dispensational scheme and even the names of the dispensations are relatively minor matters. Presumably one could have four, five, or seven...and be a consistent dispensationalist as long as the scheme is true to three essentials"[10] I would like to propose a scheme with four dispensations and then to restate the three essentials.

First, Four Dispensations

The number of dispensations follows from the natural stages that advance God's purpose to fulfillment. Since the canon consists of God's story, the stages, when introduced, follow God's pursuit of His purposes to conclusion.

The Introduction of God's Purposes

The Setting of the story, Genesis 1–11, *introduces* God's purposes in history. God's purposes include the creation of man to mediate God's rule in the realm of the earth (Genesis 1), and then the redemption of fallen man (Genesis 2–3). Rather than God immediately pursuing action to realize His purposes, He allows mankind to pursue their own way (Genesis 4–11). The only actions God initiates are to choose an elect line (Gen 5:1-32; 11:10-32) and to bring judgment to restrict the spread of evil (the flood and the division of languages).

The Four Dispensations

- *Promise*—purposed to introduce God's plan
- *Law*—purposed to identify within Israel the one who would meet the responsibilities of the Law to partner with God to complete the plan
- *Grace*—purposed to bring redemptive blessings to all nations through the governance of the ascended Christ through the Church
- *Kingdom*—purposed to restore the mediatorial reign of Christ through Israel, along with the Church, in the realm of the earth

Second, Three Essentials

- A distinction between Israel and the Church—The question raised here concerns whether promises addressed to Israel can in some sense be fulfilled in the Church. What is addressed to Israel will be kept distinct from what is addressed to the Church. Some of what is addressed to Israel is fulfilled in Christ, the Representative Israelite. Then the Representative enables Israel to

---

[10] Ryrie, *Dispensationalism*, p. 45.

realize the nation's calling. The Church in Christ may share in Christ's inheritance without replacing Israel.

- A system of hermeneutics involving normal language interpretation. Such normal interpretation seeks a textual meaning determined by the Author/author as expressed in the text. While the hearer is an active partner in the communication, interpreting the author's message, he doesn't determine the meaning. The author determines the meaning at the level of his whole composition, recognized as a *willed type knowledge*.[11]

- The glory of God revealed is the ultimate goal in the history of the earth. This goal is demonstrated as God achieves His purposes in spite of the permission of evil and the allowance of the enemy to set the terms of the conflict in history.

This narrative Biblical Theology will seek to adhere to these three essentials. In this introduction of the scheme, the three components of the overall narrative will focus on the essentials of the story.

Thus, the narrative takes the shape of an overall story:

Beginning: Setting
Middle: Plot conflict with three dispensations
End: Conflict resolution with a climactic dispensation

Genesis 1–11 as Setting

Five normative features are introduced. Normative indicates the revelation is foundational and complete, framing the structures for fallen human life in history.

Creation: Complete but Unrealized

The Creator speaks and the creation comes into existence. It is complete since all that is necessary to the creation is spoken into existence. No new creation would be added to the creation as though something were missing. While it is complete, the potential for the reproduction of life forms under the rule of man awaits the history of the earth to follow. Lurking in the background is the unexplained beginning found in Gen 1:2. Yet the creation holds out hope that through an effectual mediation

---

[11] E. D. Hirsh, *Validity in Interpretation*, pp. 24-67.

of God's rule, God's glory as Creator would shine forth in the lives of mankind in history.

Conflict: Between Man and His Creator

Unexpectedly, the serpent appears (Gen 3:1) to induce humanity to question God's Word which warranted rebellion against His Word (Gen 3:1-5). This conflict between the Creator and His creatures was spawned by God's enemy, the serpent. Rebellion against God's Word was rebellion against the structure that God had spoken into existence in creation. And when Adam took a bite of the fruit, his relationship with God died (Gen 2:17). When Adam listened to the serpent, the serpent's word took control of Adam and the realm he once ruled was lost to the enemy. Under God's permission of evil, His universal kingdom remained intact, from which judgment against the serpent was pronounced (3:14-15). And this verdict framed the conflict that would inform the interpretation of history.

Conflict: Between Woman and the Serpent

God permits the conflict the serpent introduced and correctly interprets it. It is not a conflict between the Creator and His creatures but rather a conflict between evil and the creatures. The first generation of conflict was between Eve (1 Tim 2:14) and the enemy of God. That would be followed by descendants of Eve who would be attacked by descendants of the enemy-serpent (Gen 3:15). Cain demonstrated that against Abel (Gen 4:1-24). Then God gave Seth to replace Abel (Gen 4:25-26). Seth introduced a line of Eve's offspring, one in each generation (Gen 5:1-32; 11:10-32). In conflict with the elect line, descendants of Cain arose and the human race was overwhelmed by evil.

A final display of the conflict was marked by the serpent's return to do conflict with a climactic descendant of the woman (Gen 3:15c). That conflict will involve death blows from each one. Since God pronounced judgment against the serpent-enemy, the serpent will be condemned but the working out of the final conflict remains unknown.

Covering before God

Adam then faced two pronouncements of judgment: one against himself (Gen 2:17) and the other against the serpent carried out by the woman's offspring (Gen 3:15c). When he named his wife Eve—mother of the living—it expressed his faith in God. This faith believed God's promise to bring an offspring from them to judge the evil one and to somehow deal with the judgment of immediate death because they ate the fruit (Gen 2:17). When God provided skin covering (Gen 3:21), the skin came from a sacrifice bearing their judgment. While Adam and Eve now had a covering to approach God (Gen 4:4; 8:20; 12:7-8), they lost the intimate relationship which the garden had provided (Gen 3:22-24).

Nations Delegated with Authority to Restrain Evil

Sin that arose in Cain (Gen 4:1-24) spread unchecked through the human race, to the point of bringing grief to the Creator (Gen 6:1-8). Only elect Noah (Gen 5:1-32) found favor and grace in the eyes of the LORD. After a worldwide flood "to bring an end to all flesh" (Gen 6:13), God established His own covenant with Noah (Gen 9:9, 11).

The Noahic Covenant would frame fallen human life. While God would never again judge with a worldwide flood (Gen 9:12-17), God remained as Judge of the human race. The new world bathed by the flood had a new environment (Gen 8:22). Humanity would be delegated with authority to judge anyone who took human life (Gen 9:5-7). This authority would be distributed among the nations.

Thus, Genesis 1–11 left a refashioned world that included the invasion of evil. God's universal reign remained unchallenged, yet the permission of evil in the realm of the earth resulted in the mediatorial reign of man lost. This realm, including mankind, was now ruled by the serpent. Jesus would call Satan "the ruler of this world" (John 12:31). This introduced the two purposes of history: the salvation of man from evil and the restoration of man's mediatorial rule of God on earth. These purposes introduced in primeval history found no resolution, yet set the stage for the history of the earth. In history, they would find resolution.

Middle: Plot Conflict

In Gen 3:15, the verdict announced against the serpent introduced a core conflict which would define the narrative interpretation of the fallen history of the earth.

The plot-conflict is delineated in the Book of Job. The conflict is introduced in the heavenlies between the Lord and Satan (Job 1:6). Job's life of righteousness was an occasion to bring honor to the Lord before Satan (Job 1:8). Yet Satan challenges the validity of his righteousness based on Job's motivation (Job 1:9-11). And the Lord allowed Satan to introduce conflict into Job's life within boundaries that the Lord maintains (Job 1:12). Satan's contention was that Job under attack would curse God and ask to die (Job 1:11).

The conflict came in disease and in criticism from friends offered as mistaken helpful counsel. Job found no comfort from his friends but only was comforted in prayer as he drew strength from a growing awareness of God and from an expressed confidence in His love and mercy. But in spite of Job's intense suffering, he never cursed God.

In the end, God spoke to Job, not to give explanations but to assure him of His own supreme sufficiency (Job 38–41). And in Job's suffering, God was glorified before a hidden Satan and in the eyes of Job's wife and friends. In God's glory, Job's well-being was restored (Job 42).

The *progressive revelation* that follows in the canon of completed Scripture focuses on the resolution of the plot-conflict. The dispensation of promise, to which was added the dispensation of law, addresses the key question: will a divinely enabled human steward resolve the conflict between God and Satan? The answer is a sad no. Chosen individuals would be entrusted with God's revelation as stewards, yet the power of evil would be so overwhelming that none would prove to be sufficient— not Abraham, nor Moses, nor David. Still God's *Word* stood firm.

In the *dispensation of promise*, God's promises stood firm because God was committed to bringing deliverance and blessing. Still, the stewards entrusted with the promises were unwilling to fully trust the One who promised. While stewards fell short, God's commitment remained firm. Somehow God would make it happen. Embedded in the promise were promised effectual agents—the Seed of the woman, the Son of David, the Arm of the Lord. Each of these anticipated agents implied God's anointing to be effectual. The name *Messiah* didn't necessarily appear but divine assurance did. An agent was promised as one to be anointed by God's Spirit to accomplish His purposes and will. So Peter interprets Ps 16:10 as David speaking concerning the resurrection of Messiah (Acts 2:31). The name Messiah is not mentioned. Then Peter adds, based on the First Advent, this prophesied resurrection is the resurrection of Jesus (Acts 2:32). This Messianic Steward of God's *Word* would cling to the truth of the promise in spite of the threats of evil and the experience of death.

Messiah was recognized in the *dispensation of law*. Law was added in the Mosaic Covenant to the promise to focus Israel's attention on their responsibility as called to be God's elect people. When their responsibility was repeatedly violated, Israel was forced to face its need for an adequate sacrifice and for a sufficient deliverer to bring the promised blessing. Thus, man's insufficiency was exposed, but at the same time, God and His promise inspired hope for the promised Agent. There undoubtedly was a remnant in each generation, as suggested to Elijah (1 Kgs 19:14, 18), and illustrated by Simeon and Anna (Luke 2:25-28, 36-38), who trusted God and believed that God's agent would come.

It was only in the incarnation that the conflict between God and Satan would be resolved. Human stewards had experienced God's blessing but in the end, each fell short. When God became flesh in Jesus the Messiah, only then did Jesus fully rely on God and what He had said as in the wilderness (Matt 4:1-11). In the power of God's Spirit anointing (Luke 4:16-37), He invaded Satan's domain by healing. These miracles demonstrated the reestablishment of the effectual mediation of God's rule under the Law as proclaimed in the message of the kingdom of heaven come near (Matt 4:17).

In time, as the nation's rejection grew, Jesus surrendered to Satan's power of death (Matt 16:21). And in His death, a sufficient sacrifice for mankind was provided. In His resurrection from the dead, as a work of the Father through the Spirit, deliverance unto eternal life was provided (Ps 2:7). Thus, the resolution of the conflict of Gen 3:15 was introduced as Messiah *overcame* the enemy of God. Yet the enemy remained since he had not yet experienced *final judgment*.

In the *dispensation of grace* and the *dispensation of the kingdom*, the resolution of the conflict would be worked out to full realization. In the dispensation of grace, as the conflict with sin and death remained for mankind, the *gospel* message carried the seed of full realization—the power of God unto salvation to everyone who believes (Rom 1:16). For the unbeliever, the gospel promises the justification of life (Acts 13:39), deliverance from the penalty of sin. For the believer, the gospel promises sanctification to new life, deliverance from the power of sin through the Holy Spirit. For the believer, the gospel also holds out hope for glorification, deliverance from the presence of sin.

End: Conflict Resolution

In the *dispensation of the kingdom*, the conflict which had been *overcome* is finally *resolved* in the Second Advent of Messiah. That resolution begins with judgment upon evil which drives the nations to oppose God, even the nation Israel who was overcome by that evil, and upon Satan who ultimately drives that evil. With nations judged and Satan bound, the kingdom of heaven come to earth would be inaugurated. Messiah would rule with a rod of iron in a fallen world to fulfill the creation design introduced at the outset (Ps 2:8-9; Rev 2:27; 19:15). Further, the saints in Israel will rule with Him on earth as the Church joins Messiah as His bride for 1000 years. This resolution is marked by conflict being overcome in the salvation in Messiah and being resolved as the conflict itself would be defeated. So in a final rebellion of Satan, evil is defeated in a *final judgment* (Rev 20:7-10). Now the creation of a new heaven and a new earth is in order (Revelation 21:1–22:5). The old had been fulfilled. The new could be introduced.

Conclusion

A Dispensational Biblical Theology is a narrative of God's governance of salvation history. That governance about which Dispensationalism is concerned is a subset of God's universal providential governance. It is within God's universal reign that God spoke creation into existence (Genesis 1). And it is within creation that God created man to mediate God's reign over the realm of the earth (Gen 1:26-28). That reign would be mediated through Adam as a steward of God's *Word*.

However, the invasion of evil in the newly created earth appeared without explanation. And Adam lost his mediated role and the reign over the earth was usurped by the serpent. In so doing, the enemy of God positioned man also as an enemy of God, which introduced death (Gen 4:8). In the breakdown of the structures of creation, the very definition of life was challenged (Gen 6:1-4). While God's judgments that followed (Genesis 6:5–11:9) limited the destructive and rapid spread of evil, they did not promote progress toward reaching God's stated purposes.

Movements toward the introduction of God's plan included the pronouncement of the final verdict against the serpent (Gen 3:15) and the election of a line of Eve's offspring through whom God's plan would be carried out (Gen 5:1-32; 11:10-32). The question was: would their conflict with evil be effective to overcome?

The plan introduced God's *Word* of promise addressed to Abraham in the elect line (Gen 12:1-3). The *Word* promised a certain outcome assured by God's commitment. But was the *Word* sufficient: outspoken in what it guaranteed, bold in holding forth the salvation, persuasive as received by spiritually enlightened elect ones?

Yet, as history would demonstrate, they would be selectively effective but none were completely effective. And collectively among the elect, it was no match for evil. That is until the *Word* that had been spoken took on human flesh. That living *Word* would hold on tenaciously to the spoken *Word* and experience the commitments of God to deliver and to bless. Only the *Word*, fully God and fully man, living and dying, would discover God the *Father* faithful through the power of God the *Spirit* in resurrection. In this coalition of the three persons of the Godhead, God's *glory* burst forth. And this coalition of persons set the paradigm of grace in salvation for unbelievers and believers that would follow in the Church. Finally, God the Son would return to judge and to rule in the name of God the *Father* through the power of God the *Spirit*. The unrealized purpose of creation would be realized. God's *glory* is fully displayed in the progress of revelation through the four dispensations of Biblical history. The purposes of God's plan have been realized in spite of the sustained, powerful challenge of evil.

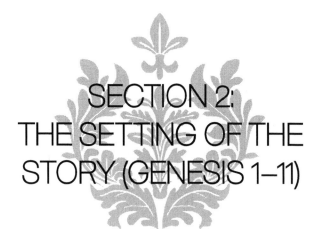

SECTION 2:
THE SETTING OF THE
STORY (GENESIS 1–11)

Introduction to the Setting (Genesis 1–11)

The shape of the canon creates the initial expectations of the role of Genesis 1–11. In the telling of a story, there are certain facts, events, and themes which *set the stage* for readers to be prepared to grasp the story that is about to be told. This role leads to a search for such *themes* that will control the flow of the plot-conflict about to unfold in the account of Biblical history. Before these themes are considered, a question needs to be asked. Are those expectations warranted based on the textual composition found in Genesis 1–11?

The answer rests in the distinctive composition of the narrative in Genesis 1–11 when compared to the composition of Genesis 12–50.[1] These distinctions provide support that the role of setting is in fact warranted.

First, there is a distinction in *the period of history* treated. Genesis 1–11 is considered *primeval-history* because of the broad chronology of the events addressed: creation, fall, flood, and Tower of Babel. This is distinct from the relatively shorter chronology of the history of the patriarchs in Genesis 12–50: Abraham, Isaac, Jacob, and Joseph and his brothers.

Second, there is a distinction in the *structure* of the themes treated. Genesis 1–11 introduces the beginnings of history, thus the name Genesis. These beginnings highlight themes that form the basis of the plot structure treated in the history developed in Genesis 12–50. There are

---

[1]   Many interpreters have recognized the distinctive nature of Genesis 1–11. For example see Peter C. Craigie, *The Old Testament: Its Background, Growth, and Content* (Nashville, TN: Abingdon Press, 1986), p. 106; Kenneth A. Mathews, *Genesis 1–11:26*, New American Commentary, ed. E. Ray Clendenen (Nashville, TN: Broadman & Holman Publishers, 1996), p. 26; and Gordon J. Wenham, *Genesis 1–15*, vol. 1, Word Biblical Commentary, ed. David A. Hubbard and Glenn W. Barker (Waco, TX: Word Books, 1987), pp. 1-lii.

three themes introduced in Genesis 1–11 that provide the necessary structure for the historical account.

1. The theme related to the point or purpose of creation

2. The theme related to the goal of creation

3. The theme related to the conflict within the plot of history

These three themes form the basic plot structure of the Biblical story.

The *first* theme introduces the rationale for the existence of the earth. The Biblical account of life is reasonable even though it fails to provide a rationalistic explanation. The beginning of the account in Gen 1:1-3 hints at a reasonable occasion for creation. Creation has a point or purpose from God's perspective, but the full disclosure of that purpose remains within God and His will to reveal them. However, mankind participates in a reasonable world.[2]

The *second* theme indicates that the Biblical account of history is not simply cyclical. At the outset, the narrative does not account for the seasons of the year and the sequence of the years, but God has a goal which is worked or accomplished through history. The story related in historical terms progresses towards the realization of a goal and this brings a basis for hope. God is superintending the process in history toward a revealed but unrealized goal of the mediated rule of God through man on the earth. This goal contributes to the meaningfulness of history and the value of human life.

The *third* theme provides an account of the *conflict* within the history of the created earth. But the Biblical account is unique when compared to other Ancient Near Eastern (ANE) explanations of creation. All other accounts include conflict from the very beginning but the Biblical account of creation explains that history begins without conflict under the absolute control of God. It is a monotheistic creation. Conflict is allowed to enter history as a challenge to God and a challenge for the survival of His creatures. But with God, man can be saved from the conflict and its consequences, as well as inherit a share in God's victory over the challenge.

In Genesis, "In the beginning God" (1:1) sets God apart from creation and in supreme control over His creatures and their place in history. While conflict is characteristic of human existence, the Creator is prior to and in control of that conflict which even serves God's own purposes. Following the introduction of the conflict in Genesis 3, the remainder of

---

2   G. K. Chesterton, *Orthodoxy* (Garden City, NY: Image, 1959).

the setting examines whether mankind can resolve the conflict by themselves (Genesis 3–11).

Third, there is a distinction related to the *treatment* of themes. Genesis 1–11 introduces anticipation of what is ahead while Genesis 12–50 begins to present the working out of what had been anticipated. Thus, Genesis 1–11 introduces unrealized purposes for creation while Genesis 12–50 is the initial stage in the administration of those purposes. And Genesis 12–50 introduces the first *dispensation*. A dispensation is a stage in God's governance in which He entrusts His Word to His steward. This unique administration of His will advances toward the fulfillment of His purposes in history during that stage. The initial administration of God's purposes features the patriarchs as stewards of God's Word of promise. Those promises frame God's commitment to act in the patriarchs' lives and in the future. And those commitments, when combined, form a plan that will encompass the history of the earth.

While there are distinctions between Genesis 1–11 and Genesis 12–50, the author himself considers both sections to be historical. This point of view sees that the people and events are true to historical reality. The claim to that perspective is expressed in the repeated *toledoth* formulation: "these are the records of…" or "these are the family records of the descendants of…" These formulations are present in both the primeval history (2:4; 5:1; 6:9; 10:1; 11:27) and in the historical period (11:27; 25:12, 19; 36:1; 37:2). The distribution in both sections indicates the continuity of the account in *Genesis*, as all is viewed as historical by Moses.

The historical continuity is further reflected in the genealogy of Gen 5:1-32 and 11:20-32 beginning in the creation of Adam and continuing through the family of Terah and Abram. While the genealogy may include gaps,[3] it still represents a historical sequence true to reality.

---

[3] Robert R. Wilson refers to these "gaps" in terms of fluidity and notes three types of fluidity: (1) changes in genealogical relationships, (2) additions of names, (3) disappearance or omission of names (Robert R. Wilson, *Genealogy and History in the Biblical World* [New Haven, CT: Yale University Press, 1977], pp. 29-36).

CHAPTER 3:
INTRODUCTION OF
THE SETTING AND THE
GOOD CREATION

The Point of Creation: To Replace the Former Ruler

The initial creation account (Genesis 1:1–2:3) introduces two controlling themes: the rationale for creation and the immediate goal of creation. The rationale for creation is not disclosed directly but is implied in the sequence of the introductory verses (Gen 1:1-3).

However, that sequence admits to disparate interpretations. In one interpretation, there is a *historical sequence*:

- First act of creation (1:1)
- Partially created earth (1:2)
- First day of creation (1:3)

Does a formless and empty (*tohu wabohu*) earth exist as created? Why is Gen 1:3 the first day of creation when creation begins in 1:1? Without adequate answers to these questions, another interpretation of the sequence has been proposed; *a reasoned sequence*:

- Title for the creation account (1:1)
- Initial judged condition of the earth (1:2)
- First day of creation (1:3)

In this proposal, the title follows the *toledoth* pattern that occurs throughout Genesis. In this view, verse 2 "must describe the state of the earth prior to verse 1, as it would be a contradiction to represent the creation as a formed cosmos and the earth as unformed."[1] So is the *reasoned sequence* view preferable? If so, why?

---

[1] Bruce K. Waltke and Cathi J. Fredricks, *Genesis: A Commentary* (Grand Rapids, MI: Zondervan, 2001), p. 60.

Genesis 1:1 provides a title for the creation account of the heavens and the earth. This is not a historical description of what God did, but a literary title of all the acts of creation which follow (1:3–2:3). It follows the *toledoth* pattern. Genesis 1:2 is a parenthetical statement introducing the condition of the *earth* when the *earth* was about to be created ("now the earth was formless"). The text, however, does not clarify how the earth ended up in that condition; an unformed and empty earth that was about to become a newly created earth. The implied explanation is that it was a *judged* earth. The judged earth will be *created* as a part of the formed cosmos. What evidence is there for such a *primordial judgment* (prior to Gen 1:1)?

Primordial judgment is suggested by both the language and the conditions of darkness and watery deep which are associated with judgment and evil. Jeremiah 4:23 uses the same phrase, "formless and empty" in a technical sense, describing the condition of "the whole land."[2]

In some Scriptures, the *sea* is depicted as hostile to God or as allied with hostile creatures that God violently subdued in history (Job 26:12-13; Pss 74:13-17; 89:9-12). The coming of the Man of Sin is associated with the sea (Dan 7:3; Rev 13:1). In Gen 1:2, the *deep* is portrayed as still and settled, because the whole chapter portrays God in absolute control as *Creator*. This is contrary to all other ANE accounts of beginnings which portray creation as conflict. In Ps 104:6-9, God rebuked the primordial deep.

In a similar depiction of hostility, *darkness* is associated with evil (1 John 1:5). Although darkness is allowed to remain as night, God always created in the *light*. There is no *moonlighting* for God, suggesting that darkness is incompatible with God and His works of creation.[3] Further, in Rev 21:25 and 22:5, there will no longer be night.

Both the language (formless and empty) and the concepts (sea and darkness) imply that Moses had in mind a primordial judgment. This implication of a judged earth existing prior to a created earth is also compatible with Isa 14:12-15 and Ezek 28:13-16.

Caird calls Isa 14:12-15 an "unambiguous example" of the prophet's *use* of metaphor.[4] The metaphor is used to compare a historic king's arrogance to a prior unnamed king's inordinate arrogance expressed toward

---

[2] Peter C. Craigie, Page H. Kelley, and Joel F. Drinkard, Jr. *Jeremiah 1–25*, Word Biblical Commentary (Dallas, TX: Word, 2002), p. 82.

[3] According to Gordon Wenham, "If light symbolizes God, darkness evokes everything that is anti-God: the wicked (Proverbs 2:13), judgment (Exodus 10:21), death (Psalm 88:13)." *Genesis 1–15*, p. 16.

[4] Caird, *The Language of the Bible*, p. 224.

God. If it is a metaphor, the question is what earlier king expressed this dramatic arrogance? If it is a metaphor, this arrogance is not described just as hyperbole. The Latin Vulgate took the pride to be that of Lucifer. The question is posed: who is this well-known instance of arrogance that would fit Isaiah's metaphor?

There are several reasons that the answer to the question was known in the ancient world and suggested in Gen 1:2. *First*, Childs posits that such an instance of condemned arrogance is found in the *language* of a Canaanite myth. "The name of the highest God was *'ēl 'elyôn* and the seat of the deity was Mount Zahon. The most plausible reconstruction is of *Helel's* (morning star) challenge to the power of Elyon who, when thwarted, was thrown down to Sheol."[5] While this language is likely reflected in Isaiah, what Isaiah had reference to was revealed in the Hebrew Scriptures. The Canaanite myth referred to conflict in creation while the implied conflict in Scripture occurred *before* creation.

Second, the Scriptural creation account in the chapter portrays the Creator in absolute control. There was no conflict. The point of the account is "to teach us that the whole world and all that it contains were created by the word of One God, according to His will, *which operates without restraint*."[6] It is as though opposition did not exist. But Cassuto says that conclusion would go beyond the text. The language "is tranquil, undisturbed by polemic or dispute; the controversial note is heard only indirectly."[7] That indirect message is the implications of the language of *formless* and *empty* and images of *sea* and *darkness* of Gen 1:2.

Third, conflict follows the completion of creation and the beginning of history. It appears as an inordinate expression of pride. This pride is manifest in the serpent *questioning and denying* God's Word (Gen 3:1, 4). And in place of God's Word, he posits the goal of becoming like God by rebelling against God's command (Gen 2:17). While the origin of the speaking serpent remains unaddressed, the identity of the serpent is without question.[8] The serpent, an animal, speaks as the *enemy of God*.

---

[5] Brevard S. Childs, Isaiah (Louisville, KY: Westminster John Knox, 2001), p. 126.

[6] Umberto Cassuto, *A Commentary on the Book of Genesis: Part One: From Adam to Noah*, Israel Abrahams, trans. (Jerusalem: Magnes, 1972), p. 7, emphasis added.

[7] *Ibid*.

[8] Later revelation makes the identification of Satan with the Serpent in Genesis explicit (Rev 12:9).

This temptation of pride corresponds with the inordinate pride expressed by the shining morning star.

"I will ascend above the highest clouds;
I will make myself like the Most High" (Isa 14:14, HCSB).

That correspondence is beyond reasonable doubt to compel identity. Further, the downfall of the star only heightens the judgment pronounced against the king of Babylon (Isa 14:12, 15). Thus, the judgment of the enemy of God prior to the creation of the heavens and earth fits the metaphor matching the fall of the king of Babylon.

Fourth, there are clues that the serpent, when judged (Gen 3:14-15), had already given account for his own rebellion. After Adam had eaten of the fruit, he gave account that Eve had given him the fruit (Gen 3:10-12). Likewise, the woman gave an account of her deception by the serpent (Gen 3:13). In both cases, God spoke as their judge. Then when He spoke to the serpent, the judge asked for no accounting, but simply said, "because you have done this" (Gen 3:14). God then pronounced judgment. The implication is that the serpent had already given an account, was guilty, and final judgment was pronounced against him in the history of the earth (Rev 20:9-10).

The figure of the serpent known in the ancient world involved arrogance and judgment. Scripture also spoke about it as the enemy of God and implied that he rebelled before creation and was judged.

In a similar fashion, Block commenting on Ezek 28:13-16 proposed that Ezekiel had delivered a powerful lesson on the self-destructive danger of hubris. "Like *ʾādām* in the Garden of Eden, the king of Tyre was not satisfied with signet-deputy-gardener status; he arrogated to himself the status of divine lord."[9]

But a question may be raised whether the reference is to the historical Adam (Gen 1:26-28) in hyperbolic language, or to a prior resident of an original garden of Eden. It seems that it was an original garden as described by Ezekiel which was far more glorious than the garden of Genesis. Support for the conclusion of a prior original garden is twofold. First, the hubris is not described directly as *of Adam*. Rather, *Eve* was tempted and fell (1 Tim 2:14). Adam sinned following her lead. Second, the garden dweller is spoken of as an angel who is glorious (Ezek 28:12-17). Thus, Ezekiel also uses a metaphorical lens through which to look at Tyre's historical king. He is like the same primordial figure that lived in

---

[9] Daniel I. Block, *The Book of Ezekiel: Chapters 25–28* (Grand Rapids, MI: Eerdmans, 1998), p. 120.

an original Eden, to whom God says, "Your heart became proud…so…I made you a spectacle" (Ezek 28:17). God judged him and God will judge the historical king of Tyre.

The later Old Testament clarifies that a shadowy evil figure first appeared in rebellious pride. While other creation accounts in the ANE see conflict between the gods influencing the creation of the earth, the Biblical account indicates no evidence of any opposition to God until after creation. However, the formless and empty earth engulfed in water and darkness bears witness to a judged earth (Gen 1:2), from which a good created earth emerged (Genesis 1:3–2:3). The prophets saw in historical kings of their day parallels to an original expression of pride that explains the reason for a judged earth (Gen 1:2). In addition, there is reason to expect the historic kings to be judged. Then, the created earth was good in spite of remnants incorporated from the judged earth (water and darkness).

In Gen 1:3, darkness engulfed the judged earth until God spoke *light* into existence out of nothing. What made the creation good was the existence of *light* which restricted the influence of darkness. *Light* governed the day and provided the environment in which God did His subsequent creative work. It provided a clear illumination in which God's works could be *known*. It further held in abeyance the realm of darkness which would pervade the night. The presence of light defined the day and the sequence of light and darkness created *time* as calendar days in history. The creation of light and time fashioned the environment of history that would follow creation.

In view of the allusions to judgment (Gen 1:2) and the prophetic metaphorical reference to a primordial display of pride (Isa 14:12-15; Ezek 28:13-16), *the rationale of creation* is clarified. Man is created to replace the primordial resident of the earth, Lucifer. Yet man, created lower than angels (Ps 8:5-6; Heb 2:5-9), would be fodder in a conflict with that original rebel. In this perspective, man would seem to be fated to be a pawn to an inevitable defeat. But, in another perspective, a *pawn* in God's hand becomes *an agent and steward* of God's creation plan. When such a *steward* would exercise his faith and confidence in God and His Word to overcome and to defeat the enemy, he would bring to full display God's glory. That is the *rationale* of creation developed in Genesis 1:3–2:3.

The Goal of Creation: to Establish the Rule of a New Ruler

Creation involves orderliness, whereas judgment had brought about disorder. The order in creation is both logical and chronological. *Logical order* concerns that which is necessary for the world to exist and that order emerges in a symmetrical scheme. The symmetry introduces form into that which was formless:

- Day one—creating light and separating it from darkness
- Day two—separating water above and below, creating space
- Day three—separating the water below from the land and calling the land to bring forth plant life to support created life

Then occupants are created to fill the emptiness of the form:

- Day four—calling for light sources[10] to rule in space and over time
- Day five—creating creatures for the air and for the water
- Day six—creating animals and man to rule on earth

This logical order argues for intelligent design by a Designer.[11]

That intelligent design included reasoned purposes. His purposes combine remnants of that which had been judged (darkness and the deep) and the objects of the new creation (light, time, space, plants, and created life). The combination indicates the intent to bring to resolution and completeness the plan for both what had been judged and what was new. Thus, God's supremacy extends over all creation.

Chronological order concerns *time*. Time is the environment of change in relation to God and to man. The relationship of time to each is distinct. God exists independent of an environment of chronological change, yet speaks within time to man. Man lives within time, participating in change himself, and being involved in the change promoted by God as a steward of God's will. So God is sovereign. He is not constrained by time and is able to work within time through His stewards.

Modern man, informed by science, criticizes the apparent equation between creation days and historical days. In both periods, a day is the light period and a day is a sequence of light and dark periods, as in

---

[10]   The creation of light sources after the creation of light might seem to be out of logical order. But that conclusion is only valid if the ultimate source of light emerges from these light sources. Rather, light exists prior to light sources (Gen 1:3-5) and exists at the climax after light sources are not needed (Rev 22:5).

[11]   This order supports a model of intelligent design as a result of the Designer without adopting the formal theory of Intelligent Design.

calendar days. Such criticism says that creation days are unreasonably short. But such a criticism arises from the measured rate of change in the historical period. However, the rate of change in history does not necessarily correlate with the rate of change in creation. There is so much that is not known about creation. Was created life introduced in embryonic form and cultivated in a process of change? Or was it introduced in an already mature created form? It would then have the appearance of age.

But even when creation involves processes of change, creation change need not share the rate of change that is observed to occur in history. Thus, in spite of time being shared in creation and history, it is not evident that God intended these temporal notations to be used to calculate the age of the earth. Rather, the sequence of days indicated an orderly creation.

Creation time may be viewed as an environment which reached completion. God spoke and it came to pass. Each day, what God called into existence was completed in the light period. On the other hand, history is an open-ended environment. God speaks in promise, committing Himself to action on behalf of His stewards and often His promises are not fulfilled immediately. Rather they are addressed to stewards who, responding in faith, *wait* for God to complete what He has promised. Thus, time in history is open. Man is conscious of time; conscious of what God has said in the past, conscious to some degree of what is happening in the present, but not aware of what the future holds, beyond what God has spoken.

The future is open from man's perspective except for what God has promised. Stewards of God's Word trust what He has said and awaits what He would do. Many times, they continue to puzzle over what God meant, because often things do not happen as expected. Time is the environment God uses to develop faith and secure hope. But as God spoke and it happened in creation, so God speaks and His stewards can expect that it will happen as God has said. Creation brings confidence that what God says will happen as He says. Time is the environment in which His people learn endurance, which produces maturity (Jas 1:4). Yet it is God's Word about the future which stewards use to manage their lives in anticipation of God intervening to accomplish His will.

The climax in the acts of creation arrived on the sixth day when God created man in His own image: "Let *us* make man in *our* image after *our* likeness" (Gen 1:26a, emphasis added). Hans Walter Wolff characterized this climax, saying, "the world of man is God's whole creation."[12] He

---

[12]   Hans Walter Wolff, *Anthropology of the Old Testament* (Philadelphia: Fortress, 1974), p. 159.

adds, "This is the case because man was created in God's image to be the steward of the world."[13] The climax of creation announces the immediate goal which would be realized in the history of the created world. Man would *rule*, as a steward, over the conflict with the enemy and over creation as God intended (Gen 1:26b, 28).

In this account of the creation of man, the dust of the earth is incorporated from the former creation. In addition, what God said was unique.

> The divine intent and purpose are solemnly declared in advance and the stereotyped formula, "and it was so," gives way to a thrice repeated avowal that God created man…Human beings are to enjoy a unique relationship to God, who communicates with them alone and who shares with them the *custody* and *administration* of the world.[14]

The uniqueness in the creation of man rests in his sharing the *image* of *God*. Wolff characterizes it in five features as developed in the context of Gen 1:26-28.[15]

First, the basic meaning of *image* is a correspondence between God and man. The term *likeness* indicates that the image is not identical to God. God is the Creator and man is the creature. Psalm 8 reflects on this, seeing God, the Creator, as primary in importance, and man as comparatively insignificant and easily overlooked.

Second, man corresponds in the sense that man "proceeds from God's address; 'let *us*…in *our* image'. God resolves to fashion mankind in the image of his Person."[16] He has a share in the personhood of God "as a being capable of self-awareness and of self-determination; he is open to the divine address and capable of responsible conduct."[17] Thus, reflecting His created image, God continues to address man and to hold him

---

[13] *Ibid.* Independent of any dispensational influence, Wolff recognized man's created role to be the steward in managing the new creation.

[14] Nahum M. Sarna, *Genesis*, JPS Torah Commentary (Philadelphia: Jewish Publication Society, 1989), p. 11.

[15] Wolff, *Anthropology*, pp. 159-161.

[16] Waltke, *Genesis*, pp. 64-65, emphasis original. The use of the first person plural "let us create… in our image" evokes in some the image of a heavenly court in which God is surrounded by His angelic host. But that court must share a common image with God which angels don't share. In addition, the focus in Genesis 1 is on the sufficiency of God alone, in contrast to other ANE sources where there is consultation with others in a divine court. These contextual factors would invite us to consider that the plural pronoun refers to a plurality of persons within the Godhead.

[17] Walter Eichrodt, *Theology of the Old Testament*, vol. 2, J. A. Baker, trans. (Philadelphia: Westminster, 1967), p. 126.

accountable for their conversation in his position as steward. Stendeback also sees mankind in this perspective: "'He spoke to them,' indicating human beings are functioning as God's *partner* in dialogue...involving man as God's counterpart, capable of responding to God."[18] The psalmist calls this his crowning glory and honor (Ps 8:5).

Third, mankind corresponds in the sense that we are appointed to have a similar relationship with the creation that God has (Gen 1:26b). As a result of this appointment, man's self-awareness is to be an agent of God and a *steward* of God's creation. The psalmist said that man is put in possession of the works of God's hands (Ps 8:6). In his stewardship, he is capable of keeping God's Word in mind to direct this work and manage his life.

Fourth (Gen 1:28), man corresponds in the sense that he is put on earth in God's *image*. "Man is set in the midst of creation as God's statue. He provides evidence that God is the Lord of creation; but, as God's *steward* he also exerts his *rule*, fulfilling his task not in arbitrary despotism, but as a responsible agent."[19] God's rule is *providential* over all creation while man's is *mediatorial* over the earth. "The text is saying that exercising royal dominion over the earth as God's representative is the basic purpose for which God created man."[20] Thus, man's created role is to be a steward of God's rule on earth having God's Word in mind. This is the *goal* of creation.

Finally, *'ādām* corresponds not only to the individual male but also to mankind, including male and female. "Dominion over the world is not to be made over to great individuals, but to the community."[21] This is the immediate goal that the completed creation establishes. It awaits the history that will follow in which that mediated rule will be realized. Two trees are highlighted "in the midst of the garden" which anticipate a role in this realization (Gen 2:9).

---

[18] F. J. Stendeback, "צֶלֶם, *selem*," *Theological Dictionary of the Old Testament*, vol. 12 (Grand Rapids, MI: Eerdmans, 1975), p. 395.

[19] Wolff, *Anthropology*, pp. 160-61. This follows the practice of ANE kings who erect statues to indicate their domain.

[20] Ian Hart, "Genesis 1:1–2:3 as a Prologue to the Book of Genesis," *Tyndale Bulletin* 46.2 (Cambridge, UK: Tyndale House, 1995): 322.

[21] Wolff, *Anthropology*, p. 162.

CHAPTER 4:
CONFLICT FOLLOWING
CREATION

THE FORMER RULER AND
THE NEW RULER

Introduction: Relationships within
Creation (Genesis 2:4-25)

God's creation of the earth had been declared to be good, repeatedly (light was good, 1:4; separation of seas from earth, 1:10; the sprouting of plant life, 1:12; the light sources, 1:18; birds and fish, 1:21; animals, 1:25). All were "good," but beyond that, the creation of man and woman, with the provisions that the garden would bring, was "very good" (Gen 1:31).

That goodness of all that God created is then explored in the *relationships* viewed in retrospect. Thus, Sarna concludes that "chapter 2 is not another creation story."[1] Rather, it looks at creation in review with a changed focus not solely on God, but on humankind and his relationships.

The first relationship is to God. As the divine Potter, He molded clay into shape; but as the Creator, He gave life. He animated the clay as He shared His own breath, creating an independent person (Gen 2:7). That is the first and foundational relationship of mankind because in it is life. And this life is auspicious because it is God's very life, yet this life is also humble, shaped from mere clay. Without the continuing presence of God, how else would man ever reach the stated goal of creation?

The second relationship was that which was provided in the garden. All the trees were aesthetically pleasant and *good* for food (Gen 2:9a). In addition, two trees at the center of the garden were highlighted. The

---

[1] Sarna, *Genesis*, p. 16.

tree of life promised immediate support for life, distinct from the food from other trees, subsequent to the life given at creation, and the tree of the knowledge of *good* and *evil* warned of man's limitation. Man was unrestricted to discover and use the good to be found in God's gifts in the garden, but man's knowledge was to be limited to the good given. The knowledge of evil was to remain hidden in God. The very name of the tree implied that evil already existed, but independent of the *good* creation. Fullness of life rested in the knowledge of *good* to be found in working and exploring the creation and in fellowship with the Creator.

Third, it was not *good for man to be alone* (Gen 2:18). Adam came to realize what was missing in his life as he named the animals. This was a preparation for his dominion as names provided an initial mental control over what was unknown in the garden. This naming suggests the logic of the patterns in creation and the rational order of naming each entity that was created, as the name corresponded to the object's identity.

But the presence of rational control did not fill the emptiness of being alone. Woman was created to meet that loneliness (Gen 2:21-25) as a "helper fit for him" (Gen 2:20). Both the time of her creation and the manner in which it happened mark the person created. Adam was created first and Eve was last. This distinction means that she was not to be mistaken for a second male. The unusual process of woman's creation adds mystery to this wonderful gift given to Adam. The logic that was reflected in the order of creation is replaced by the spontaneity of Adam's words of acceptance (Gen 2:23). The separation of a rib urges for a reuniting of the two into a unified life (Gen 2:21, 24). Marriage would be the beginning of a new family separate from the groom's family. She is a helper fit for him, psychologically, emotionally, and personally. In the end, the goodness in their creation is not lost in alienation.[2] Rather, together the good is enhanced as they share together in mutual appreciation (Gen 2:25).

Mankind's Fall in Sin (Genesis 3:1-7)

The Serpent

The last relationship to be explored is the relationship to other creatures. The creature that approached Eve was a serpent that was "the most cunning of all the wild animals" (Gen 3:1). And the serpent began a conversation with Eve. She does not seem to be surprised that a serpent could

---

[2] Victor Hamilton, *Genesis 1–17*, NICOT, R. K. ed. Harrison and Robert L. Hubbard, Jr. (Grand Rapids, MI: Eerdmans, 1990), p. 191.

speak. In the unfallen world, where life was in full bloom, a speaking animal is not unimaginable.

The Serpent Questions God's Word

But *what* the animal said would expose the real identity of *who* was speaking. The serpent questioned what God had said. But, in the question, God was misrepresented. The question acknowledged all that God had created, but suggested that He had withheld fruit from man to eat. God was powerful but stingy.

Immediately the woman defended God, but still portrayed Him as more restrictive than bountiful. There is only one tree whose fruit they shouldn't *eat* nor *touch*. Eve magnified God's strictness and diminished the appearance of all that God had given freely.

The Serpent Denies God's Word

Having gained agreement on misrepresenting God, the serpent questioned God's motives for restricting man's freedom. God was fearful that man would gain godliness by knowing good and evil. The tree that God had placed off limits to man was the tree that would disclose the knowledge of good and evil. God tested mankind with the restriction of not eating and that restriction was reinforced with a threat of death (Gen 2:17). But the serpent emphatically[3] denied that God would judge (Gen 3:4). God had made an empty threat motivated by weakness. The temptation was that *disobedience* would lead to divinity.

The Image of God in Fallen Man

Man was created in the "image of God" and had God's appointment to be His steward, having God's Word in mind. But, as the woman considered the serpent's *word* of temptation, she saw that the tree "was good for food and delightful to look at and that it was desirable for obtaining wisdom" (Gen 3:6a, HCSB). Rather than following God's instructions, she believed and followed the serpent's word. Adam joined her (Gen 3:6b). What had formerly characterized their self-awareness in relation to God was now dramatically changed. The serpent's lie, that one could be like God, controlled each one's self-awareness. The word of the

---

[3] The Hebrew construction is emphatic.

serpent was a lie. It failed to mention that mankind was unable to control the knowledge of evil. They thus would know good and evil, but would be dominated by evil. That is not like God. In this respect, the woman was deceived. Immediately, in their new self-awareness, they were overwhelmed by *shame* and *guilt* and they attempted to cover up (Gen 3:7). When God called them in the garden, in their *fear*, they sought to hide from Him (Gen 3:8-9). Hamilton states, "Rather than driving them back to God, their guilt leads them into a self-atoning, self-protecting procedure: they must cover themselves."[4] The knowledge of evil darkened their mind and the lie captured their self-determination.

Man's delegated right to rule on earth as steward was lost to the serpent. The serpent now ruled Adam and the woman in their disobedience. While the image of God as a person remained (Gen 9:6), their self-awareness radically changed. They no longer saw themselves as *stewards* of God, but rather as *enemies* of God. And as enemies, their determination was to be like God themselves. Mankind had become alienated from God. Their minds were darkened and their wills driven by the serpent's lie.

The serpent's disguise was broken. He was no longer merely seen as a clever animal; he was *the enemy of God*. As the enemy, the serpent spoke as though he were God. So, the serpent had usurped God's right to claim the allegiance of mankind. Now the serpent exercised rule over the man and the woman in their disobedience. Further, the enemy of God held God hostage to His threat of death against man if they ate of the tree (Gen 2:17). Thus, God must exercise the sentence of death on Adam and all those who share his life. As mankind would face death physically at the hand of God, so mankind died spiritually, since they would view God as their adversary, and were cast out from the garden.

Conflict Introduced by Judgment

Conflict entered the world, which had been created good, as Adam sinned. In order to clarify the actual source of the conflict, God introduced judgment involving conflict between God's enemy and His allies, and God's elect ones.

---

[4] Indeed Hamilton argues that, "the climax of the creation is, interestingly, the notation that the couple were naked and felt no shame before each other" (*Genesis 1–17*, p. 181).

Adam's Stewardship (Genesis 3:8-13)

As though nothing had happened, God entered the garden for a visit with Adam and the woman. They were *afraid* and attempted to hide, but there was no hiding from God. Through a series of questions, Adam confessed that he knew shame as they were naked. Then God asked how he knew. He knew because he ate of the tree, but it was the woman, the woman that God had given him, who caused him to eat. The woman, when questioned, blamed the serpent.

The serpent wasn't questioned, implying that he had already faced his responsibility before God. The serpent already stood condemned. But, that condemnation was not part of the story of the newly created earth. Rather, as the enemy of God, he challenged God's *goal* in creation, thereby seeking to thwart God's plan. If the plan could be thwarted, God Himself would be defeated and the enemy would gain rule over all creation and God.

The Word of Judgment in History (Genesis 3:14-19)

Without hesitation, God pronounced judgment on the serpent. The pronouncement included judgment on two sides of the tempter: the serpent-animal (Gen 3:14) and the serpent-enemy (Gen 3:15).

In the verdict on the serpent-enemy (Gen 3:15), ironically, God chose to pronounce *enmity* between the defeated and fallen woman and the serpent. The judgment was declared in three stages of enmity: the first stage involved adversity between the woman, the one who had been deceived (1 Tim 2:14), and the serpent. The second stage involved the woman's seed (*zera*^{c}) who would do conflict with the seed of the serpent. The term, seed (*zera*^{c}), would be naturally taken in its collective sense, which would anticipate an unforeseen number of generations of conflict to come. But, there is no indication of a resolution of the conflict. In the third and final stage, the serpent again returns directly to the conflict with the Seed of the woman. The singular pronoun, *He*, does not refer to the singular number of the noun (Seed, *zera*^{c}) any more than the singular pronoun *His* refers to the singular of the noun (*zera*^{c}).[5] The *He* and *His* anticipate

---

[5] Jack Collins, "A Syntactical Note (Genesis 3:15): Is the Woman's Seed Singular or Plural?" *Tyndale Bulletin* 48:1 (Cambridge, UK: Tyndale House, 1997): 139-48. The pronoun he is taken as a singular usage following the LXX translation. This syntax is compatible with a parallel usage in 2 Sam 7:13. This is relevant because it also involves a promise about offspring. Second Samuel 7:13 is a promise to David of an offspring (*zera*^{c}, v.12): *hû' yibneh-bayit lišĕmi* ("he will build a house for my name"). "From these parallel uses, it becomes

an individual future Offspring who would resolve the enmity, crushing the serpent's head.

In this climactic generation, the serpent again is addressed directly in the second person: "he will strike *your* head and *you* will strike his heel" (Gen 3:15c, HCSB). The conflict is between the serpent and the final generation of the offspring of the woman. Both combatants *strike* the other. Since the same word (*shup*) is used in both cases, *strike* refers to a death blow. Since the serpent's power is death, he apparently strikes the first blow; the serpent snipped at the offspring's heel, as serpents do, and the offspring died. Since it is a death blow, how can the offspring return a death blow? This final Offspring of the woman must somehow *overcome* the death blow before He can return a more severe death blow to the head. The answer as to how death would be *overcome* remains unrevealed at this stage in revelation. Yet, attention will be given as revelation unfolds to discover the answer to this conflict.

From the perspective of the New Testament, the Church has posited an answer. Kidner described their response:

> There is good New Testament authority for seeing here the *protoevangelium*, the first glimmer of the gospel. Remarkably, it makes its' début as a sentence passed on the enemy (cf. Col 2:15), not a direct promise to man, for redemption is about God's rule as much as about man's need.[6]

This providential rule of God will govern Biblical history until the virgin born Son does direct conflict with Satan and introduces fulfillment in what is suggested, as Jesus Christ overcomes death in resurrection. Then as a climax in history, this Descendant of Eve will strike the head wound, as "the Devil who deceived them was thrown into the lake of fire and sulfur…and they will be tormented day and night forever and ever" (Rev 20:10, HCSB). This pronouncement of conflict between the woman and her offspring and the serpent introduces the plot structures for the Biblical story within the canon as a whole.

The Conflict between God and the Serpent

The serpent spoke as God's enemy. The enemy challenged God by challenging the immediate *goal* of creation. Would man, appointed to

---

clear that, on the syntactical level, the singular pronoun *hû* in Genesis 3:15 is quite consistent with the pattern where a single individual is in view." (Collins, "A Syntactical Note," 145).

[6] Derek Kidner, *Genesis* (Downers Grove, IL: IVP, 1967), p. 70.

mediate God's rule on earth, ever rule? When Adam sinned, the enemy usurped rule over creation. Further, the enemy held God hostage in His threat to judge disobedient mankind (Gen 2:17). God's plan in creating a good earth from a judged earth seemed to be thwarted. Would God be able to accomplish His creation plan using the weak and fallen human race? The prospect seemed bleak. This is the fundamental plot-conflict in Biblical history at the macro-level.

The Conflict between the Serpent and Mankind

The macro-conflict is resolved on earth in the life of God's agent and steward of His will on earth. Rather than abandoning mankind because of Adam's fall from innocence to rebellion, a plan to *redeem* man was added to supplement the plan of creation. The plan of redemption would pit chosen descendants of the woman in conflict with the serpent and his allies. In light of the craftiness and power of the serpent, to defeat man would seem to be inevitable unless man responded to God and His promise of help. That help would come in God's acts of redemption, which appear in salvation history from the consequences of Adam's sin. Sacrifice was first provided for Adam and Eve (Gen 3:21) as a pattern of redemption.

For those called by God, *salvation* from the immediate consequence of sin came. This is also exemplified in Abram justified by faith (Gen 15:6). Those chosen to partner in service were *saved* from the conflict with evil (e.g., Noah, Abraham, Joseph, Moses, David) until their tasks were completed, but none overcame the enemy. They were covenant partners. A climactic Partner with whom God partnered in Person in the incarnation would be the focus promised in the plan of redemption and of restoration. When He faced the conflict, He surrendered to death according to God's will, but He overcame death in resurrection. At His First Advent, the day of salvation arrived. The dimensions of salvation were enriched and defined by His experience. Those called received salvation by faith. At His Second Advent, the goal of creation would be fulfilled in His rule on earth, with those who were His own. The enemy of God would be finally judged and the creation plan for mankind restored.

Would Mankind Overcome Evil in Their Own Strength?

The answer to this question is represented in the narrative of the remainder of primeval history (Genesis 4:1–11:32).[7] The answer will come as negative in repeated pronouncements of judgment. In God's pain with a population that demanded judgment, two positive genealogies are included (5:1-32; 11:10-32) which note one descendant as announced in Gen 3:15. As the numbers indicate, it is one per generation. The genealogy of elect descendants begins with Adam and his offspring Seth (Gen 5:3-5). Seth had been born to Adam and Eve *in place of* Abel after he had been killed in conflict with the evil controlling Cain (Gen 4:25-26).

In this extended narrative, God's *judgment* predominates because of the inclusion of sin into the human race. Beginning with Adam and Eve, an outline of the episodes follows:

- Adam and Eve were *judged* (Gen 3:16-19, 22-24) and blessed (Gen 3:20-21);
- Abel killed by Cain who is *judged* (Gen 4:1-16) along with his line (Gen 4:17-26);
- The elect line (Gen 5:1-32);
- The expansion of evil through the race brought *judgment* (Genesis 6:1–8:14), along with the Noahic Covenant (Genesis 8:15–9:17);
- The survivors' focus on the tower of Babel brought *judgment* in the division of languages forming nations (Genesis 9:18–11:9);
- The elect line (Gen 11:10-32).

Adam and Eve (Genesis 3:16-24)

Following the judgment pronounced against the serpent, judgment fell on both Adam and Eve. For Eve, it focused on security in her *relationship* to her husband and in her bearing children. For Adam, it addressed his significance at work.

Under threat of these judgments, Adam faced a dilemma. One word of judgment threatened immediate death (Gen 2:17). The word of God's judgment against the serpent promised to incorporate the descendants of the woman (Gen 3:15). Adam heard God's Word which anticipated the woman would live to bear children. He believed God and called her

---

[7] One can see this in the recurring "then he died" (e.g., 5:5, 8, 11, 14, 17, 20, 27, 31; 9:29).

"mother of the living" (Gen 3:20). But what about the threat of immediate death? He also believed that God would care for the apparent contradiction. And God did. He clothed Adam and Eve with the skins of
a sacrificed animal (Gen 3:21). The sacrifice took the penalty of death.
Adam and Eve had a *mediated* relationship with God even though they
lost the *immediate* relationship as they were permanently shut out of the
garden (Gen 3:23-24). They lost the opportunity to directly cultivate life
forever through the tree of life. In that sense, death set in immediately.
And in time, Adam died physically (Gen 5:1-5).

With a covering for sin provided, they could approach God again
through sacrifice. In the delay in the death penalty, they would have children. Yet Adam died when he was 930 years old (Gen 5:5).

Cain and Abel (Genesis 4:1-16)

Adam and Eve had in mind God's Word which promised offspring.
So it was not unexpected that Eve named her firstborn, Cain—"I have
had a male child with the LORD's help" (Gen 4:1, HCSB). In her mind,
Cain was that promised offspring. Abel was born without comment. Two
sons, two occupations, two sacrifices; Abel's sacrifice followed the pattern
of God's provision for his parents, but Cain's sacrifice was offered based
on his own self-interest. God accepted Abel but rejected Cain. An angry
Cain brooded over his rejection. God then warned him that sin sought
access in his life to control his actions (Gen 4:7). In spite of the warning,
Cain, with the serpent's word in mind, took Abel's life out in the field
(Gen 4:8). He acted as though he were God, ending Abel's life.

In Abel's shed blood, Cain extinguished an image of God on earth.
The life and power of the serpent now coursed through Cain's life. In that
act, the race was divided. Cain became the first descendant of the serpent
and Abel was the descendant of the woman who had died in conflict.
This division of the race introduced the structure of the plan of redemption, first revealed in the judgment of the serpent (Gen 3:15).

The Line of Cain (Genesis 4:17-24)

One line of the human race was fathered by Cain. This life was expressed
in a human culture: the city arises, smiths emerge next to shepherds.
Musicians introduce human art. The building of the city was an irrecon-
cilable contradiction to God's Word to become a wanderer (Gen 4:12).

In the city, man found his security in the collective interest of man. In that culture, there was neither mention nor place for God. Cain's culture disregarded God since Cain had left God's presence (Gen 4:16).

At the heart was the self-interest of Cain which had eliminated Abel. Now that self-interest caused by evil expressed itself in greater self-assertion. Lamech was not satisfied with the protection God had promised to Cain but exerted a form of reckless vengeance and revenge. The life of Cain's line had progressed from disregard of God's Word, to murder, and then to claim a seventy-seven fold vengeance.

The Line of Chosen Descendants (Genesis 4:25–5:22; 11:10-26)

When Alexander sought to recognize the compositional unity in Genesis he found it in the line of the seed:

> For many readers Genesis appears to be a collection of unconnected stories interrupted here and there by apparently irrelevant genealogies. Yet, the present text has been carefully shaped to highlight the importance of a family lineage which begins with Adam and is traced to the sons of Jacob.[8]

This family lineage consists of two distinct genealogies: (Gen 5:1-22; 11:10-26). Each consists of ten identically crafted paragraphs in a linear[9] structure. The feature of one chosen descendant of the woman in each generation reflects the intent of Gen 3:15. This reflection will be supported in the contents of the linear genealogy.[10]

The line does not simply consist of all the natural offspring of Seth or Adam. Adam had additional male offspring not included in the line (Cain and Abel). Rather than recording all natural offspring, one son is chosen from each father. This is indicated as Seth is included *in place of* Abel (Gen 4:25). Abel was accepted by God (Gen 4:4), but Cain was not (Gen 4:5). To include Seth is to choose Seth to be that one accepted by God (Gen 4:25-26).

---

[8] T. D. Alexander, "Genealogies, Seed and the Compositional Unity of Genesis," *Tyndale Bulletin* 44:2 (Cambridge, UK: Tyndale House, 1993): 257.

[9] The distinction between 'linear' and 'segmented' genealogies is discussed by R. R. Wilson, *Genealogy and History in the Biblical World* (New Haven, CT: Yale University Press, 1977), p. 9.

[10] Linear genealogies trace descent in a linear fashion, that is, from a singular descendent in one generation to a singular descendent in the next generation.

Further, Adam was made in the image of God (Gen 5:1), and Adam fathered a son, Seth, after *his* image (Gen 5:3). A question emerges; in what sense is Seth after Adam's image while Cain was not? In a broad sense, all three sons shared the same image as persons (Gen 9:6). But, Seth, like Adam, kept God's Word in mind while Cain did not (Gen 3:20; 4:26 in contrast to 4:7-9). "The Genesis narrative emphasizes the existence of the special relationship between God and individual members of the main family line."[11]

Seth and Enosh, his son, "began to call on the name of the LORD" (Gen 4:26). Enoch "walked with God 300 years" (Gen 5:22, HCSB) and "he was not there, because God took him" (Gen 5:24, HCSB). Then there was Noah (Gen 5:29). He was called to "bring us relief from the agonizing labor of our hands, caused by the ground the LORD has cursed." He was a "righteous man, blameless among his contemporaries; Noah walked with God" (Gen 6:9, HCSB). The story of Noah's *stewardship* will be developed in the flood narrative in which he does conflict with the remainder of the human race and the judgment upon them in the flood (Gen 6:5-8).

This distinction between Noah and the rest of "man on the earth" (Gen 6:6, HCSB), further clarifies the reflection of Gen 3:15 in the genealogy. In the linear structure of the genealogy, the age of the father, when the son was born, is included in each paragraph (e.g., Gen 5:3, 6, 9). One son is chosen to do conflict with the serpent and his allies.[12] What follows is Noah's conflict in his generation.

The Judgment of the Worldwide Flood and the Noahic Covenant (Genesis 6:1–9:17)

The conflict that appeared in Noah's day was a conflict with the lifestyle of the descendants of the serpent. That lifestyle included an increasingly deteriorating culture. It was highlighted by the "sons of God" who

---

[11] Alexander, "Genealogies," p. 263.

[12] Since these are records of history, the numbers are naturally seen as literal. The number of years when the son or grandson would be born locate a "seed of the woman" in each generation. Even though it is a patterned list (ten from Adam to Noah and ten from Noah to Abraham), the numbers argue for a tight chronology. Although Kidner would not take these numbers as literal, he concedes that "the life-spans are intended literally" (Kidner, *Genesis*, p. 83). And he reaches this conclusion in spite of the abnormally large numbers in the age of these descendants.

cohabited with the daughters of men. Their offspring were powerful and famous men of old (Gen 6:4). Vos lists ways the culture had deteriorated:

> *Firstly*: the intensity and extent of evil ("great in the earth"); *secondly*: its inwardness ("every imagination of the thoughts of his heart"); *thirdly*: the absoluteness of the sway of evil excluding everything good ("only evil"); *fourthly*: the habitual continuous working of *evil* ("all the day").[13]

Von Rad notes a progression of evil that led from the first refusal of obedience (Gen 3:6), to fratricide (4:8) and from there to a defiant self-affirmation that despised all unfamiliar life (Gen 4:23-24; Song of Lamech).[14] Then he raises a question: "Can the narrator still pursue and intensify this account of the continuous increase of sin?"[15] It was in this context of the deterioration of the human culture, that the difficult phrase "sons of God" is to be interpreted. While this phrase normally refers to angels (Job 1:6; 2:1; 38:7; Dan 3:25), this interpretation is often rejected because it seems to defy normal experience and what Jesus said about angels (Mark 12:25).[16] But von Rad sees the experience as an attack on the image of God. The author "wanted to show man's general corruption. He wanted to represent…a kind of 'demonic' invasion, and thus point out a further disturbance caused by sin."[17] The form and fullness (Gen 1:2) that God had fashioned into creation was now challenged at the most basic level. Human-kind and angel-kind were intersecting, not merely at the power level (Gen 4:6), but at the life level. The created enemy-life invaded human life and the implications brought a threat for the *protoevangelium* (Gen 3:15).[18] There would no longer be simply human descendants of the woman to confront the serpent.

The response of God indicated the strong emotion with which He faced this destructive challenge from the enemy ("And the LORD regretted that he had made man on the earth, and it grieved him to his heart,"

---

[13] Gerhardus Vos, *Biblical Theology: Old and New Testament* (Grand Rapids, MI: Eerdmans, 1948), p. 51, emphasis original.

[14] Von Rad, *Genesis*, p. 113.

[15] *Ibid.*

[16] Jesus affirms that angels don't procreate, but He doesn't say they can't.

[17] *Ibid.*, p. 115.

[18] The connection to Genesis 3 can be seen also in how the account is framed. As Waltke notes, "The Hebrew reads literally: 'saw…good…took.' Their sin repeats the pattern ('saw…good…took.') of the original sin in 3:6. They are driven by lust, not spiritual discernment" (Waltke, *Genesis*, p. 117).

Gen 6:6).[19] God must wipe off created beings from the face of the earth, yet there was one from the elect line, Noah, who found favor with the LORD. The deliverance of the image of God came through Noah and through *judgment* of the remainder of the creation (Genesis 6:9–8:22).

The *judgment* was a worldwide flood stifling the corruption of the earth (Gen 6:11) since it was filled with violence (Gen 6:13). These parameters of judgment, together with the details describing the flood, make a strong *case* for a *universal flood*.[20] Further, the LORD would establish a covenant with Noah to confront the spread of evil following the flood.

To begin with, Noah would build an ark for the deliverance of himself and his family, as well as "two of every living thing of all flesh, male and female, to keep them alive with you" (Gen 6:19, HCSB). But this deliverance did not overcome the evil, nor even directly work out God's purposes. It was for survival.

Then "God remembered Noah" (Gen 8:1). God was not finished with His creation. The bold anthropomorphism makes the freedom for divine resolve in deliverance abundantly clear (Gen 3:15). The conflict with evil would continue, but the realization of God's purposes rests squarely with God.

Of great significance, God accepted Noah's worship (Gen 8:20-21). "The Lord's resolve not to renew judgment is based on the acceptance of sacrifice (cf. 1 Sam 26:19, Col 1:20), not on man's incorrigibility."[21] The very condition that brought judgment may well appear again, "even though man's inclination is evil from his youth," (Gen 8:21, HCSB). And "the assurance goes far beyond verse 21. It does not abolish disasters, but it does localize them."[22] Weather cycles and agricultural patterns will make natural life more predictable. Expectations of what would support life were local and thus, more capable of human management.

---

[19] Concerning God's sorrow, Mathews suggests that, "God's response of grief over the making of humanity, however, is not remorse in the sense of sorrow over a mistaken creation; our verse shows that God's pain has its source in the perversion of human sin" (Mathews, *Genesis 1–11:26*, p. 343).

[20] Henry M. Morris and John C. Whitcomb, *The Genesis Flood* (Philadelphia: Presbyterian and Reformed, 1961). The case is a textual argument, understanding the use of language consistent with the creation account. The word "all" is used forty-four times "in reference to the flood." Further, the case rests on the evidence: the depth and duration of the flood; the size and need for an ark; the testimony of the Apostle Peter; and the total destruction of the human race which were widely distributed (6:1). See also, Gerhard Hasel, "Extent of the Flood," *Origins* 2:2 (Loma Linda, CA: Geoscience Research Institute, 1975): 77-79.

[21] Kidner, *Genesis*, p. 93.

[22] *Ibid.*

The Noahic Covenant

The Noahic Covenant is introduced in Gen 6:18: "I will establish My covenant with you…" (HCSB). Then the account follows Noah who will enter the ark as the flood is about to come (Gen 6:18b-21). During the flood, there is no mention of the covenant. Afterward, "My covenant" is repeated extensively (Gen 9:8-17). What is not clear from the text is when the covenant is first ratified. And, what are the terms of the covenant arrangement?

The first question originally is raised in Gen 6:18: "it is uncertain whether the governing verb means *to fashion* a covenant *anew* or to *fulfill one* already made."[23] Outside of the Flood narrative, the Biblical usages of the phrase favor "fulfilling" a covenant already made. This is the sense adopted by Covenant Theology. They take the covenant "already made" to be ratified with Adam (1:28). What was already ratified, as the Adamic Covenant, is now fulfilled with Noah (9:1). What is missing is the mention of a covenant with Adam.

The sense of "fashioning a covenant anew" is favored in the immediate context (Gen 6:18; 9:1-17). These contextual factors favor this sense. First, the blessing on Noah only involves the reproduction of offspring which are to spread over the earth (Gen 9:1, 7). The blessing on Adam involved both reproduction and the right to rule (Gen 1:26-28). This reduction in terms reflects what had been lost to the serpent. Second, while Noah has a similar position as Adam had, the conditions on earth have changed. God spoke to Adam before the fall into sin, and Noah heard God speaking after the fall. One would expect different terms of the covenant in light of the rebellion of the population. Third, the word *covenant* is not present at creation with the fiat statements nor related to the Garden of Eden. So we will see the Noahic Covenant as ratified with Noah in a fallen world.

The second question concerns the terms of the arrangement. The key term, *covenant* (*bᵉrît*) is introduced in Gen 6:18 and then repeated seven times between 9:8 and 17. This section consists of two proclamations: "I now establish My covenant" (Gen 9:9) and "the sign of My covenant that I have established" (Gen 9:17). As this translation understands the phrases, this would support the conclusion that the covenant was ratified with Noah.

---

[23] Sarna, *Genesis*, p. 53, emphasis mine.

As the Abrahamic Covenant would incorporate all the earlier promises made (Gen 12:2, 3, 7; 13:14-17) into the covenant when ratified (Gen 15:9-21), so issues God raised which precede the Noahic words of establishment are incorporated (Gen 9:1-7). The focus of this series of terms is on the sanctity of human life. Related to this focus is that every living creature will fear man and these animals will be included in the human diet.[24] But the striking feature is that violence had not been overcome in either animal nor human life. The question remains regarding what the covenant says about addressing such violence.

How would this reality of rebellion be reconciled with God's sovereign right to rule over created human beings?

> God himself will not avenge murder, and that means a loss of immediacy *vis-à-vis* God which must now be recorded. But, he empowered man to do it…that is the first feature in the institution of the authorities as the executors of the demands of moral world order and thus as God's representatives.[25]

Wolff adds that "the shedding of human blood is especially stressed as a crime against 'the image of God.'" He then summarizes:

> Everything that is said about breath and blood in the anthropology of the Old Testament is instruction in an ultimate reverence for life. But, this reverence is not derived from the manifestation of life itself; it is based on the fact that the breath and blood belong to Yahweh, and therefore life without a steady bond with him and an ultimate tending towards him is not really life at all.[26]

Thus, the *image of God* survived in Noah and his descendants.

As a consequence, God established the Noahic Covenant delegating moral authority to human governance, in the protection of human life. Capital punishment was established to respect the image of God in man. This was raised as a guard against another divine judgment. The statements and the sign concerning "My Covenant" assured mankind that such a divine judgment would not come as a worldwide flood. However, it also implied that a final judgment remained in God's will.

---

[24] The original diet was given before death had entered creation. So it is clear that a vegetarian diet is initially provided. After death entered creation animals are included in the diet.

[25] Von Rad, *Genesis*, p. 133.

[26] Wolff, *Anthropology of the Old Testament*, pp. 61-62.

The record of the Table of Nations, although it is recorded first (Gen 10:1-32), represents a world forming, following the Tower of Babel (Gen 11:1-9). "The Table presents a segmented genealogy of Noah's three sons with two biographical notes about Nimrod and Peleg, both of which foreshadow the Tower of Babel narrative. The Table does not aim to give an exhaustive list of all peoples (Gen 10:5). Rather, its intentions are theological."[27] The Table holds in tension two facts: first, all are descendants of Noah, and second, there is diversity within the human race, divided into many languages and into geographical locations, as a result of God's judgment.

Conclusion

Genesis 1–11 sets the stage for the story of God's governance over the world and of salvation history. Two historical characters dominate the setting: first Adam and second Noah. Each is a prototype in their world.

First, Adam was placed in the created world to multiply and to rule (Gen 1:26-28), and would be involved in conflict with its former occupant (Gen 1:2). It was Lucifer's strategy to defeat the Creator by tempting Adam to turn against his Creator. In Adam's subsequent sin, Adam was ruled by the serpent's word and the enemy became the ruler of this world (John 12:31). The introduction of evil then only grew—from Cain who slew Abel, to Lamech who viciously lashed out at mere lads who annoyed him, to a demonic invasion of woman to produce offspring to pervert the promised line of Eve.

Immediately following the invasion of evil, God had pronounced judgment on the serpent-enemy to ultimately come from a line of descendants of Eve. Seth was chosen in place of Abel (Gen 4:25), as was one to be selected in each generation (Gen 5:1-25). Yet the decay of sin in the human race was so pervasive that in His pain, a wronged Creator sent a worldwide flood to destroy the race (Genesis 6:9–8:19).

Second, Noah was chosen from the line of Eve to preserve life in the judged fallen world (Gen 6:18). Under the Noahic Covenant (6:18), the new world would be structured around Noah and his multiplication of life (9:1, 7). The governing covenant announced God's ultimate right to judge but the rainbow assured that judgment would not again come in a worldwide flood. The covenant was ratified with Noah representing the human race (9:15).

---

[27]   Waltke, *Genesis*, p. 162.

Moses would later record the LORD's song (Deuteronomy 32) which celebrated His providential structuring of the fallen world to impede the spread of evil. These cosmic actions involved:

- The division of the population of the earth into peoples of different language speakers

- The placing of them in the charge of His heavenly agents

- The allocation of land to form nations[28]

- The delegation of authority to nations to protect human life because "God made man in his image" (Gen 9:2-6)

- The regulating of a climate such that the race could produce food to support life (8:22)

In this fallen world, God would intervene in judgment as in Ham's disrespect for his father. That judgment fell on Canaan and anticipated God's blessing Israel with land to become a nation.

However, most amazing is God's election of Shem from whom Abram would be chosen (Gen 11:10-32). This choice and subsequent promises would introduce the dispensation of promise. In the revelation of His Word, God's purposes were introduced to begin to pursue the accomplishment of God's goals which had been introduced:

The goal of creation: to establish the mediatorial reign of *man* over creation as God's steward.

The goal of redemption: to deliver the elect from the conflict caused by the evil of God's enemy.

The working out of these purposes will involve salvation history.

---

[28] Daniel I. Block, *Deuteronomy: The NIV Application Commentary* (Grand Rapids, MI: Zondervan, 2012), p. 774.

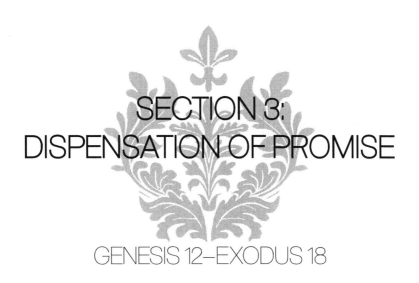

SECTION 3:
DISPENSATION OF PROMISE

GENESIS 12–EXODUS 18

Introduction to Section 3: Dispensation of Promise

The setting had oriented the story that would follow in the canon (Genesis 1–11). That orientation frames the account of the patriarchs' history (Genesis 12–Exodus 18). And that framework is seen in the *plot* structure which is introduced in the Dispensation of Promise, revelation entrusted to the stewardship of the patriarchs.

"If the characters are the soul of the narrative, the *plot* is the body. It consists of an organized and orderly system of events, arranged in temporal sequence. In contrast to life—we are invariably confronted by an endless stream of incidents occurring haphazardly and disparately—the *plot* of a narrative is constructed as a meaningful chain of interconnected events."[1]

The fundamental connection between events in a fallen world featured the tension caused by an enmity introduced in the setting (Gen 3:15). The ultimate tension is between *God* who created a *good* creation but who pronounced judgment on the serpent and fallen mankind to be carried out through the woman and a chosen line of seed, and the *serpent* and its seed who now rules over the fallen human race through its word of evil and the judgment of death.

From the line of the woman and Noah, God chose Abram and *promised* to bless him and to bless all nations through him (Gen 12:1-3). By faith in God's *promise*, Abram left Ur of the Chaldeans in search of the

---

[1] Bar-Efrat, *Narrative Art in the Bible*, p. 93.

land that the LORD had promised to show him. That *promise* progressed from the promise to see the land, to when the LORD promised to give it to Abram's seed (Gen 12:7). In unbelief, he took his father and nephew, Lot, and thus clung to some of his old ways. Such unbelief is sin with consequences such as the delay in Haran. Yet the LORD delivers Abram after his father died. And thus, the plot structure unfolds. The tension continues to structure the narrative:

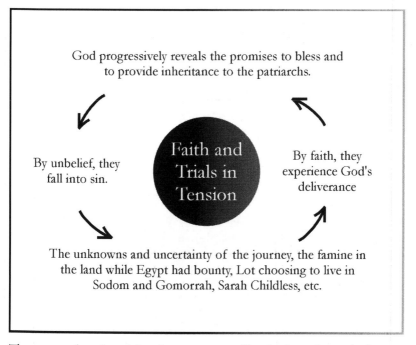

The repeated cycles of the plot are *governed* by the LORD's word of *promise*. The initial stage of the narrative features the patriarchs as *stewards* of the *promises* in both belief and in disbelief.

CHAPTER 5:
THE THEOLOGY OF THE
DISPENSATION OF PROMISE

Introduction

Biblical theology tells the story of the whole Bible. In a number of ways, the story of redemption from sin and restoration of the creation begins in Genesis 12, an account of the calling of Abram/Abraham from the family of Terah. Genesis 1–11 had set the stage through elements of hope and despair. Hope can be found in the creation account since what God created set the stage to be *worked out* in history. But despair is also found in the serpent's conquest over Adam and in mankind's inability to recover on their own from the fall (Genesis 3–11).[1] None of the creation hope had been *worked out* due to man's fall. Thus, God begins to speak to Abram (Gen 12:1-3).

As God spoke, the call came in the Word of Promise to Abram. It was not that God commanded Abram to *work out* the despair of the fallen world, but God promised Abram what He would do as Ruler to begin to *work it out*. Responding to the promise, Abram would become a *steward* of what God was doing at that stage in history. *Stewardship* of God's promises allowed God to do what He said on behalf of the steward and through the steward as a servant of God's will. These promises take the shape of a plan revealing more of who God is. As the LORD would say later, "I am the LORD. I appeared to Abraham, to Isaac, and to Jacob, as God Almighty, but by my name the LORD I did not make myself known to them." (Exod 6:2-3). God's revelation of Himself as God Almighty served several purposes.

---

[1] A Biblical revelation is unique from any other in the ANE. All ANE accounts begin with conflict. The Biblical account begins with a good world that was lost. That sets the *goal* of history to re-establish what was lost in its fullest terms.

In the first purpose, the focus rests on God who is the primary hero of the accounts of the patriarchs as Ruler of history. That focus rests on what God promised, not on what the patriarchs accomplished on their own. His Word of Promise casts a vision for the future and what He says molds the responses of the patriarchs in the midst of the cosmic conflict. As the patriarchs are transformed, God Almighty is revealed in new ways. The path of each individual patriarch is different, but none is defeated in spite of the adversity from God's enemy. As Hero, God's glory begins to shine forth in the fallen world as the sunshine peeking over the horizon.

In the second purpose, the words of God's promise mold the responses of the elect ones in their service to God's will. At the outset, this service is not as rulers on earth as the creation anticipated, but both *Abraham* and Sarah are promised kings in their lineage. So Abram is molded into a *steward* of the promised inheritance as he is known as the "father of faith." *Jacob* does not rule either, but becomes the "father of the people." His life was fashioned by a series of struggles from which he emerged with a new name, Israel, for he had "striven with God and with men, and [had] prevailed" (Gen 32:28). *Joseph* faced conflict from within his family, from his master in Egypt, and from his experiences in the Egyptian prison system, yet he overcame. In God's grace, he was elevated to become second in the ruling hierarchy of Egypt, a position which allowed him to save his family both from famine and from self-service. When Joseph remembered the divinely-given dream (Gen 42:9), he acted according to what the dream had revealed. He ruled his brothers as a steward of God's Word and solicited their repentance (Genesis 42–44).

Thus, the climax of the dispensation of promise was God Almighty's *redemption* of Israel from Egypt's enslavement. This redemption of God's firstborn son, Israel, (Exod 4:22-23) set the price of redemption to be every firstborn son in Egypt. However, God provided a Passover provision by which every household with the blood applied to the doorposts would be delivered from the judgment (Exodus 12–13).

In a third purpose, each patriarchal episode involves a plot-conflict as God's Word of Promise is challenged at every turn. The conflicts that overcame the human race with evil in Genesis 3–11 are now challenging the Word of Promise in each patriarch. This Word of Promise delivers from the final judgment of evil (justification) and prevails to overcome evil in the patriarchs' pursuit of their stewardship. While all the patriarchs will die, that temporal judgment does not negate what begins to be fulfilled in their conflict with evil. Abraham is declared righteous and thus is *delivered* from final judgment (Gen 15:6). Further, by faith, Abraham blesses (cf. Gen 12:3b) and *delivers* Isaac from premature death, and in the test, he *overcomes* the temptation to evil (Gen 22:1-2, 5, 8). Jacob *prevails* in the repeated conflicts with Esau and Laban. He is named Israel. Joseph *overcomes* the conflicts with his brothers and with Egypt. *Overcoming*, he rules in Egypt and *delivers* his brothers. In these ways, God's purpose to *deliver* and to *overcome* evil begins to be fulfilled. Similarly, the patriarchs' stewardships begin to reveal a plan of what God's promise would ultimately accomplish.

The introduction of the generations of Terah (Gen 11:27) and the revelation of God's purposes foreshadows God's plan that began with the revelation of God's promise to Abram (Gen 12:1-3). That promise looked to the future and what God committed Himself to do as He began to implement His plan. That implementation involved the beginning of deliverance from sin and its consequences[2] and the initial stages of overcoming the power of evil.

The Introduction of Deliverance

The need for divine deliverance was implicit in Gen 3:15 since the enemy and his progeny were innately more powerful than the descendants of the woman. This was illustrated with Noah. If they were to be delivered in the conflict, God must do it. What was implicit is now made explicit in the promises given to the patriarchs. They are now introduced alongside the sentence of conflict which included God's elect as Abraham, Isaac, Jacob, and Joseph. The narrative of the dispensation of promise is the story of God's revelation in the life of these patriarchs.

What Is a Promise?

Although natural language speakers understand what promises are, the field of Linguistics and Semantics can help us to think more carefully about what is involved. The early work of G. B. Caird introduced

---

[2] The pronouncement of judgment against the serpent-enemy does not promise deliverance or blessing (Gen 3:15). It is implied, however, so it is widely recognized as the protoevangelium. In addition, within the narrative there is an introduction of Adam's relationship with God. When Adam named his wife Eve, mother of the living, he believed that God would address the execution of the immediate death sentence (Gen 2:17). Through his faith, God provided a skin covering that satisfied God to admit fallen man into His presence. Abel acted on this instruction when he offered the animal sacrifice and was accepted. But the word of judgment does not express a basis for the deliverance from sin and its consequences.

this study in helpful speech-act terms.[3] In addition, the work of Willis J. Beecher demonstrated the unity of the promise theme in Scripture.[4] Walter C. Kaiser built on the work of Beecher to propose a Biblical Theology based on promise.[5] These works highlight the appropriate prominence of *promise* in Biblical revelation. Dispensationalism also incorporates God's Word of Promise in its model of Biblical theology. This particular model presents it as the first dispensation in the unfolding of God's progressive revelation in history.

A *promise* is a *performative* statement. J. L. Austin[6] named these statements performatives because they feature an author's commitment to some kind of performance in the future. Commonly, they take a form: "I will do such and such." For a promise to be viable, the author must be willing and able to perform and accomplish what has been claimed. In addition, promises are addressed to recipients. Recipients either receive the promise by faith or reject it in disbelief. The recipient must believe that the author has spoken and that he is both willing and able to accomplish what he has claimed. Thus, a promise casts a vision about the future in the recipient's imagination. A believer then responds and waits until what has been promised is fulfilled.

When the author is another human being, a promise merely concerns mutual responsibilities in a relationship. However, when the author is God, the scope of what is promised may well concern what God intends to perform throughout history. While God isn't present on earth to perform in the same fashion as humans, He acts through mediating agents—like His own Spirit, or angels, or human stewards who partner with Him. A human partner is chosen and then spoken to with various kinds of statements. In performative statements, a command expects the recipient to perform according to the direction of the command. Or in a promise, the recipient awaits God to perform according to His commitment. A partner is usually addressed in both commands and promises (Gen 18:16-21). And a partner recognizes that whatever his response may be, it is God's commitments that determine the outcome. A steward is responsible both to believe, awaiting what God has promised, and to obey according to what God expects. The steward manages what God has said in faith and in obedience. The stewardship of promise features

---

[3]   Caird, *The Language and Imagery of the Bible*.

[4]   Willis J. Beecher, *The Prophets and the Promise* (Grand Rapids, MI: Baker, 1905, 1975).

[5]   Walter C. Kaiser, Jr., *The Promise-Plan of God* (Grand Rapids, MI: Zondervan, 2008).

[6]   J. L. Austin, *How to Do Things with Words* (Oxford, UK: Clarendon, 1962), pp. 4ff.

what God has promised, but not excluding what God has commanded. Likewise, the stewardship of law features commands, but they are added alongside what has been promised and are added awaiting the completed fulfillment of promise.

Like all language statements, promises are not a picture mode of communication. In other words, all the details are not expressed the way they are in a photograph. Rather, selected aspects of meaning are expressed in the promise, but the selection forms a pattern of the picture. The essentials of the overall pattern involve a subject (what are we talking about?) and a complement (what is being said about the subject?). The pattern constitutes a message (proposition or idea). Entailed in this message is a boundary or framework which distinguishes what is meant from what is not meant. However, the message often is not precise and thus what is included and excluded may not be immediately evident.

Promises are messages from an author about what he intends to perform in the future. Promises vary in form and detail as they communicate an intention to perform. G. B. Caird[7] has illustrated five types of the promise genre. They all include a commitment about the future but all are not the promise genre. It is helpful to take note of distinctions in genre in the interpretation of promises:

1. Prediction—a promise specifies numerous details so that it has only one intended reference. God's commitment to act is not transferable to another situation or event (e.g., Mic 5:2).

2. Proverb—a statement that is not a promise in the sense of a commitment from God, but a maxim based on probable combined circumstances. Experience teaches that these circumstances combine to produce a probable outcome (e.g., Prov 3:5-6).

These two examples, (1 and 2), are extreme cases of commissive statements. Between these extremes are other examples of promises.

3. Typical prediction—a promise made in reference to a particular situation. That situation and the issues included in the promise, however, contain enough general truth to make it readily transferable to a number of situations (e.g., Isa 6:9-10; Matt 13:14-15; Acts 28:26-27). The near fulfillment is a type of the intended, ultimate fulfillment.

---

[7] Caird, *The Language and Imagery of the Bible*, pp. 57-58.

4. Situation vacant promise—a promise about an individual in some detail yet not explicit personally. The detail is distinct enough that in time, the identification can be made. At the time of the prophecy, the prophet may not know the historic person he talks about (e.g., Gen 3:15 who is the seed of the woman? Gen 22:18 who is the seed of Abraham? Isa 49:5 who is the servant of the LORD? etc.).

5. Mendicant promise—a promise using words thrown out to refer to a not fully grasped object (e.g., redemption, Exod 6:6; substitution, John 11:50-52).

All but one of these are commitment statements about the future (1, 3, 4 and 5) and all the promises are commitments based on God's predestination. The other (2) is a commitment based on the probable outworking of contingent events. What we can know about the future varies with each kind of statement. We should not claim to know more than the particular statement supports. This is valuable in recognizing the pattern of the statement. This enables the interpreter to be realistic in his expectations.

What Is a Promissory Covenant?

Weinfeld[8] is a scholar who finds support for distinguishing between types of covenantal arrangements in both the Bible and the Ancient Near East. The basic distinction between types of covenants is between a promissory and an obligatory arrangement.

A covenant in the Ancient Near East was a formal partnership arrangement, ratified by a sacrifice and/or an oath. The basic difference between a promise and a promissory covenant concerns the formal ratification sacrifice and oath. A promissory arrangement involves one party making a formal commitment in promises addressed to the other party. An obligatory arrangement consists of obligations of laws or stipulations accepted by the second party and responding to the authority of the other more powerful party.

The language we use to talk about covenants must be carefully considered because the discussion has gotten confusing. There are two separate issues: the *existence* and the *functioning* of a covenant. Our primary concern in this chapter is with the Abrahamic Covenant which is a

---

[8] M. Weinfeld, "ברת, *bᵉrîth*," TDOT, vol. 2, pp. 253-79.

promissory type covenant. Because it is promissory, it was ratified only by the LORD while Abram was fast asleep (Gen 15:8-21). The covenant came into *existence* when it was ratified. The Hebrew term, cut (*krt*), is most commonly used to refer to ratification as it is here (Gen 15:18, translated, *made*, in the ESV, NIV,[9] JPS,[10] HCSB); to cut a covenant is to make a covenant. And when the covenant is promissory, its existence is unconditional or not conditioned on Abraham or on any of his descendants. In this sense, the Abrahamic Covenant can be called, "eternal."

However, because a covenant is a partnership arrangement, its *function* is always conditioned on the participation of both partners. Different Hebrew terms are used to speak about function (*nātan*, Gen 17:2, trans. *confirm*, NIV; *establish* JPS, HCSB; *made* ESV; or *gûm*, Gen 9:9, 11, trans. *establish* ESV, NIV, JPS; *confirm*, HSCB). The variety in translation indicates the difficulty in distinguishing between existence and function. Yet the Abrahamic Covenant came into existence at the ceremony (Gen 15:8-21) but didn't begin to function until Isaac was born (Gen 21:1-7).

What is a Narrative Plot-Structure with Promise?

The primary characteristic of narrative is a plot conflict which finds resolution in the sequence of events. The conflict in promise narrative is between what God promised and that which opposes or seeks to hinder God's promises. This opposition can take the form of God's enemy, Satan. But opposition can also take other forms such as unbelief in the characters addressed with promise, opposition from foes or seed of the serpent who do not believe, and natural obstacles to the realization of what was promised (e.g., barrenness, famine, etc.).

In this narrative plot structure with promise, the *characters* are at the focus of the conflict. As the Torah became Israel's core authority, the patriarchs are the human heroes. Yet at the level of the narrative-plot, God is the ultimate Hero as His Word of Promise anticipated the outcome of each plot.[11]

In the Abram narrative, there are several conflicts: the delayed birth of a promised child (Genesis 12:7–21:7), the land promised but never

---

[9]   *The Holy Bible, New International Version* (Nashville, TN: HarperCollins, 1973, 1978, 1984, 2011).

[10]   *JPS Bible* (NP: Jewish Publication Society, 1917).

[11]   Leland Ryken, *Words of Delight* (Grand Rapids, MI: Baker, 1987), pp. 107-125.

possessed (Gen 12:2, 7; 15:8), conflict with Gentile kings (Genesis 14), conflict with the righteousness of Lot and family (Genesis 13; 18; cf. 2 Pet 2:7), the potential crisis involving Abimelech (Genesis 20) and Pharaoh in Egypt (Genesis 12). All of these contributed to a fundamental plot conflict going on within Abram's conscious self-awareness. As a descendant of Adam, his self-awareness was enslaved by a lie: "you can be like God." But in conflict were God's promises and in his responses, his self-awareness was being molded as he gradually believed more of God's Word: "leave and go...I will bless you...and you will be a blessing to others" (Gen 12:1-3, paraphrased).

The plot-conflict featured Abram's response to the two conflicting words. There are two primary plots: (1) from a divided heart[12] to faith in God's Word (Genesis 12:1–15:6) and (2) from faith to faithfulness (Genesis 15:7–22:19).

In the story of Jacob's life, the basic plot-conflict was also in Jacob's self-awareness. Not only was he a son of Adam but a self-centered awareness was learned and confirmed at home. Deception was the way they treated each other. Not only was that Isaac's awareness, it was also Rebekah's. Both had their favorites. Although both Isaac and Rebekah valued the birthright blessing, they acted as though it was under their control rather than God's.

The second plot challenged Jacob's self-centered consciousness with the dream of the ladder (Gen 28:10-15) and in his interactions with Laban (Genesis 29–31). Positively, the dream revealed what was available in God's resources. Negatively, Laban acted like God as he attempted to manipulate Jacob for his own profit. In the conflict, Jacob was weaned away from self-confidence to become more aware of God and confident in Him.

In the third plot, Jacob faced meeting Esau (Genesis 33), the brother he had wronged (Genesis 27). Jacob's thoughts of himself were finally challenged when God allowed Jacob to wrestle all night with Him (Genesis 32). In the end, God gave him a name which disclosed his historic identity—*Israel*. Later when he blessed his sons, Jacob demonstrated his transformation by speaking and acting by faith in crossing his hands to bless Joseph's sons contrary to accepted social convention (Genesis 48).

---

[12]   "The 'heart' in Hebrew describes the seat and function of the reason. It includes everything that we ascribe to the head and brain—power of perception, reason, understanding, insight, consciousness, memory, knowledge, reflection, judgment, sense of direction, discernment" (Wolff, *Anthropology of the Old Testament*, p. 51).

In Joseph's story, little is known of his conscious awareness until God reveals his dream (Gen 37:5-11). There is no doubt in Joseph's mind that what God disclosed about his family role is to be the case. So the plot in Joseph's case is not in his self-awareness, except that it was a naive faith that blurted out the dream without any consideration for others' feelings. Joseph's naive faith needed to become mature faith. And this would take place in the three plot conflicts—(1) with his jealous brothers, (2) with Potiphar who listened to his wife's lie, and (3) with the bottomless pit of Egypt's prison system (Genesis 39). While Joseph showed faith in all three, it became faith that recognized that the glory belonged to God who alone could have *delivered* Joseph (Gen 50:20).

The second part of Joseph's story is the conflict he caused for his brothers who had come to Egypt to buy grain (Gen 42:7). It was a plot instigated by Joseph's memory of the dream. Joseph managed a conflict between what the brothers claimed—"we are honest men" and what the brothers could produce to display Benjamin. The conflict was resolved by Judah who protected his father and offered himself as a substitute for Benjamin who was alleged to be guilty. In the confession of the brothers' sin and Judah's offer of himself, Joseph *saved* his family as the family had bowed before Joseph in fulfillment of the LORD's dream (Gen 45:5, 7).

The immediate conflict began between Joseph and the jealousy in his brothers' lives. Yet this was a reflection of the ultimate conflict which the LORD prophesied in Joseph's dream. That eventually led to Joseph's rise to rule in Egypt under Pharaoh. Then under Joseph's testing of his brothers, the evil in their heart was exposed. From this evil they were delivered; not merely from the famine, but from the consequences of evil in their hearts.

Conclusion

The plot-conflict is worked out in the patriarchs as stewards of God's promise. These form paradigms of stewardship for the believers who later read these accounts in Scripture.

CHAPTER 6:
ABRAHAM'S FAITH
IN GOD'S PROVISION
ACCORDING TO PROMISE

Introduction

This section will be the first consideration of *faith* but not the last. In fact, it will remain a central issue of consideration throughout the whole story. So at the outset, I'd like to raise some questions which will remain open to further consideration. Since Heb 11:1-3 and 6 speak to the answer so directly, we'll include what Hebrews has to say about *faith*.

What Is Faith?

Faith is an attitude of confidence resting on something or someone.

This proposes that faith entails both a subjective attitude and an objective ground. Hebrews 11:1 acknowledges both aspects:

> "Now faith is the *substance* of things hoped for [objective ground found in God's promise], the *confidence* of things not seen [subjective attitude]." (Author's amplified translation)

Why Is Faith so Natural?

Faith originates in our humanity. Because of our own limitations, statements of faith or assumptions are components of any field of knowledge. Unlike our Creator, humans are not omniscient.

Does the Confidence of Faith Change?

Since Faith is a subjective attitude, it is subject to change, both in the sense of development and in the sense of rejection. This answer will only consider development of faith. Abram's case considers two kinds of development: in one sense, his confidence expanded in the progress of revelation and in another sense, his confidence prompted obedient actions. His faith expanded when he eventually came to believe that his heir would come from his own body (Gen 15:4, 6) rather than being Eliezer of Damascus (Gen 15:2). In addition, his faith deepened when he offered Isaac as the LORD had said (Gen 22:9-10).

What Is the Ground or Substance of Faith?

In a Biblical worldview, God the LORD is the proper and essential object of faith. "The fear of the LORD is the beginning of knowledge" and wisdom (Prov 1:7; Job 28:28). In Abram's case, the Bible doesn't explain how Abram knew who God is or who it was who spoke to him. It simply says that the LORD said and Abram departed as the LORD had spoken to him (Gen 12:1 and 4). Explanations will become more extensive and more explicit as the story as a whole develops. For now, Abram believed what God *promised* concerning his seed.

What Role Does Faith Have in a Person's Life?

The author to the Hebrews is helpful here:

> "For by it [faith] the people of old received their commendation" (Heb 11:2).

> "without faith it is impossible to please Him, for he who comes to God must believe that He is, and that He is a rewarder of those who diligently seek Him" (Heb 11:6, NKJV).

Several issues are at stake:

> First, faith is the human cause for a relationship with God (Gen 15:6).

> Second, faith obtains a good testimony before God (Gen 18:16-33).

> Third, faith is the cause of good stewardship and is rewarded (Gen 22:16-18).

Hebrews 11:3: "By faith, we understand that the worlds were framed by the word of God so that the things which are seen were not made of things which are visible" (author's translation).

So faith must be incorporated in our field of knowledge—here of both the natural world and of God at work.

How Reliable Is Our Faith?

While Faith is not based on a comprehensive knowledge, it must be based on reliable evidence (John 20:31). Faith is "the conviction of things not seen," but nonetheless, that conviction rests on reliable witnesses. The law only authorized actions on the basis of two or three compatible witnesses. Jesus authorizes the apostles as witnesses of the unseen resurrection (Acts 1:8, 22; 2:32; 3:15; 13:31). While the apostles didn't see the event, they did see Jesus before and in death, and then after death, alive.

At the same time, as members of a fallen human race, there is a conflict in what to believe. The serpent had tempted Eve, that one can be like God, and Adam and Eve believed the lie. That belief is now instinctive to the fallen human race. This accounts for human pride and unbounded hubris. All human beings have faith but it is not necessarily faith in the true God of Scripture. Pagan gods claimed the majority populations in the ANE cultures, and idolatry continued to be a temptation for the Israelites. Even in Ur of the Chaldeans, it was a polytheistic culture in which Abram was raised (Josh 24:2). It was from there that Stephen said God called Abram (Acts 7:2).

The Faith of Abraham

"Abraham gave expression to God's provision through His promise (Gen 22:14): 'Jehovah Jireh.' The Lord had *provided* a sacrifice to keep His promise concerning Isaac. *Yera'eh* means to *provide* which is a secondary meaning of the simple verb 'to see.'"[1] The LORD *sees to it* that the promise is being fulfilled.

When Abraham and Isaac were walking together to Mt. Moriah, Isaac had the wood and Abraham the fire and knife. Isaac questioned his father

---

[1]   Kidner, *Genesis*, p. 144, clarification added.

about the sacrifice. Abraham's answer could only be generated by faith; God will "see to it," or God will "provide" (Gen 22:8).

> It might almost be called his lifetime motto; many have lived by it since. His complete certainty of God, together with complete openness as to detail, makes this a model reply to an agonizing question. God's method was his own affair; it would take them both by surprise.[2]

Abraham exemplifies the attitude of the steward toward what is promised—in the mount, it will become clear. Both senses are valid; God sees to it and the steward will see the provision. And this broad theological sense is warranted to be developed in salvation history.[3]

Fuhs develops the doctrine of providence under two broad headings: first, *experiencing God's power.* "Much more common than the immediate sight of God is the experience of divine presence in God's (*kābôd*) glory and acts in history."[4] Second, *God as Subject*: "all human apperception of God requires God's prior self-revelation."[5] Then he illustrates it in two contexts; (1) the goodness of God's work of creation is grounded in God's *seeing to it* (Gen 1:4, 10, 12, 18, 21, 25, 31), and (2) God *causing* someone *to see* or showing him something. "In the promise recorded in Genesis 12:1, the emphasis is on the assurance of God's guidance on Abram's journey from homeland to his promised land."[6]

Reformed theology has broadened the concept further in the doctrine of providence. Calvin postulated it as a corollary to creation[7] and as an implication of God's sovereignty. The theology ascribes the word as traceable to Gen 22:14. Two related clarifications are spelled out by Charles Hodge[8] that are helpful: first, "Creation…is the calling into existence what before did not exist," while providence "is continuing, or causing to continue what already has a being," and second, "in creation there is and can be no cooperation, but in preservation there is a *concursus* of the first, with the second cause." Moreland notes, "To confuse these two with a

---

[2] *Ibid.*, pp. 143-44.

[3] H. F. Fuhs, "רָאָה, *rā'â*," TDOT, vol. 13, pp. 231-39.

[4] *Ibid.*, p. 231.

[5] *Ibid.*, p. 233.

[6] *Ibid.*, p. 235.

[7] John Calvin, *Institutes of the Christian Religion*, ed. John T. McNeill, trans. Ford Lewis Battles (Philadelphia: Westminster, 1960), 1.16.1.

[8] Charles Hodge, *Systematic Theology*, vol. 1 (New York: Charles Scribner's Sons, 1899), pp. 577, 581.

theory of continuous creation leads inevitably to pantheism. However, a development of what is involved with cooperation demands a philosophical analysis."[9]

McClain, also in a Reformed perspective, posits that God's sovereignty expresses itself in universal reign. In history, the Scriptures affirm, "you rule over all" (1 Chr 29:12) and, "The LORD has established his throne in the heavens, and his kingdom rules over all" (Ps 103:19). Thus, he argues that God rules over all by both providential means and supernatural means. By providence, God rules by means of secondary causes created in creation. In addition, God rules by supernatural means introduced directly into history.

> The God of the Bible is said to be both *in* the universe and also *above* it. Therefore, at any time He may break into the so-called 'closed system' of nature (which He upholds and controls) with great exhibitions of his unveiled power.[10]

So central is the model of the kingdom to governance in history, we are proposing an analogy similar to Calvin: in creation, God spoke creation into existence, so in history, God speaks to stewards and entrusts God's Word to them so as to establish God's kingdom on earth. Stewards manage life according to the Word as they experience God's will on earth. And God's Word is progressively unfolding from patriarch to patriarch.

This universal rule could be illustrated as Abraham offers Isaac (Gen 22:1-14). Supernaturally, God interrupts Abraham: "Do not lay your hand on the lad or do anything to him; for now I know that you fear God, since you have not withheld your son, your only son, from me" (Gen 22:12, NKJV). Providentially, "Abraham lifted his eyes and looked, and there behind him was a ram caught in a thicket by its horns. So Abraham went and took the ram, and offered it up for a burnt offering instead of his son. And Abraham called the name of the place, The-Lord-Will-Provide, as it is said to this day, 'In the Mount of the LORD it shall be provided'" (Gen 22:13-14, NKJV). God's providential use of secondary agents is also expressed in God's restatement of the promise: because you have done this thing…I will bless you (Gen 22:17).

So In God's universal rule, *providential* means may be distinguished from *supernatural* means. And in the narrative plots of the dispensation of promise, God's actions may involve His direct causes and His use of

---

[9] J. P. Moreland and William Lane Craig, *Philosophical Foundations for a Christian Worldview* (Downers Grove, IL: IVP, 2003), pp. 561-65.

[10] McClain, *Greatness of the Kingdom*, p. 29.

secondary causes to accomplish His plan. In these means, God reveals Himself as Almighty.

Promise is the controlling revelation that progressively unfolds through the economy of the dispensation of promise. The continuing antecedent and normative revelation is the judicial sentence (Gen 3:15). The focus is on the promise of blessing, which God provides in an initial fulfillment of God's deliverance (Gen 15:6), followed by a call to the responsibility of the stewardship of promise (Gen 18:17-19). The outworking of God's purposes alludes to the goal of redemption already revealed (Gen 3:15) and to the role of man introduced, who will ultimately achieve the goal of ruling (Gen 1:26-28).

Abraham: The Promise to Be Blessed and to Be a Blessing (Genesis 11:27–25:11)

Surprisingly, this section begins with a series of commands followed by a series of promises (Gen 12:1-8). One is faced with two questions: (1) What is the relationship between the commands and the promises? and (2) What is the role of the commands? The answer is that the commands are the *means* by which God would fulfill what He promised. The initial promise is that God will show Abram the land (Gen 12:1d). In order to see the land, Abram had to leave his homeland as commanded (Gen 12:1a; Acts 7:2-3). For Abram to be shown the land by God, he had to separate from possible distracting influences in his familial relationships (Gen 12:1b-c). As *means*, this is distinct from *conditions*. The difference is that a condition describes an action without which the promises would not be kept. A means is one action among a number of possible actions by which the promise could be kept by God.

So Abram's action, *lek-lekā* (לֶךְ־לְךָ), "goes forth," has the force of "separating, taking leave of."[11] He left Ur of Chaldea,[12] but his father Terah took Abram and his nephew, Lot (Gen 11:31). This partial obedience was a means that God used to develop Abram's faith since God as Sovereign

---

[11] Sarna, *Genesis*, p. 88.

[12] It seems that "Terah took Abram" from the Ur of Chaldea as Gen 11:31 says. Stephen clarifies the historical sequence. The clarification was that God appeared to Abram in Mesopotamia before he dwelt in Haran (Acts 7:2). Further, Abram came out of the land of the Chaldeans and dwelt in Haran. And from there, when his father was dead, God moved him to his land in which he now dwelled (Acts 7:4). Stephen's statement that God moved him agrees with our conclusion that God drew him into a position as a steward serving God's will. The language of Genesis can be attributed to the fact that in a patriarchal society the father Terah would be seen as responsible for the initial departure of the whole family.

had other means to complete the separation. His father died in Haran on the way to the Promised Land (Gen 11:31-32) and Lot chose to live in Sodom and Gomorrah (Gen 13:5-11). So Abram's initial divided faith was being purified by events under God's providence (Gen 13:14-18).

Rather than God working directly with all nations as he did in Genesis 4–11, Abram is now chosen to be what Adam had been created to be. And so he must first be separated from his own nation to become a mediator of what God would do for and through him to the nations. In Abram's life, he mediated blessings to Lot (Gen 13:8-13; 18:16-33), to Ishmael (Gen 16:11-16; 21:13-21), and primarily to Isaac (Gen 21:8-12; 22:15-18). This introduces the dispensation of promise.

However, the climactic promise, "through *you all nations* shall be blessed" (Gen 12:3b, emphasis added), is a *situation vacant* promise. While the account of Abram unfolded, Abram was a source of blessing in his world, during his lifetime. But clearly *all nations*, even those just mentioned (Gen 10:1-23), had not been blessed yet. As a result, it is clear that the word *you* is not limited to Abraham personally. So, *who will be blessed* and *by whom* is vacant from the text at this stage in the revelation.

So from the outset, God prepares Abram for offspring: "to your offspring I will give this land" (Gen 12:7). Who would this "offspring" be? Did it mean the immediate descendant, or all offspring, or some future generation of offspring or would it be some specific future descendant? The vagueness of the language itself brings no answer, but it contributes to the identification of the vacancy to be filled.

Thus, the very promise brought hope and invited a search in each subsequent generation for the promised offspring. God's pronounced judgment on the serpent also brought the hope of a specific, future descendant (Gen 3:15c).

At the culmination of Abraham's lifetime, the "through you" (Gen 12:3) was specified further, "and in your offspring shall all the nations of the earth be blessed" (22:18). Yet, the ambiguity of language remained open: would it be either one or many offspring or both one and many offspring? The history of Israel during the dispensation of the law would be needed to clarify the ultimate referent of the promise.

The narrative begins with God's choice of Abram (Gen 11:27-32) and then the story consists in two spiritual plots in which he is molded to be God's steward in heart: (1) resolving the conflict from a divided heart to a heart of faith (Genesis 12:1–15:6), and (2) resolving the conflict from faith to faithfulness (Genesis 15:7–22:19).

The narrative in Genesis features the conflict in Abram's heart, but this theological interpretation is primarily driven by a natural conflict of childlessness. The conflict was announced in Gen 11:30 that Sarai was barren and would be resolved with the birth of Isaac in 21:1-7.

God's promise called Abram to rest in God's commitment, which focused on the future, always holding out hope. This hope was associated with another plot-conflict in Abraham's life, which was the possession of the Promised Land. It was land that would support the lives of his offspring with blessings. The conflict involved a hope to someday gain possession of the land promised, yet Abraham would live as a pilgrim and stranger in the land. This tension would be put in proper perspective through the Abrahamic Covenant. The possession was as certain as God's oath but delayed by the spiritual condition of the residents of the land. As God's unilateral gift, it was certain, but it would only be given in God's way and only be realized when the God of heaven took the initiative to provide it on earth.

There is no indication in Genesis that the nation's future would not include an actual land. The covenant was revealed to answer Abram's question (Gen 15:8). So the complexities of Abram's life told a story. That story was fashioned into a theological-spiritual plot-conflict that included natural conflicts being resolved by God's provisions received by faith.

The Plot from a Divided Heart to a Heart of Faith

Election

God's choice of Abram initially occurs in the text in which Abram's spiritual condition is unknown. There is no indication that he knows Yahweh. He is simply identified as a descendant of Terah (Gen 11:26). His familial status is equally ambiguous. Since Haran died first among Terah's descendants (Gen 11:28) and since he had a son, Lot, who was Abram's contemporary, it would seem probable that Haran was the firstborn and natural heir apparent of Terah. So Abram's election cannot be clearly attributed to his religious or familial standing.

Joshua 24:2 indicates that Terah and his family served other gods, yet the LORD chose Abram/Abraham (Josh 24:3). Genesis describes Terah taking Abram (Gen 11:31) from Ur of the Chaldeans to Haran where Terah died. Yet it was God who called Abram to leave (Gen 12:1-3) and Abram went as he had been told (Gen 12:4). Stephen later clarified that God's call came in Mesopotamia before they got to Haran (Acts 7:2).

Thus, God chose and called Abram, but because the account was about "the generation of Terah" (Gen 11:27), Terah was described as the leader. Thus, Abram recognized and responded to the voice of the LORD, but he was only beginning to know God.

Yet the question may be raised about Abram and how he recognized the voice as the LORD at all. If the genealogies in Gen 5:1-32 and 11:10-32 are closed (without any gaps), then Abram was born within one generation of Noah's death. It is possible then that Abram received direct testimony about the God of the flood from Noah's children.

Revelation

"The pattern of God's call to Abraham recalls God's pattern of creation—announcement, command (12:1), and report (12:4-9)—with an addition of God's promise (12:2-3)."[13] The additional revelation of *promise* distinguishes God's providential work in history from God's creative work in creation. In the creation account, God is the lone agent and the sole cause in speaking the earth and life into existence. In the history of the earth, God providentially incorporates Abram as a steward and a secondary cause. The report in creation was simply "and it was so." The process was left unexplained. In history, the process is of focal importance and central to the process is the Word of God and the person addressed to be a steward of that Word. Both the primary cause and the secondary cause are included in what God accomplishes in history. Although the process of cooperation is not at all capable of full description, it is essential to include the presence of both the primary and secondary causes.

A *command* is the first recorded word the LORD speaks to Abram (Gen 12:1). "Here he has to leave behind his aged father and his environment and go to a country that is unknown to him."[14] The command was counter-cultural and contrary to nature. So why did Abram leave? What was the relationship between the LORD and Abram before the *command* came? The answer to these questions is not addressed in the text although it might be inferred that the testimony Abram received or the ancient record of Semite migration influenced his departure.

But in the silence of the text, it seems best not to speculate. The fact that "Abram went, as the LORD had told him" (Gen 12:4) is revealed as the

---

[13] Waltke, *Genesis*, p. 203.

[14] Umberto Cassuto, *A Commentary on the Book of Genesis, Part Two: From Noah to Abraham, Genesis 6:9–11:32*, 1st English ed. (Jerusalem: Magnes, 1964), p. 310.

foundation of the story that follows. This foundation leaves the promises not as contingent on Abram's response but as contingent on the LORD's commitment. The relative security of living in Ur of the Chaldeans would be replaced by the promise of the little-known God. The promises alone that follow make the responses plausible and easily account for Abram's heart being divided.

The *promises* include the following (Gen 12:1-3, emphasis added):

> "…the land that I will show you.
> And I will make of you a great nation,
> and I will bless you
>   and make your name great,
> so that you will be a blessing.
> I will bless those who bless you,
> and him who dishonors you I will curse,
> and in you all the families of the earth shall be blessed."

The promises identify Abram's new stewardship. "Abram must exchange the known for the unknown (Heb 11:8), and find his reward in what he could not live to see (a *great nation*), in what was intangible (thy name) and in what he would impart (blessing)."[15]

Response

The commands were difficult and Abram's response was divided (Gen 12:4-9). In obedience, he took his wife and left his hometown. But he also took his father and nephew and stopped short of the land waiting until his father died. Nonetheless, when he arrived in the land promised, the LORD appeared and added to the promise: "to your offspring I will give this land." So Abram built an altar to the LORD (Gen 12:7).

Unexpectedly, he found the land in famine (Gen 12:10-20). Even though the land would be given and he would be blessed, the land could not support his family's life. So he turned to Egypt for help, compromising his wife and God's promise of offspring. When he left Egypt, he was shamed by his compromise as he was confronted (Gen 12:18-20). Yet God had provided rich blessings.

When the question of support for his family arose a second time, he had learned that God was sufficient (Gen 13:14-18). Abram gave Lot first choice of land and waited on God, and the LORD clarified the promise of

---

[15]   Kidner, *Genesis*, p. 114.

land to Abram. Then for the first time in this chapter, the LORD speaks to Abram and tells him to lift up his eyes (cf. Lot's lifting his eyes). He promises Abram that all that he can see will be given to him and his descendants forever, a restatement of the promise in 12:7.

The conflict created in Abram's spirit was being resolved. Did Abram have faith? Yes. Was Abram justified by faith? Not yet. The text will not mention it until 15:6. What was missing? The answer will become clear as the LORD continued their conversation (Gen 15:1).

Abram had offered sacrifices as the LORD appeared to him (Gen 12:7-8). God would care for him in the land. Now things were happening quickly. Abram delivered Lot and Sodom-Gomorrah from Chedorlaomer (Gen 14:1-16).[16] Melchizedek, king of Salem and priest of the Most High God, brought bread and wine for Abram before God, the Creator (Gen 14:17-24). Then Melchizedek blessed Abram[17] and praised God Most High on his behalf. And Abram gave Melchizedek one tenth of everything he had.[18]

What does this momentary incident mean? God is disclosing that the elect line was insufficient in itself to fully mediate God's will on earth (Gen 3:15). Abram, who represented the elect line of descendants that would follow, readily accepted the ministry of Melchizedek. The elect line had approached God through animal sacrifice on an altar (Gen 12:7-8). Now God provided an unknown king-priest to offer praise on behalf of Abram and to bless Abram on behalf of God Most High. This ministry completed Abram's thanksgiving for the victory just won and represented God's presence in the reception of the gift. For the elect line to

---

[16] Allen P. Ross notes that, "The message of this chapter has four major features. First, the land promised to Abram was plundered by invading armies who took tribute (cf. the later history of Israel and the tributes and captivities brought by eastern kings). Then Abram conquered the invading armies by the power of God, chasing them to Dan (the northern frontier of the land) and rescuing Lot and the other captives. Third, Abram's victory was an outworking of the promises of God (12:1-3), showing that he had indeed become a powerful tribal leader on the international scene and that those who shared his mission would share his blessing. Finally, Abram chose to wait for the blessing of God rather than accept anything from the king of Sodom, for he would not be satisfied with the spoils of war, especially if it put him in debt to this pagan king" (Allen P. Ross, *Creation and Blessing*, [Grand Rapids, MI: Baker, 1996], p. 294).

[17] The importance of the blessing is noted by Waltke. "Three times the important root ûrb appears. This not only alludes to Abram's name, but looks back to 12:1-3 where Abram was promised that he would be a blessing and that all families would find blessing in him. Here is the first fulfillment of that promise, as Melchizedek, one of the family of men, blesses Abram. The expected corollary of his goodwill is that he himself will be blessed. In contrast, the attitude of the king of Sodom seems to be that of disdain, and that has grave implications (cf. 12:3)" (Waltke, *Genesis*, p. 235).

[18] The significance of this is brought out in Hebrews 7.

fulfill their role, this pattern of ministry would be needed. Another clue is introduced that the divine provision will be enriched in God's time.

Yet, something was missing in what Abram believed. That becomes clear when God assured him of "protection and reward" (Gen 15:1) following his victory over Chedorlaomer. Ten years had passed since the promise of an heir had been made (Gen 12:7). With no offspring in sight, Abram questioned what this assurance meant. For a time, perhaps he had hoped that Lot would be his heir. Now he believed the heir would be Eliezer of Damascus (Gen 15:2-3). He could not figure out what God's promise assured.

In response, the Word of the LORD came to correct his speculation. "This man [Eliezer] shall not be your heir; your very own son shall be your heir" (Gen 15:4). The promise had been correct. God would bless Abram with a reward. God would bless Abram with an offspring and through his offspring would bless all nations, even though the historical referent of the offspring remained unknown. The uniqueness of this promise implied an offspring like no other: A physical descendant of Abram who, through His stewardship, God would bless *all* nations. The text states for the first time that Abram believed the content of the LORD's promise.[19] Through his faith, the LORD revealed that he was accounted righteous before God (Gen 15:6). At a generic level, this was the *gospel* (Gal 3:8).[20] All the essential components were present: faith resting in the person of the LORD, the physical offspring of Abram and the implied stewardship of this offspring to bless all the nations. The LORD revealed to Abram that now God had imputed righteousness to him, which would satisfy God regarding his final judgment of sin.[21] The first recorded case of *fulfillment* of God's plan of deliverance from the judgment of sin had occurred.

This plot-conflict was resolved at the level of Abram's personal standing with God.

The Plot from Faith to Faithfulness

This new plot-conflict concerns the stewardship of faith in spite of circumstances. Abram now believed that God would freely give him a son.

---

[19] This is the first occurrence in Genesis of the term *believe* (Heb '*âman*).

[20] James Montgomery Boice calls this "the most important verse in the Bible" (James Montgomery Boice, *Genesis: An Expositional Commentary*, vol. 2 [Grand Rapids, MI: Zondervan, 1982], p. 98).

[21] Abram is not described as doing righteousness but being declared righteous.

This is the *gospel*. And the *gospel* will be more fully stated in the progress of revelation as a message of *grace* for the reader. It was given in grace when it was first expressed. This will be true as it continues to be expressed and is finally and fully expressed in the New Testament. There is one *gospel*. In mankind's most serious problem—his conflict with evil and the consequences of his involvement in sin in final judgment—he or she can contribute nothing. Abram had not realized that. He had often tried to work out his own solution. When pressed, Abram's solutions were inadequate. He must trust in God and His solution. This solution had been included in the promises given to Abram. That is why his divided heart found resolution in an unequivocal faith in God's provision. Faith adds nothing. It is not faith in faith. Faith has no merit in itself; it simply receives God's promise on God's terms.

New circumstances do not alter the promises. From God's point of view, His character, His power, His promised solution overrides any new circumstance. His revelation includes the assurance that God is both willing and able. Faith simply receives what God has provided.

This emphasis is reflected directly in the primary piece of revelation—the Abrahamic Covenant. As a promissory covenant, it does not add any content to the promises already revealed. The formality of its ratification and assurance of the oath add to its capacity to convince over time. Thus, this piece of revelation will be examined carefully. Then circumstances which tempt different responses will be considered.

Revelation (Genesis 15:7-21)

This piece of revelation is a response to Abram's question: "how am I to *know* that I shall possess it?" (Gen 15:8). God had promised that his offspring would possess the land. Abram had heard it; he had not fully believed it. Circumstances had challenged it. He had walked as a pilgrim throughout the land and it was already occupied (Gen 13:17). God assured Abram by ratifying a promissory covenant. This assurance would not only help Abram but also future generations. The formal legal nature of the covenant reinforces the stability of what was promised and preserves it for future generations.

So God called Abram to prepare for a covenant ceremony. According to ANE custom, there was both sacrifice and oath. Preparation involved cutting animals in half by sacrifice and placing the two pieces side by side forming a path between (cf. Jer 34:18-19). The oath was to be taken by the two covenant parties as they walked between the pieces. The oath was a self-imprecation, calling upon themselves the same fate as fell on the animals if they were to fail to keep the covenant obligations (Gen 15:9-11).

After Abram completed the preparation, God put him to sleep (Gen 15:12). After explaining to Abram while he slept that the covenant would not be implemented for four hundred years (Gen 15:13-16), the LORD alone passed between the pieces (Gen 15:17). The LORD alone ratified (*kārat*) the covenant (Gen 15:18). This is called an *unconditional* covenant because its existence was not conditioned on anything Abram did because he was asleep. The covenant's very existence *assured* him that it would be inaugurated in fulfillment in the future. Then unilaterally, the LORD revealed the promise that the gift of the land was "to your offspring" (Gen 15:18). And the land boundaries were specified geographically. The covenant and not circumstances will determine the possession of the land.

Circumstantial Responses (Genesis 16:1–22:15)

Impatience (Gen 16:1-16)—Promises had been made and formal covenants had been ratified. But ten years pass without an heir for Abram. So Abram and Sarai apparently conclude that the heir would be provided through the common ANE practice of employing a concubine. Abram and Sarai acted without the LORD and Ishmael was born to Hagar. This has the predictable, but unintended, consequence of Hagar looking with contempt at Sarai (Gen 16:4).[22]

Silence and Responsibility (Genesis 17:1-21)

Another thirteen years of inactivity and silence had passed. "The two stages of covenant making, in chapters 15 and 17, not only tested Abram's faith by the long delay, but brought out two sides of the one transaction."[23] This second stage refers to covenant inauguration, which confronted Abram with his responsibility to walk before the LORD in a blameless fashion (Gen 17:1). The covenant had been ratified (*kārat*, Gen 15:18), but for the covenant to be inaugurated (*nātan*, Gen 17:2) in function, that demanded a holy walk (Gen 17:1). It had been ratified as

---

[22]   Ironically, the verb translated "despised" (*qâlal*) is the same verb used in 12:3 in one of the promises to Abram: "I will curse him one who curses (*qâlal*) you."

[23]   Kidner, *Genesis*, p. 128. The perception of "covenant making" fails to distinguish between ratification of existence and inauguration into function. Clearly the covenant existed, but it wasn't functioning.

an unconditional arrangement, but for the arrangement to function, it required an active partnership. Ishmael was not born as a covenant blessing, even though the covenant had promised many offspring (Gen 17:2). Ishmael was born of natural means.

Then Abram fell on his face (Gen 17:3). What followed was a conversation between the LORD and Abram (Gen 17:3-22). There are three sections noted, and each section states the participation of each individual.

(1) "As for Me" (Genesis 17:4-8)

First, God specifies His own role.[24] He is the covenant partner with Abram as they speak. In the future, Abram will father a multitude of nations and kings (Gen 17:4-6). As a sign of this future provision, his name is changed to Abraham, meaning the father of a multitude of nations (Gen 17:5-6). Based on what had been promised, a question arises: how does this multitude of nations relate to the one nation (Gen 12:2; 15:18)? Will nations born from Hagar, Sarah, and Keturah be included? Or will nations be understood as the "nations" given to Sarah (Gen 17:16)?

Then God adds that He will *maintain* (*qûm* as translated in JPS, or *keep*, HSCB) His covenant with Abraham and his offspring for an everlasting covenant. That will involve perpetual ownership of the land of Canaan (Gen 17:7-8). Further, such possession of the land implies that the kings will rule in the land. And the last promise will be the focus of the Mosaic and New Covenants, "I will be their God."

(2) "As for You" (Genesis 17:9-14)

The role of Abraham and his offspring is to keep God's covenant throughout the ages (Gen 17:9). This perspective is toward the future. In contrast to the twenty-three years of silence, keeping the covenant will involve the circumcision of all the males born into the family. This is God's brand as "a physical reminder of the existence of the covenant" (Gen 17:11), a covenant sign like the rainbow.[25]

This brand placed the responsibility on fathers to communicate about the reality of a relationship with God and the existence of the covenant to the next generation. God had personally revealed the covenant to Isaac

---

[24] "My covenant" occurs nine times in this chapter (vv 2, 4, 7, 9, 10, 13, 14, 19, 21).

[25] Sarna, *Genesis*, p. 125.

and Jacob. But fathers had to communicate what God no longer openly revealed to subsequent generations. According to Hamilton:

> [C]ircumcision is a means by which Abraham and his seed ratify God's lordship over them. It is their identity sign as God's covenant people. As such, circumcision is not a cognition sign, one for God's benefit, but rather a confirmation sign, one bearing witness to Abraham's belief that God would fulfill his promises with respect to progeny. Accordingly, Abraham's circumcision is as much an amen to Yahweh as was his affirmation in 15:6.[26]

(3) "As for Your Wife" (Genesis 17:15-22)

Additionally, Sarai's name was changed to Sarah because she would become a mother of many descendants. This is expressed in what the LORD promised:

> "I will give you a son by her."

> "I will bless her, and she shall become nations; kings of peoples shall come from her." (Gen 17:16).

A similar promise is given to both Abraham and Sarah. Since the two are mentioned with respect to a father and mother (Gen 17:6, 16), it is improbable that spiritual offspring of Abraham are intended. Abraham desired that "Ishmael might live before you" (Gen 17:18). In God's denial, He specifies that Isaac, the son of Sarah shall be the offspring with whom God will *maintain* (qûm, JPS) His covenant (Gen 17:19). Thus, covenant partnership is narrower than merely physical descent. Rather, covenant partnership refers to both physical and spiritual descent. Thus, a boundary is set in context that only physical-spiritual offspring will be included in the full covenant blessing.

Then, what does "nations" mean? "It is difficult to ascertain the exact definition of the term. However, if one takes the various usages into consideration, as well as some seemingly related terms, *gaw, gēw, gēâ*, the back part of the body; *gew*, Aramaic for midst; and *gewîyâ*; living body or corpse. One must conclude that the basic idea is that of a defined body or group of people, or some specific large segment of a given body."[27]

In spite of the difficulty in specifying what "nation" and "nations" refers to, the context of continuing revelation provides helpful clues. Since the

---

[26] Hamilton, *Genesis 1–17*, pp. 471-72.

[27] Gerard Van Gronigen, "חוג, *gwh*," *Theological Wordbook of the Old Testament*, vol. 1, ed. Harris, Archer, Waltke (Chicago: Moody Bible Institute, 1980), p. 153.

promises spoken referring to offspring of Abram and Sarai individually are essentially the same, the promises refer to offspring of Abram and Sarai together. However, within the natural offspring, a distinction is made with the offspring that God will maintain His covenant (*gūm*). It is offspring who recognize and believe that God is their God (Gen 17:7, 19). So the nation is composed of physical offspring of Abram and Sarai. Within the nation, there are two distinctions to be recognized. First, there is the distinction of covenant people who are physical-spiritual offspring. In the generations of patriarchs, they are all covenant people beginning with Isaac. He is supernaturally provided and spiritually responsive.

Second, the term "nations" refers to some distinction within the one physical "nation." This is a valid implication because of the sequence of promises first addressed to Abram and then addressed to Abram and Sarai. This distinction refers to the tribal distinctions within the nation. Each tribe is treated politically as a nation.

The final issue is the identity of "kings." Again, derived from the context of promises, the kings shall arise from the nations of Israel and reign in the land. In retrospect, this may refer to the division of the kingdom of Israel and the kingdom of David. Furthermore, there is a subtle indication that what was intended in the creation of man may well be realized someday in the descendant of Abraham.

Intercession (Genesis 18:22-33)

This circumstance was the impending judgment of Sodom and Gomorrah. The time of judgment had arrived, but Lot and his family lived in Sodom. Should they be judged too? The LORD included Abraham in the process of consideration for "His judgments [are] well weighed and perfectly informed."[28] So he appealed for the number of righteous to be included in the judgment of the wicked. The declining numbers reveal the LORD's spirit of mercy in concern for the city and not for his kinsmen alone. This is Abraham who is the "one chosen through whom the nations would be blessed" (Gen 12:3; 18:16-19).[29] As he prays, he realizes his own inadequacy to know a proper request. The limit was implied when the LORD went His way (Gen 18:33). But the LORD included Abraham in the role of His consideration to bless and not to judge.

---

[28] Kidner, *Genesis*, p. 133.

[29] "Why will Abraham's influence be so enormous and worldwide? The simple explanation is that God has *covenanted with* (*yāda*ʿ, lit., 'known') Abraham" (Victor P. Hamilton, *The Book of Genesis: Chapters 18–50*, NICOT, ed. R. K. Harrison and Robert L. Hubbard Jr. [Grand Rapids, MI: Eerdmans, 1995], p. 18).

Bargaining with Abimelech (Genesis 20:1-18)

The path from faith to faithfulness progresses, but not always smoothly. There are faithless relapses when faith slips into scheming (Gen 20:1-12). "At the brink of Isaac's birth story here is the very Promise put in jeopardy, traded away for personal safety. If it is ever to be fulfilled, it will owe very little to man."[30] Yet the LORD delivers him as He had when he traveled to Egypt (cf. Gen 12:10-20).

Choice Demanded (Genesis 22:1-19)[31]

After the birth of Isaac (Gen 21:1-7), Abraham is placed into what appears to be an impossible choice. Abraham's faith had grown, in spite of lapses, to love God personally. He would be called God's friend (Isa 41:8). Yet God demanded that he sacrifice his "only" son whom he also loved (Gen 22:2).[32] God's ways can be confusing—God had said that He would maintain His covenant through Isaac (Gen 17:19, 21) and now God demanded that Isaac be sacrificed (Gen 22:2).

Who did Abraham love most—God or the son God had provided? So, early in the morning, Abraham started out with his son and supplies to sacrifice his son. The decision had been made, yet he remained silent about the details of his thoughts on their journey. With whom could he share his pained thoughts? Who would understand?

Yet in Abraham's decision to love God, he allowed God *to see to it* that the sacrifice would be provided and that the offering would be acceptable to Him. Impossible demands only find their resolution in God. That resolution only occurs as God assumes the cost of evil. And that will deliver Isaac.

Abraham tells the servants that he and the lad were going to worship and said, "we will return" (v 5). The painful struggle within Abraham's heart was covered by the common experience explained by his words—a father and a son were going to worship and to return. No further explanation was asked for.

---

[30] Kidner, *Genesis*, p. 137.

[31] "The account of the sacrifice of Isaac constitutes the aesthetic and theological summit of the whole story of Abraham. It has long been admired for the brilliance of its narrative technique and for the profundity of its theology, which has inspired so much reflection by Jews and Christians" (Gordon J. Wenham, *Genesis 16–50*, Word Biblical Commentary, ed. David A. Hubbard and Glenn W. Barker [Dallas: Word, 1994], p. 99).

[32] God's threefold identification ([1] your son, [2] your only son, [3] Isaac) is rhetorically significant in that it moves from the general to the specific.

But the same is not the case with Isaac's question (v 7). It seemed odd to him that they brought no sacrifice. So when he asked his father, Abraham answered that in His providence, God would provide (v 8).[33] All Abraham knew was that he believed that the provision would be according to God's promise and demand. Isaac didn't know all that, but Abraham's faith became the ground for Isaac's faith.

As the events unfolded, Isaac was bound and laid on the altar. This could only have taken place if both father and son believed a greater good was happening.[34] The events unfolded under God's providence. Both had to believe this to act as they did.

Conclusion

Abraham served as a steward of God's revelation, as a secondary cause. His words, rather than what God had said (Gen 22:2), became the ground for Isaac's faith. This, too, is the deliverance that God's plan had intended to develop in the offspring of the woman (Gen 3:15). For Isaac, he came to believe that God would provide based on His promises, perhaps for the first time. For Abraham, his passive faith received God's promised provision when he was declared to be righteous (Gen 15:6). Faithfulness grew into active faith and obedience when God's will was expressed and followed, based on what He demanded and what was promised (Gen 22:8, 16). And God declared that He would bless Isaac *because* Abraham had done this (Gen 22:16, 18).

This is how the *secondary cause* is related to the *primary cause.* This cooperation occurs as what God says becomes what the steward believes and acts upon. Further, this is what a *steward* of God's revelation ought to be.

---

[33] "Isaac's question consists of six words (in Hebrew), and Abraham responds with an answer of six words. Isaac begins his question with *Father*. Abraham ends his answer with *son*. We have here the same phenomenon as in v. 1—special attention is drawn to the subject by placing it ahead of the verb: *God himself will provide...*'" (Hamilton, *Genesis 18–50*, p. 109, emphasis in original).

[34] As Hartley notes, "Isaac was at least in his early twenties and Abraham was more than one hundred years old. Isaac was strong enough to have withstood his father" (John E. Hartley, *Genesis*, New International Biblical Commentary, vol. 1, ed. Robert L. Hubbard, Jr., and Robert K. Johnston [Peabody, MA: Hendrickson Publishers, 2000], pp. 208-209).

CHAPTER 7:
JACOB THROUGH JOSEPH

Introduction

The next stage in fulfillment is embedded in the life of the elect family. Isaac, Abraham and Sarah's only son, was protected after the harrowing test God had put them all through. Then in protection of Isaac, Abraham sent his servant to his land and his family "to take a wife for [his] son Isaac" (Gen 24:4, HCSB). The servant would learn that God would *provide*, but Isaac did not have an opportunity to grow. Isaac loved Rebekah when they met (24:67) and they prayed for a child (25:21). But neither seemed to be mature. In fact, Isaac simply repeated many of Abraham's experiences and failed when he tried to bless the non-elect Esau with the promised inheritance. So the next phase in God's plan featured Jacob.

Jacob's challenge was the need to prevail in the relationships within his family as the elect one. Their relationships focused on the promised blessing (Gen 26:1-6) reaffirmed to Isaac, but which Isaac sought to use in his own interests. It was a heart of self-interest, inherited from Adam that all the members of the family clung to. Their selfish hearts emerged in conflict with God's call to Jacob to build an elect nation (Gen 25:22-23).

Before the twins were born, God chose the younger of the twins to be served by the elder. Esau, the elder, was rejected before either was born, yet in life, he showed that he was profane. And the story of Jacob involved the competition between the brothers—first in the womb, then in the home, and finally in the wilderness. At home, Jacob was disadvantaged, as Esau was Isaac's favorite, and in the wilderness he was exposed in the vulnerability of his young family—Leah and her handmaid with eight sons and Rachel and her handmaid with four sons.

So Jacob came to the elect family like his grandfather, with a divided heart. He wanted the firstborn's blessing, but on his own terms. Most importantly, he was woefully ignorant of God. So another challenge was introduced. Jacob was self-serving and deceptive like all members of his family. God brought him to the most ruthless member of his family, Laban—more deceitful and self-serving even than Jacob. But in the conflicts that followed, he emerged ahead of Laban because of God's promise and deliverance (Gen 31:42). As Hamilton notes, "Only God could overrule Laban's slyness, and he has."[1]

In many ways, Jacob's story is about God's governmental rule. In the wilderness, at the climax, God wins a wrestling match, yet Jacob prevails in God's mercy (Gen 32:22-32). At the outset of Jacob's story, God had appeared to him in a dream and allowed him to set the terms of their partnership (Gen 28:10-22). These terms were tested throughout his time with Laban and in his return to Esau. Jacob wanted it his way, and in the end, he hung on for anything God would give. Set free from the wrestling match, he was crippled, but with a new name—Israel. His life did conflict not only with the offspring of the enemy but also with God.[2] In God's gracious providence, he prevailed while he fathered the elect nation.

Jacob: The Elect Son

The Plot from the Youngest Son to the Elect Son (Genesis 25:22–28:22)

Election:

Mother (Genesis 25:22-23)

Jacob's mother would have been only too delighted to repeat to her favored son the word she had received before he was born. As she struggled bearing twins, the text uses "an unusual verb (*va yitrotsetsu*) which literally means 'they crushed, thrusted one another' and which foretokens

---

[1] Hamilton, *Genesis 18–50*, p. 308.

[2] "As Jacob departs Penuel (the more common name for Peniel), he leaves with two things he did not bring with him to the Jabbok River. He has a new name and a new limp. The new name will forever remind Jacob of his new destiny. The new limp will forever remind him that in Elohim Jacob met for the first time one who can overpower him" (*Ibid.*, p. 337).

the future hostile relationship between the children who are about to be born."[3]

The oracle informed her of several facts:

- she carried twins

- each would be the progenitor of a nation

- The struggle was the result of sibling rivalry for priority in birth order, God's choice rested on the younger, even though he lost the struggle.[4]

They named him Jacob, meaning:

"may he beat the heels"—i.e. "May God be your rearguard" (cf. Gen 17:19). But it also lends itself to a hostile sense of "dogging another's steps," or "overreaching," as Esau bitterly observed in 27:36. Through his own action, Jacob devalued the name into a synonym for treachery...the tenacity which was his bane secured blessing in the end (32:26).[5]

Revelation and Response

Brother (Genesis 25:27-34)

The firstborn's blessing was Jacob's desire after he lost the struggle in the womb. In Jacob's mind, the struggle continued. By bargaining for his brother's birthright, Jacob regained what was his by election. Esau failed to value what came by God's promises; Jacob valued the position. So Esau despised his birthright (Gen 25:33).

Father (Genesis 27:1-46)

Deception rested in the lap of each dysfunctional family member.[6] Isaac attempted to bless Esau in secret even though he would have been aware of God's election. He attempted to use divine powers for his own interests. *Esau* agreed to the secret delivery, even though he had sold his birthright. *Rebekah* sought to subvert her husband's plan by deceiving him in Jacob's dress and her prepared meal. *Jacob* agreed to deceive but only tearful separation followed his deception. What was at issue in the

---

[3] Sarna, *Genesis*, p. 179.

[4] *Ibid.*

[5] Kidner, *Genesis*, pp. 151-52.

[6] "The narrative is full of pathos as each parent seeks to fulfill deep longings in regard to the favorite son" (Hartley, *Genesis*, p. 246).

firstborn's blessing was the promised national destiny, but, unfortunately, each family member was more interested in their personal desires.

Dream at Bethel (Genesis 28:10-22)

The partnership involved in the promise was revealed by God to Jacob. Alone, fearful of an attack from Esau, Jacob lays his head on a stone to get some rest that night. "The dream permits an alternative to enter his life. The dream is not a morbid review of a shameful past, but rather an alternative future with God."[7] This dream was nothing less than the drawing back of the curtain to expose the providential presence of God extending to earth. The revelation features a repetition of the terms of the Abrahamic Covenant. God would be present in Jacob's life through the otherwise unseen presence of angels, ascending and descending.

The vow that followed is the first extended personal response of Jacob to God. Both Waltke[8] and Kidner support the intent of the vow: "The vow was no more a bargain than any other vow (the 'if' clause is inherent in the form); it would be fairer to say that Jacob was taking the promise of 15 and translating the general into the particular."[9]

However, Sarna highlights what is objectionable: "all the desired conditions have already been unqualifiedly promised by God."[10] Jacob wanted God to be obligated to him in providing the blessing rather than Jacob being obligated in love for God.

The Plot from Being the Son of Rebekah to Being the Son of Promise (Genesis 29:1–31:55)

Responses to Laban

Jacob is not the only one to need an uncle like Laban to make deception painful. Von Rad notes:

> That Laban secretly gave the unloved Leah to a man in love was, to be sure, a monstrous blow, a masterpiece of shameless treachery, by which he for the time being far outmaneuvered Jacob who was not exactly dubious either. It was certainly a

---

[7] Walter Brueggemann, *Genesis: Interpretation: A Bible Commentary for Teaching and Preaching*, International Biblical Commentary (Atlanta: John Knox, 1982), p. 243.

[8] Waltke, *Genesis*, pp. 394, 397.

[9] Kidner, *Genesis*, p. 158.

[10] Sarna, *Genesis*, p. 200.

move by which he won for himself far and wide the coarsest laughter. Jacob's anger in the morning could accomplish
nothing. After this night he was legally bound to Leah, and,
therefore, Laban does not need to exert himself in his explanation to Jacob. Laban's statement, however, that in his country
one did not give the younger before the elder, has a very serious aspect, in spite of the disregard with which it is thrown
to Jacob. No one understood better than Jacob, for he himself as the younger son had crossed the finishing line before
his older brother. Thus, the narrator shows how in this droll
story of the coarsest kind a nemesis is at work.[11] It is ultimately
God's decree against which Jacob's pent-up passion bounds
(Fr.). Without Leah, *Reuben, Levi* and *Judah* would not have
been born, and neither *Moses nor David* would have appeared.
God's work descended deeply into the lowest worldliness and
there was hidden past recognition. The narrator leaves it at that
and does not bring it into the open with pious words.[12]

God's providential workings are at the heart of God's promise that
Jacob would father a nation. The LORD opened Leah's womb, "but
Rachel was barren" (Gen 29:31). "Then God remembered Rachel, and
God listened to her and opened her womb" (Gen 30:22). The LORD was
present to influence what happened. Jacob's vow did not obligate God to
do it Jacob's way. But sons were born and a family grew. It wasn't pristine
but what God had promised was happening.

When Jacob desired to leave with his growing family, Laban tried to
negotiate a plan of compensation to assure Jacob would stay (Gen 30:27-
28, 31). So Jacob proposed a plan of wages. It was a scheme based on
an ANE breeding technique which Jacob would use to transfer some
of Laban's flock to himself (Gen 30:31-33). However, Jacob experienced
such success that he later acknowledged God's providence (Gen 31:4). It
was not the result of a scheme, it was divine blessing.[13] Laban's sons also
saw what was happening. Laban's flock was becoming Jacob's flock.

---

[11] "Jacob, once the subject of deceit, now becomes the object of deceit. The perpetrator of
subterfuge becomes its victim. The nemesis is made all the more pungent by the fact that
Jacob is caught in the same device he himself had once used. He pretended to be Esau in
front of Isaac. Leah pretends to be Rachel next to Jacob. While Jacob's ruse was pretending
to be his older brother, Leah's ruse is pretending to be her younger sister. Jacob is deceived as
he deceived his father" (Hamilton, *Genesis 18–50*, p. 262).

[12] Von Rad, *Genesis*, p. 286.

[13] "Do one-colored animals produce bicolored young simply by looking at a bicolored object in
their mating time? This interpretation borders on sympathetic magic. Jacob's rods function
much as do Rachel's mandrakes. It is not the mandrakes that produce fertility, and it is not

So Jacob gathered his family to flee to Bethel and to God who called him (Gen 31:13). He escaped in spite of Laban's displeasure. Not only was God forming a family to be a nation, he was also transforming Jacob to become a steward of God's Word of Promise.

The Plot from Being Merely the Brother of Esau to Being Named Israel (Genesis 32:1–33:18; 35:1-7)

Responses to Esau

God appeared to Jacob and called him to return to Bethel (Gen 31:3), a trip that would not require passing through Edom. However, Jacob realized that to return to God at Bethel he must first be restored to his brother Esau. Therefore, his growing family and all the flocks set off to meet Esau.

Jacob anticipated taking his time and making his way to meet at Edom. But on the way, he received word that Esau was on his way to meet him with four hundred men (Gen 32:6). Fear struck Jacob at the heart. No other schemes remained to deceive Esau and survive meeting this wronged brother. Further, four hundred men traveled with Esau. What could that mean? Jacob had been unexpectedly pushed into a corner. Only God could deliver him as God had delivered him from Laban (Gen 31:29).

For the first time, Jacob attempts to pray. But by no means did he abandon planning (Gen 32:7-32): he plans (vv 7-8), he prays (vv 9-12), he plans (vv 13-21), and he prays (vv 22-32).

That night, before their meeting, he took his wives and eleven children to separate them from his property. If the property was taken, then perhaps his family would be overlooked in an attack. Jacob was a man of contingencies.

Then Jacob was alone (Gen 32:24).

The great encounter with God came when Jacob knew himself to be exposed to a situation wholly beyond him...the form that the night struggle took, indicated a hunger now for God

---

Jacob's white rods that produce the right kind of offspring for Jacob—although perhaps that is what Jacob wanted Laban to think. It is God who opened Sarah's womb, and in 31:10-12 Jacob testifies that it was God, not magic, that brought about the desired results" (Hamilton, *Genesis 18–50*, p. 284).

Himself; a hunger awakened by the crisis but not determined by it.[14]

Jacob was being molded by the continuing conflict and God's promise.

As God takes the form of Jacob's equal, Jacob's faith is active. Unexpectedly, the man initiated a wrestling match that lasted until morning. This experience with God symbolized his lifelong conflicts. Though his foes, Esau and Laban, were the offspring of the evil one, the way Jacob battled included battle with God. His schemes and deception set him in conflict with God's providential plans based on truth. In reality, when you do conflict with God, the best you can do is hang on.

> The conflict brought to a head the battling and groping of a lifetime, and Jacob's desperate embrace vividly expressed his ambivalent attitude to God, of love and enmity, defiance and dependence…The crippling and the naming show that God's ends were still the same; He would have all of Jacob's will to win, to attain and obtain, yet purged of self-sufficiency and redirected to…God Himself.[15]

The meeting with Esau marks a reconciliation arranged by God. The stream of gifts gives some idea of the load on Jacob's conscience and the sheer grace of Esau's reply.

Finally, Jacob reaches Bethel. He had now come full circle in spite of his repeated compromises; this last one at Shechem where Dinah suffered the consequences of another compromise by Jacob as she was raped. "Jacob's memories of the two experiences at Bethel (chaps. 28 and 35) will recall for a long time to come what the God of Jacob encountered there, rather than recall Bethel as a divine residence, a holy site."[16] This was his growing knowledge of God. He was now known and experienced in His providential acts of deliverance, in fulfilling Jacob's call to father a family.

Joseph: Promise to Lead, Recognized by His Family (Genesis 37:1–50:26)

The active presence of evil in the elect family also influenced the behavior of Jacob's sons. This raises the question: *what is the status of God's plan?*

---

[14] Kidner, *Genesis*, p. 163.

[15] *Ibid.*, p. 169.

[16] Hamilton, *Genesis 18–50*, p. 380.

The plan of redemption and of restoration was introduced in Gen 3:15. God had declared judgment upon the serpent. This judgment involved conflict between the enemy of God and his allies and the chosen seed of the woman. As a climax, the serpent would return to the conflict to directly battle with a single Descendent of the woman. That Descendent would be delivered to overcome the serpent and rule over the serpent.

With the patriarch, Abram, the plan began to see fulfillment. Abram not only saw the land God promised, but he and his seed received the promise to be a source of blessing to all nations. So at the climax of his story, Isaac was blessed with faith and the promise of blessing for his descendants through Abraham.

In the generation of Joseph, the answer took two separate turns. On one side, Jacob's family had inherited the deception and self-interest that had plagued their father for much of his life. On the other side, a young boy was born to Rachel to join a family of ten brothers. His story was different with only a hint of possible evil in the record. There was an understandable youthfulness in his early responses, but none of the divided faith of Abraham or the self-interest of his father Jacob.

The legacy of Jacob thus raised another question: could the sons of Jacob mediate blessing to all nations, let alone themselves? The four eldest brothers illustrate the point. The eldest son and natural heir, Reuben, tried to claim his inheritance by sleeping with his father's concubine (Gen 35:22). In weakness, he failed to confront his brothers to defend Joseph (Gen 37:21-29). When his father needed assurance for Benjamin traveling to Egypt, his offer of his sons was lacking in compassion and unconvincing (Gen 42:37). Reuben had not demonstrated appropriate spiritual character to be the future leader of Israel's family.

Similarly, Simeon and Levi prove to be spiritually inadequate candidates. They deceitfully avenged Dinah's rape by Shechem (Gen 34:25-31). When the men of Shechem agreed to be circumcised, as a basis for intermarriage and trade, as they were healing, the brothers went into the unsuspecting town and slayed all the men.[17] But this was after Jacob was silent and failed to confront Hamor and Shechem for the rape. While their issue was just, their approach was evil.

The natural leader, but the most egregious offender of the family heritage, was Judah. It was Judah who hatched the plan to sell Joseph into slavery in spite of his father's affection for the boy (Gen 37:26-32). The

---

[17] It is troubling that circumcision, the sign of the Abrahamic Covenant, is used not as a pretext for blessing but as the context for murder.

heartless plan that had the promise of a financial return convinced all the brothers whose hearts were as self-centered as Judah. While Jacob had fathered twelve sons, there was little evidence of spiritual interest in the family except for Joseph.

The hope arose from a dream Joseph had about his brothers and then about all his family (Gen 37:5-9). It portrayed Joseph as the one that his family would bow down before. His brothers hated him for imagining the dream was true and his father, although he loved his son, was also incredulous. No one understood what the dream meant, but Joseph clung to it by faith—even if a naïve faith.

Yet God used the conflict in the circumstances to mold his naïve faith into an active, more mature faith. There were two stages. The first stage was a faith to be delivered from his brothers, from a false accusation as a slave by Potiphar's wife and finally from the injustice of Egypt's prison system. The second stage was an active faith in God's dream to see how God wanted him to deliver his brothers (Gen 42:9). Not only was Joseph delivered but he overcame the conflict to become second in Egypt. From his overcoming evil, he ruled Egypt second only to Pharaoh. The one delivered became the deliverer.

The Conflict from the Offspring of God's Enemy from Which Joseph Is Delivered and His Faith Is Matured (Genesis 37:1–41:57)

Election and Promise

The role of promise in the life of Joseph is more difficult to trace. At the outset, Joseph embraced the dream (Gen 37:5-11). "The account of the dreams, coming at the outset, makes God, not Joseph, the 'hero' of the story: it is not a tale of human success but of divine sovereignty."[18] It contained a promise that included the whole family as elect, but Joseph was chosen for a role in the family. He would be recognized by the family as in authority and in a position deserving due respect. The position was a delegated rule under God. In a limited and typological sense, it represented a fulfillment of God's creation and redemption goals.

As Joseph described the dream to his family, there is every indication that he believed that what God had shown him would be true. However, it was a naïve belief, seen both in the way he thrusts it in the face of his

---

[18] Kidner, *Genesis*, p. 180.

brothers and in the lack of sensitivity of what it meant to his family. As he would struggle with the evil he would experience from the hands of others, there is indication that he saw a relationship between the dream and his suffering. In the sufferings, it seems apparent that he never loses heart. He always has his eye on the LORD.

The next mention of the dream came when his brothers bowed down before him in Egypt (Gen 42:6). At that time, he remembered the dream and his memory of the vision indicated the direction he should take with his brothers as he put them through a series of tests (Gen 42:10ff).

Joseph's faith, however, is implied in each episode he faces. Each episode involves the consequences of his brothers' sin and constitutes a test of Joseph's faith. Acting in a naïve faith, he went in search of his brothers and was delivered from their anger and rejection. He had faith to reject the advances of Potiphar's wife. He had faith to interpret dreams in prison. Through these experiences his faith matured. The truth, that would later be expressed by James, is here evident: tests of faith produce endurance, which in time produces wisdom (Gen 41:33-36; cf. Jas 1:2-5). A summary of the three tests will seek to highlight the presence of Joseph's faith.

His Response to Suffering and His Deliverance

The Test of Rejection by His Brothers (Genesis 37:3-36)

Joseph's struggle would not cause him, like Abram, to question what God had said, nor would it produce the ambivalent attitudes toward God that Jacob experienced. Rather, the test focused on the hatred and jealousy experienced at the hand of his brothers (Gen 37:3, 8). He and his father were almost oblivious to their envy when Joseph went in search for them (Gen 37:12-17). They immediately conspired to kill him (Gen 37:18, 23-24). While Reuben attempted to save him, Judah won the hearts of his brothers as he proposed to profit from him (Gen 37:26). They only had to deceive their father in explaining his absence. Joseph's pleas for mercy never betrayed a loss of faith. So Joseph was sold as a slave.

The Test of Slavery in Egypt (Genesis 38:1–39:20)

Joseph was sold to Potiphar, an Egyptian officer and captain of the guard (Gen 39:1). The narration includes a strange interruption in Joseph's story. Judah had emerged as the leader in the hostility of the brothers against Joseph (Gen 37:26). Now his pursuit of marriage was told in some detail in contrast to Joseph's story in Potiphar's house with his attractive wife (Gen 39:6-7). Judah abandoned Jacob and sought a wife through Hirah. His wife's name was not even mentioned, but the wickedness of two of his sons was, and God took their lives. Oblivious to the evil in his sons, he blames their wife, Tamar. So he delayed giving her to his youngest son. Tamar, knowing the lusts of Judah, claimed her right to bear Judah's heir by seducing him. After she disclosed her pregnancy, Judah recognized that Tamar was more righteous than he was (Gen 38:26). Such was the condition of the elect family. How will they mediate divine blessing?

Joseph was a sharp contrast (Genesis 39). His master could see from the effectiveness of his work "that the LORD caused all that he did to succeed in his hands" (v 3). When he was pursued by Potiphar's wife (vv 6-12), he responded, "How then can I do this great wickedness and sin against God?" (v 9). In spite of his past performance and moral certitude, when Potiphar's wife accused Joseph, Potiphar had him imprisoned. The third test, unjust as it was, was then introduced.

The Test of Imprisonment in Egypt (Genesis 39:20–41:14)

The depth of this test is reflected in the description of the prison as a pit (Gen 41:14). Nonetheless, "the LORD was with Joseph and showed him steadfast love and gave him favor in the sight of the keeper of the prison" (Gen 39:21). He was put in charge of all the prisoners and he needed no supervision. Again the narration includes the explanation: "because the LORD was with him. Whatever he did, the LORD made it succeed" (Gen 39:23).

Most striking was Joseph's *interpretation* of dreams. He testified, "Do not interpretations belong to God?" (Gen 40:8). When speaking to Pharaoh, he confessed, "it [interpretation] is not in me, God will give Pharaoh a favorable answer" (Gen 41:16). Then in his interpretation, he prefaced it with these words: "God has revealed to Pharaoh what he is about to do" (Gen 41:25). As in his own pair of dreams, he explained Pharaoh's pair as communicating that the thing is fixed, and God will shortly bring it about (Gen 41:32).

Joseph is clearly a man whose faith had matured to faithful obedience. To the extent that he understood God's promise found in the dream, he was a *steward*. In his faithful obedience, God established him as second in command over the whole of Egypt: "I have set you over all the land of Egypt. Then Pharaoh took the signet ring from his hand and put it on Joseph's hand" (Gen 41:41-42a). "Pharaoh now performs a series of ceremonial acts that, in effect, constitute Joseph's investiture as 'Grand Vizier of Egypt.'"[19] Joseph thus was ruled by God, and God then began to rule through Joseph's presence in Egypt of the ancient world. God's plan was intended to work out in this way as illustrated in Joseph's reaching the goal to a limited degree. How God would establish his rule over his brothers will be demonstrated as Joseph tests his brothers.

The Plot from His Brothers in Need and in Guilt to Deliverance in Egypt (Genesis 42:1–47:31)[20]

Response to Deliver and to Rule

When Joseph's family finally was touched by the famine, ten of the brothers arrived to buy grain from the supply Egypt had stored. As Joseph saw his brothers bow down, he remembered his dream (Gen 42:6, 9a). Now it began to make sense. "At first sight the rough handling which now dominates the scene to the end of chapter 44, has the look of vengefulness. Nothing could be more natural, but nothing further from the truth."[21] Joseph believed dreams and *interpretations belong to God* (Gen 40:8). As God had given Pharaoh two dreams to save Egypt from an impending famine (Gen 41:17-32), so God had given him two dreams to rule over his brothers, who were the elect line of Jacob. "God is the prime mover here. Joseph, the wise administrator, works with this providence to unite the brothers."[22] Joseph is not only the steward of God's provision for Egypt, but also the steward interpreting the promise included in his dream.

Joseph's stewardship involves testing his brothers with "severe mercy."[23] He charges them from his position as governor concerning matters of state security.[24] In addition, he uses his knowledge of the family to test their response to his charge that they have come to spy out Egypt (Gen 42:14-15). Their response is both true (Gen 42:10-11, 13a) and false (Gen

---

[19] Sarna, *Genesis*, p. 286.

[20] Concerning 42:3, Wenham notes that "Jacob's sons are called 'Joseph's brothers,' thus foreshadowing their role in the next scene" (Wenham, *Genesis 16–50*, p. 405).

[21] Kidner, *Genesis*, p. 199.

[22] R. E. Longacre, *Joseph: A Story of Divine Providence: A Texttheoretical and Textlinguistic Analysis of Genesis 37 and 39-48* (Winona Lake, IN: Eisenbrauns, 1989), p. 50.

[23] Waltke, *Genesis*, p. 550.

[24] Sarna, *Genesis*, p. 292. In matters of affairs of state, a government has the authority to use deception and spying to protect their security.

42:13b) when they claim to be "honest men." Their assertion would be tested by bringing their younger brother, Benjamin, who had been left at home when they returned for grain. They claimed to have one more brother and an old father. Was this claim true?

So all ten were jailed, but in mercy nine were released to return to their father while Simeon remained in jail. In addition, Joseph tested their honesty in mercy by returning their payment for the grain (Gen 42:27-28). As they discovered the money, they recognized God was at work. Upon their return home, the brothers had to explain to Jacob where Simeon was and what conditions were set for them to return and buy more grain. They were forced to revisit old and unpleasant memories with their father, which served to highlight their guilt and reveal their long-held secret.

In time, the supply of grain ran low. They had to return to Egypt and to Joseph. In order to demonstrate their honesty, they had to bring Benjamin. Jacob had been deeply wounded by his sons and still held resentment toward them. "In clutching his advantage over those who had wronged him, he was jeopardizing himself and them—including his beloved Benjamin, whom he must lose in order to save him (cf. 27:41-46). It betrays his self-absorption that he still saw the threat of Benjamin primarily in terms of himself: 'Why did you treat me so ill...?'"[25] In light of what the account has told about Judah, it might seem strange that he convinced his father. What was convincing was that he was willing to sacrifice himself (Gen 43:8-9). Reuben was only willing to sacrifice others.

So the brothers returned to Egypt with Benjamin, whose presence proved that the brothers had spoken truthfully. When they attempted to return the money to Joseph, they added evidence that they were honest. Joseph already knew all this, but he had one more test for his brothers. Would they have compassion for their father? Joseph wanted to place Benjamin in the same position he had been placed by his brothers so many years earlier. Would the brothers sacrifice Benjamin? Or would they sacrifice themselves?

In order to highlight the issue, Joseph built suspense. He invited his brothers to his private residence and seated them according to their age (Gen 43:33). Benjamin was seated as the youngest. Then he lavishly honored them all but honored Benjamin with five times more (Gen 43:34). Would the brothers display any jealousy? They feasted to each individual's satisfaction, even though Joseph knew more than he was disclosing.

---

[25] Kidner, *Genesis*, p. 203.

From that high honor, they started to return home. Unknown to them, the money of each one had been returned again, along with Joseph's divining cup, which had been hidden in Benjamin's sack (Gen 44:1-2). It was that cup, when it was found in Benjamin's sack, that set the trap for the final test.

> The sudden threat to Benjamin was a thrust to the heart: in a moment the brothers stood revealed when the steward converted their challenge of verse 9 into a chance of freedom at Benjamin's expense, all conditions were present for another betrayal, at a far more compelling price—their liberty—than the twenty pieces of silver they had once shared out.[26]

Their response by its unanimity (Gen 44:13), frankness (44:16), and constancy (44:18), indicated that they joined Judah in his repentance. It was Judah who spoke for the group:

> "What shall we say to my lord? What shall we speak? Or how can we clear ourselves? God has found out the *guilt* of your servants; behold, we are my lord's servants, both we and he also in whose hand the cup has been found" (Gen 44:16).[27]

Then Judah pleaded for the release of Benjamin. While earlier he had disregarded his father's sorrow, now he was concerned about the pain that the loss of Benjamin would bring. It could even bring about his death. Judah even offered to remain in Egypt, substituting himself in place of Benjamin. "Judah's speech proves beyond doubt that the formerly hateful, selfish brothers are now motivated by love for one another and integrity within themselves and with one another."[28] Such genuine love and integrity can only flow from repentance and from faith in God. Joseph then made himself known to Benjamin and to his brothers whom he had *delivered*. Joseph, in his personal experience of deliverance and in his test of his brothers to deliver them, became an example of the full scope of stewardship necessary to God's plan.

---

[26] *Ibid.*, p. 205.

[27] This confession probably works at two levels. It is at one level made about the cup. But at another level it probably relates to their earlier mistreatment of Joseph. On this point Wenham notes that, "probably Judah was confessing to the much greater crime of their maltreatment of Joseph, which on an earlier visit they had concluded caused them to be treated so harshly (42:21-23)" (Wenham, *Genesis 16–50*, p. 425).

[28] Waltke, *Genesis*, p. 562.

Conclusion to the Dispensation of Promise

The dispensation of promise shapes a vision of God's plan. That vision included both a historic component and a future component. The historic component featured the formation of faith matching the content of what was promised. While faith is the response of an independent creature, it is also related to what God promised. It is involved with the cooperation of God's providence in the lives of His chosen stewards.

A steward's response is formed by revelation, as what God promises was heard, received, and acted upon. There is no merge of the divine Person with the human person. Faith is not God's faith that somehow is given to replace a human's unbelief. Nor is faith formed independently by the human person alone. Rather, faith appears as an independent person confesses his own sin and turns to receive what God has promised.

The future component features a promise whose scope transcends what has been fulfilled in the lives of the patriarchs or in history. Such a comprehensive promise anticipates a future Seed of Abraham, or a Descendent of Israel through whom the promise would be realized. This is the hope of Messiah.

However, promises alone fail to emphasize the steward's responsibility. Abraham was blessed even though he deceived Pharaoh. Jacob was blessed even though Isaac was deceived. Jacob's sons gained even though they lied to their father. That fact necessitates the addition of the revelation of the Law.

What then is the shape of a *steward*? That question is the focal issue in the narrative accounts of the patriarchs. God was molding the patriarchs by His Word in the reality of a fallen world to become His *stewards*. The patriarchs are then models for Israel who could learn about their heritage found in national promises.

A Steward Who Is Faithful

Abraham was the model of faith in receiving the promised blessing and of faithfulness in mediating blessings to others. The model of Abraham involves both the blessing of justification by faith and the inheritance mediated by faithfulness. Delay in terms of what is expected by promise is a characteristic in the development of faith. The model of Abraham is what stewardship ought to be.

And in Abraham's struggles of faith, God providentially leaves clues of how evil will be *overcome*:

- In Melchizedek and his offering to the God Most High, Abram found pure worship which alone expresses the gratitude necessary for victory over evil. In addition, Melchizedek blessed Abram after he had delivered others. While those of the elect line are the necessary stewards of God's will, another priest-king is needed for them to fulfill their role as worshipful stewards.

- In a substitute, Abraham found that God was satisfied when Abraham surrendered what God had given him. Only then does God provide a substitute sacrifice which satisfies Himself and His demand of love.

A Steward Who Prevails

Jacob provides the model of Israel who prevails in spite of intense struggles with evil. The story of Jacob is no accident because as God's chosen people, they will also be the object of intense struggles with evil. Jacob had struggled against men (Esau and Laban) and Jacob had struggled against the LORD and prevailed (Gen 32:28). Yet the proverb correctly cautions: "No wisdom, no understanding and no counsel will prevail against the LORD" (Prov 21:30, HCSB). This does not promote success, but what will enable Israel to prevail?

Only history will tell how much Israel will fail, yet on the basis of his name Israel, he will prevail. Hebrews 11:21 selects Jacob's expression of faith which highlights the future of each tribe of the nation (Genesis 48–49). "It has the quality, praised in that chapter [of Hebrews] of reaching out towards the promise, even in the face of death, 'having seen it and greeted it from afar'"[29]

A Steward Who Overcomes

Joseph completed the role of steward, at least in typology.[30] As a type of ultimate stewardship, Joseph's historic account anticipates the ultimate

---

[29] Kidner, *Genesis*, p. 212.

[30] Typology is a type of meaning in Biblical progressive revelation. The validity of recognizing typological meanings rests on both the nature of language and on the Biblical use of language. The type-token nature of language and of reality fashions our thought and communication in categories of meaning. Types of meaning are equivalent to speaking of typology in

steward, the antitype Jesus Christ. The goal of creation is reached in type, as Joseph overcomes the conflict with evil and is raised by God to a position as ruler in the life of the nation. He overcomes hatred and jealousy from Israel, a false charge from a Gentile nation, and finally indifference, in being delivered from the pit of Egyptian prison.

At each stage, he is delivered from evil so that in the climax he overcomes any conflict with evil. Evil has no claim over him as he rules as second in the land of Egypt. This is the model which reflects the stages in the humble decline of Jesus Christ on the path to *overcoming* death and evil. Therefore, God has highly exalted Him and has given Him a name second to none—He is Lord (cf. Phil 2:5-11). In type, Joseph *overcame*.

In the position as the overcomer, Joseph delivered his brothers in spite of their struggle with evil. While the people of Israel prevailed, Joseph delivered them from the power of evil as a type of Christ's Second Advent deliverance (Acts 7:9-16). Like Joseph, Christ will deliver Israel from death and from their rejection of Him at His First Advent (Rom 11:26).

---

certain statements in the Bible. Such a Biblical type of meaning may refer both to a historical reality and to a future reality. The two references share the same type of meaning, but the historical type, which in some sense is incomplete and based on an antecedent promise, anticipates a full future type of meaning. Thus, typology may be summarized as prophecy through history. And the antitype is the *sensus plenus*.

SECTION 4:
DISPENSATION OF THE LAW

Introduction

Revelation of the Dispensation of the Law

The revelation entrusted to the descendants of Israel expanded as the Law was added to the promises already given to them. So in the progress of revelation, the focus changes as the Law was added alongside the promise. The meaning of the promise is not changed. An unconditional promise exists as a commitment of God to bless according to His Word while the Law serves to highlight the obligations of the steward of a given generation as he awaits the fulfillment of that promise. So while the promise is unchanged, there is a change in the reception of the promise in a given generation. What was heard in *faith* resting in the One who promised, is now heard in a call to be *active in obedience* in response to the Law.

Relationship between Promise and Law

The two types of revelation (promise and law) are compatible even though they are different. *Law* and *promise* are both performative types of a language.[1] While performative statements commonly communicate *information*, their intent involves *performance*. In the promise, the intent is a commitment to perform on the part of the one making the promise. In the Law, the intent is a commitment to perform on the part of the subjects. Laws are legal precept statements which depend upon the response of the subjects addressed for their effectiveness. The validity of the laws

---

[1] Caird, *The Language of the Bible*, pp. 21-22.

rests on the authority of the law-giver who gives expression to what is right. But the effectiveness of the law depends upon the subjects' obedience. Otherwise, the law will only have an unintended, in terms of what is written, effect of rendering the subjects guilty.[2]

As a result, God revealed both types of revelation in the dispensation of promise. At that time, as the name suggests, the focus was on promise. When Abraham interceded on behalf of Lot dwelling in Sodom, the LORD confessed:

> Should I hide what I am about to do from Abraham? Abraham is to become a great and powerful nation, and all the nations of the earth will be blessed through him. For I have chosen him so that he will command his children and his house after him to keep the way of the LORD by doing what is right and just. This is how the LORD will fulfill to Abraham what he *promised* him. (Gen 18:17-19, HCSB, emphasis added)

By keeping the way of the LORD, Abraham would be in step to receive God's blessing and to mediate blessing to others.

Thus, the promise and the Law are different because they call for different commitments. But the two are both included in God's overall plan of redemption and restoration of man's rule.

The appropriate response to the Law is important to consider. An appropriate response to any precept involves obedient service rather than a legalistic liability. An obedient response to precepts acknowledges God's right to rule and the steward's responsibility to *serve*. To treat the Law as a legalistic liability turns the obligation into service to man rather than God. A person only attempts to manipulate God by legalistic obedience. That liability is to mankind rather than God, the Law-Giver. When Judaism was believed to be defined by the Law, the result was what the Pharisees practiced. Jesus confronted them as hypocrites. Their promotion of themselves and their keeping of the Law was intended to impress men, but God considered it hypocrisy.

The Mosaic Law and Covenant

The law is revealed as the core of the Mosaic Covenant. As such, the Law and the covenant may be distinguished. Laws prescribe the obligations of the servant-partner. A covenant summarizes the arrangement

---

[2] *Ibid.*

between the two parties. The arrangement may be promissory as in the Abrahamic Covenant. Or the arrangement may be obligatory as in the Mosaic Covenant.

These two types of covenants are distinguished at the ratification. A promissory covenant is ratified by one party alone. This was the case in the Abrahamic Covenant when Abram slept in a deep sleep and the symbolic Presence of the LORD passed between the pieces of the sacrifice. As the LORD did, He assumed the oath by which He alone took responsibility for the terms of the covenant. Thus, it is not conditioned on Abraham or any of his descendants. It is an unconditional covenant in its existence.

By distinction, the Mosaic Covenant is obligatory. At the ratification (Exod 24:1-11), both altars to the LORD and 70 of Israel's elders were sprinkled with the sacrificed blood. Israel took the oath: "all that the LORD has said we will do" (19:7; 24:3, 7). This covenant is conditioned upon Israel keeping their oath.

Purpose of the Law

In the preamble to the Mosaic Covenant, its *purpose* was introduced (Exod 19:5-6). That purpose expanded the climactic promise given to Abraham (Gen 12:3b), "through you all nations will be blessed." The Mosaic Covenant posits that this purpose will be realized *through Israel* only as they are servants of the LORD. The preface says:

> Now if you will *listen* to Me and carefully *keep* my covenant, you will be My own possession out of all the peoples, although all the earth is Mine, and you will be My kingdom of priests and My holy nation. (Exod 19:5-6, HCSB, emphasis added)

Effect of the Law

As the Law is stated, the curses are intentional (Lev 26:16-45). Disobedience by Israel to the Law will necessarily result in judgment. That was soon expressed, when Israel compelled Aaron to make a god, figuratively taking them back to Egypt (Exod 32:1). The effect on disobedient Israelites was the pronouncement of guilt and the divine execution of judgment. There are scarce mentions of the nation itself pronouncing judgment upon itself. But clearly the Law included the threat of judgment.

Of course, Israel's disobedience does not prevent the LORD from blessing the nations, but Israel fails to be the steward of blessing. Thus, Israel fails to share in God's glory.

One might conclude that the effect of the Law, addressed to subjects fallen in sin, fates them to condemnation. But the covenant also provides for the LORD's tabernacle (Exodus 25–40). The law outlines the appropriate sacrifices for Israel to live with the LORD in their midst and to approach Him in the mercy of these sacrifices (Leviticus 1–7). Thus, condemnation would be inevitable for members of the fallen human race, but mercy and grace were also available in God's presence among Israel.

Revelation of Law

James Houston discusses "'Double Knowledge' as the Way of Wisdom."[3] He does not talk about the Law as the particular source of this double knowledge but what he says applies to the Law. Calvin introduced this idea in his *Institutes of the Christian Religion* (1559): "Nearly all wisdom we possess, that is to say, true and sound wisdom, consists of two parts: the knowledge of God and of ourselves."[4] The Law is a source revelation of such double knowledge. It speaks directly of God and His will and indirectly, based on the people's response to the Law, speaks of the people themselves. Houston quotes Blaise Pascal: "To know God, and yet know nothing of our wretched state breeds pride: to realize our misery and know nothing of God is mere despair…"

An equilibrium comes between knowing God and knowing oneself. This is the direct result of the double knowledge in the revelation of the Law. In what was revealed in the Law, Israel could learn of the righteousness of God. In the tabernacle and in the priestly ministry, Israel could learn of the mercy of God. Moses, as a representative of the people, came to know the LORD. When he asked to know God's ways (Exod 33:13), the LORD revealed two things. First, His name, which reflected the way He acted (Exod 33:19-20; 34:5), but second, He allowed Moses a glimpse of who He Himself was (Exod 33:20-23; 34:6-7). God was compassionate and gracious, while at the same time loyal in His love and true to reality.

In crossing the Jordan River, when Joshua's generation in obedience set their feet in the land (Josh 1:3), God blessed them with land as He

---

[3]   James M. Houston, "The 'Double Knowledge' as the Way of Wisdom," *The Way of Wisdom*, ed. J. I. Packer and S. K. Soderlund (Grand Rapids, MI: Zondervan, 2000), pp. 308-326.

[4]   John Calvin, *Institutes of the Christian Religion* (MacDill, FL: MacDonald, n.d.), 1.1.1, 7.

had promised. Thus, through obedience to the command, Israel is in the place to experience the blessing.

On the other hand, in Israel's response to the Law, she would learn of her own unrighteousness and sin. In addition, in pursuit of God through the sacrificial system, mediated in the tabernacle and in the priesthood, Israel experienced forgiveness and acceptance by God in spite of who they were. This balance in knowledge would be challenged by the enemy of God to tempt them to wander to an extreme—either to lose faith in preoccupation with themselves or to attempt to manipulate God in their religious practice.

In the best of Israel's spiritual heritage, Psalm 1 calls the one who delights in the law of the LORD blessed. What the Law says is worthy of meditation day and night (Ps 1:2). The meditator's life is like a fruitful tree that yields fruit in season while it remains in bloom year round (Ps 1:3). This is a prosperous life. The LORD knows the way of righteousness and those who walk in this way (Ps 1:6). At the heart of Israel's worship is this introductory psalm which celebrates a relationship with God through the Law.

Outline of the Dispensation of the Law

The addition of the Mosaic Covenant declares God's claim and rule over the descendants of Jacob living and coming out of Egypt. "Such a covenant is a declaration of God's kingship, consecrating the people to himself in a sovereignly dictated order of life."[5] This is called the *theocratic rule of God* over Israel. And with the revelation of the Law, the restatement of God's rule over a chosen people, lost at the fall, is introduced through Moses.

---

[5] Meredith G. Kline, *Treaty of the Great King: The Covenant Structure of Deuteronomy* (Grand Rapids, MI: Eerdmans, 1963), p. 17.

This claim to rule His elect people through the Law describes the parameters of the dispensation of law, which unfolds in stages:

Pure Theocratic Reign (Exodus 19–Judges 21)

"All the words that the LORD has spoken we will do" (Exod 24:3).

Monarchical Theocratic Reign (Samuel–Jeremiah)

"Now appoint for us a king to judge us like all the nations." (1 Sam 8:5b).

Times of the Gentiles (Ezekiel–Gospels)

"Jerusalem will be trampled underfoot by the Gentiles, until the times of the Gentiles are fulfilled" (Luke 21:24).

The Son of Man, Ruled by the Lord (Gospels)

"Do not think that I came to destroy the Law or the Prophets. I did not come to destroy but to fulfill" (Matt 5:17, NKJV).

These four stages of the dispensation of law each relate to a different expression of God's rule over His people. The *pure theocratic stage* features the tabernacle as the focus of the LORD's presence among the people. His precepts would be known through the Law rather than through an executive leader following Moses and Joshua. Judges characterizes this historic period in the LORD's rule according to the Law.

The *monarchic theocratic* stage will feature a king mediating God's rule over Israel. The effective king will focus the people's attention on the LORD. Psalms features such a focus. David led in this fashion. In spite of the stability ordering his successors, none shared his heart after God. Each king's failure, in the context of God's promises, led to an inference that a future king would arise and be faithful as a steward of God's Word. Many of these inferred conclusions were prophetically expressed in Psalms and in the Prophets. But the immediate consequence of disobedience by the king led to Israel's captivity among the Gentiles. In addition, the prophets announced that Israel had broken the obligatory Mosaic Covenant (Jer 31:32; Hos 1:9).

During the *times of the Gentiles*, Gentiles ruled over God's people dispersed into captivity (Luke 21:24). Some seventy years later (Jer 25:11-12), Cyrus, king of Persia, inaugurated a remnant's return to the land. Yet the remnant remained under Gentile rule and it was from this remnant that a virgin would "conceive and bear a Son" (Isa 7:14). This One, named Immanuel, introduced a divine partnership in human flesh, in the Person of Jesus. While He announced the rule of God from heaven was at hand, Jesus would live under the jurisdiction of Roman rule and die on a Roman cross.

At the same time, the Son of Man chose to live and be ruled by God according to the Jewish law (Matt 5:17). So it was that Jesus was ruled by Caesar and by God (Mark 12:17). In the face of angry Jewish opposition, He challenged them: "Which one of you convicts me of sin? If I tell the truth, why do you not believe me?" (John 8:46). His innocence of sin was displayed under the jurisdiction of the Jewish Sanhedrin and under the Roman trial. Yet, in spite of this injustice, Jesus submitted to their verdict of death, and so the Son of Man, "this Jesus, delivered up according to the definite plan and foreknowledge of God, you [Jews living in Jerusalem] crucified and killed by the hands of lawless men [Romans]" (Acts 2:23).

CHAPTER 8:
THE LORD'S THEOCRATIC
REIGN OVER ISRAEL

EXODUS THROUGH DEUTERONOMY

Introduction

The story begins some four hundred years after Jacob had come to Egypt at Joseph's beckoning. Much had changed in Egypt. Yet the works of the LORD focused "on *continuity with both creation* and *promise themes in Genesis.*"[1] Without creating anew, the LORD *forms* a people redeemed by *promise*. This *formation* of people is to become a nation. While the objective seems straightforward, the people are fickle—they say one thing but do another. So the revelation of the Law, which constitutes them to be a nation, is given twice and the covenant renewed two times. God calls Israel to serve Him as a nation by entrusting the Law to their keeping.

At the heart of each story is the presence of the prophet Moses. He must both mediate the necessary covenant revelation and shepherd a rebellious people until they stand poised to enter the land. Then Joshua completes the formation of the nation as they lay hold of the land. Once the nation is formed in *Joshua*, the question is raised concerning how the theocracy will work. Judges provides an answer to that question. The story unfolds through progressive revelation until the theocracy is formed.

The stages of this revelation are as follows:

1. Transition: Redemption from Egypt to Mt. Sinai (Exodus 1:1–19:1)

---

[1] Terence E. Fretheim, *Exodus: Interpretation: A Bible Commentary for Teaching and Preaching* (Louisville, KY: Westminster John Knox, 1991), p. 24, emphasis in original.

2. Mosaic Covenant Ratified at Mt. Sinai: Covenant Ratified (Exodus 19–24), Covenant Renewed (Exodus 32–34), Sacred Space and Service in the tabernacle (Exodus 25–Leviticus 27)

3. Kadesh Barnea (Numbers 13–14)

4. Second Mosaic Covenant in the Wilderness Renewed (Deuteronomy)

[Parts 5-6 are covered in the following chapter.]

5. The Gift of the Land Received and Occupied by the Tribes (Joshua)

6. The Outworking of Theocracy in the Land (Judges)

Transition: Redemption from Egypt to Mt. Sinai (Exodus 1:1–19:1)

In order for God to form a nation, initial fundamental changes must take place. And these changes involve transitions:

- a geographical transition from Egypt to Mt. Sinai

- a political transition from servitude to Egypt to service to the LORD

- a revelational transition from promise to law/promise

To implement these transitions, God raised up Moses to lead the people through the changes. But before Moses could lead on God's behalf, he himself had to be changed by God.

With the passage of four hundred years, the number of Israelites had grown enormously. "Pharaoh was compelled to recognize that all his attempts at suppression had been in vain"[2] (cf. Exod 1:22). Thus, a more severe decree was issued claiming the lives of all baby boys born to the Jews. Each son born must be thrown into the Nile. Moses' mother attempted to creatively follow the decree and saved him by putting him into a basket, then throwing the basket into the Nile. Providentially, he was discovered by Pharaoh's daughter and rescued. Further in God's providence, in his early years he was nurtured by his mother. As a consequence, God's promise of election of the Jewish people gripped his soul. So some forty years later, after being educated in Pharaoh's house, he associated himself with the bondage of his own Hebrew people.

---

[2] Umberto Cassuto, *A Commentary on the Book of Exodus* (Jerusalem: Magnes, 1967), p. 16.

As a result, he had to flee the wilderness to wait on the Lord for forty more years. In the wilderness, having lost any anticipation for change, God met him in a burning bush (Exod 3:2-6). There, to his surprise, God revealed Himself by name to Moses in a personal fashion.

God revealed Himself by the verb *hāyâ* (to be). Cassuto appropriately relates this name to what had been introduced in Genesis. "There is also implicit in this interpretation the thought of implementing the promise: 'I am who I am always,' ever alike and consequently I am true to my word and fulfill it."[3] While Waltke emphasizes a pragmatic sense, "I can be counted on,"[4] Fretheim asserts:

> This statement that is to be God's name for all time makes two points: it speaks not only of what people are to do, but also of a divine *commitment* to being a part of this people's history. The God who goes by this name will participate in the story forever...The name shapes Israel's story and the story gives greater return to the name.[5]

This dual contribution means that God's promises are entrusted to Israel, His steward, and Israel will be molded into becoming what God promised, even as Jacob had. Israel, in history, will prevail over Egypt and other peoples.

As the Lord prepared Moses to lead a people in an exodus, he entrusted particular promises to mold Moses in leadership:

- I will *bring* you *out* from under the burdens of Egyptians.

- I will *deliver* you from slavery.

- I will *redeem* you...with great judgments. (Exod 6:6)

These promises are of one type which the Lord will summarize: "You have seen what I did to the Egyptians and how I carried you on eagles' wings and brought you to me" (Exod 19:4, HCSB).

These promises simply involve a passive faith to receive what God alone accomplished. Such passive faith, while genuine, does not call forth any

---

[3] *Ibid.*, p. 38.

[4] "In its function God's name suggests a pragmatic presence. This sense of God's being can be captured in the English phrase 'I am who I am for you'. His simplicity shows there is no shadow of variability in him. God is dependable; he can be counted upon." (Waltke, *An Old Testament Theology*, pp. 366-67).

[5] Fretheim, *Exodus*, p. 24, emphasis in original.

response except to accept what God would provide. The last promises are of a second type:

- I will *take* you to be my people.
- I will *be* your God...whom you shall know.
- I will *bring* you into the land I swore to give.
- I will *give* it to you for a possession. (Exod 6:7-8)

These promises are a second type which is reflective of what God said: "Now if you *listen* and carefully *keep* my covenant..." (Exod 19:5a, HCSB, emphasis added). This involves *active faith*. The subject participates as a partner in what God is giving. What God has promised is still given and participation neither replaces nor contributes to the gift: "You will be My own possession out of all the peoples...you will be My Kingdom of priests and My holy nation" (Exod 19:5b-6, HCSB). *Active faith* is involved in becoming His people, in knowing God, and in occupying and possessing their inheritance of the land.

In the Exodus out of Egypt, the works of God involved more than merely might to overpower Egypt. Might was involved in the first nine plagues. These hardened Pharaoh's resistance to letting the people go to worship (Exod 11:10). The final plague involved the promise, "I will redeem you."

"I will redeem you." The action is a work of God. The object is a singular pronoun, "you," indicating a collective redemption as a people. The term *redemption* means to purchase "from foreign slavery and [being] made God's own possession."[6] In the brevity of the promise, several questions are answered in the corresponding Passover ceremony. A price is set to be paid, family by family. The price is a sacrificial lamb that each family offered and applied to their own family by placing the blood on the doorposts. So it's an individual sacrifice for each firstborn son, but a collective redemption.

The Passover meal continues to be celebrated year by year as a remembrance of the original Passover and redemption from Egypt and from oppression. As this celebration is partaken of by faith, this generation and subsequent generations also may experience God's work of redemption. In the first generation, the redemption is from Egypt's sinful oppression, but subsequent generations will experience redemption from sin as the enemy of God.

---

6   Helms Ringgren, "גָּאַל, *gā'al*," TDOT, vol. 2, p. 354.

In the completed redemption, the corporate deliverance was finally received through Moses' faith at the Red Sea.

> The sacrifice is the means used for bringing Divine retribution on the wicked and for delivering the righteous from their hand (Isaiah 1:9): "Awake, awake put on strength, O arm of the Lord; awake, as in days of old, the generation long ago. Was it not Thou that did hew *Rahab* in pieces;" (Psalm LXXXIX 10) Thou didst crush *Rahab* like a carcass; Thou didst scatter enemies with Thy mighty arm.[7]

Thus, the Biblical writers speak of redemption (Exod 6:6; 15:13), combining the offering of the sacrifice in Egypt and the crossing of the Red Sea fleeing from Egypt. And the enemy was not merely Egypt but the sea monster, *Leviathan*, the serpent of old (Isa 27:1). Thus, redemption is from evil in Egypt and from the enslavement of the enemy of God.

In this redemption and the pilgrimage that follows to Mt. Sinai, Waltke recognizes the LORD's role as Warrior King:

> This is a change in role from a tribal deity in Genesis. In addition, the triumph over Egypt is entirely I AM's, for his deliverance does not depend on human strength. When Moses seeks to free his people in his own strength, God remains silent. When Moses recognizes the limits of his own strength, God calls him. In the plague incidents, Moses battles with Pharaoh as a prophet with a staff, not as a warrior imbued with physical strength and cunning.[8]

God's role will change under the dispensation of law, but at the outset Israel's faith was passive.

The second kind of promise to be considered relates to the climax of partnership with God: "you shall know that I am the LORD your God" (Exod 6:7b).

> *Yd'* is a key term in *Exodus* narratives, occurring over twenty times in the first fourteen chapters. The usual rendering "to know" hardly does justice to the richness of its semantic range. In the biblical conception, knowledge is not essentially or even primarily rooted in the intellect and mental activity. Rather it

---

[7]   Cassuto, *Exodus*, p. 81.

[8]   Waltke, *An Old Testament Theology*, p. 395.

is more experiential…so that it may encompass such qualities
as contact, intimacy, concern, relatedness and mutuality.[9]

So in the experiences under the Law, there will be a greater emphasis on
mutuality in Israel's response to the Law and the LORD's providential
working according to promise. Such mutuality occurred with Abraham,
"because you have done this…I will surely bless you" (Gen 22:16-17).
Mutuality doesn't imply equality but partnership in which each has a role
under the promise. And the faith is *active*.

Mosaic Covenant (Exodus 19–Leviticus)

The Mosaic Covenant was to be ratified with a corporately redeemed
people. They had been a people who *served* Egypt and they now would
be a people who *served* the LORD. The covenant spelled out that service.

> Sinai is neither just law nor properly a treaty. It represents a
> *confluence* of these two, producing a further facet in group
> relationships, namely, social-political-religious covenant…"re-
> ligious" in servicing its deity through worship: "social" in that
> the mandatory content of the covenant is rules for practical
> living (law); and "political" in that the deity has the role of
> exclusive sovereign over the group.[10]

The service may be described based on the purpose of the covenant
in Exod 19:5-6. Israel is called to be a treasured possession because they
serve as a kingdom of priests and live as a holy nation. Within the theocracy, the people were to serve the will of the King, the interests of the
fellow-partners, and the needs of the nations. Their realization of these
goals would be contingent upon obedience to the Law.

When God first introduced the idea of service to Abraham, "it opens
with grace (*I have known him*) directed toward the firm discipline of
law (*command…way…justice…righteousness*)."[11] This is the same order as
Israel arrived at Mt. Sinai. It was grace providing redemption from Egypt
and law in the gift of the Mosaic Covenant. "And out of the amazing
stillness that prevailed after the fearful storm are heard the words of the

---

[9] Sarna, *Exodus*, pp. 32, 35.

[10] Kenneth Anderson Kitchen, *On the Reliability of the Old Testament* (Grand Rapids, MI:
Eerdmans, 2003), p. 289.

[11] Kidner, *Genesis*, p. 133, emphasis in original.

Lord, who speaks to His people and makes known to them the fundamentals of His Torah (teaching, instruction) Exodus 19:25."[12]

Covenant Ratification (Exodus 19:4–24:18)

The Purpose of the Covenant (Exodus 19:4-6)

God had promised that Abram would mediate blessings to all nations (Gen 12:3). The force of the promise remains intact, yet under the dispensation of law, the role is treated as contingent (if…, then…). What had hindered the patriarchs from fully realizing this role was personal sin. Thus, to implement the role, God highlights the people's responsibility. And that responsibility would be encoded in the Mosaic Covenant.

The Mosaic Covenant is an obligatory covenant and the obligation is to righteousness. "Righteousness portrays a way of living in community that promotes the life of all its members, a life promoting social order in recognition of God's rule."[13] Yet in the contingency statement, the obedience in righteousness is not the end. Rather this is a condition for intimacy in relationship with God. It is a condition for partnership in mediation of blessing to the nations. It is a condition for sharing God's holiness in the world. This portrays the *stewardship* of Israel under the Law.

The Content of the Law (Exodus 20:1–23:33)

Cassuto recognizes the absolutely distinctive character of the covenant content as he compares this revelation to the content found in other ANE treaties.[14]

With respect to the Book of Exodus, the Ten Commandments are placed in a pivotal position in the book (Exodus 20). What precedes is preparatory for the revelation of the Law (Exodus 1–19). What follows are the statutes and ordinances, which are case laws (Exodus 21–23). Further, what follows in the development of the holy space in the tabernacle and priestly service (Exodus 25–40) is dependent on the distinct truth of the Ten Commandments.

---

[12] Cassuto, *Exodus*, pp. 234-35.

[13] Waltke, *Genesis*, p. 269.

[14] Cassuto, *Exodus*, pp. 235-52. The summary of the content presented here depends upon his considerations.

Moses and his generation are confronted with a new conception of spiritual revelation. Other treaties do include law collections which rest upon foundations of ethical and moral principles.

What is new is the concept of one transcendent God. "The first commandment is a prohibition against preferring other gods over *I AM*. It comes first both numerically and conceptually: it is the first principle. The remaining commandments rest on this foundation: there is no other authority than *I AM*."[15] It is not a concession that in fact there is a plurality of gods, but a recognition that the nations that will be in the land will perceive that there are other gods. For Israel, the One revealed in Genesis and in the events early in the Exodus, the LORD by name, is the only true God. He is revealed to be the Creator who is distinct from all creatures. It is He who irrupted into Israel's history to effect the Exodus.

Second, a practical corollary follows: who/what can depict this God? And the implied answer is only His self-revelation. It is not a restriction on artistic representations but an affirmation that it is impossible to represent Him in what is created. He had revealed Himself in the burning bush. This was determinative (Exod 3:2-14) as found in His name: Yahweh.

Third, another corollary includes the use of His name (Exod 20:7). It should not be used for self-serving purposes but only to honor and respect and worship Him.

Fourth, "remember the Sabbath Day to keep it holy" (Exod 20:8-11). Kline makes an interesting proposal that the Sabbath sign presented in the midst of the Ten Commandments may be equivalent to a suzerain's dynastic seal affixed to the obverse of international treaty documents.[16] Since the second command forbids any representation of the LORD, there can be no representation on the seal. Since the "sign of the covenant" is the Sabbath, which pictures the pattern of creation, the LORD is proclaimed as absolute Sovereign of creation. By keeping the Sabbath, Israel acknowledged God's sovereignty over her, and thereby pledged covenant consecration to God.

The next five commands are related to mankind, created in God's image. They express principles without which no organized, moral society can exist (Exod 20:12-16), thus, they are stated in absolute form. While there may be contextual qualifications given later, as time and

---

[15] Waltke, *An Old Testament Theology*, p. 415, emphasis in original.

[16] Meredith Kline, *Treaty of the Great King* (Grand Rapids, MI: Eerdmans, 1963), pp. 18ff. Kline follows the proposal that the partnership between the Lord and Israel is parallel in many respects to the Suzerain and vassal partnership found in ANE. From this proposal he attempts to match elements in the Mosaic Covenant to the international treaty.

place may warrant, here they are stated without qualification. First, the respect deserved by parents is based solely on position and not on performance. This is a way to express the value of the family as the foundation of an enduring society. The breakdown of the family, based on parental irresponsibility, or on the redefinition of marriage based on personal preference, will soon bring decay to a society. Second, human life is treated as an absolute value in the next commandment. Yet, based on reflection, the consequences due to the distinction between willful murder and unwitting manslaughter are expressed in different penalties. That doesn't change the value of human life, but the consequences differ based on intent. Thus, in the Ten Commandments, the principle was expressed with unqualified absoluteness because of the importance of moral order in a society. Yet as that order deteriorated because of sin, that reality of sin would be taken into consideration to protect the victims.

The framing of the Ten Commandments rests on what rightfully is possessed by God and by subjects in the community. What is rightfully God's is different from what is rightfully man's, though both have rights. There are rights of the Creator and Sovereign and rights of those created in His image. But they are revealed as rights to be respected in others, not as rights to be claimed for self-interest.

Finally, the last commandment features an attitude and not an action alone. Do not yearn for, nor strongly desire, what belongs to another. In effect, be satisfied with what is given at creation and what God grants throughout life. This command is not to remove ambition, but to challenge ambition driven by a selfish and destructive competitive motivation. A desire for all that God provides in partnership with Him is the appropriate perspective in which to value all possessions.

The Ratification of the Covenant (Exodus 24)

A covenant is a formal partnership arrangement. It is formal because it is *ratified* at a ceremony. That ceremony involves a sacrifice and/or an oath. In the Bible, the arrangements are determined solely by the LORD. It is never an agreement reached by negotiation, but a *unilaterally* imposed arrangement. Ratification concerns the formal acceptance of the partnership with God.

An *obligatory* covenant is ratified by both partners. It is an arrangement *conditioned* on the recipient partner's participation in ratification. Otherwise, it does not come into existence. In the case of the Mosaic Covenant,

Israel accepted the terms, "All the people answered together and said, 'All that the LORD has spoken we will do.'" (Exod 19:8; cf. 24:3, 7). This was not negotiated, but it was accepted. The acceptance was unanimous, was inclusive, and expressed a willingness to act in obedience. This was the oath. In addition, in the ceremony Moses threw half the blood against the altar (Exod 24:6) and the other half on the people (Exod 24:8). This formally acknowledged a bilateral arrangement.

However, was this appropriate? In one sense it was. What other response would they give for what God gave them? But in another sense, based on the double knowledge that would come with the revelation of the Law, it wasn't reflective. In accepting, they had a naive comprehension of God and an unreflective consideration of the evil they had in their hearts. Both aspects of knowledge will be a focus of Israel's stewardship under the Law.

Nonetheless, Moses ratified the covenant by blood at the foot of Mt. Sinai. Then Moses and Aaron and the seventy elders went up the mountain and saw the God of Israel (Exod 24:9-10).

Covenant Renewal (Exodus 32–34)

It had only been forty days since Moses left the community to receive the blueprint for the tabernacle. Growing impatient with God's silence and Moses' absence, the people urged Aaron to make a god to bring them back to Egypt. Aaron agreed and failed to restrain them. This was the first test of whether the LORD would annul the covenant partnership because Israel violated the terms of the Law. The covenant was now functioning and there were consequences for their covenant violation.

Moses in the Mountain (Exodus 32:7-10)

The LORD informed Moses that the people had turned aside quickly from the way (Exod 32:8). At issue was the first commandment—Israel made a god for themselves. It was not that Israel was *unable* to wait. They were *impatient, stiff-necked*, and *unwilling* to wait for God. This is the focus of covenant violations.

The LORD proposed that the covenant with the people had been voided[17] and that Moses alone stood in covenant faithfulness (Exod 32:10). There

---

[17] Brevard Childs, *Exodus* (Philadelphia: Westminster Press, 1974), p. 567. "[T]here is a harsh dissidence as if he had suddenly broken off…"

is evidence that the covenant no longer existed because the people violated their acceptance. The people had become "your people" (Exod 32:7) rather than "My people" (Exod 6:7). When Moses broke the two tablets (Exod 32:19), he regarded the covenant as broken. Therefore, he believed God would consume the people (Exod 32:10), in which case, Moses would become a great nation (cf. Gen 12:2).

Mediation (Exodus 32:10ff)

God's final word invites a response. "'Let me alone that I may consume them.' The effect is that God himself leaves the door open for intercession. He allows himself to be persuaded. That is what a mediator is for!"[18] In addition, the LORD announces the violation and pronounces the verdict ahead of time. This gives Moses something to appeal.

Moses Mediates a Covenant Renewal (Exodus 32:11–34:10)

Intercession (Exodus 32:11-13)

Moses' appeal begins with what God has promised— they will be "My people" (Exod 6:7). Second it rests on the harm that would come to God's reputation in Egypt if Israel were unable to enter the land promised. Third, his appeal rested in the patriarchs to whom God had promised many descendants. No appeal was made on the merit of the people or on their faithfulness.

God Relented (Exodus 32:14)

With respect to this threat to annihilate the whole population, God changed His mind.[19] The judgment proposed was withdrawn.

Forgiveness (Exodus 32:15-35)

Moses recognized that the status of the covenant remained unresolved while there is sin that has not been forgiven. So Moses took two courses of action.

An Immediate Course to Be Taken for Sin (Exodus 32:15-29)

Moses burned the golden calf, ground up the gold veneer, and forced the participating people to drink it, mixed with water. In addition,

---

[18] *Ibid.*

[19] God's change of mind (*nāḥam*) concerns no more than what course of action he had proposed in context. This ought not to be generalized to suggest that God's character changes nor that this provides a pattern for prayer requests. Unlike in a prayer request, there was a tentative course of action proposed by God.

against those who were wildly unrestrained, there was immediate, physical death. Sons of Levi joined Moses to administer death on brothers and even on sons (Exod 32:29).

An Ultimate Course to Be Considered for Forgiveness of Sin (Exodus 32:30-35)

Moses then proposed to the rest of the people that he would intercede for their forgiveness. The elliptical word order of his prayer (Exod 32:32) indicates how uncertain Moses was as he approached a holy God. First, he made a confession on behalf of the people, hoping for forgiveness, but then fell silent in uncertainty. If this confession did not gain forgiveness, he requested to be blotted out of the LORD's book.[20] The meaning of Moses' words is difficult to interpret. It appears that if a sacrifice is needed beyond an animal sacrifice, he offered himself to spare the nation. Such sacrifice appears to call for his immediate death so that the remaining people would be forgiven and live.

God Rejects Moses' Proposal (Exodus 32:33-34)

Sarna says:

> There must be an individual accountability. But the people also bear collective responsibility. Divine promises of national territory to the people of Israel are immutable, but total absolution for sin of the golden calf cannot be given. Israel receives a suspended sentence; the people are on probation.[21]

As Sarna noted, what Moses had addressed in prayer was not personal sin, but collective accountability within the Mosaic national partnership. However, a better way to look at Israel's status is not as on probation. *Probation* suggests they could regain a proper status themselves. Rather, the future status of the nation is based on the Abrahamic promise. The Mosaic Covenant was added alongside and is thus temporary. There will be a final covenant judgment, but the time of national accounting is appointed for a future day. Thus, Beecher is probably correct to interpret

---

[20] The sense of blot may suggest lighten in color or remove. That sense is also influenced by the meaning of "your book." Driver posits that the book should not be understood as the New Testament "book of life" which portrayed figuratively as a register of all the names of the saints who are redeemed and will inherit eternal life. Here it refers to the names of those who are living and serving in this life, whose names, it was imagined, were on the roster in the heavenly courts as belonging to the living. Moses would rather die than live if these people are not forgiven (S. R. Driver, *Exodus*, Cambridge Bible [Cambridge, MA: Cambridge University Press, 1911], p. 356).

[21] Sarna, *Exodus*, p. 210.

the future day when God said, "I will visit" as the Day of the LORD.[22] At the same time, God sent a plague against that generation as judgment on the guilty (Exod 32:35). Thus, the Day of the LORD's visitation is introduced to which the prophets will later make reference.

Moses Completes the Task of Mediation (Exodus 33:1–34:7)

Moses adds two intriguing questions: first, would God accompany that generation? That would indicate that He was their God and they were His people. The LORD in time agreed and He added the promise to give them rest (Exod 33:14).

The second question: would God show him His ways? Then Moses could know the LORD and find favor in God's sight by understanding what to request (Exod 33:13). The answer the LORD revealed focused on their relationship. Moses had already found favor and the LORD knew his name (Exod 33:17). Going back to the creation account, this was God's way in creating mankind in His own image (Gen 1:26-27). Knowing God is sharing life, not understanding God's life.

Yet Moses wanted to go deeper (Exod 33:18). "It is clear that Moses here asks to comprehend God's essential personality, the attributes that guide His actions in His dealings with humankind, and the norms by which He operates in His governance of the world."[23] This is "the ways of God" which he had asked to know.

Now Moses expressed it as "seeing your glory." Glory expresses the ideas of "weight," of "standing," and of "honor." "כבוד [glory] is by and large that asset which makes people or individuals, and even objects, impressive and usually this is understood as something that can be perceived or expressed."[24] The LORD's answer is to reveal an aspect of Himself, but not everything. In addition, the revelation is not static but personal as He passed before Moses. Knowing the LORD is a living relationship in which He is trusted but not controlled. First, God will reveal His goodness (33:19). The word *good* (*tov*), is shared as the description of the original, unfallen creation. Second He will reveal His name (Exod 33:19), which invites conversation and trust. But it is a conversation in which choice remains with God, for, "I will be gracious to whom I will be gracious, and will show mercy on whom I will show mercy." What remains undisclosed

---

[22] Willis J. Beecher, *The Prophets and Promise* (Grand Rapids, MI: Baker, 1963), p. 307. He also recognizes that although the explanation is probable, it is hardly capable of conclusive proof.

[23] Sarna, *Exodus*, p. 213.

[24] Von Rad, *Old Testament Theology*, vol. 1, p. 239. Sarna translates it, "let me go behind your Presence" (*Exodus*, pp. 213-14) while others see it more literally, "to glimpse the Divine Presence."

is God's face (Exod 33:20), even though Moses was granted a glimpse of His back (Exod 33:25).

The experience in which God reveals His goodness is the covenant renewal. The LORD's goodness is evident. He is "merciful and gracious, slow to anger and abounding in steadfast love and faithfulness, keeping steadfast love for thousands, forgiving iniquity and transgression of sin…" (Exod 34:6-7a). But this is not at the expense of righteousness, for He "will by no means clear the guilty" (Exod 34:7b). In the covenant renewal, glory rests in God's overwhelming goodness displayed in different aspects of Moses' prayer, but not at the cost of allowing unrighteousness. Mercy and righteousness are compatible in the nation's present survival with accountability, and in the nation's future final reckoning.

Ratification of a Renewed Covenant

The section concludes with a report: "I am making [*kārat*] a covenant" (Exod 34:10) and "I have made [*kārat*] a covenant with you" (Exod 34:27). The voided covenant has been ratified a second time in its renewal with the people following Moses' mediation.

Sacred Space and Service (Exodus 25–Leviticus 27)

After the ratification of the covenant, God said, "make me a sanctuary, that I may dwell in their midst" (Exod 25:8). Then again, based on Moses' intercession, Yahweh agreed, "My presence will go with you" (Exod 33:14). Eugene Merrill summarizes Israel's cultic[25] community as including four elements: "(1) sacred space, (2) sacred persons, (3) sacred seasons, and (4) sacred acts."[26]

Sacred Space

Sacred Space on earth began with the Garden of Eden. Here the Creator met face-to-face with the creature in the creation. After man's fall into sin, man was forced out of the garden and prohibited from re-entry. Subsequent communication was mediated. Jacob's dream opened up his eyes to envision this mediation according to the Abrahamic arrangement. It was a stairway between God in heaven at the top, and Jacob, His elect,

---

[25] Cultus is a theological term which "describes any system of religious beliefs and rituals as well as its adherents" (Eugene H. Merrill, *Everlasting Dominion: A Theology of the Old Testament* [Nashville, TN: Broadman and Holman, 2003], p. 374).

[26] *Ibid.*, p. 351. Merrill's development will guide the organization of this section.

on earth. Angels ascended and descended mediating God's presence and will on earth. It was not until Moses that a sacred space appeared on earth in the burning bush. And so Moses was cautioned that the ground upon which he stood was holy. He must remove his sandals.

So now the LORD was about to irrupt into history for a final time with Israel to dwell in the sacred space of the tabernacle. For the people, this provided refuge to draw near in grace and to live in a community within His presence because of His loyal love. The yearly sacred times would be celebrated nationally in the tabernacle and later in the temple. *Miškān* (dwelling) was the technical name for the tabernacle. "This is an important idea because it provides a note of intimacy or immediacy in the larger context of God's overwhelming power and glory. The great Sovereign of heaven—the wholly inconceivable and unapproachable One—would, in some sense at least, dwell in an earthly structure among fallen mankind."[27]

Not only was the tabernacle the dwelling place of the LORD, it was the core of the theocratic reign of God over Israel and mediated through Israel to the nations. This is the theocratic era of the dispensation of law. The covenant expression of law was the stewardship of Israel to participate in the tabernacle.

Within the tabernacle was furniture that further clarified the dwelling of the LORD. The residence of His glory is *the Ark of the Covenant*, located in "the Most Holy Place" (Exod 26:34). The ark's cover (*kappōret*), where God was enthroned, is the place of National atonement, once a year (Leviticus 16–17). The LORD had promised, "I will meet with you" (Exod 25:22). The terms for approaching the LORD in a respectful fashion were specifically enumerated. But when Nadab and Abihu attempted to approach God on their own terms, fire from heaven dramatically demonstrated God's displeasure (Leviticus 10).

Adjacent to and just in front of the Most Holy Place was the Holy Place. Two primary pieces of furniture portrayed Israel's fellowship in God's presence. On one side is *the table of showbread* set before the LORD (Lev 24:7-8). "Thus the table was in the truest sense, a place where the Lord and his people, represented by the priests, symbolically broke bread together."[28] On the other side, was *the golden lampstand*. "And the lamps shall be set up so as to give light on the space in front of it" (Exod 25:37). The priests served in an otherwise dark room, in the light provided by what God specified. Fellowship with God occurs

---

[27] *Ibid.*, p. 352.

[28] *Ibid.*, p. 355.

in the light as God had created during the day, in an expression of light suitable to be shared by man.

The Most Holy Place and the Holy Place combined to form the tabernacle. The outer court surrounded the tabernacle and provided gradated accessibility to holiness. Access into the outer court was provided through the *altar of burnt offering*. The function of the altar was introduced to Adam and passed on to Cain and Abel, Noah, and the patriarchs. There was a prescribed construction of the altar. There was an appointed substitute, animal life. There was a sacrifice of that life in the shedding of blood. The offered sacrifice provided the only access to God. Different sacrifices had specific meanings.

Sacred Persons

Priests represent the community in approaching God in the *sacred space*. The priests are organized in a hierarchy ultimately directed by the high priest. But before they attempt to approach God, they consecrate themselves in anticipation of the LORD's imminent self-disclosure. In addition to an elaborate ritual of consecration, they are qualified to serve when they wear special symbolic priestly attire (Leviticus 8–9). The tabernacle "became a sacred space, an extension of heaven on earth, and its officiants were His special servants, His representatives who made possible a vital and living contact between a holy God and His people who came to proffer Him adoration and praise at this sacred place."[29]

Sacred Times

Times are specified both according to the calendar and according to individual spiritual needs. When the sacrifices were introduced, they were specified according to spiritual need. Two means of access were available. Individual worshipers with a spiritual need could bring and offer sacrifices through priestly service. In addition, each morning and evening, various representative sacrifices were offered by the priest. So Daniel, while in captivity in Babylon, illustrated how a worshiper prayed at a distance from the tabernacle or temple. At the hour of the morning or evening sacrifices, the believing Jew would pray to God in heaven based on the sacrifices offered in the presence of the LORD.

---

[29] *Ibid.*, p. 364

The yearly times are specified in Leviticus 23 according to the calendar. In these sacred times, Israel was reminded and taught about God's role in the nation's yearly needs and in the nation's historical needs.

This chart may help to provide a brief overview:

Times Schedule	Scheduled Theological Meaning	Scheduled Historical Meaning
Passover	redemption	birth of a people
Unleavened Bread	separation from evil	separation from Egypt's provision
Firstfruits	resurrection to life from the dead	initial provision in harvest
Pentecost	gift of the Holy Spirit	climactic provision in harvest
Trumpets	call to prepare	prepare for national cleansing
Day of Atonement	national atonement	national cleansing
Booths	await occupation	land inheritance of blessing

Sacred Acts

Acts include prayers, offerings, and sacrifices within Israel's system of cultus (beliefs and practices). This cultus, prior to its revelation, nonetheless caused issues for Egypt.[30] Israel's worship was defined by making sacrifices and "the offerings we shall sacrifice to the LORD our God are an abomination to the Egyptians" (Exod 8:26). Sacrifices were culturally offensive in Egypt. When Pharaoh wanted to limit those who would go, Moses insisted that young and old go (Exod 10:9). Worship involved the whole community and must include flocks and herds for sacrifices (Exod 10:25-26).

Thus, at the core of their worship were the acts (sacrifices) that are prescribed in Leviticus 1–7. It is helpful "to distinguish between the 'basic

---

[30] *Ibid.*, p. 375. Merrill clarifies what is distinctive.

idea' in the sacrificial act and the reason for its performance.'"[31] "Here Jahweh was within the reach of Israel's gratitude, here Israel was granted fellowship with him in the sacred meal. Above all, here Israel could be reached by his will for forgiveness."[32]

As Israel lived during the dispensation of law, double knowledge was at the heart of their stewardship.

The righteous demands of the Law revealed a knowledge of God and His will. Israel's response to those demands exposed a knowledge of who they were. The gracious provisions of the sacrifice also revealed knowledge of God. Participating in the sacrifices helped the Israelites come to know forgiveness and mercy from God.

Kadesh Barnea

Charge to Enter the Land

Kadesh Barnea was the gateway to the land that had been promised to Abraham (Gen 15:8-20) and to Moses (Exod 6:7). But it also provided the climactic test after the Law had been ratified. Several questions emerge in the narrative:

What would the people decide about entry into the land?

What are the consequences of their decision?

How do these consequences compare to consequences due to Abraham's decisions?

What does this account indicate about the theocratic rule of the LORD?

There are two accounts of the experience (Numbers 13:1–14:45; Deut 1:19-33). The first word was Moses' charge as the people arrived at Kadesh Barnea: "See, the LORD your God has set the land before you. Go up; take possession, as the LORD…has told you" (Deut 1:21).

---

[31] Von Rad, *Old Testament Theology*, vol. 1, p. 253.

Act	Basic Idea (Sacrifice)	Reason
Burnt	whole animal	to draw near and gain a hearing
Meal	same gift for all	to give thanks
Peace	animal to be shared by all	public thanksgiving and shared blessing
Sin	various animals	atonement for unintentional sins
Guilt	animal and restitution	atonement and payment of restitution

[32] *Ibid.*, p. 260.

People's Responses

The people proposed an alternative approach of sending spies ahead, which the LORD accepted (Deut 1:22). Apparently, Moses inquired of the LORD and the LORD spoke to Moses saying, "Send men to spy out the land of Canaan which I am giving to the people of Israel." (Num 13:2). Moses then specified what they were to report about to the people (Num 13:26-33). Twelve leaders, one from each tribe, spied out the land.

Upon their return, their report not only answered the people's questions but provided their own assessment of their ability to accomplish what God had promised to give them (Num 13:26-33). The report agreed on one thing: "we came to the land to which you sent us. It flows with milk and honey, and this is its fruit" (Num 13:27). But the assessment of their ability to accomplish what God had promised was not as positive. The majority assessed their ability based on several facts: "the people who dwell in the land are strong, and the cities are fortified and very large," and the land is fully occupied (Num 13:28-29). These facts seemed to imply that the task would be impossible.

Caleb then offered an opposite assessment: "Let us go up at once and occupy it, for we are well able to overcome it" (Num 13:30). This is active faith. The majority gave a direct denial: "We are not able to go up against the people, for they are stronger than we are" (Num 13:31). Their report turned into a bad report: "The land, through which we have gone to spy it out, is a land that devours its inhabitants, and all the people that we saw in it are of great height...we seemed to ourselves like grasshoppers and so we seemed to them" (Num 13:32-33).

The people were overcome by unbelief. Their assessment rested only on their own inability. Their desire was to return to Egypt (Num 14:1-4), just as it had been at Sinai. This was an instance of despair in failing to know themselves under the Law. For Israel to live as God's people would involve a supernatural effort in the conquest of the land.

Moses assessed the people's response as unbelief. The LORD was going before them and would fight for them as He had done in Egypt. In the wilderness, the LORD had carried them from Mt. Sinai to Kadesh Barnea, "yet in spite of this word, you did not believe the LORD your God" (Deut 1:32).

The people's unbelief had unavoidable consequences. Ten times they had put the LORD to the test and had not obeyed His voice (Num 14:22). The consequence: "not one of these men of this evil generation shall see the good land that I swore to give to your fathers, except Caleb...and

Joshua" (Deut 1:35-38). The unbelievers were disinherited. In the dispensation of the law, in the theocratic era, the LORD Himself will dispense judgment against high-handed sin. For each of the 40 days they had spied out the land, they would wander a year aimlessly in the wilderness. The children whom they had lamented would perish (Num 14:3), would ironically survive the wilderness (Num 14:32-34). The years in the wilderness would prepare them to enter the land.

A marked difference in God's treatment of unbelief had emerged as the dispensation of law took effect. Israel's rejection of the LORD at Kadesh Barnea delayed the progress in God's plan for a whole generation. That is strikingly different than God's treatment of Abram in his unbelief (Gen 12:10-20; 20:1-18). While Abram was humiliated as a consequence of his unbelief, God allowed the events to progress without delay while protecting Sarah for the promise.

This difference in God's dealing with sin may be tied to the change in dispensations. Under the dispensation of promise, sin was not ignored, but the priority rested in establishing a vision and in forging out the purposes in God's plan of redemption. This priority continued in the Passover, in the Exodus from Egypt, in the divided sea, in the provision of manna, and in the provision of water. These gifts, given by the LORD, were not contingent upon obedience in the same way the gift of the land would be. They were received in passive faith.

Under the dispensation of law, obedience became the necessary response God used to give the gift of the land: "I have given you every place where the sole of your foot treads." This became the issue with Achan and the subsequent conquest of Ai (Joshua 7–8). The positive presence of obedience became the occasion for the LORD giving the Amorites over to the Israelites, in Joshua's prayer for added time of warfare (Joshua 10). The administration of God's will through His steward had changed with the change in dispensation. God would incorporate the people's active faith in God and His promise as a condition for blessing.

Balak the Moabite and Balaam

At the conclusion of their wilderness wanderings, Balak the Moabite summoned Balaam to curse Israel (Numbers 23–25). It would seem to be an opportune time for the LORD to be relieved of the burden of carrying this people. But to curse Israel would be to violate the Abrahamic Covenant (Gen 12:2). The covenant exists in spite of Israel's repeated sin. The promises of God are stable in spite of the instability of Israel in history. As a result, "Balaam blesses Israel instead of cursing them. And in the fourth oracle he predicts the eventual doom of Moab at the hands of Israel: Balak's curse, intended for Israel, will instead be inflicted by Israel on Moab."[33] That is the irony involved in nations challenging God's elect people.

While God would not curse Israel because of His promise, Israel will again deny the LORD, in spite of her oath (Exod 19:7-8; 24:3, 7). Her denial took the form of sexual immorality with the women of Moab at Peor, leading to the worship of Baal. "Baal-peor is the punishment for the sin and the fulfillment of the sentence for the golden calf...Ironically, yet justifiably, the coup de grâce to the generation of the Exodus is executed when they commit apostasy for the second time. In a real sense, Baal-peor is but an extension of the golden calf."[34] The completion of the judgment eliminates the first generation. This sin affecting 24,000 contributed to the need for a covenant renewal with the new generation.

Deuteronomy

The contemporary study of Deuteronomy is fraught with unresolved questions:

What is the relationship to Moses? Even those who take the book to have been composed by a later narrator still see the framework as the combined three valedictory addresses of Moses.[35]

What is the point of view of Deuteronomy? The question envisions the presence of two distinct points of view (the later narrator and Moses) or the presence of simply one voice (Moses).

> There is a clear historical consciousness of recollecting the past, reflecting upon the future, and choosing in the present. Key words include "today" with reference to time, and "Jordan" with reference to space. "This day" is the decisive time for Israel to identify with God's past promises and workings with Israel in order to commit themselves to accomplish the will of God for their future.[36]

---

[33] Jacob Milgrom, *Numbers*, JPS Torah Commentary (Philadelphia: Jewish Publication Society, 1990), p. 185.

[34] *Ibid.*, p. 211.

[35] Waltke, *An Old Testament Theology*, pp. 479-503.

[36] *Ibid.*, p. 498.

What is the reason for composing a second law? When some argue that this is a supplement to the first ratified covenant (Exodus 19–24), they neglect the fact that the covenant was ratified as a conditional covenant. The existence of the covenant was conditioned on the vow that Israel took, "all that the LORD has said we will do." When that vow was clearly broken in four recorded incidents, Exodus 32, Leviticus 10, and Numbers 13–14 and 25, then it followed that the covenant needed to be renewed. It seems that this renewal also was occasioned by a new generation who themselves needed to take the vow (Deuteronomy 26:16–27:8; 29:1-15) and by a transfer of leadership to Joshua (Deut 31:1-22).

Changes in the Covenant

Two rather different answers have been posed. Merrill suggests that the new generation and the new circumstances occasion the changes. "The great King would expand upon, elaborate, or even reinterpret the text in order to make perfectly clear his expectations of his junior partner…"[37] The circumstances also pose changes from wilderness and nomadic life to entering and populating a city-state culture.

Waltke, on the other hand, posits a more fundamental change: "the covenant renewal documents pertain to a spiritual, not legalistic commitment."[38] What is striking in his proposal is not the spiritual emphasis but the deemphasizing of the national issues which remain as the focus in God's dealings in history.

When the oath of the renewed covenant is about to be taken (Deut 29:10-15), the words of the covenant in the land of Moab are compared to the covenant made with them at Horeb (Deut 29:1). Thus, the two covenants are comparable and naturally involved with the theocratic reign of the LORD during the dispensation of the law. To disregard this historical relationship is a move toward a simply ideological covenant. Rather, both the first generation and the second generation must make a spiritual commitment. It was the first generation's failure in its spiritual commitment that led to the covenant renewal. It also could have contributed to Moses' emphasis on spiritual commitment in the new generation.

The Ten Commandments are recorded in essentially the same form. The only changes involve the Sabbath law, now motivated by the exodus

---

[37] Merrill, *Everlasting Dominion*, p. 390.

[38] Waltke, *An Old Testament Theology*, p. 499.

rather than creation, and greater emphasis placed on coveting a neighbor's wife in the pagan Canaanite culture.

What is highlighted is the basic principle and foundational tenet of the Decalogue called the *Shema'* (Deut 6:4-5). It consists of (1) a declaration of who God is, He is one in essence, and (2) a command about how to respond individually and in the home in light of the declaration. It is addressed to Israel, the LORD's covenant partners. The fact that the LORD alone is their God (Deut 6:4) is significant because the people were about to enter a polytheistic culture. An example, Baalism at Shittim where the Moabites worship was the "Baal of Peor" (Num 25:3). And so there were similar worship localities scattered throughout the land. For Israel, the LORD alone was their God.

As a result, Israel was to be totally committed to the LORD, as a nation and individually, with a wholehearted love. And such love is to be taught in the various experiences of the home, one generation to the next. Such an exclusive love is then characterized by an uncompromising obedience. Within the development of Deuteronomy, "the *Shema* is to the Decalogue what the Decalogue is to the whole covenant text."[39] The obedience expected in the Decalogue is amplified in the particular argument of Deuteronomy 6–26.

Such an exclusive identity of God is then related in the land to how, when, and where He can be reached. "The book of the covenant had made allowance for God to be worshiped at a multiplicity of sites— 'where I cause My name to be remembered' (Exod 20:24)—but clearly not in opposition to the central sanctuary of the tabernacle."[40] This was certainly the case in the wilderness. But Deuteronomy looked forward to occupation of the land and the necessity to remove pagan shrines and even syncretistic expressions of the LORD's worship (Dan and Bethel). Therefore, God specifies one place, "you shall seek the place that the LORD your God will choose out of all your tribes to put his name and make his habitation there. There you shall go…" (Deut 12:5). This central sanctuary served as a place of national assembly and the place of the theocratic throne of the LORD in His reign.

Another emphasis emerged from an anticipation to occupy the land. In the ANE, there were cultural means of gaining access to the ways of the gods in a polytheistic world. Deuteronomy 18:9-14 speaks against

---

[39] Merrill, *Everlasting Dominion*, p. 396.

[40] *Ibid.*, p. 400.

divination and incantations. Divination was a way of eliciting the purposes and plans of the gods. Incantations were attempts to manipulate these gods.

Rather, the *prophet* served the role to deliver the revelation from the LORD. Deuteronomy 18:15-22 had much to say about true prophecy. In addition, Moses spoke of himself as a prototype of a true prophet and intimates that a line of prophets would follow him. That line would reach a climax in a Supreme Source of Revelation. To this One, Israel was to pay careful attention (Deut 18:15).

Clearly Deut 27:10-15 is calling for a spiritual response and a heart-based commitment in taking the oath, but the *commitment* is also *national* and *judicial*. This is evident from two strains of revelation. The first strain is the laws of social life in the land (Deuteronomy 16–18), in particular, the judge and the anticipated king who administer God's reign over Israel in the land. During the period of the theocracy, the judge has prominence (Deuteronomy 16:18–17:13). Theocracy is mediated by the rule of law and the stewardship of that administration rested in the *šōpᵉṭîm*, the judges.

> [The section which] deals with the responsibilities of public officials, begins here in Deuteronomy 16:18 and continues through 21:9. It introduces four main types of human authorities: judges, kings, priests and prophets…Prominence is given to the limits established by God on the rights of each authority…Deuteronomy seeks to prevent the development of a single, strong focus of prestige and power.[41]

That focus belongs exclusively to the LORD. One type of human authority is the judge. They are to be appointed as local officials (Deut 16:18-20); there are judicial procedures to be followed in case of apostasy (Deut 17:2-7) and conditions for referral of difficult cases (Deut 17:8-13). Although the role of the judge in the Book of Judges is primarily military, Deborah indicates that the essential role is judicial.

---

[41] Dr. Jeffrey H. Tigay, *Deuteronomy*, JPS Torah Commentary (Philadelphia: The Jewish Publication Society, 2003), p. 159.

Land Inheritance

"The land plays a most important role in the book of Deuteronomy."[42] This emphasis further supports the idea that this renewed covenant has a national and judicial commitment. The first deliverance of the Law constitutes the recipients a people. When they occupied the land, the people would become a nation. Deuteronomy anticipated the people's entrance into and taking possession of the land (Deut 6:18; 8:1; 11:8-9, 11-12; 16:20). Moses explained why Israel failed to enter the land at Kadesh Barnea, "in spite of this word, you did not believe the LORD your God" (Deut 1:32).

"In reality, this land belongs to Yahweh."[43] Thus, it is given to Israel by the LORD. While the "land symbolizes the transition from disordered existence to ordered structures,"[44] it has actual substance as well. It is a rich land in every respect: a land of grain, wines and all sorts of fruits as well as of natural resources such as iron and copper (Deut 8:7-9). It is given to become a means through which God's blessings may be given to sustain Israel's life. Further, "the Deuteronomic law is given to the people for observance after entrance into the land (Deuteronomy 12:1)."[45] And it specifies idolatry as the principle sin for which Israel could lose the land (Deut 11:16-17, cf. 4:25-28; 29:23-28; 30:17-18). The temptation of polytheism, not addressed when Israel took possession of the land, would surround their lives, and would tempt generation after generation.

In the days of the patriarchs, the land was *promised* as a perpetual, unconditional gift (Gen 13:5; 17:8; 48:4). The conflict that they experienced was either from within or from other sources of evil. Now added alongside of promise was the covenant of *law* (cf. Deut 4:25-27; 8:19-20; 11:8-10, 13-17, 22-25; 28:63; 29:24-27; 30:17-18). The added *condition* only intensified the conflict within. Yet the idea of the inheritance of the land is most prominently expressed in the Book of Deuteronomy. Inheritance refers to blessings bequeathed by the Father to those who share His life. It refers not only to conquest but also its possession after the conquest (Deut 16:20). "'Life' in the full sense of the word is possible for Israel only in its land."[46] The Deuteronomic expression, "to lengthen

---

[42]   Moshe Weinfeld, *Deuteronomy 1–11: A New Translation with Introduction and Commentary* (New York: Doubleday, 1964), p. 57.

[43]   Magnus Ottosson, "אֶרֶץ, *ĕrets*," TDOT, vol. 1, p. 401.

[44]   Waltke, *An Old Testament Theology*, p. 534.

[45]   Weinfeld, *Deuteronomy 1–11*, p. 59.

[46]   *Ibid.*, p. 60.

one's days," is usually accompanied with "upon the land" (Deut 4:40; 5:33; 11:9; 25:15; 32:47).

In fact, the whole Book of Deuteronomy is considered a witness against Israel in the case of disobedience (Deut 31:26). Chapters 4 and 30, as well as 31:16-29, may then be seen as a kind of bookends for Deuteronomy, which conveys the basic message for the audience to which the book addresses itself.[47] And that message promises restoration to the land, only if the nation returns to its God with sincerity.

The fact that Israel had broken the covenant repeatedly during Moses' lifetime does not speak well for the nation's long-term viability in the land. What should Israel watch out for and hope for in the future in the land?

After a review of Israel's history from Sinai to Moab (Deuteronomy 1:6–4:40), an explicit warning and assurance occurs (Deut 4:25-31). The warning anticipates some future day when the people will be taken up in idolatry. Then the LORD will scatter them among the nations. There a few survivors will be left and forced to worship lifeless gods. Then an assurance is given. First, they will search for and find the LORD. Then, when experiencing distress, that generation will return and obey Him. As a compassionate God, He will remember the Abrahamic Covenant.

The last threat of dispersion came in the curses (Deut 29:16-28). Their responsibility extends to what has been revealed (Deut 29:29) and ends there. Then the people will be scattered among the nations. Their memory of their past covenant experiences will motivate them to return to the LORD and His law. Again an intensified conflict will draw a remnant to repent. In compassion, the LORD will restore them to the land (Deut 30:1-10). It will be God Himself who will remove the sinful impediment and restore wholehearted love (Deut 30:5-6). This theology of repentance, based on the promise of God's enablement, will prompt the people to seek restoration (1 Kgs 8:44-53; Jer 29:12-14; Neh 1:5-11).

Conclusion

The dispensation of the law was introduced in the Torah—the first five books of Moses. They provided foundational teaching for Israel. In Deuteronomy, Moses introduced the fact that judgment and dispersion among the nations would be inevitable (Deut 4:25-27; 29:1-29), and Amos would later reveal how severe the people's condition would be. Yahweh

---

[47] *Ibid.*, p. 216.

had turned them over to the worship of angels and idols (Amos 5:26). Only time in history would force Israel to face the reality of their own depravity. To gain such knowledge of themselves was necessary, but Israel, like all fallen humanity, came by it reluctantly. In fact, the fall had made seeing themselves as god seem like a good and natural perspective. So history will cycle forward with seeming progress interspersed with downward movement. All of this was necessary because of man's blindness.

CHAPTER 9:
THE LORD'S THEOCRATIC
REIGN OVER ISRAEL

JOSHUA THROUGH JUDGES

Introduction

The transition from the Torah to the historical books is not reflected in the dispensation of the law. This is the case because no new revelation is added to what Moses introduced. The issue is not *what* God says—promise and law—but *how* Israel stewards God's revelation. And this historical period is divided between possessing the land and merely living in the land.

Joshua

Introduction

While the prophet Moses had spoken with assurance that Israel would enter the land (Deuteronomy 31), the question remained, how? No new revelation is given. Since the time of Abraham, the promise of the land had been a matter of family hope. For Joshua's generation, it was "just as I promised to Moses" (Josh 1:3b). It had been a reality accepted as a matter of fact, until Kadesh Barnea. Then the people failed because of *unbelief*. Now entrance was not simply a matter of *faith*; it was an issue of *active faith*: "I have given you every place where the sole of your foot treads" (Josh 1:3a, HCSB). If they didn't claim it by walking on a piece of land, it would not be given to them. Moses said it this way, "The LORD your God himself will go over before you. He will destroy these nations before you" (Deut 31:3a). That sounds like God would complete the task. But

Moses adds, "and you will drive them out" (Deut 31:3b, HCSB). It is a shared task. That is *active faith*. But in the end, Joshua will say, "It was not by your sword or bow. I gave you a land you did not labor for, and cities you did not build, though you live in them, you are eating from vineyards and olive groves you did not plant" (Josh 24:12-13, HCSB). Moses had described it: "God is the One who will cross ahead of you...Joshua is the one who will cross ahead of you" (Deut 31:3, HCSB). That's the task of a steward who appropriates what God had entrusted to him, the promise to inherit the land.

> The Book of Joshua represents this transition in position.

> The connection between Deuteronomic History (Judges through II Kings) and *Deuteronomy* is not long in coming. Immediately after Moses' death the LORD handed over the reins of theocratic administration to Moses' delegated successor, Joshua.[1]

But how are we to view the transition? Is the possession of the land the *climax* of the Abrahamic Covenant? That's von Rad's view.[2] Or, is it the *initial* phase of an unfinished history? That is the position of the Hebrew canon, and it is our view. That is because it is only a partial fulfillment of the Abrahamic Covenant. These events reveal the LORD who keeps His covenant promise to the extent that the people obey the Law and any historic directions from God. However, while the scope of the covenant goes beyond what the LORD had promised, it is not independent of His promises.

Preparation for Holy War (Joshua 1–5)

Preparation to Take the Land

The stewardship of God's revelation of promise and law featured Joshua but did not rest on the leader alone. Rather, all the people were stewards as the situation at Kadesh Barnea made clear (Deut 1:29-31). The new generation had been prepared in the wilderness (Deut 29:5-8). It was "all Israel" that was called to "keep the words of this covenant and do them"

---

[1]   Merrill, *Everlasting Dominion*, p. 414.

[2]   Von Rad, *Old Testament Theology*, vol. 1, pp. 3-5.

(Deut 29:9). Then the LORD would establish them as His people and He would be their God (Deut 29:13).

> God would raise up the Israelites to be a *people for himself*, that is, God willingly and freely took upon himself certain obligations toward his chosen people. The people, in response, were bound to him as their God...Thus both "parties" to the covenant undertook obligations...[3]

This is a people who are prepared spiritually to take the land (Joshua 1–5) and then, by *active* faithful obedience, to occupy the land (Joshua 6–12), to allot the land (Joshua 13–21), and to be prepared to retain the land (Joshua 22–24).

This is not preparation for a simply natural task: there is no map of the land, no sharpening of armaments, no training in military warfare. Rather, it is a spiritual preparation for what God would accomplish.

This preparation focused on:

- A review of what God had said (both promise and law);

- A spying of the land to bring back a report on the fear among the people and the immediate lay of the land at Jericho;

- A crossing of the swollen Jordan based on active faith, stepping into the water before anything in the river had changed;

- An establishing of stone memorials of the LORD's provision in crossing the Jordan;

- A circumcision to confirm their faith in the Abrahamic Covenant promise and then a remembrance of the Passover.

This spiritual preparation alone would prepare Israel to be a partner in the Law of holy war (Deut 7:1-6, 17-26). Holy war means: "(1) The LORD himself would lead Israel into the land, and he would drive out the nations (vv. 1-2a). (2) Israel must totally destroy...annihilate the people (vv. 2b, 24) and demolish their cultic apparatuses (vv 5, 25)."[4]

---

[3] Peter C. Craigie, *The Book of Deuteronomy*, NICOT (Grand Rapids, MI: Eerdmans, 1976), p. 357, emphasis added.

[4] Merrill, *Everlasting Dominion*, p. 415. God's justification for such wholesale slaughter rests in the iniquity of the pagan culture. In Gen 15:13, Abraham was told that occupation of the land would be delayed for four hundred years. This delay was related to the full display of the guilt of the people in the land. So when the time of judgment arrived, Moses explained to the people: "It is not because of your righteousness or your integrity that you are going to take possession of the land; but on account of the wickedness of those nations" (Deut 9:5). Leviticus 18:24-30 records those abominable Canaanite practices which prompted God to vomit out its inhabitants.

Conquest of the Land (Joshua 6–11)

In the concluding summary of the period of conquest (Josh 12:1-24), there is a list of the many kings defeated by Moses and then by Joshua. The Book of Joshua selects four incidents in the period of conquest to highlight God's revelation of promise to which was added the covenant of law and any immediate historic revelation as at Ai. The addition of the Mosaic Covenant does not change the promise from an unconditional gift to a conditional gift. The focus of the promise is emphasized to Joshua as he anticipated Jericho. A man appeared before him with a drawn sword. Joshua asked, "Are you for us or for our adversaries?" Unexpectedly, he answered, "No; but I am the commander of the army of the LORD" (Josh 5:13-14). The promise indicated that the battle is the LORD's. The critical point is "that it is not a matter of whether God fights for Israel, but whether Israel fights by faith for God."[5] Israel fights for God when they take possession of the land promised by *acting* in faith and obedience required in the covenant. It is the appropriation of what God promised that demands obedience. What the command demands is the condition for fulfillment because God has chosen to address each generation with that tension. What the promise commits God to do is in tension with what the commands require of man. Since God chose this tension, it does not imply that man is able to perform on his own. Rather the tension of God's choices is to be met by faith, knowing who God is and all that He has said. The tension between God's revelation and *active* faith is reflected in each historical conquest. That tension may be reflected in the following questions:

Concerning Jericho, would the city fall when Israel followed the LORD's unconventional and seemingly inadequate strategy? Would Israel obey and avoid the temptation of conscribing booty from Jericho?

Concerning Ai, must God be involved when the outcome of the battle seemed to be obvious based on their own strength?

Concerning Gibeon, must God be considered when the evidence brought by the Gibeonites seemed so convincing?

Concerning the southern and northern campaigns, does conquest of these coalitions involve simply following what God said and following Joshua? Is there more that needs to be done?

The fact that Jericho had been devoted to destruction (Josh 6:21; Deut 7:2) set the stage for Achan's disobedience. Yet it was "the people of

---

[5] Waltke, *An Old Testament Theology*, p. 518.

Israel" who "broke faith in regard to the devoted things" (Josh 7:1), and they were defeated (Josh 7:2-5). This didn't invalidate the promise as it would be appropriated later (Joshua 8). But the disobedience did bring defeat in that attack (Josh 7:4-5). When the sin was exposed, the LORD judged Achan (Josh 7:25). Then the LORD was "turned from his burning anger" (Josh 7:26).

Then the LORD gave Joshua a detailed strategy to follow as a test in appropriating the promise (Josh 8:4-8). It was a test because earlier spies had concluded that Ai was insignificant and only needed a few forces to capture the city (Josh 7:3). Israel obeyed (Josh 8:9-13) and took possession of the land, and the promise was fulfilled as Ai was conquered (Josh 8:24-26). Care must be taken not to change the promise to a conditional promise as some interpreters do: "From the outset it was made clear that the land is given to the people of God (i. 2, 6), but the *gift is conditioned* upon the faithful observance of the Torah (i. 7f)."[6] Rather, the gift promised remains a gift promised. The condition of judgment of sin and obedience in attack became God's means of reception and appropriation. Lipinski confirms this tension: "the gift made in perpetuity did not become a qualified bequest, it did imply obligations that the recipient had over against the donor."[7]

The Gibeonites' deception also involved the tension. They came in a clever deception seeking to avoid what they saw as inevitable annihilation. They lied intending to manipulate the perception at their falling under God's judgment which they did when Joshua failed to consult God. Israel believed their lie and made a Covenant of Peace with them (Josh 9:15). As a result, the LORD accepted Israel's word as His word. Israel's failure to consult God was foolish but it was not rebellion. God treated Israel as His chosen steward and accepted their decision as His decision, even though it was made without prayerful consultation.

The extended southern and northern campaigns showed that *active faith* includes more than obedience. It also involves *wisdom* arising from "the fear of the LORD." Joshua chose Gilgal as a base camp in which the families could temporarily dwell during the extended battle. In addition, the base camp added further advantages: a base for growing food, a lookout against a potential attack from Ammon or Moab, and a gateway for trade for needed supplies from beyond Jordan.

---

[6] Abraham Cohen, ed. *Joshua and Judges*, Sconcino Books of the Bible, vol. 2 (London: Soncino, 1961), p. XIII

[7] Lipinski, "נתן, *nātan*" TDOT, vol. 10, p. 101.

Joshua led in the execution of war that took advantage of Israel's strengths. They fought no defensive war since they had no strongholds. They employed field warfare which depends upon mobility, which was their great asset. They anticipated pending attacks by an attack of their own (Josh 10:9; 11:7). They established a provisional camp near Makkedah (Josh 10:21), enabling them to use their momentum in pursuit (Josh 10:16-21) without allowing the enemy time to recuperate. Wisdom concerns decisions within the realm of obedience and promise.

Finally, Joshua maintained the unity of their military force throughout the full conquest. The Canaanites had a technical advantage, but Israel needed to maximize their strength based on unity. Yet Israel's military strength was never the deciding factor. The Canaanite city-states were geographically and politically separated so that when they corroborated together, a unified military force was wise. And the two and one-half tribes beyond Jordan joined in the battle even though they did not derive immediate benefits for themselves. The unity also reinforced their common worship of Yahweh.

The Possession of the Land (Joshua 13–21)

The possession of the land by the tribes reflects an even greater messiness than had been evident under Joshua in the conquest. Caleb forthrightly claimed the land that had been promised to him in the territory of Judah (Joshua 14:6–15:19). Judah's inheritance was clearly and definitively allotted to them, and, except for Jerusalem, they claimed their territory. The boundaries between Ephraim and Manasseh were less clear and cities in the territory of Manasseh were allotted to the Ephraimites. Simeon was given space in the territory of Judah, and Dan lost his allocation and settled outside the boundaries allotted to the nation. The narrative accounts reflect the reality of a sinful yet elect steward, Israel. With the LORD promising, one might expect a pristine uniformity. These historical realities only anticipate the people's willfulness in the increasing problems the nation will face in the following 300 years, recorded in the Book of Judges.

At the same time, the simplicity of the affirmation in the section's summary is true (Josh 21:41-43). At first reading, "the LORD gave to Israel all the land" (Josh 21:43) may seem to be in conflict with Josh 13:2, "This is the land that yet remains." This apparent contradiction has been reconciled in various ways.

Boling and Wright assert that "the first sentence (Josh 21:43) of the summary forms the strongest possible *inclusio* with 1:6. In other words, what the LORD promised at the outset of Joshua, was fulfilled when Joshua's ministry was completed."[8] What the summary affirms is appreciated in the contextual sense of *nātan*: "*entrusted…to give…subjected.* The verses (21:43, 44) display three uses of the verb *ntn*, with three distinct nuances, thus underscoring the free and gracious initiatives of Yahweh toward the house of Israel."[9] Thus, what land had been *taken* in a military sense (Josh 12:1) under Joshua had been *entrusted* as a covenant inheritance to the tribes to use. The tribes had *taken possession* in a political sense (*yāraš*) of the territory in which they would live in the history that follows. The conquest was extensive. Each tribe was to annihilate the Canaanites in the land. The land had been given rest.

Finally, "not one word of all the good promises…had failed" (Josh 21:45). L. Daniel Hawk looks critically at the veracity of this summary.[10] However, to clarify the meaning of the statement, one must specify when a promise fails. A promise fails when it is received and *acted upon* (appropriated) and the commitment God made is broken. It does not fail when a promise is not acted upon. It does not fail when the gift of promised territory is delayed because the population does not need the space yet (Deut 7:22). Thus, even though territory remained to be occupied, it does not mean that the promises had failed.

> Although not a single written will survives from ancient Israel, it is certain that a father before his death 'set his house in order' (II Samuel 17:23; II Kings 20:1 par. Isaiah 38:1), i.e., he determined the division of the property he was leaving behind (Deuteronomy 21:16; Jeremiah 14:13; 33:24)…This text distinguishes clearly between a gift to a son, who thus becomes

---

[8]   Robert G. Boling and G. Ernest Wright, *Joshua*, Anchor Bible (Garden City, NY: Doubleday, 1988), pp. 498-500.

[9]   *Ibid.*, emphasis in original. This resolution is based on the range of meaning in the term *nātan*. A gift also depends on the reception experienced. This is the position I follow. B. Waltke suggests the summary includes the hyperbole common to the ANE style of conquest narratives. "The section concludes with the summary refrain (21:43-45). In truth, however, as the section progresses, 'the focus becomes non-possession and non-fulfillment.'" (Waltke, *An Old Testament Theology*, p. 524). Furthermore, he adds that there are parts of the land that are already fulfilled and other parts that are not yet fulfilled. While this is clearly the case, partial fulfillment does not mean that the same promise is already fulfilled and yet not fulfilled in the same instance of land.

[10]   L. Daniel Hawks, *Every Promise Fulfilled: Contesting Plots in Joshua* (Louisville, KY: Westminster John Knox, 1991).

legal owner of part of the inheritance, and a gift to a servant, who merely has right of *usufruct*.[11]

Israel took possession of the land (*yrš*) as legal owners.

Later in the progress of revelation, Jeremiah would describe the land as the "inheritance of Yahweh" (Jer 2:7; 16:18, author's translation). "Israel is to think of itself as a guest lodged by Yahweh in a land that is Yahweh's own possession and therefore holy."[12] And thus, the land occupied by Israel and received as an inheritance is to be used for God's glory according to the terms of the Mosaic Covenant. This is Israel's stewardship both in occupying and in retaining the land (Josh 1:7-8). Israel's strength is present as they are careful to follow all of the Law. Deuteronomy is to be the continual object of their meditation so that they may be conscious of all that they are responsible for doing.

Retaining the Land (Joshua 22–24)

There are already indications that individuals and some tribes were experiencing conflict with obedience to the Law. The final three chapters come from Joshua, who had been faithful to serve the LORD (Josh 24:15), both as a steward of promise and of the Mosaic Law. He now speaks about three issues:

1. To release the Eastern tribes (Joshua 22)

2. To announce his personal farewell (Joshua 23)

3. To call the next generation to ratify a renewed Mosaic Covenant as a people (Joshua 24)

The release of the tribes included an expression of gratitude for their service in the conquest of the land. Further, to avoid civil war, these tribes were to be allowed to serve God in the central sanctuary at Shiloh (Josh 19:51).

Joshua's personal farewell features his testimony about what he had seen God accomplish and a summary of what has not yet been accomplished. At the heart of his message is that Israel needs to cling exclusively to the LORD their God (Josh 23:8). They had seen strong nations driven out by the LORD under Joshua's leadership (Josh 23:9-11). The LORD's warfare is so effective that one man can put to flight a thousand. On the

---

[11] Lipinski, "נחל, *nāḥal*," TDOT, vol. 9, pp. 321-22. Usufruct is, "the legal right of using and enjoying the fruits or profits of something belonging to another."

[12] *Ibid.*, p. 332.

other hand, if they allow it, a remnant of the Canaanites will become a trap to add conflict for Israel.

Finally, Joshua called the people to Shechem for a covenant renewal (Joshua 24). The stage is set with a summary of the history of the people, from the days of Abraham to the occupation of land and cities which they had not built (Josh 24:1-13). He called them to serve (mentioned eight times in Josh 24:14-24), reflecting the purpose of the Mosaic Law. They are called to obey the Law's demands. Then he mentions the *double knowledge* which comes through the Law (Josh 24:27).

He concludes with a warning. Unless they find forgiveness in Him, they won't be able to serve the LORD who is holy and jealous (Josh 24:19-20). If they forsake Him for other gods there will be no forgiveness. Joshua warns that already they had failed to recognize their sin because of the messiness of the occupation of the allotted land. But the people insisted that they would *serve* the LORD (Josh 24:21-24). This is the same commitment that the first generation had made (Exod 19:7; 24:3, 7). So Joshua ratified (*kārat*) the covenant that day (Josh 24:25).

Judges

Introduction

The people of Israel were settling into the land. The messiness that the tribes experienced in the occupation of the land allotted to each tribe was a harbinger of the problems ahead. No longer would God choose a central leader like Moses and Joshua to provide some unified national identity. The danger in reading the Book of Judges is to assign the problem solely to political structure. God had provided for a unified people through the central sanctuary where the LORD resided at Shiloh. But there is no mention of the tabernacle in the Book of Judges. So questions emerge: will the theocracy survive? How will the revelation be passed on to the next generation?

The people settling into the land did not need any central political force. Rather, their problem was the Canaanites among whom they lived. Barry Webb notes that at first the victorious Israelites allowed the Canaanites to live at a distance (Judg 1:22-26); then the Israelites no longer tried to drive out the Canaanites, and the Canaanites lived among the Israelites (Judg 1:27-30); then the Israelites lived among the Canaanites (Judg 1:31-33); and finally, the Canaanites pressed back against the Israelites and did not allow the Israelites among them (Judg 1:34-36).[13] The idolatry that had overwhelmed Canaan now became the sin that was overwhelming to the stewards of the Mosaic Covenant, the Israelites.

The revelation of the theocratic King did not change. The promise of the LORD remained front and center when the people of Israel inquired of God for His direction (Judg 1:1-4).

> However, both Judah and Joseph fail to execute herem (holy war) against the contagious Canaanite cities, contrary to Torah (Exodus 34:15, 16; Deuteronomy 20:16-18). Instead of executing Adoni-Bezek ("Lord of Bezek"), the men of Judah cut off his thumbs and big toes, a Canaanite practice, as the pagan king confesses (Judges 1:6-7).[14]

Since the king remained alive, he could promote his pagan way of life. The strongest response to possess their land came from the tribe of Judah. And so the Book of Judges presents twelve cycles of judgment on tribe after tribe. These judgments do not void the covenant but do discipline the people to learn about themselves and their need for the LORD's deliverance. This is the presence of the LORD's theocratic reign. The *judge* is central to represent the need to apply the truth of God's revelation in a fresh fashion in each generation. The *Levites* emerge because each generation must teach the truth. And the Book of Judges provides that message for later generations.

Even though this is an account of the experience of the tribes, the book's message pertains to all of Israel. John Goldingay says, "Judges goes on to emphasize the essential oneness of Israel by the same means as Joshua. Events that literally involve individual clans or combinations of clans implicate the whole nation."[15] The name *Israel* occurs more often in this book than in any other book in the Hebrew Bible. As Achan's sin affected the whole nation, so individual tribes affect the whole nation.

Consistent with this emphasis on a tribal level of experience is a type of local official featured in the book. The term is *šāpaṭ* but its meaning is debated.[16] However, the term was introduced in Deuteronomy

---

[13] Barry Webb, *The Book of Judges: An Integrated Reading* (Sheffield, UK: JSOT Press, 1987), p. 99.

[14] Waltke, *An Old Testament Theology*, p. 594.

[15] John Goldingay, *Old Testament Theology, Volume 1: Israel's Gospel* (Downers Grove, IL: IVP, 2003), p. 531.

[16] Niehr, "שׁפט, *šāpaṭ*," TDOT, vol. 15, pp. 415-19. *Šāpaṭ* glosses a basic meaning from ANE comparative languages. In these cognate languages the primary sense is *ruler*. Waltke, deriving the meaning in the context of his role as military deliverer, glosses the terms as *warlord* (*An Old Testament Theology*, p. 588). However, in the context of the Lord's theocratic rule

(Deut 16:18-20; 17:8-13) as *judge*. The role of this individual was to mediate judicial rule under the authority of the Mosaic Covenant. Further, judges were local officials appointed town by town. The role of deliverance took place as the LORD raised up and empowered the individual judge to deliver tribes from God's judgment. This emphasis on a judicial power is validated in the case of Deborah (Judg 4:4) and is distinguished from the military leader in Barak (Judg 4:6). The importance of highlighting the role of judge is that he was basically responsible for administering justice under the Mosaic Covenant. And the rule of the LORD through the Law was absolutely essential for the subsequent generations to experience the theocracy. The judge was the primary steward of the revealed law in Israel in a political sense. In that political sense, he was also raised up to administer judgment against the oppressors. In those instances, mercy came to the people who had been tested by oppression.

The other role emphasized in the Book of Judges is the Levite. He too was a steward of the Mosaic Covenant as he was responsible for teaching the Law in a personal and spiritual sense.

The book reaches its climax with the account of two Levites who reflected the spiritual condition of the culture and the necessity for spiritual renewal within Israel.

The Book of Judges consists of three sections:

Failure of the Tribes (1:1–3:6)

Twelve Judges (3:7–16:31)

Failure of the Levites (17:1–21:25)

Failure of the Tribes (Judges 1:1–3:6)

The individual tribes had the initial responsibility to annihilate the Canaanites, tribe by tribe (Judg 1:1-36). Their failure here opened the door to an overwhelming spread of the power of evil. That evil propelled each tribe toward a destiny about which they had been warned. Because they failed to remove the Canaanite pagan lifestyle around them (Judg 2:1-5), they were fated to repeated cycles of spiritual defeat (Judg 2:6-23). "First, Israel dismembered itself from I AM…This violation of the first of the Ten Commandments functions as a synecdoche for Israel's disobeying

---

through the Mosaic Law, the most appropriate gloss is *judge* who administers and establishes justice for God's people.

the Law *en toto...*"[17] (cf. Judg 2:10-13). The judgment that necessarily followed was a covenant curse which did not void the covenant. There is no record of a covenant renewal but the presence of a judge maintained a testimony to the LORD's law, and the use of a judge to serve as mediator provided evidence of the LORD's rule when His people came to Him. The judge then administered the rule of the Law as long as he lived.

Twelve Judges (Judges 3:7–16:31)

The Book of Judges *covers* about 300 years of history (c. 1350–c. 1050 BC). The twelve judges are scattered across this period, about one per generation. From the twelve, seven are arranged to display the progressive deterioration of Israel. The first three cycles display judges who judge and deliver. Gideon is the central judge whose personal weakness in fear is clearly evident. The lives of each of the final three judges display the presence of evil, yet God uses them to deliver in spite of themselves. Each individual will be listed and characterized briefly to demonstrate the deterioration.

Othniel	A judge from the generation of the conquest who provided a pattern of the normative ideal (Judg 3:7-11).
Ehud	A left-handed deliverer raised by the LORD to deliver the people who cried out to the LORD. He used deception to deliver judgment against Eglon (Judg 3:12-30) while the stone images of Moab were powerless (Judg 3:19, 26).
Deborah	A pattern of making judgments based on her prophetic gift, yet her strengths and faith highlighted the weakness of men like Barak. Still Barak was willing to go with Deborah, yet Heber's wife Jael strikes a decisive blow and gets the glory in the battle (Judges 4:1–5:31).
Gideon	He struggled personally to believe God, yet with a little faith and a few resources, he delivered Israel with a decisive victory. The comparatively meager three hundred troops underscore the idea that the LORD alone brought the victory (Judges 6:1–8:32).

---

17   Waltke, *An Old Testament Theology*, p. 595.

Abimelech	Abimelech was born of Gideon's concubine and therefore not recognized as the heir of Gideon. Yet he claimed the role of deliverer by following the custom among the pagans to kill off rivals. In the end, Abimelech was killed by a woman of Thebez who dropped a millstone on his head (Judges 8:33–9:56).
Jephthah	He followed the superstitious attempts to manipulate God, whom he also believed in, and the Spirit of the LORD empowered him to subdue the people of Ammon. Yet he suffered a high cost in the death of his daughter (Judges 10:6–12:7).
Samson	Born gifted and blessed but he squandered his strength in repeated self-serving tumbles with women, only to eventually fall before Delilah. Yet in grace at the end he judged the Philistines decisively, killing more in death than in his life (Judges 13:1–16:31). "The most striking parallels in the alternating structures point both to God's ordered providence in Israel's history and to Samson's stubborn willfulness. Like Israel, he never learns."[18]

Failure of the Levites (Judges 17:1–21:25)

The tribe of Levi was chosen to serve the LORD. Those located at Shiloh would serve the priests in the tabernacle functions. And those scattered throughout the land in Levitical towns were to teach the populace the Law. If the truth of the covenant was to influence the nation to holiness, the Levites were responsible for teaching and living that truth. These final episodes show how "the fatal contagion of the Levites infects all the tribes."[19]

In the first episode, an opportunistic young Levite served in the installation of a family shrine. Micah's family made a carved image with stolen money. Then the family shrine was forcibly stolen and installed as a tribal shrine for Dan. The young Levite who served the family shrine was seduced again by a bribe to serve the whole tribe of Dan in false worship, which continued until the Assyrian Captivity. But the greatest irony is

---

[18] *Ibid.*, p. 609.

[19] *Ibid.*, p. 614.

that the young Levite is none other than Moses' great-grandson, Jona-than (Judg 17:10-11; 18:30).[20] "Thus, the problems of religious syncretism and spiritual decay have infected the very institution designed to combat these problems, not to mention one of the most revered households in ancient Israel."[21]

While in the first episode, a family situation is raised into a tribal situation, in the second, a callous and violent Levite family situation is raised to national proportions. The Levite had recovered his concubine, who had apparently fled to her father because of his abuse. But her father had provided her no refuge. On their return, rather than staying in a Canaan-ite town the Levite and his concubine traveled further to a Benjaminite town. That night, the young men of Benjamin desired to rape the Levite. Instead, his concubine was so abused by these town bullies that she died on the doorstep where the Levite had been taken in. Incensed against Benjamin, he sent pieces of her dead body throughout the land to incite the whole nation against Benjamin. The battle that ensued stopped short of annihilating Benjamin. But then to repopulate the tribe, the tribes conscribed virgins from Jabesh Gilead to mother offspring for Benjamin. And all this transpired at Shiloh. "There is little doubt that the tremen-dous moral depravity exhibited in this final conclusion to Judges con-firms the inherent moral dangers in idolatry and polytheism."[22]

Conclusion

The dispensation of law and the rule of the LORD in the theocracy seemed to present a promising focus. If God's chosen people only *knew* what was right, surely they would do it. And they were not only told what was right, they agreed to it (Exod 19:7; 24:3, 7). Education is widely rec-ognized as instrumental for setting the human race on the right course.

Yet, when this stage of the story is told and the last chapter unfolds, the men of Benjamin act as the men of the condemned cities of Sodom and Gomorrah. The allusion to the visitors at Lot's house is unmistakable. This demanded judgment. The Levite's response to the guilt of the men of Benjamin also alludes to Abraham's response in intercession. The Levite's self-justification, rather than concern for his concubine, incited national

---

[20] For the textual and conceptual difficulties of this identification, see Daniel I. Block, *Judges, Ruth*, NAC (Nashville: Broadman and Holman, 1999), pp. 511-12.

[21] K. Lawson Younger, *Ancient Conquest Accounts: A Study in Ancient Near Eastern and Biblical History Writing*, JSOT Sup. 98 (Sheffield, MA: JSOT Press, 1990), p. 342.

[22] Younger, *Judges*, p. 348.

judgment that almost obliterated the tribe of Benjamin. On the other hand, Abraham sought mercy for the people of Sodom and Gomorrah to avert judgment. Then the plan to repopulate the tribe of Benjamin had a less than righteous and good design due to the other tribes' oath, "anyone who gives a wife to a Benjaminite is cursed." What had happened to the rule of law which is righteous, just, and good?

The power of evil had overwhelmed God's elect people so that their lives showed little difference from the descendants of Cain or of Noah. Yet in spite of the evil of the people, the LORD had begun to fulfill the promises first spoken to Abraham. At the core was the promise of a nation (Gen 12:2). A nation consists of three necessary components, outlined below.

First, there was a *chosen people* who were descendants of Abraham. This election was the feature of the families' celebration of circumcision and redemption from Egypt at Passover. These celebrations provided fathers with the occasion to communicate their faith in God's promise with their families. The gospel (of Gen 12:3) was naturally spread from generation to generation.

Second, under Moses, the people willingly received a *national constitution* in the form of the *Mosaic Law*. Israel welcomed the obligatory covenant, not once (Exodus 24), not twice (Exodus 34), not even three times (Deuteronomy 29), but four times in four generations (Joshua 24). The people were willing, but when tested by the assault of evil, they were weak. Within three hundred years after they occupied the land, during the time of the judges, they were scarcely recognizable as God's people.

Third, under Joshua, the people entered, occupied the *land*, and then distributed it tribe by tribe. Yet they failed to remove their enemies that remained in the land. They failed to fear God, and they failed to take the evil of pagan idolatry seriously. These failures soon overwhelmed them with that same evil.

So God's promise of a nation had been fulfilled—a people, a constitution, and a land. Yet the stewardship of Israel remained scarcely evident in the people of God. Had they fallen to a level that was beyond redemption? In the messiness of the story being told, that impression seemed to be the case. The prophet who wrote Judges gave an assessment: "in those days there was no king in Israel; everyone did whatever he wanted" (Judg 21:25, HCSB).

CHAPTER 10:
THE INCEPTION OF THE
MONARCHY THROUGH DAVID

Introduction

> [I]t matters little from a theological standpoint whether Deuteronomy be assigned to Moses and an early date (to which we hold) or not, for the history of Israel covered by Joshua through Kings was in any case, a product of the late sixth century BC in its final canonical form. It does matter, however, that the historical narrative, though fundamentally theological and interpretive in character, be regarded as an accurate account of events as they actually occurred.[1]

It is quite reasonable that the historical books would bear the imprint of Deuteronomy, since the historical books are historically and theologically antecedent to Deuteronomy. Emphases that are found in both Deuteronomy and Joshua–Kings have led most scholars to call these latter books the Deuteronomic history even though there is some debate about the nature and extent of the influence of Deuteronomy. In any case, Merrill posits that there are theological influences which are independent of the historical reconstruction. His assessment is one that we share. There are three theological influences that emerge to prominence in a Dispensational Biblical theology: the role of the prophets, the role of the king, and the role of the people of God. Each is addressed in the following pages.

The Role of Prophets

One important addition in Deuteronomy is the people's source of knowledge and understanding: the prophet. Of course, they had the Torah, which

---

[1] Merrill, *Everlasting Dominion*, p. 413.

provided foundational knowledge. But once in the land, what was needed was immediate knowledge concerning the transitional changes that God was implementing. Pagan occult and idolatrous practices were detestable to the LORD. Indeed, this was a primary reason for God's judgment of the Canaanites that Israel was to displace in the land. These detestable practices were tempting because they were viewed as a means to manipulate the gods in order to gain control over the unknown (Deut 18:9-14). Those who followed these practices sought knowledge from evil sources.

Rather, God would raise up a prophet who would speak on His behalf without having a personal gain in the truth of the message. He was an independent voice. The model of the prophetic voice was Moses. Moses also claimed that another prophet like him would follow. (Deut 18:15). Although some understand that Moses had only Christ in mind, this seems unlikely since the need for a prophet arose soon after they entered the land.[2] Thus, the promise is not limited to one prophet, but will be fulfilled as warranted by the adaptations in God's dealings in a generation. Samuel appears as the first prominent example, but he is not alone (1 Sam 2:27-36). Such prophets would speak on behalf of the LORD in His theocratic rule when the form of God's rule changed to a monarchy. In addition, God raised up prophets to record and interpret the historical period (former prophets) and to prophesy about their day and the future (latter prophets). The writings of these prophets constitute books included in the Hebrew canon. But the common factor is that each prophet spoke on behalf of God as Ruler over Israel.

The prophet, as a direct voice, would express the authoritative word of God's governance of the events in history. The king would mediate God's rule over the nation of Israel. The two need not be in opposition, but they were when the king pursued evil in his policies and personal life. In addition, the prophet identified God's choice of each new king and would *anoint* each one to identify God's choice publically.

The Role of the King

One major change in God's ways was the change in governmental structure. Deuteronomy spelled out the leadership that would be involved both

---

[2] Many would interpret this as simply a prophecy of Christ, "a prophet like me" (John 1:21, 25, 45; Acts 3:22; 7:37). This interpretation is true in a final sense but the promise is not limited to one. The promise implies a continuing voice which will add to and explain what Moses said in relation to the developing history. Each prophet is a partial fulfillment and Jesus Christ is the final and complete fulfillment (Rev 1:1; the revelation both from and about Jesus Christ).

in the *theocracy* and the *monarchy*. Moses had asked, "please teach me Your ways, and I will know You and find favor in Your sight" (Exod 33:13, HCSB). God never disclosed *how* He would do things to bring about historical change. God reserved His ways for Himself: "I will be gracious to whom I will be gracious, and I will have compassion on whom I will have compassion" (Exod 33:19). The way He sovereignly acts remains within the LORD's own control, but His ways are *always* consistent with His character. Thus the LORD "proclaimed His name Yahweh" reserving His right to sovereign control. Yahweh then disclosed His character—a "compassionate and gracious God, slow to anger and rich in faithful love and truth" (Exod 34:5-6). Thus, the leader was to act by faith, administering according to God's character, in the role in which he was assigned.

Judges administered the righteous judgments expressed in the Mosaic Law. That was central to the theocracy. They had no delegated authority as the priestly office did. The priests had authority to represent themselves and the people before the LORD. This was mediated through the prescribed tabernacle services.

The king also had delegated authority in his office to mediate the LORD's rule on earth over Israel. So Moses instructed the king "to write a copy of this instruction for himself on a scroll...then his heart will not be exalted above his countryman..." (Deut 17:18-20). He was a steward of God's revelation in the administration of his role as he ruled on behalf of the LORD. God's sovereign rule in history *universally* expressed remained as the providential control. This rule of God was never challenged nor changed in history. However, God's rule would be *mediated* on earth over Israel through the chosen kings. Thus, the form of the LORD's mediatorial rule would change, but not the fact of the LORD's sovereign rule.

It was this change that was stated in Judges after more than 300 years under a *theocracy*. Although the Mosaic Law had been revealed, and judges were raised up to apply righteous judgments, the people did whatever they wanted.[3] Added to this was another observation: "In those days there was no king in Israel" (Judg 21:25). The text doesn't say that a king would prevent the people from such lawlessness, but as long as a judge lived, the people lived in peace (cf. Judg 3:11). The form of government did not cause Israel's lawlessness, however, it was mentioned as a factor. When this actual change in governmental structure would occur, the LORD allowed the people to reject Him as King (1 Sam 8:7). "Samuel considered their demand sinful" (1 Sam 8:6), and it was. In the LORD's

---

[3] Cf. Judg 17:6; 18:1; 19:1. Daniel Block refers to this as the "Canaanization" of Israel (Block, *Judges, Ruth*, pp. 71-72).

permission of evil, Israel will in time learn what they actually needed. But the LORD would not abandon them. "Even though you have committed all this evil, do not turn away from following the LORD..." (1 Sam 12:20-22, HCSB). God's permissive will does not imply that the monarchy will accomplish what the people anticipated based on the model of other nations (1 Sam 12:20-22). But it was a return in form to God's creation goal (Gen 1:26-28) of an individual mediating God's rule.

This common ground between the people's sin and God's goal had been anticipated in Deut 17:14-20. Moses outlined the framework of the monarchy:

- God would choose the king from within Israel.

- Israel, as a people, would receive God's choice and enthrone him.

- The resources the king used to reign would differ from other nations (e.g., gold and horses).[4] Rather, the primary resource is God Himself.

- Finally, the enthroned king was to make a copy of the Law in order to learn to fear the LORD.

Since the LORD was the king's primary resource, a repeated issue with the king was to wait for God to provide as Abraham had. This had been an issue with Abraham and Sarah. It would be an initial issue for Saul (First Samuel 13–14). David's preparation to be king featured waiting in faith until Saul would be removed (First Samuel 16–31). Twice he was tempted to remove Saul himself in circumstances that seemed to facilitate that removal (First Samuel 24, 26). So there was a tension between *active* faith and *waiting* on the LORD.

In the historical books, three criteria appear in the text by which the king would be assessed:

- Was he *chosen* by the LORD?

- Had the LORD *gifted* him?

- Did the king *serve* the LORD?

And at the conclusion of Deuteronomic history, prophets would condemn the kings for the same wickedness as found in the people. However, during the *monarchy,* greater focus emerged within Israel to highlight the problem of sin within the nation, as king after king fell short. As a result, the prophets announced, based on the Mosaic Covenant, that

---

[4] Israel's king was not to rely on typical expressions of wealth and power, although he may make use of them.

the nation was destined for dispersion from the land, both the Northern Kingdom (722 BC) and the Southern Kingdom (586 BC).

In addition, the existence of a historic king, in spite of sin, lead David (in Psalms) and the prophets to long for an ultimate King. God would provide a King who would fully accomplish His will (Psalm 22; Isaiah 42–53). The expectation became prophetically evident in the king's failures and in the LORD's stable promises of blessings.

The Role of the People of God

In Deuteronomy, a corporate election remained for the new generation. Moses spoke "to *all Israel*" (Deut 1:1, HCSB, emphasis added). "Moses told the Israelites everything the LORD had commanded him to say to them" (Deut 1:3, HCSB). At the conclusion of the book, "These are the words of the Covenant the LORD commanded Moses to make with the Israelites in the land of Moab, in addition to the Covenant He had made with them at Horeb" (Deut 29:1, HCSB). The words translated *Israelites* were *bᵉnê yiśrā'ēl* (children of Israel), speaking of them as a unified community (Deut 1:3; 3:18; 4:44-45; 23:17 [18]; 24:7; 29:1; 32:49, 51-52). Theologically, they were chosen to be *stewards* in the service of God through the Mosaic Covenant. "The election of all Israel to represent I AM's rule among the nations remains a primary datum of Deuteronomic history."[5]

In the historical books, a distinction is recognized among the people based on the people's response to God's revelation. It wasn't new. At Kadesh Barnea, only Joshua and Caleb responded in active faith among the twelve leaders from the tribes (Numbers 13–14). A mixed multitude (Num 11:4, HCSB, "contemptible people among them") was noted during the Exodus. But nowhere is the concept of a remnant mentioned in the text of the historical books, as Covenant theology is tempted to identify.[6] God can make these distinctions but not the human interpreter. So God mentions to Elijah that 7000 had not bowed their knee to Baal (1 Kgs 19:18). But these believers Elijah had failed to see. No textual term makes a distinction between those with true and those with no faith. Theologically, there is a distinction between election to service, which incorporated the whole nation, and election to relationship. Elijah saw none in his generation as he lumped them all with Ahab

---

[5] Waltke, *An Old Testament Theology*, p. 738.

[6] *Ibid.*, pp. 739-40.

and Jezebel. Elisha will minister to some of the 7000 in that generation, which includes Naaman, the Gentile (Second Kings 2–8).

The term for "remnant" occurs primarily in the writing prophets for "survivors from judgment:" *šeʾār* (Isa 10:19-21) and *šeʾērît* (Isa 37:4). This term is used to refer to Israel, a remnant within Egypt (Gen 45:7). There is little question that there is a distinction between election to service (all the people) and election to relationship (those who actually know God). But Deuteronomy does not make that distinction under the Mosaic Law. And as with Elijah, human observations are likely to make an incorrect distinction.

Monarchy

The treatment of this extended period of Israel's history will need to be selective. The following considerations will be emphasized:

TRANSITION FROM THE THEOCRACY TO A
MONARCHY

First Samuel 7–8

First Samuel 12

DAVIDIC KINGDOM

Second Samuel 7

Psalms (2; 16; 51; 22; 110)

SOLOMONIC KINGDOM

First Kings 1–11

Wisdom: Proverbs, Ecclesiastes, and Job

DIVIDED KINGDOM

Northern Kingdom—First and Second Kings

Ninth Century Prophet—Joel

Eighth Century Prophets—Amos and Hosea

Southern Kingdom—First and Second Kings

Sixth and Seventh Century Prophets—Isaiah and Jeremiah

Transition from Theocracy to Theocratic Monarchy

Baldwin sees the unity of this historical period to be found in a theological theme:

> The very concept of a Deuteronomic History designates the books from Deuteronomy to II Kings as one such section (of the canon), bound together by a theological theme. Scholars who prefer to think in terms of "Prophetic History" equally clearly declare that they recognize a theological purpose which is common to these books.[7]

In my construction, that theme or purpose is the *mediation of God's universal rule.* Deuteronomy introduced Israel's responsibility *to mediate* God's presence and rule among the nations. That role in Deuteronomy 7–11 was developed from the restatement of the Law in 5–6. Mediation would focus on the central sanctuary in 12–17 and would be expressed through the leadership structure that would mediate His presence in 17–21. Even though Israel would disobey, the way God would govern the nation would *mediate* the glory of God in chapters 4 and 29–30.

That unifying theological theme became evident in the historical transition introduced in First and Second Samuel. Baldwin proposes that "there are three chapters which stand out as markers, characterized by their interpretation of historical changes taking place in Israel's leadership structure. They are I Samuel 7, 8 and 12 and II Samuel 7."[8]

Governed Transition (First Samuel 7–8)

The transition from theocracy to the prophesied theocratic monarchy involves a remarkable account of the LORD's governance. First Samuel begins the story in the tabernacle where one would expect God's presence to be displayed. He is, but in an unexpected way. Through the worship of the relatively unknown Elkanah and his wives, God's glory became evident. One would have expected this glory to be in the family of the high priest, Eli, but they led the nation in sin. It was Elkanah's barren wife,

---

[7] Joyce G. Baldwin, *1 and 2 Samuel,* Tyndale Old Testament Commentaries, (Downers Grove, IL: IVP Academic, 1988), p. 33.

[8] *Ibid.*

Hannah, who prayed for a son and returned that son, Samuel, to God with thanksgiving (1 Sam 2:1-10).[9]

Hannah is portrayed in contrast to Peninnah and to Eli. Peninnah mocked her because she was barren and not enjoying the blessing of God. Eli misjudged her, failing to see a woman with a broken heart. Refusing to be comforted by her husband, she poured out her anguish to the LORD in the temple.

Soon after, when honored by the LORD, she returned to honor and praise the LORD in prayer (1 Sam 2:1-10). Preeminently, He is the Holy One who lifted up the insignificant one. Against the backdrop of an evil world, where right is not right, the Holy One emerges as distinct. And those blessed by the LORD share in His distinctive glory.

Samuel was dedicated to the LORD at the tabernacle and it was his ministry that continued to mediate God's glory. He joined the man of God to prophesy judgment on the house of Eli (1 Sam 2:27-33). Samuel received God's call to replace Eli and his family (1 Sam 3:10-21). Samuel remained as *judge* over all the house of Israel (1 Sam 7:3-4), and as *prophet* called them to serve the LORD alone, who then delivered them from the Philistines. In a distinctive way, he became a "prophet like Moses" (Deut 18:15).

As a *priest*, Samuel prayed for Israel and offered sacrifices on behalf of the people (1 Sam 7:5-10). Then the warriors went out and subdued the Philistines so that they no longer encroached on Israel's land (1 Sam 7:11-14). Then he established a memorial, Ebenezer—the stone of help—to remind Israel to *wait on* the LORD. Sadly, Samuel's sons, as judges, did not walk uprightly as their father had (1 Sam 8:1-3).

So "all the elders of Israel" were not willing to *wait* for God to raise up another judge after Samuel. When Samuel grew old, they came to him saying, "Now appoint us a king to judge us like all the nations" (1 Sam 8:5). While Samuel was disappointed, the LORD said, "Obey the voice of the people in all that they say to you, for they have not rejected you, but they have rejected me from being king over them" (1 Sam 8:7). Moses had anticipated His approval of Israel's desire in Deuteronomy (Deut 17:14-20). While their request reflected the absence of faith, God in His governance chose to use the request to help Israel focus attention more clearly on human *mediation* of the LORD's reign. That focus will ultimately rest on the Anointed One, the final Mediator and Steward to

---

[9]   Hannah's prayer reflects the spirit of a righteous worshiper under the Mosaic Law. Mary's prayer expressed the same spirit (Luke 1:46-56). It is a spirit of one insignificant and oppressed under the law who turns to the Lord for relief. The prayer exalts in the Lord.

mediate the LORD's reign on earth. In David, and in the prophets, that anticipation would be clarified.

Yet Samuel warned them what they would lose. By centralizing power and authority in a king, individual freedoms and responsibilities to the LORD would be limited. "But the people refused to obey the voice of Samuel" (1 Sam 8:19). So in order to further challenge the people's insistence on their own way, the LORD chose Saul to be their first governor and prince (1 Sam 9:17; 10:24).

Saul appeared to be spiritually unaware when he went in search of his father's donkeys. It was Saul's servant who knew of Samuel and provided the payment for his service.[10] But the LORD told Samuel to anoint a ruler over Israel (1 Sam 9:16) and identified Saul directly (1 Sam 9:17). After anointing Saul (1 Sam 10:1) to reign over the people and to save them from the hand of their surrounding enemies, he gave Saul a series of confirming signs (1 Sam 10:1, 7, 9). So having heard that the LORD would be present with several gifts (1 Sam 10:2-8), Saul turned to leave without any objection. Then "God gave him another heart" (1 Sam 10:9). "Compare the turning of Saul into another man in verse 6 above; the two expressions are about equivalent in import."[11] God chose Saul and changed him into a man who knew the LORD, although not well yet. It was the people who proclaimed him to be *king* (1 Sam 10:24), although God had called him *prince* (1 Sam 9:15), *restrainer* or *governor* (9:17). And Samuel introduced the theocratic monarchy as Moses had introduced the theocracy. This is the particular way they were alike.

The LORD's Assessment of the Transition (First Samuel 12)

Now that all Israel had accepted Saul as king (1 Sam 11:15), Samuel withdraws as the theocratic leader, though his prophetic ministry continues. In his farewell address, he sets the record straight.[12] He had been a

---

[10] Robert Bergen also argues that, "Saul's unfitness to serve as the shepherd of the Lord's flock is further suggested in the unusual narrative recounted here. Semitic leaders throughout ancient times were often referred to as shepherds; the Torah's most significant patriarchs— Abraham, Isaac, Jacob, Moses—were also depicted as skillful shepherds. Yet here Saul is portrayed unflatteringly as an incompetent shepherd. So great was his ineptness that he could not even find a few large animals (v. 3; Hb. *hā 'ătōnôt*, "she-asses") that had wandered away from his father's house—ones that ultimately returned home without Saul's assistance even as he was searching for them (9:20; 10:2)!" (Robert D. Bergen, *1, 2 Samuel*, New American Commentary, vol. 7, [Nashville, TN: Broadman & Holman, 1996], p. 121).

[11] P. Kyle McCarter, Jr. *1 Samuel*, The Anchor Bible, vol. 8, (Garden City, NY: Doubleday, 1980), p. 183.

[12] Baldwin, *1 and 2 Samuel*, p. 99.

faithful steward in administering the rule of the LORD within Israel and the people were the ones who had been wicked (1 Sam 12:6-18). Both the people and the king were to follow and serve the LORD (1 Sam 10:20-25). Gerhard von Rad sees kingship under the Law as a responsive institution, rather than an independent institution like the nations.

> [T]he one-sidedness of this law concerning the king consists in the fact that Deuteronomy sees in kingship not an office which Yahweh could use for the welfare of his people, but only an institution in which the holder must live in a sphere of extreme peril because he is tempted by his harem or his wealth either to turn away from Yahweh or to "lift up his heart above his brethren." Intimate knowledge and daily study of Deuteronomy, of which he must always have a copy at hand, can alone preserve him from his behavior.[13]

This harsh assessment of theocratic monarchy fails to appreciate the role that sin plays in blocking the king's mediation of God's reign. Theocratic monarchy is not the independent office seen in other nations. Rather, it is a position to be filled by one chosen by God. Then the chosen one is anointed to serve the LORD in *active* faith. In this way, the king would *mediate* God's rule. Would Saul serve the LORD in the direction that the Law would give?

Saul, being weak in faith and fearful in heart, almost immediately disqualified himself from being king. First, in conflict with the Philistines (First Samuel 13), his son Jonathan provided a foil, showing that active faith gains conquest in the LORD's provision (First Samuel 14). Second, in judgment against Amalek, Saul's disobedience, influenced by his people, resulted in his rejection from the office (First Samuel 15). As Robert Gordon notes:

> [T]he dominant feeling in chs. 13–15 is not success, but of failure. For the biblical writer (or compiler) the victories are immaterial as compared with the importance of understanding why Saul did not earn Yahweh's approval so as to be able both to deliver Israel in its time of greatest danger and also to establish a dynasty that would earn the loyalty of its grateful subjects.[14]

---

[13] Gerhard von Rad, *Deuteronomy* (Philadelphia: Westminster, 1966), p. 120.

[14] Robert P. Gordon, *I & II Samuel: A Commentary*, Library of Biblical Interpretation (Grand Rapids, MI: Zondervan, 1986), p. 131.

Samuel, representing the LORD, anointed David with the Holy Spirit (1 Sam 16:13), after which the Spirit departed from Saul (16:14). So following Saul's failures, Samuel established the *theocratic monarchy* in David.

Immediately, David displayed his qualification to be king in serving Saul and the LORD (1 Sam 16:15-23) in active faith: defeating Goliath and routing the Philistines (First Samuel 17). However, when the women celebrated David's victories as greater than Saul's, Saul turned against David (First Samuel 18–20). In Saul's family, only Jonathan accepted, by faith, God's choice of, and blessing on, David. When David escaped the court of Saul to visit Samuel for an explanation of what God was doing, the prophet was silent. Samuel established the monarchy but Nathan would define the mediatorial kingdom. This posed a dilemma. David was chosen to be king by the LORD, but Saul rejected him. In God's silence, David was being taught *to wait*, by faith, on the LORD. While David wavered at times, he served the LORD and Saul, His anointed, twice by saving his life (First Samuel 24, 26). In time, God removed Saul in battle with the Philistines (First Samuel 31). Jonathan, the son loyal to David, died alongside his father in battle, even though he had desired to join David's kingdom following his father's reign.

At the same time, David's faith had deepened to actively pursue God's will and to that extent, he genuinely lamented the death of both Jonathan and Saul (Second Samuel 1). With Saul's removal, Judah anointed David to be their king (2 Sam 2:1-7) at Hebron. The conflict with the Northern tribes had not ended. They attempted to make Ishbosheth king after Saul. Abner, Saul's commander, supported this succession, but David's claim to the nation's throne lasted beyond Joab's cowardly murder of Abner. As a result, Israel also anointed David to be king over all the tribes (2 Sam 5:1-5).

With all the tribes unified, David took the impregnable stronghold of the Jebusites at Jerusalem (2 Sam 5:6-12). The Philistines in response immediately attacked. Following the LORD's directions, David struck down the Philistines, who never again challenged the nation (2 Sam 5:17-25).[15]

The history of the Ark of the Covenant is important to the books of Samuel. It is the object over which the LORD's glory resided. David's heart's desire was to restore the presence of the LORD to the heart of His

---

[15]   Gordon asserts that, "The defeat of and expulsion of the Philistines, following two separate engagements on Israelite soil (vv. 17-25) was also a notable achievement, and one which most of all proved his fitness to sit upon the throne of Israel (cf. 3:18)" (*ibid.*, p. 225).

kingdom, to Jerusalem (2 Sam 6:12-15). Jerusalem, the capital city of David's kingdom, would also be the place which the LORD chose to place His name (Deut 12:5). "By enshrining the ark, the symbol of God's presence, there, David transformed the old Jebusite stronghold into the place where the One God was pleased to make himself known, the centre of the earth, the site of his throne, the connecting link between earth and heaven."[16] What David envisioned was reflected in the language he used to describe himself. The LORD would be enthroned as King and he would be appointed as prince *to mediate* God's reign (*nāgîd*, 2 Sam 6:21; 7:8).[17]

Davidic Theocratic Monarchy

The LORD's Kingdom (Second Samuel 7)[18]

To accomplish that end, Nathan had a Word from the LORD. "His joy at that achievement was soon tempered by his comparison of the tent structure with his own glorious palace [2 Sam 5:11], thus explaining his desire to erect a temple commensurate with the majesty and glory of God…"[19]

However, the LORD rejected David's proposal to build God a house (temple) and instead promised that He would build David's house (royal dynasty). God's proposal included promises concerning David (2 Sam 7:9-11), concerning David's immediate descendant (2 Sam 7:12-15), and concerning a line of David's descendants (2 Sam 7:16). These promises are:

1. David's name (reputation) would be great (7:9).

2. A safe and secure land would be procured (7:10-11).

3. David's immediate descendant would occupy David's throne and his kingdom would endure forever (7:12, 13b).

4. This descendant would build a house for the LORD's name (7:13a).

---

[16] Baldwin, *1 and 2 Samuel*, pp. 205-206.

[17] Robert Chisholm likewise asserts that, "It is appropriate that the Lord reside in a central sanctuary in the city, for he is the one who possesses ultimate authority over Israel and has chosen David as his vice-regent (2 Sam. 6:2, 21)" (Robert B. Chisholm, Jr., *1 & 2 Samuel*, Teach the Text Commentary Series [Grand Rapids, MI: Baker Books, 2013], p. 212).

[18] Gordon notes that "2 Samuel 7 is rightly regarded as an 'ideological summit,' not only in the 'Deuteronomistic History' but also in the Old Testament as a whole" (Gordon, *I & II Samuel*, p. 235).

[19] Merrill, *Everlasting Dominion*, p. 434. Some contend that David is asserting his legitimacy as Israel's king since temple building was a royal prerogative. Arvid Kapelrud, "Temple Building: A Task of God's and Kings," *Orientalia* 32 (1963): 56-62.

5. He would be adopted as a son so that God would discipline him if he committed iniquity (7:14).

6. The LORD's loyal love would not depart from him as it had from Saul (7:15).

The tension between what these promises affirmed and the contingencies the Law introduced (Deut 17:14-20) remained unresolved. "The question is whether David's descendants will 'keep Covenant', and if they do not fulfill their obligations how God can achieve his purpose of blessing."[20]

The LORD anticipated a resolution. He made an absolute promise that would be permanently operative:

7. The LORD would establish an enduring line of descendants and kingdom so that the Davidic throne would be established forever (7:16).

An enduring line implies the survival of David's descendants in spite of God's possible discipline. An enduring kingdom does not presuppose that it would not be interrupted but such interruptions would not be permanent. The throne "established forever" focuses on its perseverance into the future.

David applied the covenant promise to Solomon (1 Chr 22:9-10; 28:2-5), Solomon claimed it to himself (1 Kgs 5:17-18; 8:17-20), it is confirmed to Solomon (1 Kgs 9:4-5), and it is repeatedly affirmed that, in spite of the sins of individual kings, the kingdom shall not be withdrawn from David's house for David's sake (1 Kgs 11:31-34; 15:4-5, 2 Kgs 8:19). Psalm 89 repeats the promise and pleads with God that it should not be frustrated (89:3-4, 28-32, 33-37). A Jewish commentary concludes, "this promise of an everlasting kingdom of the house of David powerfully influenced the development of the Messianic hope in Israel."[21]

Not only does the scope of the covenant extend into the unimaginable future, but there are aspects of the promises that relate to the covenants that precede it. Most evident are allusions to the Abrahamic Covenant. First, David's name would be great as was Abraham's name (Gen 12:2). Second, God would provide land through David's line as God had promised to Abraham and his descendants (Gen 12:7; 13:15). Third, the promise to provide blessing through Abraham (Gen 12:3) would find leadership in the line of David. The Davidic restoration of the Ark of

---

[20] Baldwin, *1 and 2 Samuel*, p. 36.

[21] S. Goldman, *Samuel: Hebrew Text & English Translation*, Soncino Books of the Bible (London: Soncino, 1951), p. 229.

the Covenant and the future building of the temple set the stage for the nation being a blessing to all nations. Finally, the promise to Abraham and Sarah that they would parent kings (Gen 17:6, 16) finds fulfillment in David and his descendants.

In speaking of discipline, the Davidic Covenant certainly alludes back to the Mosaic Covenant. It seems valid to conclude that the promise implies that one Descendant would not be entangled in sin. This is the hope of the ideal King based on promise.

At the outset, the tension between promise and law was addressed in David's prayer of gratitude (2 Sam 7:18-29). David confessed that since God has promised to build his house, David has taken courage to pray that it will be fulfilled (2 Sam 7:27). His hope rests on God's choice of Israel "in order to redeem a people for Himself, to make a name for Himself, to perform for them great and awesome acts…" (2 Sam 7:23). David's faith rested in the fact that God's words are true and God Himself has promised this good thing to His servant (2 Sam 7:28).

Continuing Second Samuel's account of David's reign is a list of military conquests and an account of the kindness David showed to Jonathan's son, Mephibosheth (Second Samuel 8–10). Then, unexpectedly, in an unguarded moment, David fell into sin, raped Bathsheba[22] and murdered her husband, Uriah the Hittite. Nathan, giving voice to the condemnation of the Law, confronts David. A curse would fall on David's family and on the nation due to David's weakened reign. David's sons would now do in public what David had done in private and tried to keep hidden.

Amnon, one of David's sons, raped his sister, Tamar. Absalom, David's favored son, murdered Amnon. Then Absalom tried to usurp David's throne and was murdered by Joab. David was broken.

In spite of a broken heart, his final hymn celebrated that the LORD alone delivered him from all his enemies (Second Samuel 22).[23] His

---

[22] While some would disagree with this judgment, David had no right to another man's wife. Otherwise, David would not have tried to cover it up. While Bathsheba does not seem to resist it should be remembered that David was the king. Bathsheba's consent may not have been considered. This could therefore be viewed as coercion. In Psalm 51, David speaks of his bloodguiltiness, although it is unclear whether he is referring to his sin concerning Uriah, or Bathsheba, or both.

[23] David's discipline is seen by some as a metaphor for Israel's later exile. As Bergen notes, "If David's sin with its dread consequences is a metaphor of judgment for the nation of Israel through the exilic period, it is also a metaphor of hope. As chap. 20 concludes, David has returned to the environs of Jerusalem and is successfully engaged in the arduous task of rebuilding a nation. The Lord graciously brought David back from exile east of the Jordan, and the Lord would graciously bring Israel back to Jerusalem from its Babylonian exile" (Bergen, *1, 2 Samuel*, p. 361).

final words (2 Sam 23:1-7) recalled his hymns which were prompted by the Spirit who put words on his tongue. David left a legacy as "the sweet psalmist of Israel" (2 Sam 23:1). In David's psalms, we discover that David addressed the *conflict* with sin as condemned by the Law and exposed by the prophet. He also gave expression to the *hope* which God's promise encouraged. In the prophecy that came to his lips, we gain a glimpse of God's resolution of the *conflict*. And the portion of Psalms from "the sweet psalmist of Israel" introduces the worshipper to a rich corpus of revelation, along with the worship of a man deeply touched by God. David's psalms contain the clearest expressions of the Messianic hope.

Hymnic Literature

The Resolution between Promise and Law (Psalms)

In the progress of revelation, David found rest, if not understanding, in his personal *conflict* between sin, condemned by law, and hope, expressed in promise. As a consequence of this theological point of view, two broad types of themes in the Psalms were included in the Psalter. *Lament* repented of sin which the Law condemned and pleaded for mercy from the consequences of sin. *Praise* honored God for who He is and gave thanks for the hope based on what He promised to do and on what He had done on David's behalf.

We will examine the central message of five of David's psalms. However, before we examine these particular psalms, a brief overview of the Psalter may give greater perspective. The Psalter has been described as a collection of collections. In the present form of the collection, there are five books (1–41; 42–72; 73–89; 90–106; 107–150). The books are distinguished by the concluding doxology in the last psalm of each book (see 41:13; 72:19-20; 89:52; 106:48; and all of 150). Bruce Waltke proposes an intriguing description of the five books which feature the Davidic king and his covenant.[24]

Books 1 and 2 (Psalms 1–72)

Psalm 72:20, "The prayers of David, the son of Jesse, are ended," suggests that this is a collection from the time of David. "Psalm 2 introduces

---

[24] Waltke, *An Old Testament Theology*, pp. 870-96. We will summarize his theological treatment. In his development, he relies on Gerald Henry Wilson, *The Editing of the Hebrew Psalter* (Chico, CA: Scholars, 1985), p. 20.

the principle subject of the Psalter, the king in prayer."[25] Psalm 2 includes a summary variation of the Davidic Covenant: "Ask of me, and I will make the nations your heritage" (Ps 2:8). Then in the concluding Psalm, the prayer is directed on behalf of "the royal son" (Ps 72:1).

Book 3 (Psalms 73–89)

The concluding psalm (Psalm 89) introduces a new perspective. "The Davidic covenant is viewed as established in the dim past, and more important, it is considered as fractured...But there is hope!"[26]

Book 4 (Psalms 90–106)

These hymns do not mention a mediating king in Israel. Rather, the worshiper looks to Israel's heritage in Moses and to the LORD as King. Psalms 93–99 are the so-called enthronement psalms.[27]

Book 5 (Psalms 107–150)

Psalm 106:47 prays: "gather us from among the nations." Then at the beginning, Ps 107:2-3 says, "Let the redeemed of the LORD say so, whom he has...gathered in from the lands." The regathering for these worshipers has been accomplished. In this book, there is prominent Messianic hope in the Davidic psalms. Most prominent is Ps 110:1, David "foresees a King greater than himself: 'I AM says to my Lord.'"[28]

This overview suggests that the LORD's covenant with David and his line provides a foundation of hope for Israel. As David, so the worshipers in Israel find a resolution of their sin in the hope provided in the covenant. To consider what David, himself, gave expression to, five of his psalms will be examined.

The LORD and His Messiah (Psalm 2)

The Messianic hope is a central focus in the Psalter, and nearly half (73) of the Psalms have the note *ledāwid* (belonging to David). The New

---

[25] Waltke, *An Old Testament Theology*, p. 885.

[26] *Ibid.*, p. 886.

[27] Psalm 45 is also often identified as an enthronement psalm.

[28] *Ibid.*, p. 887.

Testament cites about fifteen in connection with the LORD's Anointed and Psalm 2 is the first.

> As early as Psalm 2 it presents him in terms which leave the limitations of local kingship far behind. The psalm would serve well enough (and doubtless did) as a regular enthronement anthem for a new king, when its language would be construed as courtly rhetoric, treating the modest empire of David as though it were the world. But there is more than rhetoric here. The poem draws out the logic of the fact that the Davidic king reigns on behalf of God, whose throne is in the heavens (2:4). The uttermost parts of the earth are therefore his by right, and will be his in fact.[29]

Messiah (*māšîah*) is the title give to the Davidic king. Anointing implies consecration to an authoritative office and empowerment for his task by the gift of the Spirit. The decree of Ps 2:7 builds upon the pledge of adoption given to the Davidic heir in 2 Sam 7:14, "I will be his father and he shall be my son." Psalm 2:7 announces the LORD's decree: one day the Father will beget Him. In the New Testament's application to Christ, it is the announcement of His resurrection (Acts 13:23). He is begotten to eternal life as the Son, and as Heir of an eternal kingdom.

Personal Sin (Psalm 51)

The issue in interpreting this psalm rests in the historical reliability of the superscription.[30] If this is David's prayer following Nathan's confrontation, it is clear that the depth of his sin overwhelms him. "This is the fourth and surely the greatest of the seven 'penitential psalms.'"[31] This is understandable because David had raped another man's wife and then had her husband murdered. These are intentional sins, sins which defy God, and the Law provided no sacrifice (Leviticus 4; Ps 51:16).

Appeal (Psalm 51:1-2)

David appeals to God who is loyal in His covenant love to Abraham's heirs. He is merciful, as Moses had discovered in desiring to know God

---

[29] Derek Kidner, *Psalms 1–72* (London: IVP, 1973), pp. 18-19.

[30] While many modern commentators have rejected the originality of the superscription it seems credible to affirm its historical reliability.

[31] *Ibid.*, p. 189. Penitential psalms are prayers "by one who is deeply troubled and alarmed" (*Ibid.*, p. 60). The discussion of these Davidic psalms relies on the work of Kidner and Delitzsch.

as a covenant partner (Exod 34:6-7). There is a basis in God for his desperate appeal. Forgiveness involves cleansing.

Confession (Psalm 51:3-5)

Once David faced his guilt, sin loomed as an accusing presence. While his actions affected both Uriah and Bathsheba, his sin was only against God. To a holy God, there was no possible excuse for his actions.

> The new perspective on his sin, as self-assertion against God, opens up a new self-knowledge. This crime, David now sees, was no freak event: it was in character; an extreme expression of the warped creature he had always been, and of the faulty stock he sprang from.[32]

Restoration (Psalm 51:6-9)

"Purge me with hyssop," alludes to the cleansing of a leper, sprinkled with sacrificial blood (Lev 14:6-32).

Inward Renewal (Psalm 51:10-13)

"Create in me," calls for what only God can do. "Both David's early history and the language of 11b, 12a show that this is not an unregenerate man's request, but a prayer for holiness (cf. 11b)."[33] David prayed as a covenant partner which involved service and led to humble worship (Ps 51:14-17). This provided an example of double knowledge. The people of God, learning about themselves as sinners, were drawn to a greater intimacy and knowledge of God in prayer, based on who God is and what He alone does.

Personal Suffering (Psalm 22)[34]

An issue in the interpretation of this Davidic psalm is that there is no known experience of David which matches its language. David speaks of himself as suffering, yet the description of this suffering speaks of *execution*.[35] Referring to himself, David is a type of sufferer. Speaking in terms of execution, David alludes prophetically to Another. Franz Delitzsch categorizes this type of psalm as *typico-prophetically Messianic.*[36]

---

[32] *Ibid.*, p. 190.

[33] *Ibid.*, p. 192.

[34] Many interpreters classify this psalm as a lament with elements of prayer and declarative praise.

[35] Aage Bentzen, *King and Messiah* (London: Lutterworth, 1955), p. 94, n. 40.

[36] Franz Delitzsch, *The Psalms*, vol. 1 (Grand Rapids, MI: Eerdmans, 1871), p. 69.

In light of Gen 3:15, it would not be unexpected that David would suffer in his role as the LORD's anointed *mediating* God's rule. In addition, it would not be unreasonable that David would have realized that there would be an ultimate Sufferer in the Seed of the woman who would do conflict with the serpent. Thus, as he goes to prayer to find resolution from his own suffering at the hands of God's enemies, it is plausible that he would envision an ultimate Sufferer as Gen 3:15 anticipated. And as the psalm declares, in this final Sufferer, "You have rescued me" (Ps 22:21b). Second Samuel 23:2, "the Spirit of the LORD speaks by me; his word is on my tongue," explains what David is doing and the prophecy he includes in the psalm.

> This part of the psalm is marked by a throbbing alternation of "I/me"-sections, of increasing length (verses 1–2, 6–8, 12–18), with "Thou"-sections of increasing urgency and immediacy (verses 3–5, 9–11, 19–21). The pattern will change at verse 22 from this alternation to a rapidly expanding circle of praise and vision.[37]

The Sufferer has *overcome* the conflict and death in God's time and in God's way.

The Power of Darkness (Psalm 22:1-21)

The cry *why* "is not a lapse of faith, nor a broken relationship, but a cry of disorientation as God's familiar, protective presence is withdrawn…"[38]

The response initially appeals to God as *holy*. When David approached God from the depths of his own sin, he appealed to God's mercy and compassion. There is an incompatibility between a holy God and the power of darkness. This darkness violates His glory and reputation. The flow of the alteration may be summarized:

> *Yet I* am under attack and accused that I would seek God only for my convenience, if at all.

> *But You* had been present in my personal lifelong existence.

> *Yet I* am under attack—"the strong closing in on the weak, the many on the one."[39]

> *But You* are urgently needed as my enemies close in for the kill.

---

[37]   Kidner, *Psalms 1–72*, p. 105.

[38]   *Ibid.*, p. 106.

[39]   *Ibid.*, p. 107.

You Have Answered Me! (Psalm 22:22b)

God's answer only comes in His time and in His way. As it happened, when the suffering extended beyond being urgent, then God responded, but not necessarily in the way the sufferer anticipated. Joy is the appropriate response for the delivered sufferer, and that joy is shared by others seeing God's answer (vv. 22-31). This one is *overcoming* suffering and death by execution, which was suggestively anticipated in Gen 3:15.

Personal Hope (Psalm 16)

David begins with a plea for preservation and endurance in life. Some commentators take the plea as a cry for survival in sickness, but the theme for the whole psalm is "having one's affections centred [*sic*] on God..."[40] in active faith. This is more than a cry for survival. It is an expression of the focus of all of the psalms, whether in lament or praise. As David considers himself a faithful servant (Ps 16:1-6), the psalm speaks of some aspect "of throwing in one's lot with God in the realms of one's security (1), welfare (2), associates (3), worship (4) and ambitions (5f)."[41] In considering his ambitions (16:5-6), the faithfulness of the LORD emerges as the issue of this psalm (16:7-11). David's hope for his future rested on the promise of the Davidic Covenant. Two aspects of the promise are open to question: who will succeed the king? And how will the king's line of successors be everlasting? In meditating on the answer to the first question, each generation will have a descendant chosen by God to be enthroned. But the descendants are not equal, nor will they rule with equal effectiveness. In fact, the expectation of discipline anticipated that they would not be equally righteous. It only claims that the line will survive without violating God's elective choice.

An answer to the second question implies more. *Everlasting* implies more than survival. *Everlasting* implies a heritage in the future that even includes David himself. This is evident in his meditation, "the LORD... gives me counsel" (Ps 16:7). "At my right hand" (Ps 16:8) suggests a person who will stand by to help in whatever contingency the future may bring. That may occur in court against some accusation, or in battle against some foe (Gen 3:15).[42] "Several times in the Psalms the sense of being

---

[40]　*Ibid.*, p. 83.

[41]　*Ibid.*

[42]　"The place at the right of a person was where his defender in a trial would stand (see 109:31)" (Robert G. Bratcher and William D. Reyburn, *A Translator's Handbook on the Book of Psalms,* UBS Handbook Series [New York: United Bible Societies, 1991], p. 145).

already face to face with God grows into certainty of enjoying this intimacy for ever...for God is not one to *give...up* his friends."[43] That hope expresses itself in words of prophecy (Ps 16:10). And that hope speaks of his own resurrection: "For you will not abandon my soul to Sheol" (Ps 16:10a). But the language of the second line goes beyond David's personal hope to a hope of an immediate resurrection: so that "you will not...let your holy one see corruption" (Ps 16:10). This line is not speaking of an antitype but is actually prophetic. *The path of life* leads without break into God's presence and into everlasting fulfillment.[44] And this Psalm gives expression to *overcoming* death in resurrection that is immediate. The resurrection that Ps 22:21-22 implies is expressed prophetically in Psalm 16.

David's Spirit-led meditation answered the first question of a descendant whose soon resurrection would fulfill the hope of the Davidic Covenant. This will also fulfill the prophecy: "Great salvation he brings to his king and shows steadfast love to his anointed, to David and his offspring forever" (2 Sam 22:51).

Ultimate Hope (Psalm 110)

"Nowhere in the Psalter does so much hang on the familiar title *A Psalm of David* as it does here; nor is the authorship of any other psalm quite so emphatically endorsed in other parts of Scripture."[45] The issue in this Davidic psalm is an important question that has been implied in the typological prophetic character of Psalms 22 and 16: would the Davidic descendant to come be merely a man at his best (Solomon) or more?

What are the full consequences of *overcoming* the enemy? This question is further complicated by the recognition that the genre of the psalm is an *enthronement oracle*. So it is similar to oracles given to other kings at their anointing or crowning (cf. 1 Sam 10:1f; 2 Kgs 11:12). But the difference has led scholars to propose one of two solutions. If, in fact, it is an enthronement oracle of the Messianic King, then David could not be the author. Or, if David is the author of this enthronement oracle, then Solomon must be the descendant honored. But both of these alternatives miss the point of the psalm. What is unique in this psalm is that a royal person addresses a more-than-royal Person, "My Lord." David repeatedly approached God with the *tension* of the condemnation of every

---

43 Kidner, *Psalms 1-72*, p. 86, emphasis in original.

44 *Ibid.*

45 Kidner, *Psalms 73-150*, p. 391.

human chosen by God under the Mosaic Covenant and of the promises expressed in the Davidic Covenant. That tension could only be resolved by a more than human Person. Solomon could not be even a type of such a descendant. Rather, David is given a vision of a Person equal with God. He is designated by two direct oracles from the LORD to share a position of equality with God and to exercise a role of Priesthood on behalf of man in the presence of God Himself. Further, David recognizes this Person as his personal Lord in the role in which He functions. Delitzsch then identifies the vision given expression in the psalm as "directly eschatologically Messianic."[46] Thus, in distinction to Psalms 22 and 16 which are typico-prophetic, Psalm 110 is exclusively prophetic.

The vision portrays the Descendant of David as the King (Ps 110:1-3), the Priest (Ps 110:4), and the Warrior (Ps 110:5-7).

Sit at My Right Hand (Psalm 110:1-3)

This is the first oracle. "The authority and power conferred by such an address will be illustrated in the remaining verses of the psalm..."[47] The first feature is "how fully at one are the Lord (Yahweh) and this King. It is the Lord who wields the sceptre, it is the King who is urged to rule—for human authority is enhanced, not diminished, by such a partnership."[48] Now in prophetic vision, David receives a glimpse of the initial realization of the One who has *overcome* God's enemy (Gen 3:15). It is a partnership anticipated in the covenants but realized in His Person, both divine and human. The divinity of the LORD partners with His humanity.

The second feature that is recognized is the nature of this rule. It is a rule in the midst of enemies (Ps 110:2) in which obedience is enforced.[49] But it is also rule over "Your people" (Ps 110:3) who voluntarily and freely conform to His will. Thus, it is a rule shared on the throne of the LORD's universal reign. But this is not yet a mediatorial reign.

The Priest (Psalm 110:4)

The second oracle is a direct oracle from God appropriately translated as a quotation. The oracle is certain and that certainty is reinforced by stating the fact that the LORD has sworn and that He will not change His

---

[46]   Delitzsch, *Psalms*, vol. 1, p. 68.

[47]   Kidner, *Psalms 73-150*, p. 393.

[48]   *Ibid.*, pp. 393-94.

[49]   Kidner suggests that, "The word for *Rule* has a certain sternness, which suits the contrast between the enforced obedience of enemies in this verse and the glad response of volunteers in the next" (*Ibid.*, p. 394, emphasis in original).

mind (v 4a). The relationship between the vision and the Davidic Covenant is suggested since the Priest shall serve "forever." Like the Davidic
line which will reign "forever," this Priest-King shall serve "forever." Further, the order of this ministry is as *Melchizedek* (Gen 14:18-20), king
of righteousness and king of Salem (or *Jerusalem*, whose shortened form
brings out the meaning, "peace"). So what Melchizedek anticipated in
providing an additional link between elect man and God, the Person of
the LORD realized. The LORD is both David's Lord, as the elect human
Descendant of David, and the LORD's equal because of His divinity.

The Warrior (Psalm 110:5-7)

"Realistically, the psalm ends on the note of fierce battle and strenuous
pursuit, since the Priest-King's enthronement is not the final scene but
the prelude to world conquest."[50] This is evidenced by the terms *shatter,
wrath, judge,* and *corpses.* So a fuller portrayal of the resolution of the tension is being fleshed out in the visions of David, the prophet. The One
who has *overcome* the enemy of God will judge that enemy in finality.

---

[50] *Ibid.,* p. 396.

CHAPTER 11:
SOLOMONIC THEOCRATIC
MONARCHY (FIRST KINGS 1–11)

Introduction

The Davidic Covenant had promised that David would have a son to be enthroned, but it did not specify which son that would be. Absalom had attempted to gain popular support to claim the throne before Joab killed him. Now Adonijah sought the throne by garnering the support of two leaders in David's government, Joab and Abiathar the priest. But he lacked a prophet's support. The prophet Nathan initiated support for Solomon. The LORD had named him Jedidiah (loved by the LORD) as the text had said, "The LORD loved him" (2 Sam 12:24). The term *love*, in a covenant context, bears the primary connotation of election or choice (cf. Mal 1:2-3). David and Bathsheba, the parents, had understood it this way and Bathsheba reminded David of his promise made at the time of Solomon's birth (1 Kgs 1:11-14). So with the support of Nathan, Zadok the priest, and Benaiah, David swore that Solomon should reign after him (1 Kgs 1:30). Nathan and Zadok then anointed Solomon as the next king (1 Kgs 1:34) to be enthroned by the people.

Wisdom but High Places

The prophet assessed Solomon: "Solomon loved the LORD, walking in the statutes of David his father…" (1 Kgs 3:3a).[1] Love has reference to covenant obedience that characterized his early reign. As Deuteronomy had pronounced, the king was to write for himself a copy of this law,

---

[1] Volkmar Fritz suggests that, "'To love God' is the main principle of Deuteronomistic theology; this love has to be understood as sole and complete loyalty to Yahweh to the exclusion of worship of any foreign gods (see Deut 6:5; 11:1; 13:14)" (Volkmar Fritz, *1 & 2 Kings*, A Continental Commentary, [Minneapolis: Fortress, 2003], p. 34).

according to the tutelage of the Levitical priests (Deut 17:18-20). This is how Solomon's reign began. But the prophet added a caveat, "only he sacrificed and made offerings at the high places" (1 Kgs 3:3b). The caveat followed the description of his "marriage alliance with Pharaoh, King of Egypt" (1 Kgs 3:1-2). Such offerings characterized his later years (1 Kgs 11:1-8), but it was a problem from the beginning. Solomon loved the LORD but also loved many foreign women (and their gods), including the daughter of Pharaoh. Solomon ruled with an increasingly divided heart.[2]

Early in his reign, he "went to Gibeon to sacrifice there, for that was the great high place" (1 Kgs 3:4).[3] At that sacrifice, "the LORD appeared to Solomon in a dream by night, and God said, 'Ask what I shall give you'" (1 Kgs 3:5). Solomon did not ask with his own interests in mind, but with the task God had given. He recognized his youth and immaturity and so asked for wisdom "to govern this your great people" (1 Kgs 3:9). Waltke suggests that the request "comes as a surprise, for he already knows the Law and shows himself wise."[4] The law had taught him to correctly assess himself and to recognize God's glorious greatness. Thus, *to mediate* God's rule demanded an "understanding mind to govern your people, that I may discern between good and evil" (1 Kgs 3:9). "Wisdom in Proverbs has a threefold dimension: sapiential (a way of knowing reality [1 Kgs 4:29-34]), ethical (a way of conducting oneself [First Kings 3:16–4:28]), and religious (a way of relating to the divinely designed order or to God)."[5] Solomon acknowledged the first two dimensions. That is what his request and God's gift brought to his reign. It is the religious dimension that the Law particularly addresses and that Solomon would struggle with most.

---

[2] Iain Provan comes to a similar conclusion noting that, "At the very least, then, the authors are again asking us to see (as in 3:1a) that Solomon's love for God, even at this early stage in his career, was not entirely wholehearted" (Iain W. Provan, *1 and 2 Kings*, New International Biblical Commentary [Peabody, MA: Hendrickson, 1995], pp. 45-46).

[3] Eugene Merrill correctly clarifies that this was not included in the caveat. "The high place here refers to the location of the Mosaic tabernacle at Gibeon, the only authorized central sanctuary available to him since the great bronze altar was there (1 Kings 3:4-5; cf. 2 Chron. 1:2-6). David had, of course, erected a tabernacle in Jerusalem to house the ark (2 Sam. 6:17), but until the ark and tabernacle (that of Moses) were joined, the central sanctuary as envisioned in Deuteronomy 12 could not exist" (Merrill, *Everlasting Dominion*, p. 442).

[4] Waltke, *An Old Testament Theology*, p. 708.

[5] Richard J. Clifford, *Proverbs: A Commentary*, The Old Testament Library (Philadelphia: Westminster John Knox Press, 1999), pp. 19-20.

Temple but His Own House (First Kings 6:38–7:1)

Another caveat introduces a further division in Solomon's heart.[6] While it is likely that Solomon focused on building the temple first, the effort expended on his own palace probably delayed the temple's construction. The contrast in the text implies Solomon's affection was divided between his wives and the Lord.

Still, the building of the temple expressed a message that communicated God's glory.

> Various decorative motifs such as the cherubim, palm trees, and flowers were reminiscent of the paradisiacal setting of the first holy space, the garden in Eden, where the LORD had first made his presence known and where he had provided access to those created as his image to enjoy fellowship with him (1 Kgs 6:29, 32).[7]

When the building of the temple was completed, "the glory of the LORD filled the house of the LORD" (1 Kgs 8:10-11). This paralleled the original construction of the tabernacle (Exod 40:34-35). Then Solomon blessed the LORD (1 Kgs 8:12-21) and dedicated the temple (8:23-61). The prayer addressed two substantial questions: how could God limit Himself to dwell in a building (8:27)? The God of Scripture exists independent of creation and cannot be contained by creation. Solomon does not answer the question but raises it to recognize that God is greater than the building and that the building does not control nor limit God. God's answer to His people's prayers still rest with Himself. Solomon asked God, "listen in heaven your dwelling place, and when you hear, forgive" (8:30).

The second question relates to foreigners who make requests through the house which bears God's Name (1 Kgs 8:41-43). It reflects God's design which He first expressed to Abraham in Gen 12:3. So Solomon's request is consistent with God's previous revelation. His request is that the Lord "hear in heaven…and do according to all for which the foreigner calls to you, in order that all the peoples of the earth may know your name and fear you…" (1 Kgs 8:43). In these two issues, Solomon discerns God's will from the Law and prays for what is good.

---

[6] Provan suggests that this is an indication that Solomon's priorities were out of order (Provan, *1 and 2 Kings*, p. 69).

[7] Merrill, *Everlasting Dominion*, p. 443.

A Divided Heart and a Divided Kingdom

Solomon had wisdom to discern between good and evil, but wisdom does not always guarantee a person will do what is right. The law stated that kings were not to multiply wives nor horses (Deut 17:16), but Solomon multiplied both. His disobedience to the Law became even more acute at the end of his life. Second Kings 11:4 notes, "When Solomon was old his wives turned away his heart after other gods, and his heart was not wholly true to the Lord his God, as was the heart of David his father."[8] The result was divine anger (1 Kgs 11:9), and Solomon was disciplined according to the Davidic Covenant (2 Sam 7:14). However, the discipline was delayed for the sake of his father David (1 Kgs 11:10-11), and was carried out at the conclusion of his reign through the division of his kingdom, a symbol of his divided heart. Rehoboam, his son, inherited the tribes of Judah and Benjamin and Jerusalem while Jeroboam, Solomon's servant, was given the other ten tribes.

Wisdom Literature

Part of Solomon's legacy was a core of wisdom literature.[9] What David left in hymnic literature, Solomon left in wisdom literature. Hymnic literature explores before the Lord the revelation of God and, for David in particular, the tension between promises and law. Wisdom literature observes human experience in a created but fallen world. That literature also contrasts the way of wisdom and the way of folly in actions, attitudes, and values common to humanity.

Sapiential terminology includes wise/wisdom, fool/foolishness, knowledge, understanding, and discipline.[10] Thus, the observations of human experience are not without presuppositions: "the fear of the Lord is the beginning of knowledge" (Prov 1:7) and "the fear of the Lord is the

---

[8] "In other words, his heart was no longer wholly God's. The Lord had ceased to be the major factor in his life. Once this shift occurred, the next steps into idolatry became more natural and easier to accept." (Paul R. House, *1, 2 Kings*, NAC, vol. 8 [Nashville, TN: Broadman & Holman, 1995], p. 167).

[9] There is widespread agreement that wisdom literature consists of Job, Proverbs, and Ecclesiastes and some Psalms. Solomon is directly identified in historic titles as author of Proverbs 10:1–22:16 and 25:1–29:17. Ecclesiastes contains reflections of an old man, "the Preacher" whom it is plausible to identify, if only indirectly, as Solomon. This is because the author identifies himself as having been "king over Israel in Jerusalem" (Eccl 1:12) and as having "taught the people knowledge, weighing and studying and arranging many proverbs with great care" (Eccl 12:9).

[10] Gerhard von Rad, *Wisdom in Israel* (Nashville, TN: Abingdon, 1972), pp. 53–54.

beginning of wisdom" (Prov 9:10). Whereas law begins with special revelation (the will of God), wisdom begins with natural experience. Such
wisdom presupposes a relationship with God and a knowledge of His
will. This presupposition helps evaluate natural experiences as a way of
wisdom or a way of folly.

Proverbs

Observation

> Starting from a profound reverence for Yahweh, the wise
> teachers of ancient Israel reflected on what they observed in
> various areas of life. As they reflected on what they saw, they
> discerned patterns of acts and consequences that could serve
> either as wise examples to follow or foolish errors to avoid.[11]

This profound reverence included knowledge of the Law. "Deuteronomy presents the Law as 'your wisdom and your understanding in the
sight of the peoples' (Dt. 4:6), and sets before Israel the same two ways,
of life and death, which are a favorite theme of Proverbs."[12] Thus, the
Mosaic Covenant framed Solomon's reflection about human experience.
Yet the sayings which understand life based on the Law create new revelation,[13] not merely applications of the Law.

Maxims

"A proverb is a *brief, particular* expression of a truth. The briefer a statement is, the less likely it is to be totally precise and universally applica-
ble…So the proverbs are phrased in a catchy way, so as to be learnable
by anyone."[14] Thus, a proverb is a guideline, not a formula. "Wisdom is a
configuration of soul; it is *moral character*."[15]

---

[11] Estes, *Handbook on the Wisdom Books and Psalms*, p. 213.

[12] Derek Kidner, *Proverbs* (Downers Grove, IL: IVP, 1964), p. 16.

[13] Bruce K. Waltke, *The Book of Proverbs: 1–15* (Grand Rapids, MI: Eerdmans, 2004), pp. 76-88.

[14] Gordon D. Fee and Douglas Stuart, *How to Read the Bible for All Its Worth* (Grand Rapids,
      MI: Zondervan, 1993), pp. 217-18.

[15] Michael V. Fox, *The Anchor Yale Bible Commentaries: Proverbs 1-9* (New Haven, CT: Yale
      University Press, 2000), p. 348.

Limits in Wisdom

Maxims express truths that reflect typical human experiences. These maxims may be arranged on a spectrum. On one end of the spectrum are normative truths that are always repeated and on the opposite end are general truths that are commonly repeated.

The normative truth incorporates God in such a fashion that His presence and providence assure that the experience is repeated. Proverbs 16:1 is one such maxim. To man belongs "'the arrangements of the mind', the framing of plans, the constant planning in advance...But the projects of the mind still do not accomplish anything...But God is there precisely in this incalculable element...he has taken the whole affair out of your hands."[16] This maxim illustrates one dimension of the limitations of human wisdom. "Its aim is...to put a stop to the erroneous concept that a guarantee of success was to be found simply in practising human wisdom...Man must always keep himself open to the activity of God, an activity which completely escapes all calculation..."[17] While Proverbs encourages the acquisition and application of wisdom, it does not promote a personal godless autonomy. Such an autonomy would cancel out the benefits of wisdom (Prov 3:5-6; 26:12; 27:1; 28:11, 26).

On the other end of the wisdom spectrum are general truths. This exemplifies a second kind of limitation of human wisdom. General truths must be applied with discernment. There are proverbs which express the general truth that haste makes waste (Prov 16:12; 19:2; 21:5; 28:20). While this is generally true, there are circumstances that warrant haste such as a crisis, a battle, or an athletic competition. In such circumstances, deliberation or thoughtful consideration are best considered before the crisis arrives.

Thus, human wisdom is limited by the universal rule of God which ultimately controls, and human experience that occurs within a fallen and unpredictable world. Evil may demand a rapid or unexpected response.

Ecclesiastes

Ecclesiastes supplements the practical wisdom found in Proverbs. That supplement is expressed in the presupposition Solomon adopts for himself as he reflects back upon his own experiences. He intentionally brackets his reflections to exclude the presence of God in his presuppositions

---

[16] Von Rad, *Wisdom in Israel*, pp. 99-100. See also Prov 16:2, 9; 19:14, 21; 20:24.

[17] *Ibid.*, p. 101.

which colors his observations of experience. However, such bracketing is temporary, only to remove the brackets to see God in life (Eccl 3:2-8) and to find meaning with God's presence (Eccl 12:13-14; cf. 2:24-26; 5:18-20; 8:15). He also limits his observations to that which is expressed most fully by the motto: *hăbēl*.

Motto

A summary of Solomon's basic search and his conclusion is expressed in an *inclusio* at the beginning and at the end of Ecclesiastes (1:2-3; 12:8). That summary and motto is, "'Absolute futility' (Heb. *hăbēl hăbālîm*), says the Teacher, absolute futility, everything is futile…under the sun" (Eccl 1:2-3, HCSB). There are three aspects to this motto. The first relates to the author's chosen perspective on human experiences. That perspective is *under the sun* (Eccl 1:3, 13) a phrase that likely means to view the world in its natural existence apart from God. This includes not only what he looks at but also how he looks at it. Thus, he brackets his own reflection and limits his observations to the natural world. A second aspect relates to the scope of his conclusion. That scope, based on observing the natural world, is that *all* is futility; all is meaningless. This leads to the third aspect, namely, the conclusion that such a world is *hăbēl*. The literal sense of *hăbēl* is "vapor" or "breath," and in its metaphorical and abstract uses in Ecclesiastes, it refers to "anything that is superficial, ephemeral, insubstantial, incomprehensible, enigmatic, inconsistent, or contradictory."[18] His conclusion is that when an experience under the sun is transferred to the role of God, then this human experience is *hăbēl*. Two alternative senses of *hăbēl* have been suggested: either a neutral sense of "emptiness"[19] or negatively of the "absurdity of life."[20] But a more suitable sense awaits further consideration.

Fallen World

The literary structure of the book corresponds to the role of the motto. Sections, most often identified as the prologue and epilogue, 1:1-11 and

---

[18] Choon-Leong Seow, *Ecclesiastes*, Anchor Bible, vol. 18 (New Haven, CT: Yale University Press, 1997), p. 47.

[19] J. Stafford Wright, "The Interpretation of Ecclesiastes" in *Classical Evangelical Essays in Old Testament Interpretation*, ed. Walter C. Kaiser, Jr. (Grand Rapids, MI: Baker, 1972), p. 140.

[20] James L. Crenshaw, *Ecclesiastes: A Commentary*, Old Testament Library (Philadelphia: Westminster, 1987), p. 24.

12:8-14 are stated in the third person expressing a conclusion. But the intervening section of 1:12–12:7 is stated in the first person and gives an account of the author's experience. This central section provides the validation for the motto's accuracy.

The author describes the fallen world of human experience. Inevitable death is evidence of the senselessness of human experience. Human death came into the created world when mankind ate of the tree of the knowledge of good and evil (Gen 2:17). And the fallen world provides no explanation for itself. While death and suffering seem to be the enemy of all human life, it is particularly meaningless when infants are born to die prematurely, or children get terminal illnesses. Why were they even born? In this perspective, life is puzzling and even nonsensical. Yet *conflict* is part of God's curse that mankind might search for an answer outside of the fallen world, an answer that goes beyond what is "under the sun." Conflict is also a part of the permission of evil with the presence of God's enemy.

> Within the context of the book, 3:11 is crucial text for understanding Qohelet's message…the verse suggests that divinely given *dissonance* between the sense of the eternal and life within the confines of time is intended to produce *frustration* that compels humans to turn to God as the source of meaning.[21]

Thus, the fallen world has a built in conflict with evil, death, toil, and purpose for life that, like the author, we may abandon the brackets to see God.

Meaningful World

The longing in the heart of one created in God's image can be resolved in God and in His special revelation of Himself. Removing the bracket that excluded God, one finds the reason for death in the presence of sin and a means to address sin in the Law. Thus, "When all has been heard, the conclusion of the matter is: fear God and keep His commands, because this is for all humanity. For God will bring every act to judgment, including every hidden thing, whether good or evil" (Eccl 12:13-14, HCSB).

---

[21] Estes, *Handbook on the Wisdom Books and Psalms*, p. 314, emphasis added.

Job

As previously noted, wisdom literature operates in the world of human experience. One of those experiences is suffering, an experience profoundly portrayed by Job. Since the idea of plot-conflict and the resolution has already been examined, that exposition will not be repeated here. Instead, attention will be given to the contribution of Job to the wisdom corpus.

Job's enigmatic experience of suffering motivated him to pursue a claim to be heard by God. From his point of view, the traditional retribution formula of wisdom advanced by his friends did not suffice or apply to his situation. Therefore, the contribution of Job to the wisdom corpus relates to the appropriate response to suffering when one does not fully know God's sovereign plan. What the book says is that ultimately, knowledge of God's justice and mercy is sufficient to be faithful to His will. The question of "why" was never answered for Job. What he did learn was that he as the creature could trust his Creator without knowing why. Wisdom literature that is based on knowledge and understanding must also deal with experiences that transcend both knowledge and understanding. Ecclesiastes and Job both deal with experiences in which adequate knowledge is missing or in which the maxims in Proverbs alone do not provide the answers.

CHAPTER 12:
DIVIDED THEOCRATIC
KINGDOM, PART 1:
THE NORTHERN KINGDOM
(FIRST AND SECOND KINGS)

Introduction

Solomon's divided heart ultimately led to a divided kingdom as stipulated in the Davidic Covenant (2 Sam 7:14). This covenant is unconditional in existence (ensuring a continuity of the Davidic line and a partnership in function) yet the covenantal benefits were contingent upon the continuing faithfulness of the Davidic representative. This covenant reflects the initial stewardship of both David and Solomon. David's heart after God and his faithfulness to the Mosaic Covenant with respect to worship resulted in an extension of his reign into eternity as spelled out in the Davidic Covenant. Solomon's divided heart enjoyed, on one side, the building of the temple and an extension of his reign geographically according to his wisdom. Then, on the other side, in unfaithfulness of worship (1 Kgs 11:1-8), Solomon had ten tribes torn away from his kingdom.

The presence of God's *mediatorial* reign through the kings was varied. In the Northern Kingdom of Israel, the theocratic presence was snuffed out in the apostasy of each king. In light of this, God's providential control was now carried on through prophets. The text of First and Second Kings highlights that prophetic ministry.[1] In addition, the writing proph-

---

[1] Waltke, *An Old Testament Theology*, p. 745. In a summary chart, Waltke lists the prophetic passages and the passages indicating fulfillment. The combination indicates God's providential reign in the Northern Kingdom. The following list of passages indicates prophecy and fulfillment:

1 Sam 2:35; 2 Sam 7:13 and 1 Kgs 2:26-27; 8:20;

1 Kgs 11:29-31 and 1 Kgs 12:15b;

First Kings 13 and 2 Kgs 23:16-18;

1 Kgs 14:6-10, 15 and 1 Kgs 15:29; 2 Kgs 17:21-23;

ets Joel, Amos and Hosea are speaking to this kingdom about God's reign in the present and in the future.

In the Southern Kingdom, the *mediatorial* kingdom continued through the house of David over Judah and the temple. God's reign would be negatively affected by the disobedience of the majority of Davidic descendants, but the theocratic presence is still evident in Hezekiah and Josiah, whose reigns were assessed in unqualified approval. In the South, the writing prophets predominate with their message about God's reign (e.g., Isaiah, Micah, Jeremiah etc.).

In view of the breakdown of the LORD's *mediatorial* reign in the North, in Israel, the revealed presence of the LORD in His Word will be selectively examined.

The Non-Writing Prophets

Abijah the Shilonite

In the breakdown of Solomon's kingdom, a prophet arising from the original residence of the tabernacle (Shiloh) presented God's plan to Jeroboam (1 Kgs 11:29-40). The LORD promised Jeroboam a kingdom, offered on conditional terms, which He had promised David on unconditional terms (1 Kgs 11:38). As a judgment upon Solomon, the descendants of David will be temporarily afflicted (1 Kgs 11:39).

So Ahijah, meeting with Jeroboam, tore his cloak into twelve pieces to represent the twelve tribes and offered ten pieces to Jeroboam (1 Kgs 11:30-31). However, Jeroboam, having received the ten tribes, violated the conditional terms of God's provision when he established alternate worship centers in Bethel and Dan (1 Kgs 12:29) rather than worshiping in Jerusalem as the LORD had chosen. The faith demanded from Jeroboam by continuing to worship in Jerusalem, in spite of the political division, was too great for him to exercise.

---

1 Kgs 16:1-4 and 1 Kgs 16:11-12;
Josh 6:26 and 1 Kgs 16:34;
1 Kgs 22:17 and 1 Kgs 22:35-38;
1 Kgs 21:17-24 and 1 Kgs 21:27-29; 22:37; 2 Kgs 9:25-26, 30-37;
2 Kgs 1:6 and 2 Kgs 1:17;
1 Kgs 17:1 and 1 Kgs 18:41-46;
2 Kgs 7:1 and 2 Kgs 7:16;
2 Kgs 7:2 and 2 Kgs 7:19-20;
2 Kgs 8:12 and 2 Kgs 9:14, 16; 10:32; 12:17-18;13:3, 22;
2 Kgs 21:10-15 and 2 Kgs 24:2;
2 Kgs 22:15-20 and 2 Kgs 23:30.

A Man of God from Judah

A forceful demonstration of Jeroboam's rebellion came while the altar was being built at Bethel. An anonymous prophet condemned the altar and the king's hand was withered in his sacrifice as a judgment (1 Kgs 13:4). Not only did the power of God's word of judgment appear at Bethel, but the man of God himself became a further object lesson of judgment that followed disregarding God's Word. Having been forbidden by God to remain or to eat, the man of God refused Jeroboam's offer to stay. But when an old prophet deceived him and told the man of God to stay, he stayed. Since he disregarded the word of the LORD, he was attacked by a lion and killed, but his body remained uneaten with the lion and his donkey standing over his body (1 Kgs 13:24). The violation of the word and will of the LORD had consequences which were supernaturally enacted. The circumstances did not determine what ought to be done.

Elijah

In the North, God raised up Elijah to confront the house of Omri in the reign of his son, Ahab, and Jezebel, Ahab's pagan wife (First Kings 17). Ahab achieved a high water mark for covenant violation. "He set up an altar for Baal in the temple of Baal that he had built in Samaria. Ahab also made an Asherah pole" (1 Kgs 16:32-33, HCSB). "Moreover, at the instigation of his wicked wife, he attempted to extirpate the worship of the LORD from his kingdom (18:4)…"[2] As a judgment, the LORD sent three years of famine at Elijah's word (1 Kgs 17:1).

That precipitated a test to reveal the true God at Mt. Carmel. The LORD decisively demonstrated by fire, consuming the sacrifice, that He is the true God (1 Kgs 18:20-40). Further, the LORD sent rain to break the drought in response to Elijah's prayer.

While such a demonstration would appear to be decisive, Jezebel responded by threatening Elijah's life (1 Kgs 19:2). In despair and depression, Elijah ran to Mt. Horeb (Sinai) to demand that Israel receive immediately what they deserved—the covenant curses for such blatant violations. While perhaps at the same spot that the LORD had shown grace and mercy to Moses and punishment to the guilty, the LORD does announce

---

[2] Merrill, *Everlasting Dominion*, p. 455.

total destruction of the guilty majority, but also showed grace in delay for 7000 who had not bowed down to Baal[3] (1 Kgs 19:9-18).

When Elijah's ministry had been completed, the LORD translated him into heaven (2 Kgs 2:9-14). Elisha then cried out, "My father, my father, the chariots and horsemen of Israel!" (2 Kgs 2:12, HCSB). The cry announced the strength of Israel had been taken away in this respected prophet. No longer did Israel have national access to the LORD. Elijah had provided that national link as he confronted Ahab and Jezebel, but now that had come to a conclusion.

Elisha

Although the national covenant link had been severed and judgment on the nation was inevitable, God sent a successor in grace. Elisha claimed the rights as Elijah's first born heir and takes Elijah's cloak to complete his ministry with believers in the LORD (2 Kgs 2:13). When the LORD denied the immediate judgment that Elijah demanded, He chose to deal with the remnant in mercy. Through Elisha, mercy fell on the widow of a prophet, the Shunamite's son (2 Kgs 4:18-37), and was shown in the poison curses in the prophet's pot and the feeding of one-hundred hungry people (2 Kgs 4:40-44). In addition, Elisha healed the leprosy of Naaman, the Syrian Gentile (Second Kings 5). At the same time, he struck dead children at Bethel who mocked that he was bald, having lost his covering, namely Elijah (2 Kgs 2:23-25). The LORD, in Elisha, provided grace for believers as He delayed what had been anticipated to be inevitable judgment for the Northern Kingdom.

The Writing Prophets

Some seven hundred years of Israel's history had passed since Moses had completed the *Torah*. Writing Prophets appeared in the ninth century. Their message helped refocus the nation's attention on the *goal* of creation and the *plan* of redemption of that which had been lost to the enemy of God.

With the Mosaic Law as a backdrop, the writing prophets would announce the Day of the LORD's judgment. *Joel* focused on the significance of a locust plague (cf. Deut 28:38-42). This historic locust plague, which occurred as a curse of the Law, became the occasion to announce

---

[3] Waltke, *An Old Testament Theology*, p. 718.

the coming Day of the LORD (Joel 1:15; 2:1, 31-32). *Amos* gave attention to the fact that judgment must fall on all nations, however, Israel is uniquely deserving (Amos 1:3–2:16). This is because "I have known only you out of all the clans of the earth" (Amos 3:2, HCSB). This alludes to the Mosaic Covenant (Exod 19:5-6). The term "know" is used here in the sense of "recognize in a special way" which may be taken as a metonymy for partnership (Deut 4:5-8). Hosea took a similar emphasis as the covenant was analogous to his marriage to a prostitute. The imagery is telling concerning the people of Israel. The divorce represents the breaking of the covenant and this has the consequence that Israel is "Not My People" (Hos 1:8). Hosea's covenant lawsuit (chaps. 4–9) deals with the violations of the ten basic commands found in Deut 5:6-21.

The judgment would take the shape of what the people feared (cf. Judg 21:25). They would be dispersed to be ruled by Gentiles who worshiped pagan gods. Ironically, the elect people who had chosen to live like the enemy now lived among descendants of the enemy in the Gentile nations. But rather than experiencing acceptance, the Jewish people were hated and experienced persecution and separation. Moses foresaw this persecution with suffering and pain at the conclusion of Deuteronomy: "When all these things have happened…and you come to your senses, while you are in all the nations" (Deut 30:1). This experience of suffering would help Israel realize that life with God was better than living like the nations.

But there are two more themes that would be clarified by failure under the *theocratic monarchy*. One theme had already been introduced when God announced that a descendant of Eve would *overcome* the enemy of God (Gen 3:15). That theme was further specified when God promised a Descendant to Abram who would *mediate* blessings to all nations (Gen 12:3b). Such a striking promised Descendant had not appeared in the historical books. The Davidic Covenant had alluded to a King who would *reign* in the *everlasting* kingdom (2 Sam 7:12-16).

The prophet Isaiah prophesied about this unrealized theme in relation to two historic kings, Ahaz and Hezekiah (Isaiah 7–11 and 40–53 respectively). The prophet announced the sign of Immanuel and foresaw the Servant who would serve the elect servant nation (Isaiah 42:1-9; 49:1-13; 50:4-10; 52:13–53:12). The sign was given to Ahaz who refused it and the Servant was prophesied to accept what Hezekiah failed to accept. He, having died, would be given as a *covenant* to Israel (Isa 42:6; 49:8).

That covenant was the second theme. Jeremiah had named it "the new covenant" to replace the old Mosaic Covenant (Jer 31:31-34). The New Covenant promises to form the nation as a servant of the LORD.

In this immediate history, the prophets held out a warning of imminent judgment. This warning of pending judgment had been announced from the very first national violation of the covenant (Exod 32:34). The warning was vague in reference to time in that it could happen at any time, "on the day I settle accounts, I will hold them accountable" (Exod 32:34, HCSB). At the time of that Exodus rebellion, those leading the rebellion were immediately judged (Exod 32:33, 35). Those who were involved without intent against God, in other words, in ignorance, would live with a threat of pending judgment. Each generation lived with that threat. Now the prophets announce what was pending as imminent: "the day of the LORD is near" (Obad 15; cf. Isa 13:6; Ezek 30:3; Joel 1:15; 2:1; 3:14; Amos 5:18; 8:9-14; Zeph 1:7, 14).

Willis Beecher proposed an interesting conclusion to be drawn from this repeated reference to the Day of the LORD:

> This representation is made by prophets who lived many generations apart, and therefore by prophets who knew that other prophets had made it generations before. Perhaps this indicates that the prophets thought of the day of Yahweh as generic, not an occasion which would occur once for all, but one which might be repeated as circumstances called for it.[4]

If the term should be understood as generic, then one would expect certain repeated facts each time it would appear. Note these recurring elements.

1. The LORD would intervene in judgment, yet it would not simply be divine judgment. The Noahic flood was not called the Day of the LORD. The repeated disciplinary covenant curses in Judges were not this day either.

2. The judgment concerned a national covenant violation in which *the very existence of the covenant* with the Northern or Southern tribes was at issue.[5]

---

[4] Beecher, *Prophets*, p. 311.

[5] In Exodus 32, the covenant had been broken by the people as a whole. As such, it ceased to exist unless it would be renewed as in Exodus 34, through Moses' mediation. "The day of settled accounts" was delayed.

3. The judgment would have a "pedagogical effect."[6] That effect would be combined with a call to repentance for those who had learned.

4. The LORD would deliver the repentant who endured the judgment at the outset of the Day. Then in the climactic experience in history, those delivered would be blessed.

Joel: Ninth Century BC[7]

In a number of ways, this prophet had a generic message. That message may be stated: covenant discipline anticipates covenant judgment. Further, he does not relate his ministry to any king in Jerusalem. Some relate his ministry to the time after captivity when the house of God had been rebuilt (Joel 1:16). Others date the prophet early, proclaiming this generic message to any generation of Israel, God's people, deserving judgment.[8]

The Historic Locust Plague

Kaiser proposes that the purpose of Joel is to explain the cataclysmic plague of locusts (Joel 1:2-4).[9] The Deuteronomic curses warned that a locust invasion was discipline for covenant violation (Deut 28:38-42). This covenant curse is treated as a token anticipating a greater Day of the LORD (Joel 1:15-18). The devastation of the locusts was further exacerbated by drought and fire (Joel 1:19-20). As a result, drunkards wept for the destruction of vines (Joel 1:5), priests mourned because there were no animals to sacrifice (Joel 1:9), and farmers despaired (Joel 1:11). Therefore, the nation needed to repent (Joel 1:13-14).

---

[6] Kaiser, *The Promise-Plan of God*, p. 193.

[7] Although the dating of Joel is highly debated, it seems that the traditional ninth century date should be affirmed.

[8] Walter Kaiser advances plausible reasons for an early date: (1) the location of the book in the Hebrew canon; (2) Judah's foes mentioned among the nations are neighboring regions; (Joel 3:4); (3) over half of the seventy-three verses in the book are quoted elsewhere in the prophets; (4) the book mentions no events that can be dated to a time when the house of God still remains, and the locust plague has affected the land (*Ibid.*, p. 158).

[9] *Ibid.*

The Day of the LORD

A watchman warns that the Day of the LORD is near (Joel 2:1). The sense of *near* is not clarified in chronological terms. Rather, the covenant discipline may alone anticipate a covenant judgment for that generation.

The day promises to be dark, gloomy, and destructive for the nation (Joel 2:2). The prophet describes it as an invading army or as a consuming wall of fire (Joel 2:3-5). The effect it would have on the people would be terrifying (Joel 2:6-9). It even extended to dramatic signs in the heavens, indicating the LORD directing His army (Joel 2:10-11). In climax, the prophet asked a rhetorical question: "who can endure it?" (Joel 2:11).

The implied answer that no one could endure leads the prophet to urge the people to return wholeheartedly to the LORD (Joel 2:12-14). The reason for even making the appeal rests in the LORD's characteristic attributes of grace and mercy, slowness to anger, and steadfast love. Moses had learned this when the Mosaic Covenant was first renewed (Exod 34:6-7). Another reason for the appeal involved the possibility that God would relent.[10] This possibility alluded to Moses' original intercession for the nation when they made the golden calf (Exod 32:14). In response to Moses' intercessory prayer, God relented from the proposed extinction of the nation.

The appeal to return (Joel 2:12-14) does not suggest that the Day of the LORD would be postponed, but that a blessing would be left for the remnant who survived (Joel 2:14, 17). This call to return is the *turning point* in the chapter.

Joel then calls for a solemn assembly of the people in Zion to fast and pray (2:15-17).

The prophet announces the LORD's response in blessing their land so that the people will be known as the LORD's people (Joel 2:18-27). Then, "afterward...I will pour out my Spirit on all flesh" (Joel 2:28). The question is: after what?[11]

---

[10] H. J. Fabry, "נחם, *nāḥam*," TDOT, vol. 9, pp. 342-52. The term refers to "an alteration of Yahweh's decision." This concept will appear frequently in the prophets.

[11] Robert Chisholm contends, "The Lord moved beyond the immediate future and announced that sometime after the restoration of blessing depicted in verses 19-27 he would pour out his Spirit upon the covenant community (vv. 28-29)" (Robert B. Chisholm, Jr., *Handbook on the Prophets* [Grand Rapids, MI: Baker Academic, 2002], pp. 371-72). While textually this is possible, the appropriateness of blessing the land in the near future before the people are blessed makes this interpretation implausible. Kaiser proposes: "The time set for the outpouring of the Spirit was left indefinite, 'after this' (*'aḥ'rêkēn*). Of course, the 'after this' could refer back to 2:23b, where the former and latter rains would come 'as before' (*bāri'šôn*); then somewhat later 'after this' would the Spirit be poured out." (Kaiser, *The Promise-Plan of God*,

If the focus of attention in the announcement of the Day of the LORD is on the people to whom the warning comes (Joel 2), who are called to return (Joel 2:12-14) and to pray (Joel 2:15-17), then the ultimate blessing of the gift of the Spirit comes *after the people return and repent*. It is to "everyone who calls on the name of the LORD" (Joel 2:32a). It is also "those who escape, as the LORD has said, and among the survivors shall be those whom the LORD calls" (Joel 2:32b). "This expression [remnant] represents a stereotypical formula with an indefinite subject in the sense of 'one left over/remaining.'"[12] Thus, the remnant involves those who call on the LORD, those who are called by the LORD among the people who would face the coming Day of the LORD. After the Day of Judgment has passed, those left over will be blessed.

However, the scope of the Day of the LORD not only concerns Israel but also Gentiles (Joel 3:1-16). In particular, the nations are only included when the fortunes of Judah and Jerusalem would be restored (3:1). Then the nations are called to the Valley of Jehoshaphat and the LORD will enter judgment against the nations on behalf of His people (Joel 3:2-3). Within this scope of Gentile judgment, the LORD would now be a refuge for His people (Joel 3:16-21). This passage has become a "classic passage for the rest of the Old Testament on God's final judgment on all nations."[13]

Amos: Eighth Century BC

Amos, a shepherd and a farmer from Judah, spoke on the LORD's behalf against Israel. Having disassociated itself from Jerusalem, Israel was now stung by the words from Judah.

Against the Nations

In Amos's first recorded prophecies, it might have sounded like he was supporting Israel's national optimism.

> He announced that the Lord was coming to judge the surrounding nations. The litany of judgment starts with outright foreigners (the Arameans, Philistines, Phoenicians), moves to

---

p. 159). He ultimately settled for Peter's interpretation "I will pour out my Spirit, in those days" (Joel 2:29) as having an eschatological fulfillment. However, this fails to explain when 2:18-27 would appear in history.

[12] B. Kedar-Kopfstein, "סרף, *śārap*," TDOT, vol. 14, p. 217.

[13] Kaiser, *The Promise-Plan of God*, p. 161.

distant relatives (the Edomites, Ammonites, and Moabites) and appears to culminate with Judah.[14]

The people may well have agreed with the first seven judgments. The number seven may have even implied that God's judgment of the nations was completed.

Unexpectedly, he added an eighth judgment oracle aimed at Israel. All eight oracles were introduced with the phrase, "for three transgressions and for four." In the first seven oracles, two examples of transgressions were included, but for Israel, seven transgressions are listed. Judgment on Israel was deserved and inevitable in covenantal terms.

Against Israel

The pronouncement of deportation into captivity, forty years in advance of the judgment (722 BC) was consistent with the LORD's policy to do nothing without first "revealing his secret" (Amos 3:7). Now, the Lion roars, who can not fear (Amos 3:8; Joel 3:16)? As Amos speaks, the roar shouts out from Judah to scorch all the landscape in its hearing. Seven rhetorical questions invite the reader to recognize the justification for such judgments (Amos 3:2-6). "Israel would not be 'rescued' from the coming judgment: only a ripped and shredded remnant would be 'salvaged'"[15] An unnamed adversary prepares to surround and invade Israel.

Restoration of Jerusalem

Yet, in that day of future destruction, the fallen house of David will be restored (Amos 9:11-12). The decapitated condition of David's house at the time of Amos did not mean that it had no future. Rather, in some future day, it will be repaired and restored as in the days of old.

Thus, the future of the ten tribes of Israel would depend on the restoration of the Davidic Kingdom. Election of the descendants of Abraham involved the whole nation of twelve tribes of Jacob. In addition, Edomites, known as distinct ethnically and nationally, will share in God's restoration of David's reign and prosperity. Kaiser notes:

> [The condition of the Davidic reign] surprisingly did not cast
> Edom in the role of being vanquished by David's or Israel's

---

[14]   Chisholm, *Handbook on the Prophets*, p. 378.

[15]   *Ibid.*, p. 387.

military machine; rather it speaks of its spiritual incorporation into the restored kingdom of David along with all those Gentiles who were likewise "called by his name."[16]

Hosea: Eighth Century BC

Hosea alone, of the early writing prophets, both lived and prophesied in the Northern Kingdom of Israel. He identified his ministry with Jeroboam II during the period of expansion and prosperity and mentioned four kings in Judah who remained under the covenant of mercy (Hos 1:7). This message of Hosea will specify in no uncertain terms the covenant status of Israel,[17] already symbolized in Elijah's translation.

Hosea's Married Life

Living in Israel, Hosea's personal life with Gomer, his wife, illustrates the LORD's covenant partnership with the house of Israel (Hosea 1, 3). That is then reinforced with a legal charge of covenant unfaithfulness to the LORD directed against the house of Israel. That is concluded by the day of redemption (Hosea 2) based on the LORD's promise in the Abrahamic Covenant.

Hosea took Gomer as his wife because God had commanded him to take a "promiscuous wife" (Hos 1:2, HCSB).[18] "Hosea was to select a woman who was recognizable as a harlotrous...A common prostitute would satisfy the public symbolism, but not as eloquently as one whose sexual promiscuity was a matter of the very harlotry of Israel in the cult of Baal."[19]

While Gomer was married to Hosea, she bore three children. That marriage looked back to Mt. Sinai when all the people affirmed: "all that the LORD has spoken we will do" (Exod 19:8; cf. 24:3, 7). This was

---

[16] Kaiser, *The Promise Plan of God*, p. 166.

[17] James Luther Mays, *Hosea: A Commentary*, The Old Testament Library (Philadelphia: Westminster Press, 1969). This treatment will guide the presentation in this text.

[18] There is debate whether that describes her status at the time of marriage to Hosea, or anticipates that Gomer would become an unfaithful wife. While the anticipation would certainly be true, the description in the present also seems correct. That better explains the children of unfaithfulness (Hos 1:2) born to Hosea and Gomer. In the historical analogy, it would describe the people in the wilderness journey leaving Egypt (Exodus 16–18) and the lack of mention of spiritual experiences in Egypt (Exodus 1–11).

[19] Mays, *Hosea*, p. 26.

Israel's vow. Now, some eight hundred years into this partnership, the house of Israel gave birth to offspring whose behavior reflected their loyalty to the LORD.

> In Jeroboam's kingdom the long process of syncretism had reached a culmination in which the worship and understanding of Yahweh had been Canaanized and there was outright practice of the Baal cult. Baals were adored as deities of the land at state shrines [Dan and Bethel] and local high places ([Hos] 2.13, 17; 9.10; 11.2; 13.1).[20]

The consequences of their unfaithfulness to the Mosaic Covenant partnership with the LORD were expressed in Hosea's children's names. They had not been what the LORD had Called them to be; they were not a holy people, nor were they mediating blessings to the nations, nor were they His valued possession (Exod 19:5-6). "Yahweh is known through his acts for Israel and his declaration of his will for them. Israel is defined, identified, and judged in the context of those deeds and instructions."[21] So in their disobedience, the LORD is known by what He does to bring judgment. Interestingly, Israel served to display God's glory in her disobedience, just as she would have in obedience.

The first offspring of the LORD's partnership with the house of Israel was expressed in the name of the firstborn son, *Jezreel*, "God sows" (Hos 1:4).

The product was judgment, both of the kingship, independent from the house of David, and of the people. They will be deported from the land by a nation from the north, Assyria.

The second child, *Lo-ruhamah*, "no mercy," speaks of cessation of covenant mercy (Exod 34:6). The LORD had revealed to Moses that the Mosaic Covenant would survive because God would be merciful and gracious, slow to anger. This name harkened back to Israel's original rebellion (Exod 34:5, 7) even as the Day of the LORD had. Now in the Northern Kingdom, after some two hundred years of continual covenant violations, that mercy would no longer be available. However, that mercy would continue with the house of Judah (Hos 1:7).

---

[20] *Ibid.*, p. 11.

[21] *Ibid.*, p. 7.

The final consequence of the violation of their partnership with the LORD was named *Lo-ammi*, "Not My People" (Hos 1:9).

> "My people" (*'ammî*) is an expression drawn from the vocabulary of Yahweh's covenant with Israel. The basic relational formula which describes the covenant founded at Sinai is: "You are my people, and I am your God" (cf. Ex. 6.7; Lev. 26.12; Deut. 26.17ff.; II Sam. 7.24; Jer. 7.23; 11.4; etc.). The name and the sentence which interprets it is an outright declaration by Yahweh that the covenant is no longer *in force*.[22]

The Mosaic Covenant had been voided for that generation as the translation of Elijah symbolized, but the intent of the covenant arrangement remained unfulfilled.

The next oracle (Hos 1:10-11) announced a future reversal of the judgment so that the Abrahamic Covenant will be fulfilled. The Mosaic Covenant will be replaced by an arrangement in which "the children of Judah and the children of Israel shall be gathered together, and they shall appoint for themselves one head" (Hos 1:11). "It is in Jezreel that disaster comes…Appropriately, it will be a great victory at Jezreel."[23]

The change in Israel's status with God is so spectacular that one illustration with a prophetic oracle is not enough. A collage of oracles is added to review the change: Israel's unfaithfulness demands judgment (Hos 2:2-13), and the LORD's mercy revisits Israel to restore the nation (Hos 2:14-23). Then the illustration is completed to match the change as Hosea remarries Gomer (Hosea 3).

The consequences of Israel's unfaithfulness are portrayed in images of law, marriage, and romance. The introductory speech "begins with a call to the Israelites to bring charges against (*rîḇ*) their mother, 'for she is not my wife and I am not her husband.' There follows a long indictment charging unfaithfulness"[24] (Hos 2:2-13). That case will be the governing image to carry the message for the second half of the book (Hosea 4:1–14:9). The use of this legal image is striking because it declares that a "declaration of divorce"[25] has been filed and Israel ceases to exist as a nation in covenant relation to the LORD.

---

[22]   *Ibid.*, p. 129.

[23]   *Ibid.*, p. 32.

[24]   H. Ringgren, "רִיב, *rib*," TDOT, vol. 13, p. 477.

[25]   Mays, *Hosea*, pp. 37-38.

However, based on the LORD's election of the offspring of Abraham, the LORD's mercy in that day will restore their national identity. The same images reappear, as a Covenant of Peace (Hos 2:18 and Ezek 34:25) will be ratified and the LORD will allure Israel, speaking "tenderly to her" in the desolate state of the people's exile (Hos 2:14). The betrothal will last forever as the collective people will know the LORD (Hos 2:19-20).

Hosea's Prophetic Ministry

Again we find a loose anthology of speeches collected which present God's case against the residents of the land (Hosea 4:1–14:9). This case is directed to the house of Israel, but at times includes Judah.

> When Hosea uses normative terms to specify what is demanded of Israel, he bypasses *righteousness* and *justice* emphasized by Amos and Isaiah...in favour of *knowledge of God, devotion,* and *faithfulness* (4.1; 6.4, 6; 12.6)...In his vocabulary [these] are the qualities of living in relation demanded by Yahweh. It is this breakdown at the personal level which grieves the prophet most.[26]

This relationship in Israel's case involves covenant partnership.

"Each of the three charges in 4:1 was then taken up in reverse order, and each section closed with a bright picture of a better future when God's love would break through the barrier of Israel's persistent sin."[27]

No Knowledge of God (Hosea 4:1–5:15; 6:1-3)

"'Not to know Yahweh' appears in combination with parallel verbs as a way of expressing apostasy and religio-ethical decline."[28] To know expresses a relationship. Life is shared in a personal relationship in which the other person is known at some depth. Thus, to swear, to lie, to murder, to steal, to commit adultery (Hos 4:2; Exod 20:13-17), is not to know the LORD in these behaviors. Hosea specifically charges that the people do not know God (Hos 4:6; 5:4). And the charge is first directed at the priest, who supposedly represents Israel before the LORD (Hos 4:4-5).

---

[26] *Ibid.*, pp. 12-13.

[27] Kaiser, *Promise*, p. 169.

[28] G. J. Botterwick, "עַדָּ, *yāda* '," TDOT, vol. 5, p. 469.

This break in relationship would continue until the people confess their guilt and seek the LORD (Hos 5:15). The prophet speaks of such a return to the LORD (6:1). Then Israel can progress to know the LORD (Hos 6:3).

No Steadfast Love (Hosea 6:4–10:15; 11:1-11)

The components of meaning involved in *hesed* are not common to any single English translation. Zobel[29] proposes three components. (1) It is *active in preserving and promoting life; goodness, grace, kindness, love.* (2) it is *social* in belonging to a community including God and others. (3) It is enduring and reliable. Thus, Hosea indicts the whole nation (Ephraim and Judah). "Your loyal-love is like a morning mist…like dew that vanishes" (Hos 6:4, author's translation). As a consequence, Hosea announced that the house of Israel was to be exiled into captivity. From a historical perspective, the prophet identified Assyria as the invading enemy. It seems strange when he says that they would be exiled in Egypt (Hos 7:16; 8:13; 9:3), but that is specifically where they had come from theologically. Spiritually, they are returning to where they began. Ephraim as a whole is not a redeemed people. They are no longer a covenant people. When Israel would be redeemed, they would need a second exodus.

So when the restoration would be considered, (Hos 11:1-11), Hosea remembered their original call out of Egypt, "out of Egypt I called my son" (Hos 11:1). In the wilderness they resisted, yet the LORD taught them to walk even as they were about to enter the land (Hos 11:2-4). They won't return geographically to Egypt, but will go to Assyria, because they refuse to return to the LORD (Hos 11:5). The Holy One must execute wrath, but God's heart recoils because He must judge (Hos 11:8-9). In time, the LORD will roar like a lion and the people "shall come trembling…from Egypt, and like doves from…Assyria" (Hos 11:10-11).

Israel will return to captivity because they are losing their inheritance. Israel, as God's son, is God's heir. In a later interpretation (Matt 2:15), Jesus is Israel's representative Heir who will fulfill Israel's exodus when He departs from Egypt to eventually receive the promised inheritance from the Father (Acts 2:33). In time, Israel will receive the Son to share His inheritance.

---

[29] H. J. Zobel, "חֶסֶד, *hesed*," TDOT, vol. 5, pp. 46-64.

No Truth (Hosea 11:12–13:16; 14:1-9)

Israel's departure from the temple in Jerusalem doomed them as separated from their principle source of truth. Ephraim was surrounded by lies ("Behold your gods," 1 Kgs 12:28) while Judah still walked with God (Hos 11:12) in their midst. While there is a distinction in their daily access to truth, both Judah and Jacob are indicted because of their ways and their deeds (Hos 12:2ff.), which reflect the falsehoods they appropriated. Both appropriated lies in the way they lived.

Eventually, the LORD will call them to return and then they will realize that Assyria cannot save them (Hos 14:1, 3). The wise will discern that the ways of the LORD are right (Hos 14:9).

CHAPTER 13: DIVIDED THEOCRATIC KINGDOM, PART 2: THE SOUTHERN KINGDOM (FIRST KINGS 11–SECOND KINGS 25)

Introduction

The story of the Southern Kingdom features the unfolding of the Davidic Covenant. Twenty descendants are heirs of Solomon until captivity when the throne of David will be no longer occupied. To many in Judah, captivity could not happen if the terms of the covenant hold true (2 Sam 7:11-16). Thus, two questions come to mind. First, what does the LORD guarantee? Second, what is contingent upon the king's response? Four principles have been constructed comparing the nature of divine revelation and the unfolding events of history.

First, the Davidic Covenant is being fulfilled because there is a descendant of David chosen in each generation and he reigns on David's throne, yet the covenant is not entirely fulfilled.

There are four features which the LORD guarantees.

1. A natural descendant of David would be chosen by God in each generation.
2. There would be an anointing by a prophet
3. The king would assume the throne responsibilities to reign as the people enthroned him.
4. The throne of his kingdom would be established forever.

In each generation, for twenty descendants, the covenant was being fulfilled when the descendants assumed the throne. Generation after generation, king after king, there was a historical fulfillment for that generation.

But no individual king, nor the combination of the twenty, fulfilled the covenant because the scope was to be forever. Death marked the end for each descendant and another descendant would need to follow.

Second, within the unstated latitude that the covenant allowed, the foolishness and rebellion of individual kings had destructive consequences on the kingdom, yet without abrogating the Davidic dynasty.

The Kings of Judah

When the kings of Judah are compared with the kings of Israel, there is far more stability in Judah. The Southern Kingdom lasted some 350 years with twenty kings. The Northern Kingdom lasted only about 200 years with twenty-one kings. In the South, there was one dynasty while in the North, there were nine dynasties. That stability, under essentially the same international conditions, is best explained by the stability that the LORD established in the Davidic Covenant.

Within what God guaranteed, there was latitude for considerable diversity among the kings. The prophetic author of Kings evaluated each king against the standard of David's response to the Mosaic Law. Hezekiah and Josiah were assessed as reigning righteously without any mention of direct disobedience to the Law. Six kings received a qualified approval of their rule. There was some good and some evil and twelve were assessed as evil.

Jehoshaphat is an example of one who received a qualified approval. Positively, he removed shrine prostitutes (1 Kgs 22:43, 46), but negatively, he did not remove the high places (1 Kgs 22:43). Foolishly, he formed a marriage alliance with the house of Ahab as his son Jehoram married Athaliah, Ahab's daughter (2 Kgs 8:16-18). Athaliah nearly destroyed the Davidic house. Jehoram introduced the depraved religions of the house of Omri into Judah.

As revenge for Jehu's slaughter of her Baal-worshiping son, Ahaziah, Athaliah determined to kill off the house of David (2 Kgs 11:1). She succeeded in killing all but the infant Joash. Jehosheba, Ahaziah's half-sister, stole Joash and had him provided for and protected. When Joash was six or seven years old, Jehoiada the priest had Athaliah killed and had Joash anointed to be king (2 Kgs 11:7-20; 2 Chr 23:1-15). The Davidic line survived even though an heir was not on the throne without interruption. Sovereignly, God used individuals who actively sought to honor His will. He also assured that a chosen heir would exist without interruption.

Third, kings were responsible for *how* they ruled as recognized in the prophetic assessment, yet no matter how well they ruled, no king fulfilled the covenant.

Hezekiah was recognized as doing what was right before God (2 Kgs 18:3). The international context of Assyrian domination formed the issues of his reign. He began his reign in coregency with Ahaz, his father, (729 BC) and became the sole king in 715 B.C. In his fourteenth year on the throne (701 BC), Assyria besieged Jerusalem and demanded a complete surrender. After Hezekiah failed in an attempt to buy off his attacker, at the aqueduct of the Upper Pool (Isa 7:3), the commander demanded of Hezekiah: "What are you relying on?" (2 Kgs 18:19, HCSB). This issue would characterize his reign. The commander dismissed any options; Egypt was powerless (2 Kgs 18:19-21), his own army was powerless (2 Kgs 18:23-25), he had undermined the worship of the LORD (2 Kgs 18:22), and Assyria claimed the LORD had sent them (2 Kgs 18:25). He turned to the people, listening on the wall, and challenged their faith. Hezekiah, with Isaiah's support, withstood the pressure of Assyrian propaganda and waited on the LORD. The Angel of the LORD killed 185,000 Assyrians (2 Kgs 19:35-36) and Assyria withdrew.

Two years later, Isaiah had predicted that Hezekiah would die (2 Kgs 20:1). However, Hezekiah prayed to be healed, reminding God of his walk before Him (2 Kgs 20:2-3). Isaiah returned with the LORD's answer; He had heard his prayer and added fifteen years to his life (2 Kgs 20:4-7). Further, Isaiah prescribed a poultice to heal his boil. Some seven hundred years later, a Davidic Heir would accept premature death as the LORD's will and fully satisfy the Mosaic Covenant on behalf of all mankind. The Davidic Covenant would be fulfilled through Jesus' resurrection and return to reign.

Following Hezekiah's healing, the king of Babylon sent a gift to induce him to rebel against Assyria. In pride, Hezekiah showed him his armory and his treasures as a support for any alliance (2 Kgs 20:12-14). As a result, Isaiah prophesied the Babylonian exile, taking captive the wealth he displayed (2 Kgs 20:15-19). Later Isaiah prophesied the total destruction of Jerusalem (2 Kgs 21:10-15). While Hezekiah did what was right before the LORD, his pride drove the nation into captivity.

Josiah, the son of the wicked King Manasseh, like Hezekiah, did what was right and was approved by the LORD (2 Kgs 22:1-2). He was a true son of David as he "walked in all the way of David his father, and he did not turn aside to the right or to the left" (2 Kgs 22:2).

During the fifty-five year reign of his father, Manasseh, the Law had been lost in the decay and neglect of the temple. This would become the issue that defined Josiah's reign. Ten years after it began, the Book of the Law was found as the workmen repaired the temple (2 Kgs 22:8-10). Josiah repented when he heard what the Law demanded. He had the priest inquire what the LORD would demand of them. Huldah, the prophetess, predicted that the LORD would bring disaster on the temple and the inhabitants of Jerusalem as the Law required (2 Kgs 22:14-16). Manasseh's pagan ways demanded judgment (2 Kgs 22:17a), but because of Josiah's repentance, this judgment would be delayed (2 Kgs 22:18-20).

Josiah then initiated reforms and gathered the people to renew the covenant. This covenant renewal was patterned after Joshua's generation, a generation called to take the covenant oath. In addition, Josiah destroyed the Baal worship that had been in the temple (2 Kgs 23:4-14), destroyed the altars and worship at Dan and Bethel (2 Kgs 23:15-20), and rid the land of mediums and spiritists (2 Kgs 23:24). As far as reformers were concerned, "[b]efore him there was no king like him…nor did any like him arise after him" (2 Kgs 23:25). "Still the LORD did not turn from the burning of his great wrath, by which his anger was kindled against Judah, because of all the provocations with which Manasseh had provoked him" (2 Kgs 23:26). Thus, the Davidic Covenant was not fulfilled, in spite of the spectacular reformation. And Josiah was killed in battle at Megiddo, by the Egyptians and Pharaoh Neco. It was a battle that Josiah probably initiated for political reasons.

Fourth, while the covenant guaranteed that a descendant of David would be chosen in every generation, it does not guarantee that any particular chosen descendant would be established on the throne.

The final years in the collapse of the kingdom of Judah were chaotic at the least. Jehoiachin had not been on the throne for more than six months when he joined Ezekiel and was taken captive to Babylon (597 BC). The prophetic account uncovered the hope that the Davidic Covenant sponsored. Although Jehoiachin was not on the throne in Jerusalem, he was chosen by the LORD and was given a seat of honor in Babylon, higher than any of the other captive kings (2 Kgs 25:27-30). The Davidic Covenant was recognized by a pagan king, even though its future seemed uncertain. Matthew records the descendants of David, chosen in each generation, who were never enthroned (Matt 1:12-16). This line of heirs preceded Joseph who adopted Jesus, Son of Mary.

Isaiah: Seventh Century BC

Commentators agree that "[t]he preaching of Isaiah represents the theological high water mark of the whole Old Testament."[1] Within the canon of Scripture, Isaiah addressed basic, as of yet unresolved, theological tensions. In history, he delivered oracles following the death of Uzziah, the king of Judah, in that uncertain time. In the interpretation of his message, both the literary and the historical contexts will be considered.

Isaiah's Ministry

Isaiah's call to ministry is recounted in Isaiah 6. The question of the historical location of the call finds diverse answers.[2] What is clear historically is that it came after the death of King Uzziah, which caused suspense in the nation. Literarily, it follows an introduction which Ewald called, "the grand arraignment."[3] More recently, it has been identified as a covenant lawsuit[4] which, in literary form, Isaiah shares in common with other prophets. Thus, the call of Isaiah came not only in politically uncertain times but in a context of established national guilt. At the same time, Jerusalem would have a future (Isa 2:1-4; 4:2-6).

> This schema [chapters 2–5] would correspond well with the thought of ch. 1 and indeed the whole book: proud, self-sufficient Israel can become the witness to the greatness of God only when she has been reduced to helplessness by his just judgment and then restored to life by his unmerited grace.[5]

In his call, Isaiah saw the LORD enthroned as an absolute King of all creation. In His glory, Seraphim praised Him as holy, holy, holy. This is the essence of the *theocracy* as the LORD is seated on His universal throne. But in the year King Uzziah died, it also concerned the *monarchy* and the *mediated* reign of the LORD through the throne in Jerusalem. Isaiah's response was personal and noted his own lack of purity to communicate the message of a holy God.

---

[1]   Von Rad, *Old Testament Theology*, vol. 2, p. 147.

[2]   See John N. Oswalt *The Book of Isaiah: Chaps. 1–39*, NICOT (Grand Rapids, MI: Eerdmans, 1986), pp. 171-76.

[3]   See Georg Heinrich August von Ewald, *Prophets of the Old Testament*, 5 vols. J. F. Smith, trans. (London: Williams and Norgate, 1875–1881).

[4]   See Herbert B. Huffmon, "The Covenant Lawsuit in the Prophets," *Journal of Biblical Literature* 78 (1959): 288-95.

[5]   Oswalt, *Isaiah 1–39*, p. 113.

After his lips were cleansed, he was commissioned to a ministry of hardening to result in Israel's judgment. "Jahweh himself was to bring about Israel's downfall, his conception of the creative word of Jahweh (Is. IX. 7 [8]), and, finally, his concept of Jahweh's 'work,' [spoke of] the far-reaching nature of God's designs in history."[6] His ministry will both *display* God's dazzling glory and *harden* people in the face of that glory.

Featured in his ministry will be a message to clarify the grandeur of the LORD's ways in governing history, which would be rejected and not understood. Individuals would view the LORD's glory as a challenge to the independence of their ways. King Ahaz and King Hezekiah illustrate this in Isaiah's ministry.

Israel had grown to oppose God's ways and to be in conflict with God's will. These theological conflicts had remained unaddressed in Jerusalem. Oswalt identifies three issues to be considered.[7]

First, the Creator had allowed man to fall in sin. As a result, God's creation *goal* remained unrealized. In view of man's repeated failures, and Israel with all its blessings having failed, what would happen to God's creation goal?

Second, the LORD chose Israel to become a priestly nation among the nations, yet Israel had sought to become like the other nations. Was the LORD about to reverse His choice and replace Israel?

Third, the LORD had given Israel a king, yet the kings were no better than the people. Was God about to admit failure in the Davidic Covenant? Such an admission would imply that God was unable to keep His guarantee in the face of conflict with evil and the enemy. It seemed as though many of the people and kings of Judah were acting as offspring of the enemy (Gen 3:15). Was God incapable of keeping His plan and meeting His goal?

Isaiah's Message

Isaiah's message points to the glorious, universal sovereignty of God in history. There are decisive and clear answers to the questions just raised. The answers are both expected and perhaps unexpected. As we would expect, the opposition will be judged. And the scope of that judgment will include the nations, starting with Israel, but will extend to the enemy. As

---

6   Von Rad, *Old Testament Theology*, vol. 2, pp. 154.

7   Oswalt, *Isaiah 1–39*, pp. 54-60. (These will be adapted in our model.)

one perhaps may not expect, the Promised One,[8] first introduced as the descendant of the woman (Gen 3:15), will also be a descendant of David. And in the Promised One, God will unite with humanity to become the solution. The answers are reflective of God's holiness, both righteous and gracious, truthful and loving.

Judgment of All Who Oppose

The Nations

This began with Jerusalem and Judah. The covenant lawsuit laid the foundation (Isaiah 1–5). Isaiah's ministry of hardening will help to precipitate guilt in the nation (Isaiah 6). An oracle concerning Jerusalem joins with the messages against the other nations (Isaiah 22). And the nations in immediate proximity to Judah are enumerated nation by nation (Isaiah 13–23). So the descendants of the serpent will be judged (Gen 3:15).

The Enemy

While the interpretation of God's ultimate enemy has been debated in Isaiah, the mention of "the fleeing serpent" and "the twisting serpent" (Isa 27:1) seems to be an intended and clear allusion to Gen 3:15. This figure seems to appear twice in the judgment oracles.

Isaiah 14:12-15

This passage has already been considered in the interpretation of Gen 1:1-2. The issue in Isaiah concerns how the prophet addressed the king of Babylon. The church fathers first proposed that the one expressing rebellion was Lucifer. The Reformers contended that this was simply a reference to the historical king. The two proposed interpretations can be combined if the historic king was addressed metaphorically.

The historic king is addressed as a rebel, but the terms of the rebellion were first expressed by a prototype rebel, the enemy of God. That rebellion is described in the language of an ANE myth.[9] But the Biblical account of creation is radically different from the Canaanite myth of creation. In the myth, the conflict is in creation while the Biblical account

---

[8] See Kaiser, *The Promise-Plan of God.*

[9] "[W]ith the discovery of the Ugaritic texts, the evidence mounted for seeing a far closer parallel with Canaanite mythology...The most plausible reconstruction is of *Helel's* challenge to the power of Elyon who, when thwarted, was thrown down to Sheol. The myth depicts a cosmic battle between Helel and Elyon in the brilliant rise of the morning star in the heavens and its sudden dimming before the strengthening rays of the sun" (Childs, *Isaiah*, p. 126).

portrays a sovereign, Almighty God in complete control of creation. Such an account presupposes control over rebellion. Genesis 1:2 implies that a prior judgment of rebellion had occurred which was now followed by a good creation. Thus, the enemy of God had been defeated although not eliminated (Genesis 3). The Biblical account states that this enemy will be overcome and will be defeated in judgment. While not specifying the enemy as primordial, Oswalt recognizes the conflict in general terms. "Ultimately, the battle is between Creator and creatures, and the issue is whether we will accord him the right due him as Creator and bow to him in glad service or will continue to insist that we are as he is."[10]

Isaiah 27:1

At the climax of the same section of judgment of historic nations is a distinct section often called, "The Little Apocalypse" (Isaiah 24–27). The section begins with a description of God's devastating worldwide judgment (Isa 24:1-3). The judgment falls because "they have transgressed the laws, violated the statutes, broken the everlasting covenant" (Isa 24:5). But what is that everlasting covenant to which all nations are responsible? Chisholm posits:

> Perhaps Isaiah's language is intentionally ambiguous and designed to encompass both Israel and the foreign nations. If so, then the 'everlasting covenant' is, from Israel's perspective, the Mosaic law...from the perspective of other nations, the 'everlasting covenant' is the Noahic mandate.
>
> However, it seems that one covenant is being spoken about. In addition, the Mosaic Covenant is not spoken of as "eternal." Rather, all nations, including Israel, are responsible for protection of human life and of ecology in the Noahic Covenant.[11]

At the conclusion of the section on national judgment (Isa 27:1), a more direct reference to God's ultimate enemy appears using both Biblical language (serpent) and mythological language (Leviathan). "So the language of myth could be bent to new purposes, as here, where Isaiah, in need of strong imagery to cap his vision of God's victory over sin, oppression, and death, seizes on the Leviathan story and makes it say something much more profound than it had ever said before."[12] While identification of the enemy was recognized by Gunkel from the creation tradition of Israel

---

[10]   Oswalt, *Isaiah 1–39*, p. 321.

[11]   Chisholm, *Handbook on the Prophets*, p. 66.

[12]   Oswalt, *Isaiah 1–39*, p. 491.

(serpent),[13] the Ugaritic texts clarified who the dragon was. "It recounted the battle of Baal, lord of the earth, to conquer the sea god, Yam, Lotan, and the seven-headed dragon."[14] Yet the battle Isaiah describes does not occur at creation as the battle of Baal did, but prior to creation as the Biblical account of creation suggests. That early defeat is a precursor to the climactic judgment.

Blessing through the Promised One

The Promised One had been introduced when God introduced the *plan* of the judgment verdict (Gen 3:15). Now an Individual will be introduced who will have a definitive role in reaching God's *goal* and completing God's *plan*. And this Individual will be introduced in relation to the Davidic Kings, Ahaz and Hezekiah.

Ahaz and Immanuel

The house of David in Jerusalem faced a crisis from a pending invasion from Syria and Israel (Isa 7:2). That caused Ahaz, the Davidic king, and the people of Jerusalem to fear for the survival of the house of David. The LORD told Isaiah to take Shearjashub to meet Ahaz, in his fear, at the end of the conduit of the upper pool (Isa 7:3). God disclosed the enemy's scheme and assured Ahaz that what he feared would not happen (Isa 7:4-7) because the source of their scheme was human (7:8). Then he warned the whole house of David[15] and Ahaz, as its current king, that faith in God's Word alone would keep Ahaz secure (Isa 7:9). That was immediately followed by the command, to Ahaz alone, to ask for a sign, a sign that God's Word was reliable, a sign that he had good reason to believe (Isa 7:10-11). Ahaz refused to comply, and in that, disobeyed (Isa 7:12). He was unwilling to believe no matter what his excuse. Ahaz tried the patience of Israel and God, seeking Assyria's help (Isa 7:13). In view of the warning (Isa 7:9), Ahaz would not stand secure (Isa 7:12). What would that mean? Would the invasion of Syria and Israel come in spite of the earlier word that said it would not?

---

[13] Hermann Gunkel, *The Legends of Genesis*, trans. W. H. Carruth (Chicago: Open Court Publishing Co., 1901).

[14] Childs, *Isaiah*, p. 197.

[15] *NET Bible*, p. 1238. "The verb forms are second plural; the Lord here addresses the entire Davidic family and court. (Verse 4 was addressed to the king.) There is a wordplay in the Hebrew text, designed to draw attention to the alternatives set before the king."

In view of Ahaz' unbelief, the LORD Himself promised a sign to the house of David (Isa 7:14).[16] The meaning of the promise includes an implication that Ahaz would not stand. It was a statement of promise concerning the birth of a son: "The virgin shall conceive and bear a son, and shall call his name Immanuel." Several things are noteworthy:

- The word 'almâ denotes a "virgin" in the Scriptures in every case in which its meaning can be determined.[17]

- It has a definite article, "the virgin," indicating an identifiable young woman, not an anonymous woman.

- The verb *to call* is second person feminine and not third person feminine, "you (virgin) shall call his name." The change from third person to second person makes the statement conform to older prophetic statements.[18]

- The young woman shall conceive as an 'almâ, not simply be identified as a virgin about to conceive at the time of this prophecy.

"[T]he *sign* given to Ahaz consisted in repeating to him the familiar phrases used in promising the birth of a son."[19] It was a promise similar to that given to Hagar (Gen 16:11) and to the wife of Manoah (Judg 13:5). In each case the mother's role is prominent and the father's role is disregarded. This is also a sign to the house of David that the line of David survives this pending crisis with Syria and Israel. For Ahaz, the conception of a virgin would set him aside and exclude him from fathering in the line of succession. It is in this sense that Ahaz would not stand secure, meaning he would be judged.

Who then was this child? He could not have been one of the sign-children born to Isaiah. Such a son would not concern the "house of David"

---

[16] Isaiah 7:14 is a well-known *crux interpretum*. The goal here will not be to survey the various approaches but rather to present the approach that we believe is the most compelling.

[17] Willis J. Beecher, "The Prophecy of the Virgin Mother," *Classical Evangelical Essays in Old Testament Interpretation*, ed. Walter C. Kaiser, Jr. (Grand Rapids, MI: Baker, 1972), p. 181. The use of 'almâ in Biblical texts often conveys or implies the ideas of virgin: the account of Rebekah (Gen 24:43), that of the sister of Moses (Exod 2:8), "the way of a man with a virgin" (Prov 30:19) and then a series of plurals (Ps 68:25; Song 1:3; 6:8; and 1 Chr 15:20) which are difficult to determine.

[18] "The phraseology of this verse is quoted from older phraseology...the statements made concerning the birth of Ishmael (Gen. 16:11), the birth of Isaac (Gen. 17:19), and that of Samson (Judg. 13:5, 7)" (Beecher, *The Prophecy of the Virgin Mother*, p. 181).

[19] Kaiser, *Promise*, p. 179, emphasis added.

(Isa 7:13) and its survival from the pending invasion.[20] He could not be Hezekiah, Ahaz' son, since he had been born five years earlier.[21]

The most direct piece of evidence is His name, Immanuel—God with us. In what sense is that His name? Does it mean in a miraculous sense? He is God with us because God has provided Him. That has been true of a number of sons of promise, like Isaac, Esau, Jacob, etc., but they were not named that. More naturally, the name reflects a personal sense. He is named God with us because God is personally present in Him. In addition, He is born of the virgin. He is the offspring of the woman (Gen 3:15). That would be a most remarkable work of God, given the unbelief of Ahaz. And if that is the point, then He would be the One through whom the Davidic Covenant would be fulfilled. He would be human as the Son of the virgin. God, who made the promise, would Father this Boy. He would be a divine/human Son.[22]

The Book of Immanuel

This conclusion about the identity of the Son (Isa 7:14) is supported by the development in the "Book of Immanuel"[23] in Isaiah 7–11.

Isaiah 9:6-7

This announcement oracle (9:1-7) features the birth of a son in the house of David (9:6-7). "The titles underscore the ultimate deity of this child-deliverer."[24] That is the issue in the identity of Immanuel. Two questions emerge. What is the evidence to support the conclusion that this Son is divine? And what indication is there that these oracles are intended to be read together?

The second question will be addressed first. All three passages (7:14; 9:6-7; 11:1-5) start with the question of origins. All three passages deal

---

[20] The improbability of this option is further emphasized by the absence of a persuasive argument of any one of his sign-sons. None fits the parameters of this sign-promise.

[21] Eugene H. Merrill, *Kingdom of Priests* (Grand Rapids, MI: Baker, 1987), pp. 404, 426, n. 102.

[22] How does this son satisfy the reference in Isa 7:15-16? Ephraim, as the people of Israel, would be broken in sixty-five years (Isa 7:8). But Pekah would be deposed much sooner as a result of Assyria's invasion of Syria (732 BC). To whom does Isa 7:15 refer? One possibility is Shear-Jashub, identified by gesture. Although this is not the natural grammatical antecedent, it does provide a reason for God commanding that he join his father. The other possibility is the future Messiah whose growth would not be observed but imagined, based on the natural growth process. This would conform to the imagined perspective of promise.

[23] C. F. Keil and F. Delitzsch, *Biblical Commentary on the Old Testament: The Prophecies of Isaiah*, James Martin, trans. (Grand Rapids, MI: Eerdmans, 1969), IV-VII; 2v.

[24] Oswalt, *Isaiah 1-39*, p. 246.

with the house of David and reigning, and the three passages read in
sequence deal with a progression: fact of Immanuel's birth, the demonstration of Immanuel by descriptive names, and ultimate fulfillment
of Immanuel described in reigning. "All of this points to a remarkable
congruence with the Immanuel prophecy. Somehow a virgin-born child
would demonstrate that God is with us."[25]

Isaiah 9:6 introduces titles that identify an ideal king. What evidence
do the titles provide that the Child is divine? These are truly extravagant
titles which argue for the saving character of His reign. In the ANE and
in Israel, such a name might be given at coronation or enthronement, but
not as a birth announcement as it is here.

"Mighty God" most directly refers to His being divine. This is a reference
to God. "Apart from the attempt to deny deity to the person in question,
however, there is no reason to depart from the traditional rendering."[26]

"Everlasting Father" also is unique.[27] Many kings in the ancient world
claimed to be fathers of the realm they ruled and even of their captives,
but such a claim only applied during their reign. It was not "everlasting."[28]

"Prince of Peace" speaks to a condition of a ruler of a realm producing peace. David never achieved this. Solomon experienced it before the
conclusion of his reign. But at the conclusion, division emerged in his
kingdom. This One will be greater than David. None of David's sons
found in First and Second Kings were able to live up to this title even
though the Davidic Covenant pointed to a fulfillment of this ideal (see
2 Sam 7:10-11).

Isaiah 11:1-16

"In 11:1–16 the Messianic hope which began to be expressed in 7:14 and
which was amplified in 8:23–9:5 (Eng. 9:1-6) comes to full flower. The
Messiah is not merely promised or announced but is depicted as ruling."[29]

---

[25] *Ibid.*, pp. 246-47.

[26] *Ibid.*, p. 247.

[27] As Gary Smith notes, "'Father' is a relatively rare way of describing God in the Hebrew Bible
(Deut 32:6; Jer 3:4,19; Isa 63:16; 64:7; Mal 2:10) and a rarer way of describing a king (1 Sam
24:12), though the Israelites are frequently called God's sons (Exod 4:22-23)" (Gary V.
Smith, *Isaiah 1–39*, New American Commentary, ed. E. Ray Clendenen [Nashville: B & H,
2007], p. 241).

[28] Interestingly, "'Everlasting' is a title that does not apply to any human ruler, except that
the Davidic promise speaks of one who will rule on the throne of David forever (2 Sam
7:16)" (*ibid.*).

[29] Oswalt, *Isaiah 1–39*, p. 277.

This oracle confirms what had been introduced as the reign of Immanuel is described:

11:1: the Davidic origin of this Ruler,

11:2, 3a: the Spirit endows Him to reign,

11:3b-5: the uncompromising justice of His reign,

11:6-9: the quality of peace which will characterize His rule,

11:10-11: in that day, the Root of Jesse will bring peace to the survivors from the nations.

These prophecies emerged in the context of Ahaz' reign and the Assyrian international influence. Ahaz, hardened in his unbelief, was disqualified from fulfilling the Davidic Covenant but that didn't discredit the promise of God. This Promised One is qualified (Isa 7:14) to rule (Isa 9:6-7) and will bring results of a kingdom of peace (Isa 11:1-11).

Hezekiah and the Servant

Hezekiah is the second king with whom Isaiah has a ministry explained in his book. Is that a ministry of hardening? At first, that does not seem to be the case (Isaiah 36–37), but the literary context (Isaiah 28–35) helps us to examine the complete account (Isaiah 38–39).

Isaiah's recorded sermons include a word to both Ephraim and Jerusalem (Isa 28:1, 14), although the primary message is to Jerusalem (Isaiah 29–35). A foundational issue is the LORD's promise to restore Jerusalem after the city has been judged. Jerusalem had made a covenant with death at the hand of Assyria (Isa 28:15). God had a different plan. He would lay "as a foundation in Zion, a stone, a tested stone, a precious cornerstone, of a sure foundation" (Isa 28:16). The only question is whether the stone is both a touchstone and a foundation stone[30] or only a tried foundation stone.[31] Regardless of which sense is intended, the *stone* either refers to Hezekiah[32] or Messiah. The subsequent passage clarifies which one.

Following the collection of sermons addressed to Jerusalem, there is a narrative account of Hezekiah's reign (Isaiah 36–39). The account involves three sections:

---

[30] Oswalt, *Isaiah 1–39*, pp. 517-18.

[31] M. Tsevat, "בָּחוֹן, *bāchôn*," TDOT, vol. 2, pp. 69-72.

[32] Israel W. Slotki, *Isaiah*, Soncino Books of the Bible, ed. A. Cohen (London: Soncino, 1961), p. 130.

First, Sennacherib invades Judah, and Hezekiah seeks Isaiah's help (36–37). The text relates Hezekiah's account to his father's treaty with Assyria. First, Rabshakeh meets Hezekiah "by the conduit of the upper pool on the highway to the Washer's Field" (Isa 36:2), which is the same location where Isaiah met his father (Isa 7:3). Second, both must deal with the same international power, Assyria. In response to Hezekiah's request, Isaiah promised that the LORD would remove Assyria (Isa 37:6-7). Even though it wasn't immediate, Hezekiah believed the LORD's Word (Isa 37:14-20) and experienced deliverance.

Second, Hezekiah became sick and Isaiah delivered the LORD's word that he would not recover (Isaiah 38). Under this trial, Hezekiah turned to the LORD in prayer. In the prayer, he reminded God of how he had lived, and he wept bitterly (Isa 38:2-3). God answered the prayer through Isaiah (Isa 38:4-6). Isaiah delivered two promises: "I will add fifteen years to your life," and, "I will deliver you…[from] Assyria."

Third, Hezekiah's recovery provided an occasion for the envoy from Babylon (Isaiah 39). The occasion exposed a degree of self-confidence as he warmly welcomed the envoy to show them all that was in his realm (Isa 39:2). Isaiah immediately challenged what he did (Isa 39:3). He prophesied that all this wealth would be carried to Babylon. What he treated as his own, God would remove (Isa 39:6). In reality, it was God's and not Hezekiah's wealth. Hezekiah took comfort since it wouldn't happen in his day.

Hezekiah was like a rock during Sennacherib's invasion. But when the warning of premature death came to him, he wilted under the personal threat. Therefore, would there be a descendant of David that would serve in God's plan (Isa 28:16)? There must be. But who is he? Was there any king that would serve the interests of others while he reigned? That question introduced in Hezekiah's reign will be answered in the final section of the book (Isaiah 40–66).

The Servant

Isaiah 40–66 explores the significance of the new situation into which Hezekiah's failure to wholeheartedly believe had brought Jerusalem and the house of Judah. It was the kind of failure that would ultimately precipitate the destruction of Jerusalem by the Babylonians.

Jerusalem, which had been chosen in David's day, and had been delivered from Assyria in Hezekiah's day, now would not be delivered from Babylon. This refocuses attention on the theological issues in Isaiah:

Was the Davidic Covenant now void?

Would Israel be replaced as the people of God?

Had evil in the human race finally defeated God?

Precisely what had been taught in Isaiah 1–39?

The Davidic Covenant would stand (Isa 7:14; 9:1-6; 11:1-11). Jerusalem would become the center of all nations (Isa 2:1-4; 4:2-5; 27:2-13; 33:1-24). Evil would not prevent God's plan of redemption from being accomplished (Isaiah 40–66). The last point required the remainder of Isaiah to provide the explanation. This explanation would raise a question that remained unanswered: how will this become a reality?

Isaiah 40:1-11

The overall prophetic message of 40–66 was introduced in a dramatic fashion. There was no stated transition between 1–39 and 40–66. The introductory word was a word of *comfort* which called out to "*My* people" from "*your* God" (Isa 40:1, emphasis added).

> Without question this is the language of the covenant (Exod. 6:7; 19:5; Lev. 26:12; Deut. 26:17-18; etc.). No more is it the scornful "this people" of 6:9 or 8:6. Whatever the breaches of covenant "this people" may have committed, and however grievous the punishments the nation will have suffered, the descendants of Abraham and Jacob need not fear that God will forget his promises to their ancestors.[33]

The climactic announcement is addressed to Jerusalem. "Her warfare is ended…[and] she has received…double for all her sins" (Isa 40:2). The future time about which this comfort speaks remains indefinite. Daniel, during the Babylonian captivity, would pray about the end of captivity (Dan 9:1-19). God's answer was that Israel's suffering wouldn't end with her seventy year captivity (Jer 25:11-12). Further, the length of time would be influenced by the nations' preparation to receive the coming of the LORD (Isa 40:3-5). It would be Israel's repentance that would prepare the people to be restored. However, no human force or condition could prevail against God's promise (Isa 40:6-8). The good news is that the LORD "comes with might and his arm rules for him" (Isa 40:10).

This prologue is then developed in two broad segments for the remainder of the book (Isaiah 40–55 and 56–66). In the first segment (Isaiah 40–55), "Isaiah assumes the perspective of the future exiles. Having

---

[33] Oswalt, *Isaiah 40–66*, p. 49. Oswalt's exegesis of Isaiah's message contributes in general to what this author understands the message to be. Thus, it will guide this development.

announced the exile, he projects himself into the future and speaks to the exiles as if actually present with them in captivity."[34] The segment may be divided into two perspectives on captivity: Isaiah 40–48: Babylonian captivity, and Isaiah 49–55: captivity in general. In the first perspective (Isaiah 40–48), the might of the LORD, and in the second, the arm of the LORD (Isaiah 49–55, cf. 53:1), are revealed.

The final segment of the book (Isaiah 56–66) features the servants of the nation rather than the Servant. It is a reminder that "along with the inability of humans to deliver themselves or to replicate the divine character, there is a countervailing emphasis on the divine ability to do what the human spirit cannot."[35] This is the dominant theme of the dispensation of law.

In *Cyrus*, king of Persia, the military might of the providential working of the LORD has been revealed (Isa 44:28; 45:1). This pagan king is conscripted by the LORD as His shepherd to restore the people from the Babylonian captivity to the land. Jerusalem shall be rebuilt and the foundation of the temple laid again.

In the *servant of the Lord*,[36] the arm of the LORD[37] will be revealed, who will redeem from the captivity of sin and its penalty.

---

[34]   Chisholm, *Handbook on the Prophets*, p. 92.

[35]   Oswalt, *Isaiah 40–66*, p. 11.

[36]   Beecher, Prophets and Promise, 263-88. Beecher's foundational study on the term *servant* provides the ground upon which our treatment will rest. The following is the summary of his argument:

  1. The term appears 31 Times in 40–66; twenty times in 40–55, always in the singular, and eleven in 56–66, always in the plural.

  2. One singular use is as an ordinary, common noun; twelve other singulars in the context are defined as denoting Israel.

  3. In all cases in which it is used in the plural, it denotes Israelites by adoption (e.g., 56:6).

  4. Israel the servant is therefore Israel regarded as the promise-people. From one point of view the servant is identical with the political aggregation known as Israel. On the other hand, Israel the servant and Israel the political aggregation are sometimes spoken of as separate, or even as having relationship with each other.

  5. There are passages in which the word *servant* is used or implied without an explicit contextual identification with Israel. If these passages represent the Servant to be a person different from Israel, and at times ministering to Israel, then this Servant is representative of Israel. According to Duhm, these uses are called Servant Songs and exhibit an atmospheric change in four passages: 42:1-9; 49:1-8; 50:4-9 and 52:13–53:12.

[37]   This figure portrays the activity of the agent of the LORD who is a distinct agent, fully sharing in the life of the Lord.

Isaiah 42:1-9

This Servant song clarifies the future ministry of the Davidic Covenant. In one sense, in the narrative of First and Second Kings, the covenant was being fulfilled, but as announced to Hezekiah it would be suspended while the people were in captivity. It had not been fulfilled in Hezekiah. And in captivity, it would not be in the process of fulfillment since no descendant of David would be enthroned. However, descendants would be born.

In Isa 42:1-9, God foretells how His beneficial order of justice (*mišpāṭ*) will come to rule over the earth. It is a prediction of the future, showing how God will rule mediatorially through His *Servant* over the world.

Then God calls His Servant to accomplish the fundamental task on behalf of both the people and the nations. Through that task, He will establish justice on earth (Isa 42:4). That task begins with the ratification (cutting) of "the covenant for the people" and their being given as "a light to the nations" (Isa 42:6).

The passage mentions several factors which describe the Servant pursuing the task. In pursuing the task, He is not self-promoting (Isa 42:2), He does not destroy anything in the process (Isa 42:3), and He perseveres until justice is established on earth (Isa 42:4). His task involves self-sacrifice.

The task arose from a righteous call (Isa 42:6a); it is in view of the unrighteous plight of the people and the nation. The call is to be a covenant given to the people. That covenant is distinct from the Mosaic Covenant which depended on the people's production of righteousness (Exod 24:3, 7) to be righteous.

The service in the task was impossible for the Servant to accomplish alone, and thus God would hold the Servant by the hand so that he would be kept until the task was completed (Isa 42:6b). In what sense is the Servant a covenant (Isa 42:6c)? The Servant's self-sacrifice would ratify or cut (*kārat*, 55:3) the covenant. The same self-sacrificial act enlightens the nations about what is necessary to bring life with God to fallen man.

Who then are the people?[38] In the promise (Isa 42:6), the people are compared to the nations. The language is similar to covenant language in Isa 40:1, in which the people refers to Israel. But the absence of the personal pronoun, *My*, indicates that unless they receive the covenant, the

---

[38]   Commentators tend to divide along theological lines; for most the Servant as an individual identifies *the people* as Israel, while those who take the Servant as Israel must identify *the people* as all nations.

people won't become "My people." So the people is Israel, given the Covenant, who, when they receive the Servant, become "My people," that is, they are saved. The nations are given the Servant as a light through whom they may be saved.

Isaiah 49:1, 50:4-9

Isaiah 49:1-9 quotes the Servant as the Person who speaks. While the language of prisoners (Isa 49:9) and of desolation (Isa 49:8) continues, neither Cyrus nor Babylon is mentioned again. The "Servant who speaks" expresses the dominant theme. The focus shifts from the physical captivity of the people to moral and spiritual captivity.

The voice of the Servant calls all mankind to listen. It was the LORD who called and molded the Servant, shaped His mouth to speak effectively, yet kept Him hidden until the time was right (Isa 49:1-2).

Then God spoke to the Servant and called Him Israel. It is through Him that God would be glorified after so many years of Israel's failure (Isa 49:3). Then, the Servant's voice spoke again. His labor had been in vain and His strength was spent, yet His confidence remained in the LORD (Isa 49:4). Then the LORD assured Him that He had been formed to bring Jacob back (Isa 49:5), even as Joseph had done so many years before. He is none other than the Servant, the Person who represents the servant people, Israel (Isa 49:5), so His service would qualify the nation to serve (Gen 12:3; Exod 19:5-6). In addition, as though that were too insignificant a task, He will be a light to the nations (Isa 49:6; restating 42:6). The LORD declared that the Redeemer of Israel, whom the people had deeply abhorred, would be worshiped by princes. That salvation will take place as the Servant is given as a covenant to the people: "to apportion the desolate heritages" to Israel (Isa 49:8).

Isaiah 50:4-9 is the testimony of the Servant's experience during His rejection which He endured while having intimate fellowship with the LORD. This experience of rejection fashioned Him to sustain others with a word (Isa 50:4). During this time, He was open to obey (Isa 50:5). He submitted to the humiliation and abuse even though no one could prove that He was guilty of any sin (Isa 50:6-9).

Isaiah 52:13–53:12

As the climax to the Servant songs is reached, the *means* is laid out by which Israel would be changed to become a servant. The Servant was not given power to crush Israel but power to be crushed in love for Israel, as a substitutionary sacrifice on behalf of all the nations. While Hezekiah refused God's call to premature death, the Servant accepts such death on behalf of others.

He was despised and rejected by men to experience death; they estimated that He was afflicted by God. In that experience of death, the LORD laid on Him the iniquity of all men (Isa 53:2-6). As the LORD's Servant, He took the unjust treatment in silence, bearing the transgression of the LORD's people (Isa 53:7-8). It was out of this anguish that He saw light (Isa 53:9-11). Therefore, having been exalted, He will share a portion of His victory with many (Isa 53:12; cf. 52:13).

Isaiah 54:1-10; 55:1-5

Israel had been called to believe that the people could be restored to God (Isa 54:1). Now Israel is restored (Isaiah 54). Isaiah speaks of the amazing love of a God who is able to dispose of His righteous anger in a moment and who then glories in the wonderful opportunities to bless His people. The barren woman, rejected under the Mosaic Covenant, can now anticipate more offspring (54:1) under the Covenant of Peace (Isa 54:10) as the LORD is now her Redeemer and her Husband (54:5). Israel is called to rejoice in the wonder of what God has done.

In Isa 55:1-5, Israelites are called to accept for themselves, one by one, all the implications of the Servant's wonderful work. The life that the Servant gained is now offered free of charge to anyone who is hungry or thirsty (Isa 55:1-2). Yet as the prophet has disclosed, it was extremely costly for the Servant (Isaiah 52:13–53:12). Then he underlines the point of what would be given and the benefits available. The two lines that describe the benefits are tersely stated:

> "I will make with you an everlasting covenant,
> my steadfast, sure love for David" (Isa 55:3).

Two questions may help to clarify: what does each line of the promise mean? What is the relationship between the lines?

The first line speaks of the covenant with Israel. It is eternal and thus its existence is unconditional with respect to Israel. The second speaks of David and the love God showed David. The two lines so tersely expressed are related, yet distinct. The common intent speaks of two sources of blessing. They are distinct because one had "you," or Israel, as partner, and the other had David as partner. The same love and loyalty is expressed to the appropriate partner, and thus each is assured of fulfillment. Those who thirst and those who hunger can be assured that they will get something to satisfy, and what they get is freely given in the

Everlasting Covenant. The same assurance is found in the Davidic Covenant which will be fulfilled through the Servant. Thus the two poetic lines are related in a synthetic development. A believer can be assured of finding food as a Davidic heir can be assured of reigning forever.

In conclusion, the three issues caused by the sinful people, confounded by the sin of the Davidic descendants, are resolved by Immanuel—God with us, who will reign in the Davidic line and minister in the Person and work of the Davidic Servant.

Jeremiah: Seventh Century BC

Jeremiah's ministry occurred in the final years of the kingdom of the house of Judah before Babylon progressively took them into captivity (deportations in 605 and 597, and destruction in 586 BC). His ministry began in the year 627 BC, in the thirteenth year of the reign of Josiah, and saw the reform movement in the finding of the Book of the Law in 622 BC. He saw the premature death of Josiah in 609 BC against Pharaoh Neco at the Megiddo Pass. His recorded messages were delivered in the precarious years that followed primarily in the reigns of Jehoiakim and Zedekiah.

Kaiser[39] characterized Jeremiah as the prophet to whom the "word of the LORD" came (Jer 1:2). This reality is highlighted in the character of his message. "Jeremiah appears to be speaking in a manner so different from the authorities that his words might appear to point to his being seditious."[40] While not denying the validity of the Davidic Covenant, he did not expect it to be fulfilled in Jehoiakim (Jer 22:18-23) nor Zedekiah (Jer 21:5-7). He did not anticipate that the deported Jehoiachin would sit on the throne of Judah again (Jer 22:24-30). In fact, the words of Jeremiah seemed to be those of a traitor or an anti-nationalistic individual. He was neither pro-Babylonian (Jer 28:4, cf. 32:2-5), nor fearful of Jerusalem's destruction since he remained in Jerusalem until it fell.

> His sole motivation in speaking as he did was that he had received Yahweh's word and was convinced that the Babylonians were the instrument of Yahweh's judgment upon Judah for her breach of covenant. Yahweh had spoken. He could but

---

[39]   Kaiser, *Promise-Plan*, p. 197. He follows James G. S. S. Thomson, *The Old Testament View of Revelation* (Grand Rapids, MI: Eerdmans, 1960), pp. 60-61.

[40]   J. A. Thompson, *The Book of Jeremiah*, NICOT (Grand Rapids, MI: Eerdmans, 1980), pp. 92-94. The following treatment is indebted to his analysis.

warn them that to resist the Babylonians was to resist Yahweh and to be destroyed.[41]

"The LORD put out his hand and touched [Jeremiah's] mouth. And the LORD said to [him], 'Behold, I have put my words in your mouth'" (Jer 1:9) with the effect to pluck up and destroy nations, as well as to plant and build them (Jer 1:10). In promising the restoration of Jerusalem, he quoted these words of this mandate (Jer 31:27-28). There are three fundamental theological questions that he addressed.

The first question is: why does God bring judgment? Following Jeremiah's call, the LORD displayed a vision of what He would be doing in Jeremiah's day and through his ministry: Jeremiah saw an *almond branch*, "I am watching over my word to perform it" (Jer 1:11-12). There are two aspects of "my word" which are intended, the Mosaic Covenant and the prophet's word.

Mosaic Covenant

There is widespread agreement that the Mosaic Covenant is fundamental to Jeremiah's message and the LORD's concern. The word *covenant* (*bᵉrît*) occurs some 23 times. All but five have reference to the Mosaic Sinai Covenant or to the New Covenant. The LORD's judgment will fall on His people for their rebellion and disobedience to His covenant. Terms like *listen* (obey), *not to listen* (disobey), and *law* (commandments) reflect covenant thinking. The kings Jeremiah knew were guilty of many breaches of the Mosaic Covenant (Jeremiah 21:11–23:2).

Yet there is the question, why now? The Mosaic Covenant had been violated forty days after it had been ratified at Mt. Sinai (Exodus 24, 32). It was now some eight hundred years later. In addition, Josiah had found the Book of the Covenant early in Jeremiah's ministry and entered a solemn covenant before the LORD to obey it (2 Kgs 23:1-4, 622 BC). There is little indication in the messages recorded in the book that Josiah's reform had caused widespread repentance among the people. Rather, when speaking about the covenant (Jer 11:1-8), a conspiracy existed among the men of Judah and the people of Jerusalem to turn back to the iniquities of their forefathers (Jer 11:9). Further, they schemed against the messenger, seeking his life (Jer 11:21). Therefore, Jeremiah was not to pray for them (Jer 11:14). The LORD had decreed disaster against them because of the evil that the house of Israel and the house of Judah had

---

[41] *Ibid.*, p. 94.

done (Jer 11:17). The time was of the LORD's reckoning, who weighed the hearts of men (Jer 11:20) and pronounced judgment after enduring in grace and mercy.

The Prophet's Word

The LORD was also watching the response the prophet's word would receive. The messages which called for repentance provided the only hope for being spared judgment. Those messages were arranged early in the book, in Jeremiah 2:1–19:15. The call to repentance occurred in Jer 3:1-10; 4:1; 8:4-7; 15:19.[42]

In Jeremiah 18, the prophet is told to go to the potter's house for a word from the LORD. The LORD then likened Himself to a potter with the right to rework a vessel into what seemed good to Him (Jer 18:4). In the application to Jeremiah's ministry, the house of Israel is like the clay in the potter's hand (Jer 18:6). Yet, it is in the conversation between the prophet and the nation that the LORD molds the vessel (Jer 18:7-10): "if that nation against whom I have spoken turns from its evil, I will relent of the disaster that I thought to bring upon it" (18:8, NKJV). This is the same language found in Exod 32:11-14.

The second question is: when will judgment come? The vision also included a *boiling pot*, facing away from the north: "Out of the north disaster shall be let loose upon all the inhabitants of the land" (Jer 1:14). The message announced that the judgment that was decreed was on its way. That expectation follows the transition in Jeremiah 20, after Pashur, the priest and chief officer of the temple, beat and imprisoned Jeremiah because he rejected his prophecy (Jer 20:1-2). From that time on, Jeremiah's message from the LORD is, "I will give all Judah into the hand of the king of Babylon" (Jer 20:4) and "I will give all the wealth of the city" (Jer 20:5). This is in fulfillment of Isaiah's words to Hezekiah (Isa 39:6). Jeremiah's messages amplify the pronouncement to Pashur (Jeremiah 20–29, 34–38) and reach a climax with the description of the fall of Jerusalem (Jeremiah 39). In addition, the nations are responsible for their treatment of God's people (Jer 10:25; 30:11, 16) and the nations will be judged

---

[42]   The other reference (Jer 36:7) occurs after Jehoiakim had burned Jeremiah's scroll. He dictated it again to Baruch and told him to read it in the temple and it may be that the people will plead for mercy and turn from their evil ways. This is not a call to repent but a stated hope for repentance.

(Jeremiah 46–51). This account is followed by another presentation of the fall of Jerusalem (Jeremiah 52).[43]

Third question: how will the house of Israel and the house of Judah be restored? There are four references to the future which influence the restoration of Jerusalem.

First, Jeremiah was to purchase the field of his cousin, Hanamel in Anathoth, with the Babylonians already overrunning the land. The LORD said, "Houses and fields and vineyards shall again be bought in this land" (Jer 32:15).[44]

Second, the letter to the exiles in Babylon (Jeremiah 29) contained the promise that the captivity would last seventy years (Jer 25:11). Part of the vision saw Israel seeking the LORD with all their heart (Jer 29:10-14).

Third was the message of hope for those who survived the sword (Jer 31:2-5, 15-22).

Fourth, in an indefinite future reference ("days are coming, declares the LORD"), the New Covenant would be ratified (Jer 31:31-34). This indefinite reference does not necessarily relate it to the soon return from captivity. That may happen, but it is not clear.

A careful examination of the New Covenant is essential for understanding the restoration prophesied by Jeremiah. Two questions need to be asked and answered.

First, what is the relationship between the Old and the New Covenants? Several similarities and differences will be noted.

Similarities:

1. Both are covenants, which mean that they are formal partnership arrangements. The two parties are the same, the LORD and Israel, except that Israel exists as divided into two houses when the New Covenant is revealed.

2. Both covenants have similar terms of revelation: law, promise of forgiveness, and promise of a covenant formula ("I will take

---

[43] "Chapter 52 is essentially the same as 2 Kgs 24:18–25:30 with two important differences: (1) chap. 52 omits the appointment and assassination of Gedaliah (41:1-3; cf. 2 Kgs 25:22-26); (2) 52:28-30 includes the number taken in the three deportations, not found in 2 Kings." (F. B. Huey, *Jeremiah, Lamentations*, New American Commentary, vol. 16 [Nashville, TN: Broadman & Holman, 1993], p. 433).

[44] As Huey notes, "Jeremiah's symbolic act expressed confidence that life would return to normal and title deeds would once again be valid. This was a remarkable statement of hope for the future to be expressed in 587 B.C." (*Ibid.*, p. 292).

you to be my people, and I will be your God," Exod 6:7; cf. Lev 26:12; Jer 30:22).

Differences:

1. Since it is to be ratified as a *New* Covenant (*kārat*, 31:31), it is not a renewal of an already existing covenant (Exodus 34; Joshua 24; Jer 31:31).

2. The former covenant has become old because "they broke" it (Jer 31:32). To break a covenant may be different than to violate a covenant. A violated covenant can still exist, as the Mosaic Covenant had continued to exist since Exodus 32. A broken covenant no longer exists as the arrangement of partnership for which it had been formed. So in the Mosaic Covenant, Israel took an oath in that they accepted responsibility for it to exist ("all that the LORD has said we will do," Exod 19:8; 24:7; cf. 24:3). This is called a conditional, bilateral arrangement.

3. The New is unconditionally and unilaterally promised and ratified ("I will make," Jer 31:31). It is clear that it is unconditional in ratification in the fact that it is promised and that the second party is divided at ratification, but at inauguration, the house of Israel and the house of Judah will function under the same arrangement as one nation.

4. An unconditional covenant is the only covenant which can assure a *relationship* with the LORD and provide what is necessary for a functioning *partnership*. There is nothing man can do to establish or merit a relationship with God, other than to accept it as a gift. And that is what is promised in the New Covenant (Jer 31:34). On the other hand, relationship with God was presupposed in the Old Covenant based on redemption from Egypt.

5. Finally, the New is an internal work of God, while the Mosaic is an external word from God. This is what is necessary for both a relationship and partnership to be provided as a gift.

It is important to appreciate what is similar and what is different in the progress of revelation. That progress highlights the point in the Mosaic Covenant given to mold Israel to be God's servant (Gen 12:3) and the point in the New Covenant given to provide life for Israel to be both God's people and God's servant-partner. The Mosaic Covenant highlighted Israel's willingness to accept, but unwillingness to follow through.

In addition, they failed to take their unwillingness (as Jeremiah had) personally, and go to the LORD to find help when their inability crippled them in sin. The point of the New Covenant builds on the lessons that could be learned from history under the first covenant. Further, the promises will take Israel further to be His people and His servant, in fact.

Second, what are the terms of the New Covenant?

1. The person's heart is to be predisposed to obey God's law. The law will be written on the heart, within them. Such a move from external to internal is a necessary move as already was urged in Deuteronomy. But under the Mosaic arrangement, what was external was placed upon the heart by the people's memory, by meditation and by applying it to life. This may well be what Moses spoke of that God gives: ears to hear, eyes to see, and a mind that understands (Deut 29:4).

   > Deuteronomy 6:6—"shall be on your heart"
   >
   > Deuteronomy 11:18—"[L]ay up these words of mine in your heart."
   >
   > Deuteronomy 30:6—"[T]he LORD...will circumcise your heart...so that you will love the LORD."

   The hardness of heart at Kadesh Barnea may have been what prompted Moses to urge Israel to change in Deuteronomy. But in the end, Moses recognized that Israel would be taken captive and only then turn to the LORD. And the LORD would change Israel (Jer 31:4).

   What was a human responsibility under the Mosaic Covenant is now given as a promised work of the LORD in the New Covenant. "In Israel, the Israelites were commanded constantly to follow the Torah and shape their *lēb* in obedience to God's Word (Dt. 30:14,17; Jer. 31:33...). The *lēb* as the organ of knowledge notes deviations from God's will."[45] The heart's predisposition provides a conscience aware of disobedience and a resonance with obedience to what is taught in Scripture. In the New Covenant, this is a work of God.

2. Covenant formula—"I will be their God, and they will be My people" is a formula common to Israel's covenants. While it was true in a national sense under the Mosaic Covenant, it would

---

[45] H. J. Fabry, "לב, *lēb*," TDOT, vol. 7, p. 426.

be true in both a national and an individual sense in the New Covenant. This partnership will realize, in a deeper and more complete sense, Israel's service.

3. The nation, individually and collectively, *knows* the Lord. Again, there is an implied contrast between the relationship under the Mosaic Covenant and that under the New Covenant promises. Jeremiah had complained on the Lord's behalf, "those who handle the law did not know (*yāda'*) me" (Jer 2:8). Again, "my people are foolish; they know me not; they are stupid children; they have no understanding" (Jer 4:22). To know is to share life in a conscious, personal relationship. Under the Mosaic Covenant, some individuals, such as Jeremiah or David, knew the Lord. But under the New Covenant, the promise "they shall all know me" indicates that an individual, personal relationship is a necessary gift of the covenant collective partnership. All shall know because all will see and believe in the Lord and His promised Messiah. That promised Messiah is not stressed in Jeremiah, but mentioned as a righteous Branch to spring up from David (Jer 33:15).

4. The individual and the nation will be forgiven of sin forever. Again there is a contrast between the two covenants. In the Mosaic Covenant, forgiveness of sin is promised with a temporal limitation. It is based on what is promised in the sin and trespass offerings. It is also implied in the provision of the Passover sacrifice received and celebrated at the Passover ceremony by faith. It is also promised on the day of Atonement, celebrated year after year. But these sacrifices are offered yearly and in the temple more frequently. Under the New Covenant, sin will be forgiven and remembered no more. In this sense, the promises are everlasting. Implied in this scope of promise is a sacrifice at ratification that is sufficient to address the guilt of human sin. What animal sacrifice provides is only a symbol of sufficiency, an IOU of an adequate sacrifice. That sacrifice in the New Covenant will be permanently sufficient as Isaiah already prophesied.

Conclusion to the Monarchy

The Lord is patient, particularly in His mercy and grace. He provides a fallen people opportunities to be taught in spite of continued sin. The apparent solution proposed in Judges provided a framework for prophesied answers but had no immediate and real answer to the nation's sin. That is the point in the literature found in Deuteronomic history.

The religious condition of the people at the conclusion of Judges showed little difference from the false worship of Jeroboam I in the Northern Kingdom, or the abominations of Manasseh in the Southern Kingdom.

The political condition under the *monarchy* realized greater prosperity, but it failed to address the fundamental problem of sin. Israel enjoyed political success as the promised land, as a whole, was either occupied by Israel or by nations ruled by David, the king of Israel.

The purpose of revealing double knowledge, for which the Mosaic Law had been given to Israel, largely was defeated among the people. Israel as a whole did not *know* God, as they pursued idol worship. Thus, they would experience captivity under pagan peoples and be forced to live among gods that neither spoke nor had life. Only such a time in captivity would challenge Israel's false knowledge of God. In their immediate captivity, the presence of widespread idolatry would be questioned.

As a corollary, a faulty knowledge of God corresponds to a faulty knowledge of man's self-awareness. The very proposal that Israel's problem was simply political provided evidence of Israel's inadequate self-awareness. It assumed that if they lived like the other nations, their problems would be solved. Captivity in Assyria and Babylon would force Israel to see themselves differently. They were not self-sufficient.

At the same time, the *monarchy* provided a structure for additional revelation about the creation *goal* and the *plan* of salvation. The revelation came through two prophetic sources. The first was David, who spoke in the psalms as a prophet. His message largely sprang from the Davidic Covenant. David's heart desire was to bless the LORD with a suitable house. God reversed the blessing and instead established David's house.

Then as David subsequently mediated on the uncertainties of the Davidic Covenant, God revealed clarifications of an ultimate Anointed One. In spite of being God's King, He would experience suffering before God's enemies. Only after extreme suffering would God deliver in His time and in His way (Psalm 22). As God's chosen King, His future is both certain and uncertain facing death. Yet God provided a promise to overcome death in resurrection (Psalm 16). Then in a spectacular vision, completely unexpected, David saw his Heir elevated as Lord to share the LORD's universal throne. In this position, David's Lord would minister before the LORD as a Melchizedekian Priest (Psalm 110). Then as David anticipated in Psalm 2, God's Messiah and Son would be established to mediate God's rule on the whole earth.

Within the structure of the monarchy, prophets like Isaiah and Jeremiah were raised up as a second voice. Isaiah spoke in contrast to Ahaz and in distinction to Hezekiah. God promised Immanuel to reign on David's throne. Immanuel would also serve as God's Servant to provide salvation and enable Israel to serve as God had promised. The service Israel would accomplish would need a New Covenant. Israel had broken the Old Covenant and Jeremiah announced the New Covenant that would enable Israel to both know God and serve God.

Prophecy had envisioned solutions, but Israel failed to adequately comprehend what God had revealed. In addition, it was not at all clear as the nation went into captivity how these provisions would be worked out. But the LORD's firm word provided an unquestioning *hope* that God would provide a resolution. In spite of the circumstances of captivity, the collection of these books and their revelation would encourage Israelites to *wait* for the LORD.

CHAPTER 14:
TIMES OF THE GENTILES:
EZEKIEL AND DANIEL

Introduction

With the house of Israel dispersed to Assyria in 722 BC and the house of Judah to Babylon in 586 BC, the work of God seemed to be defeated. Israel seems to have failed in her call to establish the creation goal of mediating God's rule on earth through man. The kings and people of Israel had refused to be ruled by God through the Mosaic Law. So the right to rule has been taken from Israel and delegated to Gentile world powers. This is the period of history that Jesus would later call the "times of the Gentiles" (Luke 21:24). Nebuchadnezzar, King of Babylon, is the first king to be given that role as stated by Daniel, "Your Majesty, you are king of kings. The God of heaven has given you sovereignty, power, strength, and glory" (Dan 2:37 HCSB).

In spite of the seeming failure of God's election of Israel to service, Ezekiel, Daniel and Zechariah, while focusing on Gentile rule, still see God fulfilling His purposes through Israel. These books are generally considered apocalyptic. The apocalyptic genre considers both the immediate historic conflict and the resolution of the ultimate eschatological conflict. So the visions in these works consider the immediate issue of Jewish captivity under Gentile rule, the ultimate outcome of Gentile kingdoms, and the rule of the righteous on earth as God's mediators. Daniel traces the sequence of dominant Gentile kingdoms until the end. God's throne will be set to ultimately decide who will reign. This right rests with the Son of Man (Dan 7:13-14), "a stone was cut from a mountain by no human hand" (Dan 2:45).

Zechariah's prophecies are concerned with both the goal of creation and the plan of redemption. As such, they will focus more directly on the

King coming to Zion (Zech 9:9), on those who mourn for Him whom they pierced (Zech 12:10), and "on that day [when] Yahweh will become king over all the earth" (Zech 14:9, HCSB). Ezekiel is also apocalyptic, highlighting both the goal and the plan of redemption of Israel. It, too, begins with the immediate judgment on Jerusalem involving a departure of the Glory of God from the temple (Ezekiel 9–11). Based on the fall of Jerusalem (Ezekiel 33), Ezekiel emphasizes what Israel failed to come to *know* under the Mosaic Law and what they will come to *know*. A series of judgments on Israel and promised acts on her behalf will bring knowledge. As the LORD states through the prophet, "and you shall *know* that I am the LORD" (Ezek 6:13; 20:42, 44; 37:13, emphasis added; cf. 12:15; 15:7; 25:17; 28:22; 30:8, 25; 33:29; 34:27; 36:23; 37:28; 39:28). Israel, as a people, will be transformed to occupy the land in peace (Ezekiel 34–37). Finally, a temple will be built as a climax of God's reign on the fallen earth (Ezekiel 40–48).

In preparation for this future for Israel, a remnant of people who survived the immediate judgment and exile return to Jerusalem. Ezra and Nehemiah narrate God's agenda for this Jewish remnant. Merrill introduced this treatment of the historical period by comparing the Deuteronomistic history with that of Chronicles, Ezra, and Nehemiah.[1] Both accounts are theological interpretations of history. Chronicles/Ezra/Nehemiah focuses on the revelation of *promise*. Ezra/Nehemiah are also related to God's immediate works in the return from captivity. Persian king, Cyrus, sets the stage by dictating a decree which expresses God's historic will for the remnant of Israel. This is a reflection of the times of the Gentiles when the status of the people is determined by God under Gentile rule. However God also sends the prophets Haggai and Zechariah when the directions from Gentiles are in conflict to His will. When enemies arise and object to the decree of Cyrus and Darius, God intervenes by sending His prophets to direct the work of the people in rebuilding the temple.

God's agenda is to establish a worshiping community. This includes rebuilding the temple, reestablishing an ethnic identity, and securing Jerusalem to provide stability for a Jewish identity and security for the temple. For this community, the Law of Moses is not regarded as a covenant, but as divinely authoritative Scripture. As such, it defines the order of a Jewish religious community under Gentile political authority. Nehemiah, under the mandate of Artaxerxes, brings social order to the community by rebuilding the wall of Jerusalem and initiating reforms.

---

[1] Merrill, *Everlasting Dominion*, pp. 465-66.

Malachi speaks to this religious community of Jews to *wait* for God to accomplish His purposes.[2] The waiting is not that of a covenant partner, but of an elect people[3] who await the promise of His coming: "the Lord you seek will suddenly come to His temple…" (Mal 3:1, HCSB). Ultimately, the temple will be the place where Simeon and Anna are awaiting the consolation and redemption of Israel (Luke 2).

Ezekiel—Sixth Century BC

Historical Setting

Ezekiel was taken captive to Mesopotamia in 597 BC (note the expression "our exile" in 40:1), where he lived in a community of fellow exiles near the Chebar Canal. Ezekiel was from a priestly family (1:3), though it is not clear if he actually served in the Jerusalem temple prior to his exile.

His primary audience was these fellow exiles who were the cream of the population according to the policy of neo-Assyrian records, a policy followed by Nebuchadnezzar. They "suffered from intense theological shock. Even though the prophets justifiably denounced the people of Judah for their idolatrous and socially criminal ways, throughout the Babylonian crisis the people had maintained confidence in Yahweh's obligation to rescue them."[4]

Message of Ezekiel

Ezekiel's message wrestles with the same tension between promise and law noted by other prophets. The LORD had chosen Israel to bless them (Gen 12:1-3) as a change in strategy. Previously, He had worked with human beings as a whole (Genesis 6–11). Then by distinction, the LORD chose and blessed Israel, who under *law* were to disclose the LORD's

---

[2] This waiting is not to be understood as inactivity. The dialogical rebukes and exhortations make it clear that the people were to live faithfully until the age of consummation.

[3] The elect status of Israel is established at the beginning, "'I have loved you,' says the LORD" (Mal 1:2). As Eugene Merrill notes, "Modern studies of covenant language have shown that the word 'love' (*bhea', ,āhēb*, or any of its forms) is a technical term in both the biblical and ancient Near Eastern treaty and covenant texts to speak of choice or election to covenant relationship, especially in the so-called suzerainty documents" (Eugene H. Merrill, *An Exegetical Commentary: Haggai, Zechariah, Malachi* [Chicago: Moody, 1994], p. 391).

[4] Daniel I. Block, *The Book of Ezekiel: Chapters 1–24*, NICOT (Grand Rapids, MI: Eerdmans, 1997), p. 7.

revelation of Himself to the nations (Gen 12:3, Exod 19:5-6). Israel was called to be a priestly nation. It was the LORD's transition from the many to focus on the one people but with the other nations in view.

Ezekiel adopts that same provincial perspective as the LORD did in choosing Abraham and his descendants, focusing on Israel, yet with the consequence that the nations might come to know the LORD. "This accounts for the emphasis that the prophecies of Ezekiel are dominated by two profound theological formulas; the introductory formula and the divine recognition formula. The former *'ănî yhwh*, "I am the LORD" is often incorporated into the latter, *weyāde'û kî 'ănî yhwh*, "and they will know that I am the LORD."[5] In this sense of mediating a knowledge of the LORD, Ezekiel shares Isaiah's universal perspective. Yet Ezekiel's generation failed their mediatorial task in their disobedience and thus, was in need of Ezekiel's ministry. They had presumed upon the LORD's election and promise to bless. From their perspective, the LORD was obligated to bless them, yet from Ezekiel's message, it is not for Israel's sake alone that God would bless them. In fact, Israel had been chosen for the LORD's purpose that the nations might be blessed with a true knowledge of who the LORD is, even as Israel had been. "Underlying Ezekiel's usage is a keen awareness of the traditional exodus narratives, according to which one of Yahweh's primary aims in delivering Israel from the bondage of Egypt was to introduce Israel to himself..."[6] So Ezekiel's message corresponds to the dispensation of the law—the double knowledge: to come to know God and thereby know themselves. Only once this was accomplished would they become a priestly nation.

Outline of the Book

Some nine hundred years after the revelation at Sinai, Israel had failed to become either priests or a holy nation with the result that the LORD's reputation had been besmirched. Yet, even more serious, the people were not conscious of their failure. The people were self-confident and secure in their misplaced hope that the LORD would come to their aid. Thus, in Ezekiel's ministry, three questions are addressed:

1. What are the reasons behind their false sense of security (Ezekiel 1–32)?

---

[5] *Ibid.*, p. 36.

[6] *Ibid.*, p. 38.

2. As a watchman to the exiles of the events in Jerusalem, when does judgment fall (33)?

3. What reasons should give Israel hope for the future (34–48)?

Each of these questions will be addressed briefly in the summary of his message. Since Ezekiel's development of Israel's salvation is extensive, greater attention will be given to the restoration of Jerusalem and the temple.

What Are the Reasons behind Their False Sense of Security (Ezekiel 1–32)?

The fundamental reason that their security is false is that they had misconstrued their relationship—"they don't know the LORD" and what they precipitated in their partnership with the LORD was a pained response from Him. In addition, they failed to know themselves and to recognize their false security.

Qin'â is commonly rendered "jealousy," which appears to be a self-serving passion inappropriate to apply to the LORD (Ezek 5:13; 8:3, 5; 16:38, 42; 23:25; 36:5; 38:19).[7] Speaking of the love that the LORD has for His people, Block notes:

> This love is fueled not by an exploitative need to dominate but by ardor for the well-being of the object. In the OT *qin'â* is aroused when a legitimate and wholesome relationship is threatened by interference from a third party... Since the marriage metaphor provides the basic image for understanding Yahweh's covenant with Israel, the description of his response to infidelity a *qin'â* is both logical and natural.[8]

The intensity of God's jealousy, pain, and wrath concerning His relationship with elect Israel is directly proportionate to the depth of His love.

In addition, Israel's security is false because God's judgment will extend to the foreign nations whose gods' they had adopted (Ezekiel 25–32). The ultimate reality is that those gods are expressions of none other than the enemy of God, the serpent (Gen 3:1-5).[9]

---

[7] Ezekiel 36:5 referenced God's attitude to foreign nations appropriating land promised to Israel for themselves; 38:19 refers to God's anger regarding Goy and his associates invading the land of Israel when God sends an earthquake.

[8] Block, *Ezekiel 1–24*, p. 14.

[9] Ezekiel 28:11-19: Ezekiel is lamenting the king of Tyre. He is being described in terms of an historic figure in the Garden of Eden, who fell. The description is thus metaphorical,

As a Watchman to the Exiles of the Events in Jerusalem, When Does the Judgment Fall (Ezekiel 33)?

The LORD's final appointment to Ezekiel was as a watchman for Israel (Ezek 3:16-27). He would remain mute unless a word came from the LORD spoken to the exiles. No more conclusive word came to declare the authority of the LORD than the final announcement of the siege of Jerusalem: "I am the LORD. I have spoken; it shall come to pass; I will do it. I will not go back; I will not spare; I will not relent; according to your ways and your deeds you will be judged, declares the Lord GOD" (Ezek 24:14). The LORD reveals Himself in the word that determines events in history.

A watchman is appointed to bring a warning. If the people fail to respond, they are wicked and will die (Ezek 33:1-9). When the city of Jerusalem fell, a fugitive came with the report that the city had been struck down (Ezek 33:21). Ezekiel, who had been mute, except when he delivered the LORD's word, now spoke freely. This was a clear sign of fulfilled prophecy for that generation.

What Are the Reasons that They Ought to Have Hope for the Future (Ezekiel 34–48)?

> Drawing on the exodus narratives (cf. Exod 6:6-9; 7:1, 5, 17), this formula [that they will know that I am Yahweh] transforms Yahweh's oracles from mere announcements of coming events into announcements of Yahweh's self-manifestation... It is in the narrative of history that his character is proclaimed. This refrain calls on the hearer of Ezekiel's oracles to stand back and watch Yahweh act, whether it be in judgment or salvation, and then to draw the obvious theological conclusions.[10]

---

describing the king contemporary with Ezekiel in terms of "an anointed guardian cherub" (28:14). The portrayal of Eden and the description of the figure as a "cherub," with a unique access to God indicate that the figure is greater than the first man, Adam. It speaks of this figure, as having the same position as Adam but as a more grand character. Aside from the position of authority, the comparison features the career of the king of Tyre—the abundance of trade, filled with violence and sin (28:16) and with pride of beauty and corrupted wisdom guided by splendor (28:17). However, the climactic point is the destruction and judgment (28:16-19). H. G. May, "The King in the Garden of Eden: A Study of Ezekiel 28:12-19," *Israel's Prophetic Heritage*, ed. Bernhard W. Anderson and Walter J. Harrelson (New York: Harper and Bros., 1962), pp. 166-76.

10   Block, *Ezekiel 1–4*, p. 39.

Thus, Israel is serving in the role as priest, whether in disobedience or obedience. As they witness God's work based on what He said He would do, they have hope to believe what He said He will do.

The most striking example of what the LORD said He would do is the departure of His glory due to disobedience (Ezekiel 8–11) and the restoration of glory due to their prepared condition to receive what He promised (Ezekiel 40–43). Fisch adds a significant observation: "only incidentally he *hints* at universal peace by declaring repeatedly that, as the sequel of divine judgment on the nations and Israel's resultant salvation, God would be magnified and sanctified in the eyes of all peoples."[11] Thus, a pattern is reflected in Israel's history as well in these chapters in Ezekiel:

- Exodus from Egypt—*redemption of Israel* to be forged in a covenant partnership

- National judgment (Ezekiel 25–32) and Jerusalem's captivity (Ezekiel 33)—*redemption* and *restoration* to the land, to life, to covenant partnership (Ezekiel 34–37)

- Attacked in the land for *redemption* (Ezekiel 38–39)

- *Restoration* in a rebuilt temple (Ezekiel 40–48)

This pattern of redemption and restoration of Israel is renewed in the prophets. Thus, an overview of these promised blessings will be briefly considered.

Redemption and Restoration of the LORD's Flock and Covenant of Peace (Ezekiel 34)

The oracle begins with a contrast between selfish shepherds (Ezek 34:1-10) and the LORD as shepherding His flock (Ezek 34:11-24, 30-31). *Redemption* and *reconciliation* between the LORD and His people are implied. The mediation of the Davidic shepherd is also clarified (Ezek 34:20-24). This reconciliation may be attributed to the "covenant of peace" which is then considered (Ezek 34:25). The covenant will also bring peace with the nations and blessings of abundance in the land (34:25-29). Israel will then be God's people (Ezek 34:30).

---

[11] S. Fisch, *Ezekiel* (London: Soncino, 1960), p. XVI, emphasis in original.

Restoration of the LORD's Land Promise (Ezekiel 35.1–36.15)

This rather strange oracle finds its point expressed in 36:5-7. The LORD spoke out of love for His own people and spoke against adjacent nations that claim Israel's land for themselves. They regard this claim with unusual joy and contempt for Israel.

Restoration of the LORD's Honor (Ezekiel 36.16-38)

In order for the land to be restored to Israel, and in order to bring glory to God, Israel itself must be transformed. The oracle begins rather negatively toward Israel because the *restoration* was not for Israel's sake (Ezek 36:22-23). Implied is the question: who are you, Israel? Israel, as a priest, exists for the honor of the LORD! Israel exists to sanctify the LORD's holy name. That which was once holy at the Exodus (all that the LORD has said, we will do), but has been desecrated in history and in captivity, must be reconsecrated. What follows are a series of promises of what God will do that will enable Israel to realize her role as priest. But strangely, "absent also is any reference to the covenant promises."[12] This is significant only because 36:26-27 are commonly quoted to clarify what is included in the New Covenant. Many of these promises are based upon the covenant partnership, but some go beyond what the covenant promised. At issue is whether the promise of the Spirit is a covenant blessing.

The promises include two types of blessing. The first type is a promise to change the person. The second type is a promise to change a person's behavior. The first promises (Ezek 36:25-26) feature internal spiritual changes of the individual (personal forgiveness of sin), and replace the cold, insensitive, incorrigible, lifeless heart with a warm, sensitive and responsive heart. These two promises are what were promised in Jeremiah's statement of the New Covenant (Jer 31:33-34). The second type of blessing involves behavior. That promise features the gift of God's Spirit who will *cause* changes in behavior (Ezek 36:27). This is in addition to what Jeremiah stated. This will involve changed behavior as God's Spirit empowers the change. God will *cause* a change in behavior as the people appropriate the power the Spirit provides. These changes in behavior are not imposed but received as acted on by faith. So it would be fair to conclude that Ezekiel does not promise the gift of the Spirit as a part of the covenant, but as an enabling Presence to covenant partners. Only

---

12   Block, *Ezekiel 25-48*, p. 352.

through such changes in behavior will the LORD's honor be disclosed through Israelites.

Redemption and Restoration of the LORD's People (Ezekiel 37:1-14)

What has been spoken of in individual change is now revealed in corporate change in the valley of the dry bones (Ezek 37:1-2). What is important is to clarify first what the prophet is told based on what he sees (Ezek 37:3-10). To clarify, the portions will be outlined:

37:3—Question: can these bones live?

37:4-6—Answer from the LORD: Ezekiel will prophesy, and the LORD will cause breath to enter the bones and give them life.

37:7-8—Ezekiel prophesies first, and a skeleton and sinew are formed but without life.

37:9-10—Ezekiel prophesies a second time, and the breath breathes into the body to live. This includes redemption.

The second section to clarify: what is the LORD's interpretation (Ezek 37:11-14)?

37:11—The bones are the whole house of Israel, who is cut off.

37:12—The house of Israel is resurrected from the dead and brought to the land.

37:13—This restoration from the grave will disclose that He is the LORD.

37:14—The Spirit of God will cause life and they will settle in their own land.

The nation will be redeemed and restored to national existence in the two stages of the prophecy. It seems to follow that they come to life (Ezek 37:9-10) only after they are restored to the land (37:7-8).[13]

Restoration of the LORD's Covenant Nation (Ezekiel 37:15-28)

The question that this oracle addresses is: how can two houses become one nation (Ezek 37:15-17)? Ultimately, it will be that the Covenant of Peace will be an everlasting covenant (Ezek 37:26). This is the same provision as Jeremiah's New Covenant. By implication, this is in contrast to

---

[13]   Charles L. Feinberg, *The Prophecy of Ezekiel: The Glory of the Lord* (Chicago: Moody, 1969).

the Mosaic Covenant and serves the same goal as Jeremiah's New Covenant (Jer 31:31-32). And as mentioned earlier, David shall be king over them and they shall have one shepherd (Ezek 37:24; cf. 17:22; 29:21). In addition, the Lord will set up His sanctuary in their midst forevermore (Ezek 37:26-27).

Restoration of the Lord's Final Peace (Ezekiel 38–39)

Israel's final deliverance will come "after many days...In the latter years" (Ezek 38:8). This prophecy referring to a distant future has its fulfillment hidden by the names chosen to identify the nations. These names are not their historical names, but the names are chosen from the original dispersion associated with the Tower of Babel. Genesis 10:1-2 identifies people groups with geographical locations surrounding the land of Israel. At the end of the age, they will attempt to invade Israel.

However, the Lord will deliver Israel, and in that deliverance, He will prepare to return His glory to dwell among the nations (Ezek 39:21-22). The nations shall see what has happened, and then will know the Lord's purpose in history (Ezek 39:23).

Restoration of the Lord's Glory in the Temple (Ezekiel 40–48)

While there are some details that remain in question about this final temple,[14] there are also things that can be known. The attention given to the architectural structure and the careful measurement of its dimensions indicates that it is describing an actual temple. Fisch notes:

> [The holiness attributed to God in a yet fallen world] underlies all the regulations concerning the restored Temple and the regeneration of Israel. The isolation of the Temple from the outside world, with its compartments within compartments as visualized by Ezekiel, and the exclusion of certain classes from its precincts—these features have the purpose of emphasizing the purely spiritual nature of the Divine worship.[15]

At the core of the priests' ministry is the instruction of the people to make distinctions "between the holy and the common, and...between the unclean and the clean" (Ezek 44:23). If holiness "denotes self-discipline

---

[14] These details include the identity of *nāśî*, the continuing role of sacrifice after the death of Christ in redemption from sin, and in the inauguration of the Covenant of Peace, etc.

[15] Fisch, *Ezekiel*, pp. XV-XVI.

and freeing oneself from base instincts,"[16] then common is that which is normal in the fallen world. The acts of discipline and freeing oneself allow for degrees of effectiveness. Clearly the LORD is totally free from self-service and other characteristics of the fallen world. In addition, humans in a fallen world, even with the desire to obey, are still in need of the Spirit's empowerment to become effective. Thus, there are degrees of human effectiveness and levels of holiness among God's worshippers.

Daniel—Sixth Century BC

Historical Setting

Daniel was one of the sons of Judah deported from Jerusalem (605 BC), "competent to stand in the king's palace" (Dan 1:4). Having been hand-picked for government service, he served over the entire period of the Babylonian kingdom and into the reign of the Medes and Persians. His ministry, reflected in the Book of Daniel, covered the seventy-year Babylonian captivity. He is not described as a prophet, but nonetheless provides a prophetic voice of significant changes in the course and events included in the plan of the LORD.

Since he is not technically a prophet, he does not reflect on the struggle with the prior revelation of promise and law as Hosea, Isaiah, and Ezekiel had. Yet, he is at the crossroads in the progress of revelation.

According to Israel's rebellion against the LORD, as monitored in the Mosaic Covenant-Law through the prophets, Israel had been taken captive to Assyria and Judah was beginning its captivity in Babylon. In Daniel's personal life, along with the others of the captive remnant, he struggled with living true to the LORD and His law in the midst of a pagan culture (Daniel 1, 3, 6). However, God honored Daniel and used him to reveal His identity to pagan kings, and to point to what He was doing in their lives and in their kingdoms.

Message of Daniel

The LORD revealed that Gentile cities were temporarily replacing Jerusalem in the delegated world rule. And even when a remnant would return to Jerusalem, it would be under auspices of a Gentile political government as Isaiah had announced that Cyrus would issue the decree

---

[16] *Ibid.*, p. XV.

to return to Jerusalem. Daniel both interpreted dreams and visions that the LORD revealed to Gentile kings (Daniel 2, 3, 4), and received visionary dreams himself, which he interpreted further based on the interpreting angel (Daniel 7–12). This revelation, which was divinely revealed and interpreted by an angel, has been characterized as apocalyptic prophetic revelation.

Several broad, fundamental questions are addressed in the progress of God's revelation at the level of worldwide purposes.

1. What is the status of God's creation purpose in light of the judgment on Jerusalem and dispersion of the people?

2. Has what was lost, first in man's fall into sin and now in Israel's captivity, been sufficient to thwart or limit God's plan?

3. Does God still have a plan for a delegated kingdom on earth?

4. Will the mediated kingdom be restored to Jerusalem?

The answers to these questions touch on the outworking of God's purposes based on promise. Further, there are also implications based on the finality of the consequences of the broken Mosaic Covenant. All the prophets had anticipated a fulfillment of God's purposes, as they focused on the role of the Davidic Heir, on the restoration to the land, and on the revelation of a New Covenant. But these prophecies were not revealed in the scope of worldwide government as Daniel does. This revelation of Daniel is going to be treated in two ways: first, visions of immediate historical fulfillment, and second, visions dealing with a culmination of God's purposes. These visions of culmination will be considered again in the exposition of the final dispensation of the Kingdom.

Daniel 2—What Form of Delegated Rule Does God's Reign Now Take?

This initial vision came directly from the God of heaven to King Nebuchadnezzar. It was interpreted, mediated by Daniel on behalf of God, revealing "what will be in the latter days" (Dan 2:28). Thus, it indicates that God was working directly with Gentile kings as Isaiah had indicated with Cyrus, the king of Persia (Isa 45:1). God gave Nebuchadnezzar and the kings that followed him the delegated right to rule in a dominant role on earth.[17] The vision came to him as a majestic human statue representing four successive kingdoms:

1. A head of gold, which was Nebuchadnezzar and the other Babylonian rulers in Daniel's time;

2. A chest and arms of silver, which was Medo-Persian, including Cyrus;

3. A middle torso and thighs of bronze, which was Greece;

4. Legs of iron and feet partly of clay and partly of iron, with ten toes, which were Rome.[18]

The historical period represented by the statue begins with Babylon, following judgment on Jerusalem. The rule continues until "the God of heaven will set up a kingdom that shall never be destroyed, nor shall the kingdom be left to another people" (Dan 2:44). The unending kingdom was formed by a stone cut from a mountain, not by human hand, which struck the statue and became a great mountain that filled the whole earth (Dan 2:35, 45). This vision provided an overview that revealed the broad structure without many details. Each of these kingdoms has some geographical relationship with Jerusalem throughout history. This period of history when God's world rule is not mediated through Jerusalem will be called "the times of the Gentiles" (Luke 21:24). And the glorious statue presents Gentile world government in relation to Jerusalem from the human perspective.

Since the vision reveals what will be "in the latter days" (Dan 2:28), the feet of the image with toes and the stone from heaven are most important. Certain details are given. The final form of world dominion will include what is represented by "the iron, the clay, the bronze, the silver, and the gold, all together were broken in pieces...so that not a trace of them could be found" (Dan 2:35). So while Rome ruled at the conclusion, all the prior kingdoms existed in some shape. But within the rule of the stone, there was no remnant of those world ruling empires. In the

---

[17]   The delegation of Gentile nations is distinct from mediation of rule through Israel. Israel had been given the Mosaic Covenant as a revelation to guide their rule. Gentiles had not. They were only given the right to reign worldwide. Delegation deals exclusively with the right to rule. Mediation addresses both the right to rule and the expression of the rule featuring God's will.

[18]   Although there is debate over the historical kings and kingdoms, the text of Daniel at least identifies Nebuchadnezzar is the head of gold (Dan 2:37-38); Darius, following Belshazzar, son of Nebuchadnezzar (Dan 5:1-2), ruled according to the law of Medes and Persians (Dan 6:12), the second kingdom in the sequence was Media and Persia (Dan 8:20); and the following kingdom was Greece (Dan 8:21). Rome is inferred from history.

interpretation, the final form of the Roman Empire is "feet and toes, partly of potter's clay and partly of iron" (Dan 2:41). The kingdom was divided; some parts were strong like iron and some parts were brittle like pottery (Dan 2:41-42). But the strength of the iron parts does not make the brittle parts strong (Dan 2:43). The brittle parts weaken the strength of the whole (Dan 2:44). In addition, the unified kingdom has ten portions expressing its dominion at the end.

Daniel 7—How Did God View These Delegated Kingdoms?

While Nebuchadnezzar saw a stately, impressive statue, the same four kingdoms were revealed to Daniel as wild, violent beasts. His description gave the sum of the matter. The symbolism (Dan 7:2) alluded to the creation account with the wind and the waters (Gen 1:2). The watery deep from which the earth arose gave rise to ferocious beasts, mirroring a cesspool of evil in the nations. Yet these beasts fit within the plan of God's governmental dealings on earth following the judgment of Jerusalem.

The description of each reflects what Daniel had experienced in Babylon (Daniel 1–6) and what history would yet disclose in each empire. Again, the climax received Daniel's greatest attention.

In the sequence of the description, the final non-descript beast grew ten horns. And among the ten, another little horn arose by disposing of three. This was a wildly imaginative and boastful leader.

Then the Ancient of Days held court to decide who would be heir to rule His created world. On earth, the horn's boasts outlived the preceding beasts. Then unexpectedly, one like a Son of Man was ushered into the presence of the Ancient of Days to be awarded the right to worldwide rule which would not end. The saints of the Most High shared in His rule after they had been persecuted by the little horn, who assumed to himself the right to redefine both the calendar and the law.

Daniel 9—How Does Israel's Future Fit into This Plan?

Along with the visions and dreams given to Daniel, he was aware that Jeremiah had spoken earlier about Israel's captivity. His thought was triggered by the beginning of the reign of Darius, the Mede (Dan 9:1). He related this event to the prophecy of Jer 25:11, that the captivity would last seventy years. Jeremiah 29:10 added that after seventy years, Israel would be able to return to their homeland. Perhaps sixty-seven years had passed since Judah had been taken captive and Daniel began to pray, confessing the nation's sins and asking that the LORD would hear, forgive, and not delay to act (Dan 9:19).

Daniel 9:24-27

Gabriel brought God's answer that seventy sevens had been decreed in addition to the seventy years of dispersion of Daniel's people and his city. Although the seventy sevens have no length of time assigned to them, yet the seventy years of the dispersion have led most to conclude that seventy groups of seven years are decreed. The decree relates to Israel and to Jerusalem, during which time several purposes of God will be concluded (Dan 9:24). The nation's repeated sin and transgression (beginning in Exodus 32) will be concluded, that wickedness will be atoned for, the righteousness of the mediatorial kingdom will begin (Jer 23:5-6), the conclusion of the word of the prophet and the restoration of God's glory will occur (Ezekiel 40–43). These purposes demand a distant future realization (Dan 9:24).

Daniel 9:25

There are two basic periods adding up to a total of 490 years.[19] The first period begins with the decree to restore and rebuild Jerusalem and reaches a climax with the coming of the Anointed One—which Robert Anderson concluded was the Triumphal Entry of Jesus, the Anointed One. This first period totaled 483 years. Then there is a gap such that the second period, the last seven years, are not chronologically tied to the first period. This means that the total historical length of the decreed events is not 490 years but remains unknown in total length. However, the first period would be a remarkable historical period.

When does the period begin? There is only one Biblical account of a Persian decree to rebuild the city. Artaxerxes gave Nehemiah a decree to build the city and the walls in keeping with Nehemiah's request (Neh 1:3; 2:4-8). Further, there was no actual rebuilding of the city until Nehemiah

---

[19] For a defense of this view see J. Randall Price, "Prophetic Postponement in Daniel 9 and other Texts," *Issues in Dispensationalism*, ed. Willis and Master (Chicago: Moody Press, 1994), pp. 133-66; Robert Anderson, *The Coming Prince*, pp. 119-29; Harold W. Hoehner, *The Chronological Aspects of the Life of Christ* (Grand Rapids, MI: Zondervan, 1977), pp. 115-39.

arrived with the decree, issued either in the last months of 445 BC or the first month of 444 BC.[20]

When does the period end? Sixty-nine sevens of years would amount to 483 years. The prophetic year was 360 days and this is in keeping with consistent prophetical use. The Jewish calendar consisted of twelve months of thirty days each, with the provision that after enough months had accumulated, a thirteenth month would be added to correct the calendar. In prophecy, this thirteenth month is not considered.

The first segment of the first period consisted of seven sevens of years, or forty-nine years, after which it would be rebuilt with squares and a moat. According to Neh 11:1, one out of ten Jews returned to build a house in Jerusalem. This involved spreading out the rubble and building a new city on top of the old, destroyed city.

The second segment of sixty-two sevens, or 434 years, apparently involved occupation of the city and is climaxed by the coming of the Anointed One. Robert Anderson was the first to propose that the date of that coming was none other than the triumphal entry into Jerusalem by Jesus the Messiah.[21]

Daniel 9:26

What happened after the first period ended, and before the second period began?

The first period ended with the coming of the Anointed One. *After* that, "an anointed one shall be cut off and shall have nothing." In view of our historic perspective, the "cut off" refers to the cut off from life in death. Further, the "having nothing" may refer to His death alone, His burial in another's grave, and the end of His earthly life without known inheritance in Israel's acceptance of her Messiah.

The second event was that "the people of the prince who is to come shall destroy the city and the sanctuary" (Dan 9:26). From historical records, Jerusalem and the temple were destroyed in AD 70 by the Romans.[22] That Roman invasion clarifies the people of the invasion. It further identifies "the prince who is to come" as a Roman. That Roman destruction of Jerusalem in AD 70 and the later Roman prince correlate with the

[20] John F. Walvoord, *Major Bible Prophecies* (Grand Rapids, MI: Zondervan, 1991), pp. 170-71.

[21] Hoehner's *Chronological Aspects of the Life of Christ* supplements Anderson's work. However, not everyone accepts Hoehner's identification of an AD 33 date for Christ's crucifixion.

[22] F. F. Bruce, *New Testament History* (Garden City, NY: Doubleday, 1972), pp. 368-92.

Roman Empire existing when the Son of Man returns to conclude the Gentile worldwide reign (Daniel 2, 7).

Daniel 9:27—What Does the Final Period of Seven Years Include?

The period begins with the signing of a treaty.[23] This treaty will guarantee peace in the city and may enable a third temple to be built. The first temple was Solomon's, the second temple was associated with Zerubbabel and was modified and magnified by Herod the Great. This second temple was destroyed by the Roman military invasion in AD 70. The peace and stability established by the treaty will only last three and one-half years until the worship in the temple ceases.

> Further support may be found in the association of the terms *shiqqutz* ("abomination") and *meshomen* ("desolation") in Jeremiah and Ezekiel, which most likely influenced Daniel's cryptic construction of *shiqqutzim meshomem* ("abomination of desolation") in Daniel 9:27…This may be helpful in explaining why Jesus in the Olivet Discourse (Matt. 24:15; Mark 13:14a) used this expression to denote the signal event that would serve as a warning of the arrival of apocalyptic fulfillment.[24]

The idea from this cryptic phrase would be that the temple would be emptied of any true worship because of the abominable object that is placed on the altar or that replaced the altar. Thus, for the final three and one-half years, no undefiled sacrifice could be offered. The end is decreed. And that end will be poured out on the one who desolated the temple.

Daniel was given an overview of Gentile human government which affected Jerusalem in the remaining history of the earth until the climax. The times of the Gentiles are interfaced with Israel's 490 years decreed to accomplish God's purposes for the redemption from sin and death and restoration of the nation. Both Gentile rule and Israel's redemption and restoration reach a climax at the same time. The Son of Man, inheriting the final rule on earth in history, will replace the successive worldwide Gentile kingdoms and will rule without a successor from Jerusalem. And

---

[23] The treaty is ratified by two parties, indicated in the text as "he" and "the many." "The many" are the residents of Jerusalem at the conclusion of the "times of the Gentiles." "He" may have one of two antecedents: either "the people," that is the subject of the preceding sentence, and agrees in number and gender with the pronoun, or "the prince" who is to come. That is the closest antecedent but not the natural focus of the sentence.

[24] Price, "Prophetic Postponement," p. 148.

thus, the Davidic promise will be fulfilled in the Son of Man reigning over a redeemed and restored Israel in a final worldwide kingdom.

Conclusion

This model of a Dispensational Biblical theology featured God's governance in salvation history. Yet God's governance was more comprehensive. Genesis 1–11 recognizes God ruling on a sovereign throne from which He created the world and He permitted the human race to fall into sin (Genesis 1–3). While this thwarted the mediatorial rule of God through Adam, it didn't affect in any sense God's sovereign reign over creation.

Salvation history began with the choice of Abram and his seed, which was followed by God's sovereign formation of nations (Genesis 9) to govern on earth to protect human life. Salvation blessing would only arise from the nation promised to Abraham's descendants, Israel. However, when that nation deteriorated into evil, God used Gentile nations to judge and rule over the Israelites. This stage in the progress of revelation was introduced in the prophets Ezekiel and Daniel. But it is during this time of the Gentiles that God would continue salvation history with a remnant of Jews.

CHAPTER 15: POST-CAPTIVITY HISTORY AND THE MINOR PROPHETS

Introduction

This post-captivity period will introduce God's work with a remnant of individual Jews. It begins with a worshiping remnant, returning to rebuild the temple and the city of Jerusalem. This will be called the second temple period, lasting for four-hundred years.

Post-Captivity History: Ezra and Nehemiah

The period of history chronicling the return of survivors from the captivity is found in Ezra and Nehemiah. The purposes are identified as rebuilding the temple, restoring Jerusalem, and fashioning a worshiping community. Three questions are raised in the progress of revelation. The answers we propose characterize Biblical theology in this critical transitional period:

1. What does God want the remnant to do in the return to the land?

2. How is Moses' Law to be viewed?

3. How are the times of the Gentiles to be viewed?

God's Agenda for the Returning Survivors

The authors of Ezra and Nehemiah encased the chronicling of a series of events in a theological framework. At the outset, Ezra announces that in the first year of Cyrus, king of Persia, the Word of the LORD spoken by Jeremiah was fulfilled (Jer 25:11-14; 29:10-14). The LORD had said through Jeremiah: "This whole land will become a desolate ruin, and these nations will serve the king of Babylon for 70 years. When the 70 years are completed, I will punish the king of Babylon and that nation" (Jer 25:11-12a, HCSB).

It was that word Daniel remembered as he prayed about the termination of Israel's captivity (Dan 9:2). Daniel confessed his own sin and the sin of his people, Israel (Dan 9:3-19). The LORD then revealed the purposes to be accomplished before Israel's sufferings would be completed:

> "to bring the rebellion to an end,
>> to put a stop to sin,
>> to wipe away iniquity,
>> to bring in everlasting righteousness,
>> to seal up vision and prophecy,
>> and to anoint the most holy place" (Dan 9:24, HCSB).

This restoration begins with the decree of Cyrus.[1] Isaiah had announced some 100 years earlier that Cyrus, God's anointed, would say "to Jerusalem, 'She will be rebuilt,' and of the temple, 'Its foundation will be laid'" (Isa 44:28, HCSB).

In Ezra, "the LORD put it into the mind of King Cyrus to issue a proclamation throughout his entire kingdom" (Ezra 1:1, HCSB). In it, Cyrus recognized far more than might be expected: the LORD God of heaven has established him as ruler of all the kingdoms of the earth and has appointed him to build Him a house at Jerusalem in Judah. He then urged anyone willing among his people to go and build the house of the LORD (Ezra 1:2-3). Without specifying who should go, survivors who lived through the deportation were encouraged to go. Those who returned were family leaders of Judah and Benjamin, along with priests and Levites. Those who went included, "everyone God had motivated" (Ezra 1:5). Only a remnant of Israelites returned as determined by God, but "unquestionably the restored Israel is a continuation of the old."[2] So this remnant is not introduced as something new, reinterpreting Israel as the people of God.

Consistent with Israel's history, there were enemies of God who were also enemies of Judah and Benjamin (Ezra 4:1). So they hindered the building after the altar had been finished and the foundation laid (Ezra 4:5). Although Artaxerxes' letter ordered a cessation of construction, God

---

[1] Waltke notes that the Cyrus Cylinder and other records certify that what is reported in Ezra 1:2-4 (and 6:3-5) is at least analogous to what Cyrus did in the region of Babylon (Waltke, *An Old Testament Theology*, pp. 771-72, fn. 3).

[2] *Ibid.*, p. 782.

raised up the prophets Haggai and Zechariah to prompt them to begin rebuilding again (Ezra 5:1-2). "God was watching over the Jewish elders" (Ezra 5:5, HCSB) until Darius confirmed that Cyrus had, in fact, decreed that the temple should be built. So they finished building (Ezra 6:14).

The active presence of the LORD God of heaven was most evident in Ezra and Nehemiah's missions. In both cases, the king granted their request. In Ezra's case, it is noted that "the hand of Yahweh his God was on him" (Ezra 7:6, HCSB). Nehemiah prayed to the God of heaven (Neh 2:4-6) and made his request. The king responds favorably and asks how long he would be gone.

God's active presence also indicates that He is the essential Mover in the return to Jerusalem. "The point thus far is clear: the God of heaven (a favorite epithet in the postexilic period; cf. Ezra 1:2; 6:9; 7:12; Neh. 1:4; 2:4, 20; Dan. 2:18, 37, 44; 5:23) is sovereign."[3] All that has changed is the name God is commonly called. God is now commonly called "the God of heaven" rather than Yahweh, the covenantal name (Exod 3:14-15). He is identified by His providential throne in the heavenlies, rather than in His covenant keeping name (Exod 34:6-7). This is the initial clue that the Law of Moses is no longer considered a covenant.

The Law of Moses

An important issue for the returning survivors was the role of the Law of Moses. The change in the name by which God is called indicates that its role may have changed, as well, from being a divine covenant ratified with all the people. Two issues arise that affect a Biblical theology.

First, the prophetic covenant lawsuit (Hosea 4, Jeremiah 3, Isaiah 1) charged Israel with breaking the covenant. Jeremiah stated this in so many words (Jer 31:32). As a *conditional* covenant whose very existence depended on the participation of both parties (Exod 19:8; 24:3, 7), a broken covenant annulled the LORD's covenant commitments as well. Thus, the people lost possession of the land and were taken into captivity. They returned to the land according to the Abrahamic Covenant as servants of the Gentile nations (Neh 9:36-37).

Second, since the covenant represented the election of Israel as a nation to service (Exod 19:5-6), and since only a few survivors returned to the land, does God now transition to deal with a remnant in Israel alone? This is the contention of many Biblical theologies: "It was during the

---

[3] Merrill, *Everlasting Dominion*, p. 485.

period of the exile that the concept of a remnant acquired a fixed theological concept, viz. the hope of Yahweh's preserving and saving work."[4] These two issues will be addressed in the same order.

On the one hand, does the returned remnant treat the book of the Law of Moses as a covenant or as Scripture? In a Dispensational Biblical theology, the answer to this question is particularly important because it specifies how these books are considered to be within the dispensation of law.

Several recognized scholars propose that the Law of Moses ought to be regarded as a *renewed covenant*. This conclusion is reached from the theological high point in Nehemiah as Ezra and Nehemiah meet with all the people on the first day of the seventh month, the Feast of Trumpets (Neh 8:1). The purpose of the gathering, as the date already intimates was "to read this law aloud before all Israel" (Deut 31:1, HCSB). Although neither Deuteronomy nor Nehemiah state that this is *covenant renewal*, yet that is what is contended.

Waltke proposes that the covenant renewal ceremony followed Ezra's reforms in a familiar alternating pattern—Nehemiah 7:73b–8:12; 8:13-18; 9:1–10:39—even though the term *renewal* does not appear to be referring to the Mosaic Law.

> These chapters can also be analyzed according to the familiar pattern of covenant renewal, resembling the reforms of Asa (2 Chron. 15:1-18), Hezekiah (2 Chron. 29–31), and Josiah (34:29–35:19): proclamation of the law (Neh. 8), confession (Neh. 9), and renewal of commitment to the covenant with general and specific stipulations (Neh. 10).[5]

Yet, he concedes: "Though the relationship of the people to God has been restored, God has not yet acted in the definitive way he had promised in his covenants and through his prophets."[6] There was no ownership of land. There was no Davidic king and there was no New Covenant to ratify.

Merrill argues that the conjunction of the reading of the Law and the Festival of Tabernacles implies the added renewal commitment. Then he lists what these commitments were as stated in the text (Nehemiah 9:38–10:39). Yet, he too concedes that "What they wanted the Lord to do

[4] W. Günter and H. Krienke, "Remnant," *The New International Dictionary of New Testament Theology*, vol. 3 ed. Colin Brown (Grand Rapids, MI: Zondervan, 1978), p. 249.

[5] Waltke, *An Old Testament Theology*, p. 791.

[6] *Ibid.*, p. 793.

is not explicit but nonetheless most obvious."[7] When the reform of covenant renewal under Josiah occurred, the Covenant of Moses was stated directly and repeatedly.

While this is a plausible argument, there are several reasons that the Law of Moses should be considered Scripture rather than a legal covenant. These included responsibilities which Israel assumed before God, which weren't satisfied when the covenant was voided.

First, in addition to the prophets' statements about the people's status in their dispersion and captivity, when the temple was rebuilt, the glory of the LORD never returned. When the house of God was dedicated and Passover was celebrated (Ezra 6:16-22), they acted "according to what is written in the book of Moses" (Ezra 6:18, HCSB). Yet there was no appearance of the LORD's glory as there had been when the tabernacle was dedicated (Exod 40:34-35) and when the first temple was dedicated (1 Kgs 8:10-11). It is as though the second temple remained empty awaiting the coming of God's glory.

Second, the spiritual direction of the returned community reflected the vision of Ezra as a scribe. He "had determined in his heart to study the law of the LORD, obey it, and teach its statutes and ordinances in Israel" (Ezra 7:10, HCSB). This is the LORD's word without any covenant expectations in His return that Israel would become an independent nation.

Third, Nehemiah focused on what the prophets said about the response of the people scattered among the Gentiles. If the exiles return to God and carefully observe His commands, then He promises to gather them from there, saying, "I will bring them to the place where I chose to have My name dwell" (Neh 1:9, HCSB). These allusions to the prophets assumed that the covenant's consequences of occupying and possessing the land have been concluded (Deut 4:29-30; 30:1-5; Ezek 37:1-14) and a fresh opportunity, based on promise, is presented to return to the land.

Fourth, when they gathered around the book of Moses, it wasn't called *covenant*,[8] but simply, *law*. The agenda when the Israelites gathered on the first day of the seventh month was corporate worship in Jerusalem. It included:

---

[7] Merrill, *Everlasting Dominion*, p. 487.

[8] The term *covenant* does not refer to the Mosaic Covenant in Ezra-Nehemiah. Ezra refers to a covenant the remnant makes with their God. Nehemiah 1:5 speaks of God keeping covenant, as Nehemiah prepares to return to the land. Nehemiah 9:8 also refers to the Abrahamic Covenant. Nehemiah 9:32 speaks of "God who keeps covenant," and Neh 13:29 of "the covenant of the priesthood."

- Reading and translation of the words of Moses, so they could be understood as God's Word, Scripture (Neh 8:2, 18);

- Celebration of the Feast of Booths, which anticipated a permanent occupation of the land (Neh 8:17);

- Confession of corporate sin, which had resulted in their being enslaved in the land ruled by Gentiles (Neh 9:33-35).

So they gathered, not as a covenant nation in possession of the land, but as a worshiping Jewish community under Gentile rule. They were awaiting God's action on their behalf as the elect descendants of Abraham with his covenant and promises. Thus, it was important that they be *separate* from the peoples in the land whether in marriage (Ezra 10) or in ethnic purity (Neh 13:3). Further, they took a vow to be *separate* as a people (Neh 10:30) and to observe the Sabbath (Neh 10:31-39) as worshipers of the God of heaven.

On the other hand, consider the point of view regarding the remnant in the post-exilic view of Israel. Do we find the beginning of a fixed theological distinction between the spiritual and true Israel from the merely natural Israelite? It is unquestioned that Paul would introduce the remnant of Jews that believed in Jesus Christ as true Israel (Romans 9–11). The theological truth is that "not all who are descended from Israel are Israel" (Rom 9:6, HCSB). This reality is certainly true throughout history as the distinction between Esau and Jacob, as true descendants of Abraham, had already indicated (Genesis 25:19–36:30). But drawing such distinctions is not the point of much of the Hebrew historical books. It is introduced to Elijah in an unexpected and striking fashion when he saw himself as the only true believer in Israel (1 Kgs 19:15-18). In fact, God knew of 7000 that were true in their worship of Him, even though Elijah hadn't seen their true spiritual condition. As God chose survivors to return, there is no indication that they were chosen because they were true worshipers and the rest were not. The hope for the house of Israel and the house of Judah remained (Jer 31:31-32).

However, a Dispensational Biblical theology provides a framework for acknowledging this distinction in history. Traditionally, the dispensation of promise provided the basis for salvation as illustrated in Abraham, the father of faith (Gen 15:6). In reality, the *protoevangelium* provided a ground for faith (Gen 3:15). Those who believed are distinguished from those who did not believe as Abel was from Cain.

The text of *Exodus*, in which the Law is introduced, attempted to make no such distinction. Rather, the narrative emphasizes that the exodus generation would be redeemed (Exod 6:6; 12:1-13; 15:13). Each household would, by faith (as assessed by God), place the blood of the lamb on the doorpost and the death angel would pass over that household. The promise (Exod 12:12-13) was the basis of redemption. While undoubtedly all did not believe, all who were circumcised had the opportunity to believe. All who believed were true Israelites.

Then that generation, without distinction, was chosen to service when they were given the Law (Exod 19:5-6). Individually, in redemption, they were chosen to salvation. Collectively, in law, they were chosen to service. Even though no distinction was drawn, "we are told that God's purpose for the remnant is his purpose for the whole people."[9] Thus in the dispensation of law, the addition of law to promise provides the framework for recognizing a distinction between the believing true Israelite and the unbelieving false Israelite, even though the text fails to specify who is who. This portrays the people so that what is true in Paul is also true in Exodus. This avoids the following conclusion: "in the confrontation between Israel and the message of Jesus Christ, the idea of a *specially qualified remnant* became *modified* and *reinterpreted*, finding in this message its ultimate fulfillment in an unexpected way."[10] Rather, Jeremiah set forth the national hope before the times of the Gentiles began.

Times of the Gentiles

While Daniel gave a more comprehensive disclosure of the times of the Gentiles, Ezra and Nehemiah gave witness to the corresponding political situation. This is evident from the portrayal of what happened.

The Decree of Cyrus and Darius

The authority for the people of Israel to pursue what God desired for them was delegated to the Gentile government. It was not exclusively the Mosaic Law. Governmental edicts and letters had determined what the people of God had the right to pursue. It was Cyrus' decree which authorized the rebuilding of the temple for worship (Ezra 1:2-4). When that right was contended, it was the letter of Artaxerxes that halted the building (Ezra 4:18-22). While the prophets challenged the rightness of this decision, it was the decree of Darius that Cyrus had already authorized

---

[9] Günter and Krienke, p. 253.

[10] *Ibid.*, emphasis mine.

the returning remnant to build the temple (Ezra 6:6-12), that provided the authority to conclude the building.

Ezra's mission as a scribe of the Law was spelled out in general terms by Artaxerxes, king of kings (Ezra 7:14, 23). Nehemiah's desire to rebuild Jerusalem was supported by Artaxerxes the king (Neh 2:6-10). That support took the form of releasing Nehemiah from his responsibility and providing building supplies from the king's resources.

The Viewpoint of the Remnant

The people who returned recognized their situation as "slaves in the land" so that Gentiles "could enjoy its fruit and its goodness" (Neh 9:36, HCSB). They prayed about this, depending upon God to provide through the Gentile governments. This was true for the remnant in the land and the remnant in the Gentile nations.

Zechariah—Fifth Century BC

Zechariah was the son of Berechiah and the grandson of Iddo (Zech 1:1), who prophesied to the returned exilic remnant in Judah in the years 520-518 BC (Zech 1:1; 7:1). While Haggai, a contemporary, spoke primarily to the immediate demand of building the temple, Zechariah spoke to the sense of expectation that building a house for God brought. God had spoken through Persian, Gentile leaders and now was speaking through Jewish prophets. Building the house of God could bring the hearts of a worshiping people closer to God and His plans if they would only listen to Him. Zechariah both called for repentance (Zech 1:2-6), that they might hear what God would say, and built a vision in the hearts of the people of what God wanted to accomplish. The prophet picked up the hope for national Israel, introduced by Jeremiah, that would appear at some time in the future. The structure of the book (1:7–6:15: Eight Night Visions; 7:1–8:23: A Historic Question; and 9:1–14:21: Prophetic-Apocalyptic Visions of God's Plan) expresses that call and anticipation. They were to build the temple and wait for the LORD to intervene in history.

What Is the Envisioned Message?

Von Rad states:

> [Zechariah] became aware that Jahweh was jealous for Jerusalem and that he had already made all the preparations for his own advent—he had appointed his representatives and provided for and overcame all complication and oppositions... [these] are already accomplished in the sight of the world above, so that they have anticipated the course of events on earth.[11]

Baldwin agrees, "This conviction that all that remained was for the same pattern to be repeated on earth was to dominate apocalyptic, and is seen in both Daniel and Revelation."[12]

Thus, the book begins with a call to the people to return to the LORD and He will return to them (Zech 1:3). Such repentance was necessary for this small, insignificant remnant to have a part in what God would do: "Not by might, nor by power, but by my Spirit, says the LORD of hosts" (Zech 4:6).

Even though it was worked out in heaven, it was not a simple matter to be worked out for those on earth. The book presents that vision both in the immediate historical context (Zechariah 1–8) and in the ultimate future context of consummation (chaps. 9–14). In the immediate context, Israel sees that it has a role in the new era that is about to dawn. In consummation, Jerusalem's role is to be where the king of the house of David will reside in his capital. Those prophetic-apocalyptic visions (Zechariah 9–14) focus on the intervention of the LORD bringing judgment—judgment through which the Gentile power over Israel would finally be destroyed (Zechariah 9–11) and through which Israel itself and Jerusalem would be sifted and purged and transformed into a holy nation. This is the final great conflict in that day (Zechariah 12–14).[13] This is the message of the prophet that Luther called the greatest Hebrew prophet. In order to clarify the theological message, three questions about the prophecies will be raised. To fully appreciate the issues treated, one would need to be familiar with the same issues first raised in earlier prophets.

---

[11] Von Rad, *Old Testament Theology*, vol. 2, p. 288.

[12] Joyce G. Baldwin, *Haggai, Zechariah, Malachi*, Tyndale Old Testament Commentaries, (Downers Grove, IL: IVP, 1972), p. 72. This commentary, along with David Baron, *The Visions and Prophecies of Zechariah* (Fincastle, VA: Scripture Truth, 1962) will be followed in the exposition of Zechariah's revelation.

[13] Baron, *Visions and Prophecies of Zechariah*, p. 85.

What about the Battle?

From the time of Abraham, the chosen people had experienced conflict in battles with the enemy, with personal sin, and with evil in the world. The Mosaic Law given to the chosen people had exposed the battle that fallen men would have with the righteous demands of God, ultimately reckoned on the Day of the LORD. To heighten Israel's awareness of the battle, God had used Gentile nations to judge the nation's sin. Now God had begun to speak again through the Persian kings to bring the people back to the land God had given them, but which was now possessed by the Gentiles. *What was God about to do?*

The eight night visions framed their historical view of the battle. God's governance would implement among the nations what God had planned. And the oversight of this plan rested in an angelic patrol of human affairs. The angelic patrol was at the same level of power as the enemy of God. In the first vision, at night, the patrol was observing what was happening to Jerusalem. In the eighth vision, at daybreak, they were ready to do battle with the enemy to accomplish God's plan for Jerusalem. This providential level of God's activity on earth was also disclosed in Daniel 9–12.

In the final accounts of prophetic apocalypse, the first (Zech 9:1-8) and final (Zech 14:1-15) segments feature warfare. In the first segment, the LORD triumphs from the north (Zech 9:1-8). "[T]he writer is not taking any particular historical standpoint, but rather, in the manner characteristic of apocalyptic, is using past events to typify a supremely important future event."[14] Earlier, the prophets had foreseen enemies invading from the north (e.g., Isa 41:25; Jer 1:14-15; Ezek 26:7). Now it is the LORD who conquers every city and people as He makes His way south to set up camp in Jerusalem.

The final segment (Zech 14:1-15) portrays the dramatic reversal in the status in Jerusalem. "The chapter opens with a defeated Jerusalem, stripped of possessions and honour, submitting to all the indignities inflicted by the conqueror...eventually they see the intervention of the Lord."[15] When His feet stand on the Mount of Olives, the Mount will be split in two and the topography drastically changed. The city will rise to dominate on the plain created, and the LORD will set up His world government in Jerusalem. The survivors will go up to worship the King, the LORD of hosts, and to keep the Feast of Booths (Zech 14:16).

---

[14]   Baldwin, *Zechariah*, p. 158.

[15]   *Ibid.*, p. 199.

What about God's Promise?

The promise, when first stated to Abraham, seemed so simple and clear that the implementation would be forthright. But in a fallen world the implementation would be complicated by the contingencies of evil. Those who knew the earlier prophets could not fail to see the connection between king and shepherd in Zechariah.[16] This King would enter Jerusalem to claim the throne, humble and submissive to the reception of the people there (Zech 9:9-10). This Shepherd among the people would be rejected, sold for thirty pieces of silver (Zech 11:10-17) by a flock doomed to judgment. Their covenant (Zech 11:10) and their national unity (Zech 11:14) would be annulled as the foolish shepherds were doomed. The Shepherd would be struck down, and without a shepherd, the sheep would be scattered (13:7-8). In time, the inhabitants of Jerusalem will receive a spirit of grace to mourn when they see the One they pierced (Zechariah 12:10–13:1). A judgment will strike the whole land, and one-third will be spared and purified, those who call on the name of the LORD. In these incidents experienced by the promised One, the promise did not change even though its implementation was subject to assault from evil in the world.

What about Jerusalem?

Jerusalem was the city the LORD had chosen to dwell in at the time of David, yet by the writing of Zechariah, His glory had departed. So the exiles wrote a letter to those who returned to Jerusalem with a question: should they continue to fast at that time (Zechariah 7–8)? Since the LORD has begun to bless Jerusalem, "The fast of the fourth month and the fast of the fifth and the fast of the seventh and the fast of the tenth shall be to the house of Judah seasons of joy and gladness and cheerful feasts. Therefore love truth and peace" (Zech 8:19). Fasts when blessing is present are inappropriate; feasts should take their place.

Looking ahead, the LORD will make His way to settle in Jerusalem as His capital (Zech 9:9). Jerusalem is about to be seized and judged (Zech 12:1-5). In the Day of the LORD, Jerusalem will be inhabited again, and the glory of the house of David will settle there. Salvation will come to Jerusalem (Zech 12:6-9). In that day, the defeated and overrun Jerusalem will become the source of life and light (Zech 14:6-8).

---

[16] *Ibid.*, p. 172.

Malachi—Fourth Century BC

Nothing is known of the author or the exact historical occasion of Malachi. It seems best to see his location in history prior to the ministry of Ezra who came to Jerusalem in 458 BC. So his ministry challenged hypocrisy in the Jewish community (c. 470 BC).

> Whereas most of the prophets lived and prophesized in the days of change and political upheaval, Malachi and his contemporaries were living in an uneventful waiting period, when God seemed to have forgotten His people enduring poverty and foreign domination in the little providence of Judah.[17]

Many interpreters see the focus of the prophet resting in a return to the Mosaic Covenant. Baldwin says: "Fundamental to Malachi's teaching is the concept of covenant."[18] Merrill states the emphasis: "His appeal to his people was that they reorder their priorities and fall in line with the LORD's covenant requirements."[19] But both of these perspectives disregard what the prophets have said about the Mosaic Covenant lawsuit (Hos 1:2-9; Jeremiah 3:6-23; 11). In their national dispersion among the Gentiles, the function of the Mosaic Covenant had been annulled (Zech 11:10). Yet the Law-Scripture remained as a frame for worship and life.

What does this mean? The remnant had returned to their land as simply a religious community. There is no indication that a Gentile power had allowed for any more than the rebuilding of the temple and the city of Jerusalem. There is no indication that the LORD had ratified the New Covenant or renewed the Old Covenant.

The focus was primarily upon the priests (Mal 1:6; 2:1). The priesthood had become corrupt and worship had become routine. The covenant at issue with Levi (Mal 2:5, 8) was the covenant of the priesthood (Num 25:12-13). The covenant at issue with Judah involved "profaning the covenant of our fathers" (Mal 2:10) and profaning "the sanctuary of the LORD" as he "has married the daughter of a foreign god" (Mal 2:11). Through widespread divorce and marriage of pagan women, he disregarded the election of the descendants of Abraham (Mal 1:2-3, Abrahamic Covenant) and polluted the temple that had been rebuilt. Social justice was ignored and tithing was neglected. Von Rad correctly specifies

---

[17]   *Ibid.*, p. 211.

[18]   *Ibid.*, p. 216.

[19]   Merrill, *Everlasting Dominion*, p. 563.

the issues as "exclusively concerned with abuses practised by the community,"[20] rather than covenant partnership issues with the LORD.

The main issue related to their worship practices and lifestyles as God's chosen people. Their responsibility for honoring God's name before the nations as God's chosen people remained (Mal 1:11, 14). The LORD is concerned about His reputation beyond the border of Israel (Mal 1:5). And their worship is not honoring to the LORD as the prophet's disputation with the people indicates (Mal 1:2; 2:10, 14; 3:7).

What is fundamental to the message of Malachi is that the LORD Himself is coming to establish His reputation among the nations. "The Lord whom you seek will suddenly come to his temple" (Mal 3:1). The glory of the LORD will appear in the temple as Israel would rightly expect from her covenant history (Exod 40:34-38; 1 Kgs 8:10-11). Somehow, the restoration of the glory of the LORD to the temple and the ratification of the New Covenant will be related to His coming. And the coming of the LORD is "the day of his coming." (Mal 3:2; 4:5). This is "the great and awesome day of the LORD" (Mal 4:5), concerning which the prophet asks, "who can endure the day of his coming, and who can stand when he appears?" (Mal 3:2). That was the same question asked in Joel 2:11. It will be a day of refining for Israel and purification for the sons of Levi (Mal 3:2b-3). As Joseph had saved and transformed the patriarchs through testing, so Israel will be purified through the testing on the Day of the LORD.

In addition, the LORD will send His messenger to prepare the way before His coming (Mal 3:1). This is the same message that Isaiah had earlier prophesied (Isa 40:3-5). This messenger is further described as "Elijah the prophet" (Mal 4:5). As was proposed earlier, Elijah had been translated as a sign of cessation of the functioning of the Mosaic Covenant partnership in Ahaz's reign. Now he returns to address the nation's law responsibility. This had been introduced in Isa 40:1-2 when Jerusalem's "iniquity is pardoned," since "she has received from the LORD's hand double for all her sins." Daniel had also been told that the seventy-year captivity (Jer 25:11; 29:10-12) would not suffice to deal with her sin (Dan 9:24). Rather, seventy sevens of years were decreed to put an end to sin and to atone for iniquity. While the time framework is disclosed in general, it is not a tight chronology. One seven-year period was separated from the other sixty-nine, and since it has the role of concluding these purposes (Dan 9:24), one might expect that final week of years could correspond in some way to the outset of the great and awesome Day of the LORD (Mal 4:5).

---

[20] Von Rad, *Old Testament Theology*, vol. 2, p. 288.

Both will result in the preparation of the nation of Israel to become God's people in a final and actual sense.

Further, the ministry of "the messenger of the covenant" is disclosed. "He will turn the hearts of fathers to their children and the hearts of children to their fathers" (Mal 4:6). This is a call to repent, but more than merely an attempt, it is an effectual call that will accomplish the task. But is the messenger a messenger of the Mosaic Covenant? In the immediate context, the people were reminded of the Law of Moses (Mal 4:4). This would address the same issues without speaking of the covenant partnership. The reason for the response of repentance is, "lest I come and strike the land with a decree of utter destruction" (Mal 4:6). Thus, the call to repentance does not concern a covenant renewal, but protection from judgment of sin. Even though the covenant had been annulled, the seventy years captivity had not finished the people's law responsibility. Elijah will address that responsibility. But the text is silent over how that responsibility will be satisfied "to atone for iniquity." And total destruction could be averted if a remnant repented, rather than the whole nation. These issues imply questions which remain unanswered as the Hebrew Canon is closed.

Conclusion

The exilic and postexilic times in Biblical revelation are *transitional*. They involve a *political transition* from Israel's theocratic monarchy to a Gentile monarchy. While both are divinely appointed to represent God's providential rule on earth, they do so in different ways. In Israel, the right to rule on the LORD's behalf mediated the LORD's rule, reflected in the Mosaic Covenant. As the king is ruled by the righteous revelation in the Law, so his rule was to express the righteousness of the LORD. But the king's rebellion and wickedness predominated, and ultimately resulted in dispersion from the land and captivity by Assyria and Babylon.

Gentile governments did not mediate God's righteousness in their rule, but the right to rule was delegated to them. The Jewish remnant bore witness to that rule as Daniel and Nehemiah exemplified. But the prophets revealed that their reign would be judged by their treatment of Israel as God's people. Yet in spite of the unrighteousness of the Gentile rulers, the "Times of the Gentiles" would serve the sovereign will of the LORD and frame the judgment on Israel at the conclusion of the dispensation of the law.

The *theological transition* was beginning when the LORD kept His promise and "when the fullness of time had come, God sent forth his Son, born of woman, born under the law" (Gal 4:4). The "woman" alludes to the promise to Eve and to birth from the virgin Mary. The "law" refers to the revelation given to Israel at Mt. Sinai. The "Son" born was subject to the Law so that He could "redeem those who were under the law" (Gal 4:5). The life and ministry of the Son would bring the transition to a conclusion as the dispensation of the law reached fulfillment. The commitment that Israel accepted (Exod 19:5-6) would be fulfilled in the keeping of the obligation of that commitment (Matt 5:17), and in bearing the penalty for Israel's failure to keep their commitment (Gal 3:10). With the Law fulfilled, the stewardship of the Law would no longer be man's responsibility.

A final aspect of the *transition* was *geographical*. At the outset of the deportation, the population of Israel and Judah were taken captive to Assyria and Babylon. Then those whom God moved from Judah and Benjamin, as well as those among the priests and Levites, returned as servants to the land. This remnant of returnees was not represented as the only true believers, but rather as those who would represent the population of all Israel. In fact, three tribes from Persia were moved by God to return, to be used by God in the second temple period. Under Ezra, they were exposed to the Law of Moses to carry the burden of an unfinished responsibility that the people had originally accepted (Exod 19:5-6).

The portrayal of a majority dispersed among the Gentiles is compatible with what Moses portrayed concerning the dispersion: "The LORD will scatter you among the peoples...where the LORD your God will drive you" (Deut 4:27, HCSB; cf., 30:1, 3). It was this setting in dispersion from which God would restore Israel to Himself (Deut 4:30-31; 30:2, 5).

Thus, it appears that the returning remnant was not the intended culmination of God's work with the descendants of Abraham. Rather, the tribe of Judah was the people from whom the promised Messiah would be born (Gen 49:10; 2 Sam 7:16, 19). The leaders of the return were Sheshbazzar, the prince of Judah (Ezra 1:8; 5:14), and Zerubbabel (Ezra 2:2; Matt 1:13). So descendants of the line of David were part of this returning remnant, who would live through the second temple period to accomplish some kind of representative work in the near future (Matthew 1–4).

However, the prophetic books had kept the focus of the people on a worldwide perspective, although the focus of the remnant was on the Law of Moses. Ezekiel focused on the guilt of the immediate generation in captivity but focused on redemption and restoration of the people at some distant future generation. In spite of the ambiguity of that future portrayal, there are these certainties:

- Israel will *know* the LORD.

- Israel at that distant time will be dry bones, yet they will come to life as a God-breathed person.

- Israel will again house the glory of God in the temple in the land.

Daniel set the perspective of the Times of the Gentiles. Visions featured how it would begin and how it would reach its climax. The end of this period will involve the creation goal—the Son of Man will, in reality, mediate the rule of the heavenly Enthroned One on earth. In the meantime, Israel will suffer and overcome, to realize the plan of redemption from sin. And the suffering of the people in conflict with the enemy of God will only intensify as the Day of the LORD comes.

Zechariah has two focuses on Israel's future. One relates to what will happen to Jerusalem politically. The other relates to what will happen to Israel's promised Deliverer. Without a prior knowledge of the two advents of the promised One fleshed out in history, it would be difficult, if not impossible, to relate the literary structure of different visions. But knowing about the First Advent, and believing in what is said as it relates to a distinct Second Advent, will help to grasp the future.

Malachi is the final prophet who speaks before 400 years of silence within the second temple period (516 BC–AD 70). He challenges believers to live with integrity in the uncertainty of silence. His message of hope calls for the people to *wait*.

CHAPTER 16:
TIMES OF THE GENTILES:
INTRODUCTION TO
THE GOSPELS

Introduction

The four Gospels each contain a transitional message in the canon of Christian Scriptures. The Hebrew canon closed with the tension in the progress of revelation unresolved. Promises addressed to Israel held out hope that remained unfulfilled. Despair hung over the people as their repeated rebellion against the Law resulted in Gentile captivity. The returned remnant in the second temple period still lived with unresolved tension under Gentile rule.

The Christian scriptures add the four Gospel accounts. Each addresses the unresolved tension and presents Jesus, who resolves the issues. This is the focus of Biblical theology which this chapter will feature. But before we do, we want to briefly address the modern question. That question concerns *historicity*. How do we know that what is recorded in the text is in fact what happened? In particular, did miracles happen? Was Jesus raised from the dead?

The modern worldview featured a methodological naturalism. And of course, miracles are contrary to natural experiences—the blind gain sight, the lame walk, and the diseased are healed at Jesus' word. What historical evidence exists to support the claim that these miracles in fact happened? The accusation is that the Gospels are theologically biased rather than historically true.

This naturalism turns to historical-critical methods to find solutions that seem natural. Historicism establishes what seems to be historical by seeking the original account—that account which appears to be closest to the events. The Gospel of Mark was generally recognized as that account, even though historical records indicate that Matthew was composed earlier. Source criticism sought to piece together the probable sources that best accounted for the canonical Gospel. The historical writings of the Church paint a different picture.

Matthew and John are both authored by apostles. Mark composed an account of Peter's preaching. This is the historical, traditional witness. Luke 1:1-4 gives an account of his research and his intent in writing to Theophilus.

Today, this "kind of historical-critical approach that once dominated historical Jesus studies has been dealt a fatal wound."[1] His conclusions rest on the earlier work of Richard Bauckham.[2] He adopted a different approach rather than relying upon the historical-critical reconstruction. He postulated that the four Gospels are independent accounts of eyewitnesses to historical truth. This resembles the Hebrew system of jurisprudence, in which guilt of capital crimes is only established on the basis of two or three independent corroborating witnesses (Deut 17:2-7). Such a life or death decision could not be reached without reliable and independent testimony. Clearly, the historical reliability of the events in the life and death of Jesus of Nazareth is such a determinate issue. In that perspective and weighing of truth, the four Gospel accounts would be viewed as independent witnesses testifying to the truth of what happened.[3] Salmon suggests that the overall shape of the Synoptic perspective comes from the historical influence of Peter's preaching.[4] It is clear that the Gospel of John and the Synoptic Gospels share a common historicity but provide different interpretations of Jesus' life and ministry. This is the approach we will take. Pennington concludes: "We may assert that the epistemological foundation of modernistic, positivistic history is strikingly different from the biblical understanding."[5]

Thus, treating the four Gospels as four independent witnesses does not answer all the historical questions. At the same time, it confirms the historical account of Jesus' ministry, death, and resurrection. Based on this preliminary historical foundation, we can return to Biblical questions about the transitional message.

---

[1] Jonathan T. Pennington, *Reading the Gospels Wisely* (Grand Rapids, MI: Baker Academic, 2012), p. 93.

[2] Richard Bauckham, *Jesus and the Eyewitnesses: The Gospels as Eyewitness Testimony* (Grand Rapids, MI: Eerdmans, 2006).

[3] Pennington, *Reading the Gospels Wisely*, pp. 74-107.

[4] George Salmon, *The Human Element in the Gospels: A Commentary on the Synoptic Narrative*, ed. Newport J. D. White (London: John Murray, 1907).

[5] Pennington, *Reading the Gospels Wisely*, p. 93.

This transitional message includes Jesus entrusted with Israel's responsibility and Jesus rising from the dead as victorious over sin and death. As Heir to the promises addressed to Abraham and David, He enjoyed initial fulfillment. As Representative of Israel, He both fully kept the Law (Matt 5:18) and overcame the condemnation of the Law.

As a result, Jesus entrusted a new stewardship of grace to His followers. The Apostle John spoke of transition in the revelation: "the law was given through Moses; grace and truth came through Jesus Christ" (John 1:17).

In order to see the transitional message more clearly, two questions will be addressed:

1. How do the Gospels address the tension?

2. How do the Gospels see the tension resolved?

Tension Addressed in the Gospels

Historically, the Gospels reflect the tension as faced in second temple Judaism. The four hundred years of silence was reflected in the pluralism present in Judaism. "[I]t is evident that the radical pluralization of Judaism prior to Jesus is rooted in the flawed unity of restored Israel during the previous period."[6]

Pharisees saw the status of Israel resting in a rigidly held traditional keeping of the Law. Sadducees used a secular understanding of the Law to maintain their political status under Rome. Essenes separated from established Judaism and as the Qumran literature indicated, had their own view of promise and law: Simeon and Anna believed the promises of Messiah and waited for Him, serving God in the temple. Thus, it would be misleading to attempt to summarize Judaism as sharing a common point of view.[7]

This diversity in first century Judaism reflects the unresolved tension existing in the restored remnant to Jerusalem. Was Israel's identity to be defined by law or by God's promise? "For Jews of the first century the name Israel probably carried with it one or more of three basic associated ideas,"[8] an elect people, a people under law, and a people with promise of

---

[6] B. D. Chilton, "Judaism," *Dictionary of Jesus and the Gospels*, ed. Joel Green, Scot McKnight, I. Howard Marshall (Downers Grove: IVP, 1992), p. 401.

[7] D. A. Carson, Peter T. O'Brien and Mark A. Seifrid, eds., *Justification and Variegated Nomism: A Fresh Appraisal of Paul and Second Temple Judaism, Volume 1: The Complexities of Second Temple Judaism*, (Grand Rapids, MI: Baker, 2001).

[8] M. A. Elliott, "Israel," *Dictionary of Jesus and the Gospels*, pp. 356-57.

the Davidic Covenant. In other words, was Israel's vision of its destiny and responsibility found in law or in promise? Westerholm expressed it this way: "Pharisees and the earliest followers of Jesus—all Jews—stood for alternative visions of the destiny and responsibilities of Israel...the course which Israel must pursue, and that from which they must turn, if they were to fulfill their divine calling."[9]

Each Gospel developed the themes of law and promise but with a somewhat different emphasis. Mark highlights the Pharisees' claim to Israel's identity to be found *exclusively* in keeping the Law. Their adamant contention for a traditional handling of the Law aroused hostility toward Jesus (Mark 2:16, 18, 23-24; 3:2; 7:5; 8:11; 10:2-9; 12:13, 28-34). Yet Matthew included Jesus' early teaching that He had not come to destroy the Law and the Prophets but to fulfill them (Matt 5:17).

Both Matthew and Luke emphasize Israel as God's elect people of promise but from different perspectives. Matthew stressed that both John (Matt 3:2) and Jesus (Matt 4:17) preached a message that the kingdom of heaven was at hand for the first-century generation. That generation was called to be blessed with Messiah (Matt 5:3-12, promises embedded in the beatitudes) as they join Messiah in serving the Lord (Matthew 5:13–7:12, Sermon on the Mount, based on the Law).

Jesus focused His ministry and that of the Twelve on the generation of "the lost sheep of the house of Israel" (Matt 10:6). That elect generation soon confronted Jesus (Matt 11:16) and as a result, judgment was pronounced against them (Matt 12:39). At the climax of Jesus' First Advent, He again pronounced judgment on that historic generation (Matt 23:36), as the temple would be left desolate to them (Matt 23:37-39). Yet, a future elect generation would be blessed at the return of the Son of Man (Matt 24:30-31). That generation would be the nation to whom the kingdom of God would be given (Matt 21:43). From Jesus' point of view, the unresolved tension would be resolved in His own ministry in His two advents. Still, the First Advent generation sought a resolution in the Pharisees' view of the people under the Law rather than in the promised Davidic Heir.

Luke also featured Israel's election, but from a different perspective. His focus wasn't on an election of that generation of Israel to service, as Matthew's was, but on the election of a remnant within Israel to personal salvation. Whereas God chose Abraham and his descendants, Isaac was chosen and not Ishmael, Jacob and not Esau. So from the outset, the

---

[9] S. Westerholm, "Pharisees," *Dictionary of Jesus and the Gospels*, p. 614.

focus was on the believing remnant, Zechariah, Mary, the shepherds, and Simeon and Anna. These individuals were all chosen, believing ones. The story of Zechariah's initial unbelief illustrates this vividly. This perspective on a believing remnant lay the foundation for Luke's focus on Jesus' ministry, who came "to seek and to save that which was lost" (Luke 19:10, NKJV, emphasis added).

This difference in perspective is also reflected in the generation reaching faith or unbelief in the promise embodied in Messiah. In Matthew, the generation's response to Jesus unfolded until it reached a climax in the divided generation (Matt 11:14-30; 12:22-32). In Luke, the response at Nazareth was featured at the very beginning of His ministry (Luke 4:16-30). Individual responses are then repeatedly considered throughout the account. That response is featured in the parable of the prodigal son who "came to his senses" (Luke 15:17, HCSB; Deut 30:1, HCSB) and returned to his father in faith. A common response in Luke came from "sinners" (Luke 15:1-2), who recognized their guilt under the Law, and who found acceptance in Jesus' grace. Thus, the resolution of the tension came in those who realized the condemnation in the *Law* and the *promise* of salvation found in Jesus Christ.

Resolution of the Tension in the Gospels

All the Gospels agree that Jesus, in His Person and work, is the resolution. But their perspectives differ. In the past, the issue with Israel was *partnership* between God and Israel. It was a Mosaic Covenant partnership to which Israel had promised they would obey (Exod 19:8; 24:3, 7) but they did not. In the miracle of the incarnation, the covenant partnership between the people and God was resolved by a partnership within One Person, the Son and the Father.

Mark simply introduced it as "the gospel of Jesus Christ" (1:1). The good news implied a resolution.

Matthew found the miracle prophesied in the sign[10] Isaiah spoke to Ahaz (Isa 7:14). In a virgin conception and birth, the Davidic promise with Ahaz was not set aside. Rather, the Davidic promise would be realized in Immanuel. The Child born would be named God with us, in a personal

---

[10]   For Matthew to use this sign in the sense intended by Isaiah is essential to explain the fulfillment in Jesus' birth and to explain Jesus' place in Israel's history. To posit double fulfillment would be to change the meaning of the sign. The sign, in Ahaz's day, would be a sign of the *time* of his birth while in Joseph's day; the sign was the *virgin* birth to allay his concerns about his marriage to Mary and to account for Jesus' heirship to David.

presence. The Gospel account records how the Son of Man, representing Israel, would be the Father's Partner as God with Israel in ministry.

Luke unfolded the miracle in the announcement to Mary: "The Holy Spirit will come upon you, and the power of the Most High will over-shadow you. Therefore, the holy One to be born will be called the *Son of God*" (Luke 1:35, HCSB, emphasis added). Mary's response was direct: "I am the Lord's slave…May it be done to me according to your word" (Luke 1:38, HCSB). The Jewish Boy born was God's Son; the Son would serve according to the Father's Word—just as Mary had.

The Gospel of John introduced the second Person of the Godhead as the *Word*. The Word who spoke creation into existence (John 1:2-3) also spoke in history to stewards (John 1:3-11). As God, the Word made promises to Israel; God Himself made commitments to accomplish what He had promised. But how would that happen?

"And the Word became flesh" (John 1:14).

> The incarnation occurred not by conversion of divinity into flesh but by the assumption of humanity into God [Athanasius, *On the Incarn. of the Word* 14-15, *NPNF* 2IV, pp. 43-44; Heppe, *RD*, p 414]. God became flesh not by changing into another reality, but by assumption (*assumptio carnis*), by entering the human mode of being without ceasing to be God. Remaining what he was, he became what he was not. (Hilary, *Trin.* 3.16; Athanasius, *Four Discourses Ag. Arians* 1.35)[11]

The idea of the assumption of humanity into deity acknowledges the eternal existence of the Word (John 1:1, 14). The Person continues to be identified by the name *Son of God*. At the same time, the Person also has the name *Son of Man*. He is human by nature and is in the mode of human weakness, subject to suffering and death, in need of food and sleep. Still the union involves an assumption of human nature without sin. Only then could humanity and deity be combined in One Person and live in obedience to the Father.

So in John's prologue, the *resolution* may be conceived in this fashion: The Word who spoke creation into existence (1:1-3) is also the Word who spoke to stewards in history (1:4-11); and in the stewards' refusal to receive the Word (1:11), the Word became the Steward to fulfill what He originally had promised to do (1:14-18).

---

[11] Thomas C. Oden, *Systematic Theology, Volume 2: The Word of Life* (San Francisco, CA: Harper and Row, 1989), pp. 95-96.

Conclusion

Promise from the LORD had provided hope from the beginning. But it involved hope that had not been fully realized. The LORD added *law* to specify Israel's responsibility. But no descendant of Abraham, no heir of David, had experienced all that was hoped for because none had been willing to serve God (Isaiah 39 and Hezekiah). So the tension between hope and reality remained unresolved until the virgin birth of Jesus in Bethlehem (Isa 7:14).

Now God has taken on human flesh. God who made the commitment of promise (the Word, John 1:1-4) now partnered on earth with human flesh to keep His commitment. The Son of Man was fully subject to the Law in spite of temptation to disobey. So Jesus lived in the reality of God's promise and overcome demon possession, disease, and even death itself. He also died under the curse of the Law, only to experience deliverance from death according to God's promise. The resolution has been met in the Person and work of Jesus, the Messiah.

CHAPTER 17:
THE TIMES OF THE
GENTILES: MATTHEW

Introduction

Matthew's Gospel features Jesus as the heir to Israel's hope. This is highlighted in the genealogy by the references to David and Abraham (Matt 1:1-17). As the Heir to Abraham, Jesus is a member of the elect people with the promise of inheritance (Gen 12:1-3). As the Heir to David, whose name is mentioned twice, He has the right to rule over the Davidic kingdom (2 Sam 7:12-17). Jesus is thus firmly rooted in the election of God in Israel.

At the same time, Matthew explicitly states Jesus' intent to fulfill the Law and the Prophets (Matt 5:17). Moo assesses this intent:

> From what the Gospels tell us of Jesus' behavior, he was generally obedient to the Law of Moses. He attends the major feasts in Jerusalem, pays the half-shekel temple tax (Mt 17:24-27), wears the prescribed tassel on his robe (Mt 9:20; cf. Num 15:38-41) and, whatever may be said about his disciples' behavior or his teaching, never clearly violates the Sabbath. It is only in the case of Jesus' contact with unclean people...in his healing ministry (e.g. touching a leper [Mt 8:3 par. Mk 1:4 and Lk 5:13]) that he could be considered in violation of the Law of Moses. Even in this case, however, the unusual nature of Jesus' healing activities makes it difficult to identify a clear-cut violation of the Law.[1]

Thus, Matthew positions Jesus as the One who reconciles the scriptural tension which had remained unresolved. That is His appeal to that

---

[1] Douglas J. Moo, "Law," *Dictionary of Jesus and the Gospels*, pp. 451–52.

generation's expectations which Matthew will narrate. He will receive what God has promised because He will be faithful.

What Did the Prophet John Do to Introduce Jesus to Israel (Matthew 3–4)?

John the Baptist was the prophet God used to introduce Jesus as King, chosen by God. The introduction had four purposes for the people.

First, the people were called to *repent* because the kingdom of heaven was near. Repentance prepared sinners to receive what heaven was about to do. Continuation in sin must be challenged (Matt 3:2, 7-10) because it blinded men to God.

The kingdom of heaven is introduced without being defined. John expected the Jews of the second temple period to recognize what was meant based on their knowledge of the Hebrew Scripture. Heaven had become identified as the residence of God (Neh 1:4-5; 2:4, 20; Ezra 5:11; Dan 2:18), after the destruction of the first temple. Thus, it meant God's reign in heaven was about to come to earth in a sense that His providence did not include.

Rather, it would be God's reign mediated through man on earth. Such a mediatorial rule had been introduced at creation in Adam (Gen 1:26-28). That rule of God was lost when Adam rebelled against God (Gen 3:1-6). Since Adam accepted the serpent's word, the serpent now ruled on earth over man and through man who had an evil heart (Cain).

God challenged that rule when He revealed the Mosaic Law and introduced His theocratic reign over Israel. But Israel failed to mediate God's reign. When Israel asked for a king, God allowed His theocratic rule to be mediated through the Davidic King and his heir (2 Sam 7:12-16). But every king failed to mediate God's reign. Now what had been promised was announced as at hand in the One John was about to introduce.

Second, John the Baptist was introduced as the voice prophesied in Isa 40:3. He spoke to the people about being prepared through repentance. In addition, he announced that the Lord was coming (Matt 3:3). He was the One who would come after John, yet He would be more powerful than John. In fact, He would have a status in God's presence that made John unworthy to serve Him in the most menial task (Matt 3:11).

Third, he spoke prophetically about Messiah's future ministry. It was cast in a mold comparable to his own (Matt 3:11), characterized as *baptism*.

> It began as a metaphor…drawn from the symbolical significance of the rite which characterized John the Baptist's ministry—viz., as immersion in a river…the Spirit and fire are clearly elements into which people would be plunged, a river of *ruaḥ* and fire (as in the apocalyptic usage)…[2]

So when John saw the Pharisees and Sadducees coming to be baptized, he confronted them as serpents. Then he asked whether they had been warned to flee from the wrath to come (Matt 3:7). A defense that they were protected because they were Abraham's descendants was no defense before God. One baptism would be a judgment in fire (Matt 3:10) that would burn the unfruitful. Therefore, they need to bear fruit in keeping with repentance (Matt 3:8). Thus, it was a judgment that would weigh the genuineness of the heart's response,[3] not merely outward religious actions.

The presence of the image of fire in this warning of imminent judgment, and in Jesus' baptism with fire, would suggest a common judgment. The One coming will bring judgment of unquenchable fire (Matt 3:12), in which fire is the sphere of judgment (Matt 3:10). That common relationship is further confirmed when Jesus' later words are also considered. Jesus added, "I came to bring fire on the earth, and how I wish it were already set ablaze!" (Luke 12:49, HCSB). This is the imminent judgment John warned his generation to be prepared for. In addition, Jesus said, "I have a baptism to be baptized with, and how it consumes Me until it is finished!" (Luke 12:50, HCSB). Seeing these words from a historical perspective, there are two judgments in view. God would baptize Jesus in judgment on the cross (AD 33), and Jesus would baptize that generation of Israel in judgment (AD 70). Rome was the political agent of each judgment.

The second mention of baptism with the Holy Spirit is also identified clearly with the experience about three years later. Before the arrival of the day of Pentecost, Jesus reminded the disciples of the promise of His baptism with or in the Holy Spirit (Acts 1:5). Peter, reflecting on the coming of the Holy Spirit, referred to it as baptism in the Holy Spirit (Acts 11:16). This had reference to the coming of the Spirit (Acts 2:4). The language description of "baptism with the Holy Spirit" only occurs

---

[2] James D. G. Dunn, *The Christ and the Spirit, Volume 2: Pneumatology* (Grand Rapids, MI: Eerdmans, 1998), p. 107.

[3] Moses identified this as a *circumcised heart*. Since the leaders were responsible for this response, it is commanded under the terms of the Mosaic Law (Deut 10:16).

in relation to John and to Jesus, although the promise of the coming of the Spirit being poured out is referred to by the prophets (Joel 2:1–3:15; Zephaniah 1:2–3:20), and in each, the prophet relates the poured-out Spirit to judgment in the Day of the Lord for Israel. John and Jesus did not specify the Spirit's ministry on behalf of Israel.

Fourth, the last purpose is related to the water baptism of Jesus by the prophet John (Matt 3:13-17). Intuitively, John recognized it was inappropriate for him to baptize Jesus who came after him with a baptism involving confession of sins (Matt 3:6). Yet, it was Jesus who insisted that they had a purpose to accomplish together, "to fulfill all righteousness" (Matt 3:15). Later Jesus would say that "John came to you in the way of righteousness" (Matt 21:32). Together, John and Jesus recognize the need for national righteousness and Jesus was about to make provision for righteousness for all who believed. John's righteous way was to gather a repentant people, but repentance only prepared one to believe in the provision of righteousness. The repentant need to know Jesus Christ who provides righteousness to all who believe in Him, as God had declared Abraham to be righteous by faith (Gen 15:6). So through His baptism, He was introduced to the followers of John through the anointing by the Spirit and the Father's declaration of His Son. Thus, John and Jesus fulfilled what had been promised to the people by introducing the One who would be the Father's provision for righteousness.

Does this Son meet the test which the nation had failed in the wilderness (Matthew 4:1-11)?

For the first time in Biblical history, Satan emerges from the shadows on earth. In Adam's presence, he had appeared in a serpent. In Israel's history, the prophets used the names of pagan gods or allusions to the serpent, or Leviathan, rather than an individual name (Isa 27:1). But now, in the presence of the Son, there was no disguise that would hide his identity. He is God's enemy, Satan.

The temptation in the wilderness allows Jesus to set out what He will be responsible for. By quoting from Deuteronomy, He establishes Himself as the Representative of Israel. In the wilderness, having fasted for forty days, His hunger set each decision as having a cost for Him. There are three decisions:

1. Matthew 4:2-4: Jesus is a *steward* of God's Word (Deut 8:3).

2. Matthew 4:5-7: He must not *tempt* God by appropriately using the Word (Deut 6:16).

3. Matthew 4:8-11: He must only *serve* and *worship* God according to His Word (Deut 6:13).

In a Dispensational model, the responsibility of the steward is defined by what God said. He submits to God's Word, refuses to test God's will as expressed in His Word, and faithfully worships and serves God.

Jesus in Conflict with Satan (Matthew 4:17–16:20)

The narrative of Matthew repeats the phrase, "From that time Jesus began to…" (Matt 4:17; 16:21). In the wilderness, Jesus positioned Himself in conflict with Satan. This conflict took the shape that heaven's rule[4] was at hand in the presence and the pending ministry of Jesus of Nazareth.

First, Proclamation (Matthew 4:17, 23; 7:13-14, 24-27)

The initial proclamation of Jesus is the same as John's concerning the kingdom of heaven (Matt 4:17). So while the nearness of the kingdom is related to the Davidic Heir, when He begins His ministry, His presence does not change *the message*. Rather, for the Davidic kingdom to be inaugurated on earth, it not only would involve God's chosen and anointed King (Matt 3:16-17), it would also involve this generation's setting Him over them as their king (Deut 17:15). But that would involve confrontation with Rome. Thus, the question for the nation is: has Jesus brought the reign of heaven to earth as the Davidic Heir? The proclamation said that repentance would provide the only lens through which Jesus' true identity would be recognized.

Second, Teaching (Matthew 5:1–7:29)

Matthew introduced Jesus' teaching for His disciples in what is called the Sermon on the Mount (Matthew 5–7). The beatitudes are promises made to persons who shared a view of the world with Jesus. The blessing promises both inclusion into the kingdom (theirs *is* the kingdom) and inheritance in the kingdom (theirs *will be*). The promised share of future

---

[4] Heaven's rule on earth was mediated by the Messiah to challenge the rule of Satan who had just attempted to lure Jesus to serve Satan's rule.

inheritance would be for those who share in Jesus' attitude toward the fallen world and God's will (5:2-12). While in the world, these who share this attitude are to be salt and light (Matt 5:13-16).

In light of this hope, Jesus was quick to clarify His relation to the Law and the Prophets (Matt 5:17-19). The singular, *the Law*, encompassing every detail, each jot and tittle (the smallest letter or one stroke of a letter), expresses a unity which was reflected in the original Mosaic Covenant. Yet, when the revelation was called a covenant, it involved an *arrangement* between God and the people that could be annulled. Yet, the people's *responsibility* to God, expressed in the Law, had never been fulfilled. Thus, Jesus assumes that national responsibility to the Law, as the nation's Representative, and specifies His commitment, not to destroy but to fulfill it. Fulfillment of law involves a consistent, comprehensive response of obedience to the demands. Thus, the Israelites would see His good works and could give glory to His Father who is in heaven (Matt 5:16; cf. Mal 1:6, 11). This also would involve Israel's role as a priest-nation (Exod 19:5-6). Jesus' disciples, as salt and light, can have the same role.

Endorsement of the Law

Greatness in the kingdom involves doing and teaching what the Law demands (Matt 5:18-19). Jesus' exposition of the laws of murder and adultery used what is said to interpret God's full intent. That exposition of intent deepened the disciples' understanding by clarifying the full meaning. In the question of divorce, He developed the implications of the creation mandate while not removing God's permissions implied in Deuteronomy 25. He encouraged truthfulness rather than technical manipulation in the use of the religious oaths. Again, Jesus exposed the practice of using *lex talionis* as an excuse for retaliation. Thus, in proper interpretation and in considered application, the Law ought to be fulfilled (Matt 5:21-48). It is fulfilled when the disciple is like his heavenly Father, perfect (Matt 5:48).

Transcendence of the Law

Douglas Moo agrees with a Dispensational perspective toward the Law in what he said:

> Matthew makes clear that Jesus' death and resurrection mark a significant shift in salvation history...Matthew shows that

John's ministry ends the prophetic office of the OT (11:13). To some extent, then, Jesus' endorsement of the Law in Matthew reflects only its continuing validity during the period before the new era is brought in.[5]

While it is correct to recognize the historical framework of the Law and its authoritative role in Israel's history, one must also acknowledge that the Law remains Scripture. As Scripture, it speaks with divine authority to subsequent eras of God's people. Moo concludes:

> Matthew integrates his stress on the continuity of the Law—for the Law looks ahead to, and is incorporated into, the teaching of Jesus—and on its discontinuity—for Jesus, not the Law, is now the locus of God's word to his people.[6]

This is what Paul would later call "the law of Christ" (Gal 6:2).

In this context, two issues arose historically, which help the subsequent reader to better understand the appropriate use of law. The first issue was the proper use of the Sabbath. Matthew 12:1-14 incorporates two Sabbath incidents that Matthew included contrasting with Jesus' own claim to give rest to those who take His yoke and learn from Him (Matt 11:28-29). The contrast is between Sabbath-rest and Jesus-rest. The question is: what yoke brings rest?

Jesus' interpretation of Sabbath practice frequently countered second temple period interpretation adopted by the Pharisees. The first example concerned the disciples picking grain for a meal on the Sabbath (Matt 12:1-8). The Pharisees charged them with violating the prohibition to reap. Jesus critiqued that interpretation with the following considerations.

First, a precedent is given in God's refusal to judge David and his men who ate the temple showbread (1 Sam 21:1-6). That failure to incur guilt before God appeared to be related to the sinful environment in Israel in which Saul refused to recognize David's election to kingship. Had God's election been recognized, David's men would have had provisions provided by Saul. It was similar for Jesus' disciples. The religious leaders also refused to recognize Jesus as Messiah who would have the right to provisions.

The coming of the Heir of David takes precedence over the Sabbath, as the priests' temple service had precedence over Sabbath rest. The priests served on the Sabbath but weren't guilty of Sabbath violations.

---

[5] Moo, "Law," *Dictionary of Jesus and the Gospels*, p. 459.

[6] *Ibid.*

The disciples were serving the anointed Son whom the Father chose to be King.

Sabbath laws ought to be interpreted in such a way that divine mercy would be emphasized rather than strict conformity with ritual prescriptions. The Sabbath worshiper finds rest in God's mercy expressed in the sacrifices, not in ritual performances. God's mercy had come in Jesus the Messiah in whom the disciples found rest. Mercy is always expressing love for others while ritual may be self-promoting.

Another example involves healing on the Sabbath (Matt 12:9-14). Jesus' defense rested on His consistency with the common practice of compassion for an animal that fell into a ditch, rather than the stricter construction of the Law which forbade the drawing up of anything on the Sabbath. The assistance given in mercy in both cases ought to prevail. The Jews showed animals mercy as Jesus showed mercy to people in need. Such mercy honors the God of mercy. Further, one may wonder whether Jesus' unique act of healing ought to be categorized as a Sabbath work or as a gift from God in mercy. And a generous giver finds it difficult to wait to give a needed gift. Healing on the Sabbath was consistent with the worship of a merciful God.

The second issue that helps us to see how Jesus interpreted the Law concerned the issue of clean and unclean (Matt 15:1-20). Scribes and Pharisees came from Jerusalem and observed that His disciples broke tradition, "For they do not wash their hands when they eat" (Matt 15:2). The issue is not hygiene, but defilement under the Law which required purification. Unwashed hands must be regarded as susceptible to defilement, and are routinely assumed to be defiled, which affects the rest of the body.

Jesus' first defense was that a failure to wash hands was a violation not of Scripture but of extra-Biblical tradition. Pharisaic adherence to tradition as a whole often resulted in violation of fundamental Scriptures. Such was evident in their hypocrisy. Isaiah 29:13 condemned this hypocrisy which was concerned with the lips and ignored the heart. Jesus later condemned the neglect of the weightier matters of law, like justice, mercy, and faith (Matt 23:23). They are matters of the heart (cf. Matt 9:13; 12:7). The hypocrisy was concerned with how an action looked to others, whether it gained their admiration. Jesus' criticism indicates they were not concerned about God, only appearances.

The heart influence is then applied directly to the issue of clean/unclean (Matt 15:10-20). "An indifferent attitude toward matters of ritual purity is justified by noting what enters the body leaves it as well—without entering the 'heart.' The 'heart' is seen as the source of true (moral) uncleanness."[7]

Third, Miracles (Matthew 8:1–9:38)

Matthew collects the miracles in thematic order, rather than recording each in their historical occurrences. As such, they form a list of powerful displays which comment on the authority (Matt 7:29) with which Jesus taught. Each miracle is a token of His reign over Satan and Satan's influence, which ravaged human life. The kingdom of heaven will exercise such heavenly authority displayed in these tokens of His reign. This is not the kingdom come from heaven to earth to reign over Israel. A kingdom involves a ruler, a realm, and a throne rule. In these accounts, the ruler is Jesus, the Heir of David. The rule is not the exercise of the Davidic throne prerogatives, but the exercise of heavenly authority in conflict with Satan and a fallen world. The realm is the satanic realm within Israel, which at this point in the narrative is weighing the evidence of Jesus' authority. Israel is not an independent nation as they are under Roman rule.

People's Response (Matthew 11:20-24; 12:22-32)

What was the people's response? Jesus had come in God's power. There was no question about power when the demon-oppressed man, blind and mute, was healed so that he saw and spoke. But it was done in mercy; a mercy that would not defend nor promote itself. Did the mercy neutralize the power and disqualify Jesus' claim to being the son of David? Matthew had just quoted Isa 42:1-4, which described the LORD's Servant who will accomplish God's purposes—displaying both power and mercy (Matt 12:15-21). But mercy did not contradict nor disqualify the presence of power.

This miraculous display overwhelmed the crowd—this One can't be the Son of David, can He (Matt 12:23)? When the Pharisees[8] heard them consider this option, they realized they had to make a convincing rebuttal. The rebuttal was that He did this, yes, but in the power of Beelzebub, the prince of the demons (Matt 12:24).

---

[7]   S. Westerholm, "Clean and Unclean," *Dictionary of Jesus and the Gospels*, p. 129.

[8]   Westerholm "Pharisees," *Dictionary of Jesus and the Gospels*, p. 609. "Through all the polemic the significant role played by the Pharisees in Jewish life in first-century Palestine is apparent." The Pharisees are formulating a repeated explanation (Matt 9:34; 12:24), which was intended to reinforce the nation's response of rejection.

While mercy does not use power to destroy an opponent's refusal to believe, it does provide a refutation to validate Jesus' claim with irrefutable logic. The first argument rests on the premise that a lasting kingdom cannot be divided against itself and still continue to exist. Such division is self-destructive. The second argument seeks to undermine the accusation as self-serving. The same scrutiny was not applied to their own exorcists. The third argument warns the people of the consequences of disregarding the opposite conclusion. If Jesus delivered this man captured by evil in the power of the Holy Spirit and you deny that by attributing the delivery to the prince of demons, then entrance into the kingdom is closed to you along with this generation. For such a rejection of the evident presence of the merciful Spirit will never be forgiven (Matt 12:31-32). Misjudgments about the human appearance of the Son of Man can be forgiven, but not the appearance of such holiness at work.

What Are the Consequences of the People's Rejection? (Matthew 13:1-50)

Since that generation rejected Jesus and His miracle, which was a token of God's rule over evil, Jesus explained the consequence in the form of parables (Matt 13:3a). Parables taught by analogy. That hid the message to anyone who didn't know the point of comparison. And that excluded anyone but the disciples, who alone asked Jesus what the analogy intended to illustrate (Matt 13:10-23).

The parables addressed two consequences: First, the parable of the soils explained *who* would be involved in what God was continuing to do (Matt 13:3-23). Second, the parables of the kingdom of heaven explained *the form of God's rule* in the age to come (Matt 13:24-50).

Each will be considered.

The Parable of the Soils (Matthew 13:18-23)

This parable explained that only good soil *heard and understood* the word and thus bore fruit according to God's intent (Matt 13:23). The disciples alone had come to Jesus for an explanation (Matt 13:10). They alone had been given to know the mysteries (secrets) of the kingdom of heaven (Matt 13:11-12a). The rest would only hear the parable, and what they did would be taken away in judgment (Matt 13:12b). This judgment fell on them because of their rejection of Jesus and it fulfilled Isaiah's pronouncement of judgment (Matt 13:13-15, quoting Isa 6:9-10).

The parable of the sower explained the ministry of Jesus in that generation but included any sower of Jesus' word until the "end of the age" (Matt 13:40). The various soils represent the range of readiness to hear. Each good seed that is sown and germinates into a plant is a son of the kingdom (Matt 13:38). But among the sons of the kingdom, there are differences between those who understand and bear fruit according to the Father's desire (Matt 13:23).

The Parables of the Kingdom of Heaven (Matthew 13:24-50)

These parables describe the secrets of the kingdom which had not previously been revealed. The coming of the kingdom of heaven was at hand. Both John (Matt 3:2) and Jesus (Matt 4:17) had announced that. What they had announced was the Davidic form of the mediation of God's rule over Israel and through Israel over the nations. That form of the Father's kingdom would only be revealed at the end of the age (Matt 13:30, 40-43). This final harvest was also described in the parable of the large net thrown into the sea (Matt 13:47-50).

In the interim age, "The kingdom of heaven may be compared to a man who sowed good seed in his field" (Matt 13:24). "The one who sows the good seed is the Son of Man. The field is the world, and the good seed is the sons of the kingdom" (Matt 13:37-38a). At the same time, the "enemy came and sowed weeds among the wheat" (Matt 13:25). "The weeds are the sons of the evil one, and the enemy who sowed them is the devil" (Matt 13:38b-39a). The crop will be brought in at harvest at the end of the age (Matt 13:39b).

This introduced kingdom of heaven will begin in an insignificant size as a mustard seed or yeast, but will grow through the age to the size of a tree or to spread through all the flour (Matt 13:31-33).[9]

---

[9] In the parable of the mustard seed and the leaven, "the emphasis for Matthew falls upon the juxtaposition of two seemingly incongruent facts, the one being the experience of Jesus and his followers in the present (cf. the mustard seed), the other being their expectations of the future (cf. the tree in which the birds of heaven nest)" (W. D. Davies and D. C. Allison, *Matthew, Volume II: 8–18*, International Critical Commentary [Edinburgh, UK: Bloomsbury T &T Clark, 1991], pp. 415-16).

The value of the kingdom of heaven to God is like a buried treasure or a priceless pearl. The merchant on earth would sell all he has to purchase the treasure or pearl (Matt 13:44-46).[10]

Thus, even though the Davidic kingdom on earth will be delayed, the immediate expression of heaven's reign on earth when it appears will be significant and valuable.

Jesus' Subjection to Satan (Matthew 16:21–27:66)

The narrative changes dramatically with the phrase: "From that time Jesus began to show his disciples that he must go to Jerusalem and suffer...be killed, and on the third day be raised" (Matt 16:21). This change was recorded only after He promised He would form the Church out of a remnant of believers (Matt 16:18-19). It is not presented as replacing Israel but rather expressing the life of Christ as a community on earth while Israelites are scattered among the nations. The remnant-kingdom reigns over individual sons, but this remnant on earth takes the shape of the Church. While Jesus first introduced the remnant-kingdom as a consequence of the Jewish people's rejection, He next mentioned the Church after Peter, speaking for the disciples, confessed that Jesus is the Messiah, the Son of the living God (Matt 16:16). That confession and the truth it expressed would become the foundation of the Church (Matt 16:18), the rock upon which He builds. So who Jesus is (the truth in the confession), is expressed in the life of the Church. In this sense, the Church is Christ's. As the kingdom awaited Jesus' overcoming Satan after the resurrection, so the formation of the Church awaited Jesus' ascension to heaven. In the inevitable conflict between the Church and the powers of Satan, the gates of hades will not swallow up the Church. The life of Christ expressed in the community of the Church will not be overcome by death or conflict.

---

[10] In the parable of the hidden treasure and the pearl of great value, there are two primary questions: first, who is the merchant or the man that makes the purchase? It must be one who can make the purchase. This cannot be believers who purchase the kingdom. What do they have of sufficient value to make the purchase? Only the Son of David, who sacrifices Himself to make the purchase, has anything of sufficient value. The second question: what is the treasure that was held hidden in the field? And what is the pearl formed in the process of suffering in the oyster? This intense suffering is what makes the pearl of great value. John Walvoord suggests that the treasure hidden in the field is Israel. The pearl formed in the suffering is none other than the remnant (John F. Walvoord, *Matthew: Thy Kingdom Come* [Chicago: Moody Press, 1974], pp. 104-106). Since these are parables of the kingdom of heaven, these two purchased people may well be featured in different stages of the history of the kingdom of heaven.

Rather, believers will ultimately join their Lord, overcoming death in resurrection from the dead, or in rapture from earth.

Now, the Father's will in conflict with Satan had changed. Jesus would proceed to Jerusalem to submit to Satan's power of death at the hand of the elders, chief priests, and scribes. In the debate recorded in the Gospel of John at the Feast of Tabernacles, Jesus identified these leaders' desire to kill Him as the descendants of their father, the devil (John 8:44-47).

Two decisive consequences for His disciples followed this change in Jesus' conflict with Satan. First, Peter adopted the perspective of Satan in rebuking Jesus (Matt 16:22-23). This perspective was evidenced by Satan's attempt to tempt Jesus in the wilderness to avoid the Cross (Matt 4:8-9).

Second, Jesus called His disciples to follow Him (Matt 16:24-27). That involved denying fleshly desires in contrast to the Father's will. That will includes taking up one's own cross. The cross speaks of dying in the pursuit of God's call for a disciple in an evil world. Those choices are then followed by joining Jesus in historic events in the pending conflict with Satan, ending at the Cross.

In View of the Growing National Opposition, Does Jesus Abandon the Idea of the National-Kingdom? (Matthew 17–22)

Rather than backing off the theme of the kingdom, Jesus assured the disciples of the reality of the future kingdom, and confronted the people of Israel with their decision about His identity as the Davidic King.

The assurance for three disciples came six days after the announcement that some would see the Son of Man coming in His kingdom (Matt 16:28). The central reality is that the kingdom of God does not begin to exist when it comes to earth because it already exists in heaven (Matt 6:10). Rather, in Jesus' transfiguration, that rule is revealed and the experience provides a preview of what would appear on earth in a mediatorial form. But for now, the foreview was to convince the disciples of the existence of the heavenly kingdom (2 Pet 1:16-18).

The appearance of the kingdom occurred as Jesus had contact with both the earthly world and the heavenly world (Matt 17:2-8). Although Jesus stood on earth, His Person and clothes took on a radiance suited for heaven. In addition, He conversed with Moses and Elijah in the heavenly world. When they were in the earthly world, they were separated in time. Now in heaven, they were not. In their conversation, they talked about a yet future event. Jesus knew about His exodus from Jerusalem. Moses and Elijah knew. Only in time would His disciples understand. As a climax, Jesus received the Father's accolade for His readiness to accomplish the Father's will in spite of the opposition. Yet the transfiguration was a foreview, not an earthly inauguration of the kingdom. Only Jesus entered into the heavenly glory and those relationships appeared and disappeared. But when the kingdom was seen, it was the national kingdom with representative citizens from the past and the present.

The confrontation of the people of that generation, with their opportunity to make a choice, came in the triumphal entry into Jerusalem (Matt 21:1-11). The careful preparation which the Lord made indicates the Father's sovereignty over the events climaxing His First Advent. His disciples were given detailed and deliberate instructions which indicated His intent to follow the prophecy of Zech 9:9. Yet His presence, entrusted with the Father's Word, would submit to this generation's decision (Deut 17:15).

At that moment (Matt 21:1-11), the significance of His actions are recognized by the contrast with His recent withdrawal (Matt 14:13) from confrontation. Now He intentionally and openly parades into Jerusalem and into the temple in the midst of the religious leadership (Matt 21:12-17). To Matthew, it was the final and official presentation of Jesus to the people, to Israel as her Messiah. All of Jerusalem was teeming with multitudes of worshipers, having come to the city for the Feast of the Passover.

What Do Jesus' Final Words Mean for the People's Future? (Matthew 23–25)

John the Baptist had announced that judgment was at hand. Now the people had been given about three years to reach a conclusion about who Jesus may be and about the reign He had displayed in token miracles. As the people's decision was crystallized at His formal entry into Jerusalem, Jesus, in the temple, pronounced judgment on that generation (Matt 23:36). Judgment would fall on those religious leaders who were warned but failed to listen and repent. Rather, in hypocrisy they sought to convince their generation by what they taught, not by what they did (Matt 23:1-12). God's indictment was addressed against the teachers and the Pharisees (Matt 23:13-26). As a result, "your house is left to you desolate"

(Matt 23:38). The discussion is over whether "your house" refers to the temple, to Jerusalem, or to "the house of Israel." "In view of 21.13…and 24.1-2, one thinks first of the temple, which is no longer God's house but, ironically, 'your house.'"[11] And the judgment on that generation fell in AD 70.

Jesus laments this judgment as He would have had it different. Jesus never intended to establish the kingdom before He would die at the hand of Rome (cf. Matt 23:37). He only desired that Jerusalem would have allowed Him to protect them from an impending judgment from Rome, as a mother hen gathers and protects her chicks. But the people, in the hands of the Sanhedrin, were about to join Rome in condemnation against Jesus (Matt 23:3-5). Jesus' rejection of the people of Israel would not be forever—rather it would be until they recognize Him at His Second Advent (Zech 12:10-12). Then the people would be established as a nation.

With that transition in mind, Jesus left the temple to the leaders and spelled out God's judgment on Jerusalem; a judgment focused on a future temple (Matthew 24–25). If Jerusalem represented the people's hopes, then the condition of the temple represented Jerusalem. As Jesus and His disciples left the temple, Jesus shocked His disciples. The temple, where God had chosen to place His name (1 Kgs 8:17-21), would be destroyed (Matt 24:2). The structure built by Herod would be toppled, including both the temple proper (*naos*) and the temple courtyard (*hierios*). This includes the retaining wall supporting structure, also called the temple (Matt 24:1).

In response to Jesus' statement, the disciples asked three questions:

1. When will this happen?

2. What will be the sign of Your coming?

3. What will be the sign of the end of the age? (Matt 24:3)

Jesus' answer addressed the *signs* without specifying a date when it would happen. First, He described events which would be signs that *do not* herald the end, but do signify the instability of the world surrounding Jerusalem in coming days (Matt 24:4-14). What would follow would be a time of spiritual deception, with upheavals of nations in war and natural catastrophes. But this is only the beginning (Matt 24:4-8).

Then, followers of Jesus Christ would be persecuted. There would be apostasy, betrayal, and hatred. This gospel of the kingdom would be

---

[11] W. D. Davies and Dale C. Allison, *Matthew, Volume III: 19–28*, ICC, p. 322.

proclaimed worldwide. As the second person pronoun, *you* (Matt 24:9), indicates, these experiences could have appeared to that generation at least in a limited sense (Matt 24:9-14a). However, embedded in the third person reference is a promise about the end (Matt 24:13)—the one who endures will be saved. As the context indicates, the salvation is not from eternal damnation, but salvation at the end of the age from the consequences of the apostasy of that age.

Then Jesus announced the *end* would come (Matt 24:14b). With that announcement, He spoke of the sign of the end (Matt 24:15), first prophesied in Dan 9:27. The sign would appear to a later generation who would read about it. The third person pronoun referring to that future generation would then respond to those following events. So He no longer speaks in terms of an immediate generation (second person pronoun, *you*) but a generation at the end of the age. That generation would experience more severe judgment than Jesus' immediate generation was about to experience. And the point of continuity is the Herodian temple. While it would be judged in the immediate generation (as Luke 21:24 describes), it will experience a final judgment when the abominable object would desecrate the temple at the end time (Matt 24:15). This implies that the judged Herodian temple will be rebuilt as an end time temple.[12] In addition, that generation also would see the *sign* of the coming of the Son of Man (Matt 24:27). As He comes, angels will gather His elect from all directions (Matt 24:31). "Probably the reference is to all those who are chosen, that is, the saints of all ages, whether in heaven or on earth, for all these will converge upon the millennial kingdom scene."[13] The word describing coming (*erchomai*) allows for a process that would enable the whole earth in its rotation to see the splendor and glory of His coming. Yet, His descent to the earth will arrive in the area of the Mount of Olives (Zech 14:4).

The Lord's coming is also described by *parousia*, which is helpful for understanding the parable of the fig tree (Matt 24:32-44). The generation which sees these events and signs (Matt 24:15) will know that He is near, at the very gates (Matt 24:33). Yet, "you also must be ready, for the Son of Man is coming at an hour you do not expect" (Matt 24:44). This section addresses the disciples directly again in the second person pronoun (you). So it could happen to that historic generation of twelve disciples. Yet they

---

[12]   As elements of the retaining walls surrounding the temple mount still existed following the Roman captivity, the rebuilt temple will retain an identity with the Herodian temple. It is the same temple that has stones standing one upon another that Jesus prophesied would be completely destroyed (Matt 24:2).

[13]   Walvoord, *Matthew*, p. 190.

would not expect it. This seeming tension may be lessened by recognizing that the coming (*parousia*) may be an extended process, coming from the throne of God to the final arrival on earth. And the coming involves two gatherings, one unknown, and even unexpected, when men and women, forming Christ's body, will be taken from their normal activities (Matt 24:40-42), and one seen by all, both believers and unbelievers, in which the elect are gathered (Matt 24:31; cf. 13:43, 49). The first gathering has been called "the rapture" and the second gathering is at His Second Advent arriving on earth. And the two gatherings are separated by suffering in the Day of the Lord. That suffering will conclude with what is called the "great tribulation" (Matt 24:21).

This provides an expectation concerning the coming (*parousia*) of the Son of Man again, which helps to clarify the parables that follow on how to live waiting for Him to come:

- Serve faithfully while He is absent with the promise of His certain return, even if it seems delayed (24:45-51).

- Don't wait until the end to be assured that your preparation would be adequate (25:1-13).

- Use your talents given by the Lord, as a steward, in anticipation of His return and assessment of stewardly faithfulness (25:14-30).

- Final judgment will separate the sheep, who will inherit the kingdom prepared for them from the foundation of the world, from the goats, who will be cast out (25:31-46).

Thus, the elect nation of Israel has a future, even though there will be an immediate judgment on Jerusalem and an end time judgment on the temple. The election of the nation to serve will be fulfilled according to God's word of promise.

Who Does the Immediate Generation Reject? (Matthew 26–27)

Matthew's account of Jesus' birth and ministry had rooted these events in the history of the elect nation, as well as that generation's experience as the people of Israel.

Jesus was crucified as a messianic pretender, but this would not have kept Matthew's readers from perceiving a deeper significance in the repeated recital of this charge (26:63; 27:11, 17, 22, 27-31, 37). Unwittingly and ironically, the high priest, Pilate and the soldiers all proclaim the true identity of Jesus.[14]

And this true sense of His identity, referred to in the names and titles, is understood in spite of the evident evil intent of those who crucified Jesus.

These parables, and the ones in Matthew 13, reflect a national hope which features the Davidic heir for an elect national Israel. It will be based on Jesus' resurrection from the dead (Matthew 28). The resurrection is the overcoming of God's enemy, who had the power of death. Since this is developed more fully in Luke-Acts it will be addressed in the consideration of Luke.

Conclusion

The Gospel of Matthew features the announcement of the coming of the kingdom of heaven being at hand. As introduced by John the Baptist and Jesus, the kingdom would fulfill the Davidic Covenant. Heaven would rule over Messiah and then Messiah would mediate the rule of the Father over evil. Jesus defended His readiness to accept this role by resisting the devil's temptations (Matt 4:1-11). Then in the miracles that followed, Jesus mediated heaven's rule over various expressions of evil.

When the Pharisees in Galilee rejected the miracles as evidence of heaven's mercy, Jesus introduced, in parable form, the mystery of the kingdom of heaven. Heaven's reign was about to appear but in a form not anticipated in the Old Testament. The parable of the soils revealed who would be sons of the kingdom. The kingdom would be on earth in the presence and power of the Word, ruling in the lives of the sons of the kingdom. However, the rule on earth would not be the Davidic mediatorial kingdom on earth. The Davidic kingdom would be established through judgment during the period of tribulation—Daniel's seventieth week and the abomination of desolation (Matt 24:15). At the conclusion of the tribulation, the end of the age would have arrived with the sons of the kingdom harvested. That would precede the Son of Man's rule in the Davidic mediation of God's rule. So the kingdom of heaven was at hand from the providential throne which began at Jesus Christ's ascension. The mediatorial throne of the Davidic kingdom awaited the return of the Messiah, the Son of Man.

---

[14]   J. B. Green, "Death of Jesus," *Dictionary of Jesus and the Gospels*, p. 155.

CHAPTER 18:
THE TIMES OF THE
GENTILES; LUKE

Introduction

The remnant in Judaism, present at the beginning of the narrative of Luke, represents another perspective of the second temple period. Matthew had viewed the Jewish population as representing the called nation, Israel. Luke speaks of a Jewish remnant who genuinely worshiped God, the sons and daughters of Abraham. This remnant recognizes that the coming of Jesus is the coming of salvation. At the same time, Luke does not lose sight that this remnant of Israel is part of a people chosen to be a nation. Jesus' historic ministry is common to Matthew and Luke, but their distinct perspectives on Israel are what distinguishes the two Gospels. Luke's emphasis on a Jewish believing remnant transitions to Christians in the Book of Acts. The identity of the people is part of the transition. What in the beginning is a believing Jewish remnant, becomes the Church of Jews and Gentiles who also believe. What has happened to the believers in the process of the transition needs to be examined as the story is told.

Luke "has the same broad pattern of usage as the other two Gospels, but there is a special emphasis on salvation which is not found in them."[1] According to Louw and Nida,[2] the selection of salvation implies a world view. The language field of meaning of the concept of salvation relates to the experience of *danger* and *risk*. An individual may be in a state of being *safe* once having been *saved* from danger. Such danger can be either natural or spiritual. Luke's use applies this language to refer to the spiritual

---

[1]   I. Howard Marshall, "Salvation," *Dictionary of Jesus and the Gospels*, p. 723.

[2]   Louw and Nida, *Greek-English Lexicon*, vol. 1 (New York: United Bible Society, 1983), pp. 238-42.

reality of a fallen creation fated to death. Implied in Luke's worldview are the presence of God and Satan, God and mankind's enemy. In Luke's language, the condition of the human race is that they are both *dead* and *lost* in relation to God. They are *dead* in the sense that they may engage in religious activities, yet they are without life and fail to know God. They are *lost* in the sense that they can't find their way to God by themselves, and since they are dead in trespasses and sins, they are subject to judgment by God. So Jesus comes as *Savior*, seeking and saving whoever will receive Him. It is salvation from the condition and the consequences of being dead and lost. This theme will be considered in the development of Luke's Gospel account.

The Remnant and the Savior Born (Luke 1–2)

The introduction in Luke features a believing remnant in Israel who assume a vocal role at the beginning of the story. They recognize the people's need for salvation and give praise to God their Savior.

Mary (Luke 1:47)

Mary, like Hannah of 1 Sam 2:1-10, extols the Lord for delivering her and her people from their humble estate. The birth of her Son will bring down the mighty and exalt the humble so that all generations will call her blessed. Based on this experience of mercy, the nation Israel will eventually realize the goal she envisioned.

Zechariah (Luke 1:69, 71)

Following the birth of John, Zechariah also celebrated the Lord God of Israel who would summon from the house of David the Agent of salvation for His people. This Zechariah had been silenced due to his unbelief at the angel's announcement. Then at John's birth, he named his son and spoke praises to the Lord. The One who followed would deliver Israel, who has been the object of the enemy's attack throughout her history (Ps 18:18; 2 Sam 22:18). In particular, he undoubtedly implied Roman oppression.

John (Luke 1:77)

Zechariah's own son, John, would make known to his compatriots their coming salvation through the David's greater Son. This would include a spiritual deliverance found in the One who would give forgiveness of sins.

The Shepherds (Luke 2:11)

The angels gladly announced to the listening *shepherds*, the birth, on that very day, of a Savior in the city of David. Then, as if anticipating Peter's conclusion on the day of Pentecost, they proclaim Him both Anointed One and Lord (Acts 2:36).

Simeon (Luke 2:30)

Simeon, a second temple Israelite, read the Hebrew Scriptures in a way that was consistent with the Gospel accounts and received, as a watchman in the temple, word to wait for the arrival of the promised One. When this One was brought to be circumcised, he recognized the Lord's salvation in that Infant. Then in an allusion to Isa 40:5, he praised God: "you have prepared in the presence of all peoples, a light for revelation to the Gentiles, and for glory to your people Israel" (Luke 2:31-32).

Salvation and John the Baptist (Luke 3:1–4:15)

John's ministry is portrayed prophetically in Isa 40:3-5 and described historically in Luke 3:3, 7-17. John is the voice that "prepare[s] the way of the Lord" (Luke 3:4). John's message was preparatory. It addressed the obstacles in the way of people seeing the salvation of God. In the quote, Luke replaces the word *glory* with the word *salvation*, to further highlight his thematic emphasis. The obstacles are represented as topographical, but when related to a call for a response of repentance, the actual obstacle is the presence of evil. John addressed the crowds as a brood of vipers, alluding to them as descendants of the serpent. John rejected a mere physical lineage to Abraham as a sufficient source of the promised life of the woman (Gen 3:15). Rather, God's wrath was coming to judge that generation of people in the land.

John's message was a call to repent for the forgiveness of sins. Those who repented joined the remnant as they were baptized by John in the Jordan River where he ministered. Several questions are addressed in the extended discussion (Luke 3:7-17).

First, *why were Israelites called to repent?* A remarkable change had occurred in the descendants of Israel as he called the leaders a "brood of vipers" (Luke 3:7; Matt 12:34; 23:33). As already suggested, this is an allusion to Gen 3:15. In this, Jesus related this generation to the serpent. Israel, the elect people, as a whole had associated themselves with the serpent, and now they were among the descendants of the enemy of God rather than being a people of God. It was a generation whose knowledge was evil, and as a result, they could not escape the coming judgment. It was "the wrath to come," which the prophets had announced as the Day of the LORD. This judgment was a temporal judgment coming to Jerusalem.

Second, *what should they repent about?* To *repent* means to change one's mind. The mind change concerned first of all that they were descendants of God's enemy, that their thought was controlled by evil (Luke 3:7). Further, the fruit of their hearts involved actions that weren't in keeping with repentance (Luke 3:8-9). The crowd's attitudes and actions were self-serving (Luke 3:10-14). It was this knowledge of evil that blinded their eyes to recognize the expected One (Luke 3:15).

Third, *for whom were they looking?* It would be natural for their expectation to settle upon John as the Messiah. In that very expectation, they failed to recognize the preparatory elements in John's ministry. So in John's response, he attempted to compare his own preparatory ministry with the coming One's Messianic ministry. Both would baptize. But the coming One would be mightier and worthy of higher honor. That was implied in the elements of baptism: water rather than the Holy Spirit and fire. The water portrays cleansing of the body and the Holy Spirit implies a cleansing and forgiveness that involves the inner person. Further, the fire is related to the description of judgment that immediately follows. It is a judgment that will divide the wheat from the chaff. And the chaff will be burned with unquenchable fire (Luke 3:16-17).

The temporariness of John's ministry is realized when Herod the tetrarch imprisoned John. John had reproved Herod for marriage to Herodias, his brother's wife, and all the evil things he had done (3:18-20). For this, John was put to death.

Fourth, *what does John's baptism of Jesus mean?* Luke's account focuses on God's response to Jesus' submission to John's baptism. Jesus was praying.

The heavens opened so that the Holy Spirit descended on Him—in visible form for all to see—and anointed Him. Then the Father's voice from heaven identified Jesus as the Son of God and expressed His love for the Son. The baptism revealed Jesus' identity as the divine Son and the Anointed One, Messiah.

Then Luke added His genealogy. Jesus was also identified, through Mary, as the Son of David through the line of Nathan (Luke 3:31), and the Son of God (Luke 3:38) descended through Abraham to Adam. This refers to His humanity as Joseph's adopted Son, "being the Son (as was supposed) of Joseph…" (Luke 3:23). This wording provides evidence that this records Mary's line through David and Nathan.

So when Jesus announced that "the kingdom of God has come near'" (Luke 10:9), He referred to the mediated kingdom introduced in Adam. It was this reign that God had assigned to Adam which the serpent had usurped in Adam's rebellion (Gen 3:1-6). This mediated kingdom had been introduced for Israel in the Davidic eternal kingdom. This genealogical record emphasizes the Adamic reign.

Finally, *what does Jesus' temptation mean?* In light of what the Father announced in commendation of Jesus as His beloved Son, it is no surprise that the devil appeared in the wilderness to tempt Jesus to reject this difficult role (Luke 4:1-13). Adam had failed. Israel had failed. David had failed. Jesus is now tempted to renounce the Father's declaration and the role that it entailed. This is not only the devil's scheme, but it is also the Father's will as the Spirit led Him to be tempted. But Jesus resolutely rejected what the devil had gained when Adam sinned. Jesus was willing to accept the hope and the cost of being the Son of God, as Adam had not been.

When the temptation had been concluded, "he departed from him until an opportune time" (Luke 4:13). That hour and the power of darkness would come again (Luke 22:53). Lingering in the background is the enemy, at work in various expressions of evil, but waiting for the strategic moment to attack. The message of salvation included the danger of Satan's working. The deliverance provided by Jesus would include salvation from the penalty and power of evil.

Jesus and the Ministry of Salvation (Luke 4:16–19:44)

Nazareth

Jesus' ministry of salvation is introduced in a programmatic account of His sermon at Nazareth. The term *salvation* does not appear in this text (Luke 4:16-30), but there are clues from the passage of Isaiah which He reads that Sabbath day (Isa 61:1-2a). The first clue is that Jesus came "to proclaim the year of the Lord's favor" (Luke 4:19). This is an allusion to the year of Jubilee (Lev 25:10). This allusion is strengthened by two uses of the term *aphesis* in the quote, "*liberty* to the captives" and "set at *liberty* those who are oppressed" (Luke 4:18, emphasis added). This year of total forgiveness of debt is now turned into a metaphor for salvation. Jesus had come to proclaim that God was ready to forgive sin totally. This liberty, or release from sin's control, is comprehensive, both at a physical level and at a spiritual one, as the entire ministry of Jesus makes clear (Luke 1:26-28; 7:47; 24:47). Although the salvation is not final, it is real.

This time of salvation is further emphasized in light of the deliberate opening of the scroll to find the place to read and the rolling up of the scroll when He finished. For Jesus also chose to stop short of reading, "and the day of vengeance of our God" (Isa 61:2b). This is even more striking in light of John's announcement that "the axe is laid to the root of the trees" (Luke 3:9). The announcement of the beginning of judgment had been delayed for the year of Jubilee during Jesus' First Advent ministry. So judgment is imminent on that generation, but that judgment is not the final day of vengeance. In the meantime, spiritual salvation is available.

Peter's Call to Become a Disciple

It is also striking that the account of the call of His disciples in Luke is delayed until Peter acknowledged that he was a sinful man (Luke 5:8). Jesus had first called Peter when he and his brother were with John the Baptist (John 1:41-42). When the disciples returned to Galilee, Jesus again called Peter along the Sea of Galilee as he was casting a net into the sea (Mark 1:16-17). Peter had not yet left his trade to become a fisher of men. It is only when Peter realized Jesus' holiness in contrast to his own sinfulness, that "they left everything and followed him" (Luke 5:11).

Salvation by Faith

Luke's account specifies that salvation is by faith (Luke 5:20; 7:9, 50). Faith, or the absence of faith, continues to be featured (Luke 8:13, 25, 48, 50). Of the stories of faith, the most remarkable is a woman of the city, known as a sinner, who anointed Jesus' feet. Based on who she was, all sorts of motivations for that expression of affection could be suggested by what she did, but Jesus declared, "Your faith has saved you" (Luke 7:50). Her lifestyle clearly did not deserve anything, yet Jesus' pronouncement reflected God's grace. Salvation is given freely to those who believe.

Parable of the Soils

That theological truth is reinforced in Luke's account of the parable of the sower and the soils. All three Synoptic Gospels include the parable Jesus taught and interpreted, but Luke's record of the interpretation included Jesus' comment on the relationship between salvation and faith. No other account even mentioned salvation.

The reason for distinguishing between the various soil conditions and salvation is only mentioned in Luke. The basic point of the parable is fruit bearing, and only one soil bears fruit. All three Gospel accounts agree on that basic point. But of the other three responses, are they equally unacceptable? Only Luke clarifies the answer to that question with regard to salvation. This is the spiritual salvation until the final judgment comes.

The first soil was the hard-packed path and gave no response to what was sown. That opened a door to the devil. Only Luke included the devil's strategy. The untouched word was to be removed "so that they may not believe and be saved" (Luke 8:12). The controlling word of purpose, *so that*, is linked to both verbs: *believe* and *save*. Ultimately the devil acts to prevent salvation. The condition of salvation is faith. So salvation is prevented when faith is prevented. And the possibility of faith is eliminated when the Word is removed. Without the Word, there is no object for faith nor basis of salvation.

The second soil responds in faith. But the image of rocky soil implies that nothing takes root in that person. Thus, the response, even though it is joyful after hearing, only believes for a while. Now the devil changes his strategy. He cannot prevent faith and thus he can't prevent salvation. But he can now prevent enduring faith. So in the time of testing, a faith without root falls away. Based simply on Jesus' wording, this temporary faith is faith indeed rather than mere profession. It is Jesus who said the response was faith. The issue is not genuine or false faith but active or inactive faith. Inactive faith doesn't endure or produce fruit and is not what God desires. In the conflict with evil, an inactive faith stops believing. This snapshot portrayal says nothing about other possible opportunities to respond to later seed sown and cultivation of the soil. It simply affirms that the one believes.

The third soil portrays a life that is cluttered with weeds—cares, riches, pleasures. No comment is made about faith, but it is inferred to be present since the plant starts to grow. However, the competing demands of life choke out any fruit from being produced in mature form. That also is not what God desires.

The fourth soil is a good and honest heart and is in contrast to the shallow or cluttered heart. What highlights this faith is that it holds fast to the truth of what Jesus has said. That person holding on in faith produces fruit. That heart that holds fast to God's Word is a steward of God's Word: "take heed how you hear. For whoever has, to him more will be given; and whoever does not have, even what he seems to have will be taken from him" (Luke 8:18, NKJV).

The Call to Discipleship

Jesus' call was directed to His *followers*. The call (Luke 9:23-27) followed Peter's confession (Luke 9:18-20). Since the call was addressed to Peter, the point was not a test of whether his faith was genuine. Peter's confession indicated that his faith was genuine. The testing in the call was whether His disciples' faith would be active or not. An active faith of stewardship is necessary in the service of God while following Christ (Luke 9:21-22).

The call was to be a servant in imitation of Christ. It was marked by denial of self-interest (denying himself), by self-sacrifice (taking up his cross), and by joining Jesus as He determined to journey to Jerusalem (Luke 9:31, 51). Jesus' purpose anticipated His serving God at Jerusalem.

Although salvation is a valuable gift freely given, Jesus made the same costly demands that He made on Himself. Thus, these demands are not a call to salvation from the penalty of sin, but a call to anyone who would serve God as one who already shared Jesus' life. The demands are then described against an implied background of a conflict with sins' power. The value of life is lost when one attempts to save it for oneself. This is the perspective of self-interest. However, whoever is willing to lose his life for Christ's sake, Christ promises that he will save it from the power of sin (Luke 9:24). Gaining the world for one's self but losing one's life profits nothing. You cannot serve both (Luke 9:25). The ultimate value of your life is Christ having confidence in you in the glory of the Father's presence (Luke 9:26). This life has served God rather than sin. Christ will have confidence in one who lived to serve.

Then, to assure His disciples of that glory, Jesus promised to give three disciples a preview of His glory in the Father's kingdom (Luke 9:27-36). Would anyone want to think of themselves rather than His glory? Yet, that's where Peter found himself (Luke 9:33). He was thinking according to self-interest rather than in terms of Christ's interest.

The Journey to Jerusalem (Luke 9:51)

The mention of the transition in Jesus' ministry from Galilee to Jerusalem reflects a distinct Lukan emphasis. In Matthew, it was mentioned in 19:1. In Mark's Gospel, it was 10:1. In Matthew 19–20, it precedes the triumphal entry (Matt 21:1), and in Mark, chapter 10 precedes His entry into Jerusalem (Mark 11:1). Luke devotes almost ten chapters (9:51–19:28) to the journey to Jerusalem. The emphasis seems to be related to "the acceptable year of the Lord" (Luke 4:19, NKJV) related to Jesus' first Advent ministry of salvation.

There is a distinct emphasis on salvation. While the twelve were sent out before leaving Galilee (9:1-6), seventy were sent two-by-two into the towns and the villages traveling toward Jerusalem (Luke 10:1-24). They were to prepare for a follow-up visit from the Lord on His journey to Jerusalem. Upon the disciples' return, Jesus rejoiced that heaven determined those to whom things were hidden and those to whom things were revealed (Luke 10:21-24). This continuing work of God is reflected in the issues raised along the journey.

Are Many Being Saved?

As Jesus traveled to Jerusalem, someone asked if only a few would be saved (Luke 13:23). Jesus rejected giving such a forecast. Rather, He directed the conversation back to that generation's responsibility. Jesus had warned them, in effect, that "the year of the LORD's favor" will give way to "the day of vengeance of our God" (Isa 61:2). So, while it is the day of salvation, individuals ought to respond to Jesus' message as He speaks.

A lawyer (Luke 10:25-42) and a rich ruler (Luke 18:15-30) would respond and ask Jesus a similar question about their responsibility in that generation: "What must I do to inherit eternal life?" This language is shown to be equivalent to "enter the kingdom" (Luke 18:24-25) and "be saved" (Luke 18:26). Jesus' answer in both cases may seem surprising as it sounds like He is saying that one must obey the Law to be saved. That certainly seems to be at odds with salvation given by faith in God's promise. Yet in both cases, Jesus initially directs them to the Law and that which it demands (Luke 10:26-28; 18:20-24). Jesus' words, "do this, and you will live" (Luke 10:28) seems to prove the point that life is a reward for obedience. There are three reasons why Jesus is not saying salvation from God's condemnation is gained by obedience to the Law or that life is the reward for obedience:

1. In the case of the rich ruler, he addressed Jesus as "good teacher." Before He directed the ruler to the Law, Jesus wanted the ruler to face the implications of what he had observed in Jesus' life. If He (Jesus) was, in fact, good, then he (the ruler) must realize that Jesus is God who alone is good. Then what does that indicate about what Jesus would say? The ruler wasn't ready to go there.

2. In both cases, Jesus directed them to what the Law said. Both realized what it said. When Jesus expected them to do it, they balked. The lawyer wanted to define "neighbor" the way he wanted. Then he would love the ones he would choose to be his neighbors. In the parable of the Samaritan, the lawyer realized he had defined his neighbor in a selfish fashion. Both wanted eternal life out of pure self-interest. The ruler thought he already loved completely. When Jesus pointed to the fact that he loved his wealth more than God, the rich ruler went away sad, unwilling to sacrifice his wealth for the poor and come to look to Jesus as a follower of Him.

3. Jesus directed them to the Mosaic Law because that revelation was their God-given responsibility during the dispensation of law. While both thought they were obeying, self-examination showed they were not fully obeying. If they only recognized their need, in the year of God's favor, they could find favor from Him. But neither did. Under the dispensation of law, they had failed to know both God and themselves in their sin.

Jesus might well have answered the question (Luke 18:18), "as many as realize they are lost, will be found when they come to Me. They would recognize Me as God who reveals who they are in reality and wants to show them favor in salvation."

Seeking the Lost to Save Them

Luke 19:10 summarizes the purpose of Jesus' mission as, "to seek and to save the lost." This purpose will be clarified in two final pericopes that we will consider: a parable on finding what was lost (Luke 15) and an illustration of Jesus finding a seeker (Luke 19:1-10).

The Parables of the Lost

The parable was addressed to religious leaders who criticized Jesus for seeking the lost among known examples of sinners condemned in their religious culture (Luke 15:1-2). In response, Jesus told a parable (Luke 15:3), with three component stories forming the single parable.

In the first two stories, the lost sheep and the lost coin, a question, "what man of you?" or, "what woman of you?" controlled the response. The religious leaders would readily seek what either had lost; whether material possessions (sheep) or sentimental possessions (coins). In this regard, the religious leaders were like heaven rejoicing when they had found what they had lost. In the first story, there was a willingness to search no matter what the risk and even though the loss was only one percent of one's holdings. In the second story, there was a willingness to do whatever was necessary to find what was of value to the heart.

But in the third story, there was a separation between heaven and the religious leaders. The separation was reflected in the father and the eldest son who held the lost son and brother in different value. This story was more comprehensive in what is entailed in seeking and finding the lost. The lost son had a personal choice whereas the sheep and the coin did not. Seeking involves more than just searching, although that is included.

So the story begins as the father allows his dissatisfied son to leave with his portion of the inheritance. Out of sight of his family, the youngest son squandered his wealth on reckless living. When a famine struck, everything was gone including his friends. Circumstances forced him to find employment caring for pigs. He longed for something to eat to satisfy his hunger, even from the pig's food.

"[W]hen he came to himself" (Luke 15:17), he realized that living with his father was better than living with pigs. This alludes to the same response Israel would come to when they were under Gentile captivity (Deut 30:1). But returning to his father had advantages for himself but not for his father. So he prepared a speech of genuine repentance. On his way home, while he was yet a long way away, his father saw him. His waiting father ran to him and embraced him. His speech of repentance had no influence on his father since he didn't even allow him to complete it. Repentance prepared the son to admit who he was and what he had done, but this waiting father's heart was always ready to receive him. The son believed that no matter what he had done, if he returned, his father would receive him. And he did. He now was beginning to know himself and his father.

But the elder son did not share his father's heart. He was wrapped up in himself and what he thought he deserved from the father. The father tried to persuade the eldest son because the younger son had been lost and now was found, had been dead and now was alive (Luke 15:32). The parable ends with the implied comparison that the religious leaders' attitude toward lost sinners was the same as the elder brother's attitude toward his lost brother. Neither shared the life of the Father.

The Event of Seeking the Lost

Seeking the lost was what Jesus' journey to Jerusalem would be all about (Luke 9:51). It seems probable that on the journey Jesus visited those towns which received His disciples. He had sent out twelve (Luke 9:1-6) and then the seventy (Luke 10:1-12) in search of those who would welcome Jesus. Jesus arrived in Jericho, a town that had welcomed His envoys. But there was an unknown seeker who wanted to see Jesus (Luke 19:1-4). Because he was short in stature, he had climbed a tree, basically out of sight from the road below. But "when Jesus came to the place, he looked up" into a sycamore tree and found him (Luke 19:5). And Jesus said He *must* go to his house that day. While the crowd grumbled because He went to the house of a sinner, Jesus announced: "'Today salvation has come to this house, since he also is a son of Abraham'" (Luke 19:9). That was Jesus' historic mission: to seek out the lost and to save those who recognized their need for salvation. These believed that Jesus was their Savior. Zacchaeus' search didn't find Jesus but Jesus found him whom the Father had prepared (Luke 10:21-22).

Provision of Salvation (Luke 19:45–24:53)

Precipitating the Day of Judgment from Rome

John the Baptist had announced that judgment on Israel was at hand (Luke 3:7-9). The One coming after him would gather the wheat and burn the chaff (Luke 3:17). Jesus said He had come "'to proclaim the year of the Lord's favor'" (Luke 4:19). That set the order: first salvation, then wrath. The programmed triumphal entry forced the hand of the religious leaders to act immediately in regard to Jesus and His claim to be King (Luke 19:39-40). Satan acted in Judas to betray Jesus to the Jewish leadership (Luke 22:3-6). The opportune time had arrived; it was Passover.

For Jesus, His concern for Jerusalem was painful (Luke 19:41). Although He was precipitating rejection by the leaders, He desired to protect Jerusalem (Luke 13:34) and the temple (Luke 13:35a). But Jerusalem did not know what would have brought peace because it was hidden from them (Luke 19:42). Speaking to Jerusalem, Jesus said, "the days will come upon [you], when [your] enemies will...surround you and hem you in on every side and tear you down...because you did not know the time of your visitation" (Luke 19:43-44) in the First Advent. This was the near judgment which John was announcing (Luke 3:9-14). But it would not be the complete judgment on Jerusalem from the LORD that the prophets had announced (Isa 61:2b), the day of vengeance.

This became clear when Jesus announced the judgment that was about to fall on the temple (Luke 21:5-28). This announcement followed the cleansing of the temple from religious commerce (Luke 19:45-46). This Olivet Discourse speaks of two visitations in judgment. These two are distinguished when the Lukan and Matthean accounts are compared. The two visitations relate to the First and Second Advents. Luke's account emphasizes the judgment in AD 70. Matthew's account refers to the end time judgment.[3] The account in Luke was shaped by the growing

---

3 The support for such a double divine visitation of judgment on Jerusalem is validated by the following:

    1. Matthew 24:1-31 and Luke 21:5-28 are recording the same Olivet discourse. Both passages begin with the disciples' admiration of the temple structure. Both include Jesus' announcement that not one stone will be left on another of the temple. Although the questions are different, they are not incompatible. Matthew emphasizes the sign of Jesus' return and the end of the age (24:3). Luke emphasizes the sign of what Jesus said is about to take place (21:7).

    2. The two signs are distinct. Luke has Jerusalem surrounded by the enemy (21:20) as He had previously said (19:43). Matthew has the abomination of desolation (24:15) spoken by Daniel (9:27) about the end times.

storm in Jerusalem. In the Jewish leaders' cleverness, they would ally with Rome to bring about the crucifixion of Christ (John 11:47-54). That Roman display of power (AD 33) brought judgment which Jesus accepted in place of condemned mankind. Israel's guilt would be satisfied when the Gentiles would trample Jerusalem until the times of the Gentiles would be completed (Luke 21:24). The judgment on Jerusalem was what John introduced and was the Day of the LORD in that generation (AD 70). The completion would come as spoken of in Matthew as well as in Luke's conclusion (Luke 21:25-28). That completion is marked by a yet future climactic Day of the LORD (1 Thess 5:1) and by the return of the Son of Man[4] to bring "the times of refreshing" and to restore all things (Acts 3:20-21).

Ratifying the New Covenant (Luke 22:20)

As Jesus huddled for a final Passover with His disciples, He also taught about the full meaning of the Passover. He announced that He would not eat another Passover until the final exodus and redemption of Israel. The original Passover anticipated Israel's redemption and would be fulfilled in the kingdom of God (Luke 22:16). This fulfillment is an end time fulfillment, coinciding with the Son of Man returning to rule on earth (Luke 21:25-28). Then Israel's final redemption would have arrived (Luke 21:28) as the Passover ultimately anticipated.

In the meantime, Jesus introduced the Lord's Supper (Luke 22:19-20). But what do the bread and cup mean? The bread was a symbol of His body, broken in death, and broken in their place (*huper humas*). What Jesus had desired to do on behalf of Jerusalem was rejected by the political leaders (Luke 19:41-44), but He was accepted by the eleven (Luke 13:34-35). So the benefit of His death as a substitutionary sacrifice was accepted by them. After the meal, Jesus introduced the cup. Unlike the bread it was not a symbol of Jesus' body; rather, it contained wine which was a symbol of His sacrificed blood. This blood was then related

---

3. What follows the signs are distinct. Luke has "Jerusalem...trampled underfoot by the Gentiles, until the times of the Gentiles are fulfilled" (21:24). Matthew has the "great tribulation" (24:21-28) suffered by the whole world.

4. Yet both accounts conclude with the coming of the Son of Man, which the Matthean account asked about. Both *include* this end time event related to the final judgment of the temple.

4 Even though Jesus announced that the kingdom of God was at hand, He never intended to inaugurate the kingdom on earth before He died on the cross. His death on the cross was always intended to precede the inauguration of the kingdom.

to the ratification of the New Covenant. Ratification normally occurs at a formal covenant ceremony involving a sacrifice and the parties taking an oath. But the Lord's Supper does not appear to be such a formal ceremony. There are several reasons that it is not such a ceremony. First, this simple, private Passover celebration was introduced as a remembrance of Jesus' death which was about to take place. Second, the eleven disciples were not party to the New Covenant nor representatives of the house of Israel and the house of Judah. The disciples were not chosen to be, nor were they regarded as, representatives of a nation. There was no mention of the divided people becoming a unified nation. Third, the institution of the elements was to remember what was about to happen at the Cross and to remember His death until He returns. There is no indication that the covenant is ratified by the bread and wine which the Lord instituted. Rather, the ratification simply occurred as God was satisfied *by Christ's death* and Christ's death alone was, therefore, the basis on which the believers became beneficiaries of the covenant blessings (Luke 22:19-20).

Accepting the Cross (Luke 23:35-43)

As Jesus hung on the cross, words were flung at Him that were intended to express Israel's contempt for Him (Isa 53:3). The rulers scoffed, "He saved others; let him save himself" (Luke 23:35). They were intending to expose a scam. The soldiers scorned, "If you are the King…save yourself!" (Luke 23:37). One of the criminals harangued, "Are you not the Christ? Save yourself and us" (Luke 23:39). These words, spewed out with contempt, could have generated an angry response if Jesus had taken them up. But He chose to disregard them. He had saved others many times. Their harangue confirmed the reality of Jesus' ministry. If He would save the lost, He must sacrifice Himself in their place. And He chose to do that. To make the point, Luke alone included the rebuke of the other criminal and the call of faith to Jesus, "remember me when you come into your kingdom." Jesus replied, "today you will be with me in Paradise" (Luke 23:42-43). The criminal was saved by faith alone.

Resurrection—(Luke 24:1-53)

Luke's case for Jesus' victory overcoming death is historical, not primarily theological. Yet, in the historical fact, the theological consequence of *overcoming* the enemy's power of death occurred. In addition, the facts of the revelation are historical (died, buried, an empty grave, appearance to witnesses, etc.). A theological argument must await Spirit-led reflection by His apostles. By the first day of the week, the tomb was empty (Luke 24:1-3). Two angels, appearing as men, addressed the women's perplexity and reminded them that Jesus had spoken of resurrection on the third day (Luke 24:6-7). The meaning had escaped the women and the disciples at the time since they hadn't heard and accepted what Jesus said.

Luke alone tells the account of two disciples on the road to Emmaus. In their conversation, Jesus drew out from the two their hopes that had been shattered by the Cross. They even spoke of Jesus' words of resurrection without any grasp of what could be expected. Then He expounded what Scriptures said about Him (24:27). Then in the display of His hands in the breaking of the bread, Jesus turned their unbelief to faith by opening their eyes to see that He in truth was the crucified One who now was alive (Luke 24:13-35). Their sadness was turned to immediate gladness. That night they returned to the other disciples in Jerusalem.

Then Jesus met with the disciples in Luke 24:36-49. He showed them His scars of the wounds and His body they could touch. Then He asked for food to eat, "while they still were amazed and unbelieving because of their joy" (Luke 24:41, HCSB).

Following this display which caught their attention, He exposed the flaw in their thinking. They never considered seriously that "everything written about [Him] in the Law of Moses and the Prophets and the Psalms must be fulfilled" (Luke 24:44). Then He opened their eyes to see, ears to hear, and "minds to understand the Scripture" (Luke 24:45). They were called to witness to the correlation between these historical observations they saw about Him and the empty grave, and the Scripture which spoke about Him and His experiences (Luke 24:48). In addition, Jesus would send the promise of the Father upon them (Luke 24:49), the Father's promised inheritance given to His Son. God the Father promised Jesus an inheritance upon completing His First Advent mission. This would include the sending of the Holy Spirit. Luke's second volume, Acts, would describe the account of what He would send to share with the remnant of believers.

Conclusion

There are two fundamental purposes of the canon reflecting what happened in Genesis 1–3. Matthew emphasized the kingdom come from heaven to earth and reestablished the creation purpose (Genesis 1).

Luke emphasizes salvation from sin and its consequences in death. This addresses the second fundamental purpose of God (Genesis 3).

Salvation was expected in the Hebrew Scriptures as the remnant bore witness (Luke 1–2). Jesus' sermon at Nazareth proclaimed "the acceptable year of the LORD" (Luke 4:16-21, NKJV), quoting Isa 61:1-2a. This time of salvation was reflected in the works of salvation by faith (Luke 4:31–9:17) in the ministry in Galilee. This led to Peter's confession (Luke 9:18-20) and to Jesus' prediction of His death and resurrection, which would become the basis of salvation (Luke 9:21-22). At the same time, Jesus' transfiguration assured the future resolution of the coming kingdom (Luke 9:27-36) while at the same time rebuked the demon (Luke 9:37-42).

Luke 9:51 introduces Jesus' final journey to Jerusalem to fashion the remainder of His First Advent ministry, according to a final summary: "the Son of Man came to seek and to save the lost" (Luke 19:10).

CHAPTER 19:
THE TIMES OF THE
GENTILES: JOHN

Introduction

The context of the questions concerning Israel in the second temple period have influenced the Gospel of John less than the Synoptic Gospels. Yet John does feature a believing remnant as Luke had. But John writes for anyone who would consider the signs which Jesus performed and the words which He spoke. He writes that they might believe in Him. And John defines saving faith perhaps more clearly than any other Gospel account. Faith is defined by *what* is believed. The *what* finds its content summarized in John 20:30-31, that He is the Anointed One (by the Holy Spirit), God's Son (as the Father declared from heaven). This revelation about His Person, with implications about His work, was based on the promises in the Hebrew Bible. This revelation becomes the heart of the gospel displayed in the *signs* He did. And in John's Gospel, John calls this revelation of His Person a display of God's glory (John 1:14).

Raymond Brown focuses on these themes in outlining the book:

Prologue (1:1-18)

The Book of Signs (1:19–12:50)

The Book of Glory (13:1–20:31)

Epilogue (21:1–25)[1]

This outline appropriately focuses on Jesus Christ and His glory, which appeared both in the glory of the *historical signs* (John 2:11; 11:40; 17:4) and in His climactic glorification in *crucifixion* and *resurrection*

[1] Raymond E. Brown, *The Gospel according to John: I-XII* (Garden City, NY: Doubleday, 1966) and Raymond E. Brown, *The Gospel according to John: XIII-XXI* (Garden City, NY: Doubleday, 1970).

(John 7:39; 12:16, 23; 13:31; cf. 21:19). It is His glory which John relates to the other theme of faith. People ought to believe because His glory is worthy.

The Book of Signs

The theme of Jesus' glory and the theme of faith will be featured in our interpretation of John, with the desire to examine how one influences the other, how the revelation of His glory *draws* the unbeliever to believe. In order to introduce this consideration, first, we will explore the summary of the book (John 20:30-31) and the summary of the historical ministry (John 12:37-50).

Summary of the Book (John 20:30-31)

The summary is a reflection on the writing of the whole book. John 20:30 explicitly remarks that the book was merely a *selection* of the signs that Jesus had done. Then in v 31, he refers to those which had been written. Does John intend to refer only to the account of miraculous events, or does He include Jesus' explanation? Since the sign is merely a token of His glory, Jesus' explanation is needed to flesh out what the token means about Himself. Thus, "these are written" (John 20:31) refers both to the signs and to Jesus' explanation of what they mean about Him and His ministry.

Are the signs limited to the Book of Signs (John 12:37), or should Jesus' crucifixion, resurrection, and ascension be included? Brown states, "[T]here is no evidence that he thought of the resurrection itself as a sign, or that the main events of The Book of Glory, the passion and death of Jesus, were on the level of signs."[2] Yet Barrett[3] sees the crucifixion and resurrection as the greatest, supreme signs. He maintains that the death and resurrection are not called signs because they are not merely a token of something other than themselves, but *are* the thing they signify. Brown adds, "in 'the hour' of his return to his Father, Jesus is no longer pointing symbolically to his glory but is actually being glorified."[4] Yet when Jesus was asked for a sign to substantiate His claim to call the temple His Father's house, He promised a sign (John 2:18-19). That sign was, "Destroy this temple, and in three days I will raise it up" (John 2:19).

---

[2]   Brown, *John XIII-XXI*, p. 1059.

[3]   C. K. Barrett, *The Gospel According to St. John* (Philadelphia: Westminster, 1978), p. 65.

[4]   Brown, *John XIII-XXI*, p. 1059.

Whereas John did not call it a sign, Jesus did. Thus, the miracles are signs not of the kingdom of God, as in the Synoptic Gospels, but of Christ's glory. And He is glorified (John 13:31) in the climactic events of crucifixion, resurrection, and ascension. Since God, in turn, would be glorified in Him, it happens not merely in Jesus' ascension. Jesus being glorified includes all three events.

The book is written with a particular purpose in the response of the reader. Two questions follow: to whom is the book written? And, what is the purpose? The purpose is expressed in the subordinating conjunction, "in order that" or "so that." The purpose is, "that you might come to believe,"[5] but it may be best to translate the phrase more generally, "might believe." The book is written for an evangelistic purpose, so that the audience includes unbelievers. But as W. H. G. Thomas[6] has pointed out, we must evaluate the evangelist's statement of purpose in light of the fact that he relates the content of the Gospel to signs performed in the presence of *disciples*. And the disciples are repeatedly said to believe. Thus, the purpose is designed to gain a positive response, whether addressing an unbeliever or a believer. A salvific note is added at the end of the verse, "that by believing you may have life in his name," supporting the scope focused on evangelism.

Second, the relationship between the revelation of the text and the response of the reader is clarified as Jesus discussed the response of His generation following the sign of the feeding of five thousand in John 6. The people that had seen and experienced this miracle responded by searching for Him (John 6:25). But they failed to see the miracle as a sign signifying something about Jesus (John 6:26). So He challenges their response because they *worked* for the wrong thing (John 6:27). The strength of Jesus' word, *work*, indicated that they had a real responsibility in their response. They were to work for what endured, which the Son of Man *gives*.

Recognizing this responsibility, they ask what they can do (John 6:28). The appropriate response was to *believe* in the One God sent, as affirmed by the signs He performed (John 6:29). Then they asked for another sign like their ancestors received in manna in the wilderness (John 6:30-31). In response, Jesus clarified: Moses *did not give* the manna but His Father *gives* true bread (John 6:32). What is the Father *giving*?

---

[5]   Author's translation. There is a difficult textual variant in the Greek text. Some manuscripts have a present subjunctive, "that you may hold the faith" and others have an aorist subjective, "that you may come to faith."

[6]   W. H. G. Thomas, "The Purpose of the Fourth Gospel," *Bibliotheca Sacra* 125 (1968): 256-57.

The bread of God is the One who comes down from heaven and *gives* life to the world (John 6:33). The people respond—"give us this bread always" (John 6:34)!

This response seems sufficient, but the bread is not *what* He gives to satisfy their hunger, but *who* He is: "I am the bread of life...no one who *comes* to Me will ever be hungry, and no one who *believes* in Me will ever be thirsty" (John 6:35, HCSB) yet these people come but do not believe.

Why?

Everyone the Father *gives* will come to Him (John 6:37). So a relationship with Jesus only takes shape as God is involved in *giving* them to Jesus. What is involved in the Father *giving* them to Jesus? The Jews' complaint arose because of what they saw in Jesus. He claimed to come from heaven, but they knew He came from Joseph (John 6:42). Then Jesus clarified, no one comes in faith unless the Father *draws* him. That *drawing* involves *hearing* and *learning* from what the Father teaches (John 6:44-45; Isa 54:13).

So as to focus on the need to pay attention, Jesus pressed the image to become more difficult to hear and to understand: "the bread that I will give for the life of the world is my flesh" (John 6:51). That image led to two responses:

1. The Jews argued, "How can this man give us his flesh to eat?" (John 6:52).

2. Many disciples said, "This teaching is hard! Who can accept it?" (John 6:60, HCSB).

These two responses objected because the Spirit *gives* life. The flesh does not lead to comprehension. Rather, Jesus' very words are Spirit-based and life (John 6:62-63). In addition, the Father's election grants those who come (John 6:65). And many of His disciples stopped following him (John 6:66).

To clarify what was happening, Jesus pressed the Twelve, "Do you want to go away as well?" (John 6:67). Peter responded: "To whom shall we go? You have the words of eternal life, and we have believed, and have come to know, that you are the Holy One of God" (John 6:68-69). It wasn't that they understood all that was being said, but they believed that Jesus was sent from God and what He spoke was from God and was true. But then Jesus revealed God's point of view: Peter spoke for the eleven who were chosen (elect). One of the disciples is a devil who will betray Him (John 6:70-71).

What are these Spirit-based words about? It is God's work of grace. Moses had recognized that his generation needed eyes to see, ears to hear, and a mind to understand (Deut 29:4). Later, when Jesus explains why that generation did not believe (John 12:37), He quotes Isa 6:9-10, which was fulfilled (John 12:40). It means that they could not believe because God had blinded their eyes and hardened their hearts.

So the Father teaches through Jesus' words, which, when believed, give eternal life. The words are believed because the Spirit gives the hearer eyes to see, ears to hear, and a mind to understand. This gift is not regeneration (John 3:3-5), nor is it faith to respond (Eph 2:8-9).[7] Rather, the gift is the desire to listen to Jesus' words and to learn (John 6:44-45) so that they can do the work "for the food that endures" (John 6:27). They are responsible for believing in the One the Father has sent (John 6:29). This work of the Spirit is what has been called efficacious grace.

At the conclusion of the Book of Signs (John 12:27-36), the same discussion takes place about subsequent generations and their response to Jesus Christ. The focus is upon two historical acts involving Jesus (John 12:32). They both refer to the judgment of this world and its ruler (John 12:31).

First, the Son of Man must be "lifted up." The image, *lifted up*, signifies the type of death He is about to die (John 12:33). It is a portrayal of His death on the cross (John 3:14; 8:28). That *lifted up* experience also includes Jesus' words, "The One who sent Me is with Me. He has not left Me alone, because I always do what pleases Him" (John 8:29, HCSB). This, by implication, involves His resurrection. Together these events, His death on the cross and resurrection from the dead, involve the judgment of the world and its ruler (John 12:31).

Second, Jesus promises, "I will draw all people to myself" (John 12:32, HCSB). This is not the effectual drawing of the elect to hearing and learning (John 6:44-45) since it involves *all people*. Rather it has the sense of "draw the attention of all people." This would refer to Jesus as "the true light, who gives light to *everyone*, [who] was coming into the world" (John 1:9, HCSB, emphasis added). The open display of His death on the cross, His resurrection, evidenced by the empty tomb and the apostles' witness, is the most vivid display of God's glory (John 12:28). This is the glorious

---

[7]   Ephesians 2:8-9 states, "For by grace you have been saved through faith. And this is not your own doing; it is the gift of God, not a result of works, so that no one may boast." What is the gift? It is not simply faith because the gender does not agree with faith as the antecedent. The antecedent of it is the work of efficacious grace which enables one to believe.

sign to which subsequent generations are called to respond: "Destroy this temple [body], and in three days I will raise it up" (John 2:19).

Conclusion of Jesus' Historic Ministry (John 12:37-50)

This conclusion involves two segments: an evaluation of the people's response (John 12:37-43), and a summary of the essentials in His own ministry (John 12:44-50).

An Evaluation of the Generation's Response (John 12:37-43)

John, as a disciple in Jesus' generation, experienced the light shining from Jesus' ministry. Given the historic signs portraying Jesus' glory (John 9:2-3; 11:4), which seemed so convincing, how could that generation of Israel not believe in Him (John 12:37)? In the prologue, John had already said, "He came to his own, and his own people did not receive him" (John 1:11).

Thus, to evaluate that historical fact, he found the answer in the theology of Isaiah. In fact, the response of Jesus' generation fulfilled the word of the prophet Isaiah (John 12:38). That prophet foresaw that Israel would reject and crucify her Messiah (Isa 53:1-12).

John began his evaluation with the question that Isaiah raised before the prophecy of the Servant being rejected and crucified: "Who has believed our message?" (Isa 53:1, NASB). This question is appropriate because of the dramatic expression of glory provided both by Isaiah's prophecy (Isaiah 40–52) and Jesus' signs. This display of glory exceeds any other generation in salvation history.

In the Exodus generation, the people had seen the plagues directed against Egypt and Pharaoh. Further, they walked out of Egypt with wealth from the Egyptian people, yet the LORD had not yet given that generation a heart to understand, eyes to see, or ears to hear (Deut 29:4). In Isaiah's own generation, Hezekiah, along with the people, had experienced God's deliverance of Jerusalem from the invasion of Assyria (Isaiah 36–37), yet they failed to believe Isaiah's message (Isa 53:1). In each generation, these displays of God's glory were sufficient to bring condemnation when rejected but not sufficient to enlighten without an additional work of God.

Now when John speaks of his generation, he concludes that they "did not believe" (John 12:37). That happened to fulfill the word of Isaiah

(John 12:38). Then John quotes and relates two passages from Isaiah. First, in Isa 53:1, a question is raised which is the same question John raises for his generation, "who has believed our report?" (John 12:38, NKJV). Second, John concludes that they didn't believe because "they *could not believe*" (John 12:39, emphasis added). That conclusion was supported by a quotation of Isa 6:9-10. This announcement speaks in Isaiah of God the Father's work of judgment. It refers to an opposite work of God than was spoken about in Deut 29:4. "He has blinded their eyes and hardened their heart, lest they...understand with their heart, and turn, and [He] would heal them" (John 12:40). Isaiah spoke prophetically of Jesus and His glory (John 12:41).

While John used Jesus' explanation of the Father's work of grace in John 6:44-45, he now used Isaiah to speak of His work of judgment (John 12:37-39). In each case, there is a mystery only accepted by those who believe in Jesus and accept His words. The mystery includes both the unconditional election of the Father (John 6:65) and the personal responsibility only met in the efficacious grace of the Spirit (John 16:5-11).

In Isaiah's day, many commentators see this glory in the vision of the enthroned God (Isa 6:1-5). While Isaiah described what he saw, he never spoke about the enthroned God. Rather he spoke in prophetic terms about a King in contrast to Ahaz (Isa 7:14; 9:6-7; 11:1-5). Further, in distinction to Hezekiah, he spoke in terms of God's ultimate Servant (Isaiah 42:1-6; 49:1-8; 50:4-9; 52:13–53:12). In John's day, his generation saw the signs from the Son and heard the very Word from the Father. What Isaiah spoke about in prophecy, John experienced.

Even though that generation was hardened, "many believed in Him" (John 12:42, NKJV). And some believed from the most improbable group, the Jewish rulers, like Nicodemus and Joseph of Arimathaea. Yet a number kept silent about their faith for fear of the Pharisees. What was the status of their faith? It was inactive in terms of testimony but genuine in terms of response.[8]

---

[8] D. A. Carson has questioned in particular the genuineness of such a silent response. If one is ashamed to publicly declare faith in Christ, does such shame override a profession of faith? "The leaders themselves (same word as in 3:1) seem at this point to fit the pattern of inadequate, irresolute, even spurious faith that John repeatedly describes in this Gospel (e.g. 2:23-25; 6:60; 8:30 ff)" (D. A. Carson, *The Gospel According to John* [Grand Rapids, MI: Eerdmans, 1991], pp. 450-51). This response is certainly inadequate and with mixed motives. But is it without resolve or spurious?

This section is an evaluation of the Apostle John who describes the response with a construction that he regards as a technical phrase, *pisteuen eis* (12:42). Bultmann comments on the force of the construction: "The fact that πίστευεν είς is equivalent to πίστευεν ότι shows rather that πίστευεν είς arises out of the use of πίστευεν for 'to regard as credible,' as true...

Summary of Jesus' Ministry (John 12:44-50)

While John based his evaluation on the theology of Isaiah, he based his summary on Jesus' own words. This summary features three issues:

- My message is My Father's message.
- To believe in Me is to believe in My Father.
- Judgment is based on a response to My words.

Jesus' Message is Sufficient

Jesus expands upon what makes His message sufficient. It is sufficient to correspond to what the Father says (John 12:44). That correspondence rests in God's word to Moses: "I will raise up for them a prophet like you…I will put My words in his mouth, and he will tell them everything I command him. I will hold accountable whoever does not listen to My words that he speaks in My name" (Deut 18:18-19, HCSB, alluded to in John 12:49-50). The force of the word *command* highlights the idea of correspondence.

Jesus' message is sufficient because it expands upon the *signs* that Jesus did. The signs reveal God's glory. Thus, "the one who sees Me sees Him who sent Me" (John 12:45, HCSB). Brown highlights the importance of the Old Testament background for John's use of the concept of *glory*.

> [T]here are two important elements in the understanding of the glory of God: it is a *visible* manifestation of His majesty in *acts* of *power*…In Exod xvi 7-10 Moses promises the people: "In the morning you shall see the glory of God." He is refer-ring to the miracle of the manna.[9]

This view of glory is compatible with John's use of miracles as *signs*. BDAG[10] proposes two meanings for the term *sēmeion* (sign). First, it could be "a sign or distinguishing mark whereby something is known."

[in] John esp πίστευεν εἰς and πίστευεν are constantly used interchangeably in the same sense." (Bultmann, *Theological Dictionary of the New Testament*, vol. 6, ed. Kittel [Grand Rapids, MI: Eerdmans, 1968], p. 203). Thus, this assessment of Johannine usage validates the author's view of the response as genuine in spite of being inactive. The case of Nicodemus demonstrates that what is inadequate (John 3:1) is not necessarily spurious (John 7:50-51). Active faith is drawn out by God over events in history.

9   Brown, *John I-XII*, p. 503, emphasis added.

10   Walter Bauer, *A Greek-English Lexicon of the New Testament and Other Early Christian Literature*, rev. and ed. Fredrick Wm. Danker, 3rd ed. (Chicago: University of Chicago Press, 2000), pp. 920-21.

Second, it could be "an event that is an indication or confirmation of intervention by transcendent powers." Both senses are appropriate here.

Jesus' message is sufficient because it brings light in a dark world so that all who believe have light by which to live (John 12:46). In the prologue, John added that "the darkness did not overcome it" (John 1:5, HCSB). Thus, the sufficiency of Jesus' ministry is expressed because of its revelatory clarity and ability to overcome opposition in power.

A Response Is Necessary

In each mention of Jesus' ministry, an independent response is also necessary. This is reflected by the consistent appeal: come to Him, see Him, believe in Him. It is necessary because each aspect of the ministry carries with it a responsibility which is properly received or rejected.

Judgment of the Response

To believe in the Son is to believe in the Father. This response is necessary because the Father gives the blessing. To see the Son is to see the Father. This is also necessary because the Father governs salvation history.

Further, inadequate responses are considered. When the person hears the Word but doesn't keep the Word, no judgment is passed because Jesus came in the First Advent to save (John 12:47). On the other hand, one who rejects Jesus and does not accept His Word is not judged immediately (John 12:48). This judgment awaits the day of reckoning. On that day, judgment will rest on the historic rejection of Jesus' Word.

Glory of the Incarnation (John 1:14-18)

This introductory hymn in John 1:1-18 was composed by John to reflect upon Jesus' role in the creation and human history. Of course, this perception rests upon Johannine authorship. Based upon this premise, this is John the Apostle's studied conclusion about Jesus. John 1:14-18, the last strophe, introduces the community of disciples, and gives expression to the impact which the career of the Word had on them. The *real* Jesus is portrayed in four images.[11]

---

[11] Ray C. Stedman, *God's Loving Word* (Grand Rapids, MI: Discovery House, 1993), pp. 36-42.

The four images are presented in John 1:14-15. The first describes the *incarnation*—the Word became flesh.

> The Prologue does not say that the Word entered into flesh
> or abided in flesh but that the Word *became* flesh. Therefore,
> instead of supplying the liberation from the material world
> that the Greek mind yearned for, the Word of God was now
> inextricably bound to human history.[12]

This idea of bond was at the heart of the idea of covenant. A covenant
is a bond between two partners. Now the bond is personal rather than
formal. The human nature is bound to the divine nature in one Person.
And that Person shares the same essence with the Father, who is another
Person in the one Godhead. Jesus made His dwelling or pitched His tent
(*skēnoun*) among the people of Israel in human flesh. This is an allusion to
God's first dwelling on earth within the nation, residing in the tabernacle
(Exod 25:8; 29:46).

The second image is the appearance of God's *glory*. It was the glory of
God that had departed from the temple before it was torn down (Ezekiel
8:1–10:18). It was that glory which was absent from the rebuilt temple
(Ezra 6:1-22). Yet this glory was personal, as the only Son shares with His
Father. Father and Son bear a shared likeness. Philip hadn't realized this
until Jesus pointed out, "Whoever has seen me has seen the Father...Do
you not believe that I am in the Father and the Father is in me? The words
that I say to you I do not speak on my own authority, but the Father who
dwells in me does his works" (John 14:9-10). It was Jesus in glory that
cleansed the temple at the outset of His ministry and claimed it as His
Father's house (John 2:16). The second temple that had been completed
without the appearance of God's glory is now claimed as the Son's appropriate dwelling.

The third image is the display of the familial glory, as "full of grace and
truth" (John 1:14). In the fallen world, seemingly, grace appears at the
expense of truth, or truth appears only at a loss in grace.[13] In deity, these
two virtues are mutually necessary and dependent. To be truthful, God
must be gracious. If God's favor would appear to undeserving man, it must

---

[12] Brown, *John I-XII*, p. 31.

[13] It might seem that graciousness would overlook the true condition of another. Let us not
embarrass the person. Let us not put him to shame. Let us be tolerant. That is not grace, but
compromise. Such a sacrifice of truth is hurtful to the other person in the long run. Or it may
seem necessary to set aside grace to make a point of truth. But truth not clothed in grace can
be destructive. A constructive expression of truth must be capable of being heard, received,
and acted upon.

be with a truthful revelation of God's holiness in the midst of the sinful condition of man. That display is fully present as the mark of deity. This is divine life and "that life was the *light* of men" (John 1:4, HCSB, emphasis added). Thus, Jesus' glory and Jesus' light are the same inward presence of what displays itself outwardly as grace and truth (Exod 34:6-7).

The final image is His rank compared to God's prophet, John. John's statement may sound puzzling: "He who comes after me ranks before me, because he was before me." Rank on earth is commonly measured by historical sequence; the elder ranks higher than the younger. But this is reversed because of the heavenly order. Heavenly order measures rank in essence; eternal ranks higher than temporal. Implied in John's comparison is the idea that the Word is God (John 1:1) while the prophet is a man.

The Apostle John then explains what the incarnation means to every believer alive after Jesus was fully glorified (John 13:1-3). As a result, grace and truth are now revealed to the fullest extent (John 1:16-18). For those with access to the account of Jesus' glorification (John 18:20), grace has been received from His fullness—one gift of grace upon another, blessing to one and blessing to another (John 1:16). The law was given through Moses. The commandments make their demands which are righteous, just, and good. Yet, the demands provide no mercy. Law does not contradict grace, rather it supplements it. Law makes its demands, which no fallen human is willing or able to keep completely. But in condemnation, the condemned are pushed to Jesus, from whom grace is provided in truth (John 1:17). In His truthful provision of grace, God is revealed. Jesus, in His First Advent, made God known (John 1:18). In other words, sinful human beings can find grace in Jesus Christ because, in truth, He sacrificed Himself to satisfy our need before God.

Tokens of this reality of Jesus' life, shown in the darkness of fallen human life, are brightly displayed in two passages (John 7:1–8:59 and John 9:1-41). To clarify the issue, Jesus claimed to be the Light of the world (John 8:12; 9:5).

Light Shines in Darkness (John 7:1–8:59)

The Issue of Jesus' Identity (John 7:1-58)

By the time of the fall Feast of Tabernacles, the question of Jesus' identity came into full focus. The next spring, at the Feast of Passover, He would be crucified for claiming to be equal with God. There were a variety of opinions that were being discussed as people were gathering for the feast.

Jesus' Brothers (John 7:1-9)

In Galilee, Jesus' brothers had observed His miracles. They were not yet convinced that they meant anything about Him, beyond that He was their brother, who worked wonders. Therefore, they urged Him as a celebrity teacher, but He insisted that His timing was under God's plan. So Jesus delayed departing while His brothers left for the feast.

At the Middle of the Feast (John 7:10-36)

Several questions filtered through the crowd at the feast. Central to all the questions was: who do you think Jesus really is? Different answers were being entertained, generally with shallow supporting reasons. All were impressed with His teaching that He quietly initiated in the temple complex, particularly since He had received no formal rabbinic instruction. He alluded to His identity when He said He taught what God taught Him. Another question circulated: why hadn't the Jewish leaders challenged Him? The crowd knew they differed over His Sabbath healing. His teaching in response was profound, silencing the criticism. So, as a last resort, the religious leaders sent temple police to arrest Him.

On the Last Day of the Feast (John 7:37-44)

The Feast of Tabernacles had its origin in the Mosaic Law (Lev 23:33-36). Originally, it was the final of seven yearly feasts celebrating the anticipation of final occupation of the land. So for seven days the people gathered in Jerusalem to live in temporary tabernacles or booths, awaiting the fulfillment of God's promised plan for Israel. It was a Feast with eschatological expectations.

"Of particular importance for our purposes are the ceremonies that sprang up in connection with the celebration of Tabernacles at Jerusalem."[14] During the celebration, on each day, there was a procession from the pool of Siloam to pour the water around the altar. "On the seventh

---

[14] Brown, *John I-XII*, p. 326.

day there was a sevenfold circumambulation of the altar."[15] It was on this occasion that Jesus made an unexpected and bold promise.

He boldly, and without qualification, promised to quench the thirst of anyone coming to Him in faith, believing that He would bless, based on an eschatological prophecy in Scripture (John 7:37-38). Brown makes a reasoned case that this promise is based on Zech 14:8: "living waters shall flow out from Jerusalem" to the Mediterranean and the Dead Sea.[16] This promise is also expressed in the eschatological passage in Ezek 47:1-12. The water was flowing from the temple which housed the glory of the LORD (Ezek 43:3-5) where God's throne resides (Ezek 43:7).

Jesus clarified that the eschatological blessing was the Holy Spirit. However, the gift of the Holy Spirit would be available from Him following His *glorification*, after His resurrection and ascension (John 7:39). Since Jesus hadn't been glorified, the Spirit hadn't been given to quench the thirst of believers.

Following this dramatic but terse claim, the crowd was divided over His identity (John 7:40-44). Some concluded He was the Prophet, some that He was Messiah, but others objected that Messiah didn't originate in Galilee. The confusion continued.

The Sanhedrin's Response (John 7:45-52)

When the temple police returned without Jesus, the chief priests and Pharisees were arguing that none of the leaders had been persuaded by Jesus' claim. In reference to the Law, Nicodemus objected that any official judgment demanded that He be given a trial, hearing His defense. They dismissed Nicodemus with the Galilee assertion: does Messiah come from Galilee?

However, John includes an event that followed, which served the role of presenting a trial of Jesus.

---

[15] *Ibid.*, p. 327.

[16] As the Feast of Tabernacles is an eschatological feast, so Zechariah 9–14 describes aspects of Yahweh's triumph in the eschatological Day of the Lord:

- 9:9—The messianic King comes to Jerusalem, triumphant and riding on a donkey.

- 12:10—Yahweh pours out a spirit of compassion and supplication on Jerusalem…they will mourn.

- 13:1—He opens up a fountain for the house of David to cleanse Jerusalem.

- 14:8—Living waters flow out from Jerusalem to the Mediterranean and the Dead Sea.

- 14:16—When all enemies are destroyed, people come up year after year to Jerusalem to keep the Feast of Tabernacles properly.

The Test of Jesus' Claim (John 7:53–8:11)

This passage is debated among textual critics, but the translations admit to probable authenticity as reflected by the inclusion of 7:53–8:11 in most authorized translations. The unity of the text in context will be demonstrated by a proposed coherent flow of thought, and thus the testimony of the author's argument concerning Jesus' identity.

The Test

In spite of the menorahs which lighted the whole temple court, that early morning brought shadows and darkness that symbolized the religious leaders' scheme. They were bent on discrediting Jesus in the eyes of the crowd that had gathered that early morning (John 8:2). The leaders had a scheme in which they would test Jesus in a way that gave Jesus no good option in a legal decision (John 8:3-6). The test was to demand a verdict from Jesus concerning a woman caught in the act of adultery. But the test was clearly driven by bias as seemed to be evident to the people, for where was the man? They were using the woman for their destructive ends which cast its ominous shadow over the test of Jesus in the temple (John 8:6).

The Verdict

The verdict they concluded should be based on Moses' Law. Adultery deserved death (Exod 20:14; Lev 20:10), but would Jesus concur? In view of that, they attempted to create the dilemma. Were He to condemn her, the people would sense an injustice committed against her. Although she was guilty, so was the man. Selective enforcement reflects their bias. On the other hand, if He were to excuse her, Moses would condemn Him since the words of the Law left no room but for a condemnation. Would His response to the dilemma not besmirch His reputation?

An Allusion to a Precedent

Unexpectedly, and seemingly disregarding the dilemma, Jesus stooped to write with His finger in the dust of the ground. It alluded to God writing on the tablets with His finger (Exod 31:18). At Mt. Sinai, these tablets were shattered after the covenant had been broken (Exod 32:19). When the religious leaders insisted on a verdict, He rose and conceded her guilt.

The one who was without sin in using this woman, let him throw the first stone. With this, He challenged her accusers: were they free from guilt in their use of her guilt? Jesus saw through their scheme to their motive and challenged their right to execute the verdict as the Law prescribed. In this charge, He spoke in *truth*. The witnesses demanding a death penalty were to throw the first stones (Deut 17:7). But in *grace*, He stooped again as if to write on a second set of tablets (Exod 34:1-2). In stooping, He allowed the leaders, guilty of using the woman, to excuse themselves without pursuing the verdict against her or against Himself.

When all had disqualified themselves by leaving, Jesus stood from writing the law a second time (Exod 34:10-29). Jesus asked the woman about her accusers. None remained but Jesus. In *grace*, Jesus didn't condemn her either, even though she was guilty and He was qualified to judge her. Standing, He confronted her with the *truth* of her sinful choice. Challenging her, He allowed her to depart with the words, "go, and from now on sin no more" (John 8:11).

The Light of the World (John 8:12)

Jesus Enlightened All Involved

Again Jesus turned to the crowd to emphasize the presence of His light—full of grace and truth. This revealed that He was the light for both the woman and the leaders. Like the light of the menorah brought light to the temple, so Jesus brought light to those gathered around Him (John 8:12). In the light of Jesus' life, all saw the reality of a sinful and deceitful world and saw and heard the offers of grace from Jesus, spoken in truth. This Light is suitable for the whole world.

The Debate over His Claim (John 8:13-59)

Demand for Proof

The Pharisees, lingering on the fringes, demanded witnesses to verify the truth of His claim (John 8:13). Ignoring the witness of what had just happened, they call for witnesses of His claim as the Law had said. So Jesus challenged their demand with three facts (John 8:14-20). First, they did not pay attention to Him to know whether He had given proof. Second, when they do reach their verdict, they only considered superficial facts. Jesus has a heavenly perspective,[17] yet they failed to consider this. Finally, if they only had read the Scripture, they would see that the Father had already been that witness and confirmed His claim by what He was able to do. His teaching in response to the test reflected God's glory. His healing on the Sabbath was disclosed as from the Father and His Son (John 5).

Warning from a Heavenly Perspective

Yet, Jesus continued to plead with them (John 8:21-29). The language may appear to be vague and thus evasive. But as they pursued the issue of His origin, He answered and emphasized the importance of what He had to tell them. A third time He adds that after they crucify Him, they'll know He is from heaven and from God. While some of those with whom He was speaking were confused, many from the crowd believed in Him (John 8:30). They believed that He brought light to their lives, and to the situation, from His heavenly perspective.

Separating Those in the Crowd

Jesus separated those in the crowd from the believers by addressing those who believed first (John 8:31-32). He promised that abiding in His Word would bring knowledge of the truth and freedom from sin.

Unbelievers in the crowd identified themselves as they objected. Their pride was offended because they had never seen themselves as enslaved (John 8:33). Jesus was not talking about political freedom, even though the Romans ruled Jerusalem, but about sin. Everyone who sins is a slave to sin (8:34). It was true they were in Abraham's house, but they were not there as sons. They were there as slaves. And slaves do not live in the house forever. Only the son has a permanent place in the house (John 8:33).[18]

True Condition of Slaves

As slaves of sin, they are in reality descendants of the devil (John 8:36-47). And the allusion to the enmity found in Gen 3:15 displays how effective the devil had been in Israel's history, even enslaving many of the

---

[17] Jesus knew He came from the Father in heaven and was about to go to the Father in heaven. That perspective would certainly give Him a credibility to make His claim.

[18] Stedman, *God's Living Word*, p. 250.

people in Israel. While Jesus had forthrightly resisted the devil's temptation, the corporately elected descendants of Abraham had joined other nations to serve the serpent in sin.

Jesus sums up the status of their controversy with two questions (John 8:46):

1. Can you convict Me of any sin?
2. Why don't you believe if I speak truth?

Then He adds the answer: you don't listen because you are not in touch with God (John 8:47).

The Consequences of Rejection

Unable to answer His questions, they resort to personal attack and bigotry. Jesus again focused on their choice—If anyone keeps His Word, he will *never, never* see death (John 8:51). Jesus does not say never die but never *see* death. For the one who holds Jesus' Words secure, death doesn't usher one into condemnation but into the Father's presence and life. All will die physically, but sons will not be separated from God.

The Jewish leaders failed to listen carefully and took what He said as though He merely spoke of experiencing physical death. As such, for the leaders, the death of the patriarchs seemed to prove Jesus' claim to be false. They lived and they died. Does He claim to be greater than Abraham who died? But Jesus' claim anticipated what the Father would do. It wasn't Jesus who would glorify Himself, but the Father would glorify Jesus as He would overcome death. His future resurrection experience would validate His claim to be God's Son (John 8:54). Even they who boasted in Abraham did not share Abraham's response to God's promised One. Abraham rejoiced when he saw Jesus' day (John 8:56). This claim suggested Jesus' pre-existence, because He had seen Abraham. When God promised a descendant through whom all nations would be blessed (Gen 12:3; 15:4-6), Jesus was the One through whom God's word of promise would be realized. Abraham believed the promise and saw that day of blessing by faith. Thus, he saw Jesus as his descendant in the promise, who alone would bring blessings to all nations. He didn't know historical Jesus, but he knew the Promised One's role, which historical Jesus would fulfill.

The opponents of Jesus had only one tactic left, since they could not answer Him. So they picked up stones to stone Jesus, the descendant of the woman, but He slipped away. His time had not yet come (John 7:6; 8:20, 59).

Light Transforms Blindness (John 9:1-41)

Blindness

Jesus and His disciples stumbled onto a beggar whom they heard was blind from birth. The disciples asked, "who sinned…that [this man] was born blind?" Their question was very Jewish, since they assumed a direct connection between personal sin and such suffering. In Jesus' answer, He does not deny a connection, this happened "that the works of God might be displayed in him" (John 9:3). The point of Jesus' ministry is that believing is seeing, rather than the common maxim, seeing is believing. The Pharisees thought that what they saw or understood ought to determine what ought to be believed.

The last account (John 7:1–8:59) of Jesus' display of light now transitions from that willful pride that produced experiential blindness to judicial blindness, which left them unable to see (chap. 9). At the same time, a man born blind is drawn through growing faith to finally see the light of who Jesus is.

The Blind One Given Sight

Often Jesus gave physical sight instantly with a touch. But this time, He spat on the ground, formed mud to put on the blind man's eyes and sent him alone to find the pool of Siloam. Then, washing off the mud, it was implied that he would see (John 9:7). But to follow these strange directions called for faith in the One who gave the directions. So, by faith, he followed what Jesus said in spite of the difficulty of even finding the pool, and the improbability of gaining his sight this way. However, the pursuit of faith foreshadowed a process by which he would eventually come to know Jesus, in whom he believed (John 9:35-38).

The Question of a Miracle

When he returned with physical sight for the first time in his life, his neighbors wanted to know what happened. But first, they had to be assured that he was the blind man they had known because this had never been heard of before. This was not the restoring of sight that had failed in the past, but the creation of sight that had never existed. His rehearsal of what Jesus had done hardly satisfied his neighbors (John 9:8-12).

So they brought him to the Pharisees for their explanation. But the Pharisees were divided. Some said the miracle cannot be from God, since it was performed on the Sabbath. Others raised the question, "How can a man who is a sinner do such signs?" (John 9:16). So they asked the one whose eyes were opened and he said that Jesus must be a prophet (John 9:17).

This response was reasonable. Jesus' actions and words prophesied what had happened when he gained sight. But something was left unanswered, who alone could create sight? However, the proposed answer didn't resolve the Pharisees' dispute. Perhaps there really was no miracle. So they asked his parents if he was born blind. Out of fear of the Pharisees' influence, they kept their answer to basic facts: "We know that this is our son and that he was born blind" (John 9:20). At least the answer clarified that there had been a miracle. But how it happened or who did it—they ventured no opinion.

The Pharisees Oppose the Obvious

A second time, they returned to the blind man who now saw (John 9:24-25). The fact that the miracle happened on the Sabbath now controlled their discussion. So they commanded him to give God *glory* because they had concluded that Jesus was a sinner. The man who had believed Jesus and now saw continued to reason by faith. He didn't know, based on his understanding, whether He was a sinner or not. "One thing I do know, that though I was blind, now I see!" (John 9:25).

So they repeated the same questions he had previously answered (John 9:26-34). They apparently hoped that in repeating the story, he could be caught in some inconsistency. He pointedly challenged their presupposition. In sarcasm, he asked whether they wanted to be Jesus' disciples. They insisted that they followed Moses and they didn't believe what he had said repeatedly. "We do not know where he comes from" (John 9:29).

Their unbelief challenged the man who now saw to draw the only reasonable conclusion from the miracle. By faith, the obvious reality was that this miracle came from God. He had been born blind and the miracle involved the creation of sight, not simply the restoration of what no longer functioned. God does not create by the hands of sinners, but, "if anyone is God-fearing and does His will, He listens to him" (John 9:31,

HCSB). Therefore, if He were not from God, He could not have done anything. Now the man's faith had grown from merely believing what Jesus prophesied to believing the miracle God did through Him. And this man's reasoning was irrefutable. So the Pharisees rejected him based on their faulty theology; he was born in sin causing his blindness. How could he instruct them?

Believing Is Seeing

He had come to realize his faith in the One who healed him. Jesus found him to ask if he had believed in the Son of Man (John 9:35; cf. Dan 7:13-14). The man was ready to confess his faith but did not know who it was he had believed. Jesus identified Himself and the man confessed his faith. Then Jesus revealed His mission of judgment (John 9:39).

Unbelief Is Blindness

Jesus did not come in His First Advent to hold court and settle verdicts, but He came for judgment based on people's response to Himself (John 9:39-40). "That those who do not see may see, and those who see may become blind" (John 9:39). The Pharisees opposed the obvious, both in what happened to the man who now saw and in their own guilt before God. Their reasoning was protective of themselves and exposed their blindness (John 9:39-41). They were judicially blind.

The Book of Glory

Glorification of Jesus

The historic ministry viewed from a distance appeared to be confusing in terms of responses (John 1:19–12:50). The Jewish people were in disagreement. Satan blinded the leaders to cling to what they had at the expense of hearing and accepting Jesus. The Sadducees and Pharisees battled to retain their lifestyle and their own prominence which they won in the second temple period.

Instances of Jesus' glory had appeared in the signs. They were there and then passed by. The disciples were still forming their settled conclusions, which John, in reflection, expressed in the Prologue (John 1:14-18). So the *Book of Glory* is a *book of clarification* for all to see Jesus' glory (John 13–21).

That clarification came from what Jesus said to and did for His disciples, to clear their heads and help them to think straight, by faith, about Jesus' true identity and esteem. But it primarily came from what the Father did for Jesus, His Son, in the midst of confusion and disorder in an evil world; an ultimate clarity came in Jesus' resurrection and ascension to the Father from His crucifixion. The Son was glorified. The Father's esteem for His Son is the true esteem which we can begin to share in our appreciation of the One whose story is being told.

Clarification of Grace

When Jesus and His disciples gathered for their final meal, the disciples, coming off the street, were dirty and unprepared. No one cared enough to help the other. They tried to ignore it. Jesus couldn't. So, as Master, He began to wash their dirty feet. When finished, He asked, "Do you know what I have done for you?" (John 13:12, HCSB). While the answer seemed straightforward, there was something more basic that Jesus wanted them to realize.

The disciples had already begun to suggest answers when He came to Peter. When Peter objected to being served by Jesus, the *first* point came out, they would have *no part with Him* unless Jesus washed their feet. That led to a *second* point. Since washing was necessary, Peter wanted to be washed all over. Jesus clarified that they all had been *bathed* except for Judas. So they didn't need another bath. All they needed was foot washing from the dirt they had accumulated from walking in the world. A bath and foot washing were illustrations of *forgiveness*. In forgiveness there is a distinction; a bath is *relational forgiveness*, which is once for all, and *foot washing* is fellowship forgiveness, which is daily.

Forgiveness is provided by *grace*, through faith in the *truth* of Christ's finished work. He entrusted this truth to His stewards so they could have a *part* in His continuing presence on earth. They were in need of daily forgiveness to maintain fellowship with Him. Only then could they be a part of His presence on earth. In addition, they were to wash one another's feet. His presence on earth was to involve a community of stewards who were willing to forgive each other. This fellowship was based upon Jesus' entrusting of *grace*. Forgiveness of another who offends does not rest on what they deserve, but on what Christ has done on the cross. Jesus concluded, "If you know these things, you are blessed if you do them" (John 13:17, HCSB).

Clarification of Love

While a command to love has always been a part of stewardship on behalf of God, now the focus of love changes as stewards are entrusted with the truths found in Christ's finished work. Jesus called this love the "new commandment" (John 13:34-35). The old commandment had been to love others as one would love themselves (Lev 19:18). That certainly encourages the community that is protective of one another. But grace brings more. This love is *self-sacrificial* (John 13:1-3). Rather than being measured by the standard of *self-protection*, it is motivated by a heart of *self-sacrifice*. The disciples had repeatedly seen it in Jesus, such as when He conceded to His mother's off the wall request (John 2:4), or spoke with the Samaritan woman at the well (John 4:10), or in His concern for the hungry crowd (John 6:5), or the man born blind (John 9:1, 3-4), or even for disciples with dirty feet (John 13:1). It would be most evident on the cross as He cared for His mother (John 19:26-27). That love was to characterize the disciples' love so that "all people will know that you are my disciples" (John 13:35).

Clarification of Prayer

One might think that the time of miracles ended with Jesus' personal departure. It is clear that those miracles that were intended to be signs of Jesus' own identity served a focused purpose. In His resurrection, that ultimate sign had appeared (John 2:18-19), but Jesus added that His stewards would continue to do the works Jesus had done, and, in fact, would do greater works (John 14:12). This expectation was directly linked to prayer in Jesus' name (John 14:13). Praying as though He were present is prayer in His name—asking on His behalf. Jesus' most fundamental work was to do conflict with the enemy, Satan. His resurrection *overcame* the enemy's power of death. Those works must continue through the stewards of His grace. These works, in response to the stewards' prayers, the Father will authorize in bringing glory to His Son. And the works will be more in number as stewards multiply in number and service.

Stewards Empowered by God's Spirit

Stewards are entrusted to keep Jesus' commands (John 14:15). Based on the past experiences recorded in the Scripture, there were not many cases of consistent obedience, if any. It wasn't that Jesus' stewards were removed from the fallen race through regeneration, or somehow found new strength in themselves. When Jesus was with His disciples, they continued to stumble, like Peter, but Jesus promised to send *another paraklēte*. The disciples were strong and effective in Jesus' enablement. So too stewards in the future will be empowered through the gift of the Holy Spirit.

It was not as though God were withholding His enablement from His stewards in the past, but the coming of the Spirit awaited Jesus' glorification in overcoming the enemy. The Spirit had been *with* them in Jesus' presence, but He would be *in* them shortly (John 14:17).

In anticipation of that time, Jesus reminded His disciples of what would be needed to continue to grow. Life is only found in Jesus who is the true Vine. For disciples to continue to mature, they must abide in the Vine. That is the only source of life (John 15:1-17; cf. 8:31-32). They abide in Jesus' life by listening to and keeping Jesus' word (John 15:7). This is another way to describe the role of stewardship of His word, or prayer, and of service to God in bearing fruit (John 15:7-8).

The time of growth following Jesus' departure will not be free from conflict. Disciples of Jesus Christ will be hated by the world (John 15:18–16:4). In addition, as Jesus was about to depart, the Holy Spirit would be sent to convict the world and to guide His disciples toward greater comprehension of truth (John 16:5-15).

Yet, their confusion would only be intensified in the immediate days ahead. Their faith could be challenged to the point of despair. So in oblique but true terms, Jesus speaks about what was about to happen which would become clearer in retrospect. To some degree, that conversation helped (John 16:16-33), but what brought the greatest clarity was Jesus' high priestly prayer (John 17).

The Clarification of Resurrection

This moment of respite for the disciples ended all too quickly. Now the confusion of evil broke out of the seeming order. Judas, Jesus' own treasurer, betrayed Him. The temple leaders, who supposedly interceded with God on behalf of the people, served themselves and their interests on behalf of the devil. Without two witnesses in agreement, they condemned Jesus (John 18:1-27). That decision had been reached earlier and was expressed by Caiaphas (John 11:45-53). Peter denied Jesus, but Jesus was faithful to His Father. Pilate, the Gentile ruler, acted as a captive to evil, for though he found no guilt, he pronounced Jesus guilty to be crucified (John 18:28–19:16).

And Jesus was crucified (John 19:1-37). Pilate was thwarted in his political scheme to substitute and to crucify Barabbas; the cries of the mob carried the will of evil. Yet, Pilate insisted that He be crucified King of the Jews. He shamed Israel, yet Israel's rejection was declared in true perspective. They acted as descendants of the devil. Everyone was confused except Jesus who in suffering still followed the script—announcing the end when it came and giving up His spirit to His Father (John 19:30). He surrendered to the control of the Holy Spirit as He surrendered His Spirit to the Father.

He was buried by Joseph of Arimathea and Nicodemus, publicly honoring Jesus in spite of a history of only private belief. On the first day of the week, God broke death's hold upon Jesus, because it had no legal claim against Him. As had been anticipated, Jesus overcame the enemy by faith to the end. Glorified, He would now be seen in His true renown by Mary Magdalene, by the disciples, including Thomas, the last of the disciples to see and believe. Thomas was right; He is Lord and God (20:28). It is in this sense that the Father glorified the Son (John 8:54) and His glory glorified the Father. Finally, the glorified Jesus restored Peter to fellowship with a part in ministry (John 21).

Conclusion

The resurrection is the final *sign* which the beloved disciple, the author of the Gospel, finally came to know. This experience, in a sense, is a summary of how the Gospel account works.

John had forgotten that Jesus had said three years earlier, "Destroy this temple, and in three days I will raise it up" (John 2:19). Three years later, John would remember what Jesus said (John 2:22). What happened is illustrated when John entered the empty tomb.

The interpretation of the empty tomb admits to a number of different, if not disparate, understandings. Mary Magdalene concluded that someone had taken the body. Yet she hadn't seen the body, nor did she know who had taken it, nor where someone may have hidden the body (John 20:2). No one had seen the tomb being emptied. Resurrection from the dead is a miracle, admitting to no analogous experience in comparison to which it may be understood.

So discovering what happened demanded some other explanation. That is described as Peter and the other disciple visited the tomb (John 20:1-10). Together they ran to the tomb, wanting to verify what Mary had said about the empty tomb. The other disciple arrived first and stooped to look inside. He "saw the linen cloths lying there" (John 20:5). It would not seem likely that the body would be carried away and the linen cloths would be left behind. When Peter arrived, he entered the tomb immediately. Then the other disciple followed him in. Inside, he saw that "the face cloth, which had been on Jesus' head…[was] folded up in a place by itself" (John 20:7). This confirmed his earlier suspicion. The body hadn't been taken, but somehow had left. The folded wrapping by itself was evidence of a deliberate, personal action. How could that be?

"Then the other disciple…saw and believed" (John 20:8). What did he believe? Seeing the evidence of deliberate actions, he believed what Jesus had earlier promised, "Destroy this temple, and in three days I will raise it up" (John 2:19). John saw the evidence as a sign so that he believed what Jesus had promised. And believing, he knew that Jesus arose from the dead. This is the epistemology of the Gospel account. These signs have been recorded that the reader may believe what had been promised concerning Messiah, the Son of God (John 20:31).

Conclusion to the Gospels

The Gospels are *transitional* books featuring *theological* changes. On one side, the revelation of the Hebrew Bible finds fulfillment in the Person and work of Jesus the Messiah. This fulfillment was limited to First Advent issues. On the other side, new revelation concerning the mediatorial kingdom, concerning the work of salvation, and concerning the gift of eternal life, is introduced. That gift of eternal life was to be given freely so that it was received by grace and through faith alone.

Each of the four Gospels shares in common the primary themes concerning the death and the immediate resurrection of Jesus Christ. Gospel narrative genre is distinguished from other hero narratives by focusing thirty to forty percent of the book upon these themes. The emphasis concerns the fact that overcoming the enemy of God is of primary importance in fulfilling the creation goal, and is the foundation of the plan of redemption.

The new revelation introduces the dispensation of grace, which features the ascended God-man keeping the commitments of God. Every other human being in the history of the Hebrew Bible was overcome by the enemy and was ravaged by evil. Some were delivered from evil by God to accomplish God's plan at that stage in history. But the plot-conflict produced adversity between God's stewards and the allies of the enemy of God. Death, which was under the enemy's control, was the universal experience of the human race.[19] Death settled the issue until Jesus overcame death in resurrection. The fallen human race inherited a sinful nature from Adam and experienced personal sin, which resulted in death. Further, all failed in the temptation to sin until Jesus withstood the tempter in the wilderness. Deuteronomy had revealed how to respond in resistance to temptation, but no one was willing to resist temptation until Jesus, God's Son. The promises of God were sufficient to provide deliverance, as Joseph, Joshua and Caleb, and David indicate. But no one was willing to pay the price of receiving what was promised until Jesus prayed—"not as I will, but as you will" (Matt 26:39). The record of the death and resurrection of Jesus Christ is truly remarkable in human history. The resurrection has been called the first fruits of a great harvest from among the dead ones (1 Cor 15:23). As a result, believers can stand firm against the wicked one (Eph 6:10ff.). Believers can live expectantly, hoping to be resurrected from the dead or raptured in life (1 Thess 4:14-16). Believers can anticipate the judgment of God's enemy (Rev 20:1-3, 7-10). Believers have hope.

All of the basic themes of the new revelation are shared by all four Gospels. But each Gospel highlights one theme. The *kingdom of God* come to earth is the most comprehensive theme in the Scripture which alludes to the creation goal. The fulfillment will feature God's rule come to reside on earth in the person of the Davidic heir mediating God's reign. At the core is the control of God's enemy, Satan. This was present in token form in Jesus' miracles. It will reach its climax in the binding of Satan as the Davidic Heir reigns on earth. Following Christ's First Advent and prior to His Second Advent, Christ's authority on earth will be exercised in His Word and through His Spirit. Christ Himself will share the providential throne with the Father in the heavenlies. John the Apostle describes those

---

[19]   Exceptions were Enoch and Elijah who were translated from earth to heaven. While translation avoids death, it does not overcome death.

who are victorious over evil as *overcomers* (Revelation 2–3), even though they have not overcome death yet.

Salvation is also a comprehensive theme because of human enslavement to sin and death. This general theme is celebrated because of Christ's salvation from sin and the grave. That includes several aspects of salvation. When Jesus rose from the grave, He was raised from the penalty of sin to eternal life. When Jesus lived an obedient life, He was delivered from the power of evil. When Jesus was resurrected from the grave, He was delivered from the presence of evil as Satan tempted Him in the wilderness.

Each of the three aspects of salvation is available for humans. When Jesus declared the prostitute who washed His feet to be saved by faith (Luke 7:50), she was saved from the penalty of sin as she went in peace. In the parable of the soils, only the fourth soil is saved from the power of sin at work (Luke 8:15). When they bear fruit, they are saved from sin's power. That was what Jesus spoke to His disciples about following Peter's confession. A saved life is saved from sin's power (Luke 9:24). A lost life is lost to the power of sin. Only after the final resurrection will a believer be saved from the presence of sin in his/her resurrection glorified body.

The gift of *eternal life* is also a comprehensive theme. It is essential to being saved and to entrance into the kingdom. But it features the new life that a believer now has. It is not a sinless life because the body retains a connection to a believer's sinful past. It is also a body that will be buried in death. The eternal life of the believer departs from the body at death, and joins the Lord in the presence of the Father. But it is life which is indestructible. It is life capable of life with Christ. John uses the image of birth to describe its origin. It is *new* life as well as life from *above*. It is a gift given and received by faith.

These three themes introduce Jesus' new revelation found in Jesus' teaching. But the new revelation is based on His work on the cross, and on His resurrection from the dead. These themes will be developed in teaching and living in the dispensation of grace.

SECTION 5: DISPENSATION OF GRACE

Introduction

A Dispensational reading of Scripture sees the New Testament revelation in a distinctive perspective. Such a reading does not change what is written in the texts, but it does change the perspective in which it is read. Certain contextual features are kept in mind as texts are read. Those perspectives may be specified as theological, revelational, and Christological.

A Theological Perspective

A dispensation may be defined as a stage in God's governance of salvation history. While God's providence extends to all created reality, God's special revelation focuses on salvation history. And in a dispensation, the revelation is entrusted to stewards who are responsible for living and ministering by that revelation. God is actively involved according to what He has said through His stewards. That active involvement is the work of salvation. Thus, it is God who governs this age of grace. The work of salvation concerns what God has provided in Christ, and now what God is doing in and through His stewards.

A Revelational Perspective

Having reached an initial climax in the progress of revelation, this dispensation of grace reveals what God is now doing in salvation. As we remember, the progress in revelation is based upon the stage that was set in Genesis 1–11.

- Goal of creation—Adam was entrusted with the final words of creation. Adam was to multiply the human race and to rule over the creation which had been given an inherent capacity to develop free of God's further intervention (Genesis 1:1–2:25).

- Goal of overcoming evil—When Adam disobeyed God, his rule was usurped by the serpent. The chosen descendants of Eve were entrusted with the responsibility to do conflict with the serpent and its descendants. That conflict would characterize history with the goal of our being saved from, and overcoming, the serpent and evil (Gen 3:14-19).

- Norms of the Noahic Covenant—A covenant with Noah and with the human race frames the surviving creation. While God remains the Governor of salvation history, He delegates the protection of mankind's life-blood to man (national governance) and forms a climate that is manageable for man to support his life from the earth. Final judgment rests with God, although it will not be with a flood of water. The rainbow is a continuing sign of this reality through history.

This revelation sets a stable framework within which history will unfold, and revelation will be introduced and progress. *Progress* means that the initial revelation is not complete, but revealed in stages, guided by the goals of redemption and of creation.

- Dispensation of Promise—Abram is entrusted with promises of God's intervention in history. These promises would transform his own life personally, and would introduce a future for his descendants in bringing blessing to all nations.

- Dispensation of Law—His descendants, Israel, were also entrusted with the Law. Before they could mediate blessing to others, they must first face the responsibility of human accountability before God and before the nations. The prophets revealed that Israel failed to keep their responsibility.

- Jesus Christ, representing Israel, assumed the human responsibility under the Law and kept those responsibilities perfectly. Yet He also assumed mankind's burden of failure under the Law, accepted the curse of the Law at the hands of Israel's authorities, and died on the cross. At the same time, by faith in God's *promises*, He performed miracles and was delivered from death in resurrection from the dead and overcame the rule of the serpent (Satan).

Progress in revelation relates to the blessing of deliverance from evil. The revelation of God's work of salvation is now complete. The revelation of God's word of salvation is about to be revealed in the apostle's ministry and the Epistles they would write featuring the *gospel*.

The progress of revelation will be completed when the final judgment of evil and the re-establishment of God's creation purpose occur.

A Christological Perspective

The immediate context in which the New Testament is read is the finished work of Christ recorded in the Gospels. This distinguishes stewards living after Christ's First Advent from stewards of any earlier age. Of course, Old Testament believers were blessed in view of what God promised to accomplish in Christ. This, too, is grace. But the full unfolding of the meaning of grace awaited the stewardship following Christ's First Advent. Thus, this age is called the dispensation or stewardship of grace. This revelation about what Christ accomplished, and about what the gift of eternal life means, is now entrusted to these stewards. Stewards today live on the basis of what Christ has already accomplished and have hope based on what Christ has promised to accomplish in His Second Advent.

The believers in the dispensation of grace are entrusted with the word of salvation. The finished work of God entailed in the gospel will be summarized in six points constituting the Christological perspective.

Conflict with Satan

The Synoptic Gospels share the perspective that this *conflict* began following Jesus' baptism; it followed the Father's affirmation that Jesus is God's Son (Matt 4:1-11; Mark 1:12-13; Luke 4:1-13). The conflict concerned the Father's will for His Son. The Gospel of John focused on the conflict at the Cross, "the ruler of this world will be cast out" (John 12:31-32). While Satan continues to rule the children of disobedience (Eph 2:2), believers have been delivered from the power of darkness and translated into the kingdom of the Son (Col 1:13). As a result, Paul urges believers to stand against the schemes of the devil, clothed in armor provided by Christ (Eph 6:14-17).

Conflict with the World

Jesus spoke of the world's hatred of Him and of the disciples He would leave in the world (John 16:18-25). He lamented over the city of Jerusalem. He desired to defend them, but they refused (Matt 23:37-39; Luke 13:34-35). As a result, He suffered at the hand of Jerusalem and Rome, who crucified Him (Acts 2:22-23). In light of the world's animosity, Jesus prayed for His disciples whom He would leave in the world (John 17:6-19). He also prayed for those who would believe in Him through their word (John 17:20-26). Believers will suffer from the world as Jesus did, or will suffer if they walk according to the world (Eph 2:2).

He Received the Father's Judgment

Before the Cross, Jesus prayed about the Cross: "let this cup pass from me; nevertheless, not as I will, but as you will" (Matt 26:39; see also Mark 14:35). Thus, Peter could acknowledge that Jesus was delivered up by the determined purpose and foreknowledge of God (Acts 2:23). Jesus' death is at the core of the gospel: "God presented Him to demonstrate His righteousness at the present time, so that He would be righteous and declare righteous the one who has faith in Jesus" (Rom 3:26, HCSB). Before the Cross, Abraham believed God who promised a descendant through whom all nations would be blessed. God declared him to be righteous by faith (Gen 15:1-6; Rom 4:1-5). Whether by promise or by completed work, God provided a righteous standing before Himself.

Resurrected from the Dead

Jesus spoke of the hour for the Son of Man to be glorified (John 12:22-24). As the hour approached, Jesus prayed to be glorified (John 12:27-28; 17:1-5). And that glorification included both the resurrection (Matt 16:21; 17:22-23; 20:17-19) and the ascension (Acts 1:9-11). As a result, believers receive the gift of eternal life (John 12:24; 20:31). While these works of God at the First Advent explain the basis of Christ's authority to give eternal life to all who are chosen (Acts 13:30-33; John 17:2-3), the gift of rebirth is normative in all dispensations (John 3:3, 5). Now, believers have a living hope to share in Christ's bodily resurrection, since Christ's resurrection is the first fruits (1 Cor 15:20-28). Further, as Christ was raised from the dead by the glory of the Father, so believers also share in the Spirit-empowered resurrection to "walk in newness of life" (Rom 6:4).

Ascension to Receive the Son's Inheritance

Jesus Himself announced His expectation of receiving the promise of the Father, that is, the Son's inheritance (John 7:37-39; Acts 1:4-8). This announcement is confirmed by Peter, who relates the Holy Spirit being poured out with Jesus' exaltation to the right hand of the Father (Acts 2:32-34). Later, Paul would contend that this inheritance came to Jesus as the Seed of Abraham. This inheritance is now shared with Jewish and Gentile believers baptized into Christ (Gal 3:14-29). In a later Prison Epistle, Paul would call the Holy Spirit the down payment of our inheritance (Eph 1:13-14).

These are essential truths of the work of God through Christ in His First Advent. These truths will be preached in the gospel in the formation of the Church (Acts), and explained as aspects of the gospel in the Epistles addressed to the Church. This is a completed work of God which is unfolded in the words of Christ. There is no progress in revelation but rather an exposition of the revelation of the gospel of grace.

Conflict with the Flesh

Three enemies remain for the believer to do conflict—the Devil, the world, and the flesh. The flesh is the residual presence of the evil in the believer's old man (Rom 6:6). The believer's old man has been crucified with Christ as he is baptized into His death (Rom 6:3, 6). The old man was crucified with Him in Spirit baptism, in order that sin's dominion over the flesh may be abolished, so that we may no longer be enslaved to sin. In this passage in Romans 6, the flesh is a synonym with the body of sin.

Objections to this Reading of a Dispensation of Grace

Grace and Law

What does it mean that the dispensation of law has come to an end? Paul says, "For Christ is the end [or, goal] of the Law for righteousness to everyone who believes" (Rom 10:4). By speaking of *telos...nomou*, Paul is not saying that law is done away or terminated. The law remains as Scripture. Rather, Israel pursued an endless and unreachable goal in search of their own righteousness (10:2-3). Christ alone found the realization of the otherwise impossible goal or end of the Law—perfect righteousness. What Paul does say is that the believer is no longer "under law" (6:14-15).

This is what is meant by saying, "the dispensation of law has come to an end." The law was the revelation entrusted to Israel in history. It was Israel's obligation that Jesus fulfilled (Matt 5:17-18). Israel had claimed that all that God had said, they would do (Exod 19:8; 24:3, 7). Jesus met this obligation in His lifetime (John 8:46). Jesus bore Israel's failure to meet that obligation on the cross (Gal 3:13).

The Scriptural law that remains gives expression to man's responsibility before his Creator, to conform to His will. There are a number of obligations that it does not voice.

Theonomy

Rushdoony charges:

> To hold, as the churches do, Roman Catholic, Greek Orthodox, Lutheran, Calvinist, and all others virtually, that the law was good for Israel, but that Christians and the church are under grace and without law, or under some higher, newer law, is implicit polytheism.

The flaw in his reasoning is the failure to acknowledge that it is wrong to return to a prior economy in history which God entrusted to Israel. In view of Christ's finished work on the cross, believers are free from the obligation to be under the Law and free from the condemnation and curse of the Law.[1]

Interpretation of Scripture Law

Kaiser Posits, "The moral law is a *coercive force* helping the redeemed to spot moral imperfections that still cling to their lives."[2] This position rests on a common Reformed interpretation which distinguishes between the moral, civil, and ceremonial laws within the Mosaic Law. The various laws within the Mosaic Law can be roughly distinguished between these three categories. It is clear that Jesus fulfilled the sacrificial demands in His death on the cross. At least these have been terminated in their view. Jesus' fulfillment of the moral laws did nothing to terminate the moral

---

[1] Rousas John Rushdoony, *The Institutes of Biblical Law* (Nutley, NJ: Craig Press, 1973), p. 18.

[2] Walter C. Kaiser, Jr., *Toward Old Testament Ethics* (Grand Rapids, MI: Zondervan, 1983), p. 312, emphasis added.

laws. Are believers in the Church still under the moral laws as the phrase *a coercive force* would seem to imply? And what is the force of the Sabbath law (Exod 20:8-11)?

Luther posited a different force in the interpretation of the Law:

> [The law] is no longer binding on us because it was given only to the people of Israel...Exodus 20[:1]...makes it clear that even the Ten Commandments do not pertain to us...We will regard Moses as a teacher, but we will not regard him as our lawgiver.[3]

This view of interpretation matches what the Apostle Paul affirms: "*All Scripture* is inspired by God and is profitable *for teaching*, for rebuking, for correcting, for training in righteousness" (2 Tim 3:16, HCSB, emphasis added).

However, for the believer in the Church, we have the obligation of the "law of Christ" (Gal 6:2). For Christ, the payment of His life sacrificed on the cross was extremely costly. Still, it is provided freely in grace to anyone who believes. Yet one who receives such a costly gift carries an obligation to Christ—to love God and to love one's neighbor.

Grace and Antinomianism

Does the termination of the dispensation of law prompt antinomianism?[4] Such a charge against a Dispensational Biblical theology fails to grasp what Paul said about being "under grace" (Rom 6:14). In Romans 6, Paul asked two pertinent questions.

First, "Are we to continue in sin that grace may abound?" (Rom 6:1). The question is prompted by the conclusion that grace reigns (Rom 5:21). Does the reign of grace mean that grace is continuously surmounting our ongoing sinful lives? Paul's answer in Rom 6:1 is decisive—*no!* Christians have died to sin (6:2-3). This does not mean that it is impossible for a believer to sin, but sinning is no longer necessary. He is not a slave to sin any longer. Thus, it is an *inconceivable* choice.

Second, "Are we to sin because we are not under law but under grace?" (Rom 6:15). Again, the answer is a decisive, no! The implied question is that grace gives us license to sin. That question is *absurd*, for it fails to realize the real implications of sin. When we sin, we should realize that

---

[3] Martin Luther, "How Christians Should Regard Moses," in *Luther's Works*, ed. Helmut T. Lehmann (Philadelphia: Muhlenberg, 1960), pp. 164-65.

[4] Patrick Fairbairn, *The Revelation of Law in Scripture* (Grand Rapids, MI: Zondervan, 1869, 1957), pp. 29-30.

this expresses our old slavery to sin. And surrendering to a slavery to sin puts us on a path that produces death (Rom 6:16).

So, antinomianism may seem to be prompted, but this fails to grasp the reality of being "under grace."

The dispensation of grace is then expressed in the core of the revelation of the New Testament. Changes introduced by the stewardship of grace are interpreted in the historical perspective of Acts. What is entrusted in grace is then examined in the *Epistles*, authored essentially by the Apostles. While a New Testament theology[5] deserves both detailed exegesis of critical passages and evaluation of different authors' viewpoints, this Biblical theology must be more modest. It will attempt to pursue both exegesis and evaluation based on the focus of grace.[6]

---

[5]　George Eldon Ladd, *A Theology of the New Testament* (Grand Rapids, MI: Eerdmans, 1974); Leon Morris, *New Testament Theology* (Grand Rapids, MI: Zondervan, 1986); Charles C. Ryrie, *Biblical Theology of the New Testament* (Chicago: Moody, 1959). The other option is to organize the material thematically. See Donald Guthrie, *New Testament Theology* (Downers Grove, IL: IVP, 1981).

[6]　Ryrie features four doctrines: God, salvation, Scripture, and the Church. We will add the doctrine of Israel.

CHAPTER 20:
ACTS

Introduction

The Book of Acts continues the historical transition that was introduced in the Gospels. These include the transition from Christ's ministry on earth to Christ's ministry from heaven. Further, there is a transition of the people of God from Israel, who crucified Christ, to the Jews and Gentiles, who constitute the Church. Luke himself highlights the geographical and cultural transition from Jerusalem to Rome (Acts 1:8). Luke considers these transitions within a historical narrative that reflects a theological agenda.[1] The question to be considered relates to how these transitions are incorporated in the plot/conflict of the narrative.

Adolph Schlatter, in his Biblical theology, focused on essential themes which are also reflected in the Dispensational point of view in Acts.

The first is the governance of God. This governance accounts for the unity between the events in the historical outreach from Jerusalem. The Father is ultimately responsible for His promise to the Son, which is the Holy Spirit. Luke "directs the community's attention to the chain of events because he sees in them God's sovereign providence."[2] In His ascension, the Lord Jesus joined the Father on the providential throne. "The history he conveys to us presents itself to him as God's work and is recognized as such through the particular demonstrations of God that manifest themselves in the miracle and the *Spirit*-effected guidance of his messengers."[3]

---

[1] I. Howard Marshall, *Luke: Historian and Theologian* (Grand Rapids, MI: Zondervan, 1970).

[2] Adolf Schlatter, *The Theology of the Apostles: The Development of New Testament Theology*, trans. Andreas J. Köstenberger (Grand Rapids, MI: Baker, 1998), p. 339.

[3] *Ibid.*, p. 341, emphasis added.

The second theme in the transition is the evidence of the revelation being made known in periods in history. "[The] two periods are clearly distinguished: the first period, in which Jesus' proclamation takes place only for the Jews, and the second, which produces the church which is open to all."[4] In a Dispensational model, the Gospel period was the conclusion of the stewardship of law given to Israel and was addressed in the ministry of the Representative of Israel, Jesus Christ. This is what Acts summarizes as "all that Jesus began to do and teach" (Acts 1:1). The Book of Acts is the history of the completion of the transition. It begins at the Jewish Feast of Pentecost celebrated in Jerusalem (Acts 2:1), but it concludes in Rome, as the Jews were divided over Paul's message to the Jewish community (Acts 28:28-29). As a climax, Paul's ministry continued while he was under house arrest, and "he welcomed all who visited him," Jew or Gentile (28:30, HCSB). This transition is facilitated by two featured apostles: Peter, the Apostle to the Jews, and Paul, the Apostle to the Gentiles.[5] The period of ministry to the Jews includes Acts 2–12, and the period of ministry to Jews and Gentiles is Acts 10 and 13–28. As the overlap in chapters indicates, while the transition actually happens, the distinction between the two periods is not pronounced. As was reflected at the conclusion of the book, the Jewish population, whether living in Jerusalem or in dispersion, was divided, yet they nonetheless received the message of the gospel first (Gen 12:3). The Gentiles welcomed Paul's message as the gospel spread from the first Gentile church at Antioch (Acts 11:19-30; 13:1-3). This is revelation being made known as it is adapted to each new situation. The gospel is complete, as is Christ's suffering, but the apostles making it known is not (Col 1:24).

The third feature is the ministry of the gospel of grace as God's work of salvation in the perspective of Christ's finished work. Schlatter suggested this emphasis even though he would not develop it as a dispensation of grace. "The movement of events in itself becomes the subject of perception...because they revealed humanity's guilt and misery merely as a foil for the *divine grace*..."[6] The grace of God is evident against the foil of Israel's rejection of God's revelation in Jerusalem, which is particularly highlighted in the salvation of the Jewish Saul (Acts 7:60–8:3; 9:1-19). But the unmerited favor of God is also displayed in the salvation of Gentiles. Many of the Gentiles had been drawn as God-fearers who

---

[4]   *Ibid.*, p. 340.

[5]   Richard Belward Rackham, *The Acts of the Apostles: An Exposition* (London: Methuen and Co., 1957 reprint).

[6]   Schlatter, *The Theology of the Apostles*, p. 339-40, emphasis added.

responded to the Jewish worship in the synagogue. Cornelius highlights this work of grace that came to him as a righteous man (Acts 10:2), yet in need of grace in Jesus Christ (Acts 11:18). But others are pagan religious Gentiles, like those in Athens, and are in need of a broader view of God as seen in the created world.

These three themes will be developed from the text in Acts to highlight the dispensation of grace. A broad outline of Acts reflects this transition:

- Christ's final words to the apostles and ascension (1)
- Israel's rejection of the kingdom and the Church born in Jerusalem (2–7)
- The Church transitions from Jerusalem to those who had been touched by Jerusalem (8–10)
- The Church expands to the western Gentile world (13-20) from Jerusalem to Rome (21–28)

The message of the whole text of Acts may be summarized: The birth, spread, and expansion of the Church, in spite of opposition from Judaism, reveals Jesus Christ, who through the Holy Spirit, providentially draws individuals to the risen Savior from Jerusalem to Rome.

Doctrine of God

In the progress of revelation, the Persons of the Godhead had already been revealed. The focus of Biblical revelation is consistently on God, but different Persons of the Godhead have been featured at different stages. The plurality of Persons in the Godhead had been suggested in the plural pronouns from the very outset of creation: "let *us* create man in *our* image" (Gen 1:26-28, emphasis added). During the history of Israel, God revealed Himself as *Yahweh*, the covenant Lord who providentially ruled the people through a turbulent history in the land. He remained sovereign while the people were in captivity, but was called upon as "the God of heaven." God the Son, sent by the Father, was the highlight during His First Advent. Now Jesus has ascended to share the providential throne with the Father. Then, "Luke clearly shows that he sees his book as the outcome of revelations of the *Spirit* from the risen Lord to the apostles (Acts 1:2)."[7] It may be called *the age of the Spirit*. This focus will help to consider the governance of God in a discussion of each Person in Acts.

---

[7] Guthrie, *New Testament Theology*, p. 536, emphasis added.

The Father

Sovereign Grace

"Throughout the book of Acts the existence of God is assumed because of the apostolic preachers' background in the Old Testament."[8] His existence appears in the acts of history, acts which are described as both sovereign and gracious. At the Cross, Peter describes a striking juxtaposition between the sovereign decision of God, and in the same event, the presence of human decision. Jesus "was delivered up according to God's determined plan and foreknowledge" (Acts 2:23, HCSB), which incorporated the evil in Israel's use of lawless people (Rome being known for its law) to nail Him to a cross and kill Him. God's plan was determined by grace to address the evil within the human decision. This was expressed in Jesus' prayer on the cross to forgive those who condemned Him due to their ignorance of what was happening (Luke 23:34). Grace is behind the confession of the Roman centurion (Mark 15:39) and in the faith of the criminal crucified beside Jesus (Luke 23:40-43).

Christian believers who gathered in Jerusalem after the day of Pentecost perceived this same *grace*. "For, in fact, in this city both Herod and Pontius Pilate, with Gentiles and the people of Israel, assembled together against Your holy Servant Jesus, whom You anointed, to do whatever Your hand and Your plan had predestined to take place" (Acts 4:27-29, HCSB).

Luke and Paul recognized that human opportunity was related to divine appointment. At Pisidian Antioch, Luke summarized the outreach to the Gentiles: "all who had been appointed to eternal life believed" (Acts 13:48). These were *appointments of grace*. Paul summarized the Creator's appointments: "And he made from one man every nation of mankind to live on all the face of the earth, having determined their appointed times and the boundaries of their habitation" (Acts 17:26). These were appointments of grace for many. For Paul, it was the road to Damascus (Acts 9:3-5).

Inheritance

While God was described as Father of His people (Deut 32:6; Jer 3:4, 19; Isa 63:16; 64:7; Mal 1:6; 2:19), He in particular identified Himself as Father of the Davidic heirs (2 Sam 7:14; Ps 89:27). In Acts, He is so named because of His relationship to Jesus Christ, His Son. So when

---

[8] Ryrie, *Biblical Theology of the New Testament*, p. 108.

Jesus mentions "the promise of the Father," He is alluding to His own concluding words: "I am sending the promise of my Father upon you" (Luke 24:49). The question surfaces, where had this promise been declared originally?

Kaiser attempts to find the promise stated in the Old Testament but concludes that it is not directly stated. "[T]his specification in the promise doctrine of the outpouring to the Holy Spirit is not *directly* connected with the overall promise-plan given to Eve, Shem and Abraham, Isaac and Jacob."[9] That promise-plan referred to the coming Descendant who would be central to all that God promised. And that descendant was Jesus Christ, not the Holy Spirit. What was promised to that line was the Abrahamic Covenant, which promised an Heir and an inheritance. God promised Abraham blessings by which his Descendant would bless others. The Davidic Covenant was a continuation of this promised line. So, as Father to the descendant of David, the promise was a promised inheritance. Jesus revealed the inheritance and ultimate blessing to be the Holy Spirit (Luke 24:49). Paul will later call the Holy Spirit "a down payment of more to come"[10] in Eph 1:13-14. This gift is an initial installment of our inheritance. So Jesus' gift of the Holy Spirit is given as a share in His inheritance. The Book of Acts traces how the various aspects of that gift enabled the early church to accomplish her mission. Jesus had earlier breathed on the disciples so that they would receive the Holy Spirit, whom He possessed following His resurrection (John 20:22). But apparently this was temporary. This wasn't the same as His inheritance portion that He received at His ascension to the Father's throne (Acts 2:33). The inherited gift of the Spirit was that portion He shared with His own *after* He was glorified (John 7:39).

Response to Prayer

Although the dynamics of prayer are never rationally explained, instances of prayer occur and the answer often appears as part of the narrative. So the gathered believers pray for boldness (Acts 4:23-31), and the apostles stand in the temple proclaiming the words of this life in spite of having been imprisoned and put on trial (Acts 5:12-32). Or the church at

---

[9]   Walter C. Kaiser, Jr. "The Baptism in the Holy Spirit as the Promise of the Father: A Reformed Perspective," *Perspectives on Spirit Baptism*, ed. Chad Owen Brand (Nashville, TN: Broadman and Holman, 2004), p. 19.

[10]   Harold W. Hoehner, *Ephesians* (Grand Rapids, MI: Baker Academic, 2002), p. 242.

Antioch prays (Acts 13:3) and the ministry of Paul and Barnabas follows (Acts 13:4–14:28).

Jesus Christ

Post Resurrection Ministry (Acts 1:3-8)

Before His ascension, Jesus explained to His remaining disciples the import of His resurrection (Acts 1:3). First, it was important because the truth of the empty tomb would validate their message. Since they would be witnesses to the historical fact and to the theological interpretation, they needed to be assured, with persuasive evidence, that He was the same Person who was now alive. Second, His resurrection was the primary example of the kingdom of God present on earth. Jesus *overcame* death because God's reign defeated Satan's power of death. Jesus' death had been an apparent victory of God's enemy who exercised the power of death he gained in Adam's sin (Gen 2:17). But in His resurrection, Jesus *overcame* death in the righteous power of God, combating the enemy's claim. It is the overcoming power that is at work through the Holy Spirit that exemplified God's providential reign on earth in raising Jesus from the dead.

Ascension (Acts 1:9-11)

The disciples' observation of the Lord's ascension was used by the angels to explain His Second Advent. In the same way He ascended out of this world, He will descend again into this world. This experience clarified His promise to return. His ascension not only concluded the earthly portion of His First Advent but also became the prelude to His continuing heavenly ministry. Thus, the disciples needed to return to Jerusalem to await the coming of the Spirit. The Spirit would continue what Jesus Christ began and what was exemplified in the resurrection.

Spirit Baptism

Jesus had promised that the believers would be baptized with/by the Holy Spirit (Luke 24:49). Dunn contends that the metaphor, "baptized in Spirit" originated in John the Baptist's ministry.[11] He then traces a sequence of usage, which we conclude is essentially valid. First, John

---

[11] Dunn, *The Christ and the Spirit*, vol. 2, pp. 103-117.

announced the Coming One's ministry as both of judgment (fire) and of mercy (Holy Spirit). It began as "a metaphor drawn from the symbolical significance of the rite which characterized John the Baptist's ministry— viz., as immersion in a river."[12] John's prophetic announcement predicted the means by which the new age would begin. As a result, John's ministry brought to a conclusion the Mosaic age (Luke 7:26-28), which ended in judgment on Jerusalem (AD 70). On the other hand, he would prepare the way for Messiah who would baptize with Spirit.

Second, Jesus' interpretation of John's announcement is introduced in Luke 12:49-50: "I came to bring fire on the earth, and how I wish it were already set ablaze! But I have a baptism to be baptized with, and how it consumes Me until it is finished!" (HCSB). Dunn then adds, "not only does Jesus accept the Baptist's expectation as an aspect of his ministry, but he sees also that the purgative judgment which the Baptist predicted must first be experienced by himself."[13] Thus, the judgment from Rome would first fall on Jesus on the cross (AD 33) and then would fall on Jerusalem (AD 70, Luke 21:20-24).

Third, in Acts 1:5, Jesus promised that His disciples would be baptized with the Holy Spirit not many days from now. "The promise is seen as fulfilled in the experiences of the Spirit which followed Easter—specifically the experiences of Pentecost and at Caesarea (Acts 2:1-4; 10:44-46; 11:15-17)."[14] Since Jesus had been baptized with fire on the cross, those who accepted His sacrifice on behalf of the world now would only be baptized with the Spirit (Acts 1:5).

Fourth, Ladd provides a helpful explanation of the significance of being immersed in the river of the Spirit. "The contrast between the realm above and that below is the contrast between the realm of the Holy Spirit and the realm of human existence."[15]

Fifth, this connection between the two realms was first realized by Saul in his conversion on the road to Damascus. Unexpectedly, Saul's persecution of believers on earth included the persecution of Christ in heaven: "Why are you persecuting me?" (Acts 9:4). That connection was personal and simultaneous. Christ is persecuted as He is present in believers connected by the Spirit.

---

[12] *Ibid.*, p. 107.

[13] *Ibid.*, p. 110.

[14] *Ibid.*, p. 112.

[15] Ladd, *A Theology of the New Testament*, p. 292.

Finally, Paul revealed the actual connection, when he later used the same metaphor, Spirit baptism. "We all were baptized by one Spirit into one body—whether Jews or Greeks, whether slaves or free—and we were all made to drink of one Spirit" (1 Cor 12:13, HCSB). Paul thus makes a significant addition. When Jesus in heaven baptizes with the Spirit, He thereby unites believers *into one Body*. And that Body is His Body. That Body formed by being immersed in the Spirit also involves the Spirit indwelling each believer. The Spirit is both the *Location in* whom believers are immersed and the *Agent with* whom the Body was formed.

Revealing Himself from Heaven

As a means of extending the ministry of the Body, He revealed Himself selectively. Stephen saw into the heavenly presence of God with Jesus standing at His right hand. This appearance constituted a confirmation to the truth of Stephen's accusation against the nation of Israel (Acts 7:55). Saul saw a bright light shining from heaven and communicated with the Person, Jesus, whom he persecuted (Acts 9:3). In Saul's case, it provided a call to the thirteenth apostle. In this experience, Saul alone was commissioned to minister to the Gentiles. His presence was later revealed to Peter in a vision (Acts 10–11) and to Paul at Corinth (Acts 18:9).

Active in Deeds on Earth

The Lord opened Lydia's heart to hear and respond to the things spoken by Paul (Acts 16:14). He added to the Christian group (Acts 2:47; 4:12) and performed miracles (Acts 4:10; 9:34; 13:11; 16:18; 19:11).

The Holy Spirit

Morris cautions the student that the description of the coming of the Spirit involves a non-stereotyped range of speaking of what happened. They "were all filled with the Holy Spirit" (Acts 2:4; cf. 4:8, 31; 9:17; 13:9, 52). This apparently corresponds to the phrase, "full of the Spirit" (Acts 6:3, 5; 7:55;. 11:24). Other passages speak of the Holy Spirit as "coming" on disciples (Acts 1:8, 19:6) or "falling" on them (Acts 10:44; 11:15). God "poured out" the Spirit on people (Acts 2:17-18; 10:45) or "gave" the Spirit (Acts 15:8; cf. 8:18). From a human point of view, people "received" the Spirit (Acts 2:38; 8:15, 17; 10:47; 19:2). Morris concludes that "It does not appear to matter greatly how it is expressed."[16] Yet there are details that need to be explained. There are repeated terms, like *filling* or *baptism* that do take on technical meaning. When they are repeated with textual descriptions of the effects, they warrant similar technical explanation (like speaking in tongues, etc.).

Spirit of Christ's Body

In the context of the developing discussion, the ascended and enthroned Son received warrant from the Father to continue His ministry on earth. This warrant came as a sharing of His inheritance with God's sons. It may sound strange to consider the third Person of the Trinity (Acts 13:2) as an inheritance. But if an inheritance is a designated share in the Father's holdings, given with the idea of extending the Father's estate, then a Person may be so considered. He would be a holding, not as a personal possession, but as a personal resource to aid in completing the Father's service (Gen 12:3; Exod 19:5-6).

So the Holy Spirit is the Son's inheritance as a means to continue His mission on earth. The basis for a continuing ministry was accomplished in Jesus' First Advent. The Spirit is not to be viewed as a possession, but as a personal resource who will enable the believer to grow and to serve as Christ's Body on earth.

Power Source

Believers are controlled by the Spirit in the execution of their ministry (Acts 2:4). This *filling* has the sense of empowering or overwhelming someone as one may be filled with anger or sadness. This controlling work is sovereignly executed through a willing servant who believes (Acts 2:4; 4:31). This use of *pimplēmi* may be distinct from Paul's use of *pleroō* (Eph 5:18) concerning Spirit filling. *Pimplēmi* is ministry related and sovereignly controlled. Yet individuals are characterized as "full of the Spirit" (Acts 6:3, 5; 7:55; 11:24).

Sign Gifts

The ability to speak in languages unknown to the speaker provided a sign for the gathered Jews at the Feast of Pentecost (Acts 2:4). The crowd

---

[16] Morris, *New Testament Theology*, pp. 193-94.

was bewildered because each one was hearing them speak in his own language learned in dispersion (Acts 2:6). But there was a particularly Jewish slant to this sign. Isaiah had spoken of foreign invaders speaking in a foreign language as a sign that the nation was under divine judgment (Isa 28:11). That would suit Peter's contention that his generation was about to be judged (Acts 2:40). In every subsequent occurrence of tongues (Acts 10:46; 19:6), the presence of tongues speaking provided evidence to Jewish observers that God was present and active and was about to bring judgment on Jerusalem. In the case of Cornelius, the blessing that first came at Jerusalem was now shared equally by Gentiles (Acts 10:46). This was further evidence that judgment was coming upon Jerusalem. At Ephesus, those associated with John the Baptist are now completed through Jesus Christ outside of Jerusalem (Acts 19:6).

Spirit Direction

Frequently the Spirit gave direction to Paul in his missionary efforts. In a particularly decisive way, the Spirit communicated to all the leaders (Acts 13:2), when Paul and Barnabas first left Antioch. On his second journey, there was both the disagreement between Barnabas and Paul over John Mark (Acts 15:36-41) that gave direction, and the Spirit's forbidding and not permitting as they traveled (Acts 16:6-7). The vision of the man from Macedonia gave final direction (Acts 16:9-10) to Europe. At Corinth, Paul was compelled by the Spirit (Acts 18:5). In addition, the Spirit used disciples and prophets to warn Paul of the danger that lay before him in Jerusalem (Acts 21:4, 11). Yet, the Lord assured Paul that after he had testified for Him in Jerusalem, he must also witness in Rome (Acts 23:11). And an angel of God assured him that in spite of the storm at sea he would be brought before Caesar (Acts 27:24). So the means of direction are all divinely sourced but are present in diverse ways. It is perhaps impossible to conclude that there was one means of direction for the Body of Christ, but certainly the Spirit was a common means and seems to be frequently mentioned. As a take away, the Spirit seems to be the normal way.

The Doctrine of Salvation by Grace

The Message of Salvation

If the message of salvation was deserved in any sense, it would not have come *first* to Israel (Acts 3:26) or to Saul (Acts 9:3-4). Israel had repeatedly been charged with the crucifixion and death of Jesus Christ (Acts 2:23; 3:13-15; 4:10, 30; 7:51-53). This would not argue for merit. Yet, the decision to crucify Jesus was reached in ignorance (Acts 3:17), even though the prophets had foretold that Christ would suffer at the hands of His people (Acts 3:18). Therefore, it came to them because it was provided *in grace*, and the message was delivered *in grace*. It came to them *first* because they were chosen *in grace* to serve the nations (Gen 12:3; Exod 19:5-6).

The message of salvation, delivered and recorded in sermons in Acts, is worthy of exposition as these sermons appear in the text. They each express the *message of grace* and illustrate how the message was molded to communicate to the audience in various religious and cultural settings:

- Peter at Pentecost for Jewish worshipers
- Paul at Antioch of Pisidia in a Jewish synagogue
- Paul at the Areopagus in Athens

Peter at Pentecost

The Day of Pentecost arrived, and with it, something the gathered worshipers had not expected. A small band of followers of Jesus Christ began to prophesy in languages they hadn't learned. But these were the very languages of the gathered Israelite worshipers. This so surprised them that they asked, "what does this mean?"

Joel's Prophecy

Peter began his explanation to the Jewish audience by reading what Joel said would happen to Israel (Acts 2:28-32). This included:

1. God would pour out the Holy Spirit so that those endowed would prophesy.
2. God would display heavenly wonders.
3. God would judge Israel in the Day of the LORD.
4. Everyone who called on the name of the Lord would be saved.

The pouring out of the Holy Spirit came because Jesus had ascended to the Father. Jesus' ascension happened because this generation of Jews had crucified Him. But God the Father had raised Him from the dead, as the Scripture had prophesied (Ps 16:10). The apostles were witnesses of the historic fact of the resurrection. Having ascended to the Father, Jesus was elevated to the position of both Messiah and Lord, receiving what the Father promised, the Holy Spirit. He is responsible for this Spirit's display (Acts 1:5; 2:33).

Then *what must we do?*

Peter's answer reflected John the Baptist's original message to that generation: "Repent and be baptized…for the forgiveness of your sins" (Acts 2:38). The only difference was that Peter spoke after the crucifixion of Jesus. Repentance was a public confession of sin.[17] In John's case, confession of personal sin prepared them to receive Jesus as Messiah. In Peter's case, confession of sin included the guilt of the crucifixion of Christ. That was followed by water baptism. In John's case, baptism testified to their identification of a waiting remnant. In Peter's case, it was baptism in the name of Jesus Christ, publically testifying to their faith in Jesus Christ. As Jewish believers, they would receive the promised Holy Spirit (Acts 2:39).

Then Peter concluded his message, calling that generation of Israel to be saved from the pending judgment (Acts 2:40). This calling was included in the conclusion of Joel's prophecy. Though the salvation in this context is specified for that generation, and it is salvation from the pending judgment on that generation of Israel rather than the reception of eternal life, about three thousand were added to the Church (Acts 2:41-47). Thus, salvation forming the Church included a more comprehensive deliverance from judgment.

Paul at Antioch of Pisidia

This was the Gentile world in Asia Minor, yet Paul was meeting Jewish worshipers and God-fearers in the synagogue. Was the gospel available outside the Jewish world in Jerusalem?

---

[17] This definition is based on the usage in Acts. There are many Dispensationalists who base their definition on the derivation of the root, "change of mind." Then repentance means turn from unbelief to faith in Christ. But usage in the Gospels and Acts often concerns sin. That conclusion depends on the context in which the term is used.

God's Provisions for Israel

Paul assures these Jews that God had chosen Israel. As His people, God had given them gifts which reached a climax in the gift of the Savior, Jesus (Acts 13:15-25). Based on this title, Savior, salvation will be announced as available through Him.

God's Provision of Salvation

This *salvation* in grace appeared when Jesus was rejected by Jerusalem, but God raised Him from the dead (Acts 13:26-37). In His resurrection from the dead, God has *completely fulfilled* what He had promised (Acts 13:33a). The promise found its most pervasive expression in the decree of Ps 2:7, when the Father begat the Son to eternal life, to be Heir of all nations (Acts 13:33b).

Jesus' Sonship had been introduced at His birth, and He was recognized in His baptism as David's Heir and the Jewish Messiah. However, Jesus' Sonship was established as He entered the position of Heir in His resurrection to eternal life. This position as Heir only awaited the settlement of His inheritance as the nations continue to contest His right in the court of history. That inheritance included the holy and sure blessings promised to David, and in a parallel statement in the New Covenant (Isa 55:3; Ps 2:12), promised to everyone who thirsts (Isa 55:1).

Salvation Available for All

So, through Jesus' provision of this *salvation*, everyone who believes will be saved, whether in the Jewish world or now in the Gentile world (Acts 13:38-41). Jesus Christ justifies the one who believes, while the Law of Moses could not. Israel and the Gentiles are both recipients of this good news.

Paul at the Areopagus

The Areopagus was the intellectual capital of the Gentile world, yet Paul had to begin with what they didn't know. In a conversation that took place in the marketplace, he taught these intellectuals what they didn't know of Jesus or of the true God. This message at the Areopagus cast a scriptural framework on the world to help them understand the meaning of Paul's gospel. Thus, it is a pre-evangelistic, rather than an evangelistic, message.

The Unknown God

The Athenians worshiped one god they confessed they did not know (Acts 17:22-23). The pride of the human heart will never be penetrated unless the heart is willing to repent and confess its need for revelation.

God of Creation and Providence

What they worshiped in ignorance, Paul declared in the God known from creation and providence in history (Acts 17:24-28). Since God made heaven, earth, and all things, then it follows that He neither dwells in manmade temples nor needs man's service. This includes all the existing objects of worship in Athens, which Paul saw as idols (Acts 17:16-23). God's supply for natural man is comprehensive in roles of originator, sustainer, and provider of everything (Acts 17:26-27).

The argument challenged their reasoned conclusions and their practice. They were unwilling to follow what basic evidence indicates is true, so what they acknowledge in theory and what they practice are inconsistent.

The Responsibility of Mankind as Creatures

Their existence in time and space, which exceeds their span of control, entails responsibility. This responsibility is related to a relationship between God and His offspring, as their poets recognize (Acts 17:28). In this existing responsibility, man is unwilling to examine reality because it threatens his view of his own autonomy.

God's offspring will be judged regarding their moral responsibility by the resurrected One (Acts 17:29-31). The resurrection of Jesus Christ establishes God's *right* and *power* to judge man. It proves God's *right* to do whatever He purposes to do, because even death cannot frustrate His determination. It proves God's *power* to extend life beyond the grave, and so as to execute judgment as He purposed. This is a pre-evangelism message, encouraging them to hear more (Acts 17:32-34). While some responded to receive Jesus Christ, the majority questioned or mocked.

Conclusions: Salvation by Grace through Faith

A Universal Call and Grace

Since the provision is universal in the name of Jesus Christ, the call included in the message is universal. In other words, Jews are not the only ones called, but Gentiles are as well. The invitation, and thus the call to salvation, is not limited by ethnicity, nor by any other individual privilege. J. B. Green summarized that "our discussion of the narrative unity of Luke-Acts has highlighted the centrality of God's purpose to bring salvation to all."[18] A claim to a universal call is *not* a claim of universalism, in which all are saved, simply because the provision has been made for all. But a universal call implies the offer is freely given to all. No one could be found who would be deserving of the invitation while another would not be. Nor is anyone to be found who would be disqualified to receive an invitation as first given. It is an invitation that is without any condition warranting a call from man's point of view. There is only one condition to receive the gift of salvation. That condition is faith in the Giver and the One who has been given to provide for salvation.

Works and Grace

Because of the Jewish culture in Judea, some came from Jerusalem to Antioch demanding that "unless you are circumcised according to the custom prescribed by Moses, you cannot be saved" (Acts 15:1, HCSB). This is a doctrinal conclusion. Was there any condition in addition to faith necessary to receive salvation? Paul and Barnabas sharply rejected that anything must be added, even if circumcision was required to be in the covenant community in the Old Testament. There were no works necessary to receive the gospel. Salvation is by grace through faith alone. As Paul and Barnabas traveled to Jerusalem, the doctrinal issue was settled (Acts 15:2-4). The believers concurred with Paul and Barnabas.

A second question considered at the council was a cultural question (Acts 15:5): was it necessary for a believer to adopt the works of a Jewish culture (circumcision and keeping the Law of Moses)? This adoption of works came after one believed. Peter who had brought the message of salvation to Cornelius, the Gentile, said that "God, who knows the heart…

---

[18] J. B. Green, "Acts of the Apostles," *Dictionary of the Later New Testament and Its Developments*, ed. Ralph P. Martin and Peter H. Davids (Downers Grove, IL: InterVarsity, 1997), p. 17.

made no distinction between us and them, having cleansed their hearts by faith" (Acts 15:8-9).

However, without affecting the message of grace, Jewish believers could, out of a good conscience, be zealous for the Law (Acts 21:20-26). On the other hand, Gentiles should respect the conscience of Jews and limit what might be accepted in Gentile culture, but was offensive to Jews (Acts 15:22-35). This was the substance of the letter sent to the Gentile churches. Grace thus provided freedom from law, and provided the potential to be free from sin to pursue a life of love toward God and toward fellow citizens, Jews or Gentiles. Grace would fulfill this essence of the Law to be applied in a Gentile culture. But grace doesn't excuse disregarding others' consciences.

The Saved People

A confusing feature of the transition in Acts concerns the people responding to be saved. Should they be considered a remnant within Israel? What was the future destiny of corporate Israel? Does the Church replace corporate Israel? Does the gift of the Spirit represent a fulfillment in what was promised to Israel, but now fulfilled by the Church? And how does the gift of the Spirit relate to Jesus Christ's promise that He would baptize His disciples in the Spirit? In order to sort out these themes, the *doctrine of Israel* and the *doctrine of the Church* will be considered, based on the early messages by Peter and later messages by Paul in Acts.

The Doctrine of Israel

Feast of Pentecost

Pentecost was a Jewish feast as "Jews living in Jerusalem, devout men from every nation" (Acts 2:5, HCSB) had gathered to worship. In their heritage, it was the feast that worshiped God for the completed provision of the grain harvest in the land (Lev 23:15-22). But on this day, the Spirit came upon the remnant of 120 believers in Jesus Christ, and they "were all filled with the Holy Spirit and began to speak in different languages, as the Spirit gave them ability for speech" (Acts 2:4, HCSB).

Peter stood up with the eleven to explain *what this meant* (Acts 2:13-14). He rejected the idea that they were drunk, but quoted Joel to explain what was happening. In essence, this was a warning to Israel of coming judgment; *the Day of the Lord* (Acts 2:20).

This is the same context that John the Baptist had set for the same generation (Luke 3:7-19). "Brood of vipers! who warned you to flee from the coming wrath?" (Luke 3:7, HCSB). When the people debated whether John was the Messiah, John distinguished his ministry: baptism in/with water, from Messiah's ministry: baptism in/with the Holy Spirit and fire (Luke 3:15-16). Messiah's ministry in fire was about to happen as "His winnowing shovel is in His hand to clear His threshing floor," to gather the wheat and to burn the chaff with fire (Luke 3:17, HCSB).

With this prophecy of John as a background, Jesus announced (Luke 12:49-50) that He came to bring fire to the earth (as John had prophesied, 12:49) and had a baptism to be baptized with that consumed Him (as Jesus added to what John prophesied, Luke 12:50). Dunn proposed that Jesus both accepted John's prophecy to bring judgment, and Himself prophesied that He would also be judged.[19] As the Book of Acts opened, Jesus had been judged on the cross and He then promised the apostles that they would be baptized in/with the Holy Spirit alone (Acts 1:4-5).

Now Peter, on the day of Pentecost, quotes Joel to warn that "the great and remarkable Day of the LORD comes" (Acts 2:20c). This judgment was coming on that generation of Israel because they had crucified Jesus, the Nazarene (Acts 2:22-23). But God reversed their judgment of Jesus in death and raised Jesus from the dead (Acts 2:24-31). Their ability to speak in languages they hadn't learned was a witness to Jesus' resurrection (Acts 2:32). After having ascended to the Father's right hand, He received the promised Holy Spirit from the Father (Acts 2:33; cf. 1:4). "He has poured out what you both see and hear" (Acts 2:33, HCSB). So the explanation of the coming Holy Spirit is the ascended Lord and Messiah (Acts 2:34-36) and not Joel. Then what does Joel explain?

Some parts of Joel related to what was happening and some parts did not. The *first* portion of Joel speaks of the Spirit coming upon the people of Israel, and as a result, they prophesy (Joel 2:28-29; Acts 2:17-18). This explained the apostles "speaking of the magnificent acts of God" (Acts 2:11, HCSB). This did not explain the various languages, but speaking in tongues facilitated communication, catching the Jewish worshipers' attention.

The *second* portion of Joel (Joel 2:30-31a; Acts 2:19-20a) spoke primarily of heavenly wonders. These are not mentioned in Acts at the day of

---

[19]   Dunn, *The Christ and the Spirit*, vol. 2, p. 110.

Pentecost. A sign on earth is mentioned at the temple worship (Acts 3:1-10; 4:14-16). So Joel was quoted to warn the "men of Judah and all you residents of Jerusalem" (Acts 2:14, HCSB). For the Spirit enabled prophecy and the signs were to happen "before the great and remarkable Day of the Lord comes" (Acts 2:20c).

Thus, when we combine Jesus' words with Joel's words the historical construction follows:

- Jesus was judged at the hand of Israel using Rome (AD 33).

- That generation of *chaff* in Israel was about to be judged by Rome (AD 70).

The *wheat* then respond to Peter, asking, "what must we do?" (Acts 2:37, HCSB). Peter alludes to the essence of John the Baptist's message to the generation who was about to crucify Messiah: *repent* and *be baptized* (Acts 2:38a, b; Luke 3:7-8). Then Peter added that they should be baptized confessing faith "in the name of Jesus Christ." Peter's call was not the gospel. It was a call to now separate the wheat publically from the chaff of that generation who had crucified Messiah. Then the wheat, like the 120 believers, would receive the gift of the Holy Spirit (Acts 2:38c).

This promise was a national promise for Israel of inheritance shared with their Messiah (Acts 2:39). The wheat is then called in Joel to be saved from the chaff of that "corrupt generation" (Acts 2:40). The presence of wheat and chaff among Jewish residents in Jerusalem provides evidence that a *transition* from the nation was happening. A remnant of over 3000 received the Spirit and was added to the 120 believers formed into the Church. The remainder of the Jewish population awaited baptism with fire that Joel identified as the coming Day of the Lord.

National Salvation (Acts 3:12-26)

What happened on Pentecost for a remnant within the population in Jerusalem was extended to the people as a whole as Peter and John went to the temple to worship. While Peter and John approached the temple, God provided a healing to glorify His Servant, Jesus (Acts 3:6-8). That healing was also a *sign of deliverance from Israel's impotence* under Roman rule. The healing invited Israel's worshipers to look to God to address their corporate lack of power. Peter's sermon explained how that would come as seasons of refreshing (Acts 3:19) and times of restoration of all things (Acts 3:20-21)—the kingdom restored to Israel (Acts 1:5).

Many of those who heard believed (Acts 4:4). But the rulers, elders, and scribes refused to believe (Acts 4:13-21). The message called the people to repent for killing the Author of Life whom God raised from the dead (Acts 3:13-16). The absence of the national leaders' repentance resulted in no forgiveness for Jerusalem, nor the coming of the *times* of refreshing (Acts 3:19). Such refreshing ultimately would be a time of national blessing. No matter what the immediate occasion of Jesus' death had been, heaven had to receive Jesus "until the times of restoration of all things" (Acts 3:21, HCSB). Then heaven would send Jesus "who has been appointed for you as the Messiah" (Acts 3:20, HCSB), which would apparently refer to restoring the world to creation conditions (Acts 3:21). This also alluded back in time to the disciples asking the question of restoring the kingdom to Israel (Acts 1:6). What Jesus spoke of as "*times and seasons*" (Acts 1:7, emphasis added), Peter now spoke of as "*seasons of refreshing*" (Acts 3:19, HCSB, emphasis added), available for Israel.

For this to occur, corporate sin had to be addressed, and it would only be through Christ (Acts 3:16) as this healing signified. The message of salvation had to come to Israel *first* (Acts 3:26). The reason was that when God chose Abraham, He promised that through him all nations would be blessed (Gen 12:3). Peter spoke of the same scope of worldwide restoration to a blessed condition. Israel had to be blessed in order to be a blessing. This was God's election of Abraham for His plan of redemption to bring national blessing. Now, what would the national leaders decide?

A second time, the leaders rejected the stone which they, as nation builders, had rejected when they crucified Jesus on the cross (Acts 4:11). It may be that the Lord's prayer on the cross to forgive His executors (Luke 23:34) accounted for the nation builders' second opportunity.

Generational Guilt (Acts 7:51-53)

When the future of Israel is viewed from the point of view of God's promises, that future is hopeful. But, when it is viewed from Israel's generational responsibility, as Stephen saw it (Acts 7:1-50), judgment on that generation must fall. First, as Stephen would argue, every generation of Israel deserved judgment; judgment could have fallen on any generation. Disobedience started with the very beginning.

Abraham delayed his journey to the land promised when he included his father on the journey and when he waited at Haran until his father died before he left in search of the land. This began a pattern of disobedience which would characterize his descendants, and this disobedience would eventually bring judgment (Acts 7:2-8). God gave him no inheritance personally (Acts 7:4-5). Yet, the promises of an inheritance remained valid (Acts 7:6-8) for his descendants.

A second argument concerned Israel's response to two God-provided deliverers, Joseph and Moses. Joseph was called to deliver the elect family from evil but was only known by his brothers on the second advent (Acts 7:13). They saw him on their visit for food and then on their return with Benjamin to Egypt. He then delivered his family. Moses, likewise, was called to deliver the nation out of Egypt (Acts 7:17-27). In the same pattern, Moses was rejected when he initially claimed leadership (Acts 7:35). Nonetheless, God delivered the nation through Moses from Egypt (Acts 7:36) on his return to the people. The two instances of corporate rejection involve a typological pattern of Israel's acceptance of divinely chosen deliverers. The First Advent of Jesus Christ would follow the pattern. Israel would reject their Deliverer at the First Advent. It would require a Second Advent to redeem the nation (Acts 7:9-36).

A third argument rests on the serious consequences of Israel's rebellion forty days after the Law had been given (Acts 7:39). The prophet, Amos, interpreted what God did as turning and giving them over to worship the host of heaven (Acts 7:42-43). Israel, as a whole, needed spiritual redemption. That judgment followed them throughout their history as a guilt every generation bore. John the Baptist had warned his generation and Stephen now announced the judgment. This was a judgment that national dispersion had not satisfied (722 BC and 586 BC). It was a responsibility to the Law which Christ had borne (AD 33), but the people failed to keep when they rejected Him. The people soon (AD 70) must bear Israel's guilt (Acts 7:37-43).

A final argument concerned the status of God's approval as seen by the people, which was based on the existence of the temple (Acts 7:44-50). Rather than supporting the nation's attitude as though they hosted God, in fact, God rejected them. Even Solomon recognized that God was not confined to man-made buildings (Acts 7:48-50). The temple would not ultimately provide protection from the judgment of the people's sin. The temple must be judged along with people (Acts 7:44-50).

Stephen's accusers recognized the force of his argument but had no answer. So they stoned Stephen (Acts 7:57-60), as Cain killed Abel. Yet the promises given to Abraham have not been voided (Acts 7:5-8). Israel had a future in spite of the judgment of this generation (AD 70).

Then during Paul's final visit to Jerusalem, he delivered a message of grace (Acts 21:37–22:21). The gospel of grace characterizes the dispensation of grace.

The Doctrine of the Church

Pentecost and the Church

It seems fair to conclude that the Church was born on the Day of Pentecost.[20] But how did the Church come into existence? Do these promises to Israel end up fulfilled in the Church because Israel defaulted? Or how does Luke's account explain the birth of the Church?

There was the prophecy of Joel, addressed to Israel, that Peter used to explain what God was doing with Israel on the day of Pentecost. Peter explained the witness of many voices praising God (Acts 2:16-21, quoting Joel 2:28-32). Their speaking in different languages facilitated the communication to the Jews gathered from various parts of the Roman empire, but speaking in different languages wasn't what Joel said would happen. He said those influenced by the Spirit would *prophesy*. And Joel said this would announce the coming Day of the LORD for Israel.

But there was another voice speaking of the coming Spirit. The Lord had addressed His apostles, following His resurrection, reminding them that He would baptize them with the Holy Spirit (Acts 1:4-5). Peter quotes this as the Father's promise when he explains what the ascended Lord was doing (Acts 2:33). While it is impossible to find this exact context of promise in the Hebrew Bible, the Davidic Covenant describes this kind of relationship between God the Father and David's sons. Jesus, as the Davidic Heir, has ascended to join the Father on His providential throne. And Jesus spoke to those who would be Spirit-baptized as followers of Him, and not as members of Israel. Now they were all Jews, but it wasn't for that reason that He made the promise. He promised because they were His disciples and apostles. Those who accepted the message were added to them (Acts 2:41).

---

[20]   F. F. Bruce, *The Book of Acts* (Grand Rapids, MI: Eerdmans, 1964), pp. 80-81; Rackham, *The Acts of the Apostles*, pp. 31-43; Ernst Haenchen, *The Acts of the Apostles* (Oxford, UK: Basil Blackwell, 1971), pp. 190-96.

Since the promise of the Spirit is not based on promises to Israel, but based on Christ's promise to His disciples, the community of believers were Christ's, not covenant partners with God.[21]

A Body and the Church

The Church is controlled by Christ, even as a body is controlled by its head. The image of a Body is particularly suitable because Christ's bodily presence was no longer on earth. He had ascended. The life of believers may not seem distinct in a religious community like Jerusalem. But in a Gentile culture, like Antioch, the Christ-like person is so different that these disciples were first called Christians (Acts 11:26).

While they may not appear on the surface to look different, the community is surely distinct. Following Pentecost, they were described as being together and having everything in common (Acts 2:44). This unusual situation was caused by the number of Jewish believers who gathered in Jerusalem for the day of Pentecost. Their plans were for a brief journey and then a return home. On the day of Pentecost they believed in Jesus as Messiah and Lord, as Peter had said. But there was so much they didn't know, so few whom they knew were also believers. So they devoted themselves to meeting together daily in the temple (Acts 2:46). They pursued the apostle's teaching about Jesus Christ, and fellowship, and prayer together (Acts 2:42). They broke bread from house to house with gladness and simplicity (Acts 2:48). Residents of Jerusalem sold their possessions and property to distribute to any in need (Acts 2:45). This sounds like Body life (Acts 4:23-37).

Grace and the Church

Paul and Barnabas were separated to the work of establishing churches in the Gentile world (Acts 13:1-2). "They had been commended to the *grace of God* for the work that they had fulfilled" (Acts 14:26, emphasis added). This was also the description of his second mission: "Paul chose

---

[21] We have distinguished Jesus' promise from what Joel prophesied concerning the poured out Spirit. It is common in the scholarly literature to relate it to the New Covenant as they say is expressed in Ezek 36:27. There are several facts that are assumed in our conclusion: Luke does not say a covenant is involved, but a promise from the Father; Ezekiel does not describe the series of promises in Ezek 36:22-32 as a covenant, but does mention a Covenant of Peace in context (34:25; 37:26); finally, Ezekiel describes Spirit indwelling and Jesus describes it as baptism with the Spirit in comparison to John the Baptist's baptism with water. And that Spirit baptism formed Jesus' Body on earth (1 Cor 12:13).

Silas and departed, being commended by the brethren to the *grace of God*" (Acts 15:40, NKJV, emphasis added). These inconspicuous references to particular ministries have a broader application to the very nature of God's work in the Church. It may have particular reference to the Gentile world and the unmerited status of these people, as Barnabas found Gentiles as recipients of *God's grace* at Antioch (Acts 11:23). But Paul was set aside to testify to *God's grace* in his life, and particularly on the road to Damascus (Acts 20:24). Stephen is characterized as *full of grace*, marked by God's work in his life (Acts 6:8). Believers at Corinth were enabled to believe (Acts 18:27). The Jerusalem community was enabled to be generous (Acts 4:33). Believers at Antioch of Pisidia were to continue in the *grace of God* (Acts 13:43). Peter, in the Jerusalem council, spoke of Jews also as *saved by grace* (Acts 15:11) rather than through the Mosaic Law. The word of salvation, the gospel, is described as the *word of grace* (Acts 14:3; 20:32). Would it be misleading to characterize Luke's view of the mission of the Church to be a *stewardship of God's grace*? And at the core is the revelation of grace in the word of grace, *the gospel*.

Scriptures and the Church

Hebrew Scriptures played an important role in Peter's message to the gathered people of Israel on the Day of Pentecost. Likewise, Paul used the Scriptures related to the blessings brought by Messiah extensively when speaking to the men of Israel and to the God-fearers at Pisidian Antioch. The Bereans were called more noble because they examined the Scripture to validate the claims of Paul's preaching concerning Messiah (Acts 17:11). That message, spelled out at Thessalonica, involved a syllogism proving that Jesus was the Messiah (Acts 17:2-3). The reasoning followed this syllogistic pattern:

1. Based on Scripture, Messiah must suffer and rise from the dead.

2. Based on history, Jesus suffered and rose from the dead.

3. Therefore, Jesus is the Messiah.

A distinction which Acts makes must be carefully observed. The Scriptures prophesied the coming of Messiah. They didn't prophesy the coming of the Church. As was contended earlier, the Church identity was based on what the Lord taught the apostles about baptism with the Spirit. It was not based on the Scriptures predicting a people of God replacing or expanding Israel.

Conclusion

Luke and Acts both bear remarkable similarities. Both feature the theme of salvation. Both feature journeys to bring the message of salvation to the people. In Acts, it is clearly expressed as the *gospel*. Luke has a journey climaxing in Jerusalem. On the Passover Feast, Jesus' death and resurrection provide God's basis of salvation. Acts also begins in Jerusalem at the later spring Feast of Pentecost. The ascended Lord Jesus pours out the Holy Spirit on those who received the message to add them to the 120 who had followed Jesus in Luke. A Body of believers was formed to introduce the Church.

Following the leaders of Jerusalem's rejection of the gospel, judgment was pronounced on Jerusalem to fall in AD 70. Now the gospel spread north focusing on Antioch and Syria. That became the base for missionary journeys to the west, ultimately to Europe and finally, Rome. It was clear that the providential work of Jesus Christ was guiding the spread of the gospel and the growth of the Church in the Gentile world. The journey of the gospel in Acts does not overlook Jerusalem with one final opportunity. Then Paul made his way under Roman provision to Rome. But the book ends. The ministry of the gospel has only begun. By implication, many more journeys with the gospel would follow to the ends of the earth.

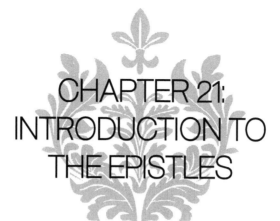

CHAPTER 21: INTRODUCTION TO THE EPISTLES

Introduction: The Nature of Epistolary Revelation

George Eldon Ladd is correct when he concludes:

> Revelation, then, is the totality of the historical event of Jesus Christ plus the apostolic interpretation of the divine meaning of the event—the apostolic interpretation being itself part of the event. This divinely initiated apostolic interpretation includes an eschatological dimension.[1]

As he develops his thought, he quotes Rom 16:25-26 as support for the conclusion that revelation is the total Christian message, not limited to the event of Jesus Christ. But what Paul said is somewhat puzzling from the view of progressive revelation we have taken. Paul said:

> Now to Him who has power to strengthen you *according* to my gospel and the proclamation about Jesus Christ, *according* to the revelation of the mystery kept silent for long ages but now revealed and made known through the prophetic Scriptures, *according* to the command of the eternal God to advance the obedience of faith among all nations. (Rom 16:25-26, HCSB, emphasis added)

The puzzle focuses on "the revelation of the mystery." What is the mystery kept silent or hidden for ages but now revealed? Is that the gospel? If so, how does that relate to progressive revelation?

The answer to these questions concerns two further questions. First, how are the three clauses related? Each is introduced by *kata* (according). Second, what does the term *mystery* mean?

---

[1] Ladd, *The Theology of the New Testament*, p. 386.

First, the three clauses are parallel, modifying the clause, "Him who has power to strengthen you." God's power is in accordance with each clause. The clauses are related but distinct: Paul's gospel, the prophetic revelation of the mystery, and God's command to advance the obedience of faith. They are distinct sources of God's power, yet they are related to the content of the *gospel*.[2]

Second, in the second clause, the mystery is introduced: "the revelation of the mystery kept silent for long ages." Gunther Bornkamm[3] posits that Paul has his thought in the stream of late apocalyptic thought. "The μυστήριον is God's pre-temporal counsel which is hidden from the world but revealed to the spiritual." Thus, in the context of Paul's uses, three distinct facets appear:

1. Written but not understood (1 Cor 2:7), so hidden from sight

2. Hidden, since it was only intimated (Eph 5:31-32)

3. Hidden, since not written (Eph 3:3-10)

Beginning with the possible range of Pauline uses of *mustērion*, what meaning does Paul intend in Rom 16:25?

Before we draw a conclusion, we need to consider Paul's use of portions of these clauses earlier in the epistle. At the outset of the epistle (1:5-6), Paul spoke of his apostolic calling: through Jesus Christ, he was to bring about "the obedience of faith...among the all the nations... including you," i.e., the Romans. So Paul's apostolic calling framed the composition of the epistle. Further, the theme of the epistle featured the Gospel (1:16-17).

The word, *mustērion*, itself appeared in Rom 11:25, in which Paul said, "I do not want you to be unaware of this mystery, brothers: a partial hardening has come upon Israel, until the fullness of the Gentiles has come in" (emphasis added). The Gentiles gained a privileged status as equal with the natural branches when they were grafted into the olive tree. Each of these portions reappears at the conclusion of the epistle (16:25-26).

In the first sense, the identity of Jesus of Nazareth was not understood "to the rulers of this age" (1 Cor 2:7). These rulers include both Roman and Jewish leaders. This would certainly include Saul of Tarsus, who didn't know the identity of Jesus until He revealed Himself on the road to Damascus (Acts 9:3-5). Then when Paul preached in a synagogue, he

---

[2]   C. E. B. Cranfield, *The Epistle to the Romans*, vol. 2 (Edinburgh, UK: T & T Clark), p. 809-814.

[3]   Gunther Bornkamm, "μυστήριον," TDNT, vol. 4, ed. G. Kittel, pp. 820-24.

"reasoned with them from the Scriptures, explaining and demonstrating that the Christ had to suffer and rise again from the dead…" (Acts 17:2-3, NKJV). Thus, the prophetic scriptures revealed and made known what the Messiah must do. This sense of the gospel as mystery is plausible for the majority in Judaism, but not for Simeon, Anna, and others in the remnant.

In the second sense, the interpretation turns on the sense of *intimation*. While the term *gospel* is not used in Gen 15:6, when Abram believed God and the substance of His promise of an heir, God declared him to be righteous. Paul referred to the gospel as preached beforehand to Abraham, "In you shall all the nations be blessed" (Gal 3:8-9 quoting Gen 12:3; 18:18; 22:18). This is more than intimation of meaning.

Cranfield believes that the gospel was fully disclosed when the full testimony of the prophets is heard in the progress of Old Testament revelation. This would be the same thing as Paul did at Thessalonica (Acts 17:2-3).

In addition, the early church, in a post-resurrection perspective, recognized Gen 3:15 as the *protoevangelium*. I believe that this is the true expression of the gospel, the content of which includes God who announced judgment on the serpent, the Descendant of the woman (He, Him) who would ultimately strike the head of the serpent to judge the evil one. The Church saw that in resurrection He had overcome the blow of the serpent. This is truly the gospel, yet it is not the final revelation of the message. It does not state that the Descendant is both human and divine (Ps 110:1, 5; Isa 7:14; 9:6-7; 11:1-2; Dan 7:13-14), or that the blessings of salvation are the result of the Servant's substitutionary atonement (Isa 53:1-12), or that David's Heir would be resurrected in a soon resurrection (Ps 16:10). So while the gospel is truly known as early as Gen 3:15 or 12:3, the subsequent prophetic scriptures enrich our knowledge. But this is not to suggest that Gen 15:1-6 is merely an intimation of the gospel. Rather it expresses the true identity of the gospel in generic form.

In the third sense, the truth is regarded as a mystery because it hasn't been revealed previously. That is not the case regarding the truth of the gospel. As Paul noted (Gal 3:8), the gospel did appear in Gen 12:3: "in you all the families of the earth shall be blessed" (cf. Gen 18:18). While Gentiles are included and will be blessed through Israel, the status of the Gentiles as equal with Israel as branches in an olive tree had not been revealed. This truth is a mystery in this third sense.

Then, reconsidering the three clauses in Rom 16:25-26, the first clause, "…*my gospel* and the preaching of Jesus Christ" (emphasis added), is the theme of the epistle (1:16-17) to the Jews first and then to the Gentiles.

The second clause, "[T]he revelation of the *mystery*," is the equal status that Gentile branches have with natural branches (Israel) in the present age (Rom 11:16-25). While Israel's rejection of her Messiah and her apostasy had been made known in the prophetic Scripture, a void was left in the silence about who would fill Israel's role (Gen 12:3; Exod 19:5-6).

Paul's call to advance obedience among the Gentiles, the third clause, which would be based on justification by faith (Rom 1:5-6), anticipated filling that void.

Two conclusions follow in clarifying the puzzle raised in considering "the revelation of the mystery." First, the gospel is not the mystery, since it was revealed in a generic form (Gen 3:15; 15:6). Yet, many rulers of this age didn't recognize it.

Second, the gospel includes both the record of the events of Christ's First Advent and the apostolic interpretation. In Paul's ministry as Apostle to the Gentiles, he featured the revelation of the mystery. While the prophetic Scripture made known Israel's rejection of her Messiah, an implied void was left in the silence that followed. Paul's revelation of the mystery filled that void in both the equality between Jew and Gentile in the Church (Eph 3:3-10) and the equal status between natural and unnatural branches in the olive tree (Rom 11:16-25). This would continue "until the fullness of the Gentiles has come in" (Rom 11:25).

As a result, the *revelation* in the Epistles features the *gospel*. Paul made this clear at the beginning and conclusion to Romans. The subject of the epistle is the *gospel* (Rom 1:16), so in the final benediction, Paul addressed it "to him who has the power to strengthen you according to my *gospel*" (Rom 16:25-26, emphasis added). This emphasis is repeated in his broader epistolary development.

First, in 1 Cor 15:1-4, the gospel refers to the historic events in Jesus Christ's First Advent death, burial, and resurrection. This is the common focus in all four Gospel accounts: Matthew 21–28; Mark 11–16; Luke 19:28–24:53; John 18–21.

Second, Paul relates these events "in accordance with the Scriptures" (1 Cor 15:3-4). This corresponds to, "according to the revelation of the mystery" (Rom 16:25). This is central to Paul's preaching ministry as recorded in Acts (at Pisidian Antioch, 13:13-41; or at Thessalonica 17:2-3). It was certainly implied in his testimony at Jerusalem as Jesus was revealed to him on the road to Damascus (Acts 21:37–22:21). That transformed the way he read the Scriptures. No longer did he read the Scriptures thinking he had eternal life in them (John 5:39) as he followed

Judaism. Rather, Saul now read them to testify of Jesus (John 5:39) as the one whom God has glorified.

Third, in Paul's interpretation of the gospel for the Church, he found God's command for obedience both *through* faith (Gal 2:20) and *based on* faith (Romans 5:12–8:39).

While the concept of gospel is viewed in a variety of ways, it has a shared common message. Pennington states it this way: "This is not a message of moralism or a call to greater religious obedience but rather is a proclamation of God's grace and the invitation to hope. This is why it is rightly called 'good news.'"[4] This range of views does not involve a progress in revelation because the gospel message is *complete*. The message of God's grace through Christ is *completed*. What is incomplete is making God's blessing known to whoever believes. This is Paul's claim in Rom 1:16: "[the gospel] is the power of God unto salvation to everyone who believes." The range of making it known relates to God's work of salvation: salvation from the penalty of sin (justification), from the power of sin (sanctification), and from the presence of sin (glorification). In Paul's Epistles, addressed to believers, he primarily makes known sanctification in obedience of faith. While all the Epistles in the New Testament do not share Paul's exact use of vocabulary, the term *gospel* is shared (Heb 4:6; 1 Pet 1:12, 25; 4:17).[5]

The Epistles: A Message of Grace

In view of the description of the dispensation of grace, what is the basis for calling the revelation of the Epistles a message of grace?

In both Paul's writings and those of the other apostles, *charis* appears 154 times. Nearly two-thirds (100) of those appearances occur in Pauline Epistles in which *charis* is normally translated "grace." In an article summarizing the use of *charis* in the other one-third of the uses, Casurella notes:

> It is difficult to discourse on all the aspects of grace in early Christian literature because there is a sense in which the entire New Testament and much early Christian writing is all about the grace of God in Christ and its outworking in the believer.[6]

---

[4]   Pennington, *Reading the Gospels Wisely*, p. 5.

[5]   *Ibid.*

[6]   A. Casurella, "Grace," *Dictionary of Later New Testament and Its Developments*, ed. Ralph P. Martin and Peter H. Davids (Downers Grove, IL: InterVarsity Press, 1997), p. 433.

Clearly, just based on the number of uses of the term, grace is a central theme in the New Testament. Yet those who address the topic of the center of Pauline Theology consider topics like justification, the mystical *in Christ*, or reconciliation and peace, but none, to this writer's knowledge, consider grace. All these topics are related to grace, but is grace a focus, as in the dispensation of grace?

Although Dunn would contend that early Judaism at its heart was a religion of grace,[7] Stephen Westerholm counters: "To say that salvation in Judaism was 'by grace' and imply that 'works' (in the 'Lutheran' sense) were excluded is simply not true to Judaism."[8] Nor, he adds, would Judaism "construe the relation between divine grace and human works in the same way Paul did."[9]

The gospel of the advent of the Son of God, and the works Jesus, the Messiah, did, corresponding to the work of the Father, displays an unprecedented revelation of grace. While grace is present throughout the Biblical canon, this display of grace is fresh and focused, alone sufficient to solve the human need. What is this revelation of grace in the Epistles?

First, and in the broadest sense, it is heavenly favor initiated by God the Father alone and provided by God the Son. In this broadest sense, all divine revelation (promise and law) is a display of heavenly favor. And Israel, as the elect people of God, is favored as well in its corporate election. While all displays of grace have this favor in common, the grace of God in Christ favors mankind uniquely:

- Favor freely initiated as a moment in history in which God alone shows concern. There is little evidence that Israel cries out for help.

- Favor of such a sort as God Himself becomes human flesh (as the last Adam, the representative Human) yet without personal sin.

- Favor in which the God-man acts on mankind's behalf in spite of Israel's rejection, to gain eternal life through resurrection, which then is freely given to whoever believes. This is the gospel in its full sense (*sensus plenus*).

---

[7] J. D. G. Dunn, "Romans, Letter to the," *Dictionary of Paul and the Letters*, ed. Gerald F. Hawthorne, Ralph P. Martin, and Daniel G. Reid (Downers Grove, IL: InterVarsity, 1993), p. 842.

[8] Stephen Westerholm, *Perspectives Old and New on Paul* (Grand Rapids, MI: Eerdmans, 2004), pp. 443-44.

[9] *Ibid.*, p. 444.

Second, the contention of Dispensationalism is that believers in the Church are now administers of the revelation of grace. Ladd proposed that those whom the administration features are primarily, if not solely, the ministry of apostles.

> The apostles are 'administrators' (*oikonomoi*) of the myster-ies of God (1 Cor. 4:1), and have received this 'divine office' (*oikonomian tou theou*) in order to bring the word of God to its completion (*plerōsai*) by making it fully known (Col. 1:25, RSV; cf. Rom. 15:19).[10]

In supporting his contention, he quotes 1 Cor 4:1. However, the servants and stewards are not only Paul the Apostle, but also Apollos, the minister of the Word. Earlier in the context, he addresses those who build upon the foundation, who is Jesus Christ (1 Cor 3:11-12). These are not limited to apostles. Further, Apollos' ministry was influenced by Priscilla and Aquila's ministry in making known the completed gospel (Acts 18:24-28). Paul himself was dependent on Ananias' ministry of the Lord's Word (Acts 9:10-19). In both of these cases, individual believers are stew-ards of the Word. What does it mean to be a steward of revelation in the dispensation of grace? It means to invest our own lives in God's grace promised in the gospel. It means to live one's life applying those truths of Christ's finished work in one's own life. It means to minister these truths to others in the world and in the community of the Church. Paul outlines that Body ministry in Eph 4:7-16. As a Body, the Church does "the work of ministry" (Eph 4:12). The goal is "to build up the body of Christ." And that goal entails both numerical growth and growth in maturity. But the roles of individual members differ depending on the gifting of the Spirit and the tasks in the stewardship of the truths. The reality is that all believers are entrusted with the truths of grace, whether made use of in one's own life, or in ministry in the lives of the other believers. While Ladd is correct to emphasize apostles as Paul mentions, he does not reflect the Scripture when he limits stewardship to apostles.

Making the Gospel Known to all Nations

Gospel

God's concerns in the dispensation of grace are both making the gospel known to those who don't know, and strengthening believers in accord

---

[10] Ladd, *Theology of the New Testament*, p. 386.

with the gospel. Thus, we would like to begin considering the role that the gospel has in the Epistles of the New Testament.

In the New Testament Epistles, the intended role of the gospel is not to evangelize, but rather to strengthen the Church in faith, and as Paul said, "to bring about the obedience of faith" (Rom 1:5; 16:26). This is a somewhat perplexing phrase. At face value, it has the sense of "faith's obedience." Based on New Testament Epistles, it is not obedience that flows inevitably from faith. Otherwise, the apostles would not need to exhort believers to obey. Nor is it obedience that is faith. Rather, it is obedience that comes from faith. Hodges correctly concludes, "it refers to the obedience that *can* and *should* be *produced* by faith."[11]

The relationship between faith and obedience is helpful to consider more deeply. In relation to Paul's own ministry, he wrote: "through whom [Jesus] we have received grace and apostleship to bring about the *obedience of faith* for the sake of his name among all the nations" (Rom 1:5, emphasis added). In the first half of Romans, the relationship can be that faith is the *means* of obedience. Faith in a relationship with Christ brings about a walk of obedience (Gal 2:20). Or as in Romans, faith is the *basis* of obedience. The terms *faith* and *believe* occur in Romans 1–5, the terms *obedience* and *obey* only occur in Romans 6–8. The salvation provided by God in Christ is received by faith. That work of God, when believed, becomes the *basis* for God to strengthen the believer in obedience (Rom 16:26).[12]

It is this aspect of the gospel that is most often featured in the Epistles, which are addressed to believers. The Epistles speak about the gospel by which believers may be strengthened to obey. Of course, this is not to say that all of the recipients of the letters are believers, but the Epistles are addressed to believers and speak about the gospel in such a way as to further establish believers in obedience. If an unbeliever reads about the gospel in the epistle, this may benefit them to believe. This is the same argument about unbelievers hearing prophecy (1 Cor 14:24-25). Even though the gospel teaching is not addressed to them, still the truth of the content may draw unbelievers to believe and be justified by faith. So, the Epistles may be used evangelistically, but that is not their intent.

Thus, we want to trace the advance of the gospel, addressed in the Epistles, book by book. While the treatment will be selective, the focus

---

[11] Zane C. Hodges, *Romans: Deliverance from Wrath* (Corinth, TX: Grace Evangelical Society, 2013), p. 29, emphasis in original.

[12] *Ibid.*

will be upon the historical advance of the churches from Jerusalem to the Roman Empire. The cultural environment of many churches uniquely influenced the testing of believers' obedience.

Conclusion

In various commentaries, little attention is given to the author's intent in expositing the gospel. The case we want to make in a Dispensational Biblical theology is that God speaks to His own people as stewards of the message. In the OT, the promises were spoken to Abram and to the patriarchs to draw them to faith. This began with an evangelistic intent to the patriarchs. Then, as subsequent generations of Israel read the Torah, these promises continued to have an evangelistic intent. The added message was then addressed to Israelites as stewards of God's Word with the intent of sanctification and ministry (Exod 19:5-6).

Now, as Paul wrote about the gospel to the churches of saints (1 Cor 1:2), his intent was not evangelistic, but rather sanctification of believers. He presupposes that the church was a gathering of those who had already been evangelized. He wrote about the gospel to the church as stewards of the message intended for their personal growth (sanctification) and for their continuing ministry of the gospel.

The premise of this Dispensational account of progressive revelation rests on this analogy: as God spoke and the creation came into existence, so God speaks in salvation history, and the purposes of God will be fulfilled. In creation, God spoke *ex-nihilo*, but in history, He speaks to His own stewards who will be the mediators of His will.

CHAPTER 22: CHRISTIANS IN THE JEWISH WORLD

Introduction

The Jewish world was a primarily religious culture that generally responded with vitriolic passion against Christianity. All three Epistles discussed below, James, First Peter, and Hebrews, consider persecution in a religious cultural occasion, while each historical occasion is unique. Yet the gospel message provides normative revelation for all canonical Christian audiences, whatever the cultural and historical occasion.

James

James is the pastor of the Jerusalem church (Acts 12:17; 15:13), who wrote to believers, scattered as twelve tribes (Jas 1:1-2). His concern is their faith response in trials: is it active and living or inactive and dead (Jas 1:21-22)? In the midst of trials (Jas 1:2-18), active faith obeys. Obedience involves being "quick to hear" (James 1:21–2:26), "slow to speak" (Jas 3:1-18), and "slow to anger" (James 4:1–5:6). Active faith is the means by which obedience emerges in the midst of trials. So we rejoice as faith is tested, because in trials faith has the opportunity to grow.

First Peter

Peter writes to many who may have been at Pentecost but who are unified by truths of the gospel—elect and sanctified by the Holy Spirit to obedience and to restoration in Christ's blood (1 Pet 1:1-2). That gospel (1 Pet 1:12) is the basis of new birth to a hope living through Christ's resurrection, a hope about a heavenly inheritance, ready to be revealed in the last days.

At the present, this is a basis for rejoicing, yet in fact, many are grieved by present suffering. That suffering purifies the genuine portion of faith, which can save the inner person from the power of sin. This salvation was prophesied but not understood in the days of the OT Prophets. Now it is heard in the preaching of the gospel (1 Pet 1:12).

Two applications follow:

- Be obedient (1 Pet 1:14) as you live before God in faith and hope, since God's Word in the gospel endures (1 Pet 1:25).
- Desire God's Word (1 Pet 2:1) to recognize the role that the Church has in the world today, as Israel had. Live as sojourners and pilgrims before the world.

This lifestyle includes submission to the government, in the workplace, in one's family, and compassion for one another (First Peter 2:1–3:12). This application of submission holds in spite of suffering, as Christ suffered for us. The goal is suffering for God's glory according to God's will (First Peter 3:13–4:19).

The elders ought to shepherd the flock of believers to submit to God and to resist the devil (1 Pet 5:1-11).

Hebrews

The third letter considered is addressed to Jewish believers, as evidenced by the following verses: "those who are to inherit salvation" (Heb 1:14), "partners in a heavenly calling" (Heb 3:1, NET), "brothers" (Heb 3:12), "we have a great High Priest" (Heb 4:14; cf. 8:1), "beloved...confident of better things...that accompany salvation" (Heb 6:9, NKJV), "do not throw away your confidence" (Heb 10:35), and "looking unto Jesus, the author and finisher of our faith" (Heb 12:2, NKJV). The words of description are important, because believers are in the throes of a decision. What the author says does not change in spite of what they decide. The indication that they are Jewish believers is that the decision is to return to Judaism, which would have significant consequences, but it would not change their identity. The consequences would involve the loss of opportunities and rewards.

There is no clue in the text that there is a divided audience. In the decision they all face, Hebrews seeks to persuade them to persevere in faith. That is obedience. They can be strengthened by looking at Jesus, the *Founder* and *Finisher* of their salvation (Heb 2:10), who is bringing many sons to glory. He is the *Apostle and High Priest* of their confession (Heb 3:1), who helps believers to persevere in faith to the end. This "word of exhortation" (Heb 13:22) concerns perseverance in two primary ways:

1. Warnings of the consequences of failure to persevere,

2. Instruction and encouragement to persevere based on what God has provided in Jesus Christ.

Warnings of the Consequences of Failure to Persevere

The interpretation of the five warnings of failure in Hebrews has generated disparate views. Schreiner and Caneday have summarized four common views on warnings and assurance in the whole New Testament that also distinguish the interpretation in Hebrews.

1. The loss-of-salvation view takes the warnings as addressed to believers who, if they fail, lose their salvation.

2. The tests-of-genuineness view sees the warnings as addressed to professors who, in retrospect, see their failures as evidence that their profession is hypocritical.

3. The hypothetical loss-of-salvation view understands that the warnings are addressed to believers as God's means to ensure perseverance in faith, since failure is yet to take place.

4. The loss-of-reward view takes the book and the warnings as addressed to believers as a means of God encouraging perseverance, but if there is failure, what is lost is an inheritance of rewards.[1]

---

[1] The loss-of-reward view will be taken as taught in Hebrews and the support for that conclusion will be advanced. The arguments against that view are presented by Thomas R. Schreiner and Ardel B. Caneday, *The Race Set Before Us: A Biblical Theology of Perseverance* (Downers Grove, IL: IVP Academic, 2001), pp. 19-45. These issues will be addressed:

First, the reward view adopts novel readings of themes like eternal life, salvation, and inheriting the kingdom of God (28). These novel readings lead to what they call double talk (27) or what they also call double use since the terms may refer both to a present possession and a future reward (24). The accusation of "novel" seeks to undermine the reading because it is not supported by a consensus. Yet, with the four positions existing, there is no actual consensus. And when compared to the other views it is only unique on what can be lost. It agrees with two other views that salvation from hell of a believer can't be lost. It agrees with each of the other views except the test-of-genuineness view that the warnings are addressed to believers. The claim that something can be lost rests on the careful contextual use of terms. The warrant for this depends on an examination of each warning.

Support in the book for a loss-of-reward view consists of these considerations:

1. The book is a "word of exhortation" addressed to brothers (Heb 13:22). The fact that this is a spiritual designation is indicated when they are addressed as "holy brothers" (Heb 3:1) and "brothers" (Heb 3:12) who have received a "heavenly calling" from which they are warned not to fall away.

2. The author applies the warnings to himself as well as to his readers (Heb 2:1; 3:14; 6:1; 10:26; 12:1). It seems evident that the author would not consider himself to be merely a professor. Rather, the ones addressed are addressed as genuine believers.

3. While the author doesn't know the actual spiritual condition of every reader, he addresses the failure and loss as though it applies to believers. So, a reader may have to disqualify himself, because he doesn't even have the right to what can be lost.

4. The determination of the failure and what would be lost must be considered contextually as each warning is interpreted. But the loss need not be equated to eternal damnation.

Loss of Salvation from the Power of Sin (Hebrews 2:1-4)

This warning concerns neglecting the message of salvation. That message was historically demonstrated to be authoritative and true, since it was first delivered by the Lord and the apostles who heard Him. God confirmed the truth with signs and wonders. The loss comes in being overcome by the overwhelming power of sin. This is implied in the

---

The fact that something can be lost (reward) certainly does not minimize its importance for the individual who would experience the loss.

Finally, the loss-of-reward view claims to read the texts in context literally. And as the three ambiguous terms are compared, it is apparent that they are not complete synonyms: *eternal life* is what God gives, *salvation* is what God does, and *inheriting* is an aspect of acquisition. If we recognize a legitimate application of an already-and-not-yet model, then to distinguish an already aspect of what God gives and does from a not-yet aspect is not novel. Further, to distinguish aspects of acquisition, an already receiving and a not-yet inheritance is to be expected. But, the validity depends on contextual interpretations.

A second criticism of the view targets the assumption that perseverance is not inevitable. If the book is addressed to believers, then it would be very strange to consider the warnings as addressed to unbelievers. There is no textual evidence for such a change in audience. Then, if the warnings are addressed to believers, the warning must concern something to be lost if in fact there is a failure. The warnings speak of something to be lost. The warnings also speak of failure that has not yet happened. There is nothing in Hebrews to indicate that God prevents failure. In fact, the author commends those who had failure and faith (e.g., Gideon, Barak, Samson, Jephthah, and even David, Heb 11:32).

examples of "every transgression or disobedience." Unlike Paul, Hebrews repeatedly uses the term *sanctification* or, *sanctified*, to speak of salvation from the penalty of sin (Heb 2:11; 9:13-14; 10:10; 13:12).

Loss of Future Inheritance (Hebrews 3:7–4:13)

Psalm 95 is addressed to the people of God. In one sense they are already the people of God, but like the original wilderness generation, they had not yet entered their inheritance of rest. Neither Moses' generation nor David's generation entered the rest. At least it is clear that Moses and David themselves never lost their relationship with God. They lost their historic opportunity on earth to enter Sabbath rest with their generation.

Loss of Growth (Hebrews 5:11–6:12)

The readers of Hebrews were dull of hearing (Heb 5:11). They ought to be teachers, implying that they were genuine Christians, but were dull of hearing (Heb 5:12). While they desired to review the basics, the author knew the way to grow. They had to leave the basics to go on to maturity (Heb 6:1-3). And as the author writes, he will do this with them if God permits (Heb 6:3). For, it would be impossible to renew to repentance someone who started well (Heb 6:4-5) and then fell away. His growth would be stunted because of his choices. He would remain a genuine, but immature, believer.

The illustration of farming a thorn-covered field which was about to be burned is not an image of damnation, but of possible restoration. After the thorns are removed, the field might be cultivated again (Heb 6:8). It was not a strategy to abandon the field, but to restore it again. So, the term *impossible* speaks of the exceeding difficulty for one who has fallen away. Yet the final illustration seems to hold open a remote possibility.

Loss of Access to God (Hebrews 10:26-31)

The fourth warning concerns deliberate sin in spite of the knowledge of Christ's sacrifice for sins. The only expectation is consequences in kind. The warning places this consequence on earth, not in eternity or in heaven. This is not eternal damnation.

The author had just called the readers, the brothers, to draw near to God (Heb 10:19-22). He was about to note that the readers were sanctified by the blood of the New Covenant (Heb 10:29). Yet, they deliberately rejected access to God through Jesus Christ. Under the Mosaic Covenant, such violations resulted in premature physical death (Heb 10:28). This consequence would be more severe. They had profaned the blood of the New Covenant and outraged the Spirit of grace (Heb 10:29). When Jesus faced God's judgment on the cross, He was alone, abandoned by God (Ps 22:1). Now believers who reject Him face consequences on earth of being alone, without God, but not eternally abandoned by God. Alone during judgment, Jesus did not lose His relationship. The implication is Hebrew Christians do not either. Unfortunately, they try to go it alone, resulting in frightening consequences.

Loss of Completing the Race (Hebrews 12:18-29)

As Mt. Sinai was an awe-inspiring scene, so the scene related to the New Covenant is even more impressive. Believers in Hebrews have come to the heavenly city, to angels and to those who share in the inheritance of the First Born; to God the Judge of all men, to Jesus the Mediator of the New Covenant, and to the sprinkled blood that demands judgment more than Abel's blood (Heb 12:22-24).

If the brothers would contemplate that destiny, they would be compelled to persevere in their calling (Heb 3:1-6). This race dare not be ignored. Reaching the goal is far too valuable.

Instruction Based on God's Son

Warnings make a powerful statement concerning the "word of exhortation" (Heb 13:22). But instruction also contributes to an exhortation. That instruction features God's Son, Jesus Christ, in His earthly advent (Hebrews 1:1–4:13) and in His heavenly session (Hebrews 4:14–13:25).

In His earthly advent, Jesus was portrayed as the archēgos, the Founder, Pioneer, or Model of the journey His brothers make, following Him. In His heavenly session, He ministers as a High Priest and Mediator of our Salvation. Perfected in His First Advent for His heavenly ministry, He now serves those whom He called to journey on earth to bring them to share in His glory.

Instruction from Our Model (Hebrews 1:1–4:13)

Hebrews begins with two ultimate questions:

1. Who speaks for God?
2. Who will inherit the right to rule the creation?

The Son with a Relational Right to Speak (Hebrews 1:1-4)

God has various spokespeople whose personalities and perspectives fashion the Word that God speaks. However, there is only One like a Son whose personality and perspective so corresponds to the Father that He gives an unaffected and perfect expression of God. In the last days, He speaks and acts for the Father.

The Heir with the Name to Rule (Hebrews 1:5-14)

The earth was created for man to mediate God's rule. That rule was lost when the serpent beguiled Adam and Eve. It was lost to an angelic power, named "Day Star, son of Dawn" (Isa 14:12). The battle lines were drawn. Who had the right to rule the creation? Who would receive the names *Son* and *Heir* designating this right to rule? Several Hebrew Scriptures were quoted to demonstrate that that name would be given to none other than Jesus (Heb 2:9); He was resurrected to be Son (Ps 2:7) and seated at the Father's right hand as Lord (Ps 110:1). No angel qualified.

The Founder of Salvation (Hebrews 2:5-9)

In this section, the question of a mediator for God's rule on earth in the age to come is raised. Psalm 8 spoke of a Son of man who was positioned, in His humanity, lower than the angels, that He might be raised to be crowned with everything in subjection to Him. That One is none other than Jesus. Although He is now crowned with glory and honor because He suffered death, He has not yet been raised to begin a final rule as King. He has overcome death for everyone that sons in time might also overcome death and share in His rule. But all His enemies have not yet been removed.

The Founder's Link with His Followers (Hebrews 2:10-18)

Many sons will follow Him in His conquest over death. He has been qualified to serve these followers because of His suffering. Jesus is the One who sanctifies and those who follow are sanctified to become members of one family. They have one Father, and Jesus calls God's sons brothers. Jesus is the *Founder* of their salvation. He is the *Pioneer* of their present salvation as they journey through a lifetime. He is the *Model* of the journey through His sufferings. In the midst of life's temptations, He is available in heaven to meet their needs and help them in their trials along the journey on earth.

Instruction from Our Mediator (Hebrews 4:14–13:39)

The first section of instruction featured the Son's completion of the First Advent journey. As such, He is a Model for the reader. With that completed, He is exalted to the position of honored Heir and awaits His destiny as mediatorial ruling King over creation. Brothers are now experiencing salvation from the power of sin and, through our journey, are being prepared for inheritance-salvation, or salvation from the presence of sin. Now as *Mediator* of our salvation, Jesus has a ministry of High Priest to the worshiper and needy traveler's journey.

Believers need a priest because they do not have an immediate relationship with God. That was Adam's experience of God in the Garden. God came to fellowship with Adam and Eve face to face. It was an intimate relationship without misunderstandings or need for a helper. That is, until Adam ate of the forbidden fruit. Then Adam knew Eve in pride, and as an object of conquest, and Eve knew Adam in fear and shame—the knowledge of evil. That knowledge drove them to cover up and hide from evil seen in the other. Leaves satisfied to cover their shame but did not cover any guilt before God. They needed mediation. God provided animal skins to cover their guilt based on the sacrifice of a substitute assuming that guilt. Animal sacrifice was passed on to Abel who sought to approach God through sacrifice and was accepted. Cain approached God on his own terms and was rejected.

The provision of a priest as mediator first came with Melchizedek interceding for Abraham. That order of ministry occurred once, until the exemplar would be followed by the ascended Son. When the nation was given the Mosaic Covenant framework, it also supported a priesthood. Mediation was provided by Aaron, the high priest, who offered sacrifices. God dwelt among His people with a mediated relationship and covenant partnership.

One Greater than Aaron (Hebrews 4:14–5:10)

The keynote, which introduces Jesus' priesthood, is that a believer may approach the throne of grace with confidence. Jesus is the Priest who can truly help (Heb 4:14-16). As a priest, His help is both sympathetically offered and fully effective. It is sympathetic because He felt the force of temptations even though He remained without sin. "Only the sinless can experience the full intensity of temptation, for the sinful yield before the limit of temptation is reached."[2]

Jesus' help is effective because the throne of grace is located at the mercy seat, the place of propitiation. In the place where God's wrath against sin is satisfied, the one who comes finds mercy; the remission of deserved judgment and grace, the supply of undeserved blessing. It was the priest who dealt with the knowledge of evil—fear, insecurity, anxiety, guilt, and shame—as he explained and offered the sacrifices and counseled the worshiper.

Jesus fulfills that role, meeting the requirements to deal with temptations of evil and to provide a basis for understanding in His sacrifice. God appointed Him to this role (Pss 2:7; 110:4). As a result of His own temptations, He can feel the believer's weaknesses and the lure of sin. It was in the Garden of Gethsemane that He faced the emotional misery which sin produced: its shame, guilt, and despair. "He saw our sins as his own, and thus fulfilled beyond any other priest's experience the ability to deal gently with other's sins since he was so fully aware of the sense of personal defilement sin leaves."[3]

Melchizedek (Hebrews 7:1-28)

The unfolding of the meaning of the Melchizedekian priesthood of Jesus had been the author's goal since he introduced the idea of priestly help (Heb 2:17). The author saw Melchizedek as a picture for which Christ is the reality. He introduced several similarities between Melchizedek in his ministry to Abraham, and Jesus in His ministry to believers: both are king-priests, both refresh and strengthen those to whom they minister, both receive what others owned. By name, both were King of Righteousness and in place were King of Peace.

Further, the Melchizedekian priesthood was superior to the Levitical order (Heb 7:4-10), and the Aaronic priesthood and law were to be replaced by a new order (Heb 7:11-19). The priesthood was the heart of mediation, while the Law set the framework (Heb 7:11-12).

The Law had made nothing perfect, so "a former commandment is set aside...[and] a better hope is introduced, through which we draw near to God" (Heb 7:18-19). Based on God's oath (Ps 110:4), Jesus is made the guarantor of a better covenant (Heb 7:22). Not only does Jesus mediate

---

[2] Ray C. Stedman, *Hebrews* (Downers Grove, IL: IVP, 1992), p. 62.

[3] *Ibid.*, p. 65.

a better covenant (Heb 8:6), but He also guarantees the covenant. The *Mediator* would assure the ratification of the covenant with God, since the house of Israel and Judah rejected Him. The *Guarantor* would affect the benefits of the covenant with those called (Heb 3:1). In this way, the Guarantor ensures that the benefits of perseverance would be present in believers' lives. These two aspects work together to promote perseverance and perfection as believers actively grow in Christ-likeness.

This guarantee rests in Jesus' resurrection-life because His life is unending. So "he is able to save to the uttermost" (Heb 7:25a). It is complete, persisting throughout the life of each believer, and is totally encompassing all who come to Him. "[H]e always lives to make intercession for them" (Heb 7:25b).

The New Covenant

The ministry of the priest rests on the arrangement of the covenant. The main point in the new arrangement features the High Priest seated in the heavenlies in the very presence of Majesty. This holiness of divine presence is incomparably better than the pattern on earth with the holy of holies (Heb 8:2). The Priest's ministry is also incomparably better since the Priest is also the mediator of a better covenant.

In order to appreciate how much better the ministry of the High Priest is, the author of Hebrews compares and contrasts the Old and New Covenants. A covenant is a formal arrangement between two parties. In the New Covenant, the parties remain the same. In the first covenant, descendants of Israel were one party, as the Hebrew Bible indicates (Exod 24:1-8; Deut 29:14-29). The New Covenant is made with the divided people, the house of Israel and the house of Judah (Jer 31:31; Heb 8:8; 10:16). It was not a New Covenant because there was a change in party. The Church did not replace Israel in her role of covenant partner. Hebrews answers three questions in making the distinction between the covenants, thus enhancing the more excellent ministry of the High Priest.

First, What Made the First Covenant Faulty? (Hebrews 8:7-8)

The descendants of Jacob received the covenant ratified (Exod 24:3, 7). These people were a redeemed people coming out of Egypt, but the covenant said nothing about redemption. God promised to redeem the enslaved people (Exod 6:6) and did so based on promise (Exod 11:12-13). The covenant itself was based solely on law (Exodus 20:1–23:35). Some, like Joshua and Caleb, believed God's promises given to the Patriarchs and acted on the basis of faith (Numbers 13–14; Joshua). But the majority failed to act in faith. Thus, the Mosaic Covenant was faulty because the people failed to obey, and so the LORD disregarded them (Heb 8:9).

Second, What Makes the New Covenant Better?

Hebrews 8:6 assesses the New Covenant as having been enacted (*nenomothentētai*, legally ratified) on better promises. The covenant not only had better promises, it was *only* a series of promises (Heb 8:10-12). The covenant was ratified (*suntelesō*, coming into existence, 8:8) as a promissory covenant. Unlike the Mosaic Covenant, Israel failed to receive the Mediator of the New Covenant in their rejection of Jesus Christ, yet it was ratified (came into existence) as the LORD received the sacrifice (Heb 9:14).

One of the promises was particularly relevant in the contrast between the covenants. This promise features a generational, personal relationship for each and every Israelite under the New Covenant. This relationship is not based on teaching but another means, which effectively brings all Israel to faith and to knowledge of the Lord (Heb 8:11). So by contrast with the Mosaic Covenant, the New Covenant only incorporates personally redeemed partners.

Third, How Does this New Covenant Impact the High Priest?

The priest enables the arrangement to function and accomplish the goal set out. The goal remains the same for both the Old and New Covenants (Exod 19:5-6). But the covenant arrangement and sacrifice differs. Jesus Christ has the essential role, both in bringing the covenant into existence (Mediator), and in the function of the covenant partnership (High Priest). Hebrews compares and contrasts both of these factors which we will follow.

Existence of the New Covenant

Mediation is at the heart of bringing a covenant into existence. Kent posits, "as mediator (*mesitēs*) he is 'middleman' who gets the parties together and makes possible the agreement."[4] Moses was involved in the mediation of the covenant ratified at Sinai (Gal 3:19). Moses represented the people to receive God's arrangements. He thus solicited Israel's response of acceptance (Exod 19:8; 24:3, 7). On the other hand, on behalf of the LORD, Moses spoke the words that had been revealed (Exod 20:19).

In a more pronounced fashion, Jesus Christ, in His self-sacrifice, is the Mediator of the New Covenant (Heb 9:14-15). "Christ is mediator in that

---

[4]   Homer A. Kent, Jr. *The Epistle to the Hebrews* (Winona Lake, IN: BMH, 1983), p. 150.

by His very person and death He accomplished the reconciliation that was needed."[5] Hebrews takes pains to specify that sacrifice. The blood of Christ represented the cost of the sacrifice. Jesus offered Himself through the enablement of the eternal Spirit. For those who are called, this sacrifice purifies their conscience to serve the living God and to receive the eternal inheritance.

The same sacrifice provides redemption from the transgressions under the first covenant. In the ratification of the New Covenant, the sacrifice satisfied what remained in the broken covenant (Heb 9:15).

Function of the New Covenant

In the ratification of the New Covenant, the LORD was satisfied by Christ's sacrifice. He was the principle Partner in the covenant. But Israel, the other partner, rather than accepting the covenant Mediator, rejected Him and put Him to death. So the partnership between the LORD and Israel had not yet begun to function. Thus, Christ is not yet the High Priest of Israel's covenant partnership with the LORD. Then how is He functioning?

The death of the Mediator (Heb 9:15) is also the death of the Testator (Heb 9:16-17). This transition introduces a strange use of the word *diathēkē*. It is clearly translated, "covenant" when the New Covenant was ratified (Heb 9:15). Then, *diathēkē* is translated, "will" or "testament" in 9:16-17. A promissory[6] covenant may be inaugurated[7] as a will and testament (*diathāsomai*, make a will, Heb 10:16). The same death ratified the arrangement as a *covenant* and inaugurated the arrangement as a *will and testament*. A will and testament begins to distribute its benefits at the death of the testator. That strange turn of events is what Hebrews puts forth as occurring (Heb 9:16-17) in view of Israel's rejection. Covenants are inaugurated while the parties are living; a will is inaugurated at the death of the testator when the beneficiaries receive their inheritance.

The High Priest intercedes on the behalf of those called, both Jews and Gentiles, and prays for the people on the basis of the benefits they have received from the New Covenant. That is the better ministry which the

---

[5] *Ibid.*

[6] A promissory covenant may exist conditioned on one party alone. So the Abrahamic Covenant was ratified as God alone passed between the pieces, and Abraham was fast asleep. The New Covenant was ratified as God alone accepted the mediating sacrifice, while Israel caused the death of the Mediator.

[7] The choice of vocabulary is deliberate, using *ratification* to refer to cutting the covenant (*karuth*) or providing the formal sacrifice to bring the covenant into existence. On the other hand, *inaugurate* refers to the covenant beginning to function.

High Priest has. The benefits of the New Covenant form the basis of His ministry of intercession as He prays on behalf of those who are beneficiaries. The benefits include the law placed upon the heart, knowledge of the LORD, and forgiveness of sins.

Faith Made Visible (Hebrews 11:1-40)

The progress of the argument of the High Priest in *Hebrews* (4:14–10:39) has come to a conclusion with the consideration of the interface between the New Covenant and the Melchizedekian priesthood of Jesus. However, the book continues with a consideration of the *faith* that appropriates the benefits from the priestly ministry of Jesus (Hebrews 4:14–13:25). This concerns the benefits of prayer, boldly drawing near the throne of grace.

The section begins with an appeal from witnesses exemplifying faith responses to God. If we are encouraged to persevere, then what does persevering faith look like? It is widely varied from Abraham to Samson. None are perfect, but each is exemplary in some respects. A formal or complete definition is not provided, but rather, an introduction (Heb 11:1-3) describes what faith does.

Faith (Hebrews 11:1-3)

The translations of the first three verses describing faith differ widely. Yet the translations can be combined to appreciate what *faith* is. The subjects upon which faith is focused are "things hoped for" and "things not seen." They are *hoped for* because God has promised that they will happen. They are *not seen* because God has spoken about things beyond our sensory experience (i.e., creation, death, etc.). Faith focuses on what God has said as a lens through which we see what is not seen (Heb 11:1).

The substance of faith is assurance because God has spoken. Conviction rests on evidence, the evidence that comes from who God is and what He has done in the past, based on His promise (Heb 11:2-3).

Such a description of faith helps the reader of Hebrews to persevere in faith following Christ's First Advent. He is the Heir of the world based on Christ's pilgrimage from earth to the right hand of God. During testing throughout His advent, He was perfected to serve the sons whom He calls to glory. Faith rests in Him and His ministry as High Priest on the behalf of believers—those who are His brothers.

So we can come boldly before God's throne of grace. We can live expecting Christ to mediate God's blessing to our generation. The witness of believers throughout history reiterate evidence to form convictions. And our assurance can rest on the Guarantor of the New Covenant blessings.

Using faith, we come to understand. Man has confronted the universe already existing. Christians come to the Scriptures, delivered from old ways which were accepted by generations in the past. Understanding the universe or the Scriptures must begin with a context set by foundational principles. These principles are often assumed or believed on the basis of evidence, but evidence that is short of rational defense. Yet, once believed, that faith framework provides the groundwork for understanding the unknown in the creation or in Scriptures. Those who believe in a universe spoken into existence by the Word of God are able to realize that what is seen does not necessarily find its origin in other material objects. They find their ultimate origin in God who spoke. Understanding begins by believing that God spoke and the world came into existence and the Scriptures came to be.

Conclusion

The framers of the canon classified these epistles addressed to Jewish audiences as General Epistles. These Jewish believers are addressed as Christians with problems in suffering for their faith and in facing a decision about the basis of their worship. While the historic occasion highlighted the Christians facing suffering from the religious community of Judaism, the testing concerned active and purified faith. While the historic occasion concerned a decision to return to Judaism, the temptation concerned the basis of their walk with God.

Hermeneutically, the interpretation and application of the meaning of these General Epistles examine the norm of *historical. Historical* refers at a minimum to the historical language and the historical occasion. The occasion of a general epistle needs to be interpreted in terms of the historical situation of the original readers but is to be applied to comparable theological circumstances. James and First Peter fit the Jewish world but are not limited to that world. Hebrews may seem to be tied more closely to a world in which Judaism is an alternative, but it is a challenge to the depth of a believer's appropriation of Christ's finished work.

CHAPTER 23: CHRISTIANS IN THE GENTILE WORLD, PART 1: ROMANS

Introduction

In making the gospel known to all nations, the gospel events had been completed. A gospel ministry was certainly introduced in the Book of Acts, in which those facts were communicated. As Ladd pointed out,[1] the revelation of the gospel also included the Epistles, which interpreted for the believers the significance of the gospel in various Gentile situations. In the next two chapters, selected Pauline Epistles will be considered in the perspective that I have introduced.

Introduction to Romans

The epistle to the Romans has a unique perspective in reference to the *gospel*. Rather than molding the message to address Christians in a particular historical or cultural situation, Paul simply speaks of the gospel and the human race. The occasion was that the audience had never been taught the obedience which is based on faith in the gospel (Rom 1:5). He rejoices about the gospel because it "is the power of God for salvation to *everyone* who believes…" (Rom 1:16, emphasis added). While we have used Paul's final words (Rom 16:25-26) to set a perspective on revelation during the dispensation of grace, now we will consider how Paul's agenda affects his letter (Rom 1:15).

Hodges[2] proposes that Rom 1:5, in effect, provides the framework for the letter. His perspective will be followed in the exposition of the epistle to the Romans. In the expository section beginning with chapter 3, there

---

[1] Ladd, *Theology of the New Testament*, p. 386.

[2] Hodges, *Romans*, pp. 29-30.

are twenty references to *faith* until we reach 5:2. Then, from 5:2–8:31, also known as the Christian life section, there are no further uses of the word *faith*. But between 5:2 and 8:31 the word *obedience* occurs twice and the word *obey* occurs three times. Neither word (*obedience* or *obey*) occurs from 3:1–5:2. This expository section is preceded by a demonstration of the depravity of the human race (Romans 1:18–2:29). This establishes the need for the gospel (Rom 1:16-17) that had been introduced. Without the realization of the spiritual condition of natural man, and the judgment of God that addresses depravity, the reason for the gospel is lost.

The argument proceeds from the subject of justifying faith to the subject of Christian obedience. In the epistle, the climactic focus on *obedience* (Romans 6:1–8:30) is the product of *faith* in Christ (Romans 3:1–4:25).

The Gospel: The Subject Matter (Romans 1:16-17)

At the outset, Paul sets forth the theme of the epistle: "the gospel is the power of God for salvation [available] to everyone who believes." This slight paraphrase is introduced to emphasize the aspect of salvation emphasized in Romans. The gospel is central because it makes available the power of God. It is the means of salvation to the believer to whom it is entrusted. This emphasis reflects the use of the term *salvation*. The noun *sōtēria* is introduced in the theme (Rom 1:16) and then not used again until 11:11. The verb *sōzō* occurs next at Rom 5:9-10. It is not used in relation to justification by faith (Romans 3–4), although it could have been used to speak of salvation from the *penalty* of sin. Rather, Paul reserved the term to speak of the one who already believed and the need to be saved from the *power* of sin. As if to emphasize the distinction in Rom 1:17, he says that through the gospel the righteousness of God is imputed to those who believe. Righteousness "is not only attained *by means of faith* but it is also *granted to faith*. *Faith*, then is the beginning and the end of this divine righteousness."[3]

As a conclusion to the theme, Paul quotes Hab 2:4. God connects imputed righteousness and life—the righteous one by faith is the one who can live. In the section dealing with obedience (Romans 5:9–8:30), Paul elaborates on the point in Habakkuk based on the finished work of Christ: "if by the Spirit you put to death the deeds of the body, you will *live*" (Rom 8:13, emphasis added).

---

[3] *Ibid.*, p. 37, emphasis in original.

The transition introducing salvation makes two aspects of the gospel clear: "having now been justified by His blood, we shall be *saved* from wrath [cf. Rom 1:18] through Him…we were reconciled to God through the death of His Son, much more…we shall be *saved* by His life" (Rom 5:9-10, NKJV, emphasis added).

What Is the Universal Problem of Mankind? (Romans 1:18–3:20)

Since the ground for salvation from the about to be revealed wrath of God (Rom 5:9) is righteous standing before God, what is the condition of mankind deserving of wrath? Paul weighs mankind's universal problem.

An outline of Paul's contention:

- Humanity Stands Under God's Wrath (1:18–2:5)
- Humanity Faces God's Impartial Judgment (2:6–3:20)
    - The nature of God's judgment (2:6-16)
    - The vulnerability of the Jews (2:17-29)
    - The decisive witness of Scripture concerning humanity (3:1-20)[4]

Humanity Stands under God's Wrath (Romans 1:18-32)

What is under review is the widespread and obvious depravity of the human race. While some would restrict this assessment to Pagans, the text treats "ungodliness and unrighteousness" as a human problem (Rom 1:18). As a result, the human race is under God's wrath both in history and at the end of history. The human problem begins with what ought to be known about God the Creator from the creation (Rom 1:19-20). Two things mankind ought to infer to be true are evident: His power and His essential existence as God, which is higher than any being in the world. This self-evident knowledge eliminates any human being from having an excuse.

Because the human response was neither respectful nor thankful, they lost the capacity to comprehend or to discern (Rom 1:21). They confused their own darkness with light, as they formed idols (Rom 1:22-23). As a result, God's wrath turned them over to their own iniquity (Rom

---

[4] *Ibid.*, pp. 39-95.

1:24-28) and they did unseemly things (Rom 1:29-31). Paul's indictment of humanity culminates in mankind's tragic effort to make evil a virtue (Rom 1:32).

The moralist quickly attempts to excuse himself. In censuring humanity, he condemns himself as he does the same thing (Rom 2:1). On this basis, God's judgment is impartial. Such a moralist view of human evil misses God's leading to repentance (Rom 2:3-5) but does not escape God's judgment on the day of wrath (Rom 2:5).

Humanity Faces God's Impartial Judgment (Romans 2:1–3:20)

As a result, God's judgment gives what mankind deserves (Rom 2:6). So the principle of judgment is considered on the one hand, God will give eternal life to anyone who deserves it, by persisting in good works (Rom 2:7).[5] The question is, does the Scripture teach that such a principal is true to anyone's experience? Scripture's teaching in Rom 3:9-20 is that the answer is no, "there is none righteous not even one." On the other hand, God's wrath is directed to whoever is selfish and disobedient to the truth, whether Jew or Gentile (Rom 2:8-9). An impartial judgment may be reached (Rom 2:11-15).[6] For those without the Law, "the law inwardly inscribed on their hearts will be made manifest"[7] through their conscience and criticism of others. Jesus Christ Himself will expose what is secret as Judge (Rom 2:16).

But does the Jew not have a distinct advantage as God's elect? As Hodges notes, Jews are vulnerable under the Law (Rom 2:17-29):

> The self-confident Jew should consider the reality that once he is a *transgressor* of the *law*, he not only has no advantage over a Gentile, but he would actually be worthy of condemnation by any Gentile who is not a *transgressor* of the *law*, even though the Gentile was uncircumcised.[8]

This is another way to demonstrate the impartiality of God (Rom 2:11), however much a Jew might imagine that God would be partial to him.

---

[5] *Ibid.*, p. 23.

[6] For those who sinned without the law, they will perish without law.

[7] Hodges, *Romans*, p. 71.

[8] *Ibid.*, p. 78, emphasis in original.

The Decisive Witness of Scripture Concerning
Humanity (Romans 3:1-20)

Paul's argument that God will give the Jew no special status on the Day of Judgment may seem to say that there is no advantage in being a Jew. That is not true. Chief among the advantages of election is having written revelation from God. "That advantage is not annulled by the fact that the Jews fail to believe their own Scriptures, since their unbelief only enhances the perfect truthfulness of God"[9] (cf. Rom 3:3-9).

This privilege that Israel has becomes the very instrument by which both Jews and Gentiles are condemned as sinful humans (Rom 3:9-20). Paul's earlier accusations against humanity (Romans 1:18–2:29) are then confirmed by numerous scriptural quotations (Rom 3:10-20).

What Is God's Provision of Positional Righteousness? (Romans 3:21–4:25)

God is the only possible source of righteousness for man. Why? God has demonstrated that all human beings share the same level of sinfulness before God (Rom 3:23). So God has *justified* freely those who believe, because Someone has paid the *redemption* price to set those believers free from enslavement under sin. How is that possible? Jesus has been set forth as the *propitiation* of God's holy character—in open display for all to observe (Rom 3:21-25).

As a result, God can both be righteous in His own character, and, consistent with His character, declare righteous anyone who believes (Rom 3:26). The law of faith is the only condition of salvation for all individuals, thus excluding anyone on the basis of personal merit, and excluding the boasting of the proud (Rom 3:27). The law of faith also establishes the validity of the Mosaic Law as it is exposing sin. Otherwise, if the Law were the means of justification, the standards of the Mosaic Law would have to be lowered (Rom 3:31).

There is a future result. The gospel fulfills what the Law and the Prophets had anticipated (Rom 3:21; 4:1-25). In an earlier epistle, Paul had specified that God had "preached the gospel beforehand to Abraham, saying, 'In you shall all the nations be blessed'" (Gal 3:8). In Romans, Paul explains how God declared Abraham to be righteous by faith (Rom 4:1-12). Then he adds that Abraham would be heir of the world (Rom 4:13-17).

---

[9] *Ibid.*, p. 88.

What is involved is that Abram believed God's promise and God declared him to be righteous (Gen 15:6; Rom 4:1-3). Then God ratified a covenant with Abram as party (Gen 15:9-21), which encompassed all promises made to Abram (Gen 12:2-3; 13:15). These were represented in the covenant with the land promise (Gen 15:18-21). However the climactic promise was that through him all nations would be blessed (Gen 12:3b). God's fulfilling this promise involved Isaac.

Isaac believed when Abraham offered him on Mt. Moriah (cf. Gen 22:9). As they walked together to the sacrifice, Isaac asked where the animal to be sacrificed was (Gen 22:7). Abraham answered, "God will provide for himself" the sacrifice (Gen 22:8). Then, when no sacrifice appeared, Abraham had to tell Isaac that God had said to offer him as a burnt offering (Gen 22:2). When Isaac allowed himself to be placed on the altar, he shared Abraham's faith in what God had said.

Following the sacrifice of the substitute ram (Gen 22:13), God restated the covenant promise with this addition: "*because* you have done this and have not withheld your son…I will surely bless you…" (Gen 22:16-17, emphasis added). This is what Paul meant when he said that the promise was confirmed (*bebaian*, made sure and certain) to all the seed (Rom 4:16). No one else in the line of descendants accepted the promises as Abraham had until Jesus did (Gal 3:16). Because Jesus received God's promises, He was delivered when offered as a sacrifice, even as Isaac had been. That gospel is now proclaimed to all mankind, both Jew and Gentile, to be received by faith (Rom 4:16).

Thus, Abraham is heir of the world to come (i.e., the millennial kingdom, Heb 2:5) to be populated—whether by Jew or Gentile—by justified believers, of whom he will be father (Gal 3:29; 4:5). Abraham's faith, on behalf of Isaac, like believers after Christ's resurrection will overcome death because God raises the dead to life (Rom 4:18-25).

What Is the Fruit of Justification in Christian Experience? (Romans 5:1-11)

The fruit featured first of all, peace with God, allows God to pour out His love in the believer's life (Rom 5:1-5; 8:31-39). The presence of His love in the presence of the Holy Spirit holds out anticipation and hope. It is an anticipation of salvation from the rule of sin, against which the rule of the wrath of God had handed over the fallen world (Rom 5:6-9). The argument supporting that hope rests in *reconciliation* (Rom 5:10-11), expressed in a syllogism: if when we were sinners, God's love could effect reconciliation through Christ's *death*, how much more, having been reconciled, we should anticipate a future salvation from sin and death based on Christ's *life*.

What Does Christ's Resurrection and Ascension Life Contribute to Salvation from the Power of Sin? (Romans 5:12–8:39)

Directly to the point, Paul makes an assessment of God's work of salvation: "For if while we were enemies we were reconciled to God by the *death* of his Son, much more, now that we are reconciled, shall we be saved by his *life*" (Rom 5:10, emphasis added). This second aspect of God's work of salvation will occupy Paul's thought in Romans 5:12–8:39. While consideration of the resurrection-life naturally follows Jesus' death on the cross, this next section is the focus of much of the New Testament literature.

The epistolary literature is consistently addressed to believers, many of whom worship in a geographically located community. Thus, it is natural to expect the letters addressed to these communities to address issues in the recipients' lives in their present existence as believers. As important as it was to ground their faith in the death of Christ on the cross (Romans 1:19–5:11), these letters are not evangelistic in nature. Rather, the letters' primary focus is related to God's current work of salvation in the lives of believers. Theologically, this has been named the present tense of salvation or salvation from the power of sin. Having been grounded on salvation from the penalty of sin, this present tense aspect of salvation features the resurrected life and ascended position of Jesus Christ. This is the same focus as Hebrews. In addition, the Epistles promise the future tense which involves salvation from the presence of sin (glorification) when the resurrected Lord will return to reign on earth. Romans will address salvation from the power of sin in the next section under consideration (Romans 5:12–8:39).

Paul explains that Christ, as the last Adam, will be the source of life, even as the first Adam was the source of the fallen nature of the human race (Rom 5:12-21). Further, the creation, fallen in Adam and subjected to futility, awaits the appearance of the children of God with their Lord, to be set free (Rom 8:20-21) from this fallen futility.

The Fallen Life in the First Adam and the Creation of Life in the Last Adam (Romans 5:12–6:14)

The Fallen Life in Adam

The first Adam was created to pass on life to the human race. When he disobeyed, sin controlled this life which he possessed. He would die, and his offspring all died, indicating that "all sinned" in his sin (Rom 5:12). The Bible didn't leave a record of what sin each individual committed, but each died, indicating that each one's judgment as a sinner was certain (Rom 2:11-16). Even before the Law specified human violations, sin was wrong because it opposed man's well-being (Genesis 4–11). Adam, and the death he passed on to others, became a type in an inverse pattern of Christ, the last Adam. As the first Adam passed on sin and death, so the last Adam would pass on obedience and life to those who receive it (Rom 5:17).

The New Created Life in the Last Adam

The coming One, Jesus Christ, broke the cycle of death in His resurrection out from among the dead. If death ruled the lives of mankind receiving Adam's life, it is more than reasonable that those to whom God's gift of grace and righteousness has come should reign in life through the one man, Jesus Christ (Rom 5:17). Through the righteous act of Jesus Christ, the righteousness of life (RSV, NAB) came for all (Rom 5:18, *dikaiōsin zōēs, righteousness sourced in life*). The justified one has life, both an imputed righteousness and an imparted life which can be righteous (Rom 5:19). Justification is not being made righteous, but a righteousness and life is given which can lead to practical righteousness. The Mosaic Law had been slipped in (*pareisēlthen*) to serve as a preparation for grace (Rom 5:20). If sin reigns in death, then the reign of grace can bring a vital experience of life (Rom 5:21). The regal language (Rom 5:14, 17, 21) suggests the spiritual presence of the kingdom of God in believers' lives, as Christ begins to reign in them from heaven. This corresponds to the mysteries of the kingdom Jesus unfolded in the parables (Matthew 13). It is not the Davidic mediatorial kingdom ruling on earth, but Christ's providential reign over believers, giving them life, experienced through the Word sown and the Spirit's fruit.

A question emerges that is yet to be answered: how does the reign of grace bring the experience of life? The answer that Paul posits begins with this question: should sin be multiplied that grace might be multiplied in repeated forgiveness (Rom 6:1)? That question assumes that grace invites sin because forgiveness is given freely. It is possible for believers to continue to sin, as the question implies, but not *live* there. Sin is not an authentic Christian experience. Believers are in fact *dead* to sin and thus incapable of being truly at home in sin. How has this *new creation* been formed? Believers are baptized by the Spirit into the death and burial of Christ[10] (Rom 6:3). Believers are united to Christ's crucified and dead body. In that spiritual sense, they are dead to sin. As resurrection began a new life for Christ, so we too can walk in newness of life (Rom 6:4). As death is the end of any master's claim on the service of a slave, so death with Christ can be seen as both the basis for our righteous status and our liberation from slavery to sin (Rom 6:7).

Now Paul has answered how grace has come to reign in the creation of the new man. But it remains to answer: how does the new creation influence behavior? The answer to this question invokes three issues. First, is to *believe* that we are alive with Christ before God (Rom 6:10). Second, is to *consider* ourselves dead to sin and alive to God (Rom 6:11). Third, is to *present* our members as instruments for righteousness (Rom 6:13) to Christ and to His reign in our lives.

Paul concludes that sin does not need to have dominion over this one who is a new creation, because this one is not under law but under grace (Rom 6:14).

Life under Grace, Not under Law (Romans 6:15–7:25)

Change of Status (Romans 6:15-23)

This change in status raises another question: Does the removal of law prompt one to sin (Rom 6:15-23)? Intuitively, the removal of legal stipulation seems to be tantamount to removal of all restraint to sin. But the question fails to consider our death with Christ. A drastic inward change has been brought about by obedience to the gospel (Rom 6:17-18). Righteousness and holiness are now the true expression and fruit of who we are. This is the consequence of grace, not of law. Law was irrelevant when dealing with the fallen nature of man. Law could not impart life nor could it compel obedience. Rather, life must be imparted by God freely as a gift. The gift of life can produce obedience (Rom 6:20-23).

---

[10] See, "Appendix 3: Baptism," in this book.

*Then, what is the consequence of freedom
from the Law (Romans 7:1-25)?*

Ironically, freedom from the Law is the key to sin's loss of power. To support this ironic assertion, Paul develops two arguments related to law.[11]

Metaphor of Marriage (Romans 7:1-6)

The authority of law lasts as long as subjects of the law live. As long as marriage partners are alive, the law of marriage has authority over the partners.[12] When one partner dies, the marriage bond is invalidated.

Now the metaphor portrays the individual married to the Law. But when the believer dies and is buried in Christ, the marriage to the Law no longer exists. The believer is dead with respect to sin and the Law. Then in an extension of the metaphor, the dead individual is free to marry another. And that marriage is to Christ, portrayed in the believer's resurrection in Christ. Now the believer lives under the authority of Christ, the new husband. This is the first argument, based on a metaphor used to express the importance of having been raised to new life in Christ.

Weak Flesh (Romans 7:7-25)

A second question is raised: although a believer is dead to sin and the Law, does that believer experience victory over sin? That answer is influenced by the fact that *dead to sin* does not mean that sin no longer exists. Rather, sin does not rule but makes its appeal to believers through their weak flesh.

First, Paul affirms that it would be wrong to conclude that since a believer is dead to the Law, that the Law is evil. Rather, the Law is like a searchlight that exposes sin and brings it to man's consciousness. In so doing, the Law assists sin by focusing a person's mind on sin (1 Cor 15:56). That is where the problem is.

The Law and sin died because they are no longer master as they had been since Adam. Now sin lies dormant in the flesh, which is the remnant of Adam's old life in the new creation. When the Law searches the person, sin is aroused. So when the Law says one ought not covet, then every kind of desire springs to mind (Rom 7:7-8). So when Paul says he was "once alive" (*ezōn*, 7:9), he signifies his early experience and consciousness as a living Christian. So the Law roused the dormant sin in his weak flesh

---

[11]   This exposition follows Hodges, *Romans*, pp. 183-202.

[12]   Most would interpret the Bible to regard two exceptions to the law of marriage: marital unfaithfulness and personal abandonment. In either case, the marriage bond is broken.

and killed his aliveness in his walk with God (Rom 7:9). When he said he died in his Christian experience, he is not saying he no longer possessed life, but he lost his life's enjoyment. And death in that sense was experienced. That was precisely the serpent's strategy in the Garden.

Now as sin works death though a good law, this diabolical strategy provides further evidence of how exceedingly evil sin is (Rom 7:9-12). It wasn't the Law that caused death, but sin did (Rom 7:13). That led Paul to realize something about himself. Paul described himself as fleshly and that realization was accompanied by inner conflict (Rom 7:14-15). Paul was stupefied by what he did. The inner conflict revealed a carnal side of Paul—the believer. This fleshly side contained no good thing. The inner wish to do good, sourced in I, found no good expressed through the flesh.[13]

This inner conflict led Paul to a sense of frustration and despair (Rom 7:24-25). But still he realized that he could be delivered from this body of death, although he had not yet experienced it. And he expressed thanks to God through Jesus Christ.

Another question emerges: how can the inner principle of the mind, which serves the Law of God, triumph over the flesh which serves the law of sin? Paul expressed the answer in Phil 3:8-10. He counted what he had gained in Judaism as rubbish, "that I may know Him and the power of His resurrection and the fellowship of His resurrection" (3:10, NKJV). The goal is knowing Christ. This experience will be explained in Rom 8:1-39.

Knowing Christ and the Power of His Resurrection (Romans 8:1-13)

No Condemnation (Romans 8:1)

Paul had experienced the condemnation of the Law when he attempted through his flesh to obey the Law. He had expressed it in the words: "Wretched man that I am! Who will deliver me from this body of death?"

---

[13] This reality of a carnal side to a believer has been challenged. But the evident description of the redemption of the person (Rom 3:24), an already dimension of salvation and a not yet redemption of the body (Rom 8:23), indicates that a remnant of Adam remains. The personal pronoun, *I* (Rom 7:14-18), has reference to the redeemed person, however, this new creation remains housed in the weak flesh. Thus, no matter how strong the inner desire to do good, the power to accomplish that desire is not present in the flesh.

(Rom 7:24). He now will explain that the one who walks according to the Spirit will be saved.[14]

Law of the Spirit of Life in Christ (Romans 8:2-4a)

What is this law? It is a principle derived from the Spirit's work in baptizing a believer into the life of the resurrected Lord. *Pneuma* speaks of the presence of the Holy Spirit vitalizing the believer's life in Christ.

The Law of Moses was inadequate because the believer's flesh was weak and unable to respond consistently in obedience. The reality of Christ's sacrifice on the cross addressed the weakness of His own human flesh, yet without sin. In resurrection, He demonstrated God's power to realize holiness in human flesh. Jesus put away sin and death as the controlling power and principle in human experience. In Spirit baptism, He distributes His own resurrection life in a way that makes life available to all believers.

Now the righteous requirements of the Law might be carried out in the obedience of believers who live in the energy imparted by the Spirit.

Walk according to or after the Spirit (Romans 8:4b-7)

How can the righteous requirement of the Law be fulfilled? The orientation of the believer's mind is vital. With the mind set on the things of the Spirit, the Spirit produces the experience of resurrection life which brings peace. That peace resolves the warfare between the inner person and the sinful flesh (Rom 7:7-24). A mind set on the things of the Spirit may be described as turned on by the Spirit.

Indwelling Spirit (Romans 8:8-11)

If a person is Christ's, then that person has the indwelling Spirit which identifies a Christian. In that state, how can a believer present

---

[14] While the majority text includes the reference to walking according to the Spirit in Rom 8:1, the majority of textual critical scholars omit it. This leads most interpreters to conclude that it is positional condemnation rather than practical condemnation. The textual reading may not be included in the best manuscripts, but the context favors this idea to be implied, even if not included. The immediate context is not dealing with one's position in justification (Rom 3:23; 4:1-12). Following the development of justification, Paul presents the consequences (Rom 5:1-11). Included as a consequence is salvation by Christ's resurrection life (Rom 5:10). That is the subject he has been developing (Rom 5:12; 7:25). At a climax, he speaks of being saved from the body of death (Rom 7:24). This experiential deliverance is what he is about to discuss: we are delivered by Christ as we live according to His Agent, the Holy Spirit. So this is what the context has introduced even if it is not explicitly present.

his members as instruments of righteousness to God? The total process includes a miracle that is not under the control of the person. But it is analogous to Christ's resurrection. In dying, Jesus' spirit had given control to God (John 19:30). The Holy Spirit took control of Jesus who was dead and without any personal power to change His position. Then the Spirit raised Him to a new order of personal life, resurrected from among the dead ones. That is being "in the Spirit" which is distinguished from the concept of walking in the Spirit (Rom 8:9-13).

Walk According to the Spirit (Romans 8:12-13)

There is an illusion in the fallen world that sin holds a mortgage on every person's body. It is the natural way to live, making payment by acting sinfully. But sin no longer reigns. It is dead. Therefore, the believer has a choice. It is possible to exist, continuing to make payments to sin, but that's not life. On the other hand, the Spirit wants to put to death the sinful deeds of the body so the believer may live. Such a living walk allows the Spirit to do His work in empowering deeds of righteousness which the believer does in obedience.

Knowing Christ and the Fellowship in His Suffering (Romans 8:14-39)

It was in the midst of Jesus' suffering at the hands of evil that the power of resurrection became a reality. Without suffering, there would be no resurrection. What is the believer's suffering? How is he sustained in the midst of suffering?

Birthright of Divine Sonship (Romans 8:14-17)

The term *huioi*, meaning *sonship*, refers to the mature status of a son, achievable by virtue of the Holy Spirit. That status is in contrast to the servanthood of a child under the tutorship of the Law (Gal 4:1-7). A Spirit-led experience is the believer's true birthright, having been accepted as mature sons. As sons, believers cry out in the midst of life's sorrows to God as Father. And the Spirit also cries out with us and in us. In this fashion, the Spirit adds His testimony to ours, that we are God's sons. With this status in mind, Paul expands the vision: a son is an heir, but a mature son can become a co-heir with the Son (Rom 8:17). Elsewhere,

Paul had said that a son has received the down payment or assurance of his future inheritance. The down payment is the Holy Spirit (Eph 1:13-14) who will not be lost, whatever the future inheritance may be. But a son may be disinherited of any future inheritance if he doesn't share with the Son who suffered rejection at the hands of an evil world. In His ascension, the Son restored *inherent* glory by virtue of His humanity and His submission to sufferings. A believer, with a birthright as a son, has an assurance in the ministry of the Holy Spirit's leading and has a hope of a future share in glory if they are willing to suffer as sons.

Glory to Come (Romans 8:18-22)

The vision of hope is enhanced by a consideration of the glory to come. A son's suffering in the present is not worth being compared with the glory that will be revealed in the future inheritance. This glory is eagerly awaited by the creation itself, since the creation became subject to vanity following Adam's rebellion. So the account in Romans returns to the theme it started with—sin entering into creation through Adam (Rom 5:12ff.). For God is progressively unfolding a plan of redemption to restore this creation, and the sons of God can share in the inheritance of this creation with the Son. Creation awaits the dominion of its glorified owners, who will bring freedom under the Son's reign (Rom 8:21). This is the creation goal. This is not the new heavens and new earth, but the culmination of God's plan of redemption and goal for the creation of Genesis 1. For now, the creation is groaning in the pain of childbirth, subject to less than discernable meaning and corruption, but with hope because of the promise of creation itself (Rom 8:22).

The Wait (Romans 8:23-30)

Sons also groan waiting in hope for the redemption of their bodies. Their wait is both eager for the inheritance to come and persevering amidst suffering at the hand of evil. As help in the midst of our weakness in suffering, the first fruits of the Holy Spirit intercede. Our groanings are His prayers and His prayers are God's thoughts according to His plan. Such prayers, when answered, can only lead to the ultimate good of those who love Christ, for whom they were made. On the basis of the Spirit's prayer and God's plan, believers can know that all things will work together for good (Rom 8:28).

God's purpose is nothing less than to bring believers into conformity to the image of God's Son. All sons will share a basic likeness of freedom from sin in a glorious resurrection body. Through the midst of suffering, persevering sons will have a greater likeness and a more extensive share in the first born Son's reign. Paul sees it as inconceivable that the predestined purpose of God should fail for any believer. All will be conformed to the image of His Son—but to varying degrees of likeness.

God's Everlasting Love (Romans 8:31-39)

Paul concludes the section where he began. The salvation of the believer rests in the love of God which has been poured out in our hearts by the Holy Spirit who was given to us (Rom 5:5). God's love sustains in our justification (Rom 5:1-9a), in our sanctification (Rom 5:9b-13), and in our suffering (Rom 8:14-30). No matter what a believer suffers, he can't be severed from God's love. Those who are included in God's plan of redemption are objects of divine love which no one can alter.

Conclusion

God chose Paul, a Jew, to be the Apostle to the Gentiles. This may seem strange, since he was "brought up in this city, educated at the feet of Gamaliel according to the strict manner of the law of our fathers, being zealous for God..." (Acts 22:3). Even though he was culturally and religiously immersed in Judaism, he was able to reason consistently from the *truth of the gospel* in spite of his heritage. Romans is the epistle that addresses everyone who believes, since "it is the power of God for salvation to everyone who believes" (Rom 1:16). So the gospel has a persuasive power to anyone who is willing to listen, is willing to consider what is said, so that anyone might understand the dispensation of grace. Thus, Romans was chosen to represent the centerpiece of epistolary revelation.

Through Christ, Paul received grace for himself and apostleship for the Gentiles, "to bring about the obedience of faith" (Rom 1:5). As a steward of grace, this is his intent to be developed in the epistle. Romans 5:12–8:31 develops the ground of *obedience* for a believer who is saved from the power of sin. Romans 3:21–5:11 explains the righteousness available by faith which reconciles us to God, who pours out His wrath on the ungodliness and unrighteousness of men (Romans 1:19–3:20).

Those acts of obedience then flow from a transformed mind (Romans 12:1–15:13). This obedience is a believer's reasonable service.

CHAPTER 24: CHRISTIANS IN THE GENTILE WORLD, PART 2: SELECTED PAULINE EPISTLES

Introduction

The gospel was at the core of Paul's ministry, whether in evangelism (Acts 13:15-41 or 17:22-32) or in teaching (Romans 5:12–8:39 and 12:1–15:13). In each of Paul's other epistles, the gospel remains at the core in teaching the churches, but it is the gospel related to various historical occasions.

First Thessalonians

Introduction

One of Paul's early Epistles featured an emphasis on the initial response of the church: their "work of *faith and labor of love* and steadfastness of *hope* in our Lord Jesus Christ" (1 Thess 1:3, emphasis added). These three responses are characteristic of the early church (1 Cor 13:13). After an unusually brief ministry (at least three weeks, Acts 17:2), Paul's message in the epistle was to the point: *stay the course.*

He describes his brief ministry, "as we [Paul, Silas, and Timothy] have been approved by God to be *entrusted* [stewards] with the gospel" (1 Thess 2:4, emphasis added). As a result of this ministry, the believers at Thessalonica had "turned to God from idols to serve the living and true God" (1 Thess 1:9). That service would also be a stewardship produced in the work of faith (1 Thess 3:1-10), and a labor of love for which Paul prayed (1 Thess 3:10-13).

Further, the believers turn to serve God and "to wait for his Son from heaven, whom he raised from the dead, Jesus who delivers us from the wrath to come" (1 Thess 1:10). This hope had become a particular issue in the months since Paul had left (First Thessalonians 4:13–5:11). They had taken Paul's quote of Jesus as speaking to them directly. In particular, "I will come again and will take you to myself" (John 14:3). Since Paul had left, some had died. Had they missed the return of Jesus? To answer their question, we will give a brief summary of the doctrine of future things in the Epistles.

Doctrine of the Future

A proper perception of the events of history and of the future is the focus of the faith spoken of in this Biblical theology. One possible criticism is that the Biblical account admits to greater continuity than reflected in the mysteries or secrets of the dispensation of grace. These mysteries in an era of grace involve added revelation not known previously and thus are not a fulfillment of Old Testament expectation. In this presentation, the case has been made that the doctrine of salvation does involve First Advent fulfillment in the Person and work of Jesus of Nazareth. The revelation of His Person is completely fulfilled. The revelation of His work has been realized in First Advent fulfillment and waits in hope for Second Advent fulfillment.

But within this revelation broadly conceived, there were aspects of fresh revelation. Both Luke and Paul saw the baptizing work of the Spirit, which formed the Church, as originating with John the Baptist and Jesus Christ Himself. The kingdom involved hidden revelation because of Israel's rejection of her Messiah. Hebrews saw the reappearance of Melchizedek, not as a fulfillment, but as a continuation of a priestly order of ministry. Because of this priestly order's superiority, it would replace the Aaronic order for now. In addition, the New Covenant was quoted as Israel's covenant, yet available to called benefactors as a last will and testament. These instances of new revelation, and thus discontinuity, will be further explored in the doctrine of Israel, of the Church, and of the use of Scripture.

For now, the question remains: what does the New Testament say is the *hope* of the Church?

Immediately we face a problem. Is Paul's thought based on second temple Judaism? Or is it derived from, and consistent with, Dan 9:24-27?

This short passage is the clearest statement of Jerusalem's future following captivity (536 BC). God revealed seventy sevens of years until God's purposes in judgment of sin would be fulfilled concerning Israel. After sixty-nine sevens, Messiah would be cast off without any apparent inheritance. Then there was a chronological gap (or parenthesis) in God's direct work with Jerusalem, until the final seven years of judgment, followed by the reign of the Son of Man (Dan 7:13-14).

When Saul of Tarsus met the resurrected Jesus on the road to Damascus, what was he expecting? Ladd sees a new understanding of salvation history as in 2 Cor 5:16-17.

> "From now on, therefore, we regard no one from a human point of view; even though we once regarded Christ from a human point of view [Judaism], we regard him thus no longer..." Because of the messianic work of Christ on the cross (vv. 15, 19), a new kind of existence has been opened up to people: existence "in Christ."[1]

His conclusion is noteworthy.

> We may not conclude that Paul interpreted this new age as being equivalent with the Jewish expectation of the Days of the Messiah that sometimes preceded the Age to Come. On the contrary, Jesus had appeared as the Messiah before the expected Days of the Messiah.[2]

This was consistent with the brief statement of Messiah being cut off and the gap in time following Dan 9:26 and preceding 9:27. Although Ladd would not call it the dispensation of grace, we believe that this was, in fact, the way Paul saw his stewardship in this age. When he looked to the future, his hope focused on two questions:

1. What happens when a believer dies?

2. What will happen when Christ comes for His people, the Church?

Hope: What Happens When a Believer Dies? (Second Corinthians 5:1-10)

Paul's answer is clear, although it is not as complete as many would like. The earthly body is described in terms of weakness and temporariness: a

---

[1] Ladd, *A Theology of the New Testament*, p. 372.

[2] *Ibid.*

"tent in which we groan," it is a "mortal body," which "will be swallowed up by life," and there is a sure expectation of a better life for believers upon leaving the body. A believer's hope is clear; to "be away from the body" is to be "at home with the Lord" (2 Cor 5:8). But the believer's form of existence in the Lord's presence is not clear. Three possibilities have been proposed:

1. Disembodied spirit, but Paul's wish is not to be found naked (unclothed) (2 Cor 5:3)

2. Soul sleep, but Paul longs to be with Christ

3. Clothed with a temporary body so as not to replace the resurrection body to be received at Christ's coming.

The hope is to be with Christ and satisfied with Him. Together, they await the Father's time for Christ to return.

Hope: What Will Happen When Christ Comes for His People? (First Thessalonians 4:13–5:11)

Paul's future expectation, in general, consisted of two ages (Eph 1:21). As in Daniel, there was the present evil age (1 Cor 1:20; 2:6, 8; 3:18; Eph 2:2). This age followed Jesus' death and ascension (Dan 9:26). Everything that remained on earth was predicated on what Jesus had accomplished. This was Paul's stewardship of grace. His hope was focused on Jesus' return (Dan 9:27). This age and this dispensation will be concluded with the coming of the Day of the Lord (1 Thess 5:2; 2 Thess 2:2) or as elsewhere called, "the day of our Lord Jesus Christ" (1 Cor 1:8; cf. 2 Cor 1:14; Phil 1:6). The dominant term describing the Lord's return, *parousia*, means both coming and presence (1 Cor 15:23; 1 Thess 2:19; 2 Thess 2:1). Two other terms are used: *apokalipsis*, meaning unveiling or disclosure (1 Cor 1:7; 2 Thess 1:7; 1 Pet 1:7, 13), and *epiphaneia* indicating the visibility of Christ's return (Titus 2:13). There is a suggestive combination of terms, *epiphaneia* of His *parousia* (2 Thess 2:8) which may imply that aspects of His coming precede His appearance.

In his early letter to the Thessalonians, Paul discussed in some detail what believers can expect when the Lord descends from heaven (First Thessalonians 4:13–5:10). As he introduced the letter, he commended them for having "turned to God from idols to serve the living and true God, and to wait for his Son from heaven, whom he raised from the dead, Jesus who delivers us from the wrath to come" (1 Thess 1:9-10). "The wrath to come" is not eternal judgment, which is not related immediately to the Son's return to earth from heaven. Rather, similar to Rom 1:18, the wrath to come is God's judgment expressed on earth, related as later mentioned in the Day of the LORD (1 Thess 5:2, 9). It begins in judgment, which ushers in Christ's reign in peace for a thousand years.

A question had arisen in the church at Thessalonica because of their lack of understanding of the Lord's promise: "I will come again and will take you to myself, that where I am you may be also" (John 14:3). They had taken it as a personal promise to historic believers on earth. When some believers began to die, the church asked, would that exclude them from being included in being taken to Christ?

Paul's answer rested on the reality of the resurrection; Jesus Christ was the first fruit of a larger harvest (1 Cor 15:20). With that as his premise, he constructed a syllogism with the following conclusion: through Jesus, God will bring with Him those who have fallen asleep (1 Thess 4:15). Then he described what would happen. The Lord Himself would descend from heaven commanding the dead in Christ to rise first. They would precede the rapture in which all living believers will meet the Lord in the air. No longer would the Body be separated from the Lord. This meeting would be unseen by the world and thus, would precede the *epiphaneia* (appearance) of His *parousia*. From that point forward, the *Body* will be treated as the *Bride* of Christ, the Church, awaiting the marriage of the Lamb.

This description of the Rapture seems clear. But the question left unanswered is *when*? Strangely, Paul adds that such a question doesn't need to be answered (1 Thess 5:1). *Why*? Perhaps Paul didn't have a specific answer. And would having such a specific answer undermine what God wanted to happen in their lives while they waited? Whatever his reason, he precedes to answer the question in general. The Rapture of believers is related to the coming of the Day of the LORD. While the time of the arrival of the day isn't known either, some general features of that time are known. First, the world won't have any idea that God is about to intervene in history. Second, the leaders of the world will think they have about reached a worldwide peace which will bring security. Then, the Day of the LORD will come and confront the world as a thief, or the timing will be as a pregnant woman who is about to go into labor. The unprepared world won't escape God's wrath.

But believers are not in the dark and ought not be surprised as the world will be. As children who have the light, they ought to be expecting

Christ's return and making preparations. One preparation involves dressing in the spiritual armament Christ has provided for their salvation (1 Thess 5:8). An essential truth that provides comfort is that God doesn't judge them for their same guilt twice. When believers died with Christ (Rom 6:3), they are identified with the wrath that God poured out on Christ. Therefore, based on God's grace and mercy, and not on their merit, they are not appointed to wrath but will be saved from God's wrath in the Day of the LORD (1 Thess 5:9).

Thus, when the question of the time of the rapture is raised, two factors are relevant. The first is that the *parousia* (coming) of the Lord will precede His *epiphaneia* (appearance). The second is that the day begins with God's wrath, from which believers will be removed in a pretribulational rapture (1 Thess 1:10).

Galatians

Introduction

This letter was probably Paul's first, written shortly after his first missionary journey (Acts 13–14). The point at issue concerned the truth of the gospel (Gal 2:5). After Paul and Barnabas departed, Judaizers had arrived seeking to interpret the gospel under the larger and previously interpreted category of Judaism. They concluded obedience should include circumcision and the works of the Law (Gal 2:3, 12-19; 3:2, 5). On the other hand, Paul saw the grace of God and the gospel of Christ as identical (Gal 1:6-7). So obedience is responding to God by faith in Christ—period. In Paul's contention for the truth, his gospel will be considered from three perspectives.

First, Paul's experience of the ascended Jesus, revealed to him from heaven, not his contact with church leaders, established the truth of his gospel. While he was advanced in Judaism, it wasn't any merit gained by these works before God, but God "was pleased to reveal his Son to me." (Gal 1:16). The grace of God's initial revelation and the provision of Christ's finished work were sufficient to distinguish Paul's standing before God in grace from something earned by what he did for God. Further, that truth was demonstrated when he corrected one of the church leaders, Peter. At the church in Antioch, Peter's hypocritical efforts to appear righteous before leaders from Jerusalem distorted the truth of God's grace. It looked like what was right depended on Peter, rather than on Christ and accepted by faith.

Second, the gospel is true because it is in harmony with what the Old Testament Scriptures said. The question introduced concerned the gift of the Holy Spirit—was the Spirit received by faith or because of works? The Scripture and Paul's gospel provide the same explanation for the blessing of justification by faith (Gal 3:6-13) and for the blessing of the inheritance of the Holy Spirit by faith (Gal 3:14-29).

Abraham's experience sets the pattern for all who are justified by faith (Gal 3:6-9). A right standing before God necessarily sets the ground to receive the gift of the Spirit. The law pronounced a curse on human attempts to obey, which Christ bore on the cross to redeem all who believe (Gal 3:10-13).

Galatians 3:14 is a transitional verse. It concludes that the blessing Abraham received comes through Christ's redemption, and that all might receive the promise of the Spirit through faith.

That is the case because the covenant promises were addressed to Abraham and to his Seed, who is Christ (Gal 3:16). This conclusion results from a historical elimination of descendants who were unwilling to fully accept God's blessing until Christ came to receive His future from God alone. This covenant promise assured Abraham of an inheritance (Gal 3:18). The purpose of the Law was added alongside the promise for historical elimination and identification. As a schoolmaster,[3] the Law would identify the Seed who is Heir, as well as eliminate anyone else's claim to be Heir (Gal 3:19-25). The schoolmaster is no longer needed once Jesus Christ has been identified as Heir.

Gentiles are united with Christ, the Heir, by two means (Gal 3:26-29). First, they become sons of God through faith in Christ (Gal 3:26). Second, they are united with Christ through Spirit baptism (Gal 3:27). Thus, if Jews and Gentiles are Christ's, then *in Christ* they are Abraham's seed and heirs according to promise (Gal 3:29). So Gentiles in the Church do not replace Israel, but Israel is still Abraham's son by birth and will by faith be his heir in the future (Gal 3:7).

Third, the gospel is true because sons of God through the gospel are positioned to accomplish the purpose of the Law through love, serving one another (Gal 5:13-14). As sons of God, believers are set free from slavery to sin (Gal 5:1). As set free, believers are now free to walk in the Spirit so that they bear the fruit of the Spirit (Gal 5:16-18, 22-23). That fruit (Gal 5:22-23) may be summarized by *love* for our neighbor, "For the

---

[3] *Paidagogos* is variously translated as, "guardian, leader, guide, tutor, schoolmaster, custodian, etc."

whole law is fulfilled in one word: 'You shall *love* your neighbor as your-self'" (Gal 5:14, emphasis added).

First Corinthians

Introduction

The gospel was central to the way Paul looked at the world. What God continues to do in the life of mankind and in the lives of believers features the gospel. And thus, it became a lens to sort out what's important and to make wise decisions. So it would not be unexpected when Paul heard about problems at Corinth, and received questions from them, to relate these to God's grace in the gospel (1 Cor 1:4-9).

Before addressing the problems (First Corinthians 5–6) and answering the questions (First Corinthians 7–15), Paul dealt with the central problem: divisions among believers in the church (1 Cor 1:10-17). They were divided in their adherence to different men who ministered in their church. Paul provided a paradigm using the gospel to address the problem (First Corinthians 1:1–4:21). At the heart of the problem is the question: is Christ divided among the ministers (1 Cor 1:13)? The answer ultimately rested in *gospel content* (1 Cor 1:18-31) and *gospel ministry* (First Corinthians 2:1–4:21).

Gospel Content (First Corinthians 1:18-31)

From God's point of view, the Cross of Christ is essential (1 Cor 1:17). From the world's point of view, the Cross is weakness and foolishness (1 Cor 1:18-25). The problem of worldliness addressed here features what makes sin look normal and righteousness seem odd. On the one hand, the Jews look for a *sign* to demonstrate the power of God. As a result, the Cross is weak. And when it is ignored, the Jews stumble over what God is doing (cf. Isa 8:14-15). On the other hand, Gentiles look for wisdom in the form of a rational argument. In this view, the Cross is foolishness. That is, unless humanity's depravity is assumed as a reality (Romans 1:19–3:20). However, from the chosen one's point of view, Christ became wisdom from God for us, since He is the source of righteousness and sanctification (1 Cor 1:26-31)

Gospel Ministry (First Corinthians 2:1–4:21)

Paul begins talking about his own ministry (First Corinthians 2:1–3:4). He speaks the gospel, which is hidden to natural man. The truth was revealed to the apostles through God's Spirit. The apostles received the Spirit to come to know the thing given to them. They speak a message not received by human wisdom but by the Spirit's working.

Recognizing how that ministry works helps to sort out the importance of ministers—Paul or Apollos. Both are servants of Christ and stewards of a message hidden in natural terms (First Corinthians 3:5–4:5). Since individual ministers are each a servant of Christ, should one divide the Body of Christ over following one servant above another?

Problems and Questions (First Corinthians 5–15)

As Paul looked at the congregation divided under various ministers, he rightly sees the congregation and ministers unified around Christ. This is the wisdom of the gospel that is then to be applied to various issues and is the source of answers to various questions. Since the gospel provides a lens of wisdom through which issues in the church may be sorted out, the following list compares the way the issue is viewed. The Corinthians looked at the issue according to a worldly value. Paul writes and looks at the same issue with spiritual discernment based on the wisdom found in the gospel.

In a similar way, the issues are clarified through the lens of spiritual discernment:

Chapters	Worldly Value	Spiritual Discernment
5	tolerance of sin	destructive influence of sin
6	personal control and satisfaction	willingness to suffer personal loss before risking another's destruction
7	satisfaction of one's personal desires in marriage	meet mutual needs, while using opportunities that circumstances bring in obedience to honor Christ
8–11	personal rights and freedoms used to satisfy oneself	use rights and freedoms to serve others in need
12–14	spiritual abilities and personal satisfaction	use abilities in love for the edification of the Body of believers
15	appeal of the novel to satisfy one's curiosities	resting on what is true as a basis for faith and hope

Second Corinthians

Introduction

In the second Corinthian letter included in the canon, at first blush, the gospel does not seem to be as prominent (2 Cor 2:12, 17). The problem among the people of dissatisfaction with the apostle seems to have captured Paul's emotions and attention (Second Corinthians 1:15–2:2). Yet, with the prominence of the gospel in the first epistle, it seems likely that it is behind the question: who is sufficient for the gospel ministry (2 Cor 2:16)? For it is one's response to the gospel that distinguishes between those being saved and those perishing (2 Cor 2:15).

New Covenant

Yet when Paul describes his ministry, he describes his ministry team as "ministers of the new covenant" (2 Cor 3:6). These terms of discussion seem to be chosen for two reasons found in the historical occasion.

First, the New Covenant provides a metaphor to explain his letter of commendation of his ministry to the Corinthians. The Judaizers came to undermine Paul's ministry and questioned whether he had such a letter of reference. Since the New Covenant promised that the law was written on the heart, clearly the Corinthian church is Paul's letter (2 Cor 3:1-3). Yet there is a twist in the metaphor, the law of love for them is also written on Paul's heart (2 Cor 3:2).

Second, Paul takes the image of a New Covenant ministry which he then contrasts with the Judaizers' Mosaic Covenant ministry. The New Covenant promised the blessings received through his gospel ministry. The contrasts concerned the agent of ministry—the letter which calls for obedience, or the Spirit who gives life (2 Cor 3:4-6). Another contrast involves glory. The glory of the Mosaic Covenant featured Moses, whose face shone with glory when he was in the Lord's presence. However, Moses put a veil over his face to cover up that the glory was fading (2 Cor 3:7, 11, 13). As a result, even to that day, Israel's mind was blinded to see that the covenant was temporary.

On the other hand, the glory of the New Covenant excelled as righteousness exceeds condemnation (2 Cor 3:9), and as the Spirit's ministry is more glorious (2 Cor 3:8, 10). As a result, even though Paul was not sufficient for the ministry (2 Cor 2:16), he spoke boldly about Christ (2 Cor 3:12, 14) who when seen takes away the veil brought by the Law

(2 Cor 3:14-15). So as believers, with unveiled faces, behold in Scripture the glory of the Lord, they are transformed into the same glory by the Spirit of the Lord (2 Cor 3:18). This ministry is subsequently described in terms of the gospel (2 Cor 4:3-6; 5:12-21). In view of this New Covenant ministry, Paul does not lose heart (2 Cor 4:1, 16).

Colossians

Introduction

The gospel message was brought to the Lycus Valley by Epaphras (Col 1:7). The distinction between the message and the personal presence of Paul further clarifies that the power of God unto salvation rests in the message. They heard "the word of the truth of the gospel" which is "bringing forth fruit." Since that day they heard and knew "the grace of God in truth" (Col 1:5-6). But now a problem arose to which Epaphras asked Paul to respond.

It began as a philosophical question. Does not the "conception of matter [provide] the origin and abode of evil"?[4] As a result, heretics sought to explain the creation and the government of the world through a series of intermediate beings. These beings would address the antagonism between God and matter.

Rather than attempting to explain the problem of evil philosophically, Paul revealed the solution Christ provided in His first Advent in God's governance of the world (Col 1:13-18). This was a theological solution implicit in the gospel (Col 1:5-7), which entailed a Biblical theology. This Biblical theology took on a narrative form encompassing the first creation (Col 1:15-17) and the new creation (Col 1:18).

The First Creation

The Son shared the exact image with the invisible God in His incarnation into the human race. As a Son, taking on human flesh, He is given the title of Firstborn as pre-eminent in rank over all creatures (Col 1:15). Yet not only does He become a member of creation, but He is the Creator of all things in heaven and on earth, things visible and invisible, found in thrones and nations, rulers and authorities (Col 1:16). There is nothing

---

[4] J. B. Lightfoot, *St. Paul's Epistles to Colossians and Philemon* (Grand Rapids, MI: Zondervan, 1965 reprint), p. 34.

excluded from the Son's universal creation. So He existed before creation, and in the history of creation, all things hold together in His authority (Col 1:17). While evil is *not* presented as directly created, it is included by permission, and it will be addressed. In the Godhead, He was the *means* of creation as He spoke, and in view of His incarnation, He is the *goal* of creation. This comprehensive narrative is the Son's story.

Of course, there is also man's side of the story. It still begins with the Son whom the Father loved (Col 1:12-13). Believers are called to have thankful hearts toward the Father, who qualified them for a partnership in the inheritance of the saints in the light. They were delivered from the authority of darkness that rules over the fallen world. This deliverance is in the redemption through Christ's blood (Col 1:14). And like Israel, having been redeemed, they are transferred into the kingdom of God's Son. Thus, the problem of evil is addressed for the redeemed, even though evil is not explained nor eliminated for the creation.

The New Creation

The first creation is complete, including the kingdom of the Son. The new creation is not the new heavens and earth but is a new creation of the Son's Body on earth. It is a historical work following the firstborn who was raised from among the dead (Col 1:18). In this new creation, He is the Head of the Body, sharing eternal life through resurrection with those who are redeemed. And the Son shares all fullness in the first creation and in the new creation. All things affected by the fall into sin are reconciled to God. So, contrary to the intermediary beings, there is One Son in whom all fullness resides.

First Timothy

The Pastoral Epistles are the last letters that Paul wrote. The gospel remained "the glorious gospel of the blessed God which was committed to my trust" (1 Tim 1:11, NKJV). Further, Paul entrusted the same message to Timothy (1 Tim 6:20; 2 Tim 2:2). Thus, there is no progress in revelation of the message. Its content and even the language used were stable as it was made known throughout the Roman world.

However, there was a change in the language used to characterize those who believed. In the first church planted in Gentile soil, Antioch, believers were first called *Christians* (Acts 11:26). They were Christ-like ones.

In Paul's final Epistles, he calls them to *godliness* (1 Tim 3:16). Yet to be God-like is hidden to the natural man. So Paul quotes what may have been a hymn celebrating Jesus Christ. It is a six line hymn featuring three couplets of two lines each. In essence, he is saying that *godliness* is *Christ-likeness* (Col 2:9), except that it is now fleshed out in Christ's life. This would be clear since "God was pleased to have all his fullness to dwell in Him" (Col 1:19).

The first couplet speaks of Christ's career, which includes both flesh and Spirit combined to accomplish God's purposes. The second couplet speaks of Christ's witness, which includes the full scope of created reality—both angels and nations. The third couplet speaks of Christ's reception, which includes both being believed on in the world and welcomed in glory by the Father.

What makes godliness hidden to the world is that Jesus combines, in the scope of His ministry, what the world separates into spheres of distinct consideration and living. Because of the complexity of reality, the world brackets off one sphere from the other. It is beyond the creature's capacity to encompass all of reality within one comprehensive worldview. These distinctions may be seen in three pairs that are commonly distinguished:

1. Matter is the focus of materialism, while the spiritual is the realm of mysticism.

2. Government frames itself in natural and legal rules, while fate incorporates superstition.

3. Analysis focuses on relationships, while imagination envisions the ideal.

These pairs of couplets are all *combined* (instead of separated) in a godly worldview and in godliness which is the pillar and foundation of the truth. And godliness is the presupposed ground of the gospel and the Church—both in life and in doctrine (1 Tim 3:14-16). The term *godliness* refers to broader comparisons between the world and the Church, while Christlikeness refers to distinctness of the Church within the world. Godliness refers to a theological worldview in distinction to a humanistic worldview.

Conclusion

The focus of the truth entrusted to Paul can be imagined in the gospel. So the gospel became the lens through which Paul viewed a believer's hope for the future, a grasp on the reality of a relationship with God, a wisdom in dealing with the church community, the blessings promised in the New Covenant, and a comprehensive way of viewing all of reality. It is the basis for believers being God-like. This scope in Paul's use of his dealing with the ancient world ought to provide a model for us to deal with the modern world, in spite of apparent changes.

CHAPTER 25:
ISRAEL AND THE CHURCH

Introduction

This chapter is going to address in Paul's writings one of the most sharply debated sine qua non that Ryrie posited to define Dispensationalism.[1] To begin with, it seems almost self-evident that both Israel and the Church are a people of God. In addition, both serve God on earth in comparable terms. Even though they served at separate times in history, Peter uses terms originally applied to Israel and addressed them to the Church: "But you are a chosen race, a royal priesthood, a holy nation, a people for his own possession, that you may proclaim the excellencies of him who called you out of darkness into his marvelous light" (1 Pet 2:9). While Glenny sees this as New Testament fulfillment language,[2] we interpret it as merely sharing a comparable role in service.

---

[1] Charles Ryrie, *Dispensationalism* (Chicago: Moody, 2007), pp. 45-48.

[2] W. Edward Glenny, "The Israelite Imagery of 1 Peter 2," *Dispensationalism, Israel and the Church* (Wheaton, IL: A Bridgepoint Book, 1993), p. 187. It is evident that Jesus Christ *fulfilled* Old Testament prophesies (1 Pet 2:6-8): Israel stumbled over Jesus' humanity and was offended at His claim of Deity (Isa 8:14). The Religious leaders rejected Jesus' work on the cross as the foundation for the people of God (Ps 118:2). God chose to lay in Zion Jesus' work on the cross so that those who believed in Him would be forgiven, not ashamed before heaven (Isa 28:16). Believers addressed are like their Lord (elect, precious, cornerstone) living stones built up into a spiritual house and are a holy priesthood to offer up prayers (spiritual sacrifices) acceptable to God (2 Pet 2:5, 9). While it is clear that prophecies of a Messiah are fulfilled in Jesus Christ, it is not evident in the language of Peter that he believed those who responded in faith fulfilled any Old Testament prophecies. None are quoted. The language only corresponds to a language used in the Old Testament to refer to Israel. In speaking of Israel, ethnicity is an issue. But is it an issue when speaking of the Church? Thus, the questions we'd like to address are: first, based on these similarities, what are the differences? And second, why are the differences claimed to be the sine qua non of Dispensationalism?

Doctrine of Israel

Introduction

One of the distinctive features of Dispensational interpretation is the distinction it recognizes between Israel and the Church. Israel appears first in Scripture and needs to be examined first. The recognition of a distinction rests on two peoples of God serving distinct purposes. How Scriptures addressed to Israel ought to be related to the Church is a debated question and will be considered in *Chapter 26: Doctrine of Scripture*. For now, a consideration of the definition and election of Israel will lay the groundwork for a consideration of Israel's role in history.[3]

Definition of Israel

By a theological definition, *Israel* refers to all the descendants of Abraham, Isaac, and Jacob; also known as the Jews, the Jewish people, Israelites, or Hebrews.[4] This definition is based on Jacob's being named Israel following his struggle with God at Peniel (Gen 32:28). His twelve sons are called, "the sons of Israel" (Gen 42:5). The term began to be used in reference to his descendants (Exod 1:7) and then to the nation that would be formed from these descendants under the Mosaic Covenant (Exod 19:5) when they occupied the land. In the uses in the text so far, ethnicity is common to every use.

Election of Israel

The identification of Israel began with the election of Abram (Gen 12:1-3). He was chosen for personal relationship with God (Gen 15:6). At the outset, Abram was chosen for service: "in you all the families of the earth shall be blessed" (Gen 12:3b). The ambiguity rests in the word *you*. To whom does the word *you* refer? Clearly it refers to Abraham personally, but the scope of those to be blessed, "all the families of the earth," indicates that his descendants are intended to serve.

---

[3]   Arnold G. Fruchtenbaum, "Israel and the Church," *Issues in Dispensationalism*, ed. Willis and Master (Chicago: Moody, 1994), pp. 113-30. His thought will form the outline for this presentation.

[4]   Lewis Sperry Chafer, *Systematic Theology*, vol. 7 (Dallas: Dallas Seminary Press, 1947), pp. 205-206.

Moses will add, "because He loved your fathers, therefore He chose their descendants after them; and He brought you out of Egypt with His Presence, with His mighty power" (Deut 4:37). God redeemed "the children of Israel" and said, "go, serve the LORD, as you have said" (Exod 12:31). Yet it seems evident that not every individual descendant believed. At Mt. Sinai, the service to which they were called is further explained in a collective sense (Exod 19:3-5).

As sin spread among the people, they asked for a king to *represent* them (1 Sam 8:3-5). In time, the prophet Isaiah prophesied that the king (Hezekiah) was willing to trust God but not serve Him (Isaiah 37–39). Then the prophet announced that the LORD would raise up a Servant named Israel (Isa 49:3; cf. 42:1-9; 49:5-8). The Servant was not to *replace* Israel but to *represent* Israel. This is evident because He will be given "as a covenant for the people, a light for the nations" (Isa 42:6; cf. 49:6, 8). By means of the covenant, the people will be fashioned into a nation, and through the Servant, they will serve as a light to the nations. Thus, through them the nations will be blessed.

This is not without significance that the Gospels identify Jesus, born in Bethlehem, as the descendant of David, the descendant of Abraham (Matt 1:1-2, 6) and the offspring of Mary (Luke 3:23; cf. Gen 3:15) through whom Jesus' ethnicity is traced to David through Nathan (Luke 3:31). However, when Jerusalem rejected and crucified Jesus, they chose to sever their relationship with her Messiah. What consequences did this have with Israel's election?

As has already been recognized, election is used in Scripture to refer to God's choice of people for various purposes. Individual or personal election is to personal salvation, and national election is to serve a role in history. When Paul speaks of the election of the patriarchs (Rom 9:6-18), he speaks of them both as forefathers of the nation and as individuals with a personal blessing of salvation from God. Their election is *personal*, to salvation, and *corporate*, to serve a purpose as patriarchs and to become a nation.

National Election of Israel

In Deuteronomy, Moses speaks of God's national election of Israel which does not guarantee the salvation of every individual in the nation. Rather, in Deut 4:36-37, God chose the patriarchs' offspring after them and brought them out of Egypt. He did this to bring them into Canaan and to give them the land for an inheritance. Israel's possession of the land would take a necessary partnership with God in conquest and occupation (Josh 1:3-7).

In Deut 7:6-8, Moses said that God had chosen Israel to be a people for His treasured possession. This choice expressed the fact that He set His love on them. The New Testament recognized this privileged position that rested on Israel in comparison to other nations (Eph 2:12; Rom 3:1-2; 9:4-5). The *purpose* of God's election of Israel was revealed in the Scriptures and recognized in the New Testament (Rom 3:2-4).

First and foremost, God revealed His will to Abram that *through him* all nations would be blessed (Gen 12:3). The people were told at Mt. Sinai that they should become a kingdom of priests and a holy nation to mediate blessings to the nations (Exod 19:5-6). But realizing this role would be contingent upon their obedience to the covenant.

Subsequently, in view of the nation's continued disobedience, Isaiah called the Servant "Israel" (49:3), not as a *replacement* for the ethnic nation, but as a *representative* of the nation, in whom God would be glorified. His individual and distinct relationship to the nation is disclosed as the Servant would be honored in the Lord's presence. The honor would come as He would bring Jacob back to God; that Israel might be gathered to Him (Isa 49:5). At length, Isaiah reveals the heart of the restoration: God will give the Servant "as a covenant to the people, to establish the land, to apportion the desolate heritages" (Isa 49:8).

At the time Paul wrote Romans, Israel had been given the Servant, who was the covenant, but Israel had not received the Servant nor had Israel fulfilled her role as a national servant (Rom 9:4; cf. 3:2). So Paul explained what had happened and how they would be restored to their national role (Romans 9:6–11:32). This explanation will be considered shortly.

God also chose Israel to be a recipient of His revelation (Deut 4:5-8; 6:6-8; Rom 3:2; 9:4; Eph 2:12). Paul acknowledged this when he wrote, "to [Israel] belong...the covenants, the giving of the law, the worship, and the promises" (Rom 9:4).

Third, God chose Israel as the people through whom Messiah would be born (Gen 22:18; Isa 49:3; Matt 1:1-17; Rom 9:5; Heb 2:16-17). Paul also confessed that "from them, by physical descent, came the Messiah, who is God over all, praised forever" (Rom 9:5, HCSB).

Since Paul recognized that the nation had not yet fulfilled her role, he noted: "But it is not as though the word of God has failed" (Rom 9:6).[5] The Scriptures had been given and Messiah had been born, yet the covenant partnership had not yet been finalized.

Remnant Election of Israel

In clarification, he described the present situation: *ou pantos hoi ex yisraēl, houtoi yisraēl* (Rom 9:6). The translation of the cryptic words of Paul must reflect his description and not say more than he intended. The HCSB reflects the terse statement: "not all who are descended from Israel are Israel." The NET translation, "not all those who are descendants of Israel are truly Israel," reflects the sense. Paul is not redefining Israel to be only the remnant but is making a distinction within Israel. Natural descendants of Israel are Israel, but only the obedient remnant truly reflects what God intended for Israel. One must consider Israel internally as well as externally to evaluate the total effects of God's election. In the explanation that follows, Paul shows how a remnant elected to salvation, continuously present within Israel's history, expresses God's love. Yet exposing the nation to God's wrath will, in time, cultivate a people who respond in faith, then "all Israel will be saved" (Rom 11:26).

Israel's patriarchal history rests in God's election. God has the right to choose some from among the fallen human race (Rom 3:23) to receive mercy. Such selective mercy is not unjust since all of fallen mankind deserves judgment. To be merciful, God provided Jesus Christ (Rom 3:22). It was "to demonstrate His righteousness at the present time, so that He would be righteous and declare righteous the one who has faith in Jesus." (Rom 3:26, HCSB). As a loving God, He can show mercy to Moses and choose Pharaoh to serve other purposes (Rom 9:14-15, 17).

But what about the ones He condemned? For who can resist His election? The one who raises this question must realize that he is questioning God. God's prerogatives as the Master Potter include the right to make some vessels of mercy and others vessels of wrath for His glory (Rom 9:20, 23). Israel as a nation was chosen as a vessel of mercy, but Israel had become a vessel of wrath when they were cast into captivity (722 and 586 BC). The same destiny was in store for the remnant that returned to Jerusalem following their restoration to the land, because of their crucifixion

---

[5] See Hodges, *Romans*, pp. 251-351. This course provides the basis of the argument.

of Jesus of Nazareth.[6] Israel had again fallen under the wrath of God. In the terms of Isa 6:9-10, they were hardened in His wrath (Acts 28:25-29). Yet, as a testimony to the Lord's love, a remnant of mercy continues alongside the collective judgment. Saul is a representative instance of mercy who didn't receive what he deserved (Acts 9:1-7).

Romans 9:30–10:21 discusses how Israel may be saved from wrath. While the truths taught have general application to anyone under God's wrath, the argument has a detailed consideration of Israel's case. A strange irony existed between the nations. Israel, having received mercy, tried to use the merciful gifts to establish its own righteousness. On the other hand, the Gentile nations, experiencing God's wrath and not attempting to establish their own righteousness, found that righteousness by faith.

Though Israel did not realize it, their pursuit was useless. Christ personally is the goal (*telos*) which men strive to reach under the Law—namely, righteousness (Rom 10:4). That is, what man sought under the Law as regards to righteousness, they actually could find in the person of Christ. *Telos* also implies the actual termination of the Law as an operative covenant system. The schoolmaster no longer has a viable function now that faith has come.

Romans 10:9 is precisely what that generation of Israel needed to hear. Israel must receive justification by faith in their heart. But, Israel must also do more. No man under God's wrath can experience the new life in Christ while refusing to acknowledge the source of that life publicly.[7]

The people of Israel, whom God had tried to reach not only by the preached message but also by the provocative kindness to the Gentiles, remained disobedient (Acts 22:1-24). This divine effort to reach Israel had failed, as Isaiah had prophesied (Isa 10:20-22; 65:1-2).

---

[6] The account of God's dealing with Israel contains the entire Book of Acts. God's decision was not arbitrary, but only at the end of his journeys to Rome does Paul pronounce judgment on "this people" (Acts 28:26-28) and salvation went to the Gentiles. (The judgment was first pronounced in Isa 6:9-10). In grace, Jerusalem was given a decision (Acts 4:18-22) after two displays of the Spirit's power. Paul, who was called to minister to the Gentiles, first brought the message to Jews in every location (Rom 1:16).

[7] Acts 2:38 includes the heart response which prompted the question: what must we do? And it includes a public response: repent and be baptized, as you confess the name of Jesus Christ. This is also what John the Baptist called his generation to do (Luke 3:3; Matt 3:5-12).

Future of Israel (Romans 9:1–11:32)

It is at this point in history that Paul came into the revelation (Romans 9:1–11:32).[8]

Introduction (Romans 9:1-5)

Paul personally is greatly grieved for Israel, his own countrymen. They have been blessed with God's presence and revelation, as well as the advent of Messiah.

Word of Election (Romans 9:6-29)

God's sovereign word of election is determinate (Rom 11:28). History shows that election has been focused on our relationship as a basis for service. However, "not all who are descended from Israel," that is, physical descendants, "belong to Israel," i.e., are chosen for relationship (Rom 9:6). So, while ethnicity is common to election to service, it is not determinative of election to relationship. However, election to relationship is determinative for final service, since in the end, "all Israel will be saved" (Rom 11:26-27).

God's word of election distinguishes between ethnic descendants of Abraham (Rom 9:2-9) and between ethnic descendants of Rebecca (9:10-13). The descendants of God's choice (Isaac and Jacob) had a relationship with God.

Israel's rejection of Jesus does not demonstrate that there is unrighteousness with God (Isa 6:9-10, quoted in Matt 13:14-17 and Acts 28:26-27). God has the right to show mercy on whom He wills (Rom 9:16) as He did at the exodus (Rom 9:17-18). But then the creature asks whether election removes their responsibility (Rom 9:19). In answer, a pot who is guilty of sin and deserving of judgment has no right to mercy from the Potter. Rather, God answered, with much longsuffering, the vessels of wrath prepared (passive voice) for destruction (Rom 9:22). At the same time, God made known the riches of His glory on the vessels of mercy which He prepared (active voice) beforehand for glory (Rom 9:23). This word of election extends to Gentiles as well as to Israel (Rom 9:24-29).

---

[8] See Hodges, *Romans*, pp. 251-351 for some of the argument.

Israel's Need for the Gospel (Romans 9:30–10:21)

How might Israel be saved from the wrath of God? Israel's case (Romans 9:30–10:21) is a special case of the overall message of the epistle (Romans 1:19–8:30)

Israel's Hardening Partial and Not Final (Romans 11:1-36)

Partial (Romans 11:1-10)

The bottom line question is, "has God rejected his people?" (Rom 11:1). A remnant remained in Paul's day as it had in Elijah's day. Elijah had made intercession *against* Israel calling for national judgment (1 Kgs 19:9-18). The LORD had 7,000 who had not worshiped Baal. God's faithfulness in Elijah's day, and in Paul's day, to His elect, Abrahamic Covenant relationship with Israel means—no. This remnant illustrates an election of grace to relationship.

Paul chooses David's words (Ps 69:21-22) in which the table God set for Israel had become their snare. The law itself was designed as a schoolmaster to prepare them for Christ and for righteousness by faith. Rather, the Law became for them a supposed means of salvation in their own doing. That was the trap keeping them from what they sought. Thus, the majority of the people had fallen and God's wrath rested on them.

Not Final (Romans 11:11-36)

Israel's rejection in spite of herself is still being used to bring salvation to the Gentiles. In other words, whether in obedience or in disobedience, God uses Israel to reach the Gentiles. In the process, the Lord seeks to arouse Israel to desire that same salvation for themselves in envy toward the Gentiles.

What Image Portrays What Is Happening as a Result (Romans 11:17)?

An offering to God (Rom 11:16) is imagined in an olive tree. If the root is holy, then what about the branches? Israel will spring from its root (Abraham) in the patriarchs. The branches are Israel. The root is likely the fathers from whom the nation has grown (Rom 11:28). In the image of an olive tree, the election of grace to relationship and service is portrayed. A special opportunity is afforded to Gentiles who are grafted into the existing tree, being blessed through the patriarchs. The natural branches that remain are the remnant that is elect to relationship. This engrafting of Gentiles is contrary to nature and so the engrafting of unnatural branches would be temporary. The reverse would naturally be expected. Unnatural branches will be cut off as they linger in unbelief. The re-grafting of natural branches (Israelites) awaits their quickening to faith (Rom 11:23). It is logical to anticipate this.

At the time of the fullness of the Gentiles, "all Israel will be saved" (Rom 11:26). Isaiah 59:20-21 anticipates the Deliverer coming to banish ungodliness from Jacob. Then the New Covenant will be inaugurated with them (the house of Israel and of Judah, the stated covenant partner) when the LORD takes away their sin (Jer 31:34). Then natural branches will be engrafted into the olive tree and the fruitful nation will be an offering to the Lord. God's promises are irrevocable. At the climax of history, Israel will realize its role in obedience and that role will be realized under the rule of the Davidic heir. Thus, the very creation goal for man's ruling will be fulfilled in the fallen world through the spiritual ministry of Israel under her Messiah's rule. And Satan, in his historic challenge of God, will be decisively bound and eventually defeated and cast into the lake of fire (Rev 20:1-10).

Doctrine of the Church

Introduction

Ephesians provided Paul's most extensive revelation concerning the Church (Ephesians 2:11–3:7). What is remarkable is the historical context of the writing of Ephesians. This is a prison epistle, written from Rome. It was now some time after Paul had faced a Jewish mob at the temple in Jerusalem (Acts 21:37–22:23). At issue was the climax of his message and his report that Jesus Christ sent him far from Jerusalem to the Gentiles (Acts 22:21). The mob's response, "Away with such a fellow from the earth! For he should not be allowed to live" (Acts 22:22).

Now Paul is arguing that God created one new man, combining Jews and Gentiles in the Church (Eph 2:15). This message is like rubbing salt into a gaping wound in the heart of the Jewish world. And Paul calls this ministry God's "dispensation of the grace of God" (Eph 3:2, NKJV). The point of this section is to summarize Paul's teaching about the Church. We will begin considering the definition of the term, *ekklēsia*, Church. Then we will follow Paul's discussion of the formation of the one new man (Eph 2:11-22) and the exposition of the mystery of Christ (Eph 3:1-7).

The Definition of the Term: *Church*

The basic sense of the term is a *gathering* of people. There are four contexts in which there are different gatherings.

- People *meeting* to exercise political privileges (Acts 19:39, 41)

- Israel *assembled* to receive God's law through Moses (Acts 7:38)

- All individual believers are *assembled* through the Holy Spirit as the Body of Christ (Eph 1:22-23). This Body is what is called the universal Church, including all justified believers in the age of grace. They are assembled, not geographically, but by a real spiritual union to Christ.

- There are also local gatherings, *assembling* in a house, or in several houses in a city. These are local churches (Rom 16:15; 1 Cor 16:19; Col 4:5; Phil 1:2).

Charles Ryrie has considered the doctrine of the Church in a way that highlights these issues in the progress of revelation.[9] Among Dispensationalists, the distinction between Israel and the Church has been debated. In an effort to recognize greater perceived continuity in the progress of revelation, the attribution that the Church is a mystery has been debated. Therefore, that discussion will be considered under the "new man" (Eph 2:11-22) and "the mystery" will be defined (Eph 3:6).

The Church Is a Mystery

Ephesians 2:19, 21-22, and 3:6 include terms prefixed by *sun* (with) which express the unity between Jews and Gentiles in the Church. The question being discussed is how much they share in common? Do they share all that was promised to Israel so that the Church replaces Israel? Do they share eschatological promises and covenants so that there is an already fulfillment in the Church? Or does the not yet expectation include the re-emergence of the nation Israel? Is the Church an actual mystery *in toto*, in which there is shared soteriological fulfillment through Christ but no ecclesiological fulfillment from the Old Testament? If that is the case, then the fulfillment of the national covenants of promise are realized with Israel, and the Church is not a covenant community. Rather, the Church was only revealed when Jesus Christ promised to build the

---

[9]   Ryrie, *Biblical Theology of the NT,* pp. 393-427. Ryrie's outline and considerations will be examined.

Church (Matt 16:18-19). Yet, covenant blessings are received "in Christ" (Gal 3:15-18, 26-29; Heb 9:16-17).

All the options include some promises that are already fulfilled at the First Advent of Christ, and some that are not yet fulfilled. These options indicate that the two advents of Christ demand a more nuanced application of the already and not-yet dimensions of fulfillment than is present in most discussions. So each image in Ephesians 2–3 will be examined.

Creating of the New Man (Ephesians 2:11-22)

The position of the Gentiles based on God's revelation in the OT was distinct. The Jews called them derogatorily, "uncircumcision," as David had called Goliath (1 Sam 17:26). They were outside the citizenship of Israel and strangers to the covenants of promise. Gentiles were without God and hopeless (Eph 2:11-12). Now Gentile believers have been brought near in their relationship with Christ. That remarkable change introduces the subject. But what does that have to do with Jewish and Gentile believers?

Jesus is the basis of peace between them, because He broke down the middle wall of separation (Eph 2:14). Later, rabbis saw the Law as a fence which protected Israel from pagan practices. "This often led to a hostility of Jews toward Gentiles and was a cause of Gentile hatred of the Jews."[10] He became peace because He took the curse of the Law on the cross and law became "inoperative for believers,"[11] since the curse of death was nullified in His resurrection from the dead. It is not that Gentiles became Jews, as Gentile proselytes, nor that Jews became Gentiles. Thus, the new man refers "to a whole new race that is formed."[12] A new race in which ethnicity is not an issue. It is not that the Law ceases to exist. The new man is under the law of Christ (1 Cor 9:21; Gal 6:2). Together, Jews and Gentiles are reconciled to God (Eph 2:16) and both have access in one Spirit to the Father (Eph 2:18). This description of reconciliation is compatible with Luke's description of Spirit baptism into one Body of Christ (Acts 1:5, 7; 2:32-33; 11:15-16).

---

[10] Harold W. Hoehner, *Ephesians* (Grand Rapids, MI: Baker Academic, 2002), p. 373.

[11] *Ibid.*, p. 375.

[12] *Ibid.*, p. 379.

Paul concludes by showing that Christ has reversed the distinct condition of the Gentiles (Eph 2:19-22):

> So then you are no longer strangers and aliens, but you are fellow citizens with the saints and members of the household of God, built on the foundation of the apostles and prophets, Christ Jesus himself being the cornerstone, in whom the whole structure, being joined together, grows into a holy temple in the Lord. In him you also are being built together into a dwelling place for God by the Spirit.

Mystery of Christ (Ephesians 3:1-7)

This new revelation of the new man is then described as a *mystery*, which Paul was responsible for making known. While there is a debate among Dispensationalists about the sense of mystery,[13] we will follow the sense that Hoehner concluded:

- A mystery hidden in God (Eph 3:9)

- Cannot be unraveled or understood by human ingenuity or study

- A revealed secret to be understood by all believers, not just apostles

---

[13]   Robert L. Saucy, "The Church as the Mystery of God," *Dispensationalism, Israel and the Church*, p. 138. Saucy, in an irenic spirit, contends with the use of the term *mustērion*. Admirably he attempts to deal with all the passages using the term. He quotes Kim favorably, that there is one broad mystery, which is Christ, but fails to show how this relates to passages that do refer to Christ and how the broad mystery explains all the particular mysteries (i.e., Eph 3:6). He concludes that mystery relates primarily to the actualization or realization through Christ of that which the prophets foretold and longingly anticipated (Saucy, *Progressive Dispensationalism*, p. 150).

He describes that anticipation in relation to the church, not only as the promised Spirit of the New Covenant that would be poured out on His people (Isa 44:3; Ezek 36:27; Joel 2:29), but he would live with them. Since the primary statement of the New Covenant (Jer 31:31-34) does not mention the Spirit, he argues for His presence as follows:

The promise of Spirit indwelling is found in Ezek 36:27 (cf. 37:14), with the effect of obedience to the law (36:27). That same indwelling is what is meant by Jeremiah's statement of putting the law upon the heart (31:33). The indwelling Spirit is related to the indwelling Christ in the Gospel of John (14:16, 18, 20). The indwelling Christ is stated in the New Testament (Rom 8:9; Acts 16:7) and gives the functional identity, "the Lord is the Spirit" (2 Cor 3:17).

In summary, "the promises concerning the salvation of the Gentiles along with Israel, a certain solidarity between the promises concerning the Messiah and his people, and, perhaps most important, the prediction of the indwelling Spirit of God, make it difficult to deny some connection between this Old Testament hope and the mystery of the union of Gentiles and Israel in Christ found in Ephesians 3" (Saucy, *The Case for Progressive Dispensationalism*, p. 149) not evident in the Old Testament. Yet, Jerusalem still has dominance (Isa 2:1-4) and Gentiles never become equal citizens of the nation Israel (Ezekiel 37).

"Despite the unrevealed time of this age," he posits the mystery in the Church has occurred when Israel as a people have been set aside.

- The Church is a steward of the mystery of Christ to the intent that now the wisdom of God might be made known (Eph 3:10)[14]

So, Paul was a steward of God's administration of grace, what is now known and freely given based on the finished work of Christ. This divine administration follows upon Israel's stewardship of the Law which held them responsible before God, so that they would be useful for realizing God's promise.

Gospel

The identity of the Church in the New Testament is based on the promise made by Jesus Christ and the work He accomplished in His death, burial, resurrection, and ascension. The Epistles interpret the significance of the Lord's promise to build the Church, and of the work for believers on earth during Christ's heavenly session. Though there is continuity with promises about the First Advent ministry of the Promised One in the Old Testament, the *new man* left on earth was not anticipated. It was *new* and a *mystery* in that it was not revealed in the Old Testament. In that sense, there is discontinuity. But Hoch is correct to say, "The church is no accident or substitute for a failed kingdom program."[15] The Lord's promise indicates that it was always included in God's decreed will, simply not revealed. The account of the formation of the organism according to Jesus' promise is compelling.

Jesus first introduced the Church in His promise to build the Church (Matt 16:18). Following Peter's confession of faith, Jesus acknowledged that the truth of the confession found both in the promises looking forward to Jesus' Person and work expressed in the Old Testament, and the corresponding ministry of Jesus would be the foundation of the Church. In other words, the foundation of the Church would rest on the Person and work of Jesus. It would take the shape of His life. The apostles' interpretation of Jesus' work of building took the shape of that foundation (Eph 2:20). Christ Himself was the cornerstone.

The shape of the Church, which reflected Jesus' work on the cross, includes the work of *reconciliation*. There was reconciliation needed between God and believers, and between believers who were Jews and Gentiles (Eph 2:11-22). The believers were now in position to be related

---

[14] Hoehner, *Ephesians*, pp. 428-34.

[15] Carl B. Hoch, Jr. "The New Man of Ephesians 2," *Dispensationalism, Israel and the Church*, ed. Blaising and Bock (Grand Rapids, MI: Zondervan, 1992), p. 126.

to each other as equals, in spite of their ethnic, religious, and cultural past. Jesus' resurrection and ascension were necessary to position Him in the heavenlies. In heaven, He will take the place as Head of the organism and as Heir, who will share His inheritance (Eph 1:20-22). He is in the position of High Priest on behalf of the organism.

The organism not only had a foundation in Christ's work, but was enlivened by His resurrection life. Jesus would submerge the believer in a living and personal river—the Holy Spirit. What would the Spirit do to those immersed in Him? Paul doesn't regard the Spirit only as the river or medium, but also as the agent (1 Cor 12:13). The HCSB and the NKJV translate it, "by one Spirit." So the translation suggests that the Person in whom we are immersed is also the Personal agent in forming the organism or the Body.

In addition, "all were made to drink of one Spirit" (1 Cor 12:13). The image may be intended to combine both the uniting of all into one medium, the Body of Christ, and the indwelling of each one with the same Holy Spirit. This would naturally combine the Spirit-baptism with the ministry of Spirit-filling emphasized on the day of Pentecost (Acts 2:4).

Paul summarizes the formation of the organism in Col 1:18: "he is the head of the body, the church. He is the beginning, the firstborn from the dead, that in everything he might be preeminent." It may be suggested that as Christ existed from the beginning of the Church, the first born in resurrection, now believers have been added to His Body as it grows in the world and in history, believer by believer.

F. F. Bruce summarizes the relationship between the water and the Spirit baptism:

> Faith-union with Christ brought his people into membership of the Spirit-baptized community, procuring for them the benefits of the once-for-all outpouring of the Spirit at the dawn of the new age, while baptism in water was retained as the outward and visible sign of their incorporation 'into Christ' (cf. Gal. 3:27). And as it was in *one Spirit* that they *were all baptized*, therefore it was *into one body* that they *were all baptized*.[16]

The doctrine of Spirit baptism is not complete unless the term *baptism* is considered as used in Rom 6:1-13. The difficulty with the use in this passage is that baptism isn't specified as Spirit baptism. Yet, the effect involving spiritual change in the lives of believers can only be the result of the Holy Spirit. Dunn further relates baptism into death as an allusion

---

[16]   F. F. Bruce, *I and II Corinthians*, p. 121, emphasis in original.

to Jesus Christ's baptism with fire (Luke 12:50).[17] As Jesus accepted such a baptism in His death, so believers are baptized into judgment in sharing His death in Spirit baptism. The believer then may experience the resurrection life of Christ, which results in a new history incorporating the experiences of Jesus' history. This reality in the lives of believers completes the image of baptism. Baptism by the Spirit is not simply immersion into the Body of Christ, although such immersion forms the Church. It is also immersion into Christ's life, sharing the death and resurrection life of Christ that we might walk in newness of life (Rom 6:4). This new organism has the potential of experiencing Christ's life on earth.

The image of the spiritual organism, the Church, is not revealed, even in a disguised or limited fashion, in the Old Testament. And a living organism is distinct from a functioning covenant nation. Yet there are problem passages which need to be considered.

Glenny proposes that the use of Old Testament images in 1 Pet 2:9-10 indicate continuity in Israel's experience as a people of God and in the Church's experience as the people of God. He concludes that "the historical meaning of the New Testament fulfillment language...is the error of those who see this context as a mere analogy between Israel and the church."[18]

Yet, an examination of the context fails to see the Church in any sense as a fulfillment of the nation Israel. As Israel had an actual house, the temple, the Church as living stones are built into a spiritual house (1 Pet 2:4-5). In the immediate context (1 Pet 2:7-8), Christ's death as a spiritual sacrifice *fulfills* the role of a rejected but living stone in Zion that will be the foundation of what God intends to build (Isa 28:6). Then believers and unbelievers are contrasted. Believers are honored. On the other hand, unbelievers joined in the leader's rejection (Ps 118:22), and the stone became something they stumbled over (Isa 8:14). Believers are then described in language that originally described Israel (1 Pet 2:8). His point is not to identify them as a fulfillment of what Israel failed to accomplish, but to simply say that believers in Christ share the role on earth today, by analogy. Though Israel was not a nation at the time Peter wrote, now the believers in the church to whom he wrote, are God's people (1 Pet 2:10) built on the cornerstone laid in Zion (1 Pet 2:7). But, clearly they are *not* a nation centered in Zion as they are sojourners and

[17] Dunn, *The Christ and the Spirit*, vol. 2, pp. 108-115.

[18] W. Edward Glenny, "The Israelite Imagery of 1 Peter 1," *Dispensationalism, Israel and the Church*, p. 187.

exiles (1 Pet 2:11) outside of Jerusalem. In their sojourn, they share the role as the people of God who mediate blessings to others.

Hebrews 12:22-23 tells us that believers will occupy the New Jerusalem in the future with believing Old Testament saints. Believers have come to Mt. Zion where Christ was crucified, and by their faith, they come to the heavenly city—the New Jerusalem where God dwells and which He prepared for His own from every age.[19] The nation Israel, as descendants of Jacob, will fulfill on earth their role as mediators of spiritual blessings to all nations as the prophets foretold. Those who lived on earth, whether earlier believing descendants of Jacob or current members of the Church of Christ, the firstborn, have a heavenly place prepared. On earth, they never fulfilled God's plan at historically distinct times. That heavenly dwelling is not the Church. Rather, the New Jerusalem is the heavenly residence of God's Bride: past generations of Israel who will be resurrected to form the Bride of Yahweh and generations of the Church who will be resurrected to form the Bride of Christ.

In closing his letter to the Galatians, Paul uses the phrase, "the Israel of God" (6:16). What counts for believers is walking as a new creation of God (Gal 6:15). Neither circumcision nor uncircumcision is relevant to our walk in this world before God. Peace and mercy are upon those who so walk "and upon the Israel of God" (Gal 6:16). A compelling case has been made that this is simply a special reference to Jewish believers who so walk in the Church.[20] Such a distinguishing of a portion of the believers in the Church was appropriate when circumcision was the issue which was so important to Jewish believers.

Conclusion

Hoehner summarizes the focal issue in Dispensationalism: "Care must be taken not to make Gentile believers a part of Israel. There is a delicate balance between what applies specifically to the nation Israel and what applies to the church."[21] The central theological concern retains the identity of Israel throughout Biblical history. God made promises to ethnic Israel which are to be fulfilled, since God's word, reflecting His character,

---

[19] Kent, *Hebrews*, p. 272.

[20] S. Lewis Johnson, "Paul and 'The Israel of God': An Exegetical and Eschatological Case-Study," *Essays in Honor of J. Dwight Pentecost*, ed. Stanley D. Toussaint, Charles H. Dyer (Chicago: Moody, 1986), pp. 183-94.

[21] Hoener, *Ephesians*, p. 447.

is true. Even though not all Israel is Israel (Rom 9:6) during the dispensation of grace, "all Israel will be saved" (Rom 11:26).

But the hermeneutical concern is not merely application. Numerous OT passages about Abraham and Israel are applied to church age believers (Rom 4:1-4; 9:24-26; 1 Cor 10:1-13; Jas 2:21-24; 1 Pet 2:9-10, etc.). Exposition of OT narratives recognize analogies between God dealing with the stewardship of Israel and God dealing with the stewardship of the Church. In fact, Paul suggests that OT narratives are written for the Church, who lives after Jesus Christ introduced the end of history: "Now these things happened to them as an example, but they were written down for our instruction, on whom the end of the ages has come" (1 Cor 10:11).

Rather, the hermeneutical concern is claiming fulfillment. Passages that address Israel in which God is committing Himself to act in the future are only fulfilled in and with Israel. Thus, Hoch goes too far when he concludes, "the creation of the church from a believing remnant from Israel, who shared the good news of their Messiah could now *share with* this remnant in their covenants and promise."[22]

Clearly the Mosaic Covenant, the Law, has been made "inoperative for believers"[23] (Eph 2:14-15). And it was stated that the Gentiles were "strangers to the covenants of promise" (Eph 2:12). The Abrahamic, Davidic, and New Covenants are promissory covenants. The Abrahamic and Davidic are addressed to the Heir of Abraham and David. And thus, they are fulfilled with Jesus Christ, the Heir. Only the New Covenant is addressed to the house of Israel and the house of Judah (Jer 31:31). Thus, Hoehner also goes too far when he interprets, "Gentiles are fellow...partakers of the promise in Christ..." (Eph 3:6) as, "it probably alludes to the covenants [plural] of promise from which the Gentiles were excluded before the New Testament."[24] The Church is not heir and partner to the New Covenant promises in fulfillment of the covenant in the same sense; as we contended in Heb 9:15-17 (pp. 411-413). Rather, they are benefactors of the blessings as a last will and testament at Christ's death on the cross.

On the other hand, Gentiles are partakers in the Abrahamic Covenant blessing of the Holy Spirit in union with Christ (Gal 3:27-29). This union is because individuals in the Church are "baptized into Christ"

---

[22]   Hoch, "The New Man," p. 120.

[23]   Hoener, *Ephesians*, p. 375.

[24]   *Ibid.*, p. 447.

(Gal 3:27). Christ is Heir to the fulfillment, and the Church, in union with Christ, shares in His fulfillment according to His will. Thus, Christ chose to pour out the promise of the Father on the day of Pentecost (Acts 1:4-5; 2:33). On the other hand, Christ will share the inheritance of the land with Israel alone according to the ratification of the Abrahamic Covenant (Gen 15:17-21). That share will come when all Israel is saved (Rom 11:26).

In a similar argument, the Church will reign with the Heir of the Davidic Covenant as the Bride of Christ (Rom 5:17-21).

CHAPTER 26:
DOCTRINE OF SCRIPTURE

Introduction

This examination of the doctrine will be focused on New Testament authors' *exegesis* of Old Testament passages. As such, it seeks to *focus* on this view of the *progress* of revelation. To begin with, this examination assumes an evangelical teaching about Scripture:

> Holy Scripture, being God's own Word, written by men prepared and superintended by His Spirit, is of infallible divine authority in all matters upon which it touches…Being wholly and verbally God-given, Scripture is without error or fault in all its teaching…[1]

Two considerations fall under our study. First, revelation is *progressive*. "Progressive revelation is the recognition that God's message to man was not given in one single act, but was unfolded in a series of successive acts and through the minds and hands of many men of varying backgrounds."[2] The progress appears in two basic forms: *additional* new revelation and *exegesis* of an earlier revelation.

Our second consideration concerns *exegesis*. An earlier revelation can be cited or alluded to. In the exegesis of that citation or allusion, does the exegesis involve a *deepening* of our *understanding* or a *transformation* of the original *meaning*? The original meaning is that meaning expressed in a text in the original and immediate context.

When a New Testament author speaks of *Scripture* he may refer to either *book level* or *idea level*. Paul refers to "all Scripture" and probably

---

[1] Chicago Statement on Biblical Inerrancy, 1978.

[2] Ryrie, *Dispensationalism*, p. 31.

had in mind the 39 books of the Hebrew canon (2 Tim 3:16). Jesus summarized the Hebrew canon as "the Law of Moses and the Prophets and the Psalms" (Luke 24:44). Peter spoke of Scripture as a type of writing which included Paul's letters (2 Pet 3:15-16).

Each book consisted of numerous ideas. When we speak of *intertextuality*, we are talking about using texts at the *idea level*. Biblical authors either cite a passage expressing an idea or allude to an idea previously expressed. It is at this level that *progress* is recognized. It is intertextual exegesis that will be our focus of consideration. Two contentions will be considered:

1. Meaning is stable.

2. Meaning is transformed.

Original Meaning Is Stable

While meaning is determinate as expressed in the immediate context, progress is seen as exegesis *deepens* our understanding of the revelation of an original stable meaning. Progress can also be seen as new revelation is *added*. This is what this model of Dispensational Biblical theology contends. Two examples will be considered.

Normative Revelation in the Setting (Genesis 1–11)

Creation

In Paul's Areopagus address, Paul alluded to the fact of creation (Acts 17:24). That fact provides an entirely different perspective from which to see the world than the Athenian culture. The world seen as a creation provides evidence of the Creator and natural revelation about the Creator. He is all-powerful and divine in being (Rom 1:20).

Man's Fall into Sin (Romans 5:12-21)

> [Paul] begins with the narrative. Sin entered the world through the first man, who disobeyed the commandment given him by God. He did this...in rebellion against his Maker, for the

serpent had cast doubt upon God's truthfulness and goodness...Adam endeavored to set himself in the place of God.[3]

Paul's exegesis of Gen 3:1-6 simply unfolds the implications in the
stable and complete textual meaning. There is no progress in revelation.

Adam, a Type of the Man to Come (Romans 5:14)

In this final implication, Paul's exegesis deepens our understanding of
the revealed meaning of Adam's fall. In view of God's purpose in the
creation of man (Gen 1:26-28), what Adam lost *necessarily* demanded
a man to come. It is *necessary* because God's purpose in the words of
creation establishes such an order in mediatorial rule. If this first Adam
lost his life and position, then a last Adam will be needed to accomplish
God's purpose of life and position to rule. "τύπος denotes a mark made
by striking...such an impression used in its turn as a mould to shape
something else...and—a specialized use in biblical interpretation—a
type in the sense of a person or thing prefiguring (according to God's
design) a person or thing pertaining to the time of eschatological *fulfillment*."[4] "Adam is a figure of Christ in just this respect: that as his one sin
brought death to all, even when there was no personal sin, so Christ's one
act of obedience brings unfailing righteousness to those who are in him."[5]
Whereas the exegesis leads to a deepened understanding of the revelation,
it isn't a changed or added revelation.

Promise of the Future Heir (Romans 4:13)

"Nowhere in the OT is the promise to Abraham couched in terms
at all close to τὸ κληρονόμον αὐτὸν εἶναι κόσμου"[6] Then what is Paul
doing? Following Adam's fall in sin, he lost his role as ruler under God.
Now Adam was ruled by the serpent's lie (Gen 3:4). Thus, the serpent had
usurped the role of Adam and laid claim to be heir of the world.

But God pronounced judgment against the serpent, and eventually the
serpent would be struck with a death blow by the Seed of the woman
(Gen 3:15). Paul exegetes this implication that, in God's declaration,
the seed of the woman would become the heir of the world. Then Paul

---

[3] C. K. Barrett, *The Epistle to the Romans* (New York: Harper and Row, 1957), p. 111.

[4] C. E. B. Cranfield, *The Epistle to Romans*, vol. 1 (Edinburgh, UK: T and T Clark, 1975), p. 283.

[5] James M. Stifler, *The Epistle to the Romans* (Chicago: Moody, 1960), p. 97.

[6] Cranfield, *Romans*, vol. 1, p. 239.

understands Abram in the position of the seed of the woman in his generation. While Abram received added revelation (Gen 12:1-3, 7), this doesn't change what had already been assured of the seed of the woman.

Progressive Revelation—Added Revelation in the Plot Conflict

Dispensation of Promise (Genesis 12–Exodus 18)

Justification by Faith (Romans 4:1-5)

Paul calls the basic promise he cites "the gospel" (Gal 3:8). This promise is repeated to the patriarchs (Gen 12:3; 18:18; 22:18; 26:4; 28:14). In Romans, Paul exegeted Abraham's response.

> Paul, after admitting that, if Abraham was justified on the ground of his works, he certainly would have a right to glory, goes on to argue that, *rightly understood*, the *basic biblical text* for the righteousness of Abraham (Gen 15.6) itself implies that he was justified apart from works.[7]

Thus, Paul's exegesis involves unfolding a stable meaning such that it could be clearly understood in the historical context of Judaism. There is no need to transform the meaning in the account in Genesis, but to challenge the understanding in Judaism by the teaching of Scripture. There is no added revelation but an exegesis that was clarified as the generic gospel was unfolded in the completed revelation of the gospel.

Abraham, Father of Faith (Romans 4:16-17)

When Paul subsequently quotes Gen 17:5, there is a question of transformed meaning. "This verse [Rom 4:16] concludes and so repeats the proposition under debate, adding some amplifying details."[8] That proposition is that the promise is to be made good by means of a faith righteousness. Faith is the central concept in the chapter (Rom 4:3, 5, 9, 11-13, 16-20, 24). Faith, as demonstrated in Abraham, is the means to receive what God has promised.

So when Paul cites Gen 17:5 (Rom 4:17), in which circumcision is introduced as a sign of the existence of the covenant, the *kathōs* introduces comparison rather than fulfillment. As the physical sign of circumcision

---

[7]   *Ibid.*, p. 224, (emphasis mine).

[8]   Stifler, *Romans*, p. 80.

marks many in the nation as descendants of Abraham, so faith marks Abraham's descendants who share spiritual life.[9]

Dispensation of Law (Exodus 19–John)

Paul specifies that law was *added* alongside promise. "Why then was the law given? It was added because of transgressions until the Seed to whom the promise was made [Gen 3:15; 22:18] would come" (Gal 3:19, HCSB). Then Paul asks whether law replaced promise:

> Is the law therefore contrary to God's promises? Absolutely not! For if a law had been given that was able to give life, then righteousness would certainly be by the law. But the Scripture has imprisoned everything under sin's power, so that the promise by faith in Jesus Christ might be given to those who believe. (Gal 3:21-22, HCSB)

Thus, in the progress of revelation, the Law was simply *added* alongside of what God had already revealed in promise. The dispensation of law was then the presence of both promise and law as entrusted to Israel as revelation progressed. The Law included an obligatory type of revelation, focusing on Israel's responsibility. Promise focuses on the commitment of the One who gave the promise. Thus, these are two different types of revelation. What the Law added was not an additional condition to receive what was promised. Rather, to receive what was promised demanded faith. Obedience to the Law positioned Israel to be used to accomplish God's plan (Exod 19:5-6).

Dispensation of Grace in Gospel Revelation

We have demonstrated, selectively, that the meaning of canonical revelation is *stable*. On the other hand, it has been charged that Dispensationalism teaches multiple ways of salvation.[10] Could this amount to a transformed *gospel*? One or more versions of the gospel were expressed in the Old Testament, and a transformed and final version was expressed in the New Testament. Is this the case in the progress of the revelation of the gospel?

---

[9] *Ibid.*, p. 81.

[10] Ryrie, *Dispensationalism Today*, pp. 110-31.

Paul offers an answer to that question in his reference to a promise given to Abraham "…preached the *gospel* beforehand to Abraham saying, 'In you shall all the nations be blessed'" (Gal 3:8, emphasis added).

This token of the text also appeared in Gen 12:3; 18:18; 22:18; 26:4; 28:14. The gospel was true as it was first expressed. There were three components which define gospel:

- *God*, who promises an agent;

- *An offspring* who would be heir, *through* whom blessings would be mediated to all nations and the inheritance would be received;

- *Blessings*, which will be received from God by faith.

While this statement is true and complete in a generic sense of the gospel, the *agent* needs to be born in history, and the *blessings* need to be revealed more completely. Who would God choose to fulfill the promise of blessings? *Blessings* are also revealed in particular in Abram's experience. Abram was promised to be shown the land (Gen 12:1), yet when he arrived in the land he was promised that the land would be given to his seed (Gen 12:7).

Most importantly, Abram, having received the promise of personal blessing (Gen 12:1d-2), was blessed with justification before God when he believed the gospel (Gen 12:3b; 15:6). Abram's faith was developing. While he believed in God from the outset (Gen 12:4), the content of his faith needed to include the promised agent. After God promised reward, Abram's inadequate belief was exposed. He believed the promise of reward was pointless because Eliezer of Damascus would be his heir. Even though God had promised a descendant, some twenty-five years had passed without the promise being kept. He was losing confidence. But God assured him that he would have a son in spite of the years of childlessness. Abram believed God and the promise of an heir. God's response was to declare him to be righteous in His sight (Gen 15:6).

Now he was in a position to mediate blessing to others. God used him to bless Lot (Genesis 13; 18). But the most fascinating example was his own son, Isaac (Genesis 22). The blessing was occasioned by a test of Abraham's affection. Which was greater, his love for God or his love for his only son, Isaac? Was Abraham willing to love and to serve God at the cost of sacrificing his son?

He left immediately in obedience. He and Isaac, joined by servants, traveled to the mountain of God's direction. Upon sight of the mountain, he told the servants to wait, as he and his son went to worship, assuring them that he and his son would return. On the way, Isaac asked his father, "Behold, the fire and the wood, but where is the lamb for a burnt offering?" Abraham's answer, "God will provide" (Gen 22:7), reflected a growing confidence in God. While it was true, it was not what God had told him. God's *agent* and *steward* was growing in faith.

Nevertheless, it was not as Abraham had expected. Nothing happened as he might have expected. So he built an altar and laid out the wood. Then he placed Isaac on the altar or Isaac got on the altar as Abraham explained verbatim what God had said. Isaac had to share Abraham's faith to get on the altar. As Abraham raised the knife to plunge it through Isaac, God spoke. Abraham's action proved whom he loved most. And in His love, God provided a ram—the agent Abraham could not provide himself. Abraham loved God supremely, and the ram died to bless Isaac, who had been under a death sentence, with life. This was God's agent.

From a New Testament perspective, the agent in completed revelation was Jesus Christ, who both loves God supremely and is the sacrifice Himself. So when He is raised from the grave, He lives with eternal life (Ps 2:7). And the gospel, which was complete in its statement to Abraham (Gen 12:3), was completed in its revelation, filled in its detail, and in the final expression in Jesus Christ.

The gospel in the age of grace has the same *self-identity* by *definition*:

- God's promise is to be received.
- Jesus Christ is the agent, as the descendant of Abraham, as the sacrificial lamb.
- The initial blessing is justification of life received by faith.

The age is the dispensation of grace since Jesus Christ has accomplished what was promised at the First Advent. It is God's message of the completed sacrificial work of Christ that is now entrusted to believers, to invest in their own lives, and to communicate to the lives of others.

Original Meaning Is Transformed or Resignified

Bruce Waltke articulated clearly this perspective as a necessary component of progressive revelation. Not only does progressive revelation involve revelation *added*, which brings about *deepened* understanding, but the meaning of earlier passages is transformed when they are exegeted. "[L]ater writers interpret earlier writings to meet new historical situations and so advance our understanding."[11] Waltke also notes, "Instances of intertextuality that involve an inner-biblical exegesis, wherein later texts *transform* earlier ones by *deepening, expanding,* or *revising* them, best serve the task of biblical theology."[12]

This contention that exegeted meanings may be transformed has been called *sensus plenior* (*fuller sense*). An exegesis of an earlier text unfolds a *fuller sense* than was originally expressed. One who holds to the doctrine of Biblical inerrancy would question that an original text could be exegeted or interpreted in a transformed or even a contradictory sense. To one who understands the ontology of language as expressing meaning in a type/token pattern,[13] the exegesis of the type of meaning originally expressed could be later understood in a *sensus plenus* (full sense).

Waltke advances two examples of Isaiah's exegesis of Genesis 1 and the creation account as a justification for his contention of meaning transformation. To demonstrate a meaning transformation, one must agree with the original sense of the passages under discussion: Gen 1:2 and 1:26. That agreed upon textual sense is then transformed.

First, in Gen 1:2, "the *tōhû wābōhû* ('*formless and empty*') state of darkness that covered the watery abyss is ambiguously represented in Genesis 1:1-3 as already in existence at the time the Creator transformed it into our cosmos."[14] According to Waltke, if darkness is ambiguously represented in Gen 1:1-3, how can Isaiah exegete the passage to conclude that God created darkness? Thus, it is posited that Isaiah's exegesis is revelation of added meaning, not the unfolding of intended meaning. What needs clarification, however, is what Isaiah meant by "create." Is it "bring into existence out of nothing" or "judgment of preexisting former creation"?

Second, of Gen 1:26-28, Waltke states, "My exegesis also leads me to draw the conclusion that the ambiguous 'us/our' in God's statement 'let us make *'ādām* in our image, in our likeness' (1:26) refers to God and his angelic court."[15] This exegetical conclusion is drawn from the ANE description of the heavenly court. Then, in Isaiah's exegesis, Waltke notes, "the prophet emphatically denies that the Creator consulted with

---

[11] Waltke, *An Old Testament Theology*, p. 126.

[12] *Ibid.*, p. 125, emphasis added.

[13] E. D. Hirsch, *Validity in Interpretation*.

[14] Waltke, *An Old Testament Theology*, p. 127.

[15] *Ibid.*

anyone ([Isa] 40:13-14) or that any creature compares to him or is his equal (40:25)."[16]

In order for Waltke's contention of transformed exegetical meaning to be valid, one must begin with the conclusion of the meaning of the pronouns "us/our." The plural pronouns could have reference to the plurality of the Godhead. Only the Persons of the Godhead could share their image which became the prototype for the creation of Adam and Eve. And that is precisely the contention that Isaiah is making. While God could have a heavenly counsel that included angels in other historical decisions (1 Kgs 22:19-23), that need not be the case in creation.

So the contention that intertextual exegesis necessarily involves transformation is not validated by either example.

Bock likewise posits such intertextual transformation of meaning at the salvation history level. His contention deals with the Davidic kingdom. He concludes:

> As a result, one can speak of *inaugurated* eschatology without denying either what the Old Testament indicates about a future, earthly kingdom or what the New Testament asserts about the arrival of the kingdom as part of *fulfillment* in the first coming of Jesus.[17]

The transformation of meaning involves an *expanded* meaning which is claimed to partially fulfill the Old Testament promise of an earthly kingdom. The Davidic Covenant promised such an earthly kingdom (2 Sam 7:12-16). Psalm 2, identified with David, acknowledged that the kingdom would encompass the rulers and nations of the world. A Davidic kingdom would mean, by definition: the Davidic heir, a realm of the Davidic kingdom, and a mediatorial throne rule located in Jerusalem. To claim *fulfillment* of the kingdom promise, all three components must be present, even if only partially.

- The *Davidic Heir* was present in Jesus the Messiah. This component of the covenant was fulfilled, but this alone is not fulfillment of the covenant, nor partial fulfillment of the kingdom.

- The *realm* of the kingdom must include the people of Israel. While the apostles were Jewish, the twelve did not represent that generation of Israel. The twelve tribes of Israel, which had

---

[16] *Ibid.*, p. 128.

[17] Blaising and Bock, *Progressive Dispensationalism*, p. 98, emphasis in original.

accepted David (2 Sam 2:4; 5:3), were the promised realm of the kingdom of David. The addition of Gentiles, who accept Jesus as Messiah, does not represent the nations in fulfillment of the Davidic Covenant (Ps 2:8).

- The *throne* of David would be a *mediatorial reign* of the heavenly rule as Psalm 2 recognized. While Jesus remains in heaven, He shares the Father's *providential throne*. This is distinct from an earthly, mediatorial throne.

Jesus ascending to the providential throne of the Father does represent an expression of His rule. This is reflected in Paul's language in Romans, "those who receive the overflow of grace and the gift of righteousness *reign* in life through the one man, Jesus Christ" (Rom 5:17, HCSB, emphasis added) and "just as sin reigned in death, so also grace will reign through righteousness, resulting in eternal life through Jesus Christ our Lord" (Rom 5:21, HCSB). So Christ is reigning in the age of grace, but it is not the Davidic reign. It is a reign in the righteous life of an obedient believer which Hebrews suggests is in the order of Melchizedek.

Conclusion

The dispensation of grace means that God continues to govern salvation in the history following Christ's finished work. As such, the message of the gospel is complete, but God's *work* of salvation is being carried out throughout the earth and throughout history. Christ's governance entrusts the gospel, which is the power of God unto salvation to everyone who believes (Rom 1:16), to the Church. Those works of salvation include three dimensions:

- An initial work of salvation from the penalty of sins for new believers

- A continued work of salvation from the power of sin, for believers in the Church

- The final work of salvation from the presence of sin at Christ's Second Advent for those He calls His own

The literature involved in the revelation of the dispensation of grace is the historic Book of Acts and the apostolic Epistles. Acts featured two apostles: Peter, who formulated the message of the gospel to the Jewish culture, and Paul, who communicated the gospel to various situations in the Gentile world. The Epistles entrust the gospel to believers in the

Church and thus concern God's work of salvation from the power of sin in the lives of believers. In Romans, Paul writes about what's entrusted as "the commandment of the everlasting God, for obedience to the faith" (Rom 16:26, NKJV). So the gospel is entrusted as God's means of sanctification through obedience in the lives of believers in the Church. Their changed lives provide honor to the Lord and a testimony to their community. In addition, they may have the opportunity to communicate the gospel in that community concerning salvation from the penalty of sin.

That all believers are stewards of the gospel does not mean that all are called to professional ministry. Rather, all are called to focus their lives and their professions on the wisdom and priorities of the gospel. In God's broader providential governance, He has gifted natural abilities to all who share His image as human creatures. This may well determine a believer's profession. But while living in the world of others who share a profession, a believer is different. Believers are not only stewards of their natural gifting, they are also stewards of the gospel. The gospel has been entrusted to bring God's work of salvation into every aspect of their lives in this fallen world, but it is entrusted for God to work through the believer in the world. What believers have to contribute to the world rests in that of which they are stewards, their natural gifts according to the gospel.

Being entrusted with the gospel, the course in life a believer is to follow is determined in prayer, based upon the gospel, as God works the work of salvation. So a believer is entrusted with two aspects of God's governance. These two aspects are not in conflict with one another but are complementary as God guides through the gospel. Providentially, God guides believers to contribute to the natural life of their generations based on their natural gifts. But the priorities of their life, whether in the family, or in the workplace, or in their place of residence, are given through Christ's governance in the gospel. Christ wants to do a work of salvation in the life of each believer but also wants to do works of salvation through believers in the lives of those their lives touch. This is the dispensation of God's governance in grace: to reach all nations with the gospel of Jesus Christ.

SECTION 6: RESOLUTION: DISPENSATION OF THE KINGDOM

Section Introduction

Paul had already anticipated the concluding stewardship of God's purposes in history. He concludes: "He made known to us the mystery of His will, according to His good pleasure that He planned in Him for the *administration* of the days of fulfillment—to bring everything together in the Messiah, both things in heaven and things on earth in Him" (Eph 1:9-10, HCSB, emphasis added). As Hoehner concludes, "When it [fulfillment] is used with reference to time, it has the idea of the state of being full in the sense of completeness or having reached its *goal*."[1] Those days of fulfillment are envisioned in the Revelation of Jesus Christ (Rev 1:1). This will be the focus of this final chapter on the dispensation of the kingdom.

The days of fulfillment feature the mediatorial kingdom of God on earth, which was introduced as the goal of the creation account (Gen 1:26-28). Man's right to rule on earth was lost when Adam accepted the serpent's proposed rebellion of man against God. The serpent now usurped the rule of earth in conflict with God.

God began to reclaim His rule in word over His chosen people when He established the theocracy over Israel in the Law (Exodus 19–24). It was a rule against God which permitted Israel to rebel (Exodus 32–34). That revelation progressed when God anticipated Israel's request for a King (Deut 17:14-20). That form of God's rule would be a monarchic theocracy. God raised up David, the anointed king (2 Sam 7:12-16). A psalm associated with David gave expression to the anticipated conflict between the nations and God's Anointed (Ps 2:1-12) in which ultimately

---

[1] Hoehner, *Ephesians*, p. 218, emphasis in original.

the nations would be given to God's Anointed as His inheritance (Ps 2:8). Ironically, the power of evil is so pervasive that even Israel opposed God's Anointed and became a participant with the nations in the conflict by putting God's Anointed to death (Acts 2:22-23).

It is in this conflict that God decreed the begetting of His Son (Ps 2:7). That decree was established after Jesus became God's *begotten* Son, that is, when He overcame death—at the hands of the nations under the power of the serpent—by the Father's deliverance (Luke 22:42; 23:46). Thus, the Son will be fathered by God when He possesses life in the resurrection, which overcomes death and endures forever. And in His resurrection, the Father ruled over His Son who fully submitted to His Father.

Daniel sees this conflict in history between the nations and Jerusalem. The conflict intensifies when Israel is taken captive into Babylon in 586 BC. The revelation given to Daniel concerns this period, called "the times of the Gentiles" (Luke 21:24), which begins with Babylon and extends to the climax of history when God awards the inheritance of the final rule on earth to the Son of Man (Dan 7:13-14).[2] This perspective on national history found in Daniel serves as the background for the Book of Revelation, in which the days of fulfillment are more completely considered. Thus, in this chapter, Daniel's perspective will precede the consideration of Revelation.

In the resolution of the conflict in earth's history, God's *glory* in the conquest and in His overcoming evil will be displayed. That *glory* will be for the good shared with the Lord's own (Rom 8:28).

Dispensationalism sets the recognition of God's glory as an essential focus of this system of interpretation (*sine qua non*). It is essential, not because this distinguishes this system from other systems, but because it is the highlight of the Biblical theology. As Moses recognized, the manifestation of God's glory is the essence of a believer's life in knowing God face to face, as one speaks with his friend (Exod 33:11, 13-14, 18-23). The Lord's word to His disciples is that He calls them friends if

---

[2] Some interpreters see this judgment as fulfilled in the Roman destruction of Jerusalem in AD 70. This view, known as Preterism, has been adequately addressed and refuted. See Arnold G. Fruchtenbaum, *Israelology: The Missing Link in Systematic Theology* (Tustin, CA: Ariel Ministries Press, 1993); David Larsen, *Jews, Gentiles and the Church: New Perspectives of History and Prophecy* (Grand Rapids, MI: Discovery House, 1995); J. Ramsey Michaels, *Interpreting the Book of Revelation* (Grand Rapids, MI: Baker, 1992); Wilber B. Wallis, "Reflections on the History of Premillennial Thought," *Interpretation and History: Essays in Honour of Allan A. MacRae*, ed. R. Laird Harris, Swee-Hwa Quch, and J. Robt. Vannoy (Singapore: Christian Life, 1986), pp. 225-51.

they do what He has commanded (John 15:14-15). And the essence of the portrayal of glory in a Dispensational system features His word progressively unfolded. As God speaks in history, His people as stewards come to know God through His Word.

CHAPTER 27:
DANIEL AND REVELATION

Introduction

The Books of Daniel and Revelation are prophetic apocalyptic genre literature. They are prophetic, which distinguishes them from cultural apocalyptic literature from the second temple period. They are apocalyptic in that they address the historical conflict (Daniel 1; 3–6; Revelation 2–3). That conflict finds the ultimate resolution in the climax of history (Daniel 2:34-35, 43-45; 7:13-14, 23-28; 8:9-14, 23-27; 9:27; 11:36–12:3; Revelation 4–22).

Daniel

Five visions in Daniel set the stage for the resolution of the conflict between the Gentile nations and Jerusalem. These visions feature different aspects of "the times of the Gentiles" (Luke 21:24).

Three of the visions are unsolicited:

- Daniel 2—Nebuchadnezzar is shown the glory of Gentile kingdoms in history, but a Stone, cut without hands, will crush the kingdoms in the end.

- Daniel 7—Daniel is shown the savagery of the same Gentile kingdoms in history, but God's final judgment awards the Son of Man the inheritance of an unending kingdom.

- Daniel 8—Daniel is shown the savagery of a little horn against Jerusalem, focused on the Sanctuary, but in the end, the Sanctuary will be restored.

Two visions are given in response to a prayer by Daniel:

- Daniel 9—Daniel is given God's ultimate purposes for Jerusalem (v 24) which will be worked out in the decreed seventy sevens of years (vv 25-27). Rome will cut off Messiah and destroy Jerusalem and will be featured in Jerusalem's final seven years of suffering.

- Daniel 10:1–12:3—Daniel's final vision details periods of Jerusalem's suffering which anticipate an end time king from the north who will occupy Jerusalem until God restores many people in the final kingdom.

Daniel 2, 7, and 9: Roman Influence at the Climax

Daniel 2 provides an overview of Gentile history using a majestic human-like statue composed of various metals to symbolize kingdoms or empires. The last part of the statue to be described are legs and feet of iron and an iron/clay mixture representing the Roman empire, the most powerful but least glamorous of the empires. In the end, this empire will have the strength of iron mixed with the brittleness of clay. In this fragile form, it will be no match for the crushing stone that will deliver heaven's final blow, the Second Advent. In this judgment, the earthly kingdoms are replaced by God's kingdom. According to Dan 2:35, "the iron, the clay, the bronze, the silver, and the gold, all together were broken in pieces, and became like the chaff of the summer threshing floors; and the wind carried them away, so that not a trace of them could be found."

In Daniel 7, the kingdoms/empires introduced in Daniel 2 re-emerge as various beasts. The final scene of the vision focuses on the Ancient of Days convened in a heavenly court. Appearing before the Ancient of Days is one like a Son of Man who is given everlasting authority to reign over every people, nation, and language (v 14). In the battle that ensued, the eleventh Roman horn was so obnoxious that it was cast into the burning fire (7:24-25). Preceding this judgment, the dominion was taken away to be "given to the people of the saints of the Most High" (7:26-27).

In Daniel 9, in response to Daniel's extended confession of Israel's sin (vv 4-19), the angel Gabriel brings Daniel understanding (vv 20-23). The people of Israel and the holy city would serve as the context for God's elimination of sin and commencement of everlasting righteousness (v 24). It was decreed by the Lord, Daniels's God.

But rather than this being realized in Israel's service under law, it will involve Messiah being cut off without inheritance. Generations later, in the final generation, Rome will make a covenant with Jerusalem but then break it, and corrupt the temple sacrifice until the decreed end. Then Messiah's kingdom will appear.

Daniel 8 and 10:1–12:3: Middle Eastern Influence from the North (Possibly Assyria, cf. Isaiah 14:24-27, Micah 5:5-6).

The vision of Daniel 8 supplements the vision of Daniel 7 (8:1, "after that which appeared to me at the first"). It focuses on the temple and the desecration that comes from the King of the North, a small horn. Antiochus Epiphanes, offering an abominable sacrifice, became a *type* of the end-time king who will set up the abomination that desolates (Dan 9:27).[1]

Daniel 10:1–12:3 specifies in great detail the same series of historical and end time events related to the desecration of the temple. However, tracing the same transition from history to the end time as Daniel 8 had, a remarkable change appeared. The historical period involves the King of the North (Seleucids) battling the king of the South (Ptolemies). The period reaches the time of Antiochus Epiphanes (Dan 11:29-35). He is the King of the North (Dan 8:9-14). Then the narrative transitions to the appointed time of the end. A climactic King of the North emerges with such bombast that he even challenges the God of gods (11:36). The description of this king follows with him acting with the power of a foreign god (11:37-39). When the time of the end arrives (11:40), his conquests of other nations are listed (11:41-45). He wars in northern Africa, and in the end, sets up his royal tents in the holy land, between the sea and the beautiful, holy mountain (Dan 11:45). Who is this end time king? Revelation provides an answer to this unknown character.

Revelation

The narrative of the Bible now reaches the climax of the history of this earth. The historic plot-conflict between the enemy and God reaches the final resolution. Prophetic revelation has a focused attention on this period of history known as the Day of the LORD. "Significantly enough, it is the one book of the Bible that begins and ends with a blessing on

---

[1] Stephen Miller has identified eleven similarities between Antiochus IV and the eschatological antichrist (Stephen Miller, *Daniel*, The New American Commentary [Nashville, TN: Broadman & Holman Publishers, 1994], pp. 237-38).

those who read and keep what is written."[2] This final chapter in this Biblical theology features a concluding characterization of the progress of revelation. As J. Scott Duvall asserts, "The book of revelation presents in colorful language and powerful imagery the final chapter in God's story, where he reverses the curse of sin, restores his creation and lives among his people forever."[3]

The Revelation Features Jesus Christ (Revelation 1:1)

Since Revelation features Jesus Christ in the climax of the history of the earth, it is a book of *hope*. The letters to the churches (2–3) are revealed as an example to be kept in faith. But the remainder (4–22) is revealed as a vision of God's completion of His plan. It is a powerful reminder that in spite of the despair that too often characterizes the human experience, and in spite of the power of sin and evil portrayed in the Scriptures, the final outcome is one of victory not defeat. That is because of Jesus Christ. We keep what we read (4–22) as we continue to grow in hope.

The Revelation Made It Known

This future historical climax is signified (*esēmanen*);[4] the visions given to John make it known by symbolic portrayal. But the interpreter is not left to his own imagination to decipher these symbols. Rather, "He made it known by sending his angel to his servant, John" (Rev 1:1). The vision is revealed for John to see and record as he saw it. The angel then explains what many of the symbols mean. For example, the vision of the prostitute riding the beast that caused John to marvel greatly is explained by an angel (Rev 17:1-8). In part, the angel explains, "the seven heads are seven mountains on which the woman is seated; they are also seven kings, five of whom have fallen, one is, the other has not yet come…" (Rev 17:9-10). Without an interpreting angel, this symbol of seven heads, and its two meanings (mountains and kings) would be unknown.

---

[2] H. A. Ironside, *Revelation* (New York: Loizeaux Bros., 1920), p. 7.

[3] C. Marvin Pate et al., *The Story of Israel: A Biblical Theology* (Downers Grove, IL: InterVarsity, 2004), p. 255.

[4] Greg Beale notes the connection between Daniel and Revelation in stating, "just as the vision of Daniel 2 is communicated through symbols (cf. σημαίνω ['signify'] in Daniel 2; John 12:33; 21:19), so in like manner are the contents of John's vision revealed to him" (G. K. Beale, *The Book of Revelation: A Commentary on the Greek Text*, New International Greek Testament Commentary [Grand Rapids, MI: Eerdmans, 1999], p. 182).

Other symbols that are allusions to the Hebrew Scriptures are explained by looking at their Old Testament contexts. For instance, what does the scroll with seven seals mean (Rev 5:1)? Ironside posits that it is a title deed like Jeremiah procured (Jeremiah 32).[5] Jeremiah was commanded to buy a piece of land from Hanamel, his cousin. They had just been told by God that the land would lie captive for seventy years. God commanded Jeremiah to purchase the land because even though its near value would be worthless, the time was coming when it *would* be worth having. The title deeds were made out, sealed, and hidden away. Someday that sealed scroll would be of great value, when restoration would take place.

So the sealed scroll of Revelation 5 was a title deed to the inheritance of earth. Jesus Christ is the rightful Heir because He had provided for redemption in His death for the saints who would rule on this previously forfeited inheritance. Positionally, He had freed them from Satan's domination. Satan had been overcome at the Cross and would be bound, but the inheritance had not yet been claimed. Thus, the terms of the title deed included the right to complete judgment on Satan, that the inheritance would be claimed in the imprisonment of Satan (Rev 20:1-6). The final judgment falls when Satan is given a final opportunity to rebel at the end of the Millennium (Rev 20:7-10).

In the vision, God made *it* known. *It* refers to the actual earth and to actual events through which Jesus Christ would claim His inheritance (Ps 110:1-2). This vision is historically literal and true.

The Revelation Is a Cryptic Summary of What Will Happen

Ironside laments that "it is certainly cause for deep regret that to so many Christians the Book of Revelation seems to be what God never intended it should be—a sealed book."[6] One reason is that it is a cryptic summary. What is meant by cryptic is reflected by several characteristics of the book. First, it is a selective summary of events. In the selection, the relationship between the events is not directly expressed. Second, the selected events are not always arranged chronologically, although there is a general chronological order—beginning, middle, and end. But this can further complicate the recognition of relationships between the particular events. Thus, the interpreter is left with the task of fashioning a sequence of events in chronological order. Further, to clarify what is

---

[5] Ironside, *Revelation*, p. 88.

[6] *Ibid.*, p. 7.

happening, relationships must be inferred from the description of events and clues of relationship mentioned in the text. Such a reconstruction of the narrative-summary will be present in this recognition of the Revelation of Jesus Christ. For instance, what is the relationship between the opening of the seals (6:1-17; 8:1-6), the sounding of the trumpets (8:7–9:21; 11:15-19), and the pouring of the bowls (15:1–16:21)? While they are revealed sequentially, they seem to occur with overlap. This overlap needs to be construed.

The book's broad structure is stated in Rev 1:19 in terms of the revelatory experience of the author, the Apostle John. First was what John had *seen* earlier in the first chapter (chap. 1), second, the things which *are*, as described in the words of the Son of Man addressed to the churches (chaps. 2–3), and finally, the things that *are to take place* after this (chaps. 4–22). The reference to the Son of Man indicates a link to Dan 7:13-14 and to Jesus' common self-references (Matt 8:20; 9:6; 10:23; 11:19; 26:64, et al.). Further, the subject matter in Daniel and in Revelation overlap. Both books talk about the climax, when the kingdoms of the times of the Gentiles become the kingdom of the Son of Man on earth. In addition, both books have a focus on these events in relation to Jerusalem. Daniel had featured 490 years (Dan 9:24-27) in reference to Israel, and seven of those years had yet to be fulfilled at the time John wrote Revelation. The 483 years were concluded at the Cross of Christ. Revelation features that seven year period as indicated by references to forty-two months, or 1260 days, or a "time, times and half a time" (Dan 7:25; 12:7; Rev 12:14). These time notations refer to one-half of that seven year period if we have thirty-day months and twelve-month years. Thus, the seventieth seven in Daniel overlaps with the events that are to take place "after this" (Rev 4:1), in Revelation 4–20.

The Book of Revelation has four sequential patterns with seven components in each. There are seven historic churches (Revelation 2–3) which are addressed in letters from the Son of Man who stands in the middle of seven golden lampstands (Revelation 1). The other three sequential patterns include descriptions of seven judgments: the seven sealed judgments, the seven trumpets announcing judgments from a heavenly point of view, and the seven bowls containing judgments from an earthly point of view (Revelation 6–16). Each sequence reaches its conclusion near or at the return of Jesus Christ (8:5; 11:15; 16:17-19). Each successive sequence of judgments brings greater intensity as it draws closer to the return of Christ. The seals introduce judgments that remove structures provided in Genesis 8:22–11:9 in the life of the worldwide population (Rev 6:1-17;

8:1-5). The trumpets announce judgments, which prepare for Israel's claim to her inheritance, as the seven trumpets of ram's horn had led Israel's conquest of Jericho (Revelation 8:6–9:21; 11:15-19). The bowls hold the final judgments poured out on Gentile rule and kingdom (Rev 16:1-21). They conclude the time of Gentile rule. These three series of judgments reveal the focus of the seven years—divine wrath in judgment against rebellious national life of Israel and Gentile nations.

The experiences of characters active in this historical time period are interspersed within this framework, either in preludes, or in interludes between the sixth and seventh judgments, and/or in postludes after the seventh judgment. This seemingly random pattern contributes to the book's cryptic appearance. However, there are four primary characters involved.

First, *Jesus Christ* is the principle character. He is introduced as a heavenly Warrior, both as the core character involved in the events of end time history, and as the One to whom the revelation was given (Rev 1:1, both a subjective and objective genitive). As Ladd suggests, "Jesus is both 'the object and content of the revelation.'"[7] Jesus then showed it to John, whose written record shows it to other servants. Jesus is both God's answer to the story of human history and the Source from whom God's answer is revealed. "For the testimony of Jesus is the spirit of prophecy" (Rev 19:10).

Second, the *dragon* is introduced as the ancient serpent (Rev 12:3, 9). Immediately, the ancient plot-conflict is brought to the reader's mind. It was initiated in Genesis 3,[8] yet the serpent remained largely in disguise during Israel's history. While the serpent speaks as God's enemy in the questions he raised to Eve, the presence of the enemy is evident in the repeated presence of temptations in the history of Israel. Israel had allowed the pagan nations and their gods to remain in the land. Isaiah had exposed that Leviathan, the dragon, who was the fleeing and twisting serpent, would be slain in that day (Isa 27:1). Isaiah both exposed the sea dragon (referenced in Revelation) as the pagan god and prophesied about his end. Yet, the Bible is silent about such direct conflict until the

---

[7] George Eldon Ladd, *Commentary on the Revelation of John* (Grand Rapids, MI: Eerdmans, 1972), p. 21.

[8] Although commentators tend to focus on the ANE context of "dragon," "The serpent as the arch-deceiver in Gen. 3 certainly provided the primary background" (Grant R. Osborne, *Revelation*, Baker Exegetical Commentary on the New Testament [Grand Rapids, MI: Baker, 2002], p. 459).

climax in history arrives in Jesus' First Advent.[9] So a question emerges from his presence in this seven year period: what is his strategy? Remember, he had been overcome at the Cross and in the resurrection of Jesus Christ. His final desperate actions to somehow avoid defeat and judgment are summarized in Rev 12:1-17. The dragon's strategy is now to oppose Israel so that God's promises would fail. If God is unrighteous in His promises toward Israel, then presumably He would forfeit the right to judge evil and the dragon.

Third, *Israel* is also a primary character. Although Israel is seldom mentioned in the Book of Revelation and has been overlooked by many interpreters, her presence is unmistakable: the 144,000 Jews from every tribe (Revelation 7; 14), the temple of God (chaps. 11; 15), the woman who gave birth to the man-child (chap. 12), the beast from the land, Israel (chap. 13), Mt. Zion (chap. 14), the great city in which the Lord was crucified (chap. 16),[10] the place that in Hebrew is called Armageddon (chap. 16). Thus, it seems inescapable that the geography and the people must include Israel. God's election of Israel marks them as a target of the enemy's attack.

Fourth, the *Gentiles*, like Israel, function as a primary character in Revelation. Gentiles are mentioned in the multitudes "from every nation, from all tribes and peoples and languages" (Rev 7:9; see also 10:11; 13:7). There is also the beast from the sea (chap. 13) with the seven heads and the ten horns. This beast is related historically to the wild animals in Daniel 7 who were Gentiles—the leopard, bear, and lion—and related contemporaneously to mystery Babylon (Revelation 17–18). After the letters to the seven churches in Revelation 2–3, there is no distinctive or clear mention of the Church. They are likely present in heaven as represented by some or all of the twenty-four elders (Rev 4:10; 5:8; 11:16).

These four characters in Revelation are also involved in the plot-conflict that forms the tension of the larger Biblical narrative. This plot began with the account of creation, which rested in man created in God's own image with the intent to mediate God's rule over the earth. That rule was drastically altered when the serpent seduced man to rebel and mankind fell under the judgment of death (Gen 3:1-18). The serpent, although

---

9   The description of demon possession is limited in the Biblical account to the Gospels, continuing until Acts 19:11-20. It was during the First Advent that the devil appeared directly to Jesus in the wilderness. The evil one functioned as a foil to reflect the Son's power. There is no other record of demon possession—none in the Old Testament, the Epistles, or even Revelation.

10 Some interpreters seek to spiritualize these elements and typically understand them as metaphors for the Church. But such an approach does not seem to do justice with the text in its historical allusions.

remaining in the shadows, claimed man's position as ruler over the earth, ruling in the place of God rather than mediating God's rule (Eph 2:2; John 12:31).

The conflict burst into the open during the First Advent of Jesus Christ. While resisting the devil face to face in his temptations (Luke 4:1-11), Jesus nonetheless followed the Father's will and submitted to Satan's power seen in the death of every human (John 13:27; Luke 21:31). In death, the Father raised Jesus out from among the dead ones as the first fruits of the Father's future resurrection harvest. In this resurrection, Satan was overcome, but the death blow was yet to be dealt. The delay in the present age was accompanied by a gracious offer to save the lost who sought deliverance from judgment through Christ.

The conflict remains unresolved during the stewardship of grace. The narrative of the Book of Revelation unfolds the final stage and presents its resolution in association with the Revelation of Jesus Christ. Three dimensions of that revelation will be examined.

Jesus Christ in Revelation

The basis of *hope* rests in Jesus Christ's central place in concluding the revelation. The scope of the book includes a revelation of Jesus Christ following His First Advent in which He is central in the Church (Revelation 1–3),[11] and then moves forward to His Second Advent and what immediately follows, in which He is also central in the defeat of evil (chaps. 4–20).[12] Then there is the creation of the new heavens and the new earth (chaps. 21–22). Jesus was begotten following His resurrection (Ps 2:7; Acts 13:33); He is positioned to be at the heart of the new creation.

First Advent Revelation (Revelation 1–3)

The book opens with a vision of the ascended One, like the Son of Man (Revelation 1). His title alludes to the vision in Daniel ("one like a son of man," Dan 7:13) which also anticipates what will happen before the enthroned Ancient of Days (Revelation 4–5). Jesus frequently used the

---

[11] Jesus is presented as standing among the seven lampstands which are clearly identified as symbols of the Church (1:20). But these seven lampstands are not mentioned in chaps. 4–22.

[12] Indeed, in the defeat of evil, the "armies of heaven" play no discernable role (Rev 19:14). The Lord alone is portrayed as defeating His enemies.

title Son of Man to refer to His right as the human heir to the Father's kingdom (Luke 22:69).

In the vision, His dress and appearance spoke of His role as Priest[13] for the Church and for the believers. And as Hebrews indicates, the priesthood for the Church is after the order of Melchizedek. Mention of Christ's appearance is found in the introductions of six of the seven messages to the churches (Revelation 2–3). "It is apparent that the appearance of Christ in this vision is designed to emphasize the aspects of His nature that are most relevant to the needs and circumstances of the seven churches who are the primary recipients of this book."[14] In a brief summary, He wears a *priestly robe* with a *golden girdle* prepared for high priestly service. As Beale states, "Although the clothing of v 13 could also resemble kingly attire, its use here evokes the image of a priest because of the clear temple atmosphere of the 'lampstands' and the angels coming out of the heavenly temple, who wear the same clothing in 15:5-8."[15] His *white hair* marks Him as ancient and identifies Him with the Ancient of Days. He is both in the middle of the throne and separated from it, both identified with God as Ruler and separated from the throne to implement His will. His eyes reflect penetrating insight that enables Him to reach righteous judgments. His *feet* like burnished bronze had walked in ways that were unyielding in righteousness. What is unholy would be stamped out in judgment. His *voice* speaks with resonating power; it speaks both salvation put forth in grace, and damnation put forth in judgment. The *seven stars* in His right hand speak of the ministry committed to the seven golden lampstands. The *two-edged sword* coming out of His mouth is His Word which cuts to the quick those to whom He speaks. And His *countenance* resembles His appearance on the Mount of Transfiguration.

On earth, the lampstands appeared first before John saw One like a Son of Man in the middle of them. These seven lampstands represented seven historic churches to whom He spoke as Judge, both in commendation and promise, and in recognition and condemnation of sin. Each letter was addressed to a historic church, but also to whoever had ears willing to hear (see Rev 2:7, 11, 17, 29; 3:6, 13, 22). As such, the messages continue to speak throughout the dispensation of grace.

---

[13] Mounce concludes: "The Greek word translated 'a robe reaching down to his feet' (*podērēs*) occurs only here in the NT. It is found seven times in the LXX, and in every case but one it refers to the attire of the high priest." Robert H. Mounce, *The Book of Revelation*, New International Commentary on the New Testament (Grand Rapids, MI: Eerdmans, 1977), p. 58.

[14] Robert L. Thomas, *Revelation 1–7* (Chicago: Moody, 1992), p. 97.

[15] Beale, *Revelation*, p. 209.

Framed within the message that continues to speak are unique histor-ical issues in each church. But each issue is framed in more normative theological language. Some issues which provide evidence of spiritual life, are commended and encouraged to continue. Other issues which involve problems of sin and of the infiltration of evil into the church are con-demned. These need to be identified, repented of, and overcome in the power of the Spirit.

Common to each letter is the promise to the *overcomer*. The believer in the Church that *overcomes* shares in Christ's *overcoming* death in res-urrection. As in Christ's resurrection, the believer overcomes the power of evil through the power of the Holy Spirit. To these are promised rewards found originally in creation and now to be experienced in the climax of history.

Second Advent of Jesus Christ (Revelation 4–19)

Jesus Christ can be both a participant in the visionary revelation and the recipient of the vision. It discloses to the Son what the Father wants Him to do. He alone is worthy, based on His First Advent, to receive and open the scroll which is the title deed to rule the earth.[16] But as the title deed, it would envision the Heir claiming His inheritance. And that claim involves Jesus Christ reaching the resolution in conquest of the plot-conflict with Satan.

So it is the Lamb that opened the first of the seven seals on the scroll (Rev 6:1). From the first sealed judgment, the Lamb rides on a white horse (Rev 6:2). Based on the symbol of the rider on a white horse at the climax of the resolution (Rev 19:11-16), there are remarkable similari-ties that indicate that the Rider ought to be recognized as Jesus Christ (Rev 19:11). Yet, many commentators argue for some other identity of the rider.[17] In addition to the symbol of Jesus Christ as the central figure in resolving the conflict from the beginning of judgment until the climax, the immediate context contributes more to that interpretation. The rider wears the victor's crown (*stephanos*) given to one who has triumphed in battle or athletic competition (Ps 45:4-5). He pursues the battle with a bow which is for distant warfare and which is appropriate for the initial stage of the conflict from the heavenlies. Finally, He "came out conquer-ing and to conquer." So stated in a vision of the near future, this does

---

[16] Although his identification of the scroll is different than what is proposed here, Thomas has a very helpful discussion of the various views (Thomas, *Revelation 1–7*, pp. 376-79).

[17] Thomas also has an excellent summary of these positions. *Ibid.*, pp. 418-24.

not simply portray intent, but pronounces the outcome of the impending battle from the start.

This interpretation of the outset of the series of judgments is confirmed at the climax concerning which all agree that the Conqueror who is "Faithful and True, and in righteousness he judges and makes war," (Rev 19:11) is Jesus Christ. His insight is described as the initial vision portrayed it (Rev 19:12; cf. 1:14). His crown is now a ruler's crown (*diadem*). He has a *sword*, which is for hand to hand combat, necessary to clean up the conquest for a concluding resolution.

The resolution of the conflict concerning rule over this earth ushers in *the dispensation of the kingdom*. It will be marked by the initial conquest and by the reign of Christ for a thousand years (Rev 20:4, 6). The enemy, who has been the focus of opposition throughout history, will be imprisoned for the thousand years (Rev 20:2-3).

These conclusions have been debated along with the other related issues. The length of a thousand years is not necessarily precise, but there are no persuasive reasons to reject that which is stated in the text. The ones who share in Christ's reign include both those who lived on earth and were not killed in judgment and those throughout history who would share in the first resurrection. These participants are mentioned in general terms. That allows for an order in the first resurrection (1 Cor 15:23) which can include the people of God from various times in the period between Christ's advents. And that generality also allows for the various roles that they will share in Christ's reign. What is decisive is the revelation which the people of God received at their stage in the progress of revelation. Israel will be the covenant people who are the means of blessing for the nations through the reign of Christ (Isa 2:1-4; 4:2-6). The Church will reign with Christ as His Bride (Rom 8:17; Rev 19:7-8). Believers in the Church will be heirs and can be joint heirs with Christ. In total, this dispensation of the kingdom provides the climax of "a plan for the fullness of time" (Eph 1:10). In essence, God's creation *goal* to have man mediate His rule over creation will now be realized in the millennial kingdom. The serpent who challenged God in this respect has been imprisoned and a final resolution nears when Satan is cast into the lake of fire. This *plan* also implies man being redeemed from his fall into sin and adversity with evil.

The Son of Man lays claim to His inheritance by confronting the enemy, his allies, and the nations on earth. It is a conquest over evil and the enemy of God (Gen 3:15).

Revelation of the Conquest over Evil (Revelation 6:1–19:16)

The conquest over evil is not recorded in a sequential narrative form in the Revelation. The content of the story is found in separate portions of the Revelation, but to fully appreciate the depth of the conflict, the conquest needs to be told in such a narrative form. Such an account is found in a book entitled, *Power to Make War* by Zane Hodges.[18] It is an interpretive account of the man of sin who was given the power to make war by Satan. The interpretation rests on texts in Daniel and Revelation. It is this construction of the narrative that will be followed in the presentation to be developed.

At the core of the narrative is the question of the strategy that the devil pursues. He lost the indiscriminate exercise of the power of death when Christ rose from the dead. But being created as an angel, his powers still exceeded the human race. In particular, he could make war with Israel and create havoc in the Middle East region as he attempted to thwart the covenants and promises which God had partnered with Israel to accomplish (Rom 9:1-6). In so doing, he could charge God with weakness and unrighteousness, since He would be unable to keep His commitments that were contingent on Israel's participation. If God failed to keep His word, would He be just in His condemnation and threatened judgment of Satan? Based on God's own standard of justice, Satan could contend that he should avoid condemnation because God had not been consistently just.

If Israel's accomplishment of what God said that they would accomplish is the central issue in history, then what the Book of Revelation has to say about Israel is crucial. Yet, many Christian interpreters minimize or even disregard the place and role of Israel in the concluding events of history. Thus, as this narrative develops, we must give careful attention to what the texts say to see if the existence and salvation of Israel is the future apologetic for the glory of God. And this is one of the essential conditions of Dispensational interpretation of the concluding texts. It is not a consideration of current events, but of Biblical revelation. The interpretation of Rev 12:1-17 is crucial to an accurate perception of Israel in history.

---

[18] Zane C. Hodges, *Power to Make War* (Dallas: Kerugma, 1995).

The King Becomes the Beast (Daniel 12:1a; Revelation 17:9-18)

The narrative in Revelation begins where Daniel concluded his account about the king from the north. The dilemma of end time opposition to Israel remains unresolved. In the early visions of Daniel 2 and 7, opposition comes from the west, from the "little horn" dominating the end time Roman Empire. At the same time, in visions which include Israel (Daniel 8, 10, 11), opposition comes from the north, from the "little horn" (Dan 8:9) of the northern empire.

As Daniel concludes his account, he announces that "at that time… there shall be a time of trouble, such as never has been since there was a nation till that time" (Dan 12:1). What Daniel called "a time of trouble," Jesus called "a great tribulation" for the Jewish people in Jerusalem (Matt 24:21), following "the abomination of desolation spoken of by the prophet Daniel, standing in the holy place" (Matt 24:15).

Daniel had revealed the abomination (Dan 9:27b) after he had spoken of some kind of treaty arrangement reached with the Western Roman Empire (Dan 9:27a). This treaty had only been in effect 3½ years and had apparently provided the political protection in which Israel could rebuild the temple. Conceivably, Israel could call upon the Roman confederation (ten horns) if they needed support. Following the ratification of the treaty, the King of the North settled in his tents just north and east of the temple area (Dan 11:41, 45). Rather than being seen by them as an unwarranted invasion, the King of the North (as the "little horn," Dan 8:9) allied with the ten kings of the Roman Empire (Dan 7:8, 24-25). How this alliance was formed is a fascinating account of spiritual intrigue.

It all arose from the aggressive King of the North, who stormed the Middle East (Dan 11:40-43) and settled between the seas and the glorious holy mountain (Dan 11:40-45). There he came to an end without any human help (Dan 11:45b), yet the Lord will break an Assyrian (from the north) in the Lord's land (Isa 14:35; Mic 5:5-6).

The beast rising out of the nations (sea), having seven heads and ten horns, will also be involved at the end (Rev 19:19-21). From Daniel, the ten-horn expression of the beast, that is, the Roman empire, will be present on earth when the Ancient of Days will be seated to make His final judgment (Dan 7:7-10, 23-27).

From Rev 17:7-11, the seven heads begin in John's day (Rev 17:9-10). "[T]hey are also seven kings, five of whom have fallen, one is, the other has not yet come, and when he does come he must remain only a little while." (Rev 17:10). This cryptic time orientation matches the time of John, if he wrote when five Roman emperors had died (Late AD 68). Then Galba would be the emperor that is (killed in January of AD 69). Ortho then would reign briefly thereafter.

The image of the beast may refer either to the king or to the kingdom (Dan 2:36-38). So it can speak of the king, "One of its heads seemed to have a mortal wound, but its mortal wound was healed" (Rev 13:3a). Then another vision is added, "As for the beast that was and is not, it is an eighth but it belongs to the seven..." (Rev 17:11). Who is this eighth that is of the seven?

The identity of the beast as the eighth is a combination of the end-time King of the North (Dan 11:45b; Isa 14:25) who was resuscitated with one of the historic seven kings—likely Augustus, Tiberius, Caligula, Claudius, or Nero—and who "rises from the bottomless pit" (Rev 11:7). Now, this Roman personage, perhaps Augustus, would reside in the body and personality of the King of the North who became the beast who would receive authority for one hour (Rev 17:12b). The confluence of personalities encourages the alliance with the ten kings (Rev 17:12-13). They will share in worldwide rule and authority with the king located in Jerusalem.

This revival of the king is also the revival of the Roman Empire. "[T]he whole earth marveled as they followed the beast" (Rev 13:3b). And "the dragon gave [him] his power and his throne and great authority" (Rev 13:2). This was a spectacular miracle of Satan, "And they worshiped the dragon, for he had given his authority to the beast, and they worshiped the beast, saying, 'Who is like the beast, and who can fight against it?'" (Rev 13:4). The satanic miracle is not resurrection to life like Jesus' resurrection to eternal life, overcoming death. This is because the beast will go to destruction (Rev 17:8, 11). But in this unexplainable miracle, the King of the North allies with the kingdom of Rome in the West as the "little horn" to claim rule and worship of all people, and particularly Israel, in search of miracles (Dan 7:8, 24).

Deification of the King (Revelation 11:3-13)

The king's career as the beast would last only 3½ years, yet civilization would be shaken to its roots. The "little horn" of Daniel 7 can be identified with the eighth head of Revelation. According to Jesus' chronology in Matthew 24, these events take place toward the end of the first 3½ years.

The beginning of this 3½ year period was marked by a treaty between Israel and the Western Roman Confederacy.[19] Coinciding with the introduction of that treaty was the start of the ministry of the two witnesses (Rev 11:1-12). Perhaps that ministry also contributed to Israel's rebuilding of the temple on the Herodian foundations. The ministry of the witnesses was invincible and reflected miracles of judgment by Moses against Egypt and by Elijah against Israel.

The two witnesses tormented those who dwelled on the earth (11:10). The beast had been given *power* to *make war* (Rev 11:7; 13:7; 19:19) and his first effort to use this power against God came precisely as the witnesses conclude their 1,260 day career. The beast killed them (Rev 11:7) and the world rejoiced as their bodies lay in the street of Jerusalem (Rev 11:10).

In this environment of worldwide approval of the death of the two witnesses, the western confederacy broke its treaty with Israel. Then the beast invaded the Holy of Holies to take a seat there and claim that he himself deserves to be god. The abomination that would bring desolation to Israel and to her temple had just been committed (Dan 9:27b; Matt 24:15). And as Jesus had instructed them, at least 144,000 believing Jews would flee Jerusalem for refuge outside the city.

The world's celebration of the witnesses' death was interrupted as the bodies of the witnesses were raised and they ascended to heaven (Rev 11:11-12). In addition, before the hour ended, an earthquake shook Jerusalem, killing 7,000 residents and 1/10th of the city fell. A wave of fear and religious awe swept through the Jewish population.

Antichrist—The King's Henchman (Rev 13:11-18)

While the designation *antichrist* is used rather broadly today, the two beasts of Revelation 13 need to be carefully distinguished. The first beast, coming from the sea (Rev 13:1-10), would be a Gentile and appropriately identified as the *man of sin* or *lawlessness* (2 Thess 2:3). He is the king. The second beast, coming from the land (Rev 13:11) would be a Jew and identified as the *antichrist* (1 John 4:1, 3).[20] His religious role would put him more directly in conflict with Christ.

---

[19]   *Ibid.*, pp. 28-31. An account of this interpretation is given.

[20]   This differs from the more common approach that holds that the first beast is the antichrist and the second is the false prophet. Here, the first beast is the man of sin, and the second beast is both the antichrist and the false prophet.

This second beast, a false prophet, was raised up to promote worship of the first beast in the temple, and particularly for Israel. Gentile invasion of the temple court caused the burnt sacrifices at the bronze altar to cease (Rev 11:2). However, apart from the claim of the first beast to be worshiped, the sanctuary itself was not occupied by Gentiles (Rev 11:1). Thus, the Gentile invasion would not affect any priestly activities inside the sanctuary itself. The Jewish false prophet would promote worship of the first beast in the Holy of Holies. The antichrist would take the role of a high priest.

The abomination was then made permanent with the formation of the image of the beast. In addition, the false prophet gave life to the image by imparting a spirit to it. It would be another kind of demon possession, this time of an inanimate object. The image then had power both to speak and to cause as many as fail to worship to be killed (Rev 13:15). When the European West would be combined with the King of the North's Middle-Eastern conquests, the Roman Empire would be reborn. The New Roman Empire would then embrace roughly the same territory that was included in the ancient empire. And in this position, the beast would be able to dominate world affairs.

So, cries of wonderment will be unanswerable: "Who is like the beast?" "Who is able to make war with him?" Such is Satan's plan. It was granted to him "to make war on the saints and conquer them" and to rule over all nations (Rev 13:7).

The Great Tribulation is Satan's final opportunity to prove God false. If he can simply eliminate from earth's inhabitants all Jews who believe in Jesus, God will have no one among men with whom to fulfill His covenants, to whom the kingdom of God could be given. Satan understands that the prophecies of the Bible declare that there will be *living* Jewish believers on earth when Christ returns. Nowhere is this fact plainer than in a great prophecy contained in Zech 12:10-14. Further, it is implied in the ratified New Covenant, which had not yet been inaugurated with the house of Judah and the house of Israel (Jer 31:31-34). At the return of Christ, the New Covenant will be inaugurated with Israel.

Suppose then, that Satan could stalemate his Maker's plans. Might he not appeal to the Most High that sentences pronounced against him in Scripture need not be fulfilled either? To accomplish this strategy, he will use the king's power to make war and the false prophet's power to deceive the Jewish people.

The Dragon Cast Out of Heaven (Revelation 12:7-14)

Sometime toward the end of the first 3½ year period, in which the two witnesses live, the dragon suffered a catastrophic defeat. For centuries, Satan had been permitted access to the throne room of heaven (Job 1–2; Rev 12:10). Since the dragon lost in a heavenly battle with Michael, he was cast out of heaven (Rev 12:7-9). Now the earth's inhabitants would suffer at the hand of Satan (Rev 12:12). In particular, Satan turned to the nation of Israel (Rev 12:13-14), for with them lies the destiny of all mankind.

It is no accident that the temple of God must become the center of humanity's new religion. Nor is it any accident that the false prophet mimics the miracle performed by Elijah long ago. Above all, Israel must be persuaded to believe this lie! Namely, who is the true God?

That lie is that the Lord is a merciless Spirit. For after all, in the lie, the Lord was vengeful against Jews over the death of the great imposter, Jesus Christ. Jesus was *not* Israel's true Messiah. The king from the north, the beast, is the nation's long-awaited savior. That claim can be proven because he *made war* against the two witnesses and overcame them. Their death exposed their true vulnerability. It also can be proven because he was raised from a mortal wound. The temple must become a temple to the king. Only if Israel agrees to this, can the world live in religious harmony.

This new religion of the king must be combined with a persecution of its Jewish opponents. And this must go forward immediately. In particular, they must search for the followers of Jesus. Jesus, in His First Advent, had warned His disciples to leave Jerusalem—quickly (Luke 17:30-37). So Israel, still largely in unbelief, resembles a rotting corpse (Luke 17:37) which collects the vultures of the new Roman military.

The number of Jewish believers in Jesus Christ remains unknown, but 144,000 would be the smallest number. However, this group is called the *"firstfruits* to God and to the Lamb" (Rev 14:4). They are associated with the proclamation of the everlasting Gospel (Rev 14:5-7). This suggested growth of believers within the Jews would lead the beast and the false prophet to realize that their net was trapping only a fraction of the followers of Jesus (Rev 12:14-15). Further actions would be required.

However, earthquake-like tremors in the wilderness would help Israel to escape (Rev 12:6). The beast's effort to prevent the flight of the godly had been frustrated, and believing Jews had fled. But the warfare launched by the beast was far from over.

The King Versus the God of Heaven (Revelation 13:6; 16:10-11)

If the believing Jews would survive, Satan's strategy could not be carried out. Effective control must be established over all mankind, if "the testimony of Jesus" (Rev 12:17) was to be blotted out once and for all.

But a survey of the severity of the trumpet judgments reveals the size of his problem. How will the new ruler cope with the situation? He, along with the false prophet, would devise a system to mark and label people in which religious and economic control could be masterfully combined (Rev 13:14-17). This would be an effective noose in which to entrap the world in general—and believing Israel in particular. Accepting the registration for commerce would be the same as accepting the religion of the beast. And this marks one as eternally damned (Rev 14:9-11).

The satanic lie had no place for believing that the Lord is Creator and Judge (14:6-7). The Lord must be seen as detached and unconcerned about the earth. He must be seen as the God of heaven alone (Rev 11:3; 13:6). Followers of this lie believe that the Lord exists, but they also believe that He was the source of their problems (Rev 16:8-11). And "They blasphemed the God of heaven" (Rev 16:11, NKJV).

Armageddon (Revelation 16:16-21)

As the 3½ years progressed, man's delusions about reality led him toward the supreme folly of all human history. Man, the creature, went to war against his Creator. Yet this is the inevitable consequence of the original sin—to attempt to be like God (Gen 3:4). It was a return to the strategy of Babel in direct defiance of God. The religious expression of Babylon would be located in Rome, because the economic/religious harlot, Babylon, was carried by the beast to power. But the beast ultimately defied the harlot and rejected her influence (Revelation 17–18). Such religious approaches to God were rejected as self-serving and restrictive. In their place was the worship of the beast and of Satan. And such ultimate defiance led to the attempt to remove the God of heaven.

If the reconciliation of God and mankind provided in Christ was rejected, then the false god under satanic encouragement must come into conflict with God. Both cannot exist as reality. The final series of the bowl judgments (Rev 16:1-21) only seemed to confirm their delusion about the Lord and their hardened hearts attempted to do battle with God even as Pharaoh had so long ago (Exodus 14).

"And I saw the beast, the kings of the earth, and their armies, gathered to make war against Him who sat on the horse and against His army" (Rev 19:19, NKJV).

Who is this one sitting on the horse? "On his robe and on his thigh he has a name written, King of kings and Lord of lords" (Rev 19:16). *This is none other than Jesus Christ.*

Such a battle is preposterous. Who could be so deluded? Three demons are successful in seducing the kings of the earth to join the beast in his war against God (Rev 16:13-16).

But the battle is a disastrous rout of the forces of Satan. The Lord Jesus Christ suddenly appears in the clouds at the head of His heavenly armies (Matt 24:30; 1 Thess 1:7-8; Rev 19:11-16). The victory is His!

Revelation and the Reign of Jesus Christ and of the New Heavens and New Earth (Revelation 19–22)

The final consideration of *Revelation* combines texts that treat both the climax of the historical heaven and earth and the introduction of the eternal, new heaven and earth. In a basic sense, eternity is distinct from time and history. This is implied in the way the heavens and earth are described. The first heavens and earth are not described as old, but as first, which introduces the time sequence of history. The new heavens and earth are not described as second, but as new, which suggests a fresh replacement of the first. God is eternal. But the first heavens and earth are historically and temporally limited. When God describes Himself as the alpha and the omega, the beginning and the end, He is describing His relation to that first heaven and earth. He created it at first, and now in Revelation, He brings it to a conclusion. The dead experience the second death in God's judgment (Rev 20:11-15). The redeemed have their names written in the book of life. That life is eternal life. They thus have a place in the new heavens and earth. And the new heavens and earth are eternal as God is eternal.[21] As a consequence, what was promised in history can only be fulfilled in history. The eternity of the new heavens and earth does not provide an appropriate realm to fulfill unrealized promises of history.[22] Rather, all

---

[21]   Gregory E. Ganssle, ed., *God and Time* (Downers Grove, IL: IVP, 2001). Christian philosophers agree that God is eternal. What that means is debated. Augustine and Aquinas used it to mean outside time. Contemporary thinkers take it to refer to the limitless nature of God's life. This treatment does not seek to probe or to resolve this problem.

[22]   This distinction between *first* and *new* is disregarded by a Covenant Theology position. In their view, fulfillment is found in the *new* rather than in the history of the *first*. (Anthony

those promises are fulfilled in the millennial reign of Christ. The first earth reaches an aspect of its culmination in the judgments of the dragon and of those dead who face the Great White Throne. Whatever follows is something *new*. In addition, persons whose names are written in the book of life already have new and *eternal* life.

Thus, to consider the conclusion of the Revelation, four themes are addressed:

- The Conclusion of History (19:1–20:15)
- The Eternal Heavens and Earth (21:1-4)
- God's Final Concern (21:5-8)
- The New Jerusalem (21:9–22:5)

The Conclusion of History (Revelation 19:1–20:15)

The conclusion features the reign of God and His Servant, Jesus Christ, as the fulfillment of God's creation *goal*. The self-serving evil in Babylon implodes upon itself as the ten evil horns destroy the evil religious harlot of the end time. This expression of evil had begun at Babel (Genesis 9–11) and had remained unresolved until the climax (Revelation 17–18). The heavenly multitude rejoices because the Lord our God the Almighty reigns (Rev 19:6).

The Reign of Christ on Earth (Revelation 20:4-6)

The heavens opened and Jesus Christ, God's Servant, rode forth in final conquest. The Faithful and True One will mediate God's *rule* with a rod of iron (Rev 19:15-16). This fulfills what God intended for the first Adam (Gen 1:26-28). This *reign* does not yet carry with it any thought of perfection or absence of evil. But *righteousness* will reign in the first heaven and earth.[23] The reign of Jesus Christ is the climax (Rev 19:11-16) of history.

In addition, the reign of the saints with Jesus Christ for a thousand years is mentioned. Ironside put it this way:

> Thus, "to Him give all the prophets witness," (Acts 10:43), not only that through His name remission of sins is now to be

---

Hoekema, *The Bible and the Future* [Grand Rapids, MI: Eerdmans, 1979])

[23] Ironside highlights the importance of righteousness. In the dispensation of grace, righteousness *suffers*. In the kingdom, righteousness *reigns*. In the new heavens and earth, righteousness is *at home* (Ironside, *Revelation*, p. 336).

proclaimed among all nations but also that He is to reign in righteousness over all the world, when He comes the second time to claim the inheritance that is His by divine fiat, as Son and Heir of all things.[24]

By contrast, God's enemies will be defeated (Revelation 19:1–20:3), whether it is the implosion of evil or the slaughter of the beast and the false prophet, with their cohorts, for the supper of God. All aggressive human evil will be defeated. In addition, during this reign, the devil, Satan, is bound for these thousand years (Rev 20:1-3), during which time Israel will reign on earth under her Messiah.

The Final Conquest of Satan (Revelation 20:7-10)

For the sake of the living on earth in the millennium, the Devil will be released to tempt and to deceive some in the population. A remnant throughout history has overcome that temptation through Christ. Their names have been written in the book of life from the foundation of the earth. But for the others who lived under the reign of Christ and experienced those blessings, they will be exposed one last time to the deception of Satan. The battle of Gog and Magog ensue as the rebels surround the saints and the beloved city (Rev 20:9). Apart from the human agency of even Christ, fire comes from heaven to consume the rebellion. Then Satan is thrown into the lake of fire and sulfur (Rev 20:10).

The Final Judgment of the Dead (Revelation 20:11-15)

For the sake of the dead from all generations, a Great White Throne will be set to judge the case of each individual dead one. The sinfulness of man is not the issue, since Christ's death on the cross was universally sufficient to propitiate God's wrath against sin (1 John 2:2). What is at issue is that they are dead. In history, they never received eternal life and thus, their names had not been written in the Book of Life (Rev 20:15). Could a righteous case be made from the works of the dead (20:12), that they deserved eternal life (Rom 2:6-7)? Not one was found (Rev 20:13). So all the dead and Hades were thrown into the lake of fire in the second death (Rev 20:14; cf. Rom 2:6, 8-9).

The New Heavens and Earth (Revelation 21:1-4)

A new eternal heaven and earth appear. The new life is distinguished from the first world existence. There is no sea, as sea reflected chaos in

---

[24]　*Ibid.*, p. 342.

the first earth (Gen 1:2; Dan 7:2). Nor is the curse of death present as a consequence of Adam's sin (Gen 2:16-17). All who inhabit the new earth had their name written in the book of life (Rev 20:15; 21:17). The pain, sorrow, and tears related to sin and death will be removed.

The holy city, the New Jerusalem, will be the residence of the Throne of God and the Lamb with Their glory and light (Revelation 21:9–22:5). There, God will dwell with the Lord's wife and with the Lamb's wife in intimate fellowship that was initiated in the garden (Gen 3:8) and was typified in the tabernacle (Exod 25:31-40). This eternal fellowship is not a fulfillment of what was anticipated in history, but a fresh experience in a city where righteousness is at home. Eternal life in a new heavens and earth is not a fulfillment of what was promised in the first heavens and earth, but the inheritance for those who believed and overcame (Rev 21:7) during their life in the first creation.

God's Final Concern in History (Revelation 21:5-8)

> John's pastoral purpose in this book is nowhere more evident than in vv. 5-8 where the personal concern of Almighty God comes into immediate view…This is the first direct utterance of the Father since 1:8, and is in fact the only time it is explicitly He who speaks except in 1:8.[25]

This pastoral concern introduces the new and distinguishes the new from the first. The new is the inheritance of those who overcome (Rev 21:7).

The New Jerusalem (Revelation 21:9–22:5)

This new city, like the gift of eternal life, appears both in history and in the eternal state.[26] The New Jerusalem is descended from heaven to be the heavenly Jerusalem which is also related to Israel on earth (Gal 4:26-27). As the gates of the ancient city are named for the destination immediately outside the gate; so the tribes of Israel will gather outside the gates in the

---

[25] Robert L. Thomas, *Revelation 8–22: An Exegetical Commentary* (Chicago: Moody Press, 1995), p. 446.

[26] The evidence in the text that the new Jerusalem first appeared in history is:

21:24, 26—The nations and kings,

22:2—The healing of nations,

22:14-15—The blessing pronounced on those who come and eat of the Tree of Life while a curse rests on those outside the city,

22:15—The picture of dogs, sorcerers, and fornicators cowering outside the city wall.

heavenly Jerusalem during the millennial history. Three tribes will be gathered at three gates on each wall. This organization is similar to that of the tabernacle of old. So during the millennium, the redeemed Israel will gather on earth to administer the rule of Christ among the nations. The heavenly Jerusalem-dwellers will be king-priests in the service of the King Jesus and His will, as the Levites were in the service of God in the tabernacle. This will happen as history is being concluded. The New Jerusalem will also have its place in the eternal state.

Conclusion

The glory of the resolution of history's conflicts with evil shines forth in the story of the *Revelation*. Readers and participants worship in God's conquest over evil. Glory shines as "salvation and glory and power" belong to our God, because "his judgments are true and just" (Rev 19:1-2). The heavenly multitude voiced their worship in their repeated refrain, "Hallelujah" (Rev 19:1, 3, 6). "[T]he Lord our God the Almighty reigns." The marriage of the Lamb has come and His wife has prepared herself. She was given fine linens to wear, bright and pure (Rev 19:6, 8).

Then John mistakenly fell down to worship the messenger—a fellow servant who also had the testimony of Jesus. The fellow messenger redirected John to worship God because together their testimony about Jesus gave expression to the spirit of God's prophecy (Rev 19:10).

Thus, it might be expected that perhaps later, in John's Gospel, his testimony of Jesus would be related to the spirit of God's prophecy. So in John's Gospel, Jesus was introduced as the Word, as with God and as God. As the eternal Son spoke the Word in creation and the world came into existence, so in history, the Son spoke through the prophets. Then the Son spoke in Person in His advent (Heb 1:1-4).

In history, the Son spoke to Israel as covenant partners. When Israel refused as stewards to invest God's Word in their national life, Israel was judged. The Son's entrusted Word now became the enfleshed Word.[27] The union between God's Word and God's people transitioned from a covenant union to a personal union. The enfleshed Word accepted God's promises in spite of the temptation from evil. The enfleshed Word readily obeyed God's obligations in spite of the cost at the hand of evil.

---

[27]　D. A. Carson, *The Gospel According to John* (Grand Rapids, MI: Eerdmans, 1991), p. 113.

In the First Advent, the Son overcame death through resurrection. In His Second Advent, He will return to resolve the historic conflict with evil. How fitting that the vision is named the Revelation of Jesus Christ— the testimony of Jesus Christ.

CONCLUSION:
THE GLORY OF GOD

"All the events of the created world are designed to manifest the glory of God."[1] This reality rests in God who desires to share His glory with His creation. And this shared glory manifests God's goodness on behalf of the creation to occasion worship.

The term *glory* is an expressive word in reference to the splendor of that person. In regard to God, His glory is manifest in creation, in His governance of salvation history, and in the provision of salvation. These three aspects of manifestation will be examined in this concluding chapter.

Glory is associated with related terms. The glory of God relates to His attributes which demonstrate His unique worth. Those recognizing His worth express their esteem in worship and thanksgiving. Those who esteem His glory recognize themselves as stewards of all they are and have and all that God reveals to them. Each aspect of God's glory introduced will be considered.

First, God's glory in creation is seen in its *goodness*. This goodness is evident in creation's design and intended role, in contrast to the earth without form and empty. God's glory will be fully manifest in the completion of this role at the climax of history.

Second, God's glory in His governance of salvation history would be evident in His *power*, *wisdom*, and *management of history*. Particularly significant is the permission of evil to invade the good creation and to challenge God's intent for the role of creation. That intent focused on man, who was created in God's image, yet who had personal independence from God. Still man was assigned to rule according to God's plan. God would be glorified in creation's successful accomplishment of its role. This

---

[1] John F. Walvoord, *The Millennial Kingdom* (Findlay, OH: Dunham, 1959), p. 92.

glory would be manifest in spite of conflict with evil and through the agency of humans, created less powerful than the evil one.

Third, the goal of the provision of salvation is His deliverance of vessels of mercy from evil and its judgment, while vessels of wrath are prepared for destruction (Rom 9:22-23). God's work of salvation will manifest this glory while dealing in justice with the whole creation and in mercy and grace with the elect ones.

God's Glory in Creation

The most widely shared manifestation of God's glory is revealed in creation. Just as winter diminishes the beauty of summer, God's display of glory in creation was diminished following Adam's fall into sin. Yet God's glory in creation remained present. Death became the common experience of all living things. Paul spoke of creation falling under "bondage to corruption," as "the whole creation has been groaning together in the pains of childbirth until now" (Rom 8:21-22). Still David saw the heavens declaring the glory of the Creator, and the firmament showing His handiwork (Ps 19:1). As the space consisting of the heavens appears transcendent, almost without limits (Job 38:4-5), so is the Creator Himself. Likewise, time passes yet does not change. Day follows day but years come and years go unchanged (Ps 19:2). So God addresses the needs of each day and yet He is eternally the same. This wordless revelation is available for all who live on earth, and so each one is accountable to recognize "[God's] eternal power and divine nature" (Rom 1:20). Since He is Creator, "life and breath and everything" (Acts 17:25) come from Him. We are truly *stewards* of the creation—our life, our abilities, our families; even the space and time in which we live in history. And the question is: do we appropriately esteem our Creator?

God's Glory in Governance of History

In spite of the continuing conflict involving sin and death, the glory of God's governance remains the central theme of Scripture. Following Adam's sin and the fall of the human race, God was reserved in inserting Himself into the resolution of the generational sin which followed. At the outset, God spoke in no uncertain terms about judgment of all of the first participants in sin (Gen 3:14-19). As the human race grew, sin spread and engulfed the whole population. The only seeming exception is the line of descendants in Genesis 5 that shared the image of Adam. So God, in response to the spread of evil brought a world-wide flood, destroying all except Noah and his family (Gen 5:28-32).

God then delegated human government to the survivors, whose principle purpose was to protect human life created in the image of God (Gen 9:6). Yet, this post-flood generation proceeded to defy God, building the tower of Babel. In order to prevent such population-wide efforts of defiance, God divided the languages of the people. This, as a result, formed nations with common language and culture (Gen 11:1-9). These displays of powerful interventions in judgment manifested the glory of the governing God, limiting the advance of evil, but stopped short of introducing any restorative actions.

Glory in the Dispensation of Promise

God's restoration began as God promised to bless an elect patriarch and to use Abraham and subsequent patriarchs to bless others. The promise forged a partnership between God and the patriarch as His steward who would manage his journey by what God had promised (Gen 12:1-3).

So through God's Word, God ruled His stewards. In God's commitment in the promise, He would in time share His goodness and His glory. So as Abraham was about to offer his son on the altar, God manifested His glory in the provision of the ram (Gen 22:1-19). God's initial fulfillment of His Word displayed what God alone had promised (Gen 22:8).

Implied in the word of promise was the promise of an ultimate Agent, through whom God would provide completed fulfillment and blessing (the Seed of the woman, the Seed of Abraham, the Son of David). As history unfolded, it became clear that patriarch after patriarch, king after king in Israel, fell short of God's glory. So within the firmness and stability of God's word of promise, the expectation of glory remained a sure hope. One human agent would someday arise who would be completely united to the God who promised, so that God's glory would be fully displayed and God's Word fulfilled.

So as the history of restoration began, the very statement of promise raises a question: who has the power and faithfulness to speak and act so boldly against the conflict that evil brought? The answer will become clear that only a glorious God would. The God who spoke creation into existence is the very God who speaks in history to stewards. While stewards along the way would be disobedient, the clarity of the affirmation in promise assures the reader that the hope of fulfillment is sure.

Glory in the Dispensation of Law

The partnership forged with the elect patriarchs through promise had fallen short due to their deteriorating disobedience. It became evident that a law was needed to hold the elect line responsible for obedience. While God's providence assured that the patriarchs survived, they ended up in Egypt, a small remnant in a foreign land. Yet the immanent presence of the God of glory at Mt. Sinai would hold Israel to greater accountability. Then, as Moses realized (Exod 33:1-18), God's personal presence would be needed to enable Israel to accomplish their role in the fallen world.

Thus, a more intimate partnership was forged at Mt. Sinai through the mediation of Moses. The law was added alongside promise (Exodus 19:6–23:33; Deuteronomy 5:1–10:23), not to replace promise but to facilitate God's fulfillment of promise consistent with His glory. The law itself was glorious as it is "holy and righteous and good" (Rom 7:12). In addition, God's glory appeared as fire yet shrouded by a cloud (Exod 16:10; 24:16-18; 40:34-38; Num 17:7). Weinfeld notes:

> [The] cloud serves as a cloak to protect against the mortal danger of viewing the deity. Only Moses, who can look upon God face to face (Num 12:8; Deut 34:10), may enter the cloud (Exod 24:18). To the other Israelites, God reveals himself wrapped in clouds. They see only the flames that blaze within the cloud (Exod 24:17). Only once, at the consecration of the Tabernacle (Lev 9:23) does God reveal himself to Israel without such protection—an event parallel in importance to the Sinai revelation.[2]

Then, in the tabernacle followed by the temple, God's glory was present, but hidden behind the veil. In time, Jeremiah would reveal Israel had broken Mosaic partnership in spite of Yahweh's patience (Jer 31:32). Ezekiel would envision God's glory gradually departing from the soon to be judged temple (Ezek 8:2ff; 10:4, 18; 11:23). When the remnant returned from captivity under Cyrus' Gentile jurisdiction, a second temple would be built. But God's glory did not return when the temple was rebuilt (Ezra 6:16-22).

---

[2] Moshe Weinfeld, "כָּבֹד, kābod," TDOT, vol. 2, p. 31.

Jesus Was Born of a Woman, Under Law

The covenant partnership, which had been broken between the Lord and Israel would be replaced by the intimate, personal partnership between God the Father and God the Son. It was still a partnership defined by the Abrahamic and Davidic Covenants and by the revelation of the Law (Matt 5:17). Jesus was born of a woman, under law (Gal 4:4).

At the birth of Jesus, the heavenly angels declare: "Glory to God in the highest, and on earth peace among those with whom he is pleased!" (Luke 2:14). The magnitude of the incarnation is difficult to overemphasize. Jesus is the promised One, the anointed Agent. At the infant's birth, human flesh clothes the second Person of the Godhead, even as fire had been clothed by the cloud (John 1:14).

Paul described the partnership of the incarnation (Phil 2:5-11). God the Son existing in the very essence as God, did not consider equality with the Father a status to be grasped (2:6). "But He emptied Himself" (Phil 2:6, KJV, or "made himself nothing," ESV). When He emptied Himself, He did not stop being God. Rather, He surrendered the independent use of His rights as divine Son, submitting them to the Father. This Jesus affirmed in His response to Satan in the first temptation (Matt 4:1-4). Although He continued being God, He lived as a man, in the form of a servant (Phil 2:7). He ate, slept, and prayed in dependence upon His Father. Then He humbled Himself further and became obedient unto death on the cross (2:8).

The Apostle John observed Him in His human flesh; His glory appeared as of the only begotten of the Father, full of grace and truth (John 1:14). These virtues manifest God's true disclosure of Himself: "Yahweh is a compassionate and gracious God, slow to anger and rich in faithful love and truth" (Exod 34:6, author's translation). The glory is in the combination of grace and truth in a fallen world where these virtues are apparently contradictory. Truth may be used to override grace and grace may appear to compromise truth. Yet without grace, fallen man could not see nor accept the complete truth about himself. And without truth, fallen man would be blind to his need for God's grace. It is glorious to resolve in His Person this dilemma of mankind in the fallen world (John 7:59–8:11).

As a result, Paul celebrated: "at the name of Jesus every knee should bow, in heaven and on earth and under the earth, and every tongue confess that Jesus Christ is Lord, to the glory of God the Father" (Phil 2:10-11). This is a shared glory as God had intended in creation. The Son, in humble obedience, did what the Father, through His own Word, had promised. And the Father raised the Son to overcome death and to enable the Son to finally judge evil in the creation. "John has a particularly strong sense of the causal connection between dying and bringing forth fruit, or between the death and the resurrection of Jesus, between suffering and the glorification of the Son of Man."[3]

Glory in the Dispensation of Grace

The personal partnership between the Father and the Son is now extended in the growing of the Body of Christ. Now it is partnership between Christ and believers. It is a living partnership based on the Holy Spirit's baptism of believers into a Body with Christ as the Head (1 Cor 12:13).

In Second Corinthians 3:4–4:6, Paul compared and contrasted God's share of glory in the dispensation of grace with the share of glory under the Mosaic Covenant. It is a comparison in ministries between Paul and Moses. When the Old Covenant law was given to Moses, the Israelites could not gaze at the glory reflected in Moses' face (3:7). As a result, Moses veiled his face so that the Israelites could not stare at the end of what was fading away (3:12-13). Then Paul applies the veil on Moses' face to represent the hardness of Israel's hearts when Moses is read. That hardness exists until Paul's day when Hebrew Scriptures are read and the hard-hearted fail to see the end of the Law. Whenever one sees Jesus as Lord, as Saul did on the road to Damascus (Acts 9:3-4; 2 Cor 3:14-16), the veil is removed. The end of the Law is evident (Rom 10:4), both in a temporal sense and in a purposeful sense (Gal 3:19-23).

Turning to the Lord Jesus, the Spirit has unveiled our face to see, to hear, and to understand "the glory of the Lord" (2 Cor 3:18a). At the same time, since the Scripture is a mirror, we also see our face. In view of the differences, we are being transformed into the image of the Lord "from glory to glory." And this progressive transformation is by the Spirit (2 Cor 3:18b) while we await a completed glorification at the Lord's return.

Glory in the Dispensation of the Kingdom

At the climax of the history of this fallen earth, the glory of God will be most vividly manifest. This most complete share of God's glory will coincide with creation ruled by the last Adam. This had been the intent of the creation from the beginning (Gen 1:24-26). What was lost by the

---

[3]   Gerhard Kittle, "δόξα," TDNT, vol. 2, p. 249.

first Adam at the fall into sin (Gen 3:1-6, 14-15) will be restored in spite of the clever and deceptive presence of the evil one.

This climax is introduced in the Revelation of Jesus Christ (4–20). It celebrates His return in glory, even as "the testimony of Jesus has been the spirit of prophecy" (Rev 19:10). This concluding revelation testifies to Christ's glory: "Immediately after the tribulation of those days...then... they will see the Son of Man coming on the clouds of heaven with power and great glory" (Matt 24:29-30; cf. Mark 13:26; Luke 21:27).

The return of Jesus Christ to the creation marks the climax of the fallen earth. While the Ancient of Days reached a judgment at the conclusion of the times of the Gentile governments (Dan 7:13-14), "authority to rule and glory and a kingdom" were given to the Son of Man. As a result, "those of every people, nation, and language should serve Him" as He will mediate the Lord's rule on a fallen earth and "his kingdom is one that will not be destroyed" (Dan 7:13-14).

The Son of Man will come with power to first judge the nations: "the Lamb would open one of the seven seals and I heard one of the four living creatures say with a voice like thunder, 'Come!' I looked, and there was a white horse. The horseman on it had a bow [for distant warfare]; a crown of pending victory was given to him, and he went out as a victor to conquer" (Rev 6:1). For seven years, tribulation will fall on the nation Israel and the nations of the earth (Dan 9:27). "His judgments are true and righteous" (Rev 19:2). At the climax, "Then I saw heaven opened, and behold, a white horse! The one sitting on it is called Faithful and True, and in righteousness..." (Rev 19:11). And, "From his mouth comes a sharp sword [for close warfare] with which to strike down the nations, and he will rule them with a rod of iron. He will tread the winepress of the fury of the wrath of God the Almighty" (Rev 19:15).

The drab winter lingers in the fallen world, as the Son of Man "... seized the dragon, that ancient serpent, who is the devil and Satan, and bound him for a thousand years...that he might not deceive the nations any longer" (Rev 20:2-3). In spite of continuing shadows, the glory of Messiah begins to shine forth as He reigns. This is a fulfillment of God's word to Adam, that he should subdue the earth (Gen 1:28). While the original account does not directly mention evil, it is implied in Gen 1:2. Now, the evil that had burst on the scene (Gen 3:1-15) has been overcome at the resurrection and is about to be finally judged. In the meantime:

> Then I heard what seemed to be the voice of a great multitude,
> like the roar of many waters and like the sound of mighty peals

of thunder, crying out, "Hallelujah! For the Lord our God the Almighty reigns. Let us rejoice and exult and give him the glory, for the marriage of the Lamb has come, and his Bride has made herself ready." (Rev 19:6-7)

While the historical reign over evil displays glory over the creatures of this creation, this reign finally awaits Satan's release for one last attempt to grasp control over the creation. That opportunity would come when Satan would be released to again deceive the nations. Then the final judgment would fall (Rev 20:7-10).

> Then I saw a new heaven and a new earth, for the first heaven and the first earth had passed away, and the sea was no more… And I heard a loud voice from the throne saying, "Behold, the dwelling place of God is with man. He will dwell with them, and they will be his people, and God himself will be with them as their God" (Rev 21:1, 3).

> I did not see a sanctuary in [the New Jerusalem], because the Lord God the Almighty and the Lamb are its sanctuary. The city does not need the sun or moon to shine on it, because God's glory illuminates it, and its lamp is the Lamb (Rev 21:22-23).

God's Glory in Salvation

In providing salvation, God wished to manifest the wealth of His glory in objects of mercy (Rom 9:22-23). These objects are elect ones (Rom 9:6-29). As God chose Isaac and not Ishmael, Jacob and not Esau, Paul raises the question: is God's choice arbitrary or unjust (9:14-16)? The answer is a resounding no!

That answer is appropriate because the choice rests totally with God. It is not found in what the creature wishes or in what they have accomplished. Rather it is grounded in God's love in sharing undeserved mercy. The Creator has the right to do what He desires in His goodness. Further, raising the very question is inappropriate because the creature with his limits intrudes into the counsel of the Creator (Rom 9:19-21). A created one is like a pot saying to the Potter, "why have you made me this way?"

However, as the creature's questions probe the Creator's counsel, the illustrated answer to our questions seems to include an objection: persons are so much more than mere clay pots. But it is God who introduced the mystery of that comparison when He created human beings "in His own image" (Gen 1:26-28). How does God share His personal image and still remain the personal God? How can God share personal responsibility with human creatures and still remain the Sovereign One? The answer rests solely with God, our Creator.

Paul sketches a further answer which excludes one explanation. While God's decree would allow for the intrusion of His enemy into the creation (Gen 3:1-5), it was Adam's choice which introduced evil into the human race (Rom 5:12). So God permits evil in His decreed will but does not create nor directly cause evil. So an explanation of predestination excludes double predestination.

Rather, Paul's explanation of predestination is contrasted in the voice of verbs in Romans 9:22-23:

> What if God, desiring to show his wrath and to make known his power, has endured with much patience vessels of wrath *prepared* [passive voice] for destruction, in order to make known the riches of his glory for vessels of mercy, which *he has prepared* [active voice] beforehand for glory. (Emphasis added)

In this fallen world, God wishes to make known two things: (1) "to show his wrath and to make known his power...[on] vessels of wrath" and (2) "to make known the riches of his glory for vessels of mercy." In order to make known His glory, He, by contrast, makes known His power against evil. The passive voice (prepared for destruction) is pointedly silent about the specific forces that prepare for destruction. In the silence, the rejection of the vessel itself is as one of the implied forces preparing for destruction. On the other hand, the active voice specifically identifies God as the direct cause to prepare vessels in need of mercy for a share in God's glory.

Some time ago, we began the Biblical quest to construe a Dispensational Biblical theology. The quest focused on God as the Hero in governing creation history and participating in the lives of chosen creatures. That participation featured the progressive revelation of His will as it would be fleshed out through chosen stewards, and would be realized as the Word became flesh to be a steward of God's will. The construal was guided by and highlighted in three *sine qua non*:

1. In a textually tied literal interpretation, we allowed God to tell His own story through His inspired human authors. And in that textual interpretation, we recognized the literary genre and the expository context as the framework of each writer's contribution.

2. We have noted the distinction between Israel and the Church. All of God's people have been incorporated into the story. However, in the incorporation in the Dispensational stages, the people did not appear in a flattened and faceless fashion, but in a demonstrative and historically sensitive form. One gospel gives unity to God's work of salvation, yet the distinguishable stewardships are reflected in the progress of revelation. And the focus of each dispensation featured the fresh appearance of the glory of God.

3. The ultimate goal of the theology presented here, the manifestation of God's glory, addressed the fundamental problem of human history—the conflict with evil. The Creator delegated to Adam to be the steward of His plan, yet following the fall, mankind found itself too weak to resist evil and too hard-hearted to avoid it. The evil one would have defeated God and His plan were it not for God Himself, enfleshed as a human, Jesus of Nazareth, overcoming and finally defeating evil. God's glory was revealed most vividly as this conflict and ultimate conquest unfolded in history.

And this revealed glory appeared in each Person of the Trinity. The *Father* was glorified in His nimble governance of the elect ones in history. His glory was fully shared on earth when the *Son* assumed Israel's stewardship to accomplish the Father's prophesied will. Further, God's glory repeatedly showed forth through the *Spirit's* presence and ministry to God's people. In the Spirit's power, they would steward their life according to God's Word until God's plan would be fulfilled.

History has been the realm in which God's glory was manifested generation after generation. The completed story fittingly highlights God's glory. In addition, the completed story of the fallen earth sets the stage for the new heavens and new earth freed from evil. The anticipation of this future creation holds out hope for God's people to have a deeper and richer experience in knowing God in His glory.

APPENDICES

APPENDIX 1:
EVIL IN THE CREATION

In order to appreciate the inevitable place that evil has in the plot-con-flict of history, the first appearance of evil will be repeatedly alluded to in the progress of revelation. Evil does not change in essence in history. It positions itself as enmity against God from beginning to end and brings accusations against God's people to discredit God. Three themes drawn from the first appearances of evil will summarize the place it has in history.

First, the temptation of Eve is the temptation that sin commonly takes throughout Biblical history. The serpent questions what God has said and whether what God has said is true. The temptation comes through a subordinate which strengthens its appeal to the superiority of man, but carries no compulsion. The temptation begins as a suggestion rather than an argument:

> The incredulous tone—"has God actually said…?"—is both disturbing and flattering: it smuggles in the assumption that God's word is subject to our judgment. The exaggeration, *ye shall not eat of any tree* (RV, RSV, rightly), is a further and favorite device: dangling before Eve, it will draw her into debate on her opponent's terms.[1]

The *second* question is a denial that God's Word is true, and the first word to be denied is that God would judge in condemnation to death. This lie is so big, it even reinterprets life. Man can be *as God* rather than be a partner under God. He can outwit God based on God's own words; love is interpreted as envy, service as servitude, and blatant disobedience

---

[1] Kidner, *Genesis*, p. 67.

as a leap into freedom. Finally, God will henceforth be viewed, consciously or not, as a rival and enemy.

Third, on earth, the enemy takes a disguised appearance. The serpent is genuinely an animal, but the substance of the words discloses that a more powerful creature is involved. Eichrodt speaks of certain passages (e.g., Genesis 3) "where there are glimmerings of the idea of a superhuman *being* hostile to God."[2] While Eichrodt attempts to discover the time and source of the appearance of this superhuman enemy, he concludes, somewhat indefinitely, that it is a rebellious angel.

Rather than being "the enemy," and not being disclosed directly until later in the progress of revelation, myth figures and images are alluded to, as found in pagan myths, to speak of "the enemy." The language and the images are not true as components of a myth, but the mythic use does form a basis for recognition. "We must still keep very clearly in mind the characteristics which differentiate [Babylonian cosmogony] from the Old Testament interpretation of the universe."[3] So figures and images recognized from the pagan myth are interpreted according to that figure or image in the Biblical revelation first introduced in Genesis 3.

Later revelation names the enemy of God and humanity to be "Satan" (Heb *śāṭān* "adversary, persecutor, or accuser," Job 1–2; Zechariah 3) and the "Devil" (Gk *diabolos*, Rev 12:9).

Finally, the role of evil in history refers back to the creation account. According to the account, God did not create darkness or the primordial deep. In history, God keeps the threat associated with the Tree of the Knowledge of Good and Evil and condemns mankind to death. The whole race inherits a fallen life from Adam and thus experiences death, even though the Law had not yet come to condemn personal sin.

Darkness is a repeated witness to contrast light in creation:

> It was not the Creator's intention that there should be perpetual light and no darkness at all, but that the light and the darkness should operate consecutively for given periods and in unchanging order. Consequently, God divided the one from the other, that is, He separated their respective spheres of activity.[4]

---

[2]   Eichrodt, *Theology of the Old Testament*, vol. 2, p. 207, emphasis in original.

[3]   *Ibid.*, p. 115.

[4]   U. Cassuto, *From Adam to Noah: Part One* (Jerusalem: Magnes, 1972), p. 26.

Sea is prominent in various creation accounts. Robert Chisholm has explored the various accounts as they reveal God's conflict with evil in history. He contends that, "God is sovereign over the sea and the sinister forces it symbolizes. Consequently He deserves the worship and trust of His people."[5] He presents three kinds of treatments of the sea.

Emasculating the Sea

In the creation account (Genesis 1:1–2:4), God is absolutely in control of the sea as it is a remaining remnant of the judged earth (Gen 1:2). Like darkness, He assigns it two appropriate spheres with an expanse between. When He judges the population with a worldwide flood, He releases the water above and below without any resistance from that which symbolizes evil. Yet, that symbol of evil would never again be used to judge evil. Then according to Exod 20:11 (cf. Pss 95:5; 146:6), God made the sea. The act of God occurred on the third day when He shaped the sea in relation to the earth.

Restraining the Sea

The creation account assures us that God is in control. His creation is determined, yet after man's fall into evil, that assurance takes on some uncertainty. How will evil change things? "The world is not devoid of danger. There is a sinister, threatening dimension present that produces conflict – between the sea and the land, darkness and light, and death and life."[6] He continues, "The surging sea proudly seeks to break through its barriers ([Job] 38:8-11) and darkness must be dispelled each new morning so that evil can be restrained again, albeit temporarily (38:12-15)."[7]

Subduing the Sea

In Ps 74:13-14, the sea, depicted in terrifying images of multi-headed, serpentine sea creatures (Leviathan), was subdued in creation. In addition, in the Exodus, subduing the sea expressed Yahweh's right hand and

---

[5]   Robert B. Chisholm, Jr. "Images of the Sea in Biblical Creation Accounts: Diversity and Unity" (paper presented at the annual meeting for the Evangelical Theological Society, Providence, RI, 2008), p. 1.

[6]   *Ibid.*, p. 10.

[7]   *Ibid.*, p. 12.

majestic power in shattering the enemy, Egypt (Exod 15:1-10). The power of the enemy portrayed as Leviathan is subdued by God and God uses the power of the enemy to protect God's people.

The Future of the Sea

The image of the sea will be excluded from the concluding creation (Rev 21:1) in the resolution of the conflict seen in Dan 7:2-3 and in Rev 12:9; 13:1-2.

APPENDIX 2: GOD'S WORKS ON THE CROSS

In the Epistles, the apostles used images to explain the consequences of God's work of salvation in the Cross. Stott identifies four principal images to explain the consequences drawn from different perspectives on life: "Temple sacrifices and legal verdicts, the slave in the market and the child in the home."[1] These images are shared by Paul, Peter, and John. The Apostle John would add the image of birth and life. These five images explain consequences that were achieved on the cross. "Moved by the perfection of his holy love, God in Christ substituted himself for us sinners."[2] Each image captures a perspective on the consequences of the Cross.

Propitiation

The word translated *propitiation* (*hilasmos*) means either, "appeasement necessitated by sin" or, "expiation" of sin and guilt.[3] In the provisions of the tabernacle, on the Day of Atonement, God's wrath or anger against the nation's sin was appeased once a year. The New Testament describes Jesus as the propitiation (*hilasmos*) in relation to our sins (1 John 2:2; 4:10). As Jesus is an advocate with the Father (2:1), this role implies displeasure, even anger of the Father, before whom Jesus pleads our case. The principle term, *hilastērion*, is used with two related emphases. Paul, in Rom 3:25, speaks of the means of propitiation (propitiatory sacrifice) while Heb 9:5 speaks of the place of propitiation (the mercy-seat).

---

[1] John W. Stott, *The Cross of Christ* (Downers Grove, IL: IVP, 1986), p. 198. This exposition found in pp. 167-203 will form the framework for this treatment.

[2] *Ibid.*, p. 167.

[3] BDAG, p. 474.

One of the most amazing facts is that Christ's death appeases God's anger, "not for ours only, but also for the sins of the whole world" (1 John 2:2). Jesus is "set forth by God as the remedy for universal human guilt under his wrath."[4] This does not mean that mankind is no longer responsible for their sin and thus not subject to judgment, but that God's judgment will come from God who is appeased. "God does not love us because Christ died for us; Christ died for us because God loved us [John 3:16]. If it is God's wrath that needed to be propitiated, it is God's love that did the propitiating."[5] As a result, the good news of the gospel can be communicated in God's love to all people. While the evangelist does not know who is God's elect, the death of Christ is sufficient to satisfy God's wrath for everyone.

David Wells elaborated on this:

> In Pauline thought, man is alienated from God by sin and God is alienated from man by wrath. It is in the substitutionary death of Christ that sin is overcome and wrath averted, so that God can look on man without displeasure and man can look on God without fear. Sin is expiated and God is propitiated.[6]

Redemption

If propitiation was introduced in the approach to God on the Day of Atonement, redemption was introduced in Israel's enslavement to Egypt (Exod 6:6). The emphasis of this image highlights the plight of Israel. The focus is on the desperate state of Israel in Egypt, representing the fallen human race's captivity to sin and the rule of the enemy. In the New Testament, the *redemption* word group is applied to the marketplace where slaves are for sale. *Apolutrōsis* means, "buying back a slave or captive, making him free by payment of a ransom (*lutrōsis*)."[7] Stott proposes three aspects involved in this work of God in salvation:

1. The human plight *from* which we can't extricate ourselves is severe. The plight of captivity to Egypt, or slavery in Roman society, provides the image that is metaphorically applied to a spiritual and moral bondage to Satan and sin. Transgressions and sins enslave the human race (Eph 1:7; Col 1:14) and "the

---

[4]   Stott, *The Cross of Christ*, p. 172.

[5]   *Ibid.*, p. 174.

[6]   David F. Wells, *The Search for Salvation* (Downers Grove, IL: IVP, 1978), p. 29.

[7]   BDAG, p. 95.

curse of the law" pronounces judgment on law-breakers (Gal 3:13; 4:5). For Christ "gave himself for us to redeem us from all lawlessness" (Titus 2:14).

2. The price *with* which we have been redeemed is Christ Himself. The price paid by Christ to ransom us is His blood. We were redeemed "not with perishable things such as silver or gold," wrote Peter, "but with the precious blood of Christ, like that of a lamb without blemish or spot" (1 Pet 1:18-19). And Christ's bloodshed refers to death.

3. The Redeemer has proprietary rights over His purchase. In the case of Israel, they were redeemed from Egypt to become God's covenant people. In the New Testament, the elders at Ephesus were told "to care for the church of God, which he obtained with his own blood" (Acts 20:28).[8]

Justification

This image is drawn from the court of law. Justification is the opposite of condemnation (Rom 5:18; 8:34). While the propitiation of God is universal, concerning all sin, redemption and justification are applied to individuals by faith. Forgiveness and justification "are surely complementary, however, not identical. Forgiveness remits our debts and cancels our liability to punishment; justification bestows on us a righteous standing before God."[9]

The sixteenth-century Reformers, who rediscovered the Biblical gospel of justification by faith, were convinced of its central importance. The Roman Catholic Church, at the council of Trent, rejected the position of the Reformers. The essential reason is that prevenient grace predisposes people "to convert themselves to their own justification by freely assenting to and co-operating with that grace."[10] After the Second Vatican Council in the early 1960s, Hans Küng sought to demonstrate that Trent's words are in accord with Barth. "In brief, God's *declaration* of justice is...at the same time and in the same act, a *making just*."[11] His

---

[8] Stott, *The Cross of Christ*, pp. 175-82.

[9] *Ibid.*, p. 182.

[10] See Council of Trent, Session VI, and its Decrees on Original Sin, on Justification and on Penance.

[11] Hans Küng, *Justification: The Doctrine of Karl Barth and a Catholic Reflection* (NP: Burns and Oates, 1964), p. 204, emphasis in original.

conclusion rests on the absence of any limitation in God's declaration of righteousness which is efficacious, not only legally, but also experientially. The Protestants believe that the declaration is limited in scope to a legal pronouncement, and as such is efficacious.

Again, Stott raises four questions which summarize the issues:

1. *What is the source?* Romans 3:24 asserts that sinners are "justified by his grace as a gift." So it is God who is the source and He acts in grace.

2. *What are the grounds?* Romans 5:9 concludes that "we have now been justified by his blood." This corresponds to his earlier assertion that justification is "through the redemption that is in Christ Jesus" (Rom 3:24).

3. *What is the means?* Romans 4:5 makes a sharp contrast to highlight the means: "to the one who does not *work* but believes in him who justifies the ungodly, his *faith* is counted as righteousness" (emphasis added). Stott emphasizes that justification is by *faith*. "Grace and faith belong indissolubly to one another, since faith's only function is to receive what grace freely offers…Further, if faith is only the means, it is also the only means."[12]

4. *What are the effects?* Clearly, through Paul's writings, God declares that one who believes has a right standing before God.[13]

However, there are other passages which also deserve consideration. Romans 5:18: "through one righteous act there is life-giving justification for everyone" (HCSB). The original text literally translates, "the righteousness of life," which seems ambiguous. Different translations relate righteousness and life differently:

- Two separate gifts given together:
  - RSV "acquittal and life"
  - NAB "acquittal and life"
  - ESV "justification and life"
- Life is the effect of justification;
  - NET "righteousness leading to life"
  - NIV "justification that brings life"

---

[12] Stott, *The Cross of Christ*, pp. 190-91.

[13] *Ibid.*, p. 182-192.

The two separate gifts received by faith deal with the grammatical construction and ambiguity better. In this way, the image that John uses, *birth* and *life*, is directly added to Paul's legal image of justification. The HCSB translation also recognizes that justification is like birth. Both bring life into existence in some sense.

Galatians 2:17 and 2 Cor 5:21 (NKJV) speak of justification *in Christ*. "To say that we are justified 'through Christ' points to his historical death; to say that we are justified 'in Christ' points to the personal relationship with him which by faith we now enjoy."[14] This way of speaking leads to a discussion of a relationship with the ascended Lord through the Holy Spirit. This is what Paul is about to develop (Romans 5:12–8:39).

One final issue arises in the consideration of the Epistles' use of justification. James and Paul use the term *justify* differently, but not in contradiction. James speaks of "justification by works" when he refers to Abraham's offering of Isaac (Jas 2:21). What Abraham did in Gen 22:1-19 made public what had previously been private, and in that active expression of faith, "the Scripture was fulfilled." It fulfilled God's declaration that he was righteous by faith (Jas 2:23 referring to Gen 15:6). So, James concludes "that a person is justified by works and not by faith alone" (Jas 2:24). The point James is making is that active faith results in works by which man may observe that another is righteous. At the same time, James agrees with Paul that one is justified before God by faith, which is legal justification before God, but not demonstrated to others. The Reformers said, speaking of justification before God, that it is never by works, but unto works. James would agree.

Reconciliation

In reconciliation, the image considers the relationships within family and between friends. To reconcile is to restore a relationship that has been broken, or to renew a friendship that had been lost. And a broken relationship is precisely what happened in the fall of mankind in Adam. When Adam chose to follow the serpent's rebellion, by viewing himself as god, he then regarded God as his enemy. The serpent, in his strategy, had caused enmity between God and mankind.

But this enmity is two-sided: "there is, on the scriptural view, a definite hostility on the part of God to everything that is evil…Thus, quite

---

[14] *Ibid.*, p. 191.

apart from details of interpretation of particular passages, there is strong and consistent teaching that God is active in His opposition to all that is evil."[15]

The work of reconciliation to God through Christ is completed and universal. At the same time, it is individual and based on an appeal to be received by faith. Again, as God was propitiated for all evil through Christ, so God is reconciled in spite of all evil through Christ. There are four basic passages dealing with reconciliation, Rom 5:9-11; 2 Cor 5:18-21; Eph 1:11-22; Col 1:15-20. Three of these are considered below.

Romans 5:9-11

For the believer, to be reconciled to God is similar to being justified before God. Justification is our legal standing before our Judge in the court; reconciliation is our personal relationship with our Father in His family. This involves an individual response of faith.

Ephesians 1:11-22

This truth also has reconciled relationships between members of the family in the Church. Culturally, great hostility had developed in the Roman world. For believers in the Church, the Jewish believers and the Gentile believers are at peace. Whatever formerly divided them now is no longer significant.

Colossians 1:15-20

This passage deals with the scope of reconciliation, irrespective of whether that reconciliation has been accepted. God accomplishes this work through Christ: "through him to reconcile to himself all things, whether on earth or in heaven, making peace by the blood of his cross" (Col 1:20). What is striking is that the realm "under the earth" (Phil 2:10) is excluded. While in the climax of earth's history, all realms will acknowledge and confess that Jesus is Lord, it is not mentioned with respect to reconciliation. On earth and in heaven may well refer to all things created that suffered some degree of ruptured relationships when Adam fell into sin. The human race experienced a break in relationship.

---

[15] Leon Morris, *The Apostolic Preaching of the Cross* (Grand Rapids, MI: Eerdmans, 1955), p. 196. Consult pp. 132-50 and pp. 186-223.

It is now God who made peace with the condemned creation. It is a peace that is related to God's work of propitiation. That which is "under the earth" had been already judged and thus was not affected by Christ's death.

APPENDIX 3: BAPTISM

Baptism is a word used to refer to related experiences of believers. It is somewhat confusing since these experiences are descriptive of different mediums: water and Spirit. What is the relation of the rite of baptism in water to baptism in the Spirit? W. H. Griffith Thomas raised the pertinent question: how can that which is physical effect that which is spiritual? This would lead to a distinction between water and Spirit baptism though not necessarily one as radical as the Pentecostal and charismatic movements contend. A simple distinction would be that the rite of *water baptism* is associated with baptism in Christ's name and the testimony that the one baptized believes that Jesus is the Christ while *Spirit baptism* is a work of the Spirit at the time of conversion (Rom 8:9). The Spirit is the agent who makes baptism what it is meant to be: actual entry into the resurrected life of Christ.

Thus, the medium of water is a symbol of the medium of the Spirit, and the two occasions are related by the work of man and of God.

Another necessary question: how do Paul's language of baptism "into Christ" (Gal 3:26-27) and Jesus' language, "baptized with the Holy Spirit," relate (Acts 1:5)?

I would conclude first, that Paul's passages (Rom 6:1-11; Gal 3:26-27; Col 2:11-12; Eph 5:26; and Titus 3:5-7) all conjoin baptism with spiritual effects and refer to Spirit baptism, not water baptism. This is the case even though 1 Cor 12:13 is the sole explicit reference to baptism in the Spirit in Paul's letters. Both Paul's and Jesus' language speak of baptism in the Spirit. Paul adds that the Spirit is the Agent to form the Body of Christ (1 Cor 12:13; Acts 1:5; 9:4-5; 11:16).

Second, Christ in heaven is the One who baptizes when He pours out the Spirit (Acts 1:5; 2:33; 11:15-16).

Third is the image of being immersed in the Spirit. The medium of the Spirit is also the Agent uniting the believer to the Head, Christ, and the fellow believers to a common Body (Acts 9:4-5).

G. R. Beasley Murray concludes, "Because baptism signifies union with Christ, Paul saw it extending the *union with Christ in his redemptive action*," or union with Christ in Death and Resurrection.[1]

Dunn puts it this way: "in his last use of the metaphor, in Rom 6:3… as a baptism not merely into Christ, but also into Christ's death…He insists that the initiating experience of the Spirit brings about not only a belonging to Christ (8:9), not only a sharing in his risen life (8:10), but also a union with Christ…"[2]

---

[1]　Gerald F. Hawthorne, Ralph P. Martin, and Daniel G. Reid, eds., "Baptism," *Dictionary of Paul and His Letters* (Downers Grove, IL: InterVarsity Press, 1993), p. 62, emphasis added.

[2]　Dunn, *The Christ and the Spirit*, vol. 2, p. 115, fn. 18.

SCRIPTURE INDEX

Romans

ABOUT BOLD GRACE MINISTRIES

Purpose Statement

Bold Grace Ministries exists to: **unite** believers under the banner of God's grace (Eph 4:3-6), **share** the gospel and aid those who will proclaim it faithfully (Rom 10:14-15), **increase** believers' confidence in the power of the indwelling Christ (Gal 2:20), **love** without hypocrisy (Rom 12:9a), **proclaim** the hope of Christ's glorious kingdom (Rom 8:18-21), and **equip** the saints to share Christ's matchless grace and love with others (2 Tim 2:2).

Our Vision

Grace is relevant. By grace God makes Himself available to men, and by grace He meets our deepest needs. Grace unites us, when we are naturally so prone to division. It frees us from pride and the tyranny of sin and effects holiness and humility.

Yet too often grace is missing or downplayed in our message about Christ, our interactions with one another, and our views on the Christian life. By God's grace, and with the help of like-minded brothers and sisters, we hope to reach out to the world with a message of God's free grace, to unite and encourage our brothers and sisters in Christ, and to teach all the ways that His grace is sufficient for us in our pursuit of Christlikeness.

Find more Bold Grace books and learn more about
Bold Grace at www.boldgrace.org.